Microsoft® Word® 2010 on Demand

Steve Johnson

Perspection, Inc.

que® Que Publishing, 800 East 96th Street, Indianapolis, IN 46240 USA

Microsoft® Word® 2010 On Demand

Library of Congress Cataloging-in-Publication Data is on file
ISBN-13: 978-0-7897-4281-0
ISBN-10: 0-7897-4281-0
Printed and bound in the United States of America
First Printing: July 2010
13 12 11 10 4 3 2 1

Que Publishing offers excellent discounts on this book when ordered in quantity for bulk purchases or special sales.
For information, please contact: U.S. Corporate and Government Sales
1-800-382-3419 or corpsales@pearsontechgroup.com
For sales outside the U.S., please contact: International Sales
1-317-428-3341 or International@pearsontechgroup.com

Trademarks

All terms mentioned in this book that are known to be trademarks or service marks have been appropriately capitalized. Que cannot attest to the accuracy of this information. Use of a term in this book should not be regarded as affecting the validity of any trademark or service mark.

Microsoft and the Microsoft Office logo are registered trademarks of Microsoft Corporation in the United States and/or other countries.

Warning and Disclaimer

Every effort has been made to make this book as complete and as accurate as possible, but no warranty or fitness is implied. The authors and the publishers shall have neither liability nor responsibility to any person or entity with respect to any loss or damage arising from the information contained in this book.

Publisher
Paul Boger

Associate Publisher
Greg Wiegand

Acquisitions Editor
Loretta Yates

Managing Editor
Steve Johnson

Author
Steve Johnson

Technical Editor
Beth Teyler

Page Layout
James Teyler

Interior Designers
Steve Johnson
Marian Hartsough

Photographs
Tracy Teyler

Indexer
Katherine Stimson

Proofreader
Beth Teyler

Team Coordinator
Cindy Teeters

Acknowledgements

Perspection, Inc.

Microsoft Word 2010 On Demand has been created by the professional trainers and writers at Perspection, Inc. to the standards you've come to expect from Que publishing. Together, we are pleased to present this training book.

Perspection, Inc. is a software training company committed to providing information and training to help people use software more effectively in order to communicate, make decisions, and solve problems. Perspection writes and produces software training books, and develops multimedia and Web-based training. Since 1991, we have written more than 100 computer books, with several bestsellers to our credit, and sold over 5 million books.

This book incorporates Perspection's training expertise to ensure that you'll receive the maximum return on your time. You'll focus on the tasks and skills that increase productivity while working at your own pace and convenience.

We invite you to visit the Perspection Web site at:

www.perspection.com

Acknowledgements

The task of creating any book requires the talents of many hard-working people pulling together to meet impossible deadlines and untold stresses. We'd like to thank the outstanding team responsible for making this book possible: the writer, Steve Johnson; the production team, James Teyler; the editor and proofreader, Beth Teyler; and the indexer, Katherine Stimson.

At Que publishing, we'd like to thank Greg Wiegand and Loretta Yates for the opportunity to undertake this project, Cindy Teeters for administrative support, and Lori Lyons for your production expertise and support.

Perspection

About The Author

Steve Johnson has written more than 60 books on a variety of computer software, including Adobe Photoshop CS5, Adobe Flash CS5, Adobe Dreamweaver CS5, Adobe InDesign CS5, Adobe Illustrator CS5, Microsoft Windows 7, Microsoft Office 2010 and 2007, Microsoft Office 2008 for the Macintosh, and Apple Mac OS X Snow Leopard. In 1991, after working for Apple Computer and Microsoft, Steve founded Perspection, Inc., which writes and produces software training. When he is not staying up late writing, he enjoys playing golf, gardening, and spending time with his wife, Holly, and three children, JP, Brett, and Hannah. Steve and his family live in Pleasanton, California, but can also be found visiting family all over the western United States.

We Want To Hear From You!

As the reader of this book, *you* are our most important critic and commentator. We value your opinion and want to know what we're doing right, what we could do better, what areas you'd like to see us publish in, and any other words of wisdom you're willing to pass our way.

As an associate publisher for Que, I welcome your comments. You can email or write me directly to let me know what you did or didn't like about this book—as well as what we can do to make our books better.

Please note that I cannot help you with technical problems related to the topic of this book. We do have a User Services group, however, where I will forward specific technical questions related to the book.

When you write, please be sure to include this book's title and author as well as your name, email address, and phone number. I will carefully review your comments and share them with the author and editors who worked on the book.

Email: feedback@quepublishing.com

Mail: Greg Wiegand
Que Publishing
800 East 96th Street
Indianapolis, IN 46240 USA

For more information about this book or another Que title, visit our Web site at *www.quepublishing.com/register.* Type the ISBN (excluding hyphens) or the title of a book in the Search field to find the page you're looking for.

a

Contents

C

C

Introduction

Welcome to *Microsoft Word 2010 On Demand*, a visual quick reference book that shows you how to work efficiently with Microsoft Word. This book provides complete coverage of basic to advanced Word skills.

How You'll Learn

How This Book Works

You don't have to read this book in any particular order. We've designed the book so that you can jump in, get the information you need, and jump out. However, the book does follow a logical progression from simple tasks to more complex ones. Each task is presented on no more than two facing pages, which lets you focus on a single task without having to turn the page. To find the information that you need, just look up the task in the table of contents or index, and turn to the page listed. Read the task introduction, follow the step-by-step instructions in the left column along with screen illustrations in the right column, and you're done.

What's New

If you're searching for what's new in Word 2010, just look for the icon: **New!**. The new icon appears in the table of contents and throughout this book so you can quickly and easily identify a new or improved feature in Word 2010. A complete description of each new feature appears in the New Features guide in the back of this book.

Keyboard Shortcuts

Most menu commands have a keyboard equivalent, such as Ctrl+P, as a quicker alternative to using the mouse. A complete list of keyboard shortcuts is available on the Web at *www.perspection.com*.

Step-by-Step Instructions

This book provides concise step-by-step instructions that show you "how" to accomplish a task. Each set of instructions includes illustrations that directly correspond to the easy-to-read steps. Also included in the text are time-savers, tables, and sidebars to help you work more efficiently or to teach you more in-depth information. A "Did You Know?" provides tips and techniques to help you work smarter, while a "See Also" leads you to other parts of the book containing related information about the task.

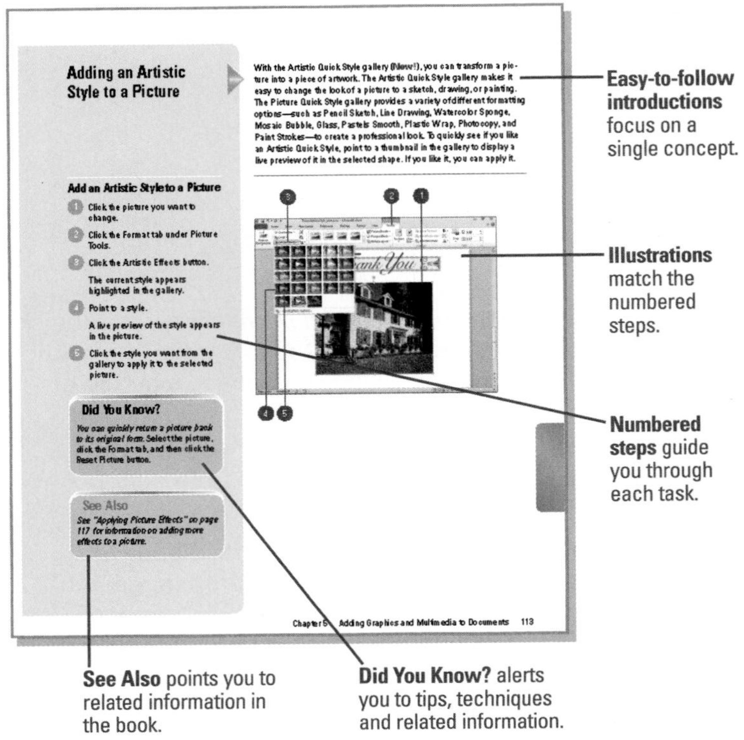

Real World Examples

This book uses real world examples files to give you a context in which to use the task. By using the example files, you won't waste time looking for or creating sample files. You get a start file and a result file, so you can compare your work. Not every topic needs an example file, such as changing options, so we provide a complete list of the example files used through out the book. The example files that you need for project tasks along with a complete file list are available on the Web at *www.perspection.com.*

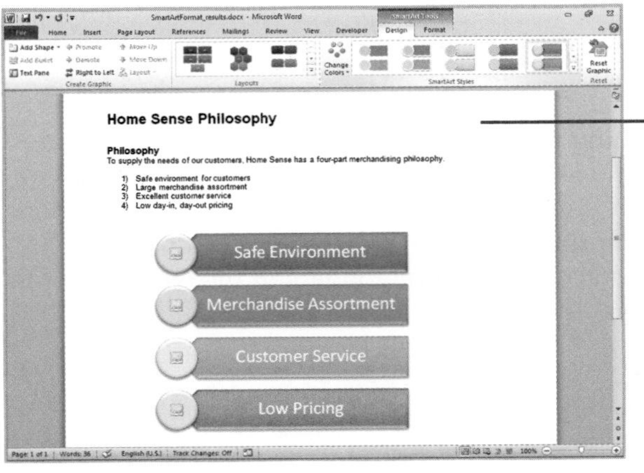

Real world examples help you apply what you've learned to other tasks.

Workshops

This book shows you how to put together the individual step-by-step tasks into in-depth projects with the Workshops. You start each project with a sample file, work through the steps, and then compare your results with a project results file at the end. The Workshop projects and associated files are available on the Web at *www.perspection.com.*

Workshops

W

Introduction

The Workshops are all about being creative and thinking outside of the box. These workshops will help your right-brain soar, while making your left-brain happy; by explaining why things work the way they do. Exploring possibilities is great fun; however, always stay grounded with knowledge of how things work.

Getting and Using the Project Files

Each project in the Workshops includes a start file to help you get started with the project, and a final file to provide you with the results of the project so you can see how well you accomplished the task.

Before you can use the project files, you need to download them from the Web. You can access the files at *www.perspection.com* in the software downloads area. After you download the files from the Web, uncompress the files into a folder on your hard drive to which you have easy access from Microsoft Word 2010.

Project 1: Creating a Form with Content Controls

The **Workshops** walks you through in-depth projects to help you put Microsoft Word to work.

Skills and Tools: Use content controls to create a form

Forms are an easy way for you to interact with users of your documents, either online or in print, and gain information and feedback from them in the process. Content controls are predefined fields or set of fields that contain information you can use throughout a document. Word includes many different types: text boxes (Rich Text and Text), picture, date picker, combo boxes, drop-down lists, and building block gallery. The fields display information you provided in Document Properties or a placeholder, which you can fill in. After you insert the fields you want, you can change field properties to customize the form. When you're done with the form, you can group the document text to the content controls to prevent a user from accidentally making changes to the document text.

The Project

In this project, you'll learn how to create a form, add content controls, change properties, and group the results to protect the document text, yet allow the content controls to change.

W

459

Microsoft Certified Applications Specialist

This book prepares you for the Microsoft Certified Applications Specialist (MCAS) exam for Microsoft Word 2010 program. Each MCAS certification exam has a set of objectives, which are organized into broader skill sets. To prepare for the certification exam, you should review and perform each task identified with a MCAS objective to confirm that you can meet the requirements for the exam. Information about the MCAS program is available in the back of this book. The MCAS objectives and the specific pages that cover them are available on the Web at *www.perspection.com.*

Microsoft Certified Applications Specialist

C

About the MCAS Program

The Microsoft Certified Applications Specialist (MCAS) certification is the globally recognized standard for validating expertise with the Microsoft Office suite of business productivity programs. Earning an MCAS certificate acknowledges you have the expertise to work with Microsoft Office programs. To earn the MCAS certification, you must pass a certification exam for the Microsoft Office desktop applications of Microsoft Word, Microsoft Excel, Microsoft PowerPoint, Microsoft Outlook, or Microsoft Access. (The availability of Microsoft Certified Applications Specialist certification exams varies by program, program version, and language. Visit *www.microsoft.com* and search on *Microsoft Certified Applications Specialist* for exam availability and more information about the program.) The Microsoft Certified Applications Specialist program is the only Microsoft-approved program in the world for certifying proficiency with Microsoft Office programs.

What Does This Logo Mean?

It means this book has been approved by the Microsoft Certified Applications Specialist program to be certified courseware for learning Microsoft Word 2010 and preparing for the certification exam. This book will prepare you for the Microsoft Certified Applications Specialist exam for Microsoft Word 2010. Each certification level has a set of objectives, which are organized into broader skill sets. The Microsoft Certified Applications Specialist objectives and the specific pages throughout this book that cover the objectives are available on the Web at *www.perspection.com.*

WD10S-1.1
WD10S-2.2

C

473

Get More on the Web

In addition to the information in this book, you can also get more information on the Web to help you get up to speed faster with Word 2010. Some of the information includes:

Transition Helpers

- **Only New Features.** Download and print the new feature tasks as a quick and easy guide.

Productivity Tools

- **Keyboard Shortcuts.** Download a list of keyboard shortcuts to learn faster ways to get the job done.

More Content

- **Photographs.** Download photographs and other graphics to use in your Office documents.
- **More Content.** Download new content developed after publication. For example, you can download a complete chapter on Groove or SharePoint Workspaces.

You can access these additional resources on the Web at *www.perspection.com.*

Working with Groove Workspaces

Introduction

Microsoft SharePoint Workspaces 2010 is a new addition to the Microsoft *Office* 2010 system that enables teams to set up collaborative workspaces. With Groove, you can bring the team, tools, and information together from any location to work on a project. After creating documents with Microsoft *Office* programs, you can use Groove for file sharing, document reviews, co-editing and co-reviewing Word documents, and for co-viewing Excel workbooks.

Instead of using a centralized server—like SharePoint Server 2010—to store information and manage tasks, Groove stores all your workspaces, tools, and data right on your computer. You don't need to connect to a network to access or update information. While you're connected to the Internet, Groove automatically sends the changes you make in a workspace to your team member's computers, and any changes they make get sent to you. Groove uses built-in presence awareness, alerts, and unread marks to see who is working online and what team members are doing without having to ask.

Groove uses tools and technology from other Microsoft *Office* system products to help you work together and stay informed. With the Groove Workspace Documents tool, you can check out documents from Microsoft SharePoint 2010 into a Groove workspace, collaborate on them, and then check them back in when you're done.

If you have access to an SharePoint 2010 site, you can use the Save to SharePoint command on the Save & Send screen on the File tab directly from Excel to access many SharePoint Server 2010 features. For example, you can create a library to work with Excel Services on a SharePoint site to share workbook data.

What You'll Do

Configure and Launch Groove
View the Groove Window
Set General Preferences
Create a Groove Workspace
Invite Others to a Workspace
Deal with Groove Alerts
Share Files in a Workspace
Hold a Discussion
Add Tools to a Workspace
Set Calendar Appointments
Manage Meetings
Work with Forms
Track Issues
Create a Picture Library
Add a Contact
Send a message and Chat with Others
Share Files with SharePoint
Share Files with Synchronizing Folders
Work with a Shared Workspace
Work with Excel Services

1

Additional content is available on the Web. You can download a chapter on Groove or SharePoint workspaces.

Getting Started with Word

1

Introduction

Microsoft Word 2010 is a powerful word-processing program that enables you to easily compose and edit documents for print or online use. Word contains new tools specifically designed to improve the way you interact with the program, and the way you collaborate with one another in preparing documents.

This chapter introduces you to the terminology and the basic Word skills you use in the program. In Word, files are called **documents**. Each new document is similar to a blank page. As you type and add additional text and other objects, your document gets longer. Unlike looking at a piece of paper, Word provides many views, such as the Reading Layout view, that helps you see the document in the best possible way for the task at hand.

With the results-oriented visual interface, you navigate through various tasks with a click of the mouse, or by using shortcut keys on your keyboard. Microsoft Word is set up with a tab-based Ribbon and dialog boxes that provide you with the tools you need when you need them to get the job done. The customizable Quick Access Toolbar gives you easy access to commonly-used commands, such as Save and Print. When working with your documents, you can view more than one document, or resize the window to compare data. Moving around in your document is made easy by the browsing function in Word. With a click of a button, you are on your way to browsing your document in various ways—by footnote, graphic, or comments, to name a few.

When you finish the design of your document, you can save it in the default XML-based format or another format; a Web page for example, to use in another office program. Microsoft also offers the Office.com Online Web site, a resource to check for updates and information on Word.

What You'll Do

Start Word

View the Word Window

Use the Ribbon and Choose Commands

Work with Toolbars

Choose Dialog Box Options

Use the Status Bar

Use Task and Window Panes

Open an Existing Document

Open Files of Different Types

Convert an Existing Document

Change Document Views

Read a Document

Get Help While You Work

Save a Document

Save a Document with Different Formats

Check Compatibility and Accessibility

Document Properties

Zoom the View In and Out

Recover a Document

Maintain and Repair Office

Get Updates on the Web

Close a Document and Exit Word

Starting Word

The two quickest ways to start the Microsoft Word 2010 program are to select it on the Start menu or double-click a shortcut icon on the desktop. By providing different ways to start a program, Office lets you work the way you like and start programs with a click of a button. When you start Word, a program window opens, displaying a blank document, where you can begin working immediately.

Start Word

1. Click the **Start** button on the taskbar.
2. Point to **All Programs**.
3. Click **Microsoft Office**.
4. Click **Microsoft Word 2010**.

   If Microsoft Office asks you to activate the program, follow the instructions to complete the process.

   TIMESAVER *To change the product key later, click the File tab, click Help, click the Change Product Key link, enter the product key, and then click Continue.*

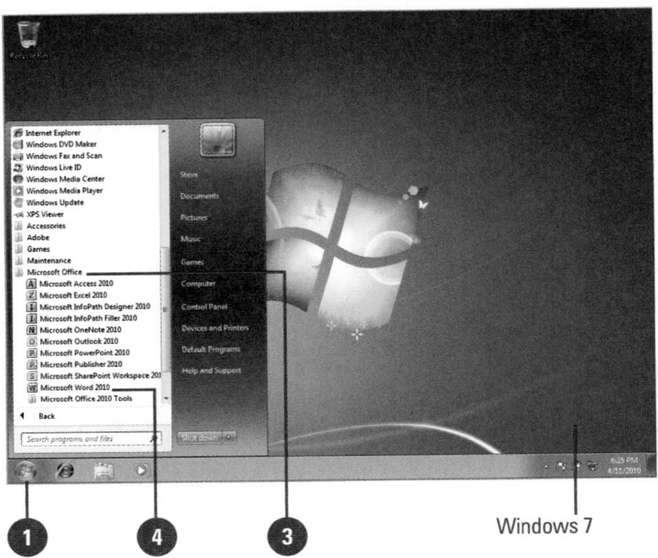

Did You Know?

You can create a program shortcut from the Start menu to the desktop. Click the Start menu, point to All Programs, click Microsoft Office, right-click Microsoft Word 2010, point to Send To, and then click Desktop (Create Shortcut).

You can start Word and open a document from Windows Explorer. Double-clicking any Word document icon in Windows Explorer opens that file and Word.

For Power Users

Need More Word 2010 Computing Power

If you're a power user or analyst that needs to create bigger, more complex Word documents, you should use the 64-bit version of Microsoft Word 2010 (**New!**). The 64-bit version of Word 2010 is built specifically for 64-bit computers. If you're using the 32-bit version, Word 2010 significantly boosts performance levels (**New!**) over previous versions for importing, filtering, sorting, copying, and pasting large amounts of data as well as opening and saving large files.

Viewing the Word Window

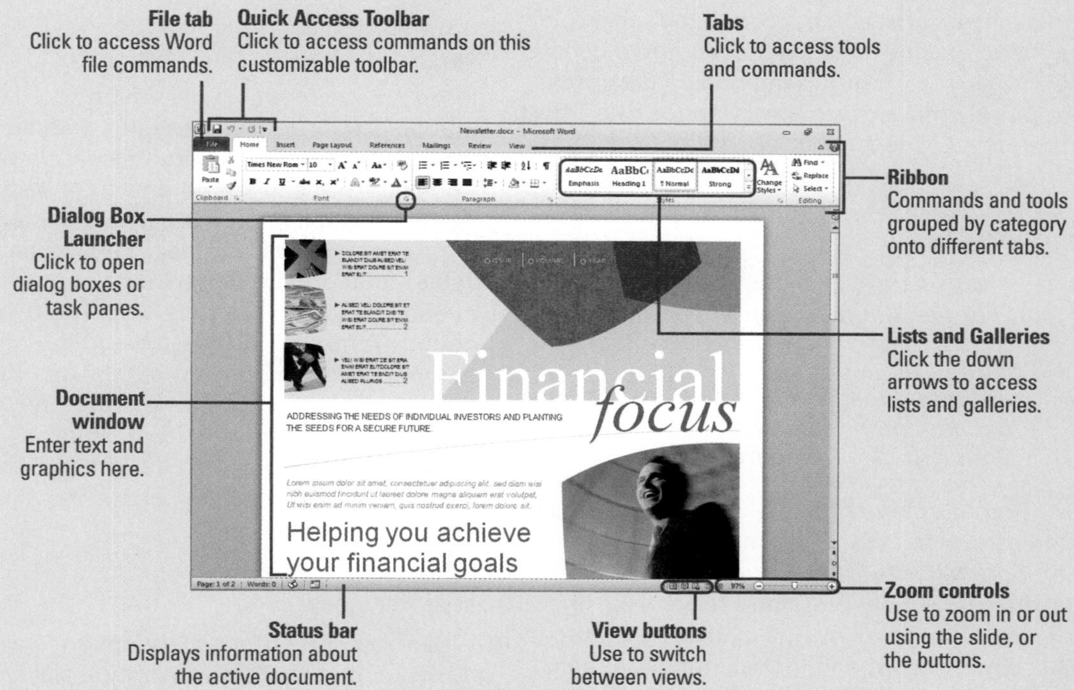

Using the Ribbon

The **Ribbon** is a results oriented way of working in Word 2010. It replaces menus, toolbars, and most of the task panes found in Word 2003. The Ribbon is located at the top of the document window and is comprised of **tabs** that are organized by task or objects. The controls on each tab are organized into **groups**, or subtasks. The controls, or **command buttons**, in each group execute a command, or display a menu of commands or a drop-down gallery. Controls in each group provide a visual way to quickly make document changes. The Office button in Office 2007 has been replaced by the File tab (**New!**), which displays Backstage view, where you can access file-related commands.

> **TIMESAVER** *To minimize the Ribbon, click the Minimize the Ribbon button* (Ctrl+F1) (**New!**) or *double-click the current tab. Click a tab to auto display it (Ribbon remains minimized). Click the Expand the Ribbon button* (Ctrl+F1) *or double-click a tab to maximize it.*

If you prefer using the keyboard instead of the mouse to access commands on the Ribbon, Microsoft Word provides easy to use shortcuts. Simply press and release the Alt or F10 key to display **KeyTips** over each feature in the current view, and then continue to press the letter shown in the KeyTip until you press the one that you want to use. To cancel an action and hide the KeyTips, press and release the Alt or F10 key again. If you prefer using the keyboard shortcuts found in previous versions of Microsoft Word, such as Ctrl+P (for Print), all the keyboard shortcuts and keyboard accelerators work exactly the same in Microsoft Word 2010. Word 2010 includes a legacy mode that you can turn on to use familiar Word 2003 keyboard accelerators.

Tabs

Word provides three types of tabs on the Ribbon. The first type is called a **standard** tab—such as Home, Insert, Review, View, and Add-Ins—that you see whenever you start Word. The second type is called a **contextual** tab—such as Picture Tools, Drawing, or Table—that appear only when they are needed based on the type of task you are doing. Word recognizes what you're doing and provides the right set of tabs and tools to use when you need them. The third type is called a **program** tab—such as Print Preview—that replaces the standard set of tabs when you switch to certain views or modes.

Live Preview

When you point to a gallery option, such as WordArt, on the Ribbon, Word displays a **live preview** of the option change so that you can see exactly what your change will look like before committing to it.

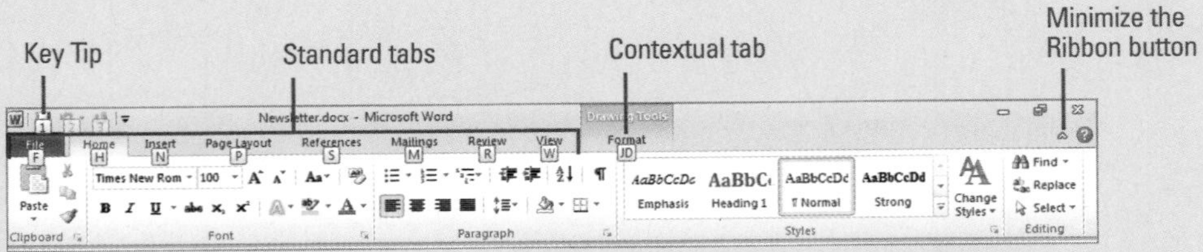

Choosing Commands

Word commands are organized in groups on the Ribbon, Quick Access Toolbar, and Mini-Toolbar. Commands are available as buttons or options on the Ribbon, or as menus on button or option arrows or the File tab (**New!**). The Quick Access Toolbar and Mini-Toolbar display frequently used buttons that you may be already familiar with from Word 2003, while the File tab on the Ribbon displays file related menu commands in Backstage view. In addition to the File tab, you can also open a **shortcut menu** with a group of related commands by right-clicking an element.

Choose a Menu Command Using the File Tab

1. Click the **File** tab on the Ribbon.
2. Click the command you want.

   TIMESAVER *You can use a shortcut key to choose a command. Press and hold down the first key and then press the second key. For example, press and hold the Ctrl key and then press S (or Ctrl+S) to select the Save command.*

Choose a Menu Command from a Shortcut Menu

1. Right-click an object (a cell or graphic element).

   TIMESAVER *Press Shift+F10 to display the shortcut menu for a selected command.*

2. Click a command on the shortcut menu. If the command is followed by an arrow, point to the command to see a list of related options, and then click the option you want.

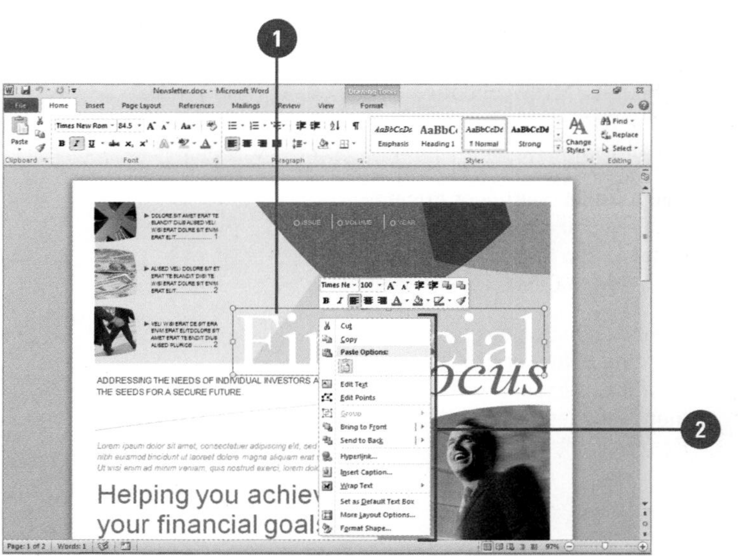

Working with Toolbars

Word includes its most common commands, such as Save and Undo, on the **Quick Access Toolbar**. Click a toolbar button to choose a command. If you are not sure what a toolbar button does, point to it to display a ScreenTip. When Word starts, the Quick Access Toolbar appears at the top of the window, unless you've changed your settings. You can customize the Quick Access Toolbar or Ribbon (**New!**) by adding command buttons or groups to it. You can also move the toolbar below or above the Ribbon so it's right where you need it. In addition to the Quick Access Toolbar, Word also displays the Mini-Toolbar when you point to selected text. The **Mini-Toolbar** appears above the selected text and provides quick access to formatting tools.

Choose a Command Using a Toolbar or Ribbon

- **Get command help**. If you're not sure what a button does, point to it to display a ScreenTip. If the ScreenTip includes *Press F1 for more help*, press F1.
- **Choose a command**. Click the button, or button arrow, and then click a command or option.

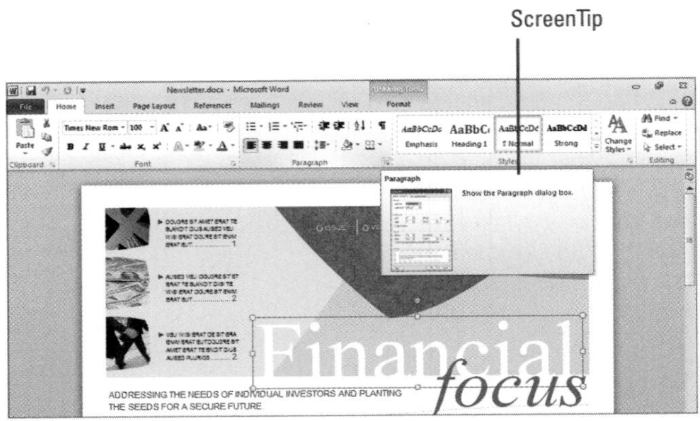

Add or Remove Items from the Quick Access Toolbar

- **Add or remove a common button**. Click the Customize Quick Access Toolbar list arrow, and then click a button name (checked item appears on the toolbar).
- **Add a Ribbon button or group**. Right-click the button or group name on the Ribbon, and then click Add to Quick Access Toolbar.
- **Remove a button or group**. Right-click the button or group name on the Quick Access Toolbar, and then click Remove from Quick Access Toolbar.

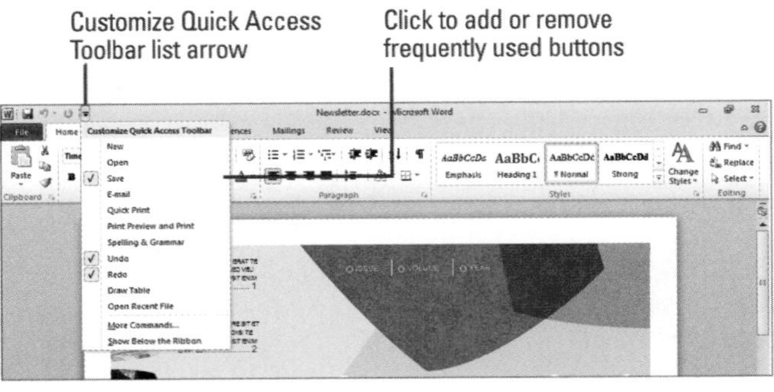

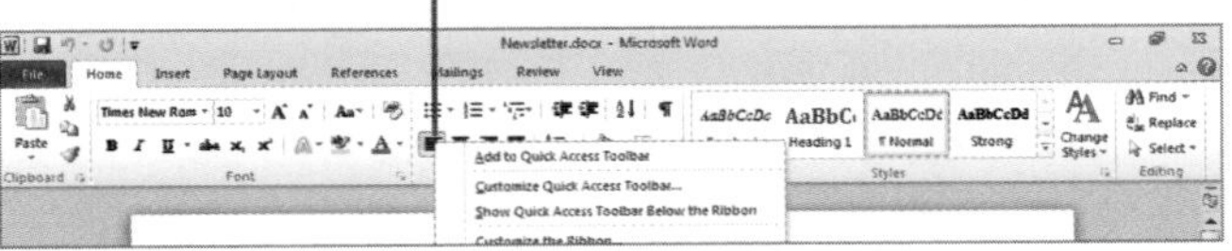

Customize the Ribbon or Quick Access Toolbar

1. Click the **File** tab, and then click **Options**.
2. Click the **Customize Ribbon** (**New!**) or **Quick Access Toolbar**.
3. Click the **Choose commands from** list arrow, and then click **All Commands** or a specific Ribbon.
4. Click the list arrow (right column), and then select the tabs or toolbar you want to change.
5. For the Ribbon, click **New Tab** to create a new tab, or click **New Group** to create a new group on the selected tab (right column).
6. To import or export a customized Ribbon or Quick Access Toolbar, click the **Import/Export** list arrow, select a command, and then select an import file or create an export file.
7. Click the command you want to add (left column) or remove (right column), and then click **Add** or **Remove**.
   - To insert a separator line between buttons in the Quick Access Toolbar, click **<Separator>**, and then click **Add**.
8. Click the **Move Up** and **Move Down** arrow buttons to arrange the order.
9. To reset the Ribbon or Quick Access Toolbar, click the **Reset** list arrow, and then select a reset option.
10. Click **OK**.

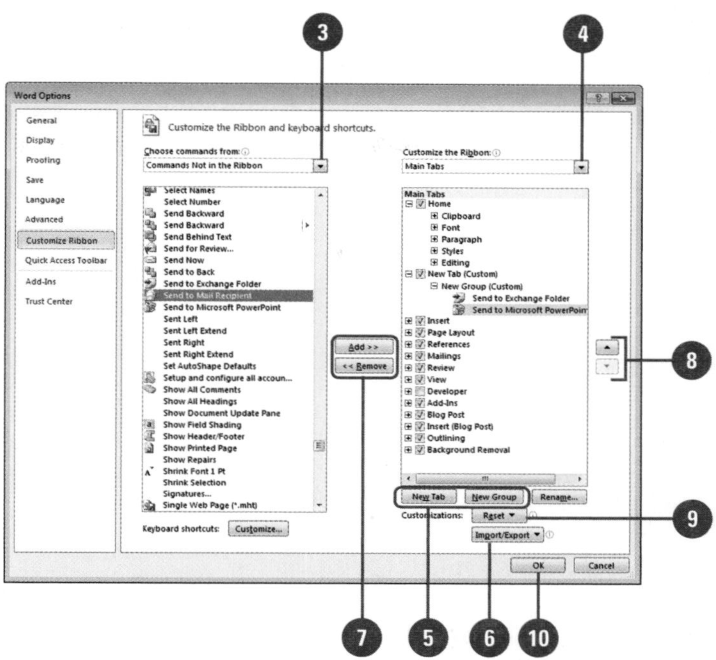

For Your Information

Moving Toolbars and the Ribbon

You can move the Quick Access Toolbar to another location. Click the Customize Quick Access Toolbar list arrow, and then click Show Below The Ribbon or Show Above The Ribbon. You can minimize the Ribbon (**New!**). Click the Minimize The Ribbon (Ctrl+F1) button on the right side of the Ribbon (to the left of the Help button). Click the Expand The Ribbon button to maximize it. When the Ribbon is minimized, you can click a tab to auto maximize it. When you click an option or in the document, the Ribbon minimizes again. Just like an auto-hide option.

Changing ScreenTips

You can turn off or change ScreenTips. Click the File tab, click Options, click General, click the ScreenTip Style list arrow, click Don't Show Feature Descriptions In ScreenTips or Don't Show ScreenTips, and then click OK.

Choosing Dialog Box Options

A **dialog box** is a window that opens when you click a Dialog Box Launcher. **Dialog Box Launchers** are small icons that appear at the bottom corner of some groups. When you point to a Dialog Box Launcher, a ScreenTip with a thumbnail of the dialog box appears to show you which dialog box opens. A dialog box allows you to supply more information before the program carries out the command you selected. After you enter information or make selections in a dialog box, click the OK button to complete the command. Click the Cancel button to close the dialog box without issuing the command. In many dialog boxes, you can also click an Apply button to apply your changes without closing the dialog box. Rather than clicking to move around a dialog box, you can press the Tab key to move from one box or button to the next. You can also use Shift+Tab to move backward, or Ctrl+Tab and Ctrl+Shift+Tab to move between dialog box tabs.

Choose Dialog Box Options

All dialog boxes contain the same types of options, including the following:

- **Tabs**. Each tab groups a related set of options. Click a tab to display its options.
- **Option buttons**. Click an option button to select it. You can usually only select one.
- **Up and down arrows**. Click the up or down arrow to increase or decrease the number, or type a number in the box.
- **Check box**. Click the box to turn on or off the option. A checked box means the option is selected; a cleared box means it's not.
- **List box**. Click the list arrow to display a list of options, and then click the option you want.
- **Text box**. Click in the box and type the requested information.
- **Button**. Click a button to perform a specific action or command. A button name followed by an ellipsis (...) opens a dialog box.
- **Preview box**. Many dialog boxes show an image that reflects the options you select.

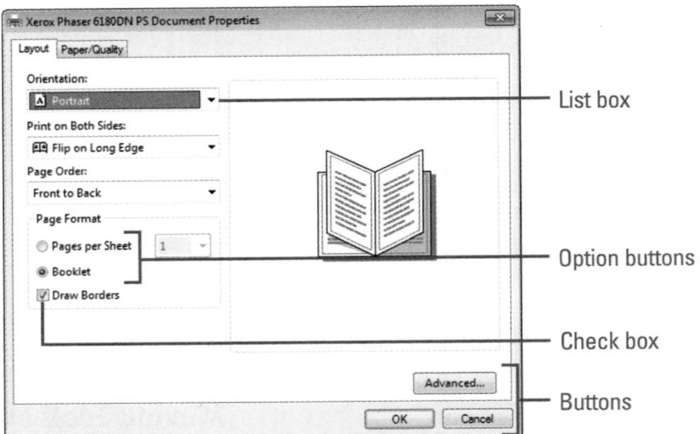

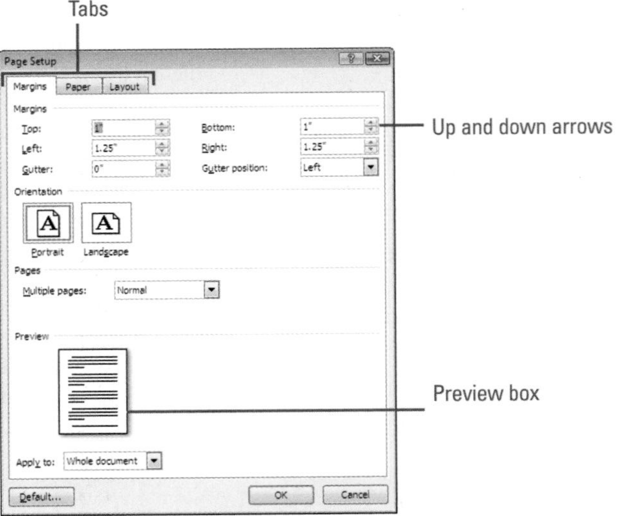

Using the Status Bar

The **Status bar** appears across the bottom of your screen and displays document information—such as word count, page numbers, language, and current display zoom percentage—and some Word program controls, such as view shortcut buttons, zoom slider, and Fit To Window button. With the click of the mouse, you can quickly customize exactly what you see on the Status bar. In addition to displaying information, the Status bar also allows you to check the on/off status of certain features, such as Signatures, Permissions, Selection Mode, Page Number, Caps Lock, Num Lock, Macro Recording and Playback, and much more.

Add or Remove Items from the Status Bar

- **Add Item**. Right-click the Status bar, and then click an unchecked item.
- **Remove Item**. Right-click the Status bar, and then click a checked item.

See Also

See "Recording a Macro" on page 411 or "Adding a Digital Signature to a Macro Project" on page 416 for information on changing the status of items on the Status bar.

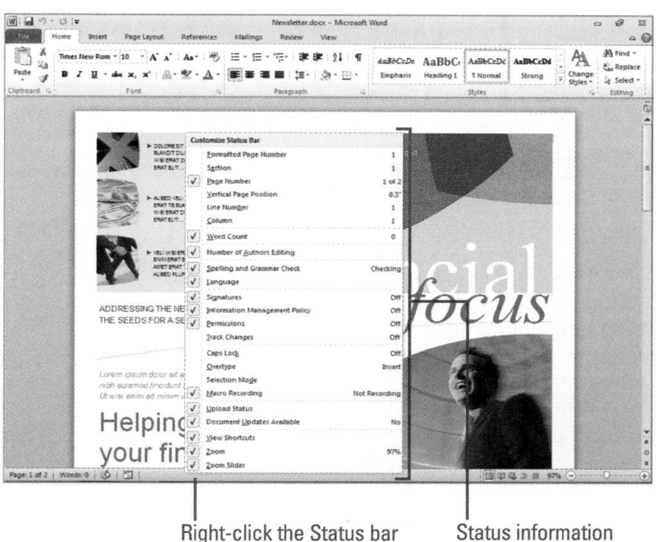

Using Task and Window Panes

Task panes are separate windows that appear when you need them, such as Navigation pane, or when you click a Dialog Box Launcher icon, such as Clipboard and Clip Art. A task pane displays various options that relate to the current task. **Window panes** are sections of a window, such as a split window. If you need a larger work area, you can use the Close button in the upper-right corner of the pane to close a task or window pane, or move a border edge (for task panes) or **splitter** (for window panes) to resize it.

Work with Task and Window Panes

- **Open a Task Pane.** It appears when you need it or when you click a Dialog Box Launcher icon.
- **Close a Task or Window Pane.** Click the Close button in upper-right corner of the pane.
- **Resize a Task Pane.** Point to the Task Pane border edge until the pointer changes to double arrows, then drag the edge to resize it.
- **Resize a Window Pane.** Point to the window pane border bar until the pointer changes to a double bar with arrows, then drag the edge to resize it.

Did You Know?

You can insert window panes. Click the View tab, click the Split button in the Window group.

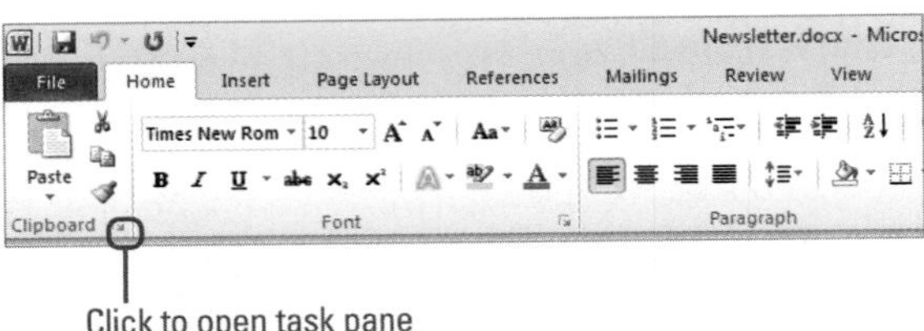

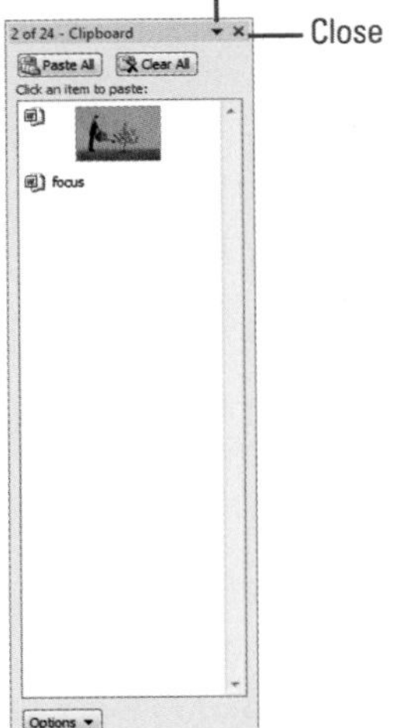

Move Task Panes

1. Open the task pane you want to move.
2. Point to the title bar.

   The cursor changes to a 4-headed arrow.
3. Drag the task pane to a new location.

   The task pane becomes undocked.
4. To redock a task pane, drag the task pane to the left or right side of the program window. Keep dragging until the task pane snaps into place.

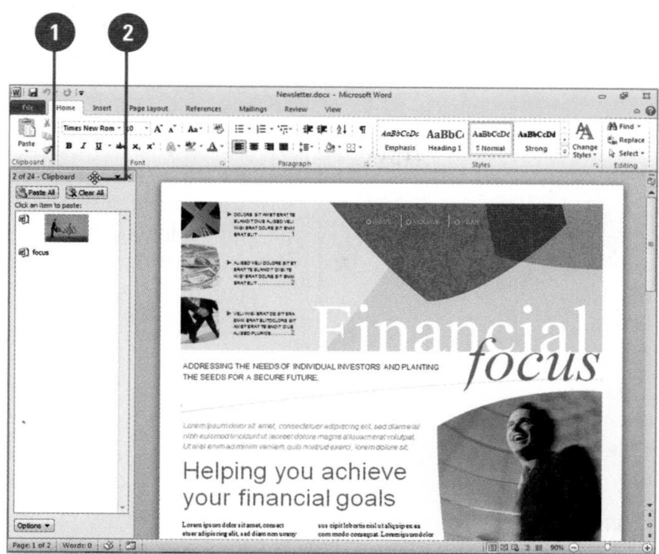

Opening an Existing Document

You can open a Word document and start Word simultaneously, or you can open a Word document or file created in another program after you start Word. You can open an existing Word document by using the File tab (**New!**). On the File tab, you can choose the Open command to locate and select the document you want or choose a recently used document from the Recent Documents or Recent Places list on the Recent screen (**New!**). Similar to the Windows Start menu, the Recent Documents or Recent Places list allow you to pin documents to the list that you want to remain accessible regardless of recent use. The Pin icon to the right of the file name on the File tab makes it easy to pin or unpin as needed.

Open a Document from the Program Window

1. Click the **File** tab, and then click **Open**.
2. If you want to open a specific file type, click the **Files of type** list arrow, and then click a file type.
3. If the file is located in another folder, click the **Look In** list arrow, and then navigate to the file.
4. Click the Word file you want, and then click **Open**, or click the **Open** button arrow, and then click one of the following options:
   - **Open Read-Only** to open the selected file with protection.
   - **Open as Copy** to open a copy of the selected file.
   - **Open in Browser** to open the selected Web file in a browser.
   - **Open with Transform** to open the selected XML file with transform.
   - **Open in Protected View** to open the selected file in protected view (**New!**).
   - **Open and Repair** to open the damaged file.

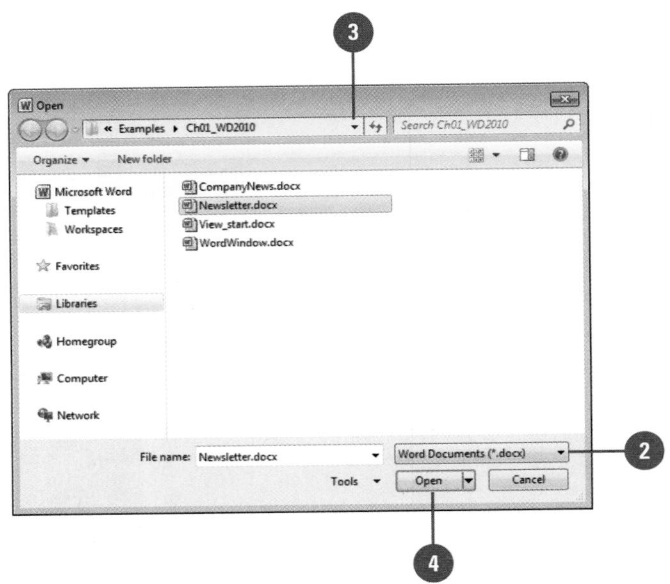

For Your Information

Using the Office Program Viewer

An Office program Viewer—PowerPoint, Word, and Excel—is a program used to open and view Office documents on computers that don't have Microsoft Office installed. The Office program Viewer is available for download from the Microsoft Office Online Web site in the downloads section. Check the Microsoft Web site for software requirements.

Open a Recently Opened Document

1. Click the **File** tab, and then click **Recent**.
2. Click the document you want to open in the Recent Documents list or a folder in the Recent Places list.
   - **Pin a document/folder**. Click the Pin icon (right-side) to display a green pin (document is pinned) on the Recent Documents or Recent Places list (**New!**).
   - **Unpin a document/folder**. Click the Pin icon (right-side) to display a grey pin on the Recent Documents or Recent Places list (**New!**).

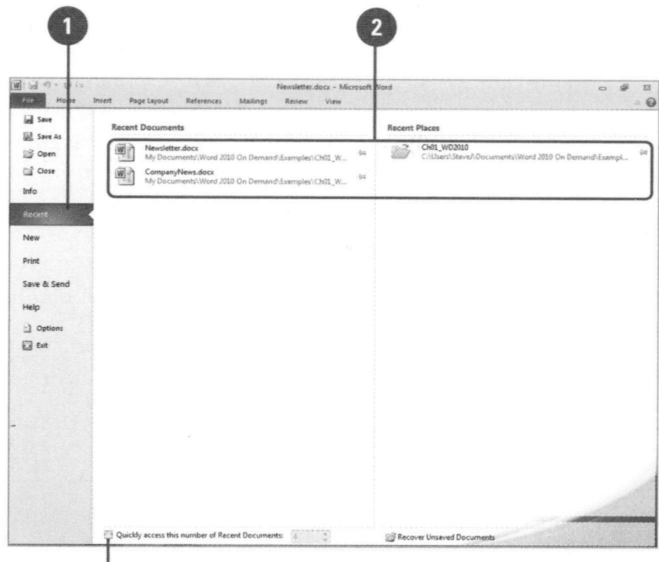

Select to add recent documents to the File tab

Did You Know?

***You can add recently used documents to the File tab* (New!).** Click the File tab,click Recent, select the Quickly Access This Number Of Recent Documents check box, and then specify the number of documents you want to display.

You can change the number of recently opened files that appear on the File tab. Click the File tab, click Options, click Advanced, change the Show This Number Of Recent Documents list, and then click OK.

You can change the default file location of the Open dialog box. Click the File tab, click Options, click Save, enter a new location in the Default File Location box, and then click OK.

For Your Information

Managing Files in the Open or Save Dialog

When you open the Open or Save As dialog box, you can manage files directly in the dialog box. You can delete or rename a file in a dialog box. In the Open or Save As dialog box, click the file, click the Tools list arrow (XP) or the Organize button (7 or Vista), and then click Delete or Rename. You can also quickly move or copy a file in a dialog box. In the Open or Save As dialog box, right-click the file you want to move or copy, click Cut or Copy, open the folder where you want to paste the file, right-click a blank area, and then click Paste.

Opening Files of Different Types

Word recognizes and can open files created in a wide variety of other programs including, but not limited to: OpenDocument, WordPerfect, Microsoft Works, Text Files, Rich Text Format, XML, and Web pages. When you open a document that was created in an older version of Word, Word opens it automatically into the current version.

Open a File in a Non-Word Format

1. Click the **File** tab, and then click **Open**.
2. Click the **Files of type** list arrow, and then select the type of file that you want to open.
3. Click the **Look in** list arrow, and then navigate to the file.
4. Select the document file you want to open.
5. Click **Open**.

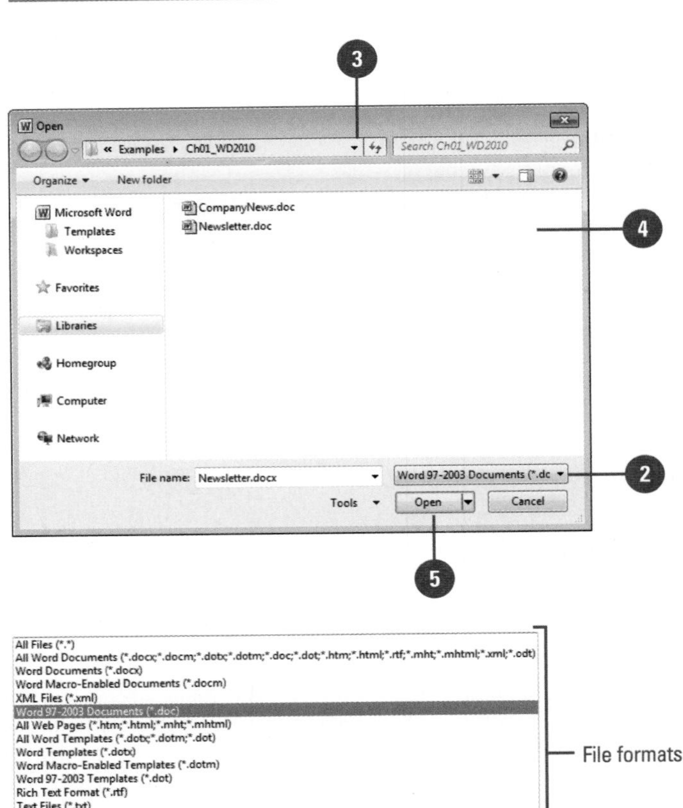

Converting an Existing Document

When you open a document from Word 97-2003 or Word 2007, Word 2010 goes into compatibility mode (**New!**)—indicated on the title bar—where it disables new features that cannot be displayed or converted well by previous versions. When you save a document, Word 2010 saves Word 97-2003 or 2007 files in their older format using compatibility mode. The document stays in compatibility mode until you convert it to the Word 2010 file format. Word 2007 and Word 2010 use the same file extensions, however there may be feature differences between the two versions.

Convert a Word 97-2003 or 2007 Document to Word 2010

1. Open the Word document 97-2003 or 2007 you want to convert to the Word 2010 file format.

   The Word document opens in compatibility mode.

2. Click the **File** tab, and then click **Info**.
3. Click **Convert**.
4. Click **OK** to convert the file to the Word 2010 format.

   Word exits compatibility mode, which is only turned on when a previous version is in use.

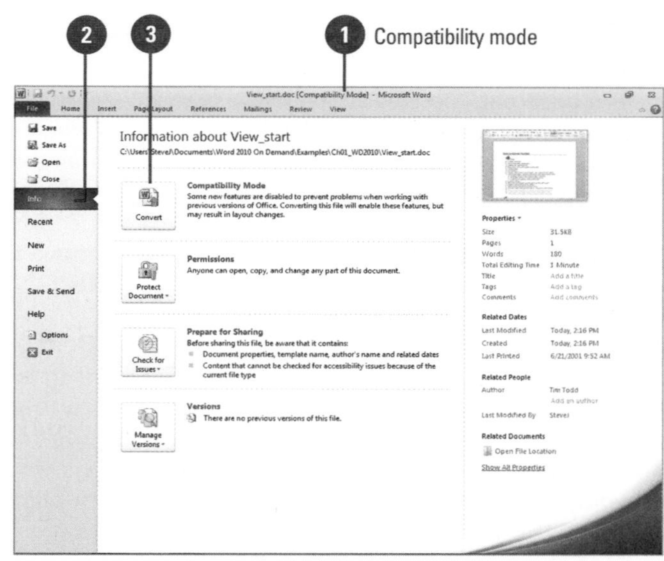

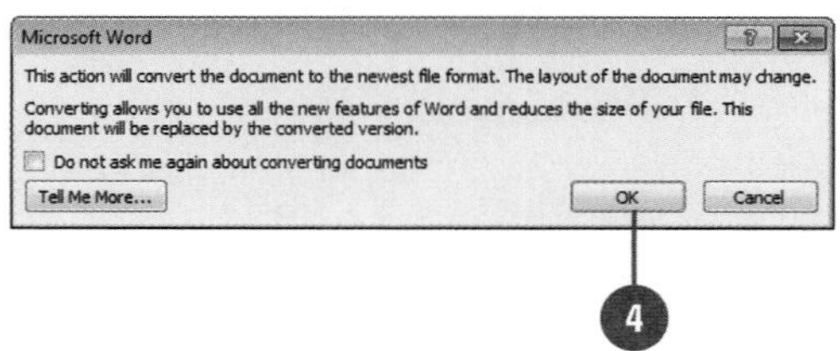

Did You Know?

You can display extensions in the Save and Open dialog boxes and Recent Documents list. Changing the Windows option also changes Word. In the Folder Options dialog box on the View tab, clear the Hide Extensions For Known File Types check box, and then click OK.

Changing Document Views

Word displays the contents of a document in different ways to help you work efficiently with your content. The available views include: Print Layout, Full Screen Reading, Web Layout, Outline, and Draft. You can change the window view from the View tab, or you can click a Document view button at the bottom right corner of the Word window.

Print Layout view displays a gray gap between each page to clearly delineate where each actual page break occurs. Word displays each new document in Print Layout view by default. This view is best for previewing your work before printing, and it works well with the Zoom feature on the View tab to increase and decrease the page view size and display multiple pages of the same document simultaneously onscreen.

Full Screen Reading view displays the full screen and removes distracting screen elements to provide a more comfortable view to read your documents. You can also display the Navigation pane (**New!**) to quickly jump to different parts of your document. When you're done, you can use the Close button.

Web Layout view displays the document as it will appear on the Web. You can save documents as HTML code to make Web content creation easy.

Outline view displays the document as an outline with headings and subheadings. When you shift to Outline view, each heading has a clickable plus or minus sign next to it to expand or collapse the content under the heading. You can drag a plus, or minus sign to move the heading and all of its associated text.

Draft view displays the document as a single, long piece of "paper," divided into pages by perforation marks. This view is fine for composition but inadequate for editing or previewing your work prior to printing or other publication.

Print Layout view

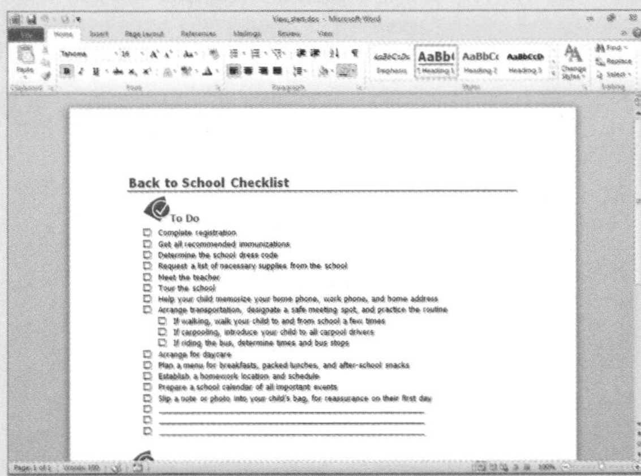

Full Screen Reading view

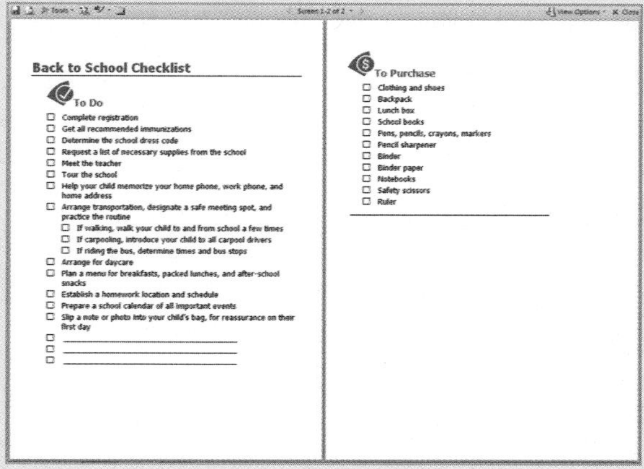

Web Layout view

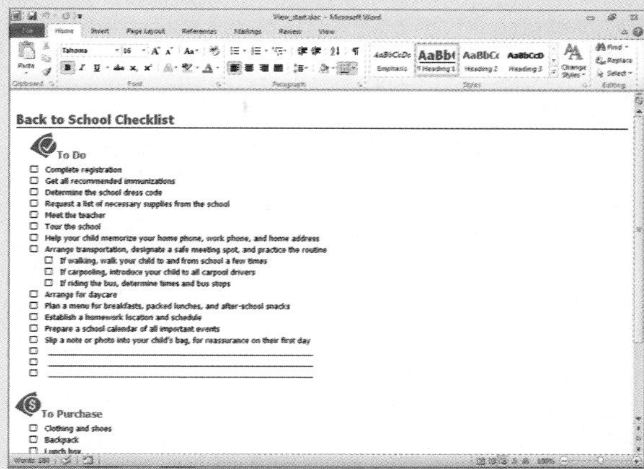

Outline view

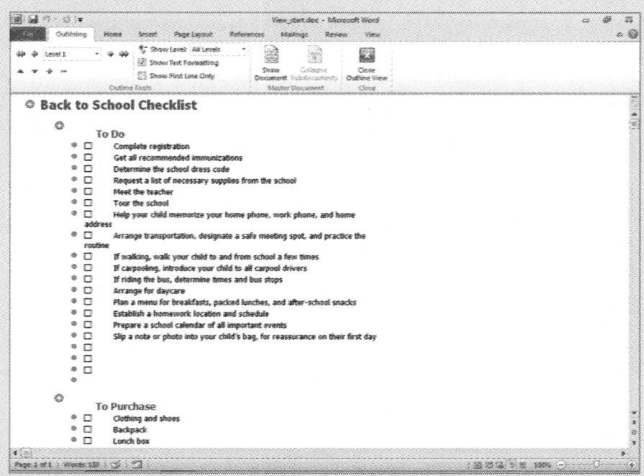

Draft view

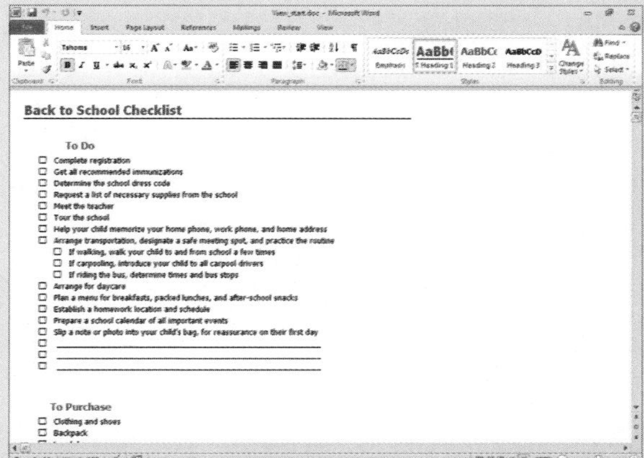

Reading a Document

You can avoid eye strain when you want to read a document with the Full Screen Reading view. The Full Screen Reading view is designed with tools optimized for reading a document. Word changes the screen size and removes distracting screen elements to provide a more comfortable view for reading your documents. In the Full Screen Reading view, you can display the Navigation pane (**New!**) with the Browse Heading or Browse Pages tab to quickly jump to different parts of your document. You can also save, print, access tools, highlight text, and insert comments. If you have a Tablet PC, you can write comments and changes directly on the page using the tablet's stylus.

Read a Document

1. Click the **Full Screen Reading View** button.
   - The Full Screen Reading View button is also available on the View tab.
2. To display the text in a larger or smaller size, click the **View Options** button, and then click **Increase Text Size** or **Decrease Text Size**.
3. To display two pages at once or a single page, click the **View Options** button, and then click **Show One Page** or **Show Two Pages**.

   TIMESAVER *Press Esc to deselect the document, type a number, and then press Enter to go to a page.*
4. When you're done, click the **Close** button.

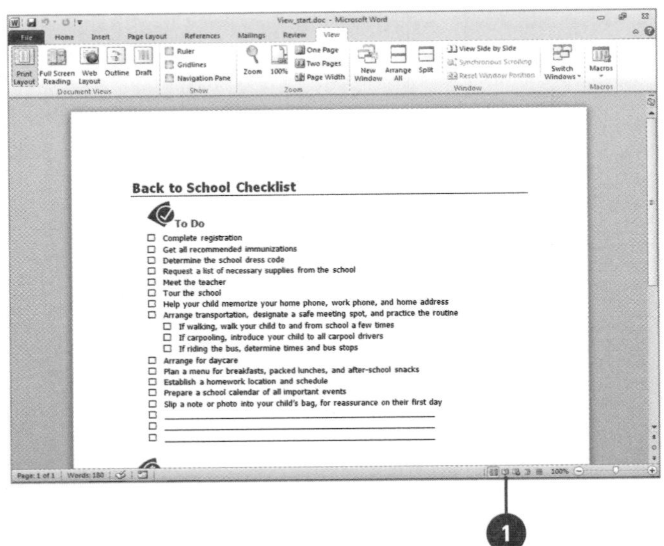

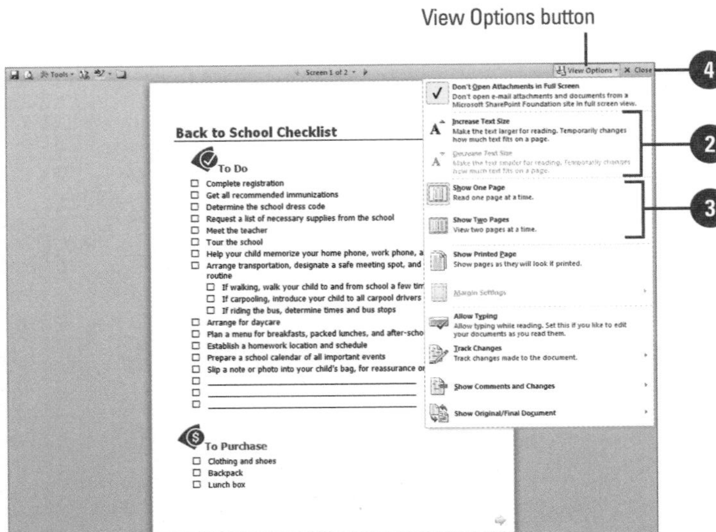

Did You Know?

You can disable open e-mail attachments in Full Screen Reading view. Click the File tab, click Options, click General, clear the Open E-mail Attachments In Full Screen Reading View check box, and then click OK.

Display Headings or Page View

1. Click the **Full Screen Reading View** button.
2. Click the **Navigation** button, and then click **Navigation Pane**.
3. Click the **Browse Headings** or **Browse Pages** tab.
4. Click a heading name or thumbnail of a page to display it.
5. To close the Navigation pane, click the **Close** button on the pane.
6. When you're done, click the **Close** button.

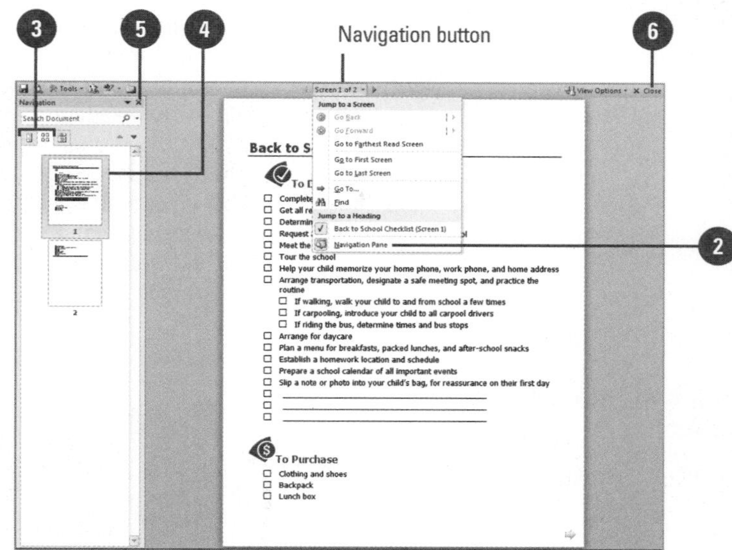

Change Full Screen Reading View Options

1. Click the **Full Screen Reading View** button.
2. Click the **View Options** buttons.
3. Click the view you want to display.
   - **Don't Open Attachments in Full Screen**.
   - **Show Printed Page**.
   - **Margin Settings**.
   - **Allow Typing**.
   - **Track Changes**.
   - **Show Comments and Changes**.
   - **Show Original/Final Document**.
4. When you're done, click the **Close** button.

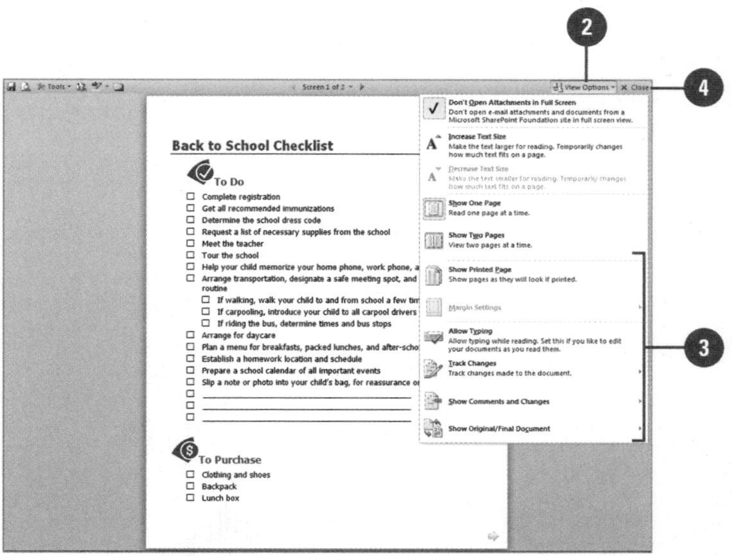

Getting Help While You Work

At some time, everyone has a question or two about the program they are using. The Office Help Viewer provides the answers and resources you need, including feature help, articles, tips, templates, training, and downloads. By connecting to Microsoft Office Online, you not only have access to standard product help information, but you also have access to updated information over the Web without leaving the Help Viewer. The Web browser-like Help Viewer allows you to browse an extensive catalog of topics using a table of contents to locate information, or ask a question or enter phrases to search for specific information. When you use any of these help options, a list of possible answers is shown to you with the most likely answer or most frequently-used at the top of the list.

Use the Help Viewer to Get Answers

1. Click the **Help** button on the Ribbon.

   TIMESAVER *Press F1.*

2. Locate the Help topic you want.
   - Click a Help category on the home page, and then click a topic (? icon).
   - Click the **Show/Hide Table of Contents** button on the toolbar, click a help category (book icon) and then click a topic (? icon).
3. Read the topic, and then click any links to get Help information.
4. Click the **Back**, **Forward**, **Stop**, **Refresh**, and **Home** buttons on the toolbar to move around in the Help Viewer.
5. If you want to print the topic, click the **Print** button on the toolbar.
6. To keep the Help Viewer window (not maximized) on top or behind, click to toggle the **Keep On Top** button (pin pushed in) and **Not On Top** button (pin not pushed in) on the toolbar.
7. When you're done, click the **Close** button.

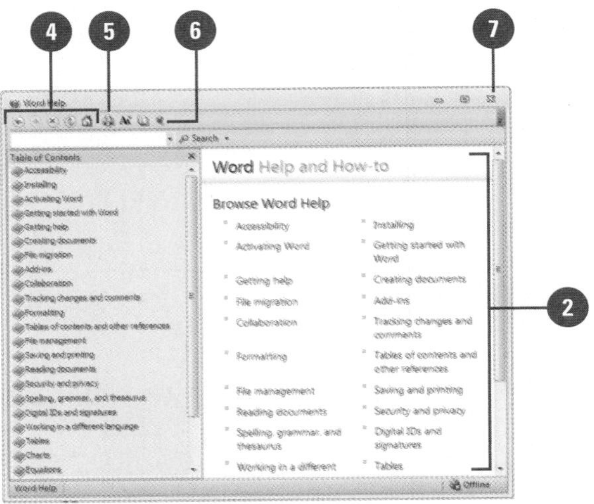

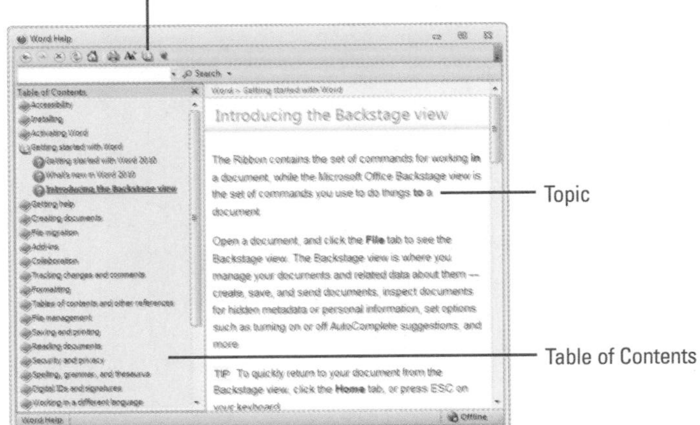

Search for Help

1. Click the **Help** button on the Ribbon.
2. Click the **Search button** list arrow below the toolbar, and then select the location and type of information you want.
3. Type one or more keywords in the Search For box, and then click the **Search** button.
4. Click a topic.
5. Read the topic, and then click any links to get information on related topics or definitions.
6. When you're done, click the **Close** button.

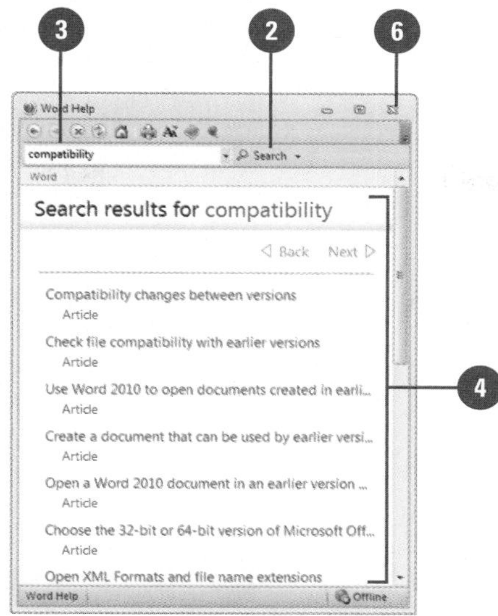

Check Help Connection Status

1. Click the **Help** button on the Ribbon.
2. Click the Connection Status at the bottom of the Help Viewer.
3. Click the connection option where you want to get help information:
   - **Show content from Office.com** to get help from this computer and the internet (online).
   - **Show content only from this computer** to get help from this computer only (offline).

   This setting is maintained for all Office 2010 program Help Viewers.
4. When you're done, click the **Close** button.

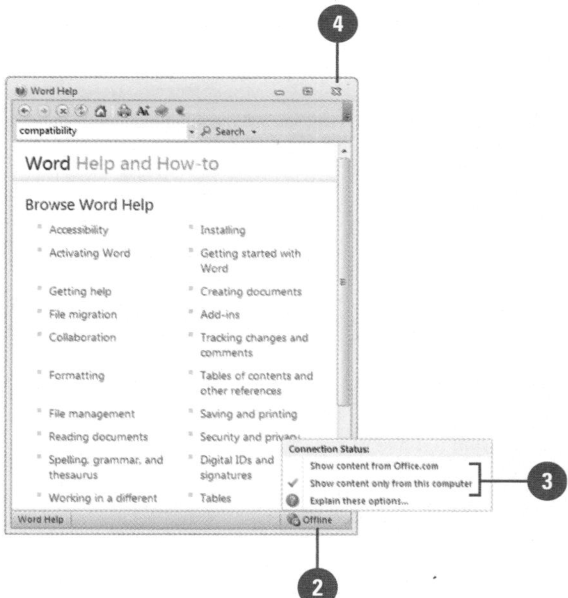

Saving a Document

When you create a Word document, save it as a file on your computer so you can work with it later. When you save a document for the first time or if you want to save a copy of a file, use the Save As command. When you want to save an open document, use the Save button on the Quick Access Toolbar. When you save a document, Word 2010 saves 97-2003 files in an older format using compatibility mode and 2007-2010 files in an XML (Extensible Markup Language) based file format. The XML format significantly reduces file sizes, provides enhanced file recovery, and allows for increased compatibility, sharing, reuse, and transportability. A Word 97-2003 or 2007 document stays in compatibility mode—indicated on the title bar—until you convert it to the 2010 file format. Compatibility mode disables new features that cannot be displayed or converted well by previous versions.

Save a Word 2010 Document

1. Click the **File** tab, and then click **Save As**.

   TIMESAVER *Press Ctrl+S to save a document in its current format.*

2. Click the **Save in** list arrow, and then click the drive or folder where you want to save the file.
3. Type a document file name.
4. Click the **Save as type** list arrow, and then click **Word Document**.
5. Click the **Authors** or **Tags** box to enter Document Properties.
6. Click **Save**.

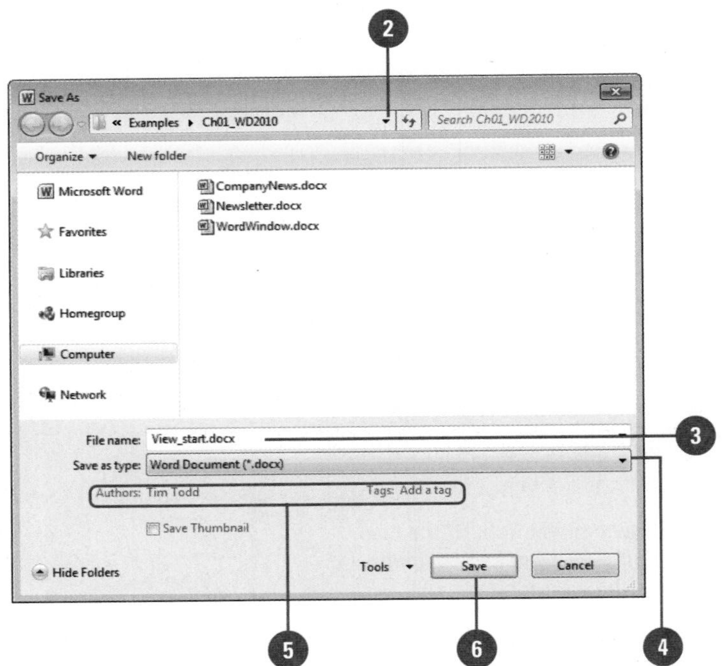

Did You Know?

You can access options from the Save dialog box. In the Save dialog box, click Tools, and then click the command option you want, either General, Web, or Compress Pictures.

Save a Word 97-2003 or 2007 Document in Compatibility Mode

1. Open the Word 97-2003 or 2007 document you want to continue to save in the 97-2003 or 2007 format.

   The Word document opens in compatibility mode.

2. Click the **Save** button on the Quick Access Toolbar, or click the **File** tab, and then click **Save**.

   Word stays in compatibility mode.

Did You Know?

You can use the Format tab under Text Box Tools in Compatibility mode. The Format tab under Text Box Tools has been integrated into the Format tab under Drawing Tools in Word 2010. However, in Compatibility mode, the Format tab under Text Box Tools is available.

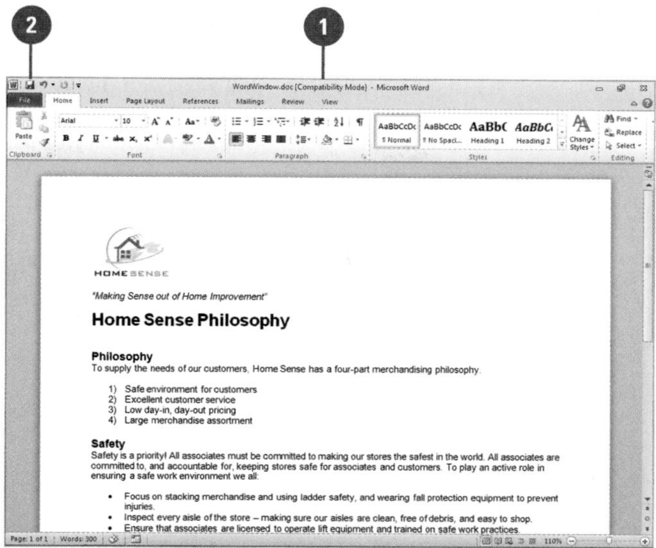

Set Save Options

1. Click the **File** tab, and then click **Options**.
2. In the left pane, click **Save**.
3. Set the save options you want:
   - **Default Save Format.** Click the **Save files in this format** list arrow, and then click the default format you want.
   - **Default File Location.** Specify the complete path to the folder location where you want to save your document.
4. Click **OK**.

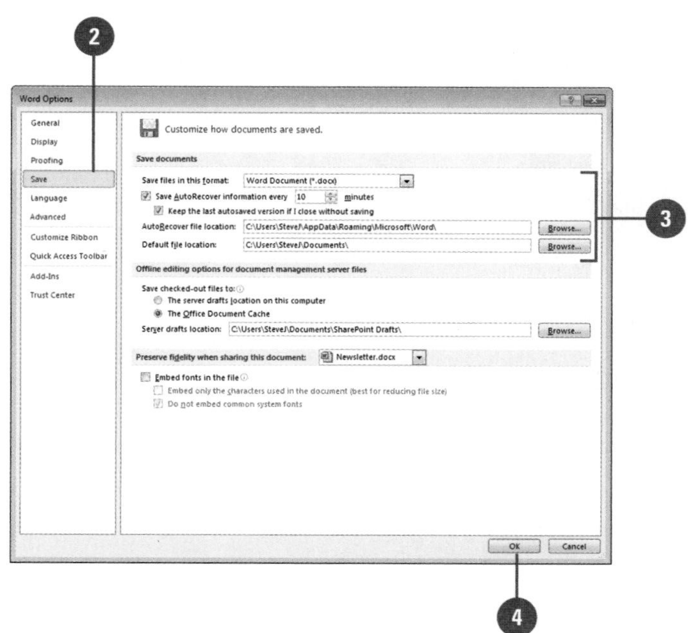

Saving a Document with Different Formats

Word is a versatile suite of programs that allow you to save your documents in a variety of different formats—see the table on the following page for a complete list and description. For example, you might want to save your document as a Web page that you can view in a Web browser. Or you can save a document in an earlier 97-2003 version in case the people you work with have not upgraded to Word 2010. If you save a document to 97-2003, some new features and formatting are converted to uneditable pictures or not retained. The format is compatible with Office 2003, Office XP, and Office 2000 with a software patch. However, for best results, if you're creating a document for someone with Word 97 to Word 2003, it's better to save it with the .doc file format.

Save a Document with Another Format

1. Click the **File** tab, and then click **Save & Send**.
2. Click **Change File Type**.
3. Click the file type you want.
4. Click the **Save As** button.

   The Save As dialog box opens with the selected file type.

   - You can also click the **File** tab, click **Save As**, and then select a file format.
5. Click the **Save in** list arrow, and then select the location where you want to save the file.
6. Type a file name.
7. Click **Save**.

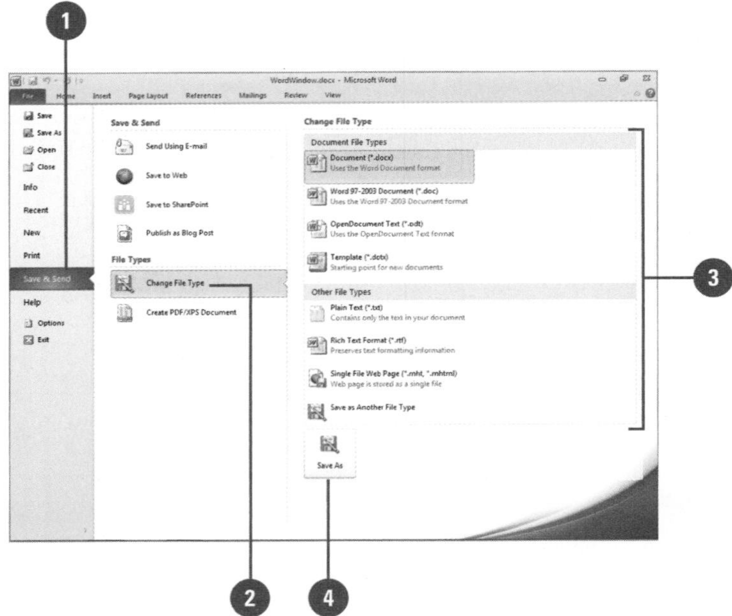

See Also

See "Creating a PDF Document" on page 376 or "Creating an XPS Document" on page 377 for information on using and saving a file with different formats.

Word 2010 Save File Formats

Save As file type	Extension	Used to save
Word Document	.docx	Word 2007-2010 document
Word Macro-Enabled Document	.docm	Word 2007-2010 document that contains Visual Basic for Applications (VBA) code
Word 97-2003 Document	.doc	Word 97 to Word 2003 document
Word Template	.dotx	Word 2007-2010 Template
Word Macro-Enabled Template	.dotm	Word 2007-2010 template that includes preapproved macros
Word 97-2003 Templates	.dot	Word 97-2003 template
PDF	.pdf	Fixed-layout electronic file format that preserves document formatting developed by Adobe
XPS Document Format	.xps	Fixed-layout electronic file format that preserves document formatting developed by Microsoft
Single File Web Page	.mht; .mhtml	Web page as a single file with an .htm file
Web Page	.htm; .html	Web page as a folder with an .htm file
Web Page, Filtered	.htm; .html	Web page as a folder with an .htm file with a reduced file size
Rich Text Format	.rtf	Text files with formatting
Plain Text	.txt	Plain text files; no formatting
Word XML Document	.xml	XML document
Word 2003 XML Document	.xml	Word 2003 XML document
OpenDocument Text	.odt	OpenDocument text document; a document created from the OpenOffice program
Works 6.0 - 9.0	.wps	Works 6.0-9.0 files

Checking Compatibility

The Compatibility Checker identifies the potential loss of functionality between a Word 2010 document and a Word 97-2003 or 2007 document. The Compatibility Checker generates a report that provides a summary of the potential losses and the number of occurrences in the document. You can also specify what versions to show (**New!**) compatibility issues. Use the report information to determine what caused each message and for suggestions on how to change it. If the loss is due to a newer feature in Word 2010—such as custom layouts or Quick Styles applied to shapes, pictures, and WordArt—you might be able to simply remove the effect or feature. In other cases, you might not be able to do anything about it. To maintain a visual appearance, SmartArt graphics and other objects with new effects are converted to bitmaps to preserve their overall look and cannot be edited. In Word 2010, the Format tab under Text Box Tools has been integrated with the Format tab under Drawing Tools. However, if you're working with a document in compatibility mode, the Format tab under Text Box Tools is still available.

Check Compatibility

1. Click the **File** tab, and then click **Info**.
2. Click the **Check For Issues** button, and then click **Check Compatibility**.

   Word checks compatibility of the document for non supported features in earlier versions of the Word program.
3. Click the **Select versions to show** list arrow, and then select one or more versions to check (**New!**).
4. View the compatibility summary information, so you can make changes, as necessary.
5. To have the compatibility checker review the Office document when the Office program saves the file, select the **Check compatibility when saving documents** check box.
6. Click **OK**.

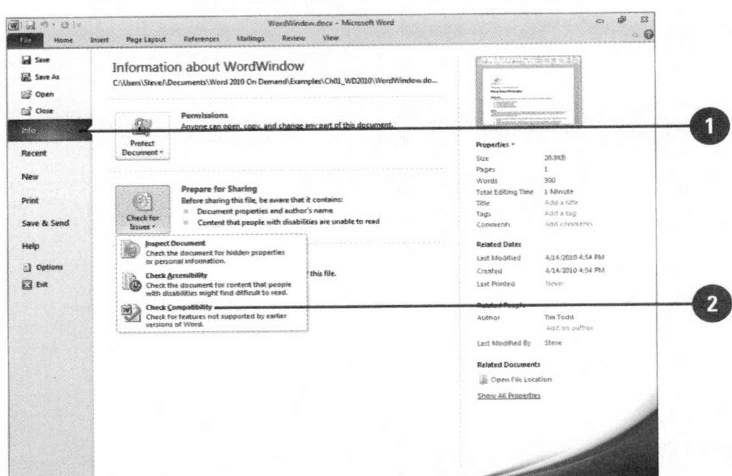

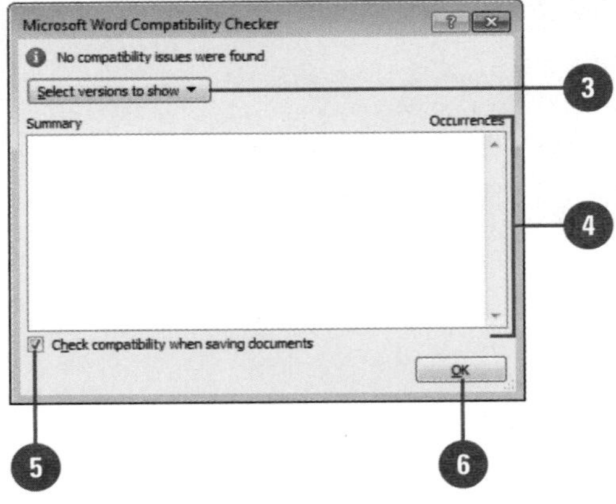

Checking Accessibility

The Accessibility Checker (**New!**) identifies potential difficulties that people with disabilities might have reading or interactive with an Office document. The Accessibility Checker generates a list of errors and warning and possible fixes in the Accessibility Checker panel. Use the information to determine what caused each issue and for suggestions on how to fix it. In addition to the Accessibility Checker, you can also add alternative text (also known as alt text) (**New!**) to objects and other items to provide information for people with visual impairments who may be unable to easily or fully see it. Alternative text also helps people with screen readers understand the content in a document. You can create alternative text for shapes, pictures, charts, tables, SmartArt graphics, or other objects. When you point to an object with alternative text in a screen reader or DAISY (digital Accessible Information System) or in most browsers, the alternative text appears.

Check Accessibility and Add Alternative Text

1. Click the **File** tab, and then click **Info**.
2. Click the **Check For Issues** button, and then click **Check Accessibility**.

   Office checks compatibility for content that people with disabilities might find difficult to read.
3. View the compatibility summary information of errors and warnings in the Accessibility Checker panel.
4. Select an issue under Inspection Results to find out how to fix it under Additional Information.
5. To add alternative text, right-click the object or item, point to a command (varies depending on the object or item), such as Format, click **Alternative Text** or **Alt Text**, enter a title and description, and then click **OK**.
6. When you're done with the Accessibility Checker panel, click the **Close** button on the panel.

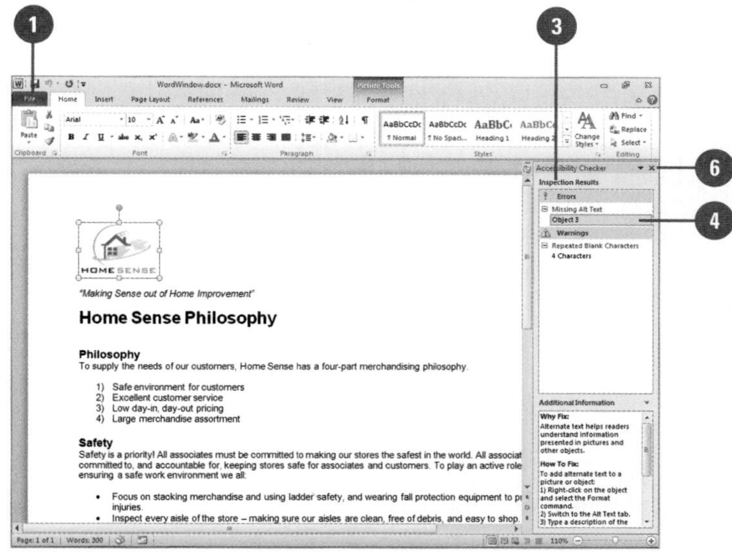

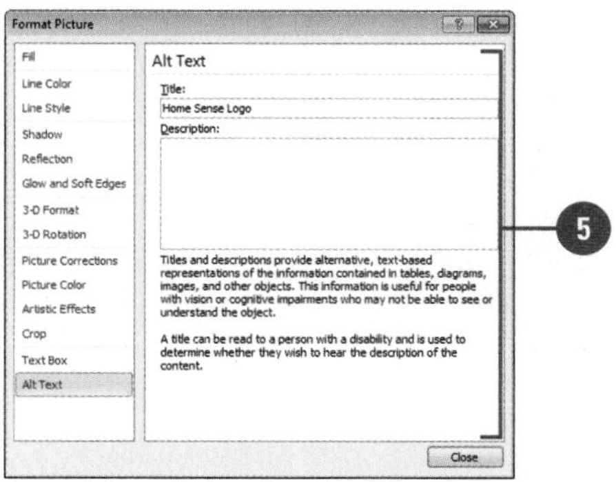

Documenting Properties

Word automatically documents properties while you work—such as file size, save dates, and various statistics—and allows you to document other properties, such as title, author, subject, keywords, category, and status. You can view or edit standard document properties or create advanced custom properties by using the **Document Information Panel**, which is an XML-based Microsoft InfoPath form hosted in the Office program. You can use document properties—also known as **metadata**—to help you manage and track files; search tools can use the metadata to find a document based on your search criteria. If you associate a document property to an item in the document, the document property updates when you change the item.

View and Edit Document Properties

1. Click the **File** tab, and then click **Info**.
2. To display other properties, click the **Properties** button, and then select an option:
   - **Show Document Panel.** Shows Document panel in the document.
   - **Advanced Properties.** Displays the Properties dialog box.
3. Enter the standard properties, such as author, title, subject, keywords, category, status, and comments.
   - **Show All Properties.** Click the link to displays more options.

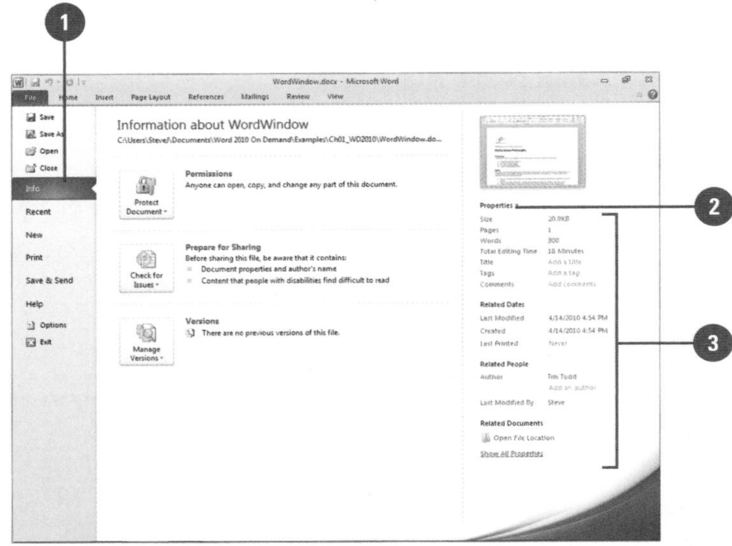

Document Panel

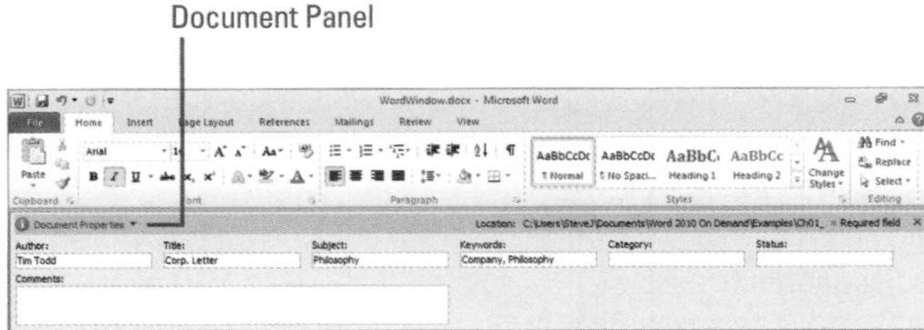

Did You Know?

You can view or change document properties when you open or save a file. In the Open or Save As dialog box, select the document you want, click the arrow next to the Views, and then click Details to view file size and last changed date, or click Properties to view all information. If you want to insert or change author names or keywords, click the Authors box or Tags box, and then type what you want.

Zooming the View In and Out

Working with the Zoom tools gives you one more way to control exactly what you see in a Word document. The Zoom tools are located in the bottom-right corner of the window. Large documents are difficult to work with and difficult to view. Many documents, when viewed at 100%, are larger than the maximized size of the window. When this happens, viewing the entire worksheet requires reducing the zoom.

Change the View

1. Use any of the following zoom options available on the Status bar:
   - **Zoom Out**. Click to zoom out (percentage gets smaller).
   - **Zoom In**. Click to zoom in (percentage gets larger).
   - **Slider**. Drag to zoom out or in to the percentage you want.
   - **Zoom Level**. Click to display the Zoom dialog box, where you can select the magnification you want.
2. For additional zoom options, click the **View** tab, and then use any of the following options:
   - **Zoom**. Click to display the Zoom dialog box, where you can select the magnification you want.

     This is the same as Zoom Level above.
   - **100%**. Click to display the view at 100%.
   - **One Page**. Click to display one page at a time.
   - **Two Pages**. Click to display two pages at at time.
   - **Page Width**. Click to display the page to the current window width.

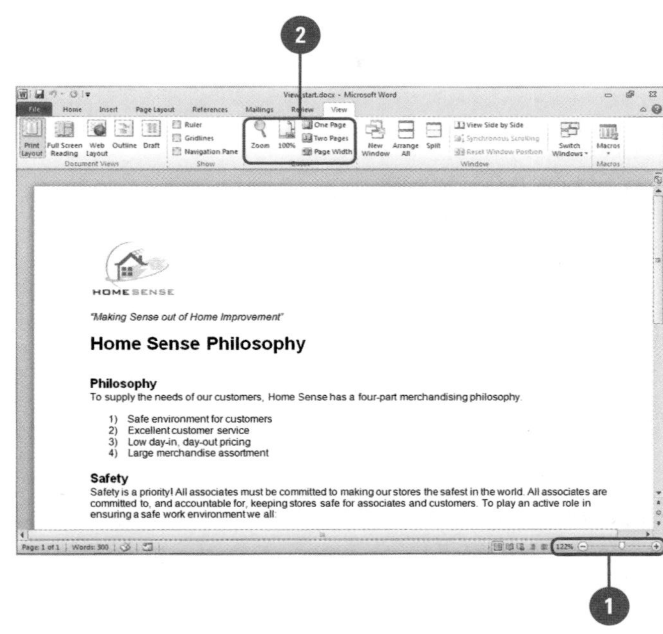

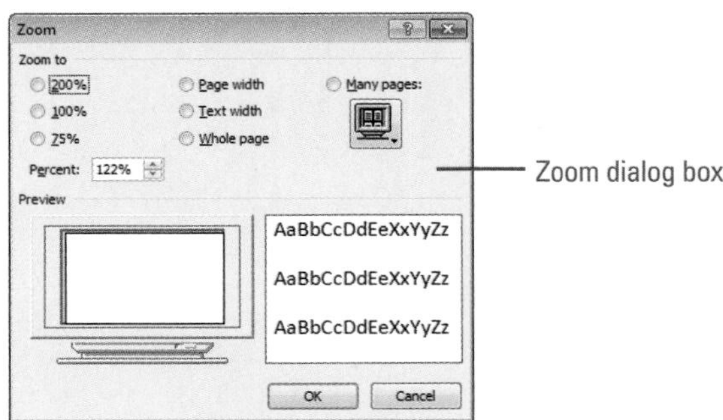

Zoom dialog box

Recovering a Document

If Word encounters a problem and stops responding, the program automatically tries to recover the file. The recovered files are stored and managed by Word. You can use the Manage Versions button (**New!**) on the Info screen under the File tab to open any available recovered unsaved files. If you have a lot of recovered files, you can also delete all file versions to save disk space. To use the AutoRecover option, you need to enable it in the Save category of the Options dialog box. You can set AutoRecover options to periodically save a temporary copy of your current file, which ensures proper recovery of the file and allows you to revert to an earlier version of a file. In addition, if you didn't save your changes when you closed a document, you can select an AutoRecover option to save your work as a safe guard (**New!**).

Recover or Revert a Document

1. Click the **File** tab, and then click **Info**.
2. To open a recovered or previous version, click a file from the available list.
3. Click the **Manage Versions** button, and then click **Recover Unsaved Documents**.

   TIMESAVER *Click the File tab, click Recent, and then click Recover Unsaved Documents folder icon.*
4. Select the file version you want to recover.
5. Click **Open**.

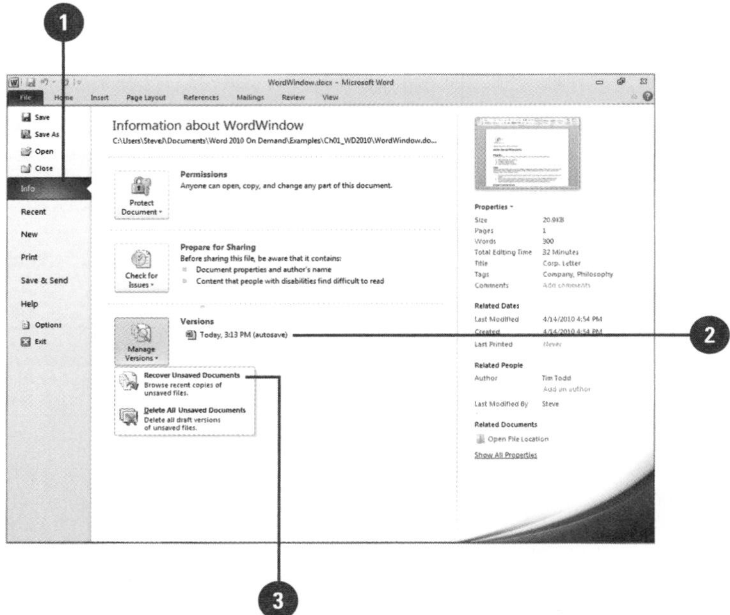

Did You Know?

You can delete all draft versions of unsaved files. Click the File tab, click Info, click the Manage Versions button, click Delete All Unsaved Documents, and then click Yes to confirm the deletions.

Use AutoRecover

1. Click the **File** tab, and then click **Options**.
2. In the left pane, click **Save**.
3. Select the **Save AutoRecover information every *x* minutes** check box.
4. Enter the number of minutes, or click the **Up** and **Down** arrows to adjust the minutes.
5. Select the **Keep the last autosaved version if I close without saving** check box as a safe guard to save your work if you don't save it (**New!**).
6. Specify the complete path to the folder location where you want to save your AutoRecover file.
7. Click **OK**.

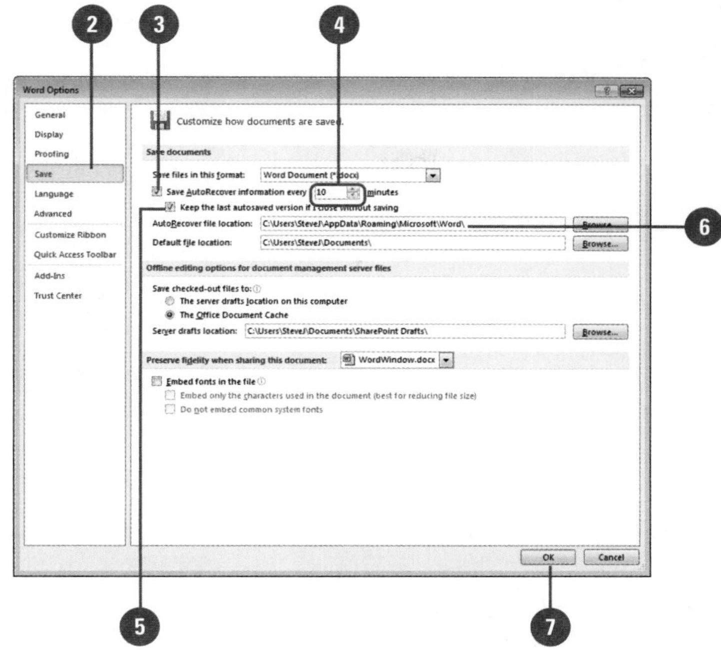

Maintaining and Repairing Office

At times you may determine that Word or another Office program is not working as efficiently as it once did. This sometimes happens when you install new software or move files into new folders. Office does the work for you with the Repair option, which locates, diagnoses, and fixes any errors in the program itself. Note that this feature does not repair personal files like documents, presentations, or workbooks. If the Repair option does not fix the problem, you might have to reinstall Word or Office. If you need to add or remove features, reinstall Word or Office, or remove it entirely, you can use Office Setup's maintenance feature.

Perform Program Maintenance

1. Insert the Office disc in your drive or navigate to the folder with the setup program.
2. In Windows Explorer, double-click the Setup icon.
3. Click one of the following maintenance buttons.
   - **Add or Remove Features** to change which features are installed or remove specific features.
   - **Remove** to uninstall Microsoft Office 2010 from this computer.
   - **Repair** to repair Microsoft Office 2010 to its original state.
   - **Enter a Product Key** to type the product registration key (located in the product packaging) for Office 2010.
4. Click **Continue**, and then follow the wizard instructions to complete the maintenance.

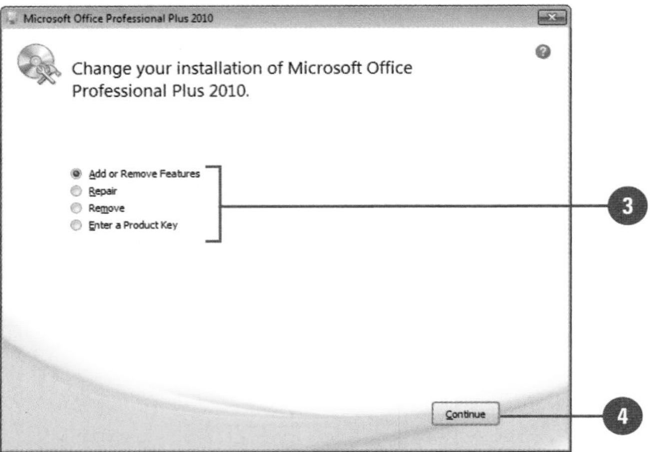

Add or Remove Features

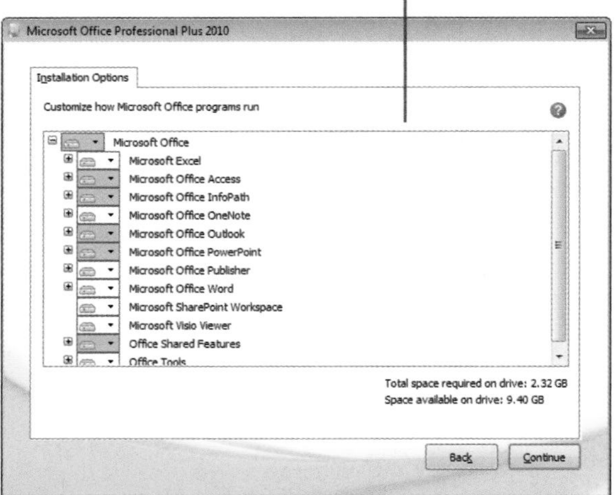

See Also

See "Working with Office Safe Modes" on page 332 for information on fixing problems with a Microsoft Office 2010 program.

Getting Updates on the Web

Microsoft offers a quick and easy way to update Word and any other Office program with new software downloads that improve the stability and security of the program. From the Help screen on the File tab, simply click the Check for Updates button to connect to the Microsoft Update Web site to have your computer scanned for necessary updates, and then choose which Office updates you want to download and install.

Get Office Updates on the Web

1. Click the **File** tab, and then click **Help**.
2. Click **Check for Updates** to open the Microsoft Update Web site.
3. Click one of the update buttons to find out if you need updates, and then choose the updates you want to download and install.

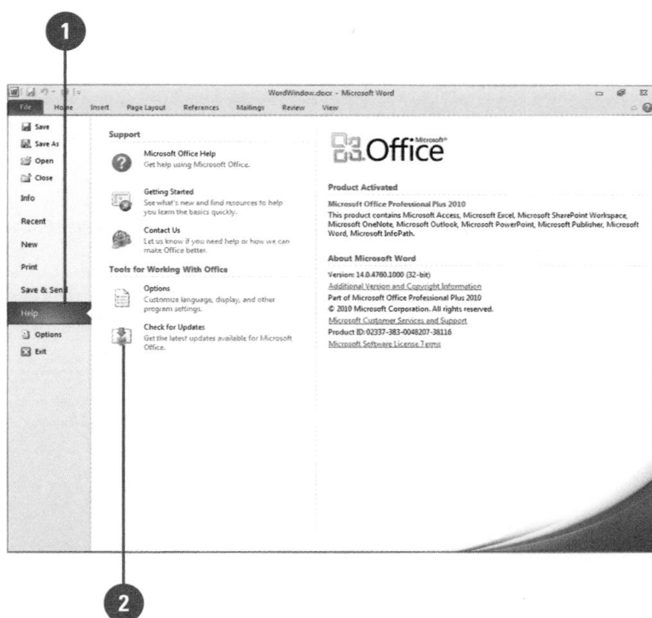

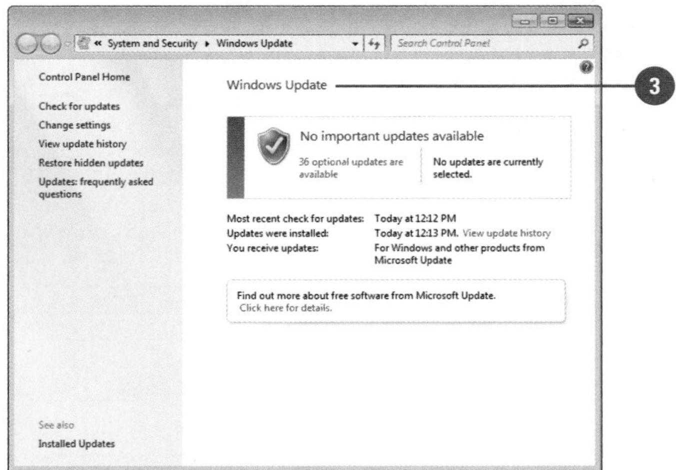

Did You Know?

You can contact Microsoft for help. You can get support over the phone, chat, or e-mail messages. To get online help, click the File tab, click Help, and then click Contact Us.

You can get better help information. At the bottom of a help topic, click Yes, No, or I Don't Know to give Microsoft feedback on the usefulness of a topic.

Closing a Document and Exiting Word

After you finish working on a document, you can close it. Closing a document makes more computer memory available for other activities. Closing a document is different from exiting, or quitting, a program; after you close a document, the program is still running. When you're finished using the program, you should exit it. To protect your files, always save your documents and exit before turning off the computer.

Close a Document

1. Click the **File** tab, and then click **Close**, or click the **Close** button on the Document window (available when documents not all shown on taskbar).

   TIMESAVER *Press Ctrl+W.*

2. If you have made changes to any open files since last saving them, a dialog box opens, asking if you want to save changes. Click **Save** to save any changes, or click **Don't Save** to ignore your changes.

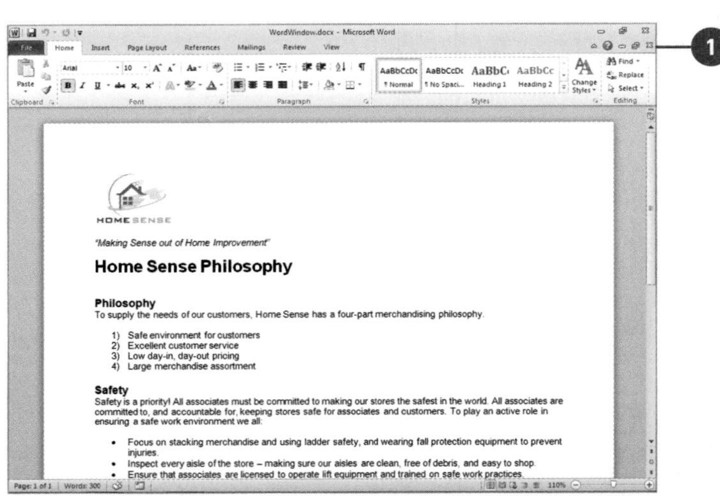

Exit Word

1. Click the **File** tab, and then click **Exit**, or click the **Close** button on the Program window (when documents not all shown on taskbar or for the last open document).

2. If you have made changes to any open files since last saving them, a dialog box opens asking if you want to save changes. Click **Save** to save any changes, or click **Don't Save** to ignore your changes.

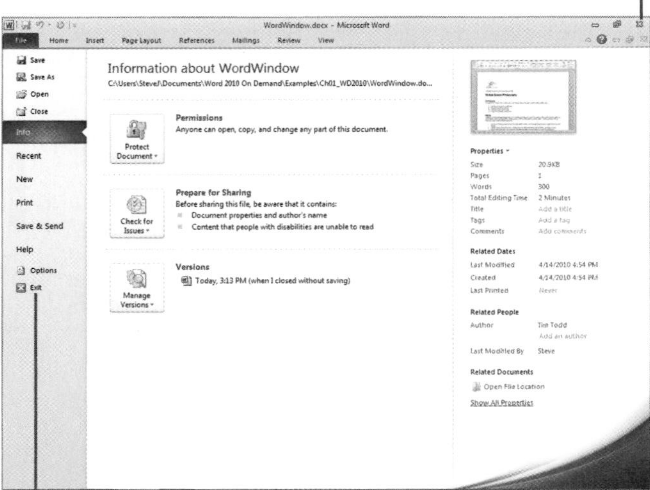

Working with Simple Documents

2

Introduction

Whether you're typing a carefully worded letter, creating a professional resume, or producing a can't-miss promotional newsletter for your business or neighborhood group, Microsoft Word is the program for you. Word contains all the tools and features you need to produce interesting documents that say exactly what you mean and that have the look to match.

Microsoft Word is designed especially for working with text, so it's a snap to create and edit letters, reports, mailing lists, tables, or any other word-based communication. What makes Word perfect for your documents is its editing capabilities combined with its variety of views. For example, you can jot down your ideas in Outline view. Then switch to Normal view to expand your thoughts into complete sentences and revise them without retyping the entire page. When you're done revising the document, switch to Reading view to read and proof your work. Finally, in Print Layout view you can quickly add formatting elements, such as bold type and special fonts, to make your documents look professional.

In addition, Word offers a Find and Replace feature that allows you to look for text and make changes as necessary. The Actions feature works with other Microsoft Office programs to enhance your documents. Contact information can be pulled from your address book in Outlook, to your Word document.

If you accidentally make a change, you can use the Undo feature to remove, or "undo," your last change. Word remembers your recent changes, and gives you the opportunity to undo them. If you decide to Redo the Undo, you can erase the previous change.

What You'll Do

Create a Blank Document

Create a New Document From an Existing One

Create a Document Using a Template

Create a Letter or Memo

Set Up the Page

Move and Resize Document Windows

Work with Multiple Documents

Navigate a Document

Move Around in a Document

Select Text

Edit Text

Copy and Move Text

Find and Replace Text

Insert Hyphens

Insert Information the Smart Way

Correct Text Automatically

Undo and Redo an Action

Creating a Blank Document

When you start Word, the program window opens with a new document so that you can begin working in it. You can also start a new document whenever Word is running, and you can start as many new documents as you want. Each new document displays a default name—such as "Document1," "Document2" and so on—numbered according to how many new documents you have started during the work session until you save it with a more meaningful name. The document name appears on the title bar and taskbar buttons.

Create a Blank Document

1. Click the **File** tab, and then click **New**.

   TIMESAVER *To create a blank document without the New screen, press Ctrl+N.*

   The New screen appears.

2. Click **Blank document**.
3. Click **Create**.

   A new blank document appears in the Word window.

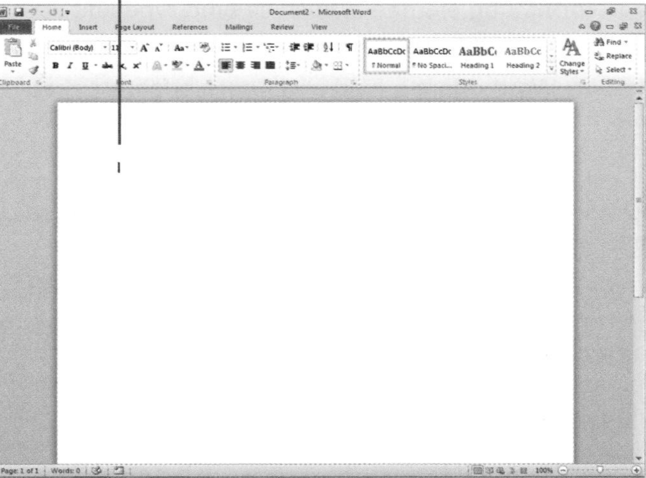

Creating a New Document From an Existing One

Instead of creating a document from scratch, you can also create a document from an existing document you already have. If you have a document that is close to what you want to create, you can use the New from existing option to create an untitled document with the contents of an existing document. You can use the New from existing option from the New screen, which opens the New from Existing Document dialog box where you can select the existing document you want to use.

Create a New Document From an Existing Document

1. Click the **File** tab, and then click **New**.

   The New screen appears.

2. Click **New from existing**.
3. Click the **Files of type** list arrow, and then select the type of file that you want to open.
4. Click the **Look in** list arrow, and then navigate to the file.
5. Select the document file you want to open.
6. Click **Create New**.

   A new document appears in the Word window.

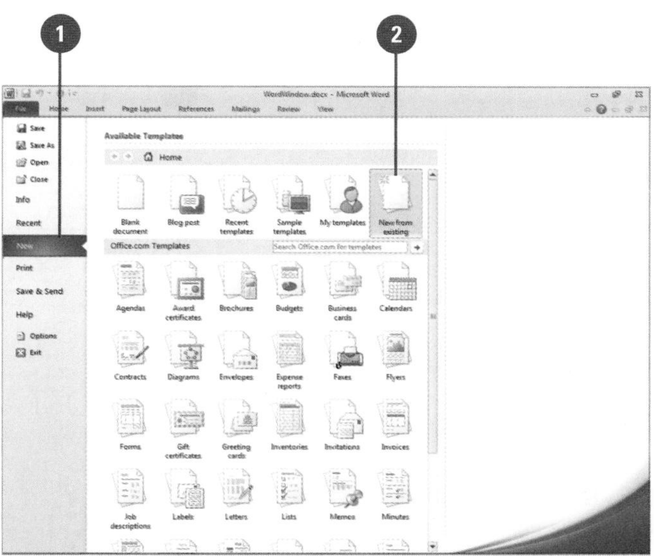

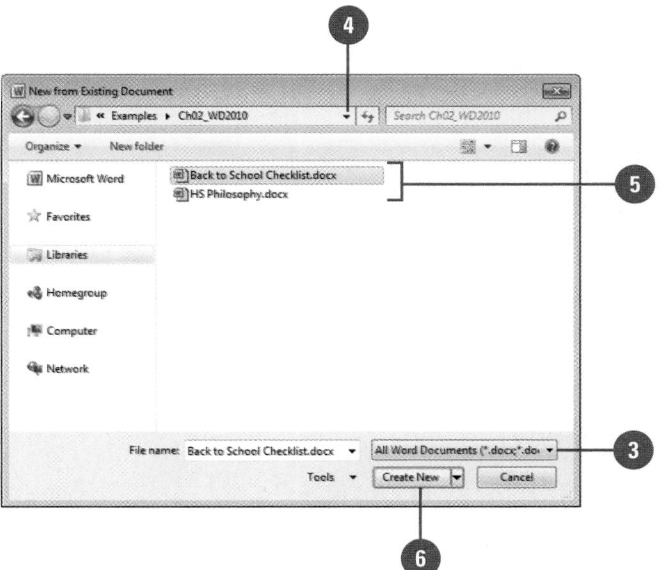

Creating a Document Using a Template

Word provides a collection of professionally designed templates that you can use to help you create documents. Start with a template when you have a good idea of your content but want to take advantage of a template's professional look. A **template** is a document file that provides you with a unified document design, which includes themes, so you only need to add text and graphics. In the New screen, you can choose a template from those already installed with Office or from the Microsoft Office Online Web site, an online content library. You can choose an Office.com template from one of the listed categories.

Create a Document with a Template

1. Click the **File** tab, and then click **New**.
2. Choose one of the following:
   - Click **Recent templates**, and then click a recently used template.
   - Click **Sample templates**, and then click a template.
   - Click **My templates** to open a dialog box.
   - Click **New from existing** to open a dialog box to select a template file.
   - Click an Office.com Templates folder (if needed), and then click a template.
3. To navigate, click the **Home**, **Next**, or **Previous** button.
4. Click the **Document** option, if available (for Create).
5. Click **Create** or **Download**.
6. If necessary, click the template you want, and then click **OK**.

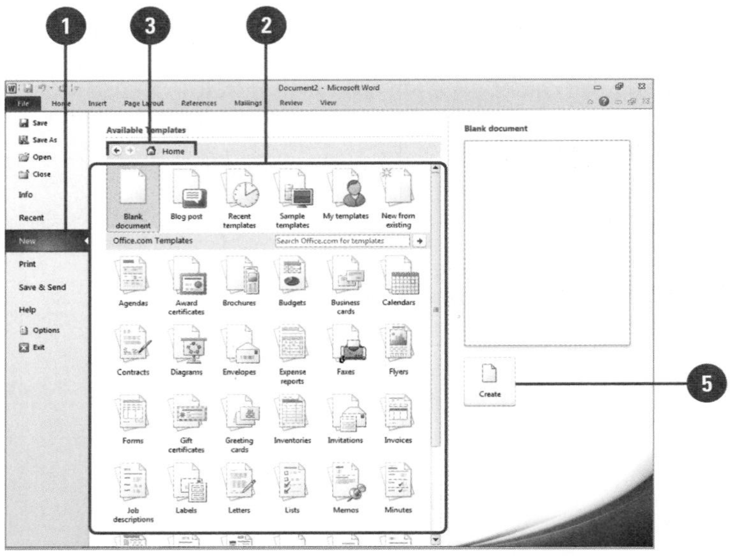

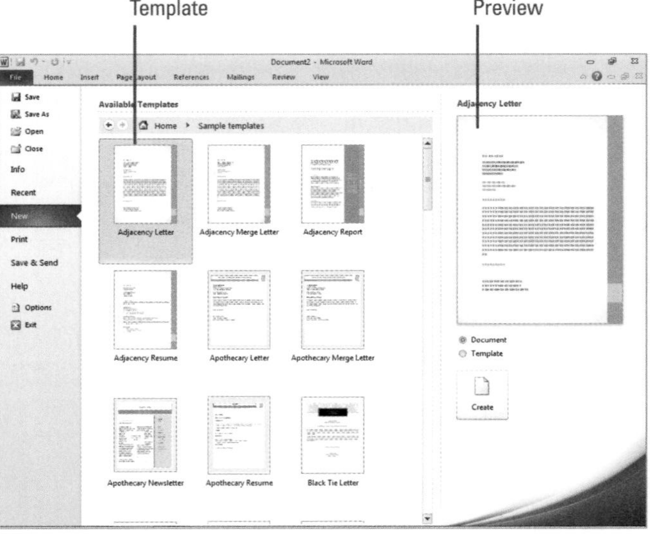

Did You Know?

You can download templates on the Web. Go to *www.microsoft.com*, click the Office link, and then search for Office Templates.

Creating a Letter or Memo

You can create a letter in Word as quickly as you can grab a pen and paper and start writing. With all of the text, formatting, spelling, and graphic features that Word has to offer, writing a letter is a very easy way to communicate with clients, friends, and family. Memos are another commonly used document whose creation has been simplified via the use of Word templates. You can create and customize a memo form all your own. Add your company logo, change font attributes, adjust line spacing, and other important parts of your document and you have a customized memo.

Create a Letter or Memo

1. Click the **File** tab, and then click **New**.

   The New screen appears.

2. Click **Letters** or **Memos**.
3. If necessary, click a folder to display the templates you want to use.
4. Click the template you want to use.
5. To navigate, click the **Home**, **Next**, or **Previous** button.
6. Click **Download**.

   A new document appears in the Word window.

7. Edit the text in the place holders to make it your own document.

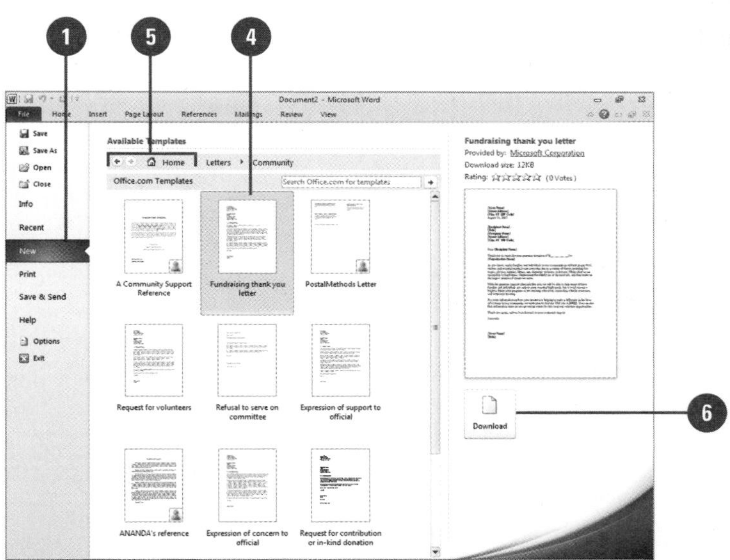

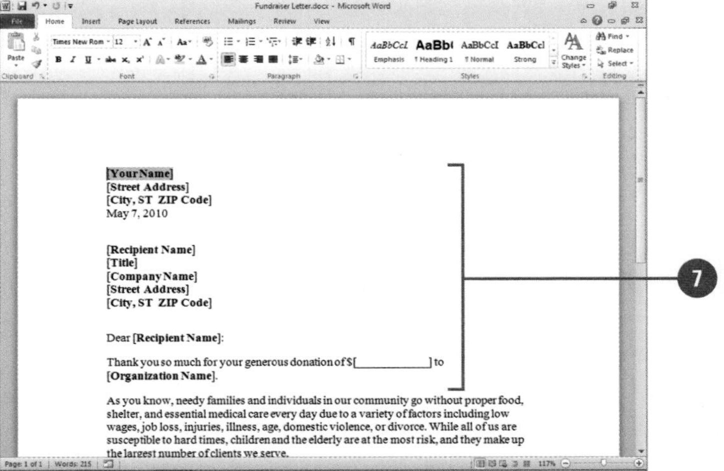

Setting Up the Page

Every document you produce and print might need a different page setup. You can achieve the look you want by printing on a standard paper size (such as letter, legal, or envelope), international standard paper sizes, or any custom size that your printer accepts. The default setting is 8.5 x 11 inches, the most common letter and copy size. You can also print several pages on one sheet. You can also select the page orientation (portrait or landscape) that best fits the entire document or any section. **Portrait** orients the page vertically (taller than it is wide) and **landscape** orients the page horizontally (wider than it is tall).

Set the Page Orientation and Size Quickly

1. Click the **Page Layout** tab.
2. To quickly change the page orientation, click the **Orientation** button, and then click **Landscape** or **Portrait**.
3. To quickly change the page size, click the **Size** button, and then click the size you want.

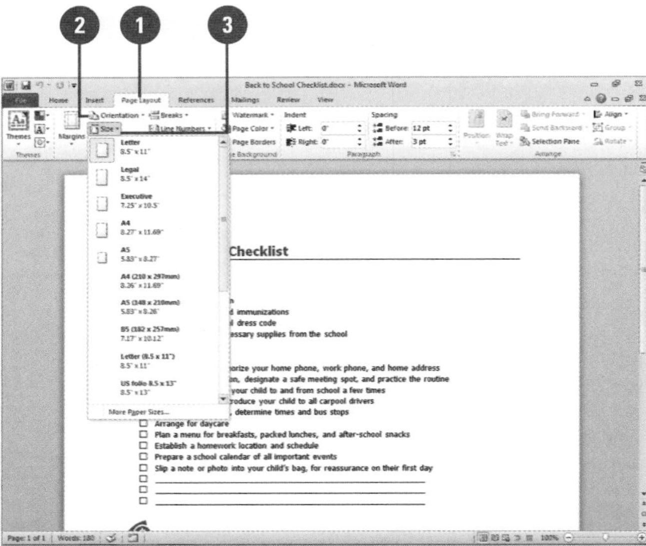

Set Custom Page Size Options

1. Click the **Page Layout** tab.
2. Click the **Page Size** Dialog Box Launcher, or click the **Size** button, and then click **More Paper Sizes.**
3. Click the **Paper** tab.
4. Click the **Paper Size** list arrow, and then select the paper size you want, or specify a custom size.
5. Select the paper source for the first page and other pages.
6. Click the **Apply To** list arrow, and then click **This Section, This Point Forward**, or **Whole Document**.
7. Verify your selections in the Preview box.
8. To make your changes the default settings for all new documents, click **Default**, and then click **Yes**.
9. Click **OK**.

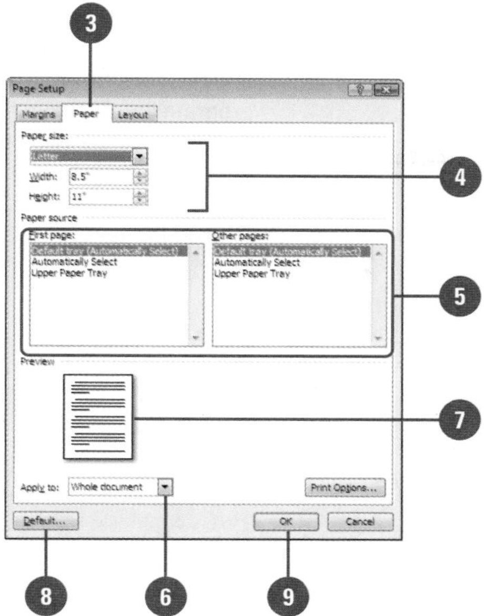

Moving and Resizing Document Windows

Every Office program and document opens inside a **window**, which contains a title bar, the Ribbon, and work area. This is where you create and edit your data. Most often, you'll probably fill the entire screen with one window. But when you want to move or copy information between programs or documents, it's easier to display several windows at once. You can arrange two or more windows from one program or from different programs on the screen at the same time. However, you must make the window active to work in it. You can also click the document buttons on the taskbar to switch between open documents.

Resize and Move a Window

- **Maximize button**. Click to make a window fill the entire screen.
- **Restore Down button**. Click to reduce a maximized window to a reduced size.
- **Minimize button**. Click to shrink a window to a taskbar button. To restore the window to its previous size, click the taskbar button.
- **Close button**. Click to shut a window.

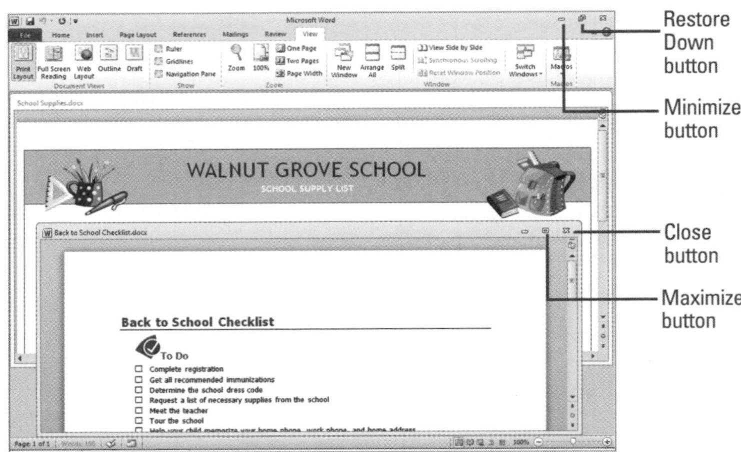

Resize and Move a Window Using a Mouse

1. If the window is maximized, click the **Restore Down** button.
2. Use the following methods:
   - **Move.** Move the mouse over the title bar.
   - **Resize.** Move the mouse over one of the borders of the window until the mouse pointer changes into a two-headed arrow. The directions of the arrowheads show you the directions in which you can resize the window.
3. Drag to move or resize the window.

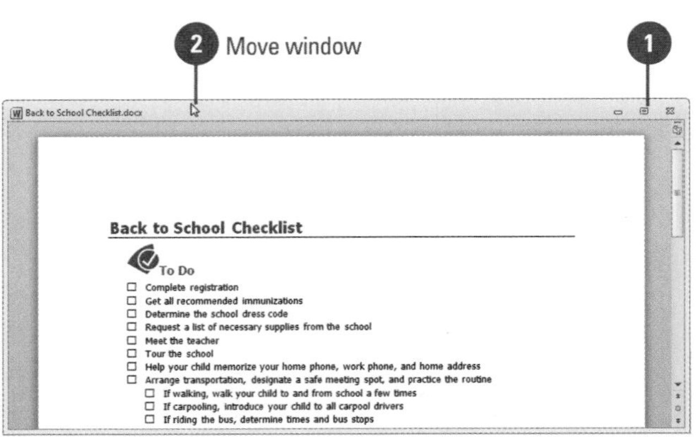

Arrange or Switch Between Windows

1. Open the documents you want to arrange or switch between.
2. Click the **View** tab.
3. In the Window group, perform any of the following:
   - Click **Switch Windows**, and then click the document name you want.
   - Click **Arrange All** to arrange windows in a horizontal arrangement.
   - Click **New Window** to open a new window containing a view of the current document.

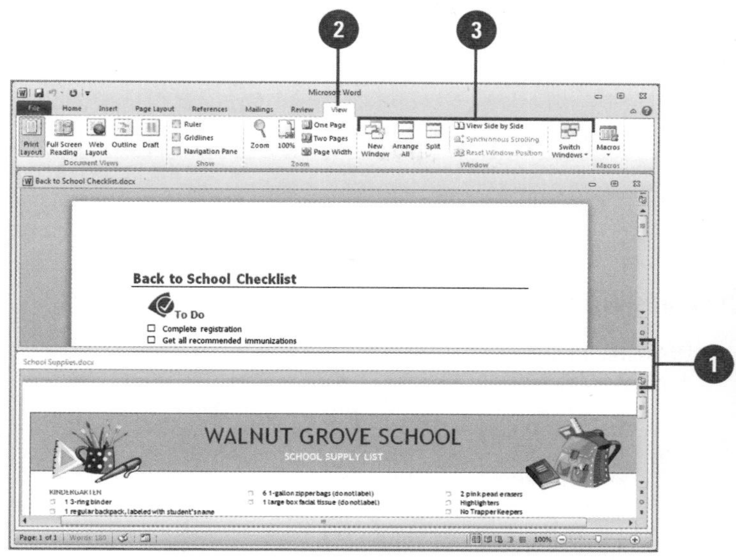

Change the Window Display

1. Click the **File** tab, and then click **Options**.
2. In the left pane, click **Advanced**.
3. Select or clear the **Show all windows in the Taskbar** check box.
   - Select the check box to display all document windows in the Taskbar. This means each document uses a separate Word program window.
   - Clear the check box to display all documents in one Word program window. This means each document uses a separate Document window. You'll see two sets of close and resize buttons, one for the Program window and one for the active Document window.
4. Click **OK**.

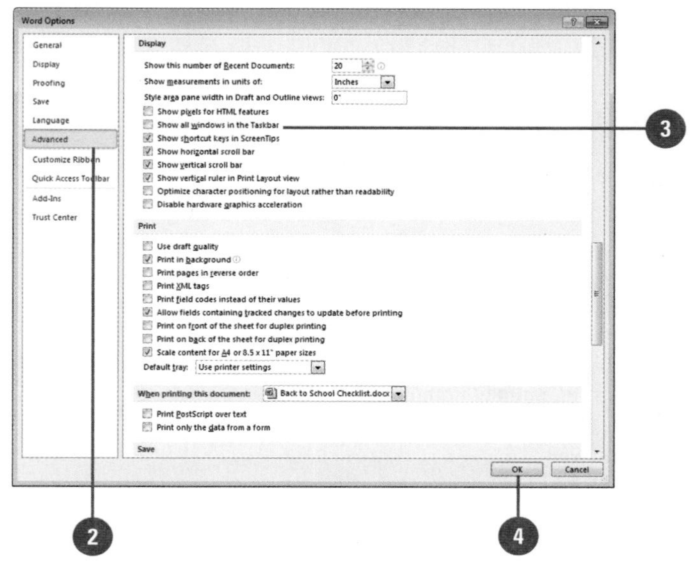

Working with Multiple Documents

If you're working on two similar documents and want to do a quick compare to see if they are the same, you can use the View Side By Side command on the View tab. When you view two documents side by side, you can enable synchronous scrolling to scroll both documents together at the same time. When you're done, you can reset the window position of the documents being compared side by side so they share the screen equally. If you want to work on two different parts of a document, you can use the Split button to create two separate scrolling sections for the same document.

Compare Windows Side By Side

1. Open the documents you want to compare side by side.
2. Click the **View** tab.
3. In the Window group, perform any of the following:
   - Click the **View Side By Side** button to compare two documents vertically.
     - To compare the documents horizontally, click the **Arrange All** button.
   - Click the **Synchronous Scrolling** button to synchronize the scrolling of two documents so that they scroll together. To enable this feature turn on View Side By Side.
   - Click the **Reset Window Position** button to reset the window position of the documents being compared side-by-side so that they share the screen equally. To enable this feature turn on View Side By Side.
4. When you're done, click the **View Side By Side** button to return to the full screen.

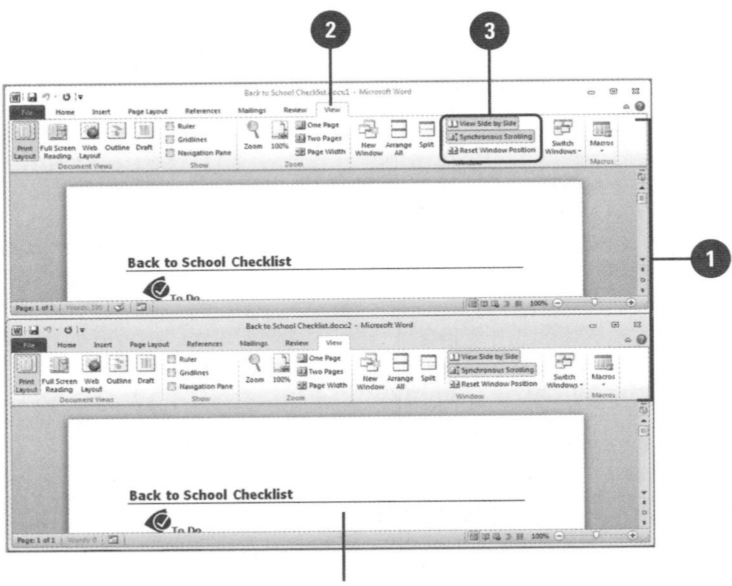

Horizontal arrangement

Split Windows

1. Open the documents you want to split.
2. Click the **View** tab.
3. Click the **Split** button.
4. Click to split the document where you want.
5. Scroll each part of the window separately.
6. To remove the split, click the **Remove Split** button or double-click the divider line.

Did You Know?

You can resize a split window. Drag the divider line to the new location you want.

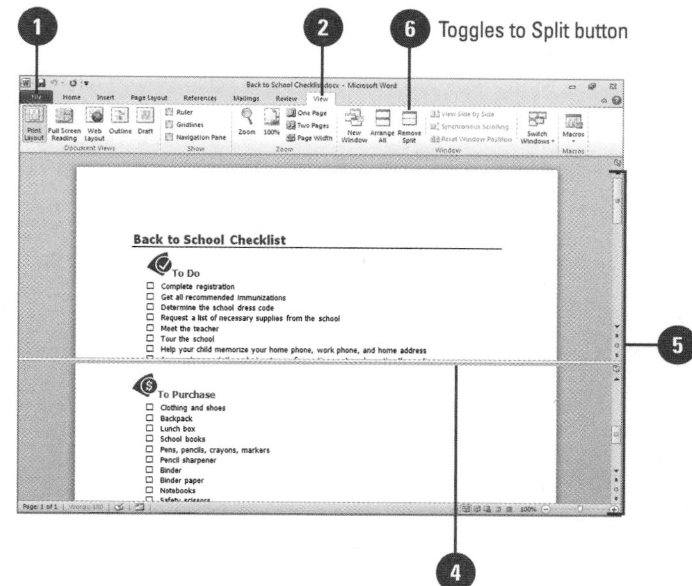

Navigating a Document

If you have a long document with headings or you're searching for keywords, you can use the Navigation pane (**New!**) to find your way around it. In the Navigation pane, you can view thumbnails for all pages, search for key phrases, quickly move between headings, promote or demote headings, insert new headings, browse headings from a co-author, rearrange heading content, and collapse/ expand heading levels of an outline. You can perform any of these tasks in the Navigation panel by using the following tabs: Browse Headings, Browse Pages, and Browse Search Results.

Navigate a Document

1. Click the **View** tab.
2. Click the **Navigation Pane** check box.
3. To work with headings, click the **Browse Headings** tab, and then do any of the following:
   - **Display a Heading.** Click the heading name, or click the **Previous Heading** or **Next Heading** button.
   - **Collapse/Expand a Heading.** Click the arrow next to the heading name.
   - **Move a Heading.** Drag the heading name to another location in the pane. The heading and its content move together.
   - **Create a Heading.** Right-click a heading name, and then click **New Heading Before** or **New Heading After**.
   - **Promote or Demote a Heading.** Right-click a heading name, and then click **Promote** or **Demote**.
4. To view page thumbnails, click the **Browse Pages** tab.
5. To perform and view search results, click in the Search box, type keywords, press enter, and then click the **Browse Search Results** tab.

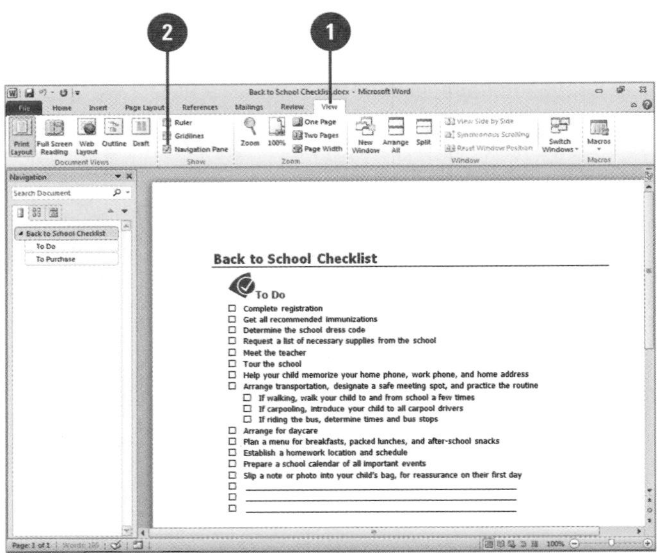

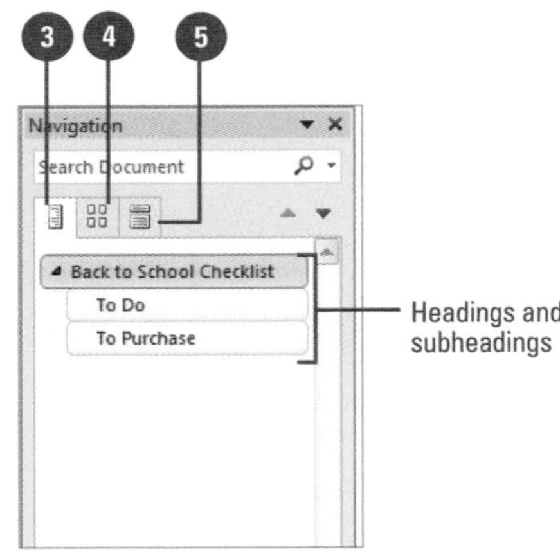

Moving Around in a Document

As your document gets longer, some of your work shifts out of sight. You can easily move any part of a document back into view. **Scrolling** moves the document line by line. **Paging** moves the document page by page. **Browsing** moves you through your document by the item you specify, such as to the next word, comment, picture, table, or heading. The tools described here move you around a document no matter which document view you are in.

Scroll, Page, and Browse Through a Document

- To scroll through a document one line at a time, click the up or down scroll arrow on the vertical scroll bar.
- To quickly scroll through a document, click and hold the up or down scroll arrow on the vertical scroll bar.
- To scroll to a specific page or heading in a document, drag the scroll box on the vertical scroll bar until the page number or heading you want appears in the yellow box.
- To page through the document one screen at a time, press Page Up or Page Down on the keyboard.
- To browse a document by page, edits, headings, or other items, click the Select Browse Object button, and then click that item. If a dialog box opens, enter the name or number of the item you want to find, and then click the Previous or Next button to move from one item to the next.

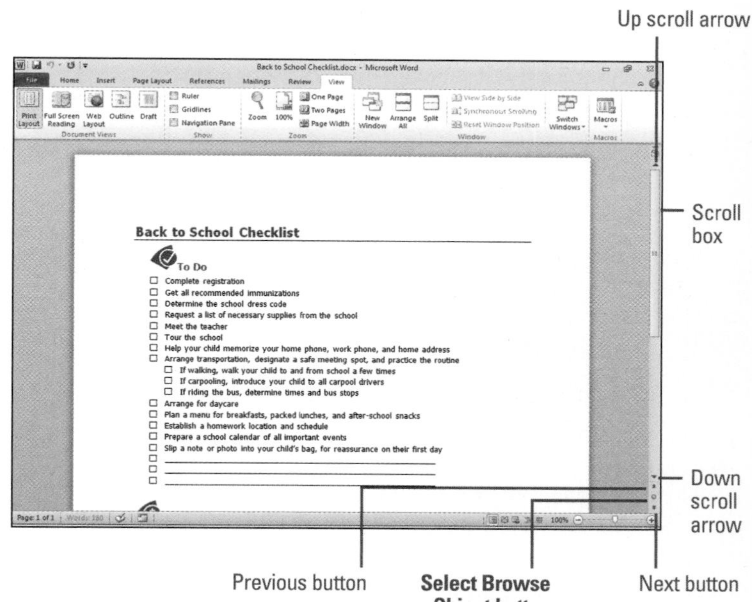

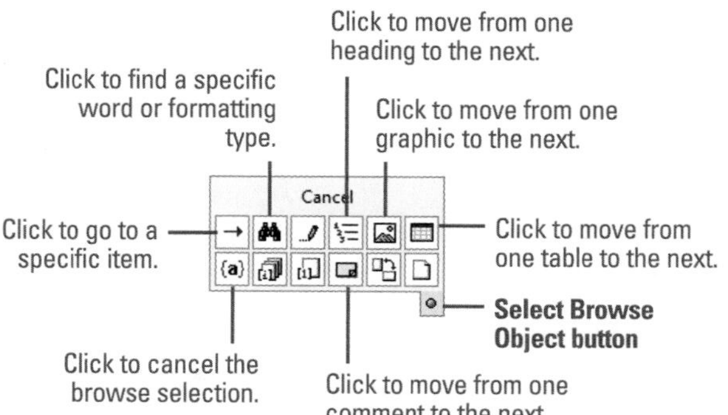

Selecting Text

The first step in working with text is to highlight, or **select**, the text you want. Once you've selected it, you can copy, move, format, and delete words, sentences, and paragraphs. When you finish with or decide not to use a selection, you can click anywhere in the document to **deselect** the text. If you need to select all or similar text or objects in a document, you can use the Select button on the Home tab.

Select Text

1. Position the pointer in the word, paragraph, line, or part of the document you want to select.
2. Choose the method that accomplishes the selection you want to complete in the easiest way.

   Refer to the table for methods to select text.

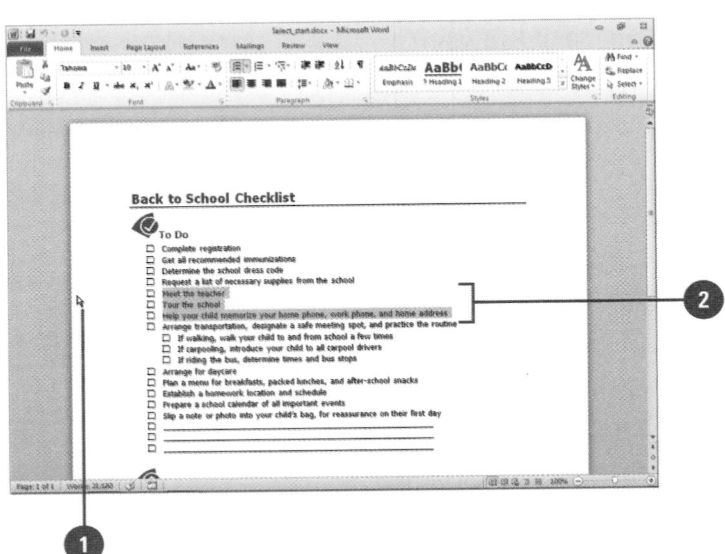

Did You Know?

AutoComplete finishes your words. As you enter common text, such as your name, months, today's date, and common salutations and closings, Word provides the rest of the text in a ScreenTip. Press Enter to have Word complete your words.

Selecting Text

To select	Do this
A single word	Double-click the word.
A single paragraph	Triple-click a word within the paragraph.
A single line	Click in the left margin next to the line.
Any part of a document	Click at the beginning of the text you want to highlight, and then drag to the end of the section you want to highlight.
A large selection	Click at the beginning of the text you want to highlight, and then press and hold Shift while you click at the end of the text that you want to highlight.
The entire document	Triple-click in the left margin.
An outline heading or subheading in Outline view	Click the bullet, plus sign, or minus sign.

Select Text and Other Items

1. Click the **Home** tab.
2. Click the **Select** button.
3. Select any of the following commands:
   - **Select All.** Click to select everything in a document.
   - **Select Objects.** Click to turn off object selection in a document. Click to select objects in the document. When you're done, click Select Objects again on the menu to turn it off.
   - **Select All Text With Similar Formatting (No Data).** Click to select all text with similar formatting to the current selection or insertion point.
   - **Selection Pane.** Click to open the Selection pane, where you can select, reorder, show, or hide objects in a document. Click Selection Pane again on the menu or the Close button to close the pane.

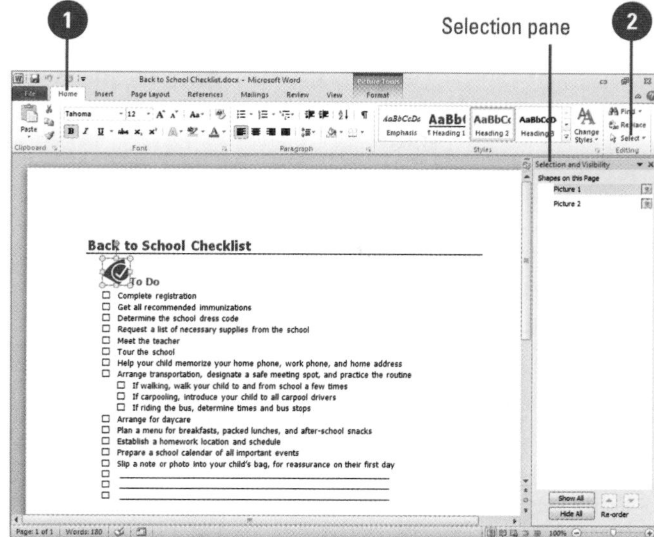

Editing Text

Before you can edit text, you need to highlight, or select, the text you want to modify. Then you can delete, replace, move (cut), or copy text within one document or between documents even if they're from different programs. In either case, the steps are the same. Text you cut or copy is temporarily stored in the Office Clipboard. When you paste the text, the Paste Options button appears below it. When you click the button, a menu appears with options to specify how Office pastes the information in the document. To copy or move data without using the Clipboard, you can use a technique called **drag-and-drop**. Drag-and-drop makes it easy to copy or move text short distances.

Select and Edit Text

1. Move the I-beam pointer to the left or right of the text you want to select.
2. Drag the pointer to highlight the text, or click in the document to place the insertion point where you want to make a change.

   TIMESAVER *Double-click a word to select it; triple-click a paragraph to select it.*
3. Perform one of the following editing commands:
   - To replace text, type your text.
   - To delete text, press the Backspace key or the Delete key.

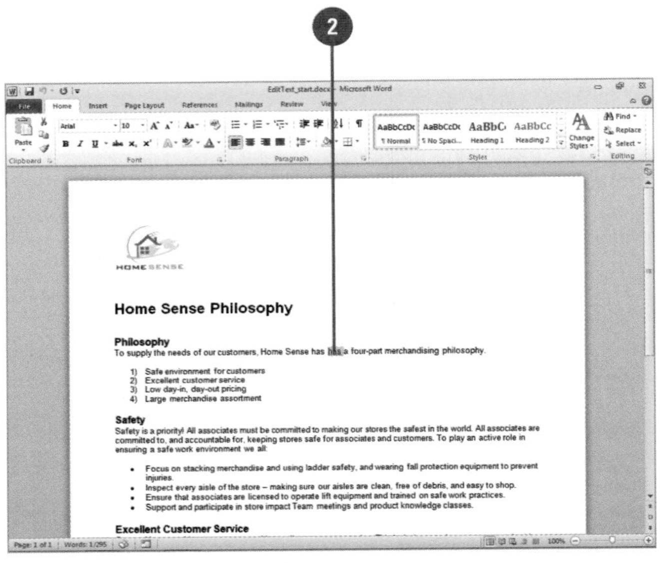

Correct Typing Errors Using the Keyboard

To Delete	Press
One character at a time to the left of the insertion point	Backspace
One word at a time to the left of the insertion point	Ctrl+Backspace
One character at a time to the right of the insertion point	Delete
One word at a time to the right of the insertion point	Ctrl+Delete
Selected text	Backspace or Delete

Insert and Delete Text

1. Click in the document to place the insertion point where you want to make the change.
   - To insert text, type your text.
   - To delete text, press the Backspace key or the Delete key.

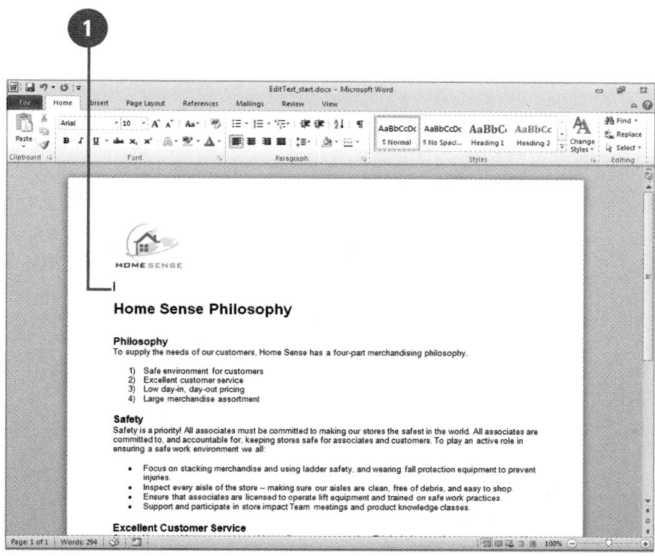

Copy or Move Text Using Drag-and-Drop

1. If you want to drag text between programs or documents, display both windows.
2. Select the text you want to move or copy.

   TIMESAVER *You can also select objects and other elements.*

3. Point to the selected text, and then click and hold the mouse button.

   If you want to copy the text, also press and hold Ctrl. A plus sign (+) appears in the pointer box, indicating that you are dragging a copy of the selected text.

4. Drag the selection to the new location, and then release the mouse button and keyboard.
5. Click anywhere in the document to deselect the text.

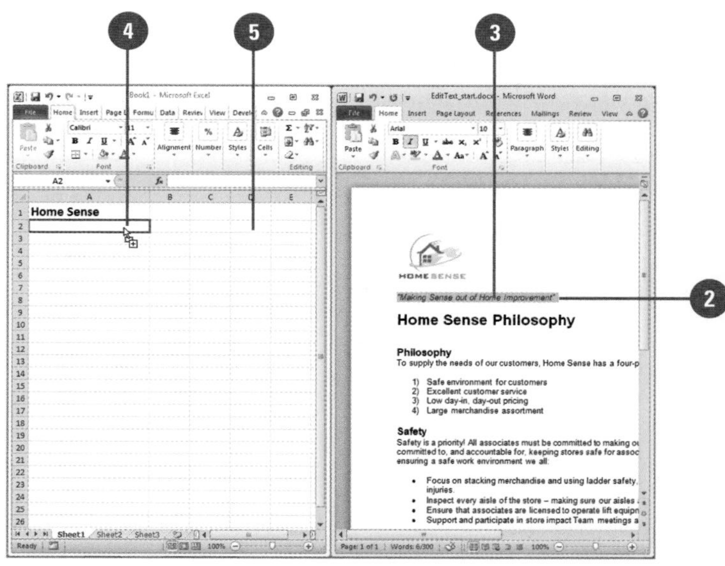

Copying and Moving Text

You can **copy** and **move** text or data from one location to another on any Office document. When you copy data, a duplicate of the selected information is placed on the Clipboard. When you move text, the selected information is removed and placed on the Clipboard. To complete the copy or move, you **paste** the data stored on the Clipboard in another location. The live preview (**New!**) on the Paste Options menu allows you to view your paste results before you actually paste it. You can use the Office Clipboard to store multiple pieces of information from several different sources in one storage area shared by all Office programs. You can paste these pieces of information into any Office program, either individually or all at once. With Paste Special, you can gain additional control over what you want to paste.

Copy or Move Using the Clipboard

1. Select the element you want to copy.
2. Click the **Home** tab.
3. Click the **Copy** or **Cut** button.
4. Click the location where you want to paste the data.
5. Click the **Paste** button or click the **Paste** button arrow, point to an option to display a live preview (**New!**) of the paste, and then click to paste the item.

   When you point to a paste option for the live preview, use the ScreenTip to determine the option.

   The data remains on the Clipboard, available for further pasting, until you replace it with another selection.

   If you don't want to paste this selection anywhere else, press Esc to remove the marquee.
6. If you want to change the way the data pastes into the document, click the **Paste Options** button, point to an option for the live preview (**New!**), and then select the option you want.

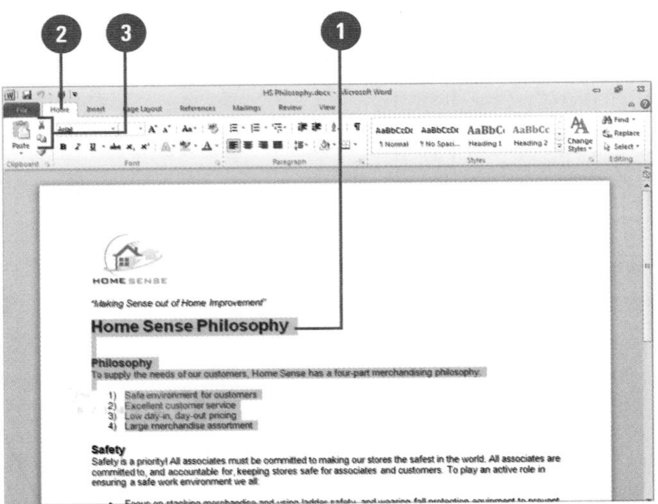

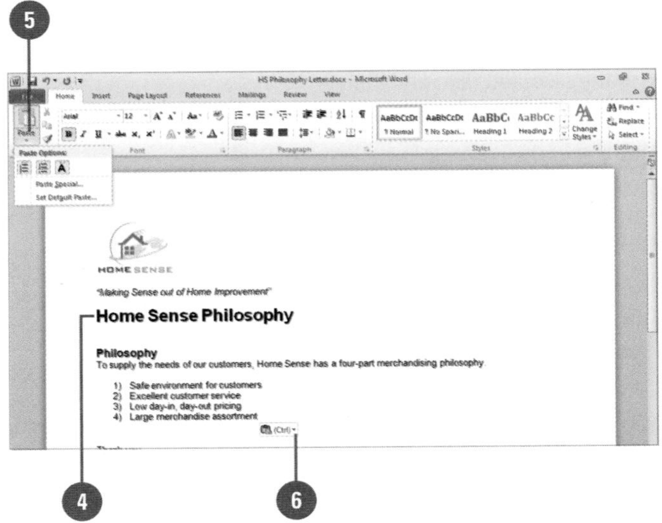

Copy and Paste Information to the Clipboard Task Pane

1. Click the **Home** tab.
2. Click the **Clipboard** Dialog Box Launcher.
3. Select the data you want to copy.
4. Click the **Copy** button.

   The text or data is copied on the Clipboard task pane.
5. Click the location where you want to paste data.
6. Click the Clipboard item you want to paste, or point to the item, click the list arrow, and then click **Paste**.

   - To change Office Clipboard options, click the **Options** button on the pane.
7. Click the **Close** button in the task pane.

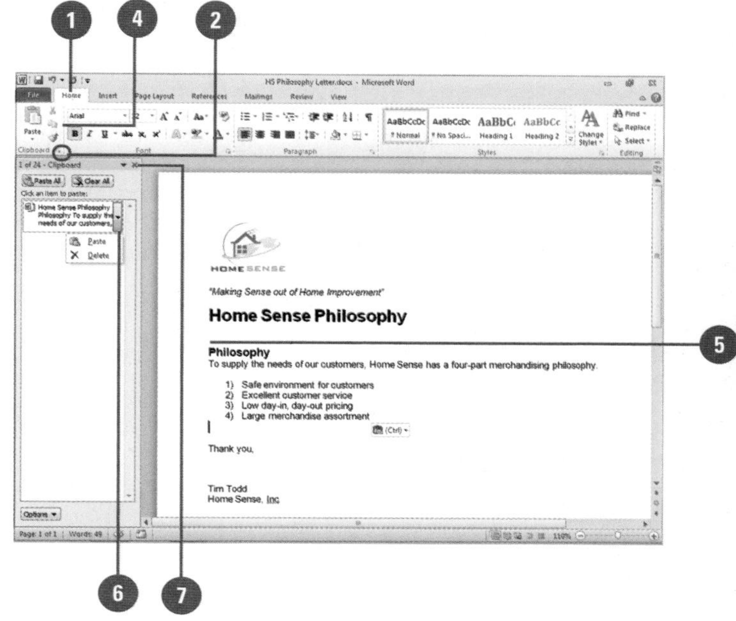

Paste Information with Special Results

1. Select the text or data that you want to copy.
2. Click the **Home** tab.
3. Click the **Copy** button.
4. Click the location where you want to paste the text or data.
5. Click the **Paste** button, and then click **Paste Special**.
6. Click the option buttons with the paste results you want.
7. Click **OK**.

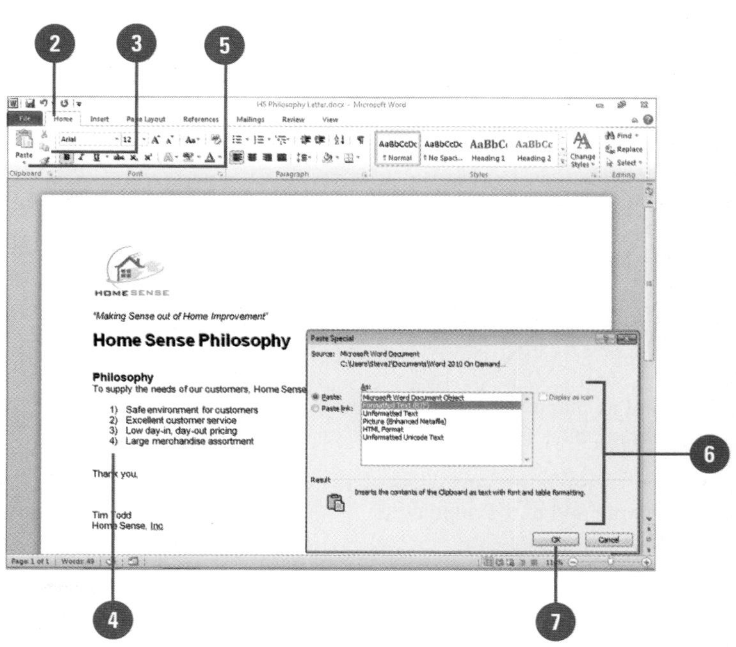

Finding and Replacing Text

The Find and Replace commands make it easy to locate or replace specific text in a document. For example, you might want to find each figure reference in a long report to verify that the proper graphic appears. When you use the Find command, Word highlights the word or phrases that it finds in the document using the Navigation pane (**New!**), which you can click to display them. You can use the Advanced Find to set more options in the Find and Replace dialog box. For example, you can use the More button to select find options, such as Match case, Format, or Special, or use the Reading Highlight button to specify whether to highlight the current find or all the items found in the document.

Find Text

1. Click at the beginning of the document.
2. Click the **Home** tab.
3. To use the Navigation pane, click the **Find** button. Click an item in the Navigation pane to highlight and go to the item.
4. To use the Find and Replace dialog box, click the **Find** button arrow, and then click **Advanced Find**.
5. Type the text you want to find.
6. To highlight all items found, click the **Reading Highlight** button, and then click **Highlight All**.
7. To specify where you want to find, click the **Find in** button, and then click **Current Selection** or **Main Document**.
8. Click **Find Next** until the text you want to locate is highlighted.

   You can click **Find Next** repeatedly to locate each instance of the content.
9. To find all places with the contents you want, click **Find All**.
10. If a message box opens when you reach the end of the document, click **OK**.
11. Click **Close** or **Cancel**.

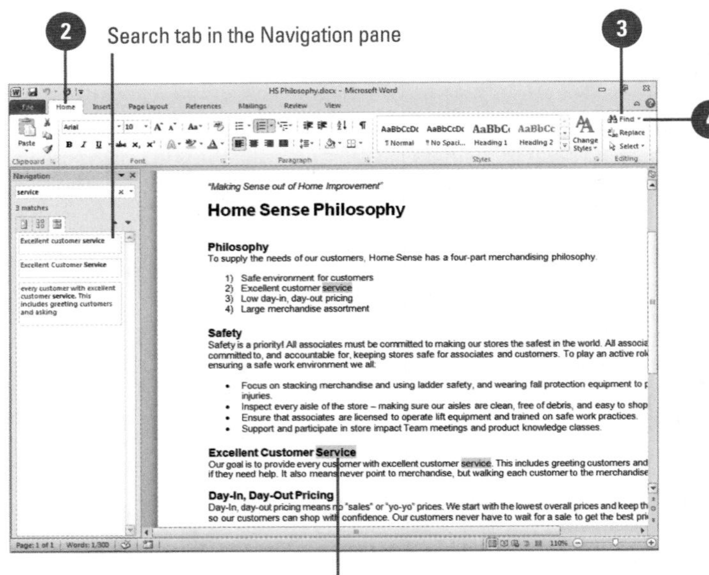

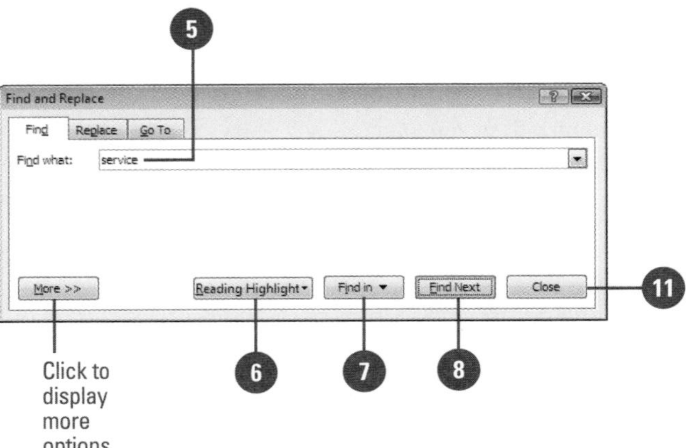

Replace Text

1. Click at the beginning of the Office document.
2. Click the **Home** tab.
3. Click the **Replace** button.
4. Type the text you want to search for.
5. Type the text you want to substitute.
6. Click **Find Next** to begin the search, and then select the next instance of the search text.
7. Click **Replace** to substitute the replacement text, or click **Replace All** to substitute text throughout the entire document.

   You can click **Find Next** to locate the next instance of the content without making a replacement.
8. If a message box appears when you reach the end of the document, click **OK**.
9. Click **Close** or **Cancel**.

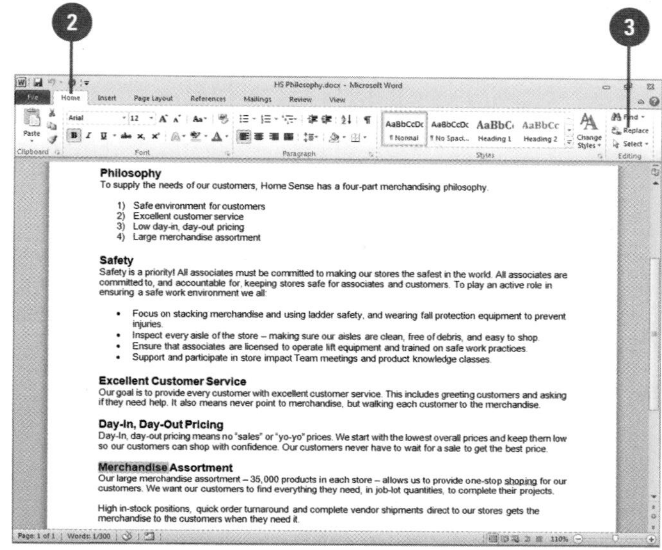

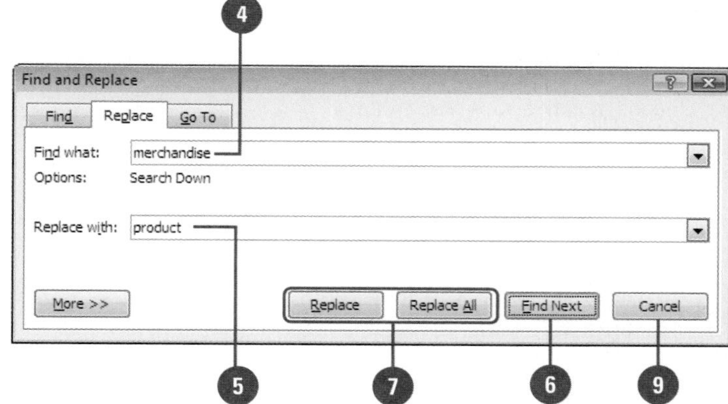

Did You Know?

You can go to different locations in Word. Click the Home tab, click the Find button arrow, click Go To, select the Go To What option you want, specify a location, and then click Next or Previous. When you're done, click Close.

Inserting Hyphens

If a word doesn't fit at the end of a line, you can set hyphenation options to hyphenate the word to display partly on one line and partly on the next line, or move the word to the beginning of the next line. You can set options to automatically or manually hyphenate words in a document, and to specify the maximum amount of space allowed between a word and the right margin without hyphenating the word. When you manually hyphenate a document, Word searches the text for words to hyphenate and asks if you want to insert a hyphen in the text. You can also manually insert an optional or nonbreaking hyphen. An **optional hyphen** is a hyphen that you specify where you want a word to break if it falls at the end of a line. A **nonbreaking hyphen** prevents a hyphenated word from breaking if it falls at the end of a line.

Set Hyphenation Options

1. Click the **Page Layout** tab.
2. To manually hyphenate part of a document, select the text you want to hyphenate first.
3. Click the **Hyphenation** button, and then click a hyphenation option:
   - **None.** Removes automatic hyphens and moves words that break on a line to the next line.
   - **Automatic.** Inserts a hyphen in a word as needed.
   - **Manual.** Word searches for text to hyphenate and asks if you want to insert a hyphen.

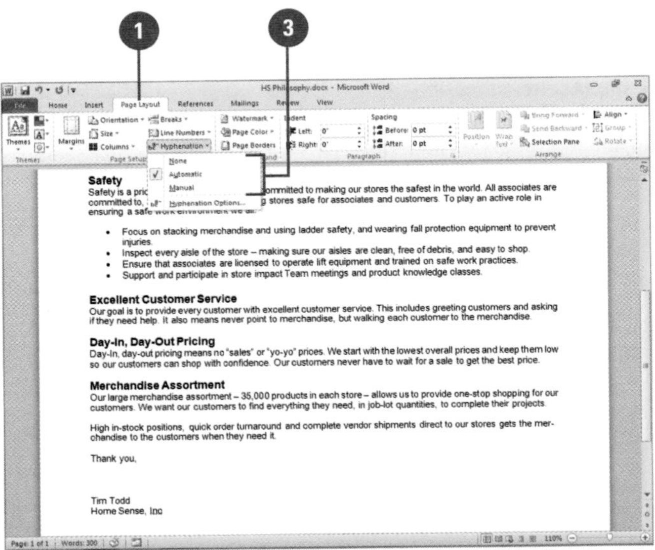

Did You Know?

You can insert an optional or nonbreaking hyphen. Click where you want to insert the hyphen. For an optional hyphen, press Ctrl+Hyphen. For an nonbreaking hyphen, press Ctrl+Shift+Hyphen.

Customize Hyphenation

1. Click the **Page Layout** tab.
2. Click the **Hyphenation** button, and then click **Hyphenation Options**.
3. In the Hyphenation zone box, specify the maximum amount of space between the word and the right margin you want.
4. Specify the limit for hyphens on consecutive lines you want.
5. Click **OK**.

Did You Know?

You can remove manual hyphens. Click the Home tab, click Replace, click More if necessary, click Special, and then click Optional Hyphen to remove manual hyphens or Nonbreaking Hyphen to remove nonbreaking hyphens. Leave the Replace With box empty, and then click Replace All.

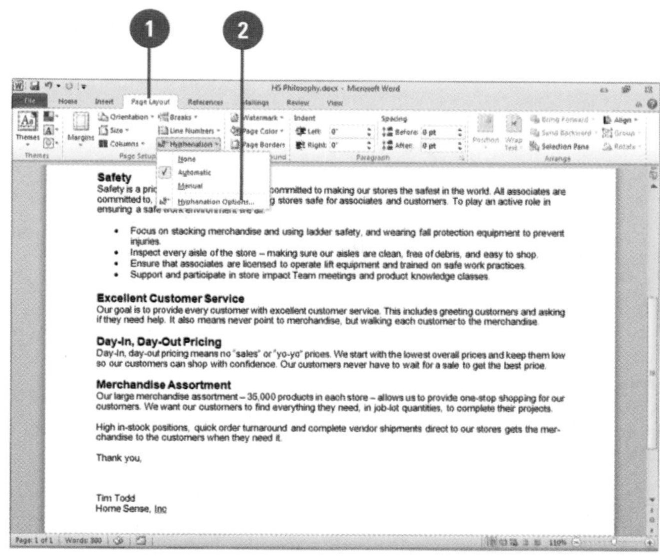

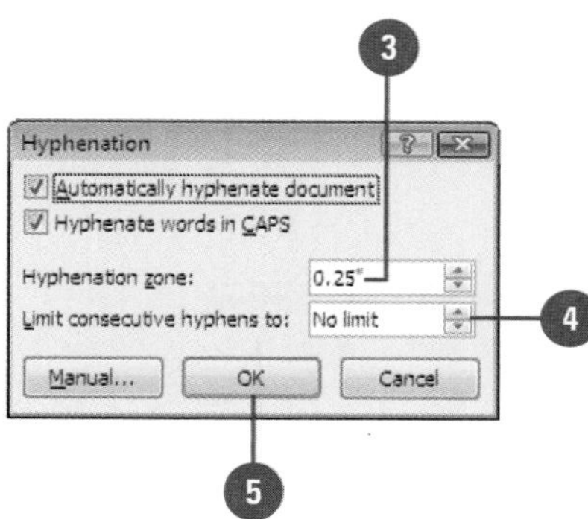

Inserting Information the Smart Way

Actions (**New!**), a replacement for smart tags, help you integrate actions typically performed in other programs directly in Word. For example, you can insert a financial symbol to get a stock quote, add a person's name and address in a document to the contacts list in Microsoft Outlook, or copy and paste information with added control. Word analyzes what you type and recognizes certain types that it marks with actions. The types of actions you can take depend on the type of data with the action. To use an action, you right-click an item to view any custom actions associated with it.

Change Options for Actions

1. Click the **File** tab, and then click **Options**.
2. In the left pane, click **Proofing**, and then click **AutoCorrect Options**.
3. Click the **Actions** tab.
4. Select the **Enable additional actions in the right-click menu** check box.
5. Select the check boxes with the actions you want.
6. To get properties about an action, select the action, and then click **Properties**.
7. To add more actions, click **More Actions**, and then follow the online instructions.
8. Click **OK**.
9. Click **OK** again.

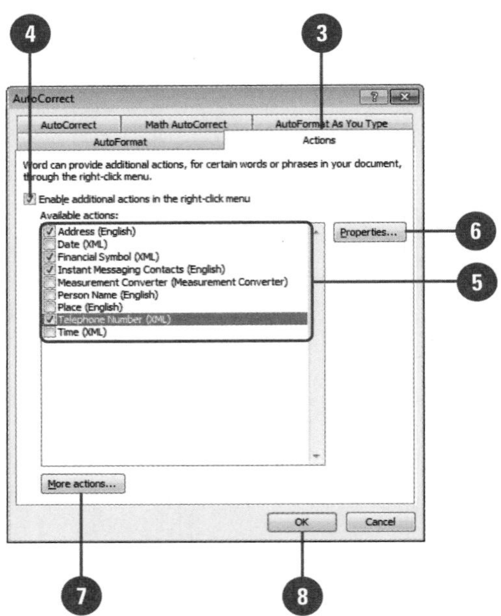

Online resources for Actions

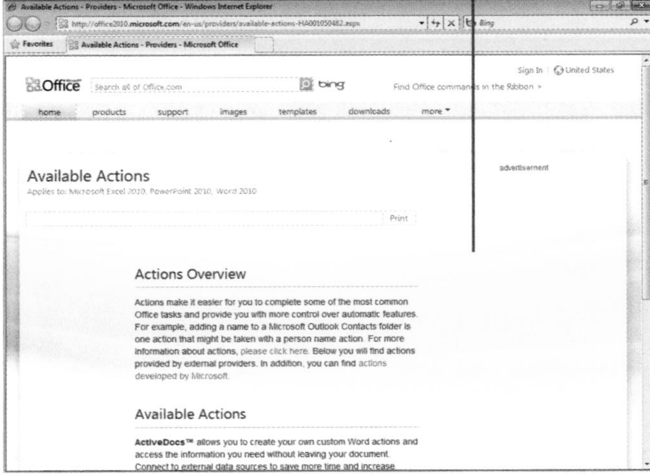

Insert Information Using an Action

1. Click an item, such as a cell, where you want to insert an action.
2. Type the information needed for the action, such as the date, a recognized financial symbol in capital letters, or a person's name from you contacts list, and then press Spacebar.
3. Right-click the item, and then point to **Additional Actions** (name varies depending on item).
4. Click the action option you want; options vary depending on the action. For example, click Show my Calendar or Schedule a Meeting.

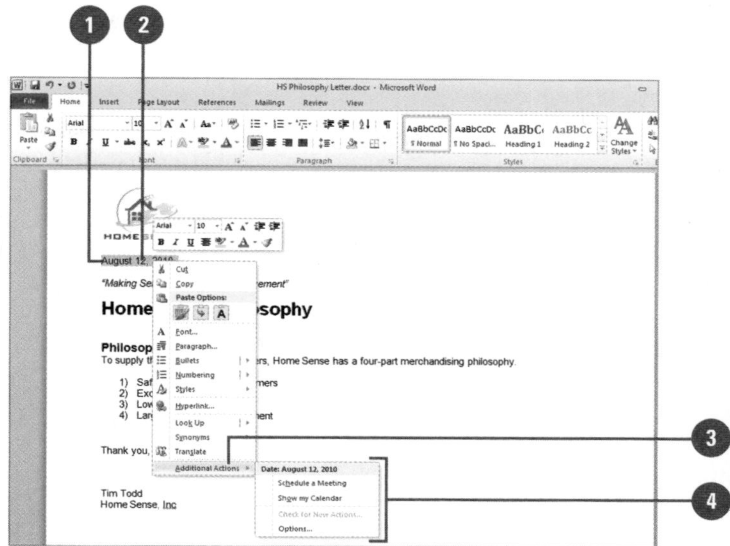

Outlook Calendar

Did You Know?

You can remove an action from text or item. Select text or item, and then press Delete to remove it.

Correcting Text Automatically

Office's **AutoCorrect** feature automatically corrects common capitalization and spelling errors as you type. AutoCorrect comes with hundreds of text and symbol entries you can edit or remove. You can add words and phrases to the AutoCorrect dictionary that you misspell, or add often-typed words and save time by just typing their initials. You can use AutoCorrect to quickly insert symbols. For example, you can type (c) to insert ©. Use the AutoCorrect Exceptions dialog box to control how Word handles capital letters. If you use math symbols in your work, you can use Math AutoCorrect (**New!**) to make it easier to insert them. It works just like AutoCorrect. When you point to a word that AutoCorrect changed, a small blue box appears under the first letter. When you point to the small blue box, the AutoCorrect Options button appears, which gives you control over whether you want the text to be corrected. You can also display the AutoCorrect dialog box and change AutoCorrect settings.

Turn On AutoCorrect

1. Click the **File** tab, and then click **Options**.
2. Click **Proofing**, and then click **AutoCorrect Options**.
3. Click the **AutoCorrect** tab.
4. Select the **Show AutoCorrect Options buttons** check box to display the button to change AutoCorrect option when corrections arise.
5. Select the **Replace text as you type** check box.
6. Select the capitalization related check boxes you want AutoCorrect to change for you.
7. To change AutoCorrect exceptions, click **Exceptions**, click the **First Letter** or **INitial CAps** tab, make the changes you want, and then click **OK**.
8. To use Math AutoCorrect, click the **Math AutoCorrect** tab, and then select the **Use Math AutoCorrect rules outside of math regions** check box.
9. Click **OK**, and then click **OK** again.

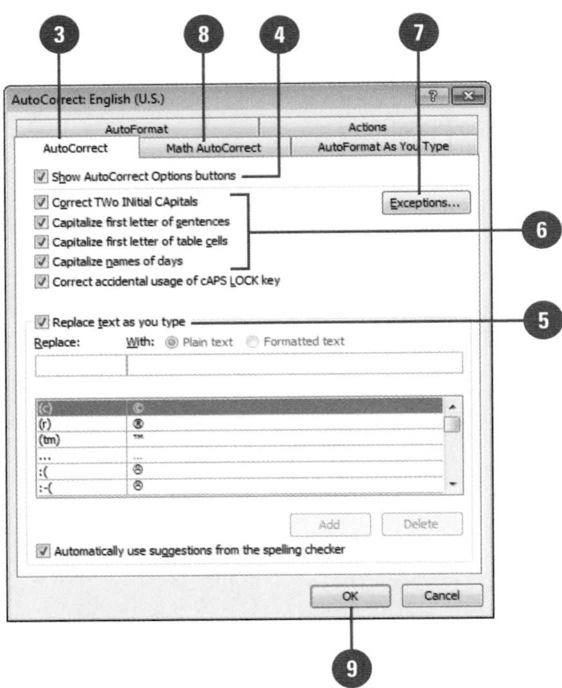

Add or Edit an AutoCorrect Entry

1. Click the **File** tab, and then click **Options**.
2. Click **Proofing**, and then click **AutoCorrect Options**.
3. Click the **AutoCorrect** tab.
4. Do one of the following:
   - **Add.** Type a misspelled word or an abbreviation.
   - **Edit.** Select the one you want to change.
5. Type the replacement entry.
6. Click **Add** or **Replace**. If necessary, click **Yes** to redefine entry.
7. Click **OK**, and then click **OK** again.

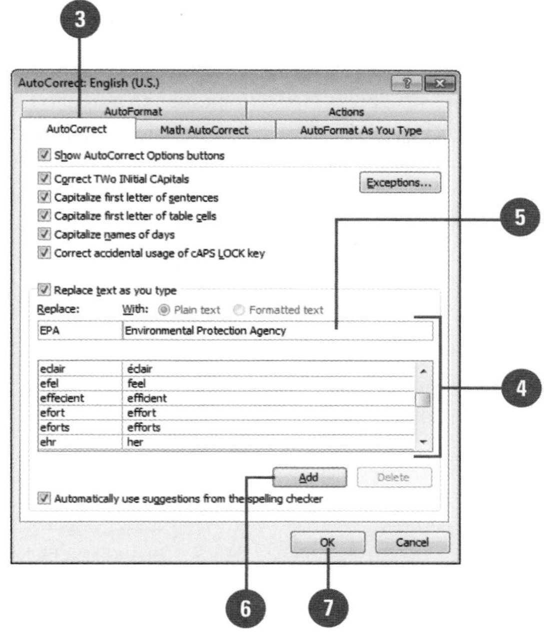

Replace Text as You Type

- To correct capitalization or spelling errors automatically, continue typing until AutoCorrect makes the required correction.

  Point to the small blue box under the corrected text, and then click the AutoCorrect Options button list arrow to view your options. Click an option, or click a blank area of the document to deselect the AutoCorrect Options menu.

- To create a bulleted or numbered list, type 1. or * (for a bullet), press Tab or Spacebar, type any text, and then press Enter. AutoCorrect inserts the next number or bullet. To end the list, press Backspace to erase the extra number or bullet.

Examples of AutoCorrect Changes

Type of Correction	If You Type	AutoCorrect Inserts
Capitalization	cAP LOCK	Cap Lock
Capitalization	TWo INitial CAps	Two Initial Caps
Capitalization	thursday	Thursday
Common typos	can;t	can't
Common typos	windoes	windows
Superscript ordinals	2nd	2nd
Stacked fractions	1/2	½
Smart quotes	" "	“ ”
Em dashes	Madison--a small city in Wisconsin--is a nice place to live.	Madison—a small city in Wisconsin—is a nice place to live.
Symbols	(c)	©
Symbols	(r)	®

Undoing and Redoing an Action

You may realize you've made a mistake shortly after completing an action. The Undo feature lets you "take back" one or more previous actions, including text you typed, edits you made, or commands you selected. For example, if you were to enter a title in a document, and then decide you don't like it, you could undo it instead of selecting the text and deleting it. A few moments later, if you decide the text you deleted was alright, you could use the Redo feature to restore it.

Undo an Action

1. Click the **Undo** button on the Quick Access Toolbar to undo the last action you completed.
2. Click the **Undo** button arrow on the Quick Access Toolbar to see recent actions that can be undone.
3. Click an action. Word reverses the selected action and all actions above it.

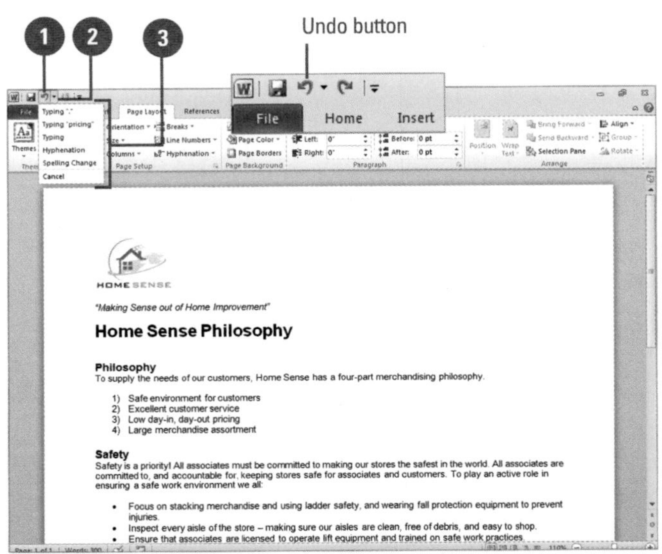

Redo an Action

1. Click the **Redo** button on the Quick Access Toolbar to restore your last undone action.

TROUBLE? *If the Redo button is not available on the Quick Access Toolbar, click the Customize Quick Access Toolbar list arrow, and then click Redo.*

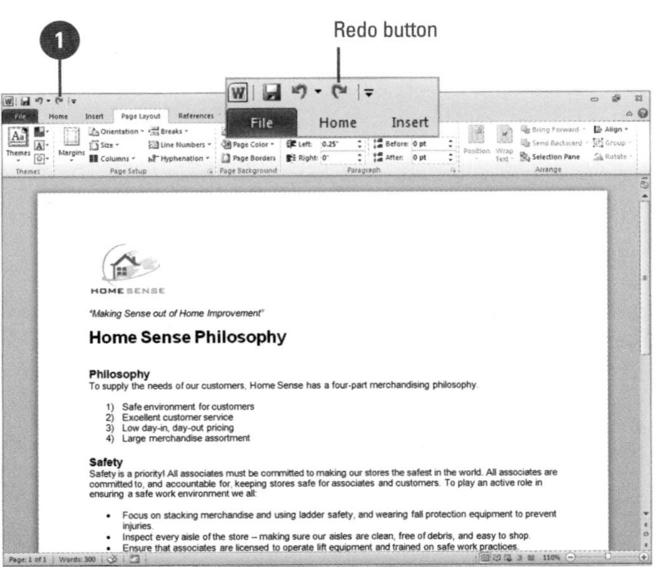

Formatting Documents

3

Introduction

Once you type a document and get the content how you want it, the finishing touches can sometimes be the most important. An eye catching document will draw the reader in, while a boring font without a lot of extra details will draw the reader away from all your hard work. To create that interest, Microsoft Word can help you change your document for a fresh look. One of the first elements you can change is your font attributes. Applying bold, underline, or italics when appropriate, can emphasize text. You might find that having different font sizes in your document to denote various topics will also enhance your document.

You can change the **kerning**—the amount of space between each individual character, for a special effect on a title or other parts of text. You can also apply a dropped capital letter to introduce a body of text, add a shading or border onto your document.

Word has various tools to help you format your document. You can search and replace formatting effects, display rulers, change a paragraph alignment, set paragraph tabs and indents, and change your line spacing. There are times when typing a paragraph will not do your text justice. Creating a bulleted or numbered list might better show your information. To further enhance the appearance of the text in a paragraph, you can quickly add a border and shading to selected text. If you have confidential information in a document or text that you don't want others to see, you can use a formatting option to hide the text.

What You'll Do

Formatting Text

A **font** is a collection of alphanumeric characters that share the same typeface, or design, and have similar characteristics. You can format text and numbers with font attributes—such as bolding, italics, or underlining—to enhance data to catch the reader's attention. The main formats you apply to text are available on the Home tab in the Font group or in the Font dialog box. Some of the formats available include strikethrough, subscript, superscript, and underline style and color. When you point to selected text, Office displays the Mini-Toolbar above it. The **Mini-Toolbar** provides easy access to common formatting toolbar buttons, such as font, font size, increase and decrease font size, bold, italic, font color, and increase and decrease list level. If you don't want to display the Mini-Toolbar, you can use Word Options to turn it off.

Format Text Quickly

1. Select the text you want to format.
2. Click the **Home** tab.
3. To change fonts, click the **Font** list arrow on the Ribbon or Mini-Toolbar, and then point for a live preview, or click the font you want, either a theme font or any available fonts.

   The font name appears in the font style.

   To change the font size, click one or more of the font size buttons on the Ribbon or Mini-Toolbar:

   - Click the **Font Size** list arrow, and then click the font size you want.
   - Click the **Increase Font Size** button or **Decrease Font Size** button.

   To apply other formatting, click one or more of the formatting buttons on the Ribbon or Mini-Toolbar: **Bold**, **Italic**, **Underline**, **Shadow**, **Strikethrough**, or **Font Color**.

   - To select an underline style, click the **Underline** button arrow, and then select a style or color.

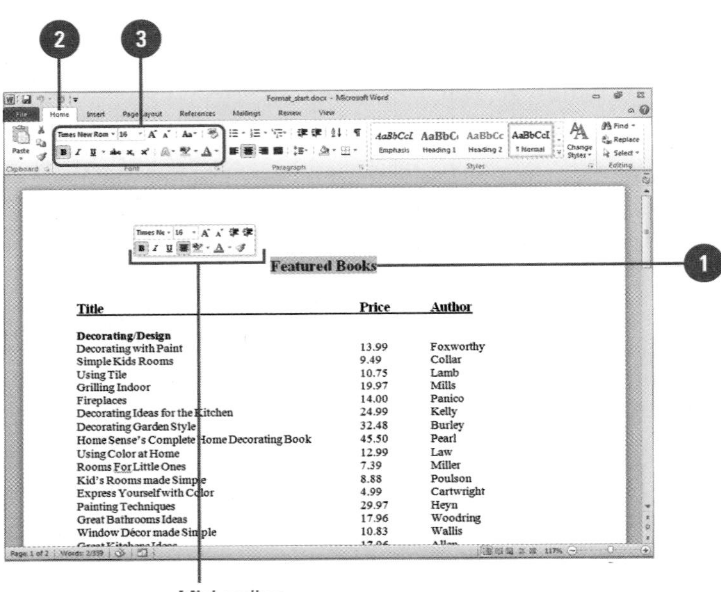

Format Text Using the Font Dialog Box

1. Select the text you want to format.
2. Click the **Home** tab.
3. Click the **Font** Dialog Box Launcher.

   The Font dialog box opens, displaying the Font tab.
4. Select the font, font style, and font size you want.
5. If you want, click the **Font Color** list arrow, and then click a color.
6. If you want, click the **Underline** list arrow, click a style, click **Underline Color** list arrow, and then click a color.
7. Click **OK**.

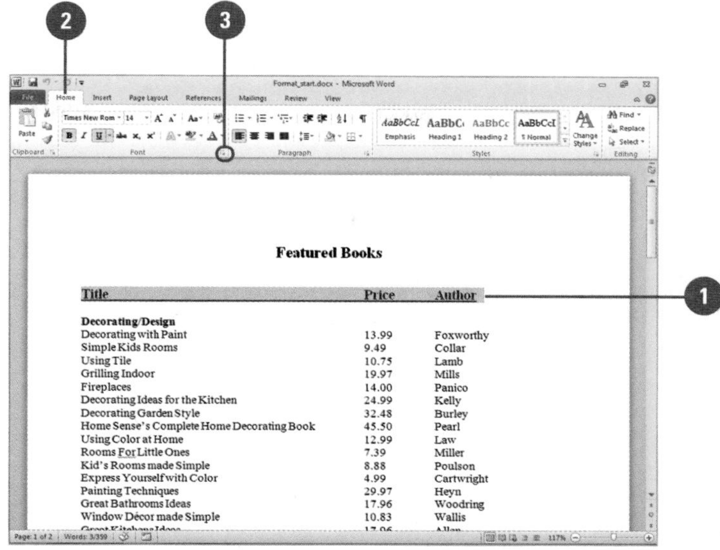

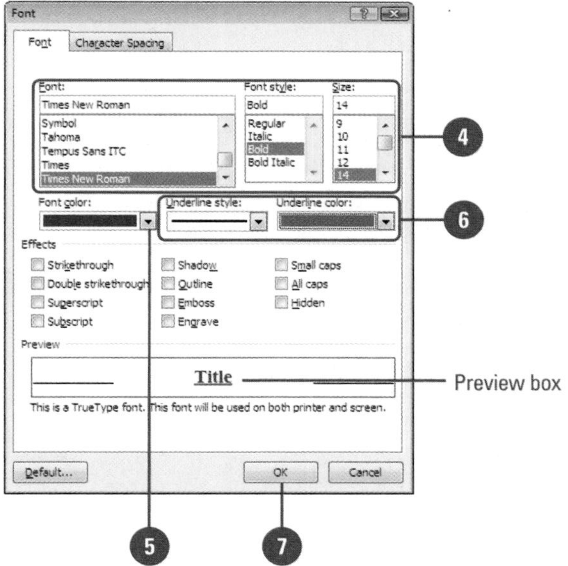

Did You Know?

You can tell the difference between a TrueType and printer font. A TrueType (outline) font is a font that uses special software capabilities to print exactly what is seen on the screen. A printer (screen) font is a font that comes only in specified sizes. If you are creating a document for publication, you need to use printer fonts.

What is a point? The size of each font character is measured in points (a point is approximately 1/72 of an inch).

Each computer has different fonts installed. Users with whom you share files may not have all the fonts you've used in a document installed on their computers.

Formatting Text for Emphasis

You'll often want to format, or change the style of, certain words or phrases to add emphasis to parts of a document. In addition to the standard formatting options—**Bold**, *Italic*, Underline, etc.—Word provides additional formatting effects to text, including Font Color, Gradient (**New!**), Shadow (**New!**), Outline (**New!**), Reflection (**New!**), Glow (**New!**), 3-D (**New!**), Highlight, Strikethrough, Superscript, Subscript, Small Caps, All Caps, and Hidden. To help you format sentences and change capitalization, you can change text case.

Apply Formatting Text Effects

1. Select the text you want to format.
2. Click the **Home** tab.
3. Click the formatting (**Font**, **Font Style**, **Size**, **Bold**, **Italic**, **Underline** (select a style and color), **Strikethrough**, **Superscript**, **Subscript**, or **Font Color** (select a color or a Gradient (**New!**)) you want.
4. To add a visual effect to text, click the **Text Effect** button (**New!**), and then click the option you want:
   - A combination text effect.
   - Outline
   - Shadow
   - Reflection
   - Glow
   - **Clear Text Effects.** Removes effect.
5. To change text case, click the **Case** button, and then click the option you want:
   - Sentence case.
   - lowercase
   - UPPERCASE
   - Capitalize Each Word
   - tOGGLEcASE
6. To highlight text, click the **Text Highlight Color** button arrow, and then click the color you want.
   - **Add highlight.** Click a color.
   - **Remove highlight.** Click **No Color.**

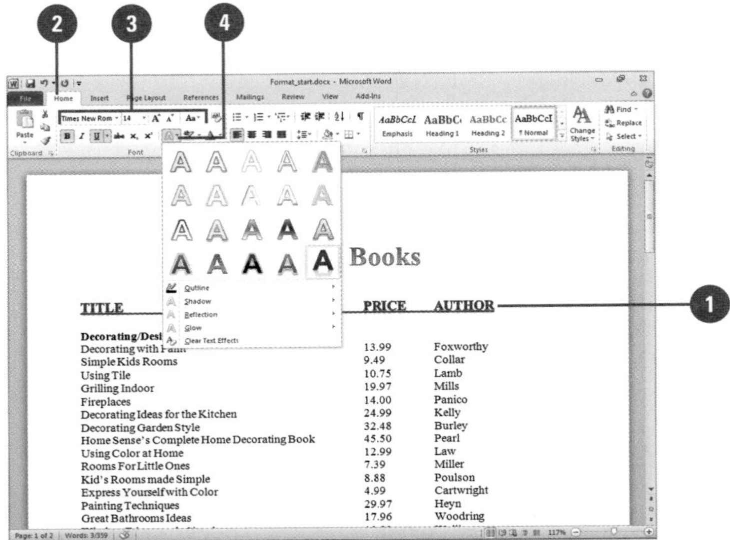

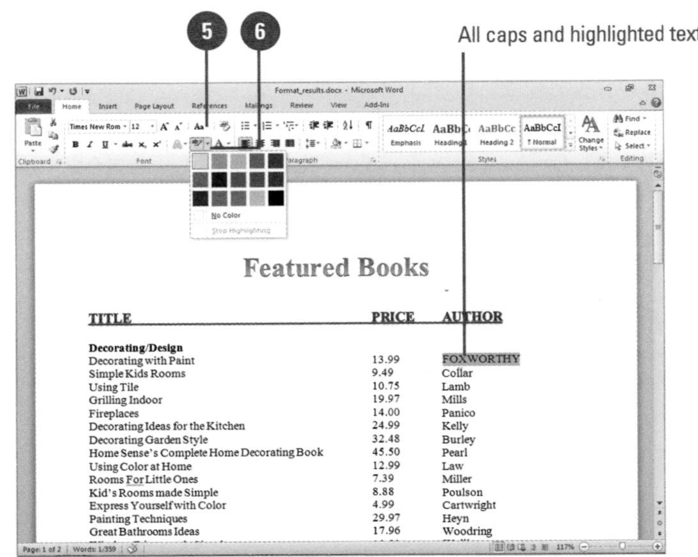

Apply Other Formatting Effects to Text

1. Select the text you want to format.
2. Click the **Home** tab.
3. Click the **Font Dialog Box Launcher**.
4. Click the formatting (**Font**, **Font Style**, **Size**, **Font color**, **Underline style**, and **Underline color**) you want.
5. Click to select the effects (**Strikethrough**, **Double strikethrough**, **Superscript**, **Subscript**, **Small caps**, **All caps**, and **Hidden**) you want.
6. To custom text effects, such as a text fill or outline with a solid or gradient, shadow, reflection, glow and soft edges, or 3-D format, click **Text Effects**, specify the options you want, and then click **Close** (**New!**).
7. Check the results in the Preview box.
8. To make the new formatting options the default for all new Word documents, click **Set As Default**, and then click **Yes**.
9. Click **OK**.

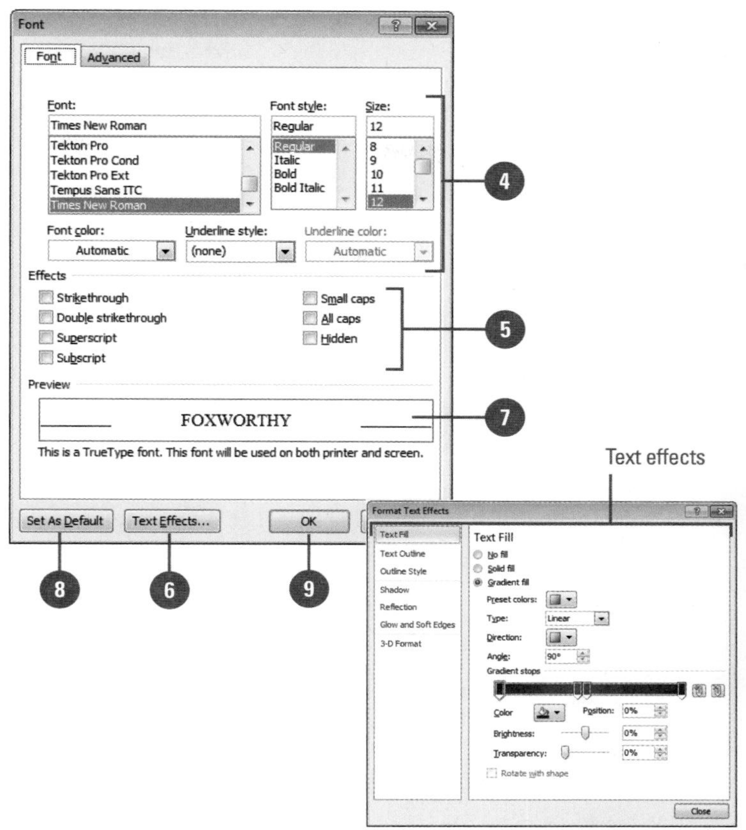

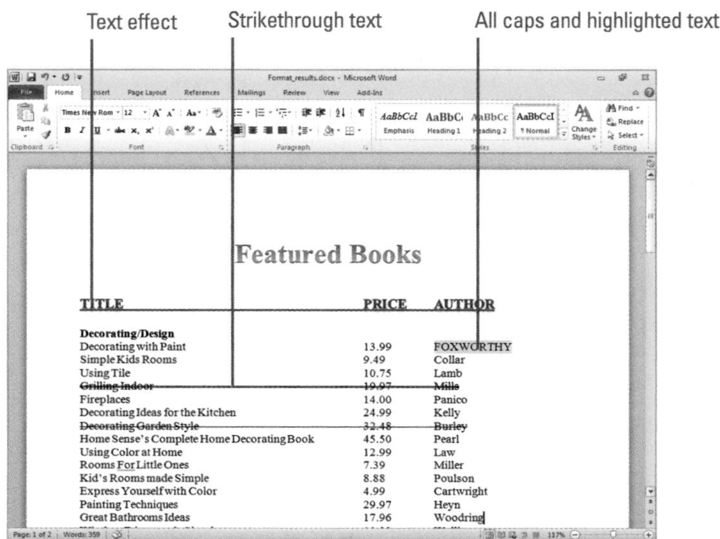

Did You Know?

You can quickly clear formatting. Select the text to which you want to clear formatting, click the Home tab, and then click the Clear Formatting button.

Changing Character Spacing

Kerning is the amount of space between each individual character that you type. Sometimes the space between two characters is larger than others, which makes the word look uneven. You can use the Font dialog box to change the kerning setting for selected characters. Kerning works only with OpenType/TrueType or Adobe Type Manager fonts. You can expand or condense character spacing to create a special effect for a title, or re-align the position of characters to the bottom edge of the text—this is helpful for positioning the copyright or trademark symbols. In addition, you can set text formatting for OpenType/TrueType fonts (**New!**) that include a range of ligature settings (where two or three letters combine into a single character), number spacing and forms, and stylistic sets (added font sets in a given font). Many of these options are based on specifications from font designers.

Change Character Spacing

1. Select the text you want to format.
2. Click the **Home** tab.
3. Click the **Font Dialog Box Launcher**.
4. Click the **Advanced** tab.
5. Click the **Spacing** list arrow, click an option, and then specify a point size to expand or condense spacing by the amount specified.
6. Click the **Position** list arrow, click an option, and then specify a point size to raise or lower the text in relation to the baseline (bottom of the text).
7. Select the **Kerning for fonts** check box, and then specify a point size.
8. Check the results in the Preview box.
9. To make the new formatting options the default for all new Word documents, click **Set As Default**, and then click **Yes**.
10. Click **OK**.

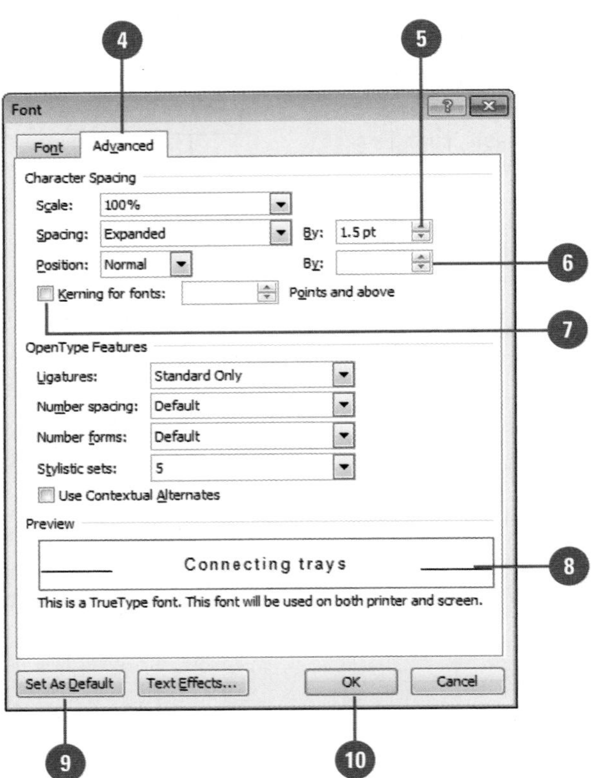

Selecting Text with Similar Formatting

A quick way to select text with similar formatting is to use the Select Text with Similar Formatting command. After you select the text with the formatting you want to find, click the Select button on the Home tab, and then choose the Select Text with Similar Formatting command. Word highlights all the text with similar formatting in the document. With the text selected, you can change the text formatting.

Select Similar Text Formatting

1. Select the text you want to find.
2. Click the **Home** tab.
3. Click the **Select** button, and then click **Select Text with Similar Formatting**.

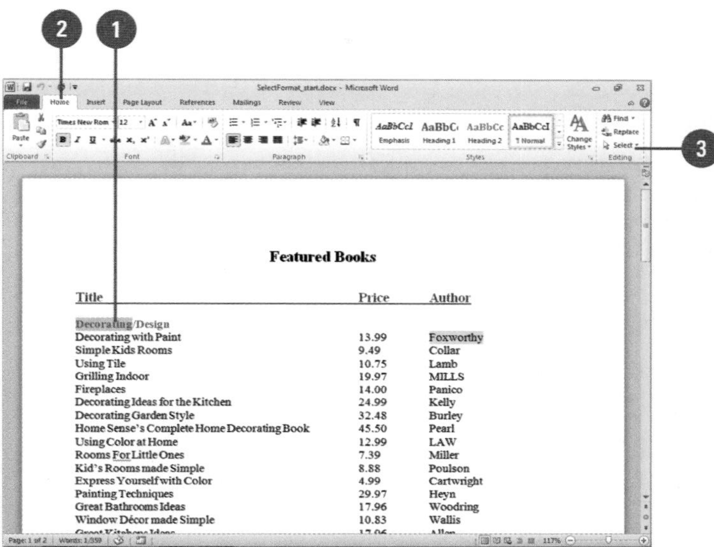

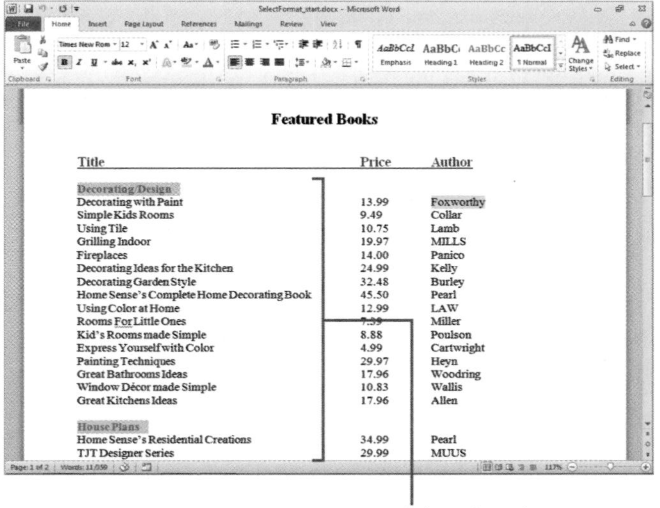

Selected results

Did You Know?

You can quickly clear formatting. Select the text to which you want to clear formatting, click the Home tab, and then click the Clear Formatting button.

See Also

See "Revealing Formatting Styles" on page 96 for more information on using the Select Text With Similar Formatting command.

Finding and Replacing Formatting

Suddenly you realize all the bold text in your report would be easier to read in italics. Do you spend time making these changes one by one? No. The Find and Replace feature locates the formatting and instantly substitutes new formatting. If your search for a formatting change is an easy one, click Less in the Find and Replace dialog box to decrease the size of the dialog box. If your search is a more complex one, click More to display additional options. With the Match Case option, you can specify exact capitalization. The Reading Highlight button highlights items found to make them easier to read. The Go To tab quickly moves you to a place or item in your document.

Find Formatting

1. Click the **Home** tab.
2. Click the **Find** button arrow, and then click **Advanced Find**.
3. To clear any previous settings, click **No Formatting**.
4. If you want to locate formatted text, type the word or words.
5. Click **More**, click **Format**, and then click the formatting you want to find.
6. To highlight located items, click **Reading Highlight**, and then click **Highlight All**.
7. Click **Find Next** to select the next instance of the formatted text.
8. Click **OK** to confirm Word finished the search.
9. Click **Close** or **Cancel**.

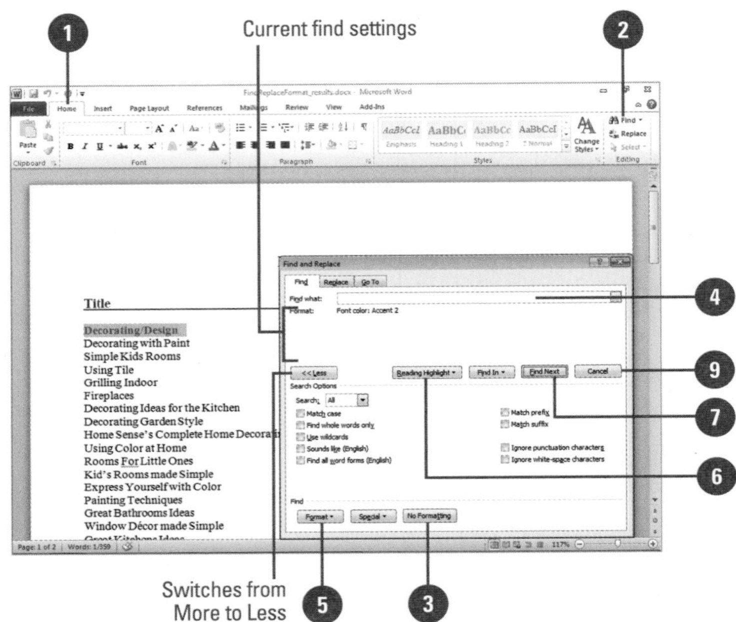

Did You Know?

You can find an item or location. Click the Home tab, click the Find button arrow, click Go To, click an item to find (an item, such as a bookmark or comment or location, such as a page or section), enter an item number or name, click Next, Previous, or Go To to locate the item, and then click Close.

Replace Formatting

1. Click the **Home** tab.
2. Click the **Replace** button.
3. If you want to locate formatted text, type the word or words.
4. Click the **More** button, click **Format**, and then click the formatting you want to find. When you're done, click **OK**.
5. Press Tab, and then type any text you want to substitute.
6. Click **Format**, and then click the formatting you want to substitute. When you're done, click **OK**.
7. To substitute every instance of the formatting, click **Replace All**.

   To substitute the formatting one instance at a time, click **Find Next**, and then click **Replace**.

   If you want to cancel the replace, click **Cancel**.
8. If necessary, click **Yes** to search from the beginning of the document.
9. Click **OK** to confirm Word finished searching.
10. Click **Close** or **Cancel**.

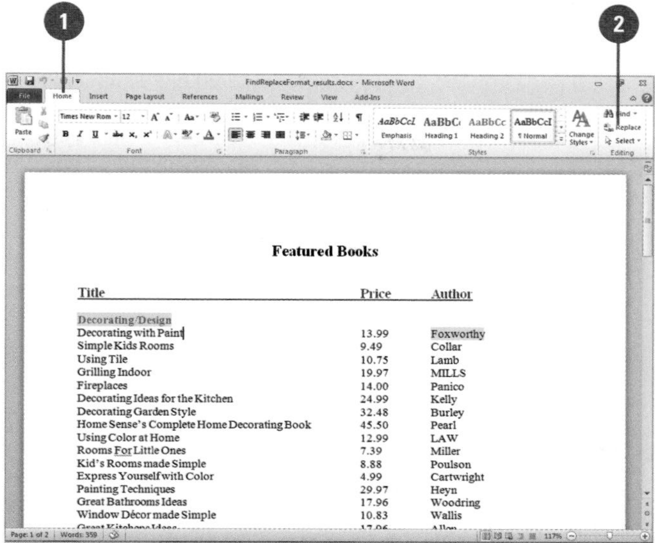

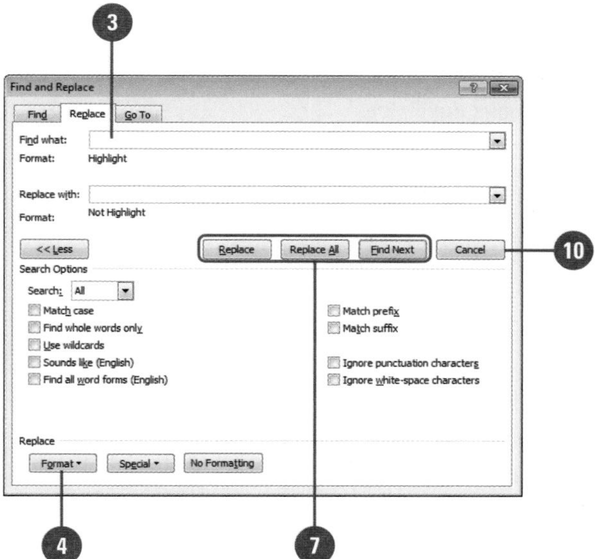

Did You Know?

You can find and replace special characters and document elements. In Word, you can search for and replace special characters (for example, an em dash) and document elements (for example, a tab character). Click More in the Find and Replace dialog box, click Special, and then click the item you want from the menu.

Finding and Replacing Custom Formatting

If your search for formatting involves a complex search for a specific type of formatted text, click More in the Find and Replace dialog box to increase the size of the dialog box and display additional options. The expanded Find and Replace dialog box provides options to find exact capitalization, find whole words only, use wildcards, and locate words that sound like English or different forms of English words. With the Special button, you can find and replace special characters and elements, such as graphics, tabs, fields, white space, and page breaks.

Find or Replace Special Formatting

1. Click the **Home** tab.
2. Click the **Find** button arrow, and then click **Advanced Find** or click the **Replace** button.
3. To clear any previous settings, click **No Formatting**.
4. If you want to locate formatted text, type the word or words you want to find and/or replace.
5. Click **More** to expand the dialog box.
6. Click **Special**, and then click the specialized formatting item you want to find.
7. Click **Find Next** to select the next instance of the formatted text.
8. To substitute every instance of the formatting, click **Replace All**.

   To substitute the formatting one instance at a time, click **Find Next**, and then click **Replace**.
9. Click **OK** to confirm Word finished the search.
10. Click **Close** or **Cancel**.

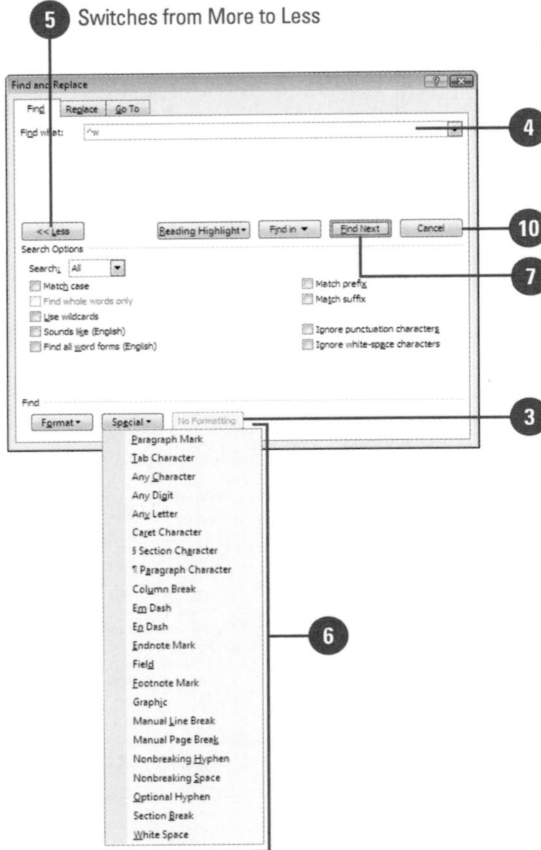

Use Find and Replace Options

1. Click the **Home** tab.
2. Click the **Find** or **Replace** button.
3. To clear any previous settings, click **No Formatting**.
4. If you want to locate formatted text, type the word or words you want to find and/or replace.
5. Click **More**, and then select or clear the options you want:
   - **Search.** Select a search direction: All, Down, or Up.
   - **Match Case.** Select to find exact capitalization.
   - **Find whole words only.** Select to find words with space on either side.
   - **Use wildcards.** Select to use wildcards, such as asterisk (*) or question mark (?).
   - **Sounds like (English).** Select to find English sounding words.
   - **Find all word forms (English).** Select to find all English forms of a word.
   - **Match prefix** or **Match suffix.** Select to find text at the beginning or end of a word.
   - **Ignore punctuation characters** or **Ignore white-space characters.** Select to ignore punctuation (periods, commas, etc.) or white space characters.
6. Click **Find Next** to select the next instance of the formatted text, or click **Replace**
7. Click **OK** to confirm Word finished the search.
8. Click **Close** or **Cancel**.

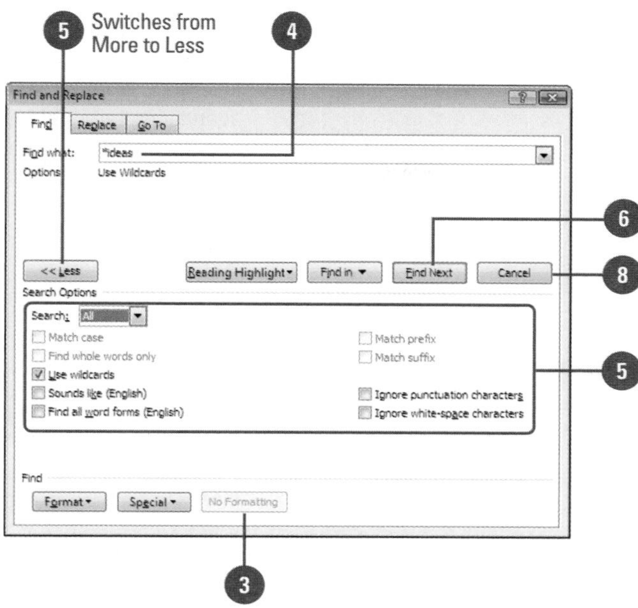

For Your Information

Using Wildcards

A wildcard allows you to search for variable text. For example, you can use the asterisk (*) wildcard to search for a string of characters ("s*d" finds "sad" and "started"), or use the question mark (?) wildcard to search for any single character (s?t finds "sat" and "set"). To search for a character that's defined as a wildcard, type a backslash (\) before the character. For example, type \? to find a question mark.

Changing Paragraph Alignment

Text starts out positioned evenly along the left margin, and uneven, or **ragged**, at the right margin. Left-aligned text works well for body paragraphs in most cases, but other alignments vary the look of a document and help lead the reader through the text. **Right-aligned text**, which is even along the right margin and ragged at the left margin, is good for adding a date to a letter. **Justified text** spreads text evenly between the margins, creating a clean, professional look, often used in newspapers and magazines. **Centered text** is best for titles and headings. You can use Click-And-Type to quickly center titles or set different text alignment on the same line, or you can use the alignment buttons on the Home tab to set alignment on one or more lines.

Align New Text with Click-And-Type

- Position the I-beam at the left, right, or center of the line where you want to insert new text.

  When the I-beam shows the appropriate alignment, double-click to place the insertion point, and then type your text.

Click-And-Type Text Pointers

Pointer	Purpose
I≡	Left-aligns text
≡I	Right-aligns text
I (centered)	Centers text
I≡ (with +)	Creates a new line in the same paragraph
▣I	Creates a text around a picture

Align Existing Text

1. Position the I-beam, or select at least one line in each paragraph to align.
2. Click the appropriate button on the Home tab.
   - **Align Left** button
   - **Center** button
   - **Align Right** button
   - **Justify** button

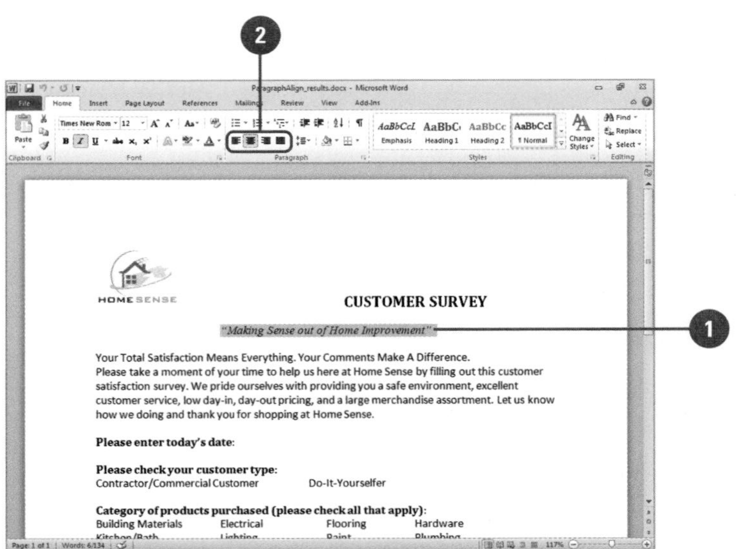

Changing Line Spacing

The lines in all Word documents are single-spaced by default, which is appropriate for letters and most documents. But you can easily change your document line spacing to double or 1.5 lines to allow extra space between every line. This is useful when you want to make notes on a printed document. Sometimes, you'll want to add space above and below certain paragraphs, for headlines, or indented quotations to help set off the text.

Change Line Spacing

1. Select the text you want to change.
2. Click the **Home** tab.
3. Click the **Line Spacing** button arrow, and then click a spacing option.
   - To apply a new setting, click the number you want.
   - To apply the setting you last used, click the **Line Spacing** button.
   - To enter precise parameters, click **Line Spacing Options**, specify the line or paragraph settings you want, and then click **OK**.
   - To apply the setting you last used, click **Add Space Before Paragraph** or **Add Space After Paragraph**.

TIMESAVER *Press Ctrl+1 for single-spacing, Ctrl+5 for 1.5 spacing, or Ctrl+2 for double-spacing.*

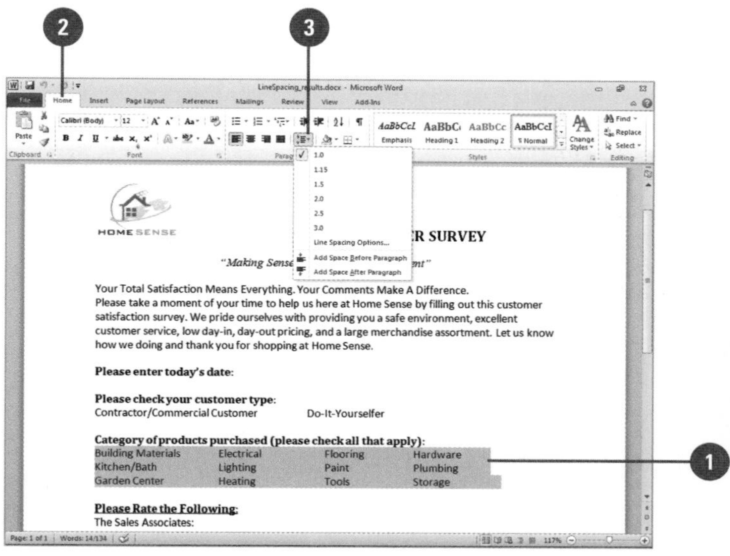

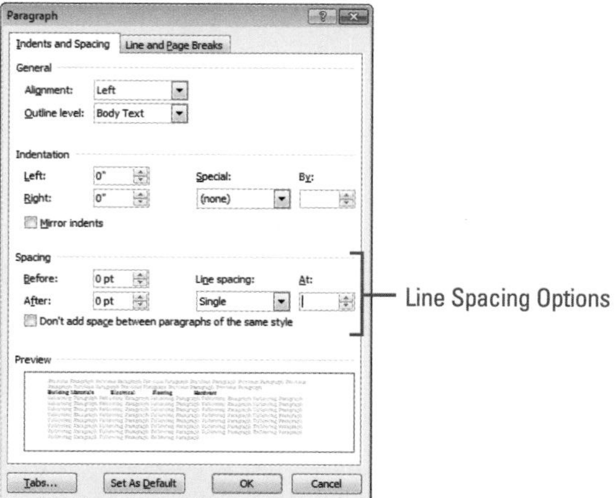

Displaying Rulers

Word rulers do more than measure. The **horizontal ruler** above the document shows the length of the typing line and lets you quickly adjust left and right margins and indents, set tabs, and change column widths. The **vertical ruler** along the left edge of the document lets you adjust top and bottom margins and change table row heights. You can hide the rulers to get more room for your document. As you work with long documents, use the document map to jump to any heading in your document. Headings are in the left pane and documents in the right.

Show and Hide the Rulers

1. Click the **View** tab.
2. Select or clear the **Ruler** check box.

TIMESAVER *Click the View Ruler button at the top of the vertical scroll bar.*

- To view the horizontal ruler, click the **Web Layout View** or **Draft View** button.
- To view the horizontal and vertical rulers, click the **Print Layout View** button.

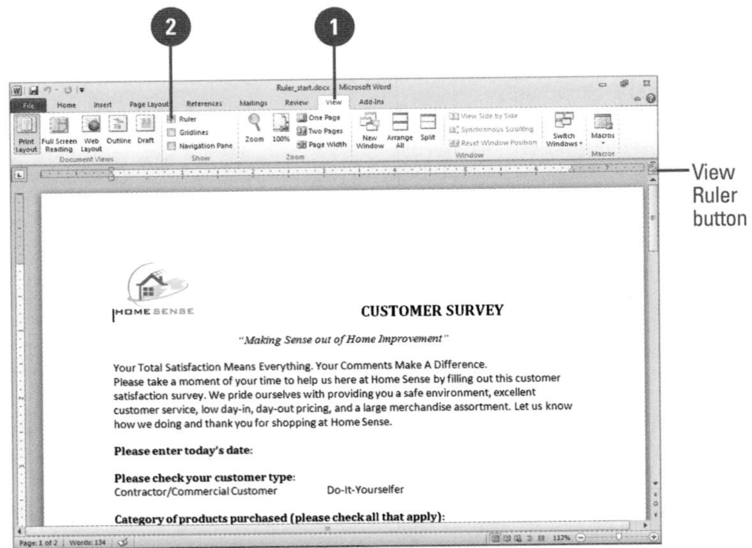

Did You Know?

You can change the ruler measurements. Change the ruler to show inches, centimeters, millimeters, points, or picas. Click the File tab, click Options, click Advanced, click the Show Measurement In Units list arrow, select the measurement you want, and then click OK.

You can set your text to be hyphenated. Hyphenation prevents ugly gaps and short lines in text. Click the Page Layout tab, click the Hyphenation button, and then click None, Automatic, or Manual, or Hyphenation Options. Click Hyphenation Options to set the hyphenation zone and limit the number of consecutive hyphens (usually two), and then click OK.

Setting Paragraph Tabs

In your document, **tabs** set how text or numerical data aligns in relation to the document margins. A **tab stop** is a predefined stopping point along the document's typing line. Default tab stops are set every half-inch, but you can set multiple tabs per paragraph at any location. Choose from four text tab stops: left, right, center, and decimal (for numerical data). The bar tab inserts a vertical bar at the tab stop. You can use the Tab button on the horizontal ruler to switch between the available tabs.

Create and Clear a Tab Stop

1. Select one or more paragraphs in which you want to set a tab stop.
2. Click the **Tab** button on the horizontal ruler until it shows the type of tab stop you want.
3. Click the ruler where you want to set the tab stop.
4. If necessary, drag the tab stop to position it where you want.

   To display a numerical measurement in the ruler where the tab is placed, press and hold Alt as you drag.
5. To clear a tab stop, drag it off the ruler.

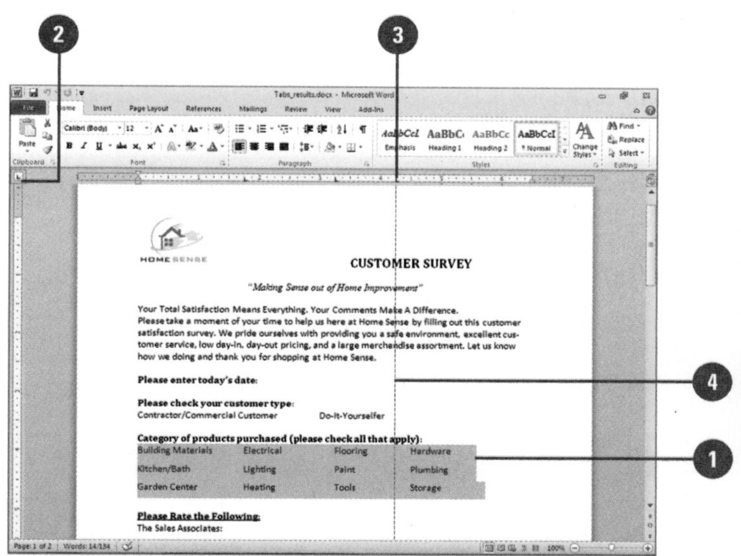

Did You Know?

You can view formatting marks. Sometimes it's hard to see the number of spaces or tabs between words. You can change the view to display formatting marks, a period for space and an arrow for tabs. Click the Home tab, and then click the Show/Hide ¶ button to toggle on and off. Click the File tab, click Options, click Display, select the formatting mark check boxes you want to view, and then click OK.

Tab Stops

Tab Stop	Purpose
└	Aligns text to the left of the tab stop
┘	Aligns text to the right of the tab stop
┴	Centers text on the tab stop
┴:	Aligns numbers on the decimal point
|	Inserts a vertical bar at the tab stop

Setting Paragraph Indents

Quickly indent lines of text to precise locations from the left or right margin with the horizontal ruler. Indent the first line of a paragraph (called a **first-line indent**) as books do to distinguish paragraphs. Indent the second and subsequent lines of a paragraph from the left margin (called a **hanging indent**) to create a properly formatted bibliography. Indent the entire paragraph any amount from the left and right margins (called **left indents** and **right indents**) to separate quoted passages.

Indent Paragraph Lines Precisely

1. Click the **View Ruler** button to display the Ruler.
2. Click the paragraph or select multiple paragraphs to indent:
   - To change the left indent of the first line, drag the First-line Indent marker.
   - To change the indent of the second and subsequent lines, drag the Hanging Indent marker.
   - To change the left indent for all lines, drag the Left Indent marker.
   - To change the right indent for all lines, drag the Right Indent marker.

   As you drag a marker, the dotted guideline helps you accurately position the indent. You can also press and hold Alt to see a measurement in the ruler.

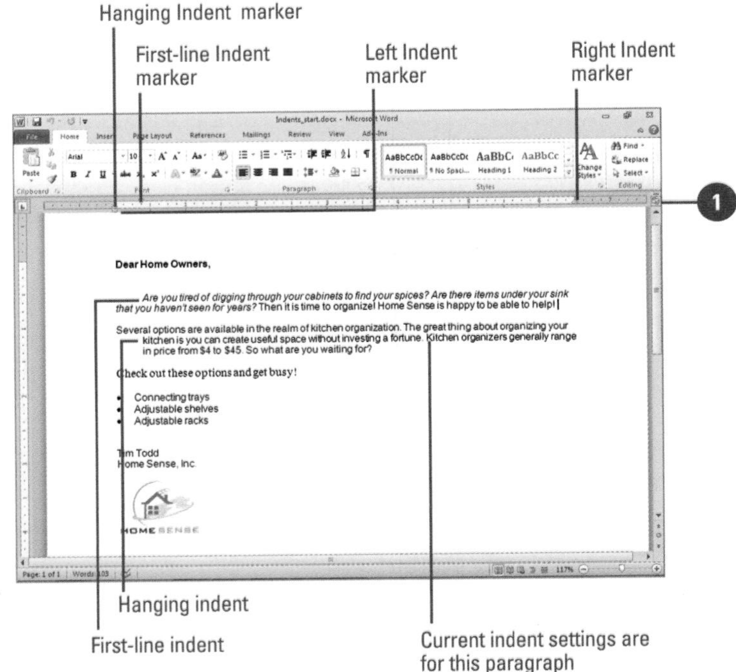

Did You Know?

You can indent using the Tab key. You can indent the first line of a paragraph by clicking at the beginning of the paragraph, and then pressing Tab. You can indent the entire paragraph by selecting it, and then pressing Tab.

Indent a Paragraph

1. Click the paragraph, or select multiple paragraphs to indent.
2. Click the **Home** tab.
3. Click the **Increase Indent** button or **Decrease Indent** button to move the paragraph right or left one-half inch.

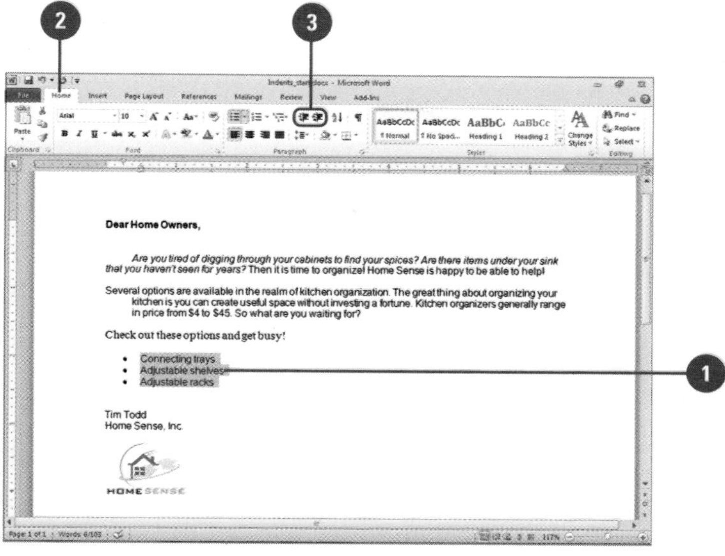

Did You Know?

You can add line numbers to a document or page. Click the Page Layout tab, click the Line Numbers button, and then click Continuous, Restart Each Page, Restart Each Section, Suppress For Current Paragraph, or Line Numbering Options.

Set Indentation Using the Tab Key

1. Click the **File** tab, and then click **Options**.
2. In the left pane, click **Proofing**, and then click **AutoCorrect Options**.
3. Click the **AutoFormat As You Type** tab.
4. Select the **Set left- and first-indent with tabs and backspaces** check box.
5. Click **OK**.

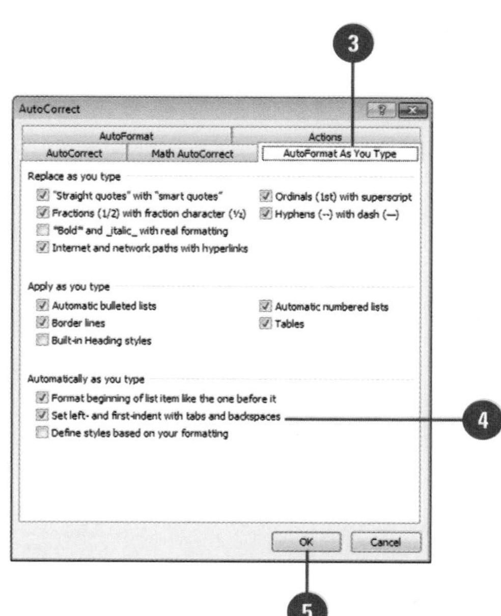

Creating Bulleted and Numbered Lists

The best way to draw attention to a list is to format the items with bullets or numbers. You can even create multi-level lists. For different emphasis, change any bullet or number style to one of Word's many predefined formats. For example, switch round bullets to check boxes or Roman numerals to lowercase letters. You can also insert a picture as a bullet or customize the numbering list style—including fixed-digits, such as 001, 002, etc. (**New!**). If you move, insert, or delete items in a numbered list, Word sequentially renumbers the list for you.

Create a Bulleted List

1. Click where you want to create a bulleted list.
2. Click the **Home** tab.
3. Click the **Bullets** button arrow, and then select a bullet style.
4. Type the first item in your list, and then press Enter.
5. Type the next item in your list, and then press Enter.
6. Click the **Bullets** button, or press Enter again to end the list.

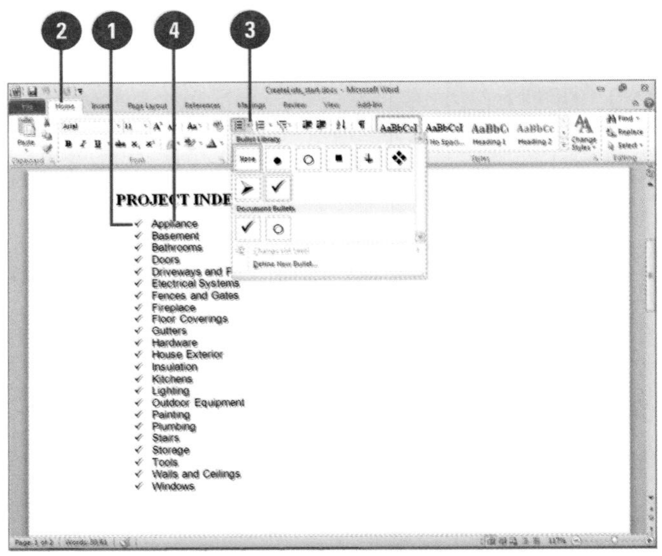

Create a Numbered List

1. Click where you want to create a numbered list.
2. Click the **Home** tab.
3. Click the **Numbering** button arrow, and then select a numbering style.
4. Type the first item in your list, and then press Enter.
5. Type the next item in your list, and then press Enter.
6. Click the **Numbering** button, or press Enter again to end the list.

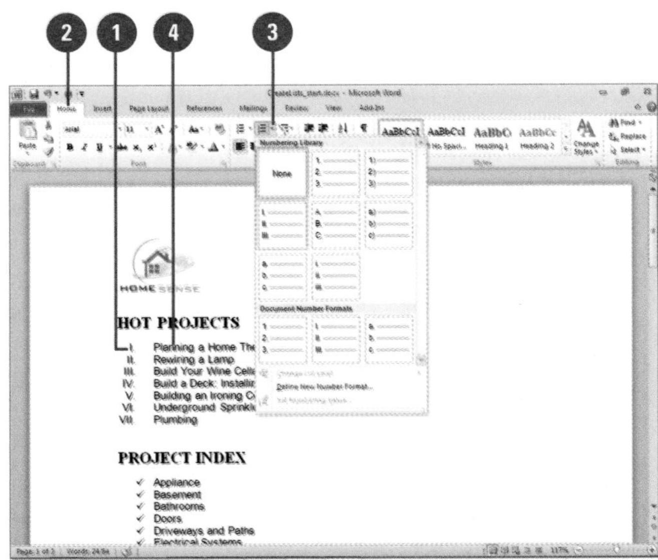

Change Bullet or Number Styles

1. Select the list, and then click the Home tab.
2. Click the **Bullets** or **Numbering** button arrow.
3. Click a predefined format, or click **Define New Bullet** or **Define New Number Format**.
4. Select the appropriate options:
   - **Bullet.** Click **Symbol**, **Picture**, or **Font**, and then select the picture you want.
   - **Number.** Select a numbering style (**New!**), font, and format.
5. Specify the alignment and any other formatting you want.
6. Click **OK**.

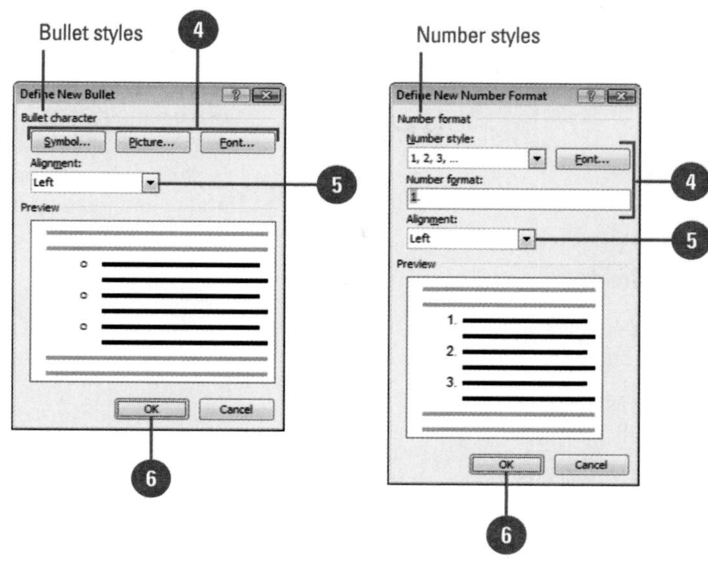

Create a Multi-Level Bulleted or Numbered List

1. Start the list as usual.
2. Press Tab to indent a line to the next level bullet or number, type the item, and then press Enter to insert the next bullet or number.
3. Press Shift+Tab to return to the previous level bullet or number.
4. To format the multi-level list, select the list, click the **Multi-Level List** button on the Home tab, and then select a format.

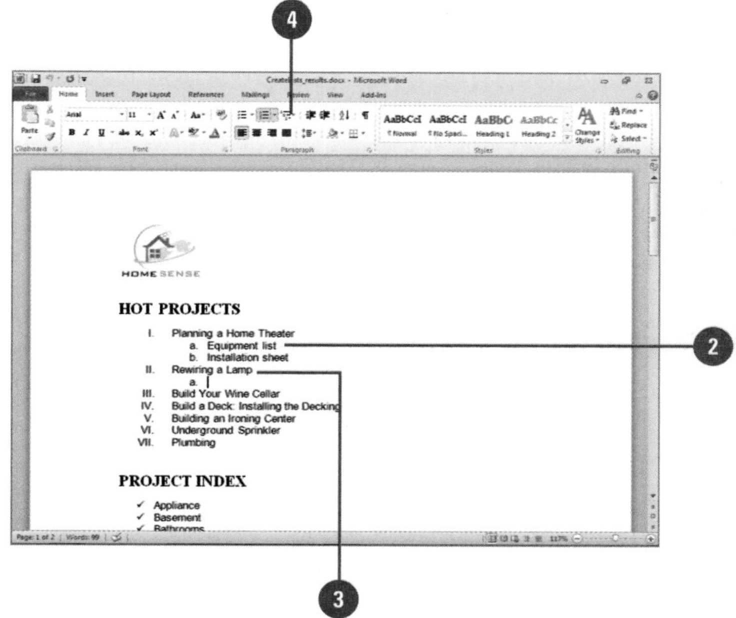

Did You Know?

You can quickly create a numbered list. Click to place the insertion point at the beginning of a line, type 1., press the Spacebar, type the first item, and then press Enter. Press Enter or Backspace to end the list.

Applying Borders and Shading

To enhance the appearance of the text in a paragraph, you can quickly add a border and shading to selected text. When you add a border, you can specify what sides you want to include or exclude. For example, you can add a border on just the top and the bottom and leave the sides open. Shading colors the background behind the selected text or paragraph. If you want to customize borders and shading by changing line style, color, and width preferences, you can make changes in the Borders and Shading dialog box.

Apply a Border

1. Select the paragraph text you want to format.
2. Click the **Home** tab.
3. Click the **Borders and Shading** button arrow, and then click to select the border commands to add or remove a border.

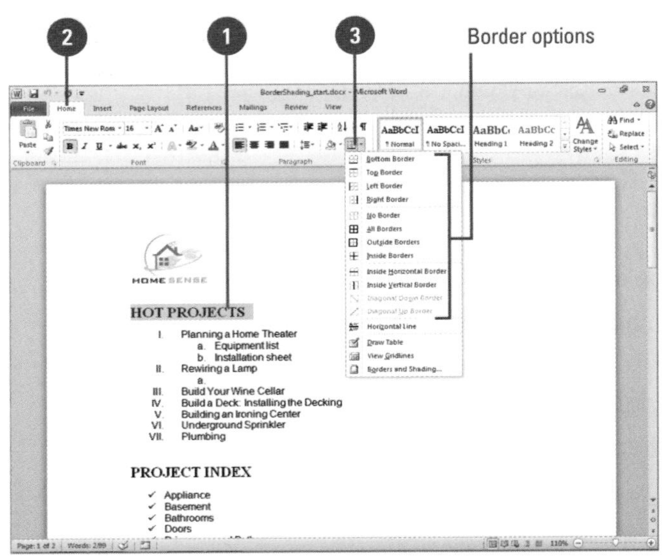

Apply Paragraph Shading

1. Select the paragraph text you want to format.
2. Click the **Home** tab.
3. Click the **Shading** button arrow, and then click to select the shading color you want to apply to the selected text.

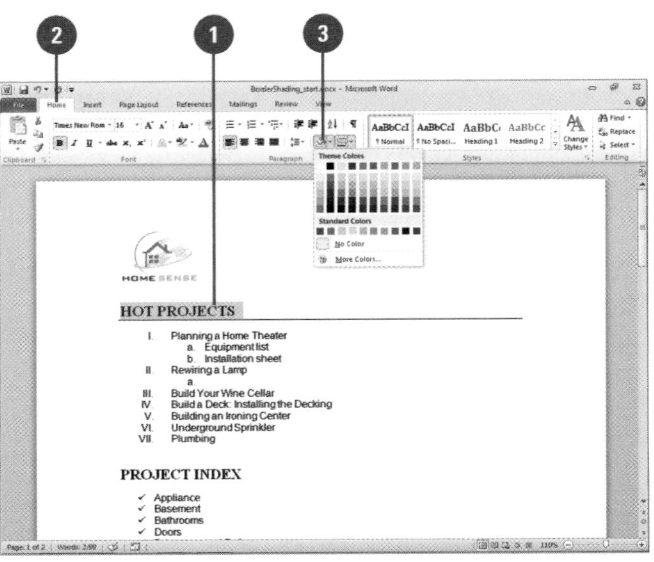

Apply Paragraph Shading and Borders

1. Select the paragraph text you want to format.
2. Click the **Home** tab.
3. Click the **Borders and Shading** button arrow, and then click **Borders and Shading**.
4. Click the **Borders** tab.
5. Click to select the type of Setting you want for your border.
6. Click to select the type of Style.
7. Apply any other options you want.
8. Look in the preview box to see the new border.
9. Click the **Shading** tab.
10. Click to select the shading fill color you want to apply to your table.
11. Apply any other options you want.
12. Look in the preview box to see the new shading color.
13. Click **OK**.

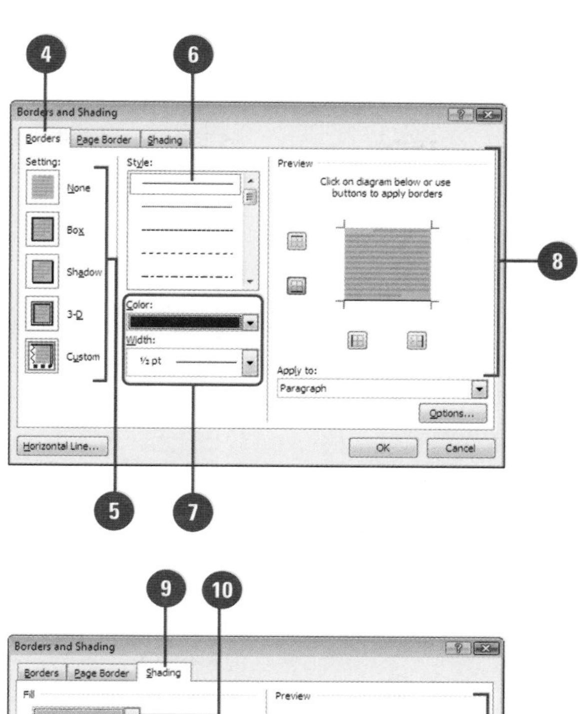

Hiding Text

If you have confidential information in a document or text that you don't want others to see, you can hide the text. When you hide text, you can't view or print the text unless you select the Hidden Text option in the Options dialog box. When you display or print hidden text, the characters appear with a dotted lined underneath. Hiding text does not protect your text from being seen, but it does conceal it from others.

Hide or Unhide Text

1. Select the text you want to hide or the hidden text.
2. Click the **Home** tab, and then click the **Font Dialog Box Launcher**.
3. Click the **Font** tab.
4. Select or clear the **Hidden** check box.
5. Click **OK**.

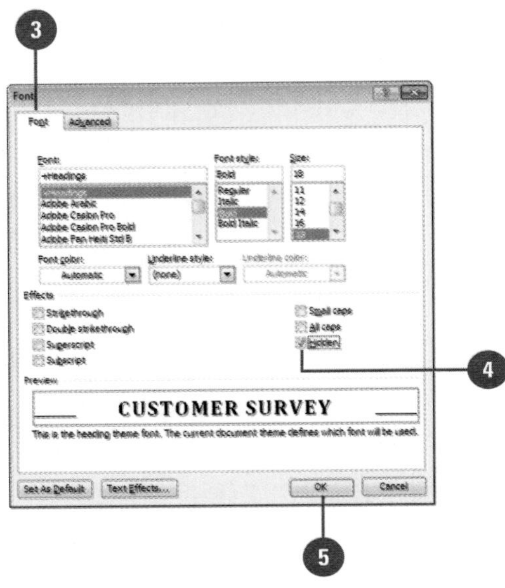

Display or Print Hidden Text

1. Click the **File** tab, and then click **Options**.
2. In the left pane, click **Display**.
3. Select the **Hidden text** check box.
4. Select the **Print hidden text** check box.
5. Click **OK**.

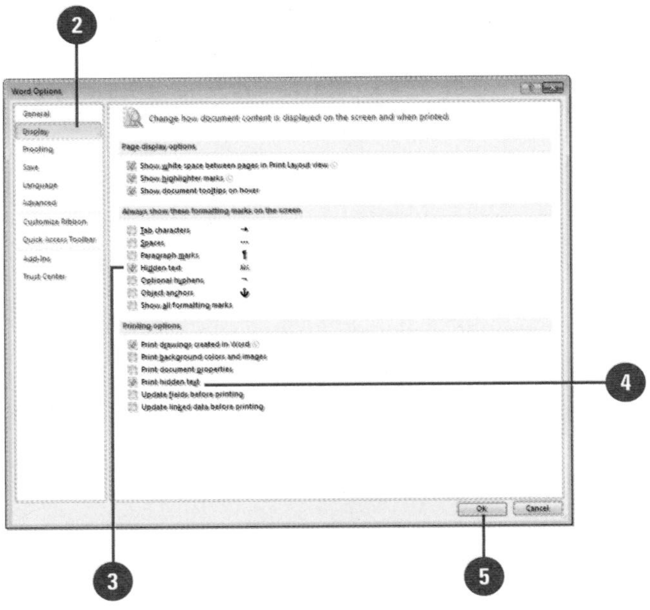

Using Templates, Styles, and Themes

4

Introduction

Microsoft Word documents are based on templates, which are predesigned and preformatted files that serve as the foundation of the documents. Each template is made up of styles that have common design elements, such as coordinated fonts, sizes, and colors, as well as, page layout designs. Start with a Word template for memos, reports, fax cover pages, Web pages, and so on. Apply the existing styles for headings, titles, body text, and so forth. Then modify the template's styles, or create your own to better suit your needs. Make sure you get the look you want by adding emphasis using italics, boldface, and underline, changing text alignment, adjusting line and paragraph spacing, setting tabs and indents, or creating bulleted and numbered lists. When you're done, your document is sure to demand attention and convey your message in its appearance.

Not everyone has an eye for color, and pulling it all together can be daunting, so Word provides you with professionally designed themes, which you can apply to any document. A **theme** is a set of unified design elements that provides a consistent look for a document by using color themes, fonts, and effects, such as shadows, shading, and animations. By using templates, styles, and themes, you can create professional looking documents in no time.

What You'll Do

Creating a Template

You can create your own template as easily as you create a document. Like those that come with Office, custom templates can save you time. Perhaps each month you create an inventory document in which you enter repetitive information; all that changes is the actual data. By creating your own template, you can have a custom form that is ready for completion each time you take inventory. A template file saves all the customization you made to reuse in other documents. Although you can store your template anywhere you want, you may find it handy to store it in the Templates folder that Microsoft Office uses to store its templates. If you store your design templates in the Templates folder, those templates appear as options when you choose the New command on the File tab, and then click My Templates.

Create a Template

1. Enter all the necessary information in a new document—including formatting and graphics.
2. Click the **File** tab, and then click **Save As**.
3. Click the **Save as type** list arrow, and then select a template format.
   - **Word Template**. Creates a template for Word 2007-2010.
   - **Word Macro-Enabled Template**. Creates a template for Word 2007-2010 with macros.
   - **Word 97-2003 Template**. Creates a template for Office Word 97-2003.

   Microsoft Office templates are typically stored in the following location:

   Windows 7 or Vista. C:/Users/*your name*/AppData/Roaming/Microsoft/Templates

   Windows XP. C:/Documents and Settings/*your name*/Application Data/Microsoft/Templates
4. Type a name for your template.
5. Click **Save**.

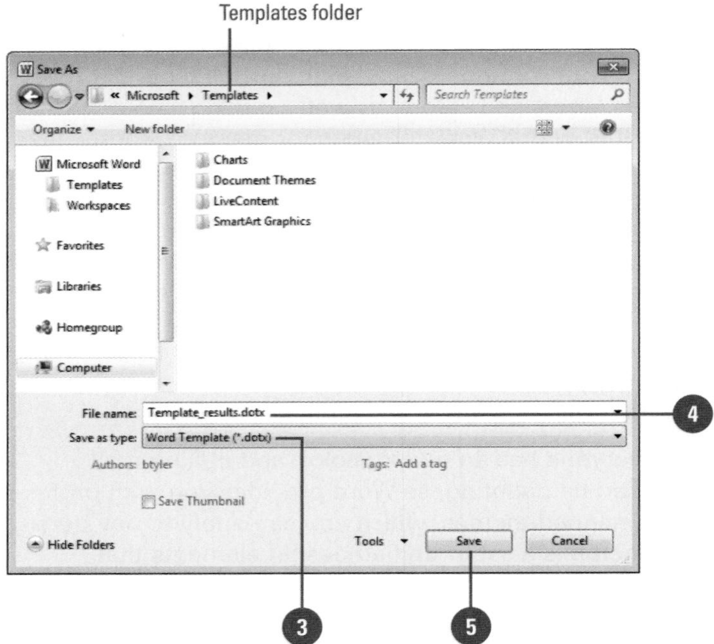

Opening a Template

You may not realize it, but every document you create is based on a template. When you start a new document without specifying a template, Word creates a new document based on the **default template**, called Normal. When you specify a particular template in the New dialog box, whether it's one supplied by Word or one you created yourself, Word starts a new document that contains the formatting, and any graphics and text contained in that template. The template itself does not change when you enter data in the new document, because you are working on a new file, not with the template file.

Open a Template

1. Click the **File** tab, and then click **Open**.
2. Click the **Files of type** list arrow, and then click **Word Templates**.
3. Click the **Look in** list arrow, and then select the drive and folder that contain the template you want to open.

   Microsoft Office templates are typically stored in the following location:

   Windows 7 or Vista. C:/Users /*your name*/AppData/Roaming /Microsoft/Templates

   Windows XP. C:/Documents and Settings/*your name*/Application Data/Microsoft/Templates
4. Click the file name of the template you want to open.
5. Click **Open**.

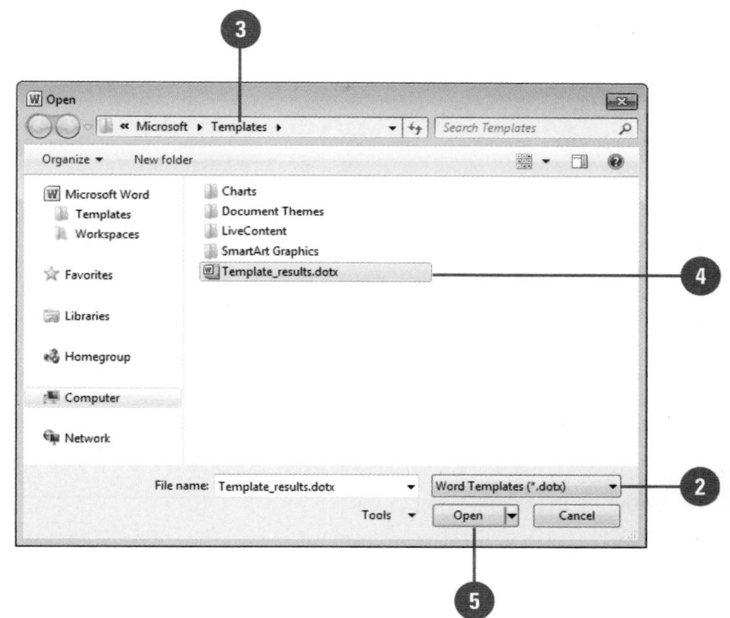

Changing a Template

Microsoft Word has a selection of pre-made templates designed for you to use. These templates are available in the New Document dialog box under the Installed Templates. If you like one of these templates, you can use it as the basis to create your own template. To customize one of the Microsoft Installed Templates, open the actual template, make the changes you want, and then save it. If you save the original template back in the same location with the same name as the original, you create a new default template. The original one is replaced by the newly saved template. If you don't want to change the original, save the template with a new name. You can also use the same procedure to change one of your own templates.

Change a Word Template

1. Click the **File** tab, and then click **New**.
2. Open the template you want to change using the following:
   - Microsoft Templates. Click **Installed Templates**, click the template you want, and then click **Create**.
   - My Templates. Click **My Templates**, click the template you want, and then click **OK**.
3. Make the changes you want to the template.
4. Click the **File** tab, and then click **Save As**.
5. Click the **Save as type** list arrow, and then click **Word Template**.

   The location defaults to the folder for My Templates.

   If you want to save your template with Installed Templates, then navigate to the following:

   C:/Program Files/Microsoft Office/Templates/1033/
6. Type a new file name or the same as the existing name to replace it.
7. Click **Save**, and then click **Yes**, if necessary, to replace the file.

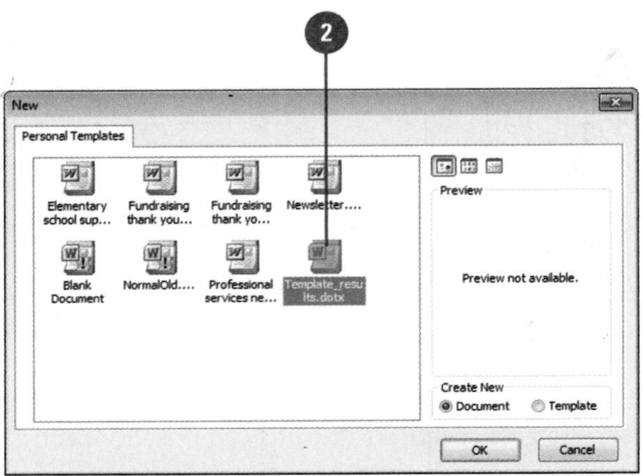

Installed Templates folder

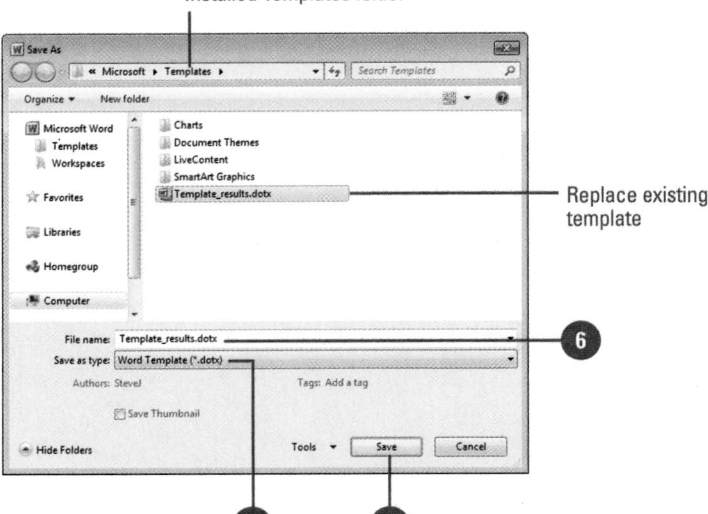

Replace existing template

Applying a Quick Style

A **style** is a collection of formatting settings saved with a name in a document or template that you can apply to text at any time. Word provides different style sets to make it easy to format text. Each style set consists of a variety of different formatting style combinations, which you can view using the Quick Style gallery. To quickly see if you like a Quick Style, point to a thumbnail in the gallery to display a live preview of it in the selected text. If you like it, click the thumbnail to apply it.

Apply a Style

1. Select the text to which you want to apply a style.
2. Click the **Home** tab.
3. Click the scroll up or down arrow, or click the **More** list arrow in the Styles group to see additional styles.
4. Click the style you want to apply from the gallery.

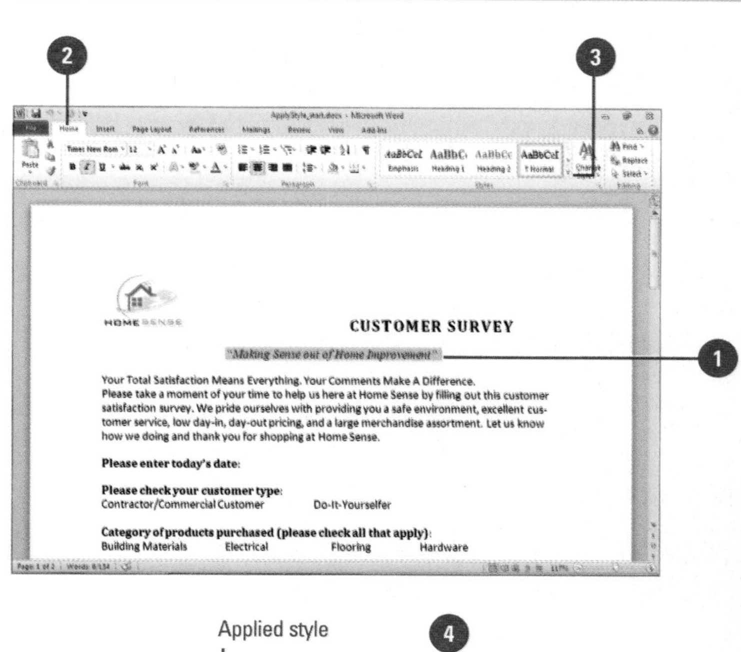

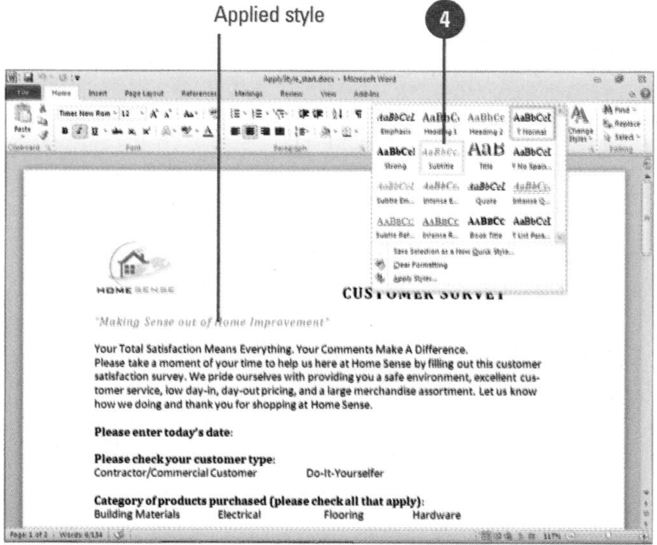

Did You Know?

You can clear style formatting. Select the text you want to clear, click the Home tab, and then click the Clear Formatting button.

You can reset the document back to document Quick Styles. Click the Home tab, click the Change Styles button, point to Style Set, and then click Reset Document Quick Steps.

You can reset the document back to document Quick Styles from a template. Click the Home tab, click the Change Styles button, point to Style Set, and then click Reset To Quick Steps From Template, locate and select the template, and then click OK.

Changing a Style Set

Not sure where to begin to create a fancy invitation or flyer? You can use style sets in Word to quickly format a document with a distinct style. Word provides predefined style sets—such as Classic, Elegant, Simple, Modern, Formal, Fancy, and Distinctive—to make it easy to format an entire document. Each style set consists of a variety of different formatting style combinations, which you can view using the Quick Style gallery.

Change a Style Set

1. Click the **Home** tab.
2. Click the **Change Styles** button.
3. Point to **Style Set**, and then click the style set you want.

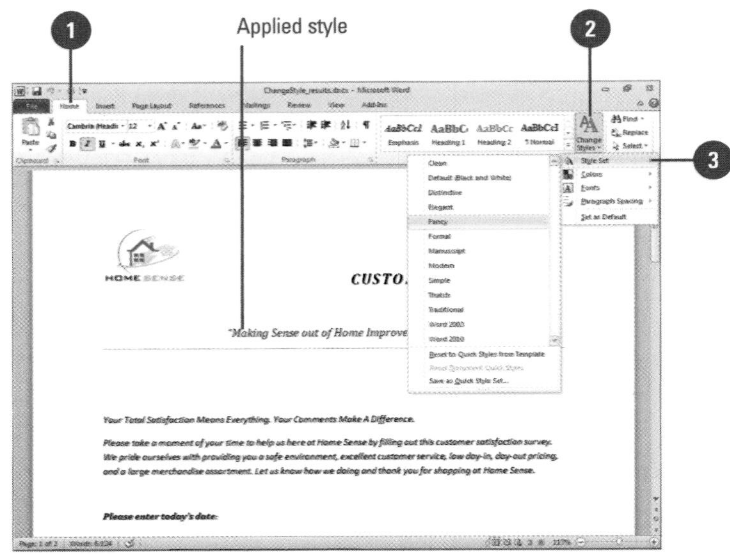

Did You Know?

You can reset the document back to document Quick Styles. Click the Home tab, click the Change Styles button, point to Style Set, and then click Reset Document Quick Steps.

You can reset the document back to document Quick Styles from a template. Click the Home tab, click the Change Styles button, point to Style Set, click Reset To Quick Steps From Template, locate and select the template, and then click OK.

Create a Style Set

1. Format a document with the style that you want to save.
2. Click the **Home** tab.
3. Click the **Change Styles** button.
4. Point to **Style Set**.
5. Click **Save as Quick Style Set**.

   The Save Quick Style Set dialog box opens, displaying the Quick Styles folder.

6. Type a file name.
7. If necessary, click the **Save as type** list arrow, and then click **Word Templates**.
8. Click **Save**.

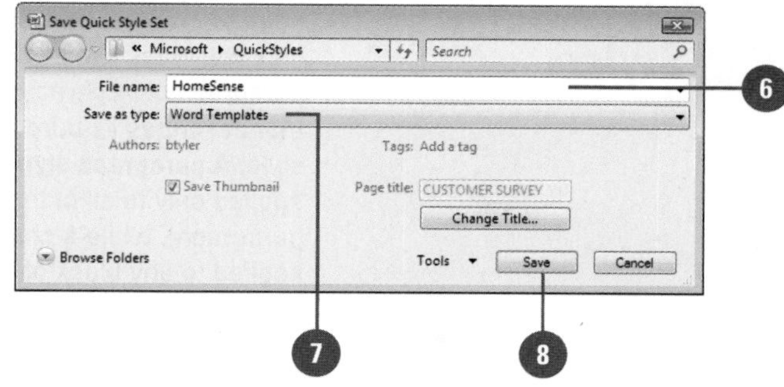

Did You Know?

You can set the default style set. Click the Home tab, click the Change Styles button, point to Style Set, and then click the style set you want to use as the default. Click the Change Styles button, and then click Set As Default.

Creating and Modifying Styles

Word provides a variety of styles to choose from. But sometimes you need to create a new style or modify an existing one to get the exact look you want. When you create a new style, specify if it applies to paragraphs or characters, and give the style a short, descriptive name that describes its purpose so you and others recall when to use that style. A **paragraph style** is a group of format settings that can be applied only to all of the text within a paragraph (even if it is a one-line paragraph), while a **character style** is a group of format settings that is applied to any block of text at the user's discretion. To modify a style, adjust the formatting settings of an existing style.

Create a New Style

1. Select the text whose formatting you want to save as a style.
2. Click the **Home** tab.
3. Click the scroll up or down arrow, or click the **More** list arrow in the Styles group, and then click **Save Selection as a New Quick Style.**
4. Type a short, descriptive name.
5. Click **Modify.**
6. Click the **Style type** list arrow, and then click **Paragraph** to include the selected text's line spacing and margins in the style, or click **Character** to include only formatting, such as font, size, and bold, in the style.
7. Click the **Style for following paragraph** list arrow, and then click the name of style you want to be applied after a paragraph with the new style.
8. Select the formatting options you want.
9. To add the style to the Quick style gallery, select the **Add to Quick Style list** check box.
10. Click **OK.**
11. Click **OK.**

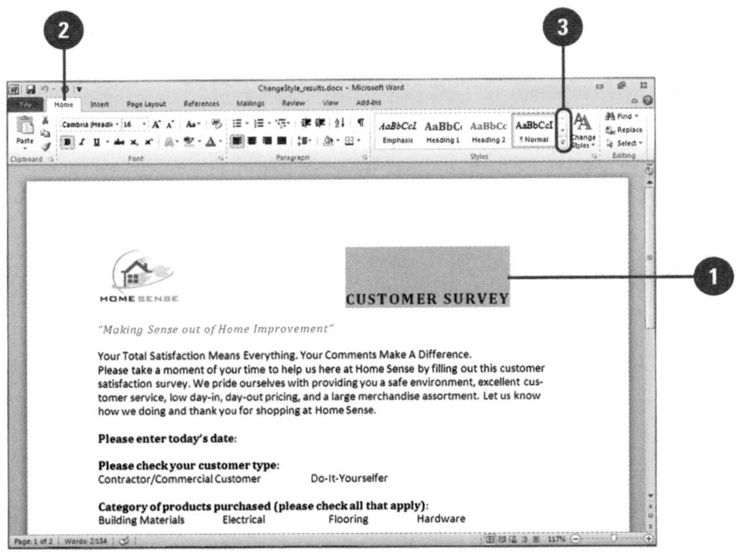

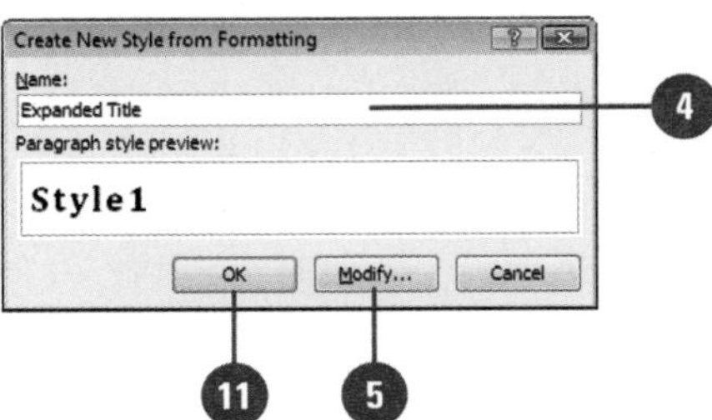

Modify a Style

1. Click the **Home** tab.
2. Click the scroll up or down arrow, or click the **More** list arrow in the Styles group.
3. Right-click the style you want to modify, and then click **Modify**.
4. Specify any style changes (Style based on or Style for following paragraph) you want.
5. Click **Format**, and then click the type of formatting you want to modify:
   - To change character formatting, such as font type and boldface, click **Font**.
   - To change line spacing and indents, click **Paragraph**.
6. Select the formatting options you want.
7. Check the Preview box, and review the style description. Make any formatting changes as needed.
8. To add the style to the Quick style gallery, select the **Add to Quick Style list** check box.
9. Click **OK**.

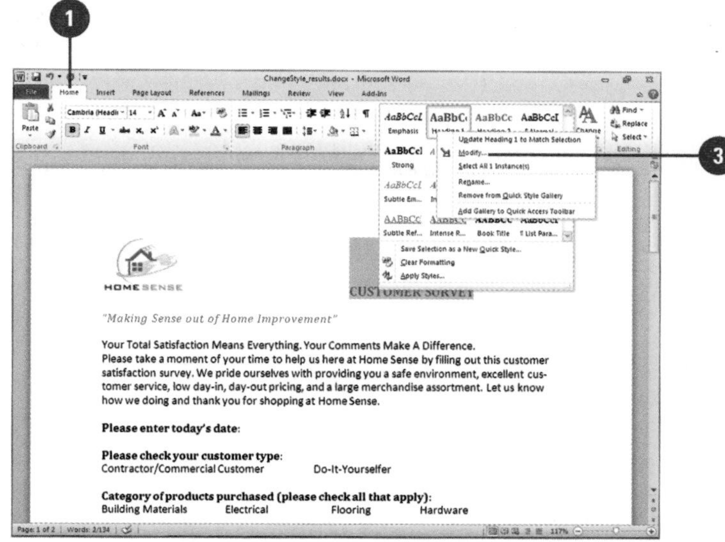

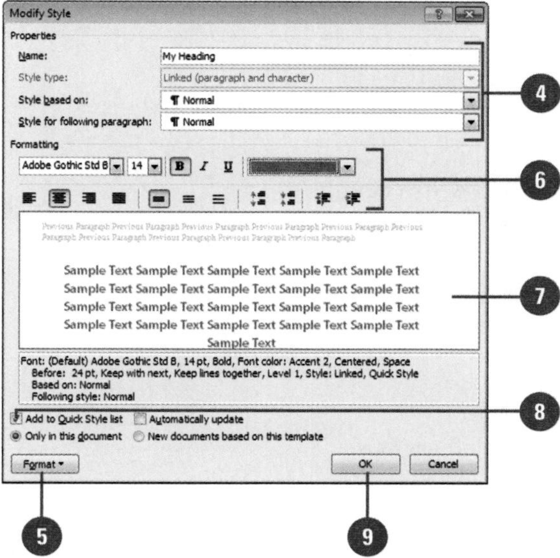

Did You Know?

You can view the list of styles. Click the Home tab, click the More list arrow in the Styles group, click Apply Style, and then click the Styles button to display the Styles list. From the Styles list pane, you can create a new style, inspect styles, manage styles, and change style options.

Managing Styles

The Styles pane give you another way to work with styles. You can view a master list of individual styles, preview styles as shown in the document, disable linked styles, and manage styles. The Styles pane allows you to work with the main document styles, such as body and heading text. You can modify or delete a style, select all instances of a style, or add a style to the Quick Styles gallery. If you want to work with the more indepth styles that Word uses to create lists, comment text, footer, header, index, tables, table of contents, and other stylized elements, you can use the Manage Styles dialog box.

Change Styles Pane Options

1. Click the **Home** tab.
2. Click the **Styles Dialog Box Launcher**.
3. Click **Options**.
4. Click the list arrows, and then select the styles you want to show and how the list is sorted.
5. Select the check boxes to show the types of formatting (paragraph, font, or bullet and numbering) you want to show in the Styles pane.
6. Select or clear the check boxes to show or hide built-in styles in the Styles pane.
7. Click the **Only in this document** or **New document based on this template** option.
8. Click **OK**.
9. When you're done, click the **Close** button on the task pane.

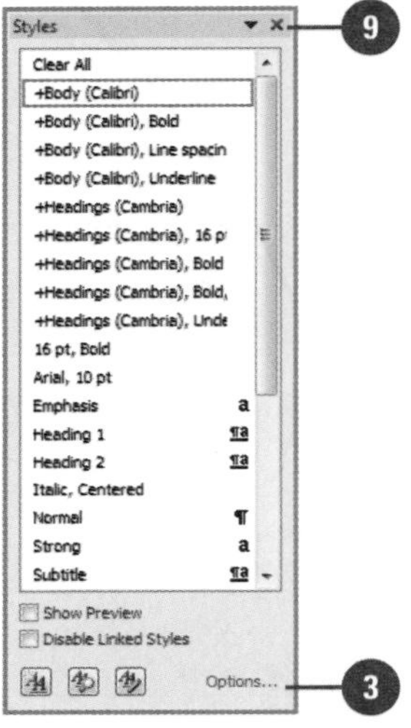

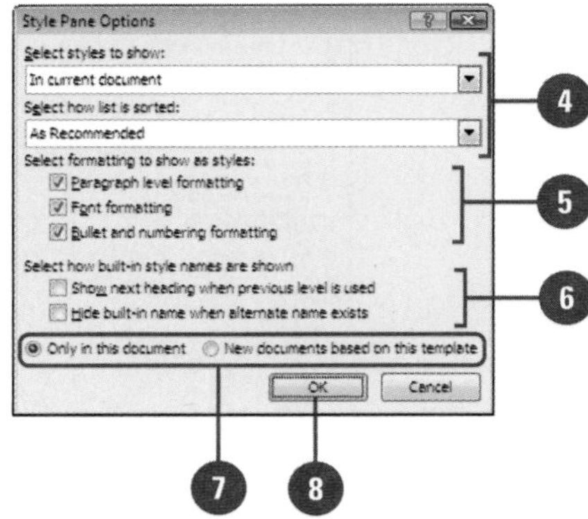

Manage Styles

1. Click the **Home** tab.
2. Click the **Styles Dialog Box Launcher**.
3. To preview styles, select the **Show Preview** check box.
4. Use the Styles pane to make the any of the following changes:
   - **Modify.** Point to the style, click the list arrow, and then click **Modify Style**.
   - **Delete.** Point to the style, click the list arrow, click **Delete**, and then click **Yes**.
   - **Select All.** Point to the style, click the list arrow, and then click **Select All x Instance(s)**.
   - **Add to Quick Style Gallery.** Point to the style, click the list arrow, and then click **Add to Quick Style Gallery**.
5. Click **Manage Styles.**
6. Click the tab with the operation you want to perform: **Edit**, **Recommend**, **Restrict**, or **Set Defaults**.
7. Click the **Sort order** list arrow, and then select the way you want to display the styles.
8. Select the style you want, and then use the options and commands to make the changes you want.
9. When you're done, click **OK**.
10. Make any additional changes, and then click the **Close** button on the task pane.

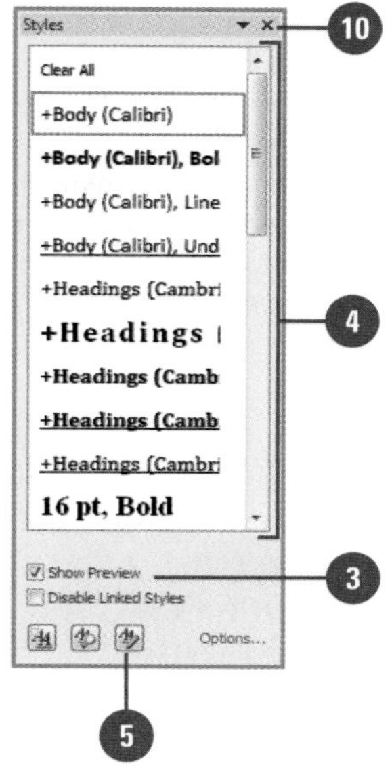

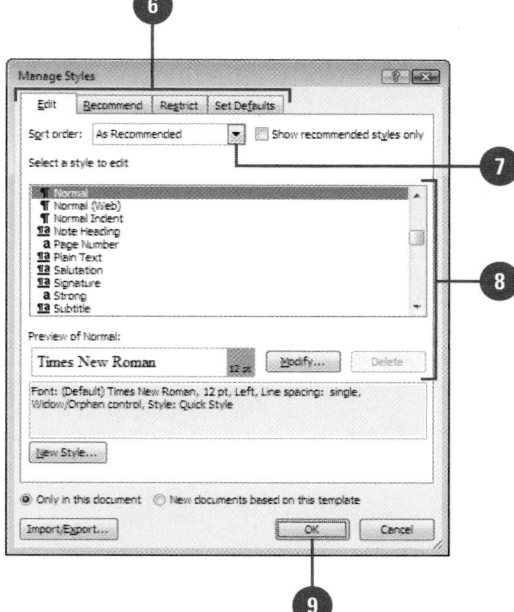

Revealing Formatting Styles

Word uses wavy blue underlines to indicate possible instances of inconsistent formatting. If you see a wavy blue underline while formatting a document, you can open the Reveal Formatting task pane to display the format of selected text, such as its font and font effects. The Reveal Formatting task pane allows you to display, change, or clear formatting for the selected text. You can also select text based on formatting so that you can compare the formatting used in the selected text with formatting used in other parts of the documents. To open the Reveal Formatting task pane, you use the Style Inspector on the Styles pane.

Select or Clear Text Formatting

1. Select the text whose formatting you want to select or clear away.
2. Click the **Styles Dialog Box Launcher**.
3. Click the **Style Inspector** button.
4. Click the **Reveal Formatting** button.
   - To provide more screen space to work, you can close the Style Inspector and Styles task pane.
5. Select the text you want to reveal.
6. Point to the Selected Text box, click the list arrow, and then click either **Select All Text With Similar Formatting** or **Clear Formatting**.
   - To apply the formatting to your surrounding text, click **Apply Formatting of Surrounding Text**.
7. When you're done, click the **Close** button on the task pane.

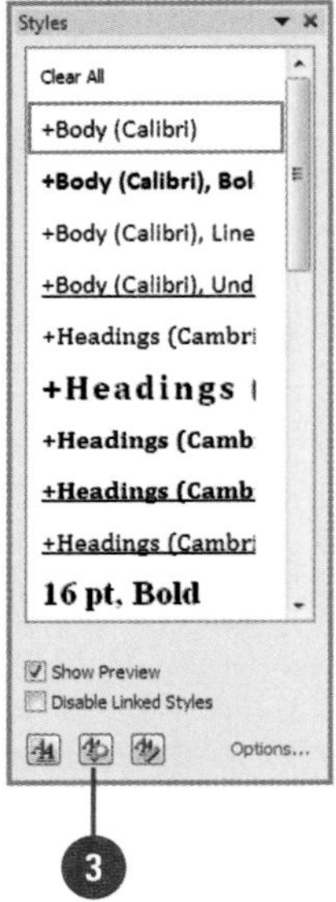

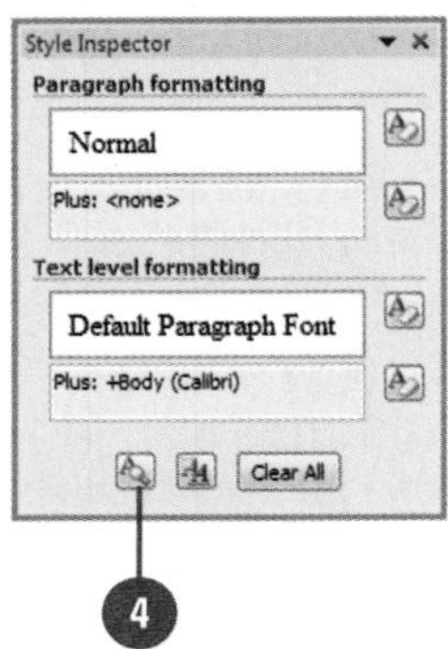

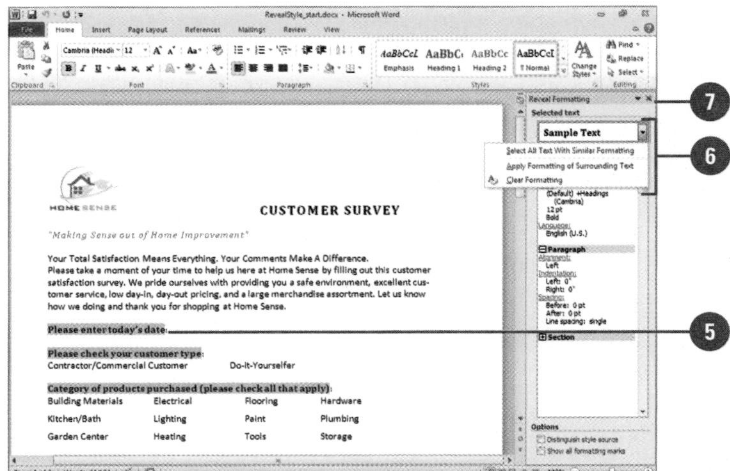

See Also

See "Selecting Text with Similar Formatting" on page 69 for information on using the Select Text With Similar Formatting command available on the Home tab.

Compare Text Formatting

1. Select the first instance of formatting you want to compare.
2. Click the **Styles Dialog Box Launcher**.
3. Click the **Style Inspector** button.
4. Click the **Reveal Formatting** button.
   - To provide more screen space to work, you can close the Style Inspector and Styles task pane.
5. Select the first instance of formatting you want.
6. Select the **Compare to another selection** check box.
7. Select the second instance of formatting to compare.
8. When you're done, click the **Close** button on the task pane.

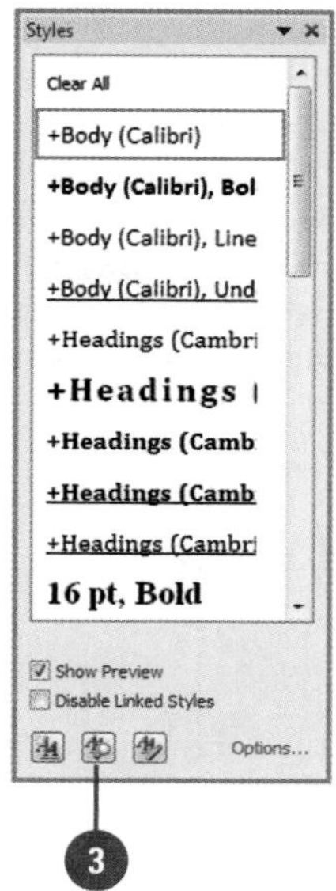

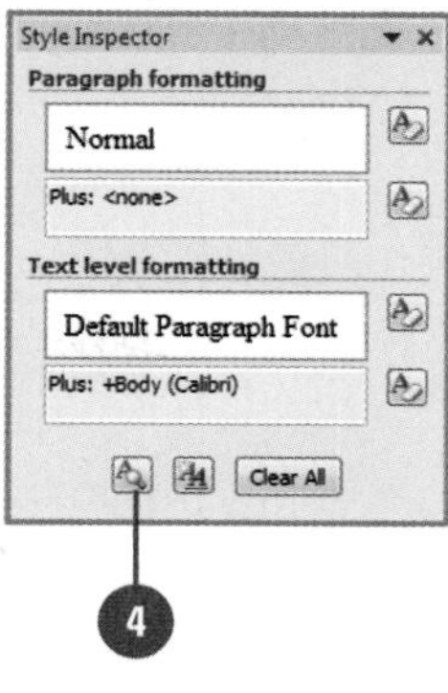

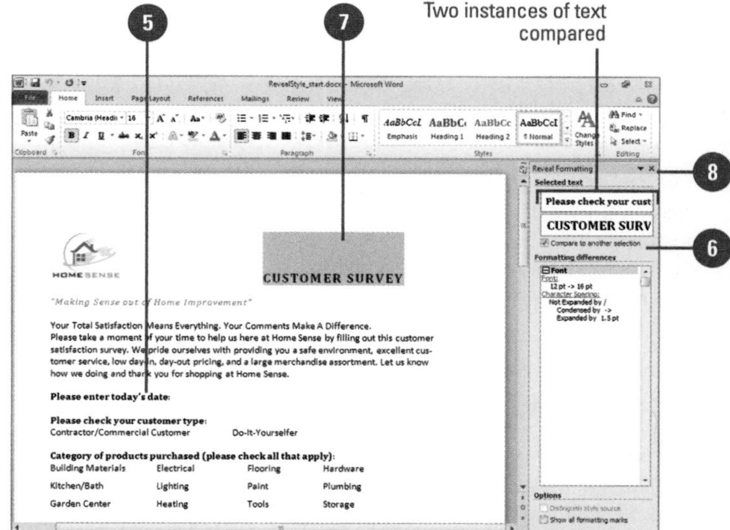

Using the Format Painter

After formatting text in a document, you might want to apply those same formatting changes to other areas in the document. For example, redoing the same formatting, you can **paint** (that is, copy) the formatting from one area to others. The Format Painter lets you "pick up" the style of one section and apply, or "paint," it to another. To apply a format style to more than one item, double-click the Format Painter button on the Home tab instead of a single-click. The double-click keeps the Format Painter active until you want to press Esc to disable it, so you can apply formatting styles to any text or object you want in your document.

Apply a Format Style Using the Format Painter

1. Select the text containing the formatting you want to copy.
2. Click the **Home** tab.
3. Click the **Format Painter** button.

   If you want to apply the format to more than one item, double-click the Format Painter button.
4. Drag to select the text or click the object to which you want to apply the format.
5. If you double-clicked the Format Painter button, drag to select the text or click the object to which you want to apply the format, and then press Esc when you're done.

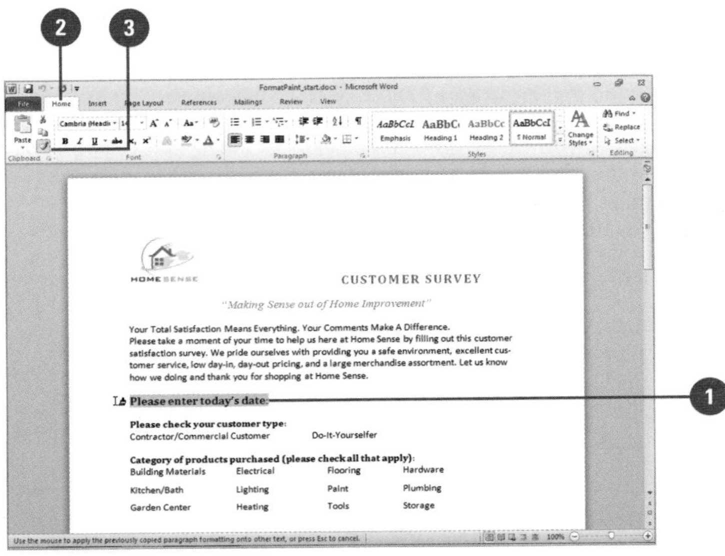

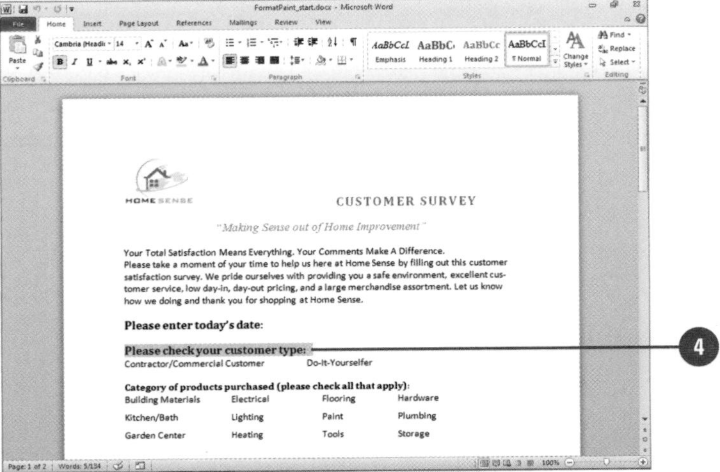

Did You Know?

You can use the Esc key to cancel format painting. If you change your mind about painting a format, cancel the marquee by pressing Esc.

Adding Custom Colors

In addition to the standard and theme colors, Word allows you to add more colors to your document. These additional colors are available on each color button palette on the Ribbon or in a dialog box, such as the Fill Color or Font Color button. These colors are useful when you want to use a specific color, but the document color theme does not have that color. Colors that you add to a document appear in all color palettes and remain in the palette even if the color theme changes.

Add a Color to the Menus

1. Click the **Font Color** button on the Home tab, and then click **More Colors**.

   This is one method. You can also use other color menus to access the Colors dialog box.

2. Click the **Custom** tab.
3. Click the **Color Model** list arrow, and then click **RGB** or **HSL**.
4. Select a custom color using one of the following methods:
   - If you know the color values, enter them, either Hue, Sat, Lum, or Red, Green, and Blue.
   - Drag across the palette until the pointer is over the color you want. Drag the black arrow to adjust the amount of black and white in the color.

     The new color appears above the current color at the bottom right.

5. Click **OK**.

   The current selection is changed to the new color, plus the new color is added to the Recent Colors section of all document color menus.

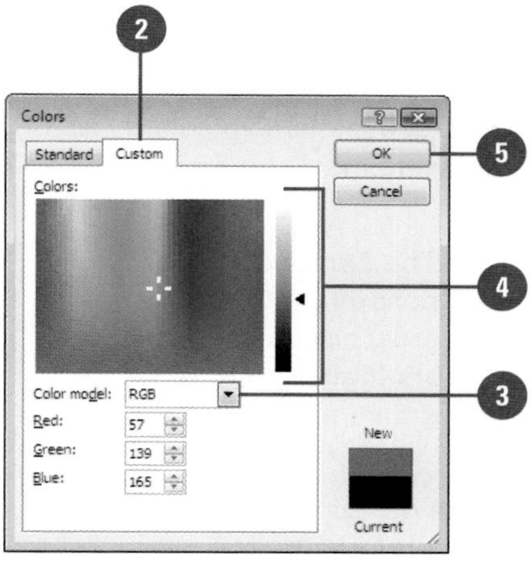

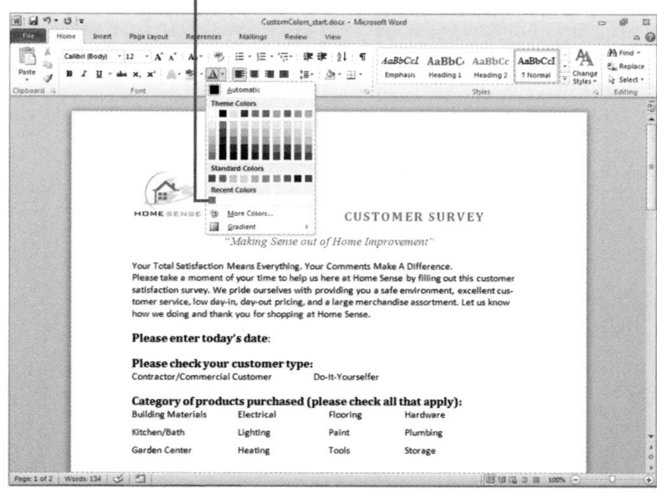

Understanding Themes

A theme helps you create professional-looking documents that use an appropriate balance of color for your document content. You can use a default color theme or create a custom one.

Themes in Office are made up of a palette of twelve colors. These colors appear on color palettes when you click a color-related button, such as Fill Color or Font Color button on the Home tab or in a dialog box. These twelve colors correspond to the following elements in a document:

Four Text and Background. The two background colors (light and dark combinations) are the canvas, or drawing area, color of the document. The two text colors (light and dark combinations) are for typing text and drawing lines, and contrast with the background colors.

Six Accent. These colors are designed to work as a complementary color palette for objects, such as shadows and fills. These colors contrast with both the background and text colors.

One hyperlink. This color is designed to work as a complementary color for objects and hyperlinks.

One followed hyperlink. This color is designed to work as a complementary color for objects and visited hyperlinks.

The first four colors in the Theme Colors list represent the document text and background colors (light and dark for each). The remaining colors represent the six accent and two hyperlink colors for the theme. When you apply another theme or change any of these colors to create a new theme, the colors shown in the Theme Colors dialog box and color palettes change to match the current colors.

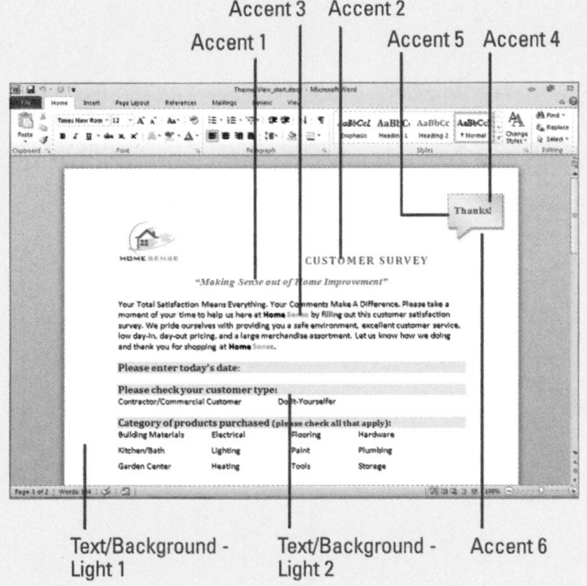

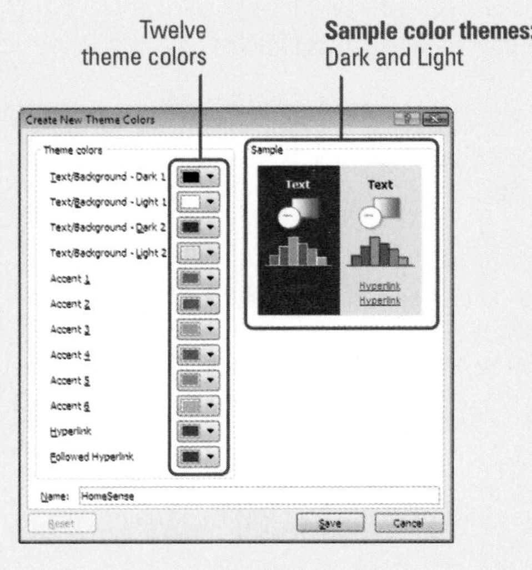

Viewing and Applying a Theme

A document theme consists of theme colors, fonts, and effects. You can quickly format an entire document with a professional look by applying a theme. Office comes with more themes and styles (**New!**). To quickly see if you like a theme, point to one on the themes gallery to display a ScreenTip with name and information about it, and a live preview of it on the current document. If you like the theme, you can apply it. When you apply a theme, the background, text, graphics, charts, and tables all change to reflect the theme. You can choose from one or more standard themes. When you add new content, the document elements change to match the theme ensuring all of your material will look consistent. You can even use the same theme in other Microsoft Office programs, such as Excel and PowerPoint, so all your work matches. Can't find a theme you like? Search Office.com online.

View and Apply a Theme

1. Open the document you want to apply a theme.
2. Click the **Page Layout** tab.
3. Click the **Themes** button to display the themes gallery.
4. Point to a theme.

   A live preview of the theme appears in the document, along with a ScreenTip.
5. Click the theme you want to apply to the active document.

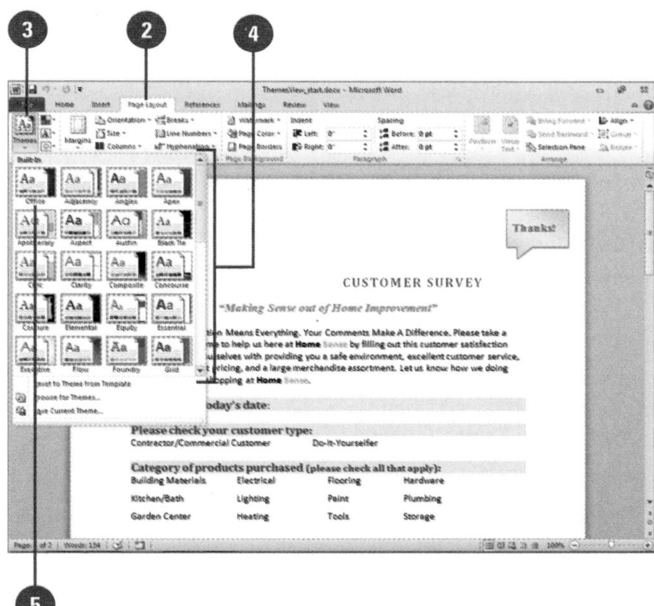

Did You Know?

You can apply themes from Office.com. Click the Page Layout or Design tab, click the Themes button, scroll to the bottom of the list, and then select an available Office.com theme. Go to *www.office.com* to download and use other online themes.

You can search for themes at Microsoft Office Online. Open your browser, go to *www.office.com*, click in the Search Office Online box, type themes, and then press Enter. Review the results list to find the theme you want. Follow the site instructions to download and use online themes.

Creating Theme Colors

You may like a certain color theme except for one or two colors. You can change an existing color theme and apply your changes to the entire document. You can add other custom colors to your theme by using RGB (Red, Green, and Blue) or HSL (Hues, Saturation, and Luminosity) color modes. The RGB color mode is probably the most widely used of all the color modes. You can accomplish this by using sliders, dragging on a color-space, or entering a numeric value that corresponds to a specific color. Once you create this new color theme, you can add it to your collection of color themes so that you can make it available to any document.

Apply or Create Theme Colors

1. Open the document you want to apply a color theme.
2. Click the **Page Layout** tab.
3. To apply theme colors to a document, click the **Theme Colors** button, and then click a color theme.
   - To apply individual theme colors, select the element, click a color button, such as Font Color on the Home tab, and then click a theme color.
4. To create theme colors, click the **Theme Colors** button, and then click **Create New Theme Colors**.
5. Click the **Theme Colors** button arrows (Text/Background, Accent, or Hyperlink, etc.) for the colors you want to change.
6. Click a new color, or click **More Colors** to select a color from the **Standard** or **Custom** tab, and then click **OK**.
7. If you don't like your color choices, click the **Reset** button to return all color changes to their original colors.
8. Type a new name for the color theme.
9. Click **Save**.

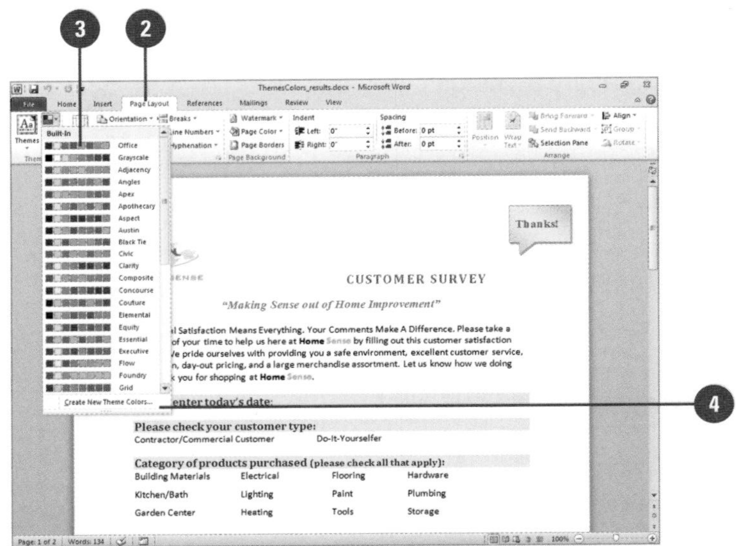

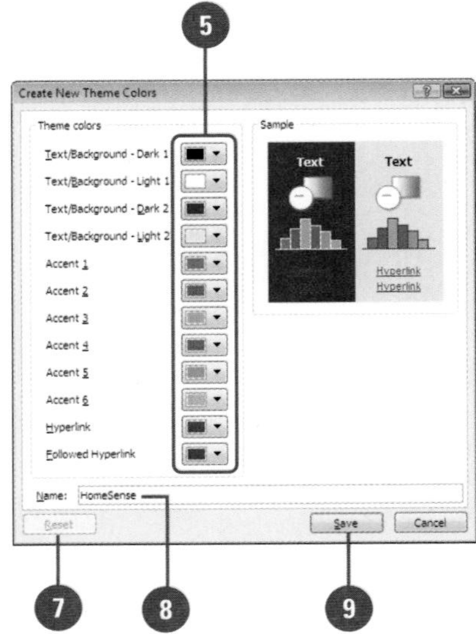

Select Custom Colors

1. Select the text you want to apply a custom color.
2. Click the **Font Color** button on the Home tab, and then click **More Colors**.

   This is one method. You can also use other color menus to access the Colors dialog box.
3. Click the **Custom** tab.
4. Click the **Color Model** list arrow, and then click **RGB** or **HSL**.
5. Select a custom color using one of the following methods:
   - If you know the color values, enter them, either Hue, Sat, Lum, or Red, Green, and Blue.
   - Drag across the palette until the pointer is over the color you want. Drag the black arrow to adjust the amount of black and white in the color.

     The new color appears above the current color at the bottom right.
6. Click **OK**.

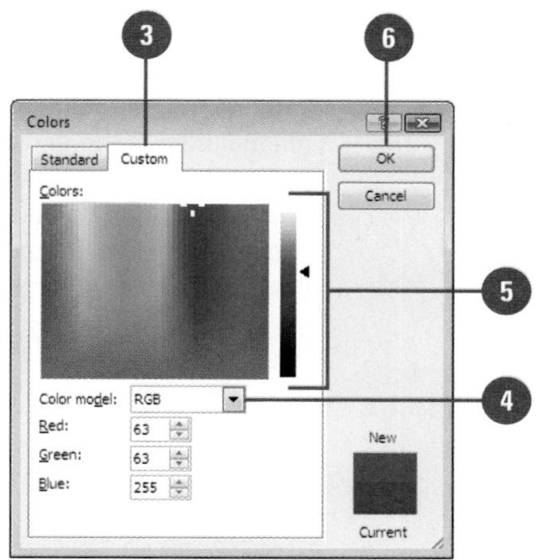

Did You Know?

You can edit a custom color theme. On the Page Layout tab, click the Theme Colors button, right-click the theme color you want to edit, click Edit, make changes, and then click Save.

You can delete a custom color theme. On the Page Layout tab, click the Theme Colors button, right-click the theme color you want to edit, click Edit, click Delete, and then click Yes.

The Properties of Color

Characteristic	Description
Hue	The color itself; every color is identified by a number, determined by the number of colors available on your monitor.
Saturation	The intensity of the color. The higher the number, the more vivid the color.
Luminosity	The brightness of the color, or how close the color is to black or white. The larger the number, the lighter the color.
Red, Green, Blue	Primary colors of the visible light spectrum. RGB generates color using three 8-bit channels: 1 red, 1 green, and 1 blue. RGB is an additive color system, which means that color is added to a black background. The additive process mixes various amounts of red, green and blue light to produce other colors.

Choosing Theme Fonts

A document theme consists of theme colors, fonts, and effects. Theme fonts include heading and body text fonts. Each document uses a set of theme fonts. When you click the Theme Fonts button on the Page Layout tab, the name of the current heading and body text font appear highlighted in the gallery menu. To quickly see if you like a theme font, point to one on the menu, and a live preview of it appears on the current document. If you want to apply the theme, click it on the menu. You can apply a set of theme fonts to another theme or create your own set of theme fonts.

Apply and Choose Theme Fonts

1. Open the document you want to apply theme fonts.
2. Click the **Home** tab.
3. Select the text you want to change.

   TIMESAVER *To select the entire document, press Ctrl+A.*

4. Click the **Font** list arrow, and then click the theme font you want.
5. Click the **Page Layout** or **Design** tab.
6. Click the **Theme Fonts** button.

   The current theme fonts appear highlighted in the menu.

   TIMESAVER *Point to the Fonts button to display a ScreenTip with the current theme fonts.*

7. Click the theme fonts you want from the gallery menu.

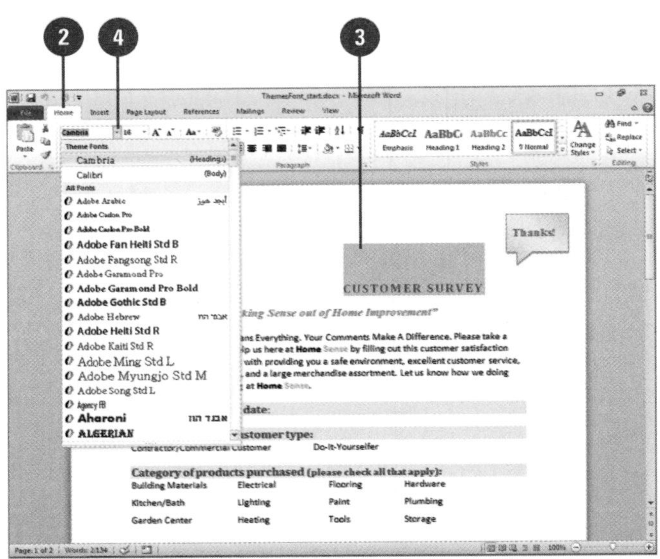

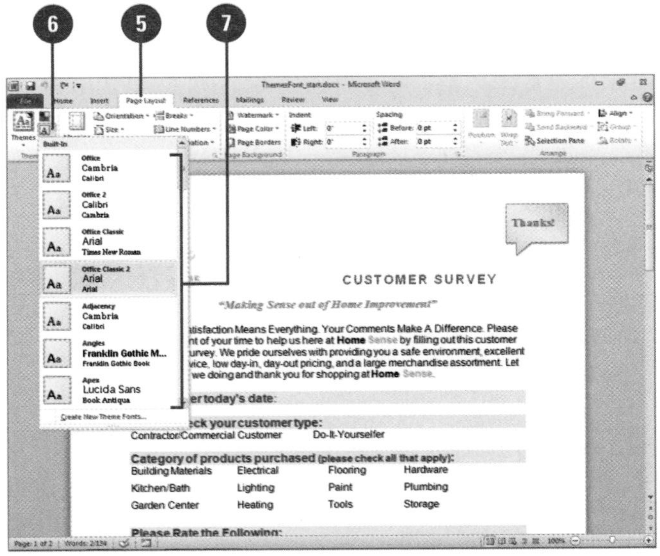

Create Theme Fonts

1. Click the **Page Layout** tab.
2. Click the **Theme Fonts** button, and then click **Create New Theme Fonts**.
3. Click the **Heading font** list arrow, and then select a font.
4. Click the **Body font** list arrow, and then select a font.
5. Type a name for the custom theme fonts.
6. Click **Save**.

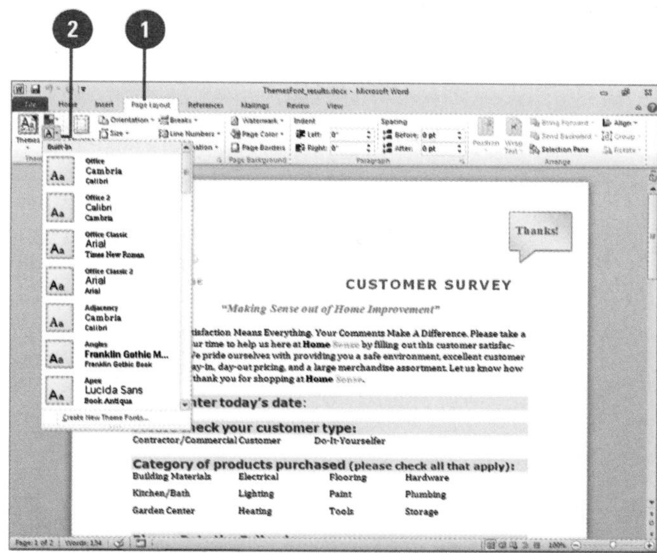

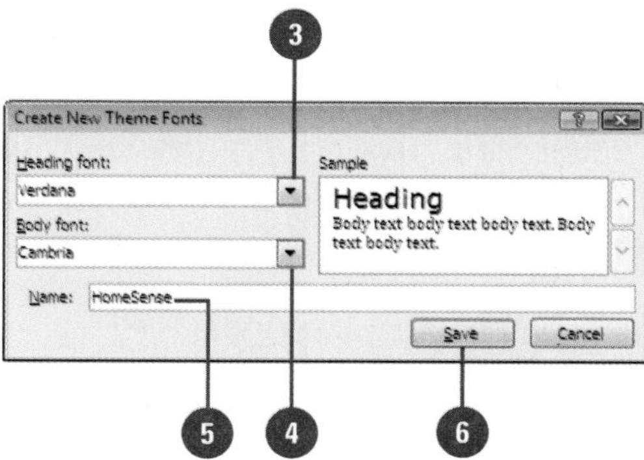

Did You Know?

The Font Color button on the Ribbon displays the last font color you used. To apply this color to another selection, simply click the button, not the list arrow.

Choosing Theme Effects

Theme effects are sets of lines, fills, and special effects styles for shapes, graphics, charts, SmartArt, and other design elements. By combining the lines, fills, and special effects styles with different formatting levels (subtle, moderate, and intense), Word provides a variety of visual theme effects. Each document uses a set of theme effects. Some are more basic while others are more elaborate. When you click the Theme Effects button on the Page Layout tab, the name of the current theme effects appears highlighted in the gallery menu. While you can apply a set of theme effects to another theme, you cannot create your own set of theme effects at this time.

View and Apply Theme Effects

1. Open the document you want to apply a theme effect.
2. Click the **Page Layout** tab.
3. Click the **Theme Effects** button.

   The current theme effects appear highlighted in the menu.

   TIMESAVER *Point to the Effects button to display a ScreenTip with the current theme effects name.*
4. Click the theme effects you want from the menu.

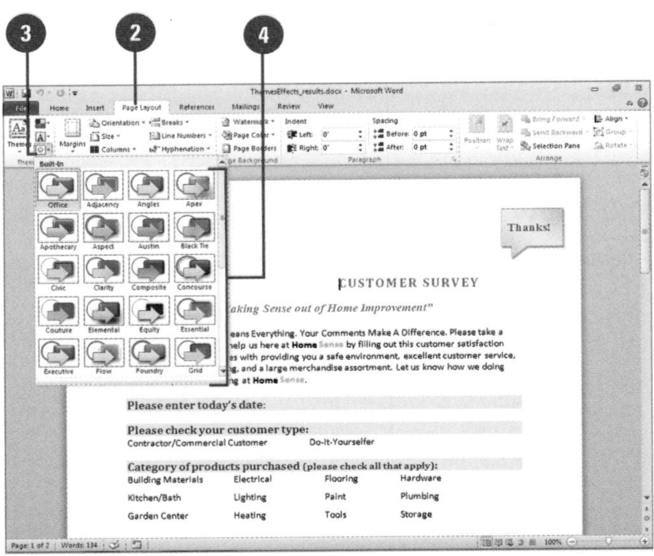

Did You Know?

You can delete a custom theme effects or fonts. On the Page Layout or Design tab, click the Theme Effects or Theme Fonts button, right-click the theme you want to edit, click Edit, click Delete, and then click Yes.

See Also

See "Viewing and Applying a Theme" on page 101 for information on applying a theme from the Themes gallery.

Creating a Custom Theme

If you have special needs for specific colors, fonts, and effects, such as a company sales or marketing document, you can create your own theme by customizing theme colors, theme fonts, and theme effects, and saving them as a theme file (.thmx), which you can reuse. You can apply the saved theme to other documents. When you save a custom theme, the file is automatically saved in the Document Themes folder and added to the list of custom themes used by Word and other Office programs. When you no longer need a custom theme, you can delete it.

Create a Custom Theme

1. Click the **Page Layout** tab, and then create a theme by customizing theme colors, theme fonts, and theme effects.
2. Click the **Themes** button, and then click **Save Current Theme**.
3. Type a name for the theme file.
4. Click **Save**.

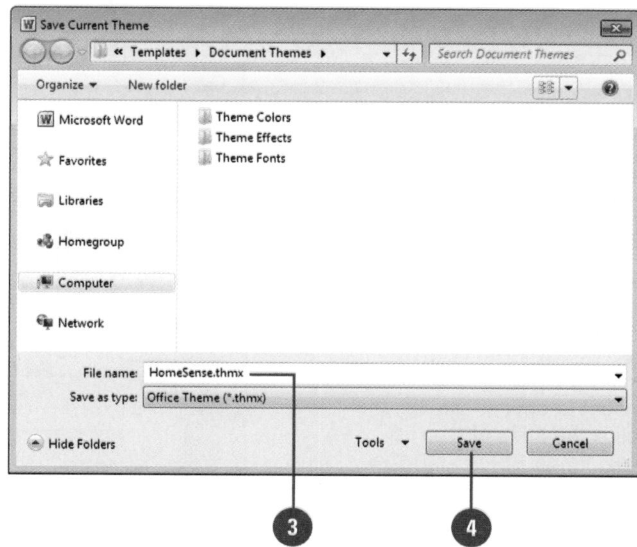

Did You Know?

You can remove a custom theme from the gallery menu. Simply move or delete the theme file from the Document Themes folder into another folder.

Choosing a Custom Theme

When you create your own theme by customizing theme colors, theme fonts, and theme effects, and saving them as a theme file (.thmx), you can apply the saved theme to other documents. When you save a custom theme file in the Document Themes folder, you can choose the custom theme from the Themes gallery. If you save a custom theme file in another folder location, you can use the Browse for Themes command to locate and select the custom theme file you want to reuse.

Choose and Apply a Custom Theme

1. Click the **Page Layout** tab.
2. Click the **Themes** button to see additional themes.
3. Point to the gallery you want to display the theme name, and then click the one you want.
4. To select and apply a custom theme from a file, click the **Themes** button, and then click **Browse for Themes.**
5. If you want to open a specific file type, click the **Files of type** list arrow, and then select an Office Theme file type:
   - **Office Themes and Themed Documents.**
   - **Office Themes.**
6. If the file is located in another folder, click the **Look in** list arrow, and then navigate to the file.

   Microsoft Office templates are typically stored in the following location:

   Windows 7 or Vista. C:/Users/*your name*/AppData/Roaming/Microsoft/Templates

   Windows XP. C:/Documents and Settings/*your name*/Application Data/Microsoft/Templates
7. Click the theme file you want.
8. Click **Open.**

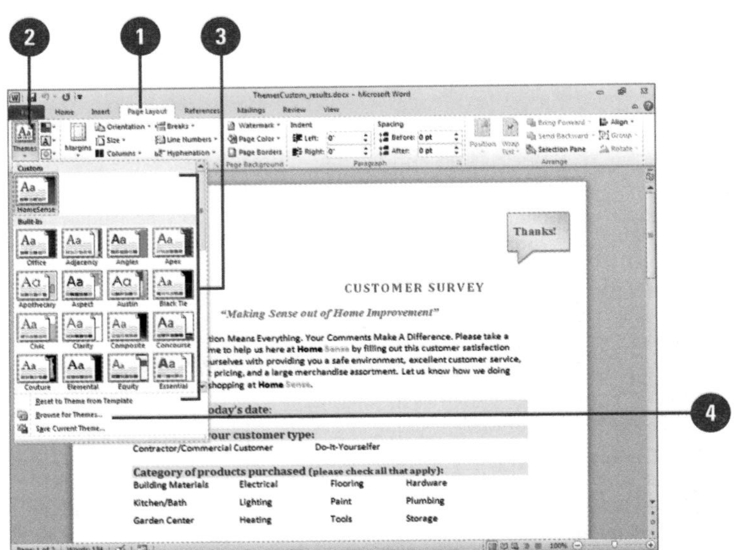

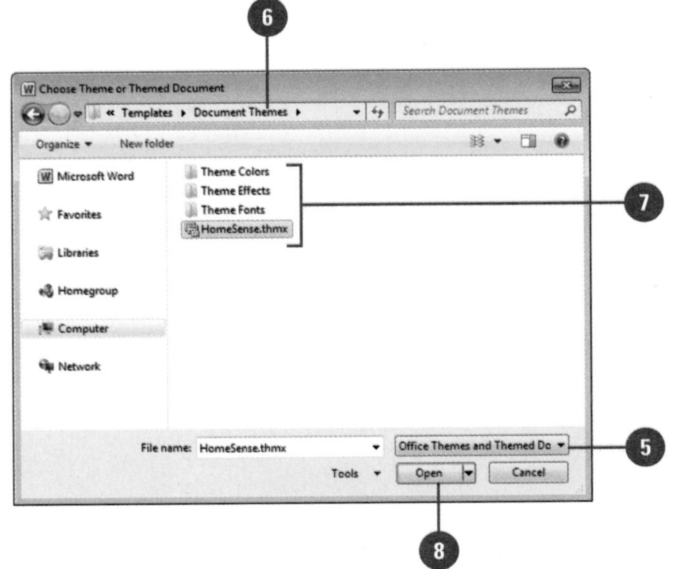

Adding Graphics and Multimedia to Documents

5

Introduction

Although well-illustrated documents can't make up for a lack of content, you can capture the attention of your audience if your documents are vibrant and visually interesting. Microsoft Office comes with a vast array of clip art, and there are endless amounts available through other software packages or on the Web. When going online to look at clips, you can categorize them so that it's easier to find the best choice for your document. You can use the Microsoft Office.com Online Web site to search for and download additional clip art.

You can easily enhance a document by adding a picture—one of your own or one of the hundreds that come with Microsoft Office. If you need to modify your pictures, you can resize them, compress them for storage, change their brightness or contrast, recolor them, or crop them.

WordArt is another feature that adds detail to your document. Available in other Office programs, WordArt can bring together your documents—you can change its color, shape, shadow, or size. Because WordArt comes with so many style choices, time spent customizing your documents is minimal.

In Office programs, you can insert SmartArt graphics to create diagrams that convey processes or relationships. Office provides a wide-variety of built-in SmartArt graphic types from which to choose, including graphical lists, process, cycle, hierarchy, relationship, matrix, and pyramid. Using built-in SmartArt graphics makes it easy to create and modify charts without having to create them from scratch.

What You'll Do

Locating and Inserting Clip Art

To add a clip art image to a document, you can click the Insert Clip Art button on the Insert tab to open the Clip Art task pane. The Clip Art task pane helps you search for clip art and access the clip art available in the Clip Organizer and on Office.com, a clip gallery that Microsoft maintains on its Web site. You can limit search results to a specific collection of clip art or a specific type of media file. After you find the clip art you want, you can click it to insert it, or point to it to display a list arrow. Then click an available command, such as Insert, Make Available Offline, Edit Keywords, and Delete from Clip Organizer.

Locate and Insert Clip Art

1. Click the **Insert** tab.
2. Click the **Clip Art** button.
3. Type the keyword(s) associated with the clip you are looking for.

   To narrow your search, do one of the following:

   - To limit search results to a specific collection of clip art, click the **Search For** list arrow, and then select the collections you want to search.
   - To limit search results to a specific type of media file, click the **Results Should Be** list arrow, and then select the check box next to the types of clips you want to find.
   - To display Office.com content, select the **Include Office.com** content check box (**New!**).
   - To access clip art on Office.com, click the link at the bottom of the Clip Art task pane. Search and download images from Office.com.
4. Click **Go**.

   Clips matching the keywords appear in the Results list.
5. Click the clip you want, and then resize it, if necessary.
6. Click the **Close** button on the task pane.

For Your Information

Understanding Clip Art Objects

Clip art objects (pictures and animated pictures) are images made up of geometric shapes, such as lines, curves, circles, squares, and so on. These images, known as vector images, are mathematically defined, which makes them easy to resize and manipulate. A picture in the Microsoft Windows Metafile (.wmf) file format is an example of a vector image. Clip Gallery also includes sounds or motion clips, which you can insert into a document. A **motion clip** is an animated picture—also known as an animated GIF—frequently used in Web pages. When you insert a sound, a small icon appears representing the sound file.

Inserting a Picture

Word makes it possible for you to insert pictures, graphics, scanned photographs, art, photos, or artwork from a DVD or CD-ROM or other program into a document. When you use the Picture button on the Insert tab, you specify the source of the picture. When you insert pictures from files on your hard disk drive, scanner, digital camera, or Web camera, Word allows you to select multiple pictures, view thumbnails of them, and insert them all at once, which speeds up the process.

Insert a Picture from a File

1. Click the **Insert** tab.
2. Click the **Picture** button.
3. Click the **Look in** list arrow, and then select the drive and folder that contain the file you want to insert.
4. Click the file you want to insert.
5. Click **Insert**.
   - To link a picture file, click the **Insert** button arrow, and then click **Link to File**.
   - To insert and link a picture file, click the **Insert** button arrow, and then click **Insert and Link**.

TROUBLE? *If you see a red "x" instead of a picture or motion clip in your document, then you don't have a graphics filter installed on your computer for that clip.*

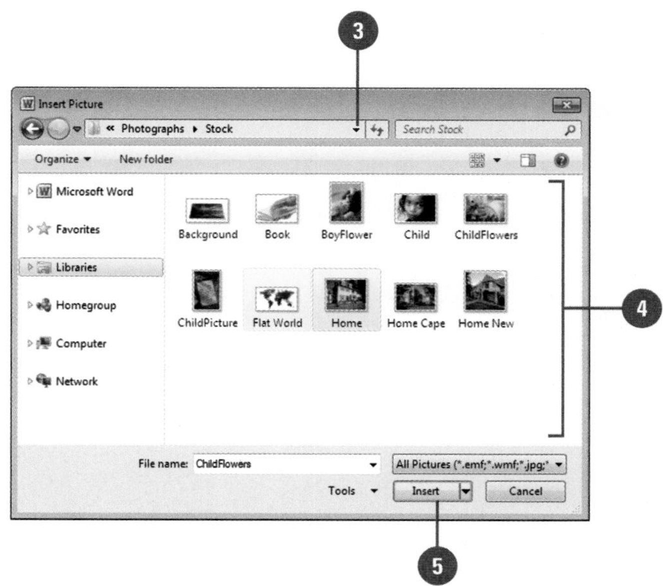

Did You Know?

You can change a picture. Select the picture, click the Change Picture button on the Format tab, select a picture, and then click Insert.

You can add graphic formats. If the graphic format you want to insert is not in the list, you can use Office Setup's Add or Remove Features option to install additional graphic formats.

Inserting a Picture Screen Shot

If you're working on a training manual, presentation, or document that requires a picture of your computer screen, then the Screenshot button (**New!**) on the Insert tab just made your life a lot easier. You use the Screen Clipping tool to drag a selection around the screen area that you want to capture, and then select the picture from the Screenshot gallery. The Screenshot gallery holds multiple screen shots, so you can capture several screens before you insert them into your document. After you insert the screen shot into a document, you can use the tools on the Picture Tools tab to edit and improve it.

Insert a Picture Screen Shot

1. Click the **Insert** tab.
2. Click the **Screenshot** button.
3. Click **Screen Clipping**.
4. Display the screen you want to capture, and then drag the large plus cursor to select the screen area to capture.
5. Click the **Screenshot** button, and then click the thumbnail of the screen shot you want to insert.
6. Use the tools on the Picture Tools tab to edit and improve the screen shot.

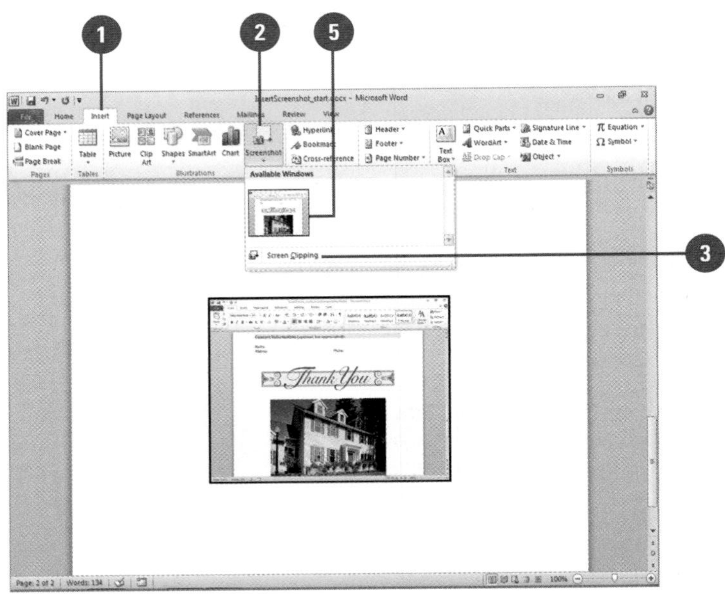

Did You Know?

You can copy the window or screen contents. To make a copy of the active window, press Alt+Print Scrn. To copy the entire screen as it appears on your monitor, press Print Scrn.

Adding an Artistic Style to a Picture

With the Artistic Quick Style gallery (**New!**), you can transform a picture into a piece of artwork. The Artistic Quick Style gallery makes it easy to change the look of a picture to a sketch, drawing, or painting. The Picture Quick Style gallery provides a variety of different formatting options—such as Pencil Sketch, Line Drawing, Watercolor Sponge, Mosaic Bubble, Glass, Pastels Smooth, Plastic Wrap, Photocopy, and Paint Strokes—to create a professional look. To quickly see if you like an Artistic Quick Style, point to a thumbnail in the gallery to display a live preview of it in the selected shape. If you like it, you can apply it.

Add an Artistic Style to a Picture

1. Click the picture you want to change.
2. Click the **Format** tab under Picture Tools.
3. Click the **Artistic Effects** button.

   The current style appears highlighted in the gallery.
4. Point to a style.

   A live preview of the style appears in the picture.
5. Click the style you want from the gallery to apply it to the selected picture.

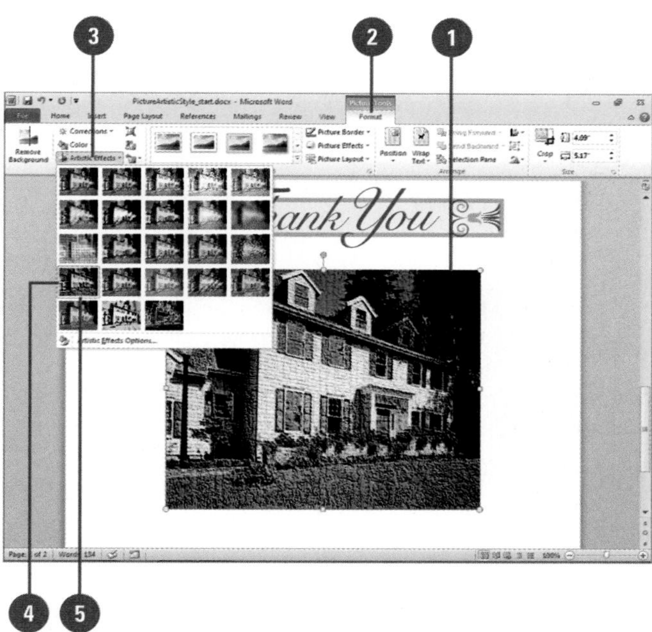

Did You Know?

You can quickly return a picture back to its original form. Select the picture, click the Format tab, and then click the Reset Picture button.

See Also

See "Applying Picture Effects" on page 117 for information on adding more effects to a picture.

Adding a Quick Style to a Picture

Instead of changing individual attributes of a picture—such as shape, border, and effects—you can quickly add them all at once with the Picture Quick Style gallery. The Picture Quick Style gallery provides a variety of different formatting combinations. To quickly see if you like a Picture Quick Style, point to a thumbnail in the gallery to display a live preview of it in the selected shape. If you like it, you can select the one you want to apply it.

Add a Quick Style to a Picture

1. Click the picture you want to change.
2. Click the **Format** tab under Picture Tools.
3. Click the scroll up or down arrow, or click the **More** list arrow in the Picture Styles group to see additional styles.

   The current style appears highlighted in the gallery.
4. Point to a style.

   A live preview of the style appears in the current shape.
5. Click the style you want from the gallery to apply it to the selected picture.

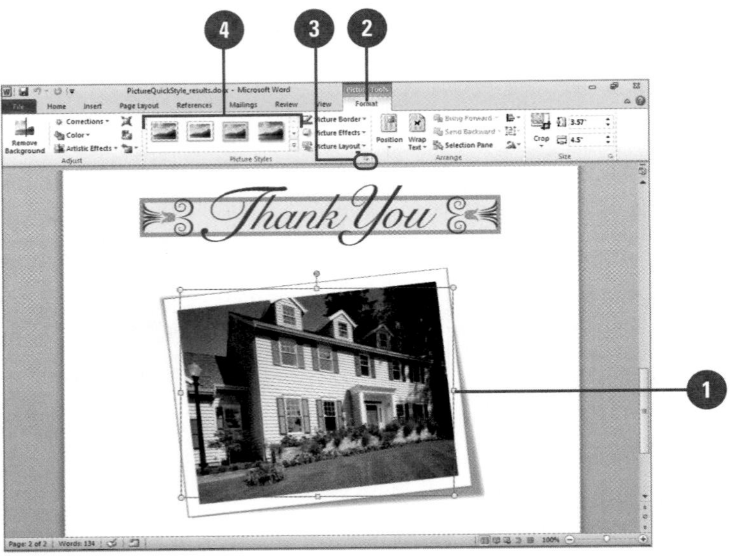

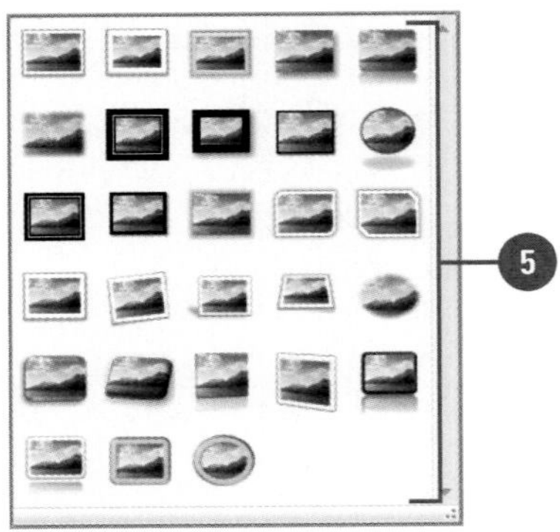

Applying a Shape to a Picture

After you insert a picture into your document, you can select it and apply one of Office's shapes to it. The picture appears in the shape just like it has been cropped. The Crop to Shape gallery (**New!**) makes it easy to choose the shape you want to use. Live preview is not available with the Crop to Shape gallery. You can try different shapes to find the one you want. If you don't find the one you want, you can use the Reset Picture button to return the picture back to its original state.

Apply a Shape to a Picture

1. Click the picture you want to change.
2. Click the **Format** tab under Picture Tools.
3. Click the **Crop** button arrow, and then point to **Crop to Shape**.
4. Select the shape you want to apply to the selected picture.

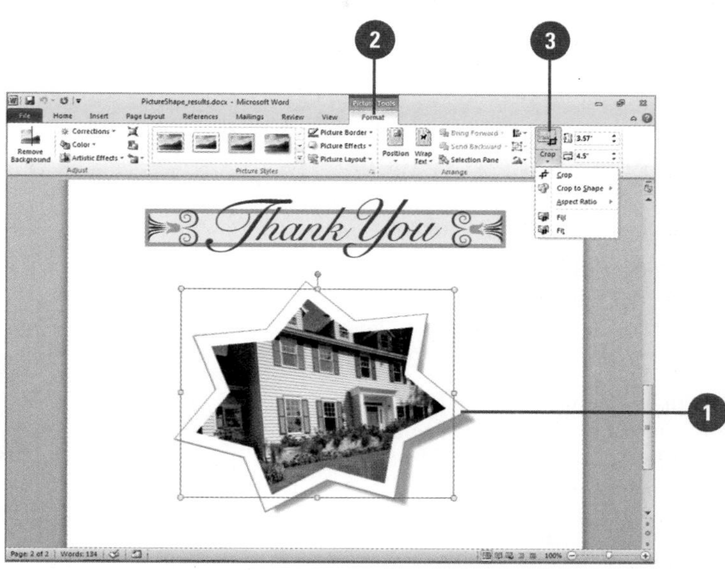

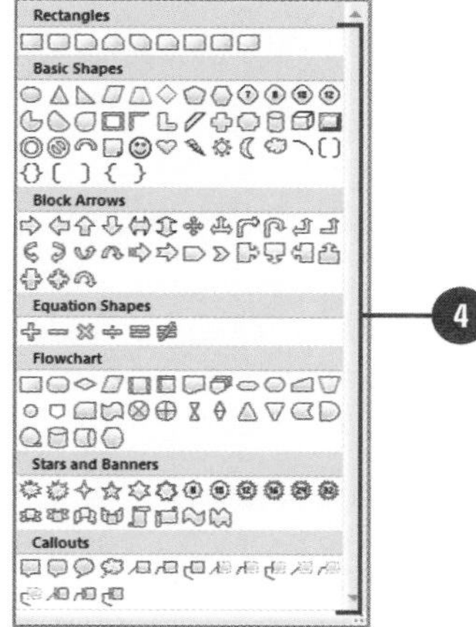

Did You Know?

You can save a shape as a picture in the PNG format. Right-click the shape, click Save As Picture, type a name, and then click Save.

You can copy the window or screen contents. To make a copy of the active window, press Alt+Print Scrn. To copy the entire screen as it appears on your monitor, press Print Scrn.

Applying a Border to a Picture

After you insert a picture, you can add and modify the picture border by changing individual outline formatting using the Picture Border button on the Format tab under Picture Tools. The Picture Border button works just like the Shape Outline button and provides similar options to add a border, select a border color, and change border width and style. You can try different border combinations to find the one you want. If you don't find one that works for you, you can use the No Outline command on the Picture Border gallery to remove it.

Apply a Border to a Picture

1. Click the picture you want to change.
2. Click the **Format** tab under Picture Tools.
3. Click the **Picture Border** button.
4. Click a color, or point to **Weight**, or **Dashes**, and then select a style, or click **More Lines** to select multiple options.
5. Drag a sizing handle to change the size or angle of the line or arrow.

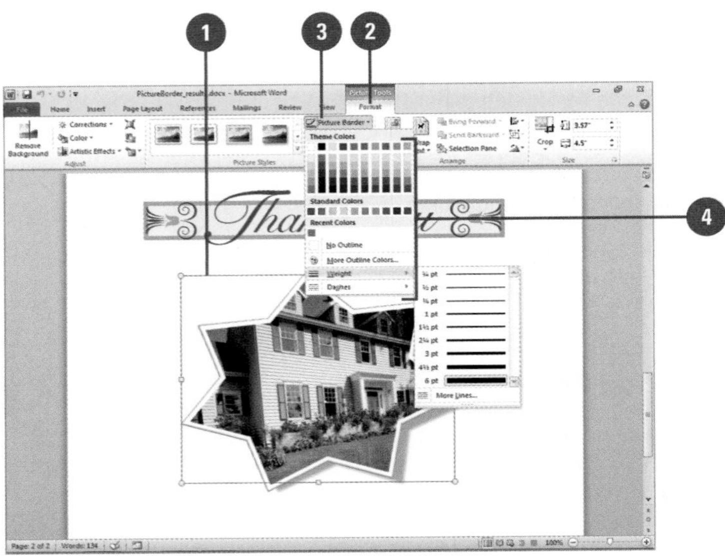

Did You Know?

You can remove a border. Select the picture, click the Format tab, click the Picture Border button, and then click No Outline.

Applying Picture Effects

You can change the look of a picture by applying effects, such as shadows, reflections, glow, soft edges, and 3-D rotations. You can also apply effects to a shape by using the Picture Effects gallery for quick results, or by using the Format Shape dialog box for custom results. From the Picture Effects gallery, you can apply a built-in combination of 3-D effects or individual effects to a picture. To quickly see if you like a picture effect, point to a thumbnail in the Picture Effects gallery to display a live preview of it. If you like it, you can apply it. If you no longer want to apply a picture effect to an object, you can remove it. Simply select the picture, point to the effect type on the Picture Effects gallery, and then select the No effect type option.

Add an Effect to a Picture

1. Click the picture you want to change.
2. Click the **Format** tab under Picture Tools.
3. Click the **Picture Effects** button, and then point to one of the following:
   - **Preset** to select No 3-D, one of the preset types, or More 3-D Settings.
   - **Shadow** to select No Shadow, one of the shadow types, or More Shadows.
   - **Reflection** to select No Reflection or one of the Reflection Variations.
   - **Glow** to select No Glow, one of the Glow Variations, or More Glow Colors.
   - **Soft Edges** to select No Soft Edges or a point size to determine the soft edge amount.
   - **3-D Rotation** to select No Rotation, one of the rotation types, or More 3-D Settings.

   When you point to an effect, a live preview of the style appears in the current shape.
4. Click the effect you want from the gallery to apply it.

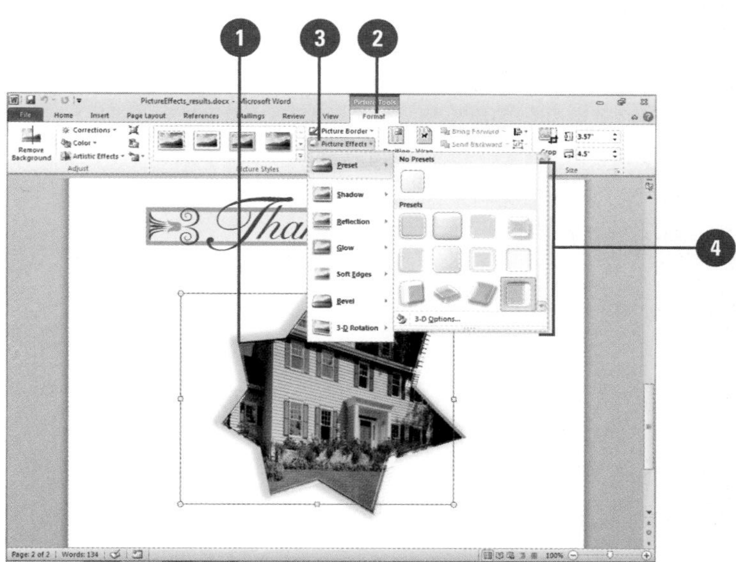

Modifying Picture Size

Once you have inserted a picture, clip art and other objects into your document, you can adapt them to meet your needs. Like any object, you can resize a picture. You can use the sizing handles to quickly resize a picture or use height and width options in the Size group on the Format tab to resize a picture more precisely. If you want to set unique or multiple options at the same time, you can use the Size and Position dialog box. These options allow you to make sure your pictures keep the same relative proportions as the original and lock size proportions.

Resize a Picture

1. Click the object you want to resize.
2. Drag one of the sizing handles to increase or decrease the object's size.
   - Drag a middle handle to resize the object up, down, left, or right.
   - Drag a corner handle to resize the object proportionally.

Resize a Picture Precisely

1. Click the object you want to resize.
2. Click the **Format** tab under Picture Tools.
3. Click the up and down arrows or enter a number (in inches) in the Height and Width boxes on the Ribbon and press Enter.

   If the **Lock aspect ratio** check box is selected in the Size and Position dialog box, height or width automatically changes when you change one of them. Click the **Size Dialog Box Launcher** to change the option.

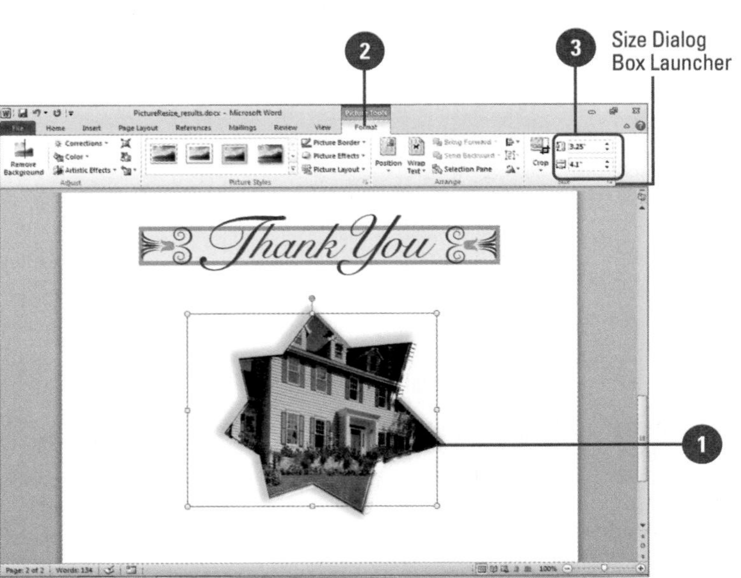

Precisely Scale a Picture

1. Click the object you want to resize.
2. Click the **Format** tab under Picture Tools.
3. Click the **Size Dialog Box Launcher**.
4. To keep the picture proportional, select the **Lock aspect ratio** check box.
5. To keep the picture the same relative size, select the **Relative to original picture size** check box.
6. Click the up and down arrows or enter a number in the Height and Width boxes in one of the following:
   - **Size.** Enter a height and width size in inches.
   - **Scale.** Enter a percentage size.

   If the Lock aspect ratio check box is selected, height or width automatically changes when you change one of them.
7. If you want to remove your changes, click **Reset**.
8. Click **Close**.

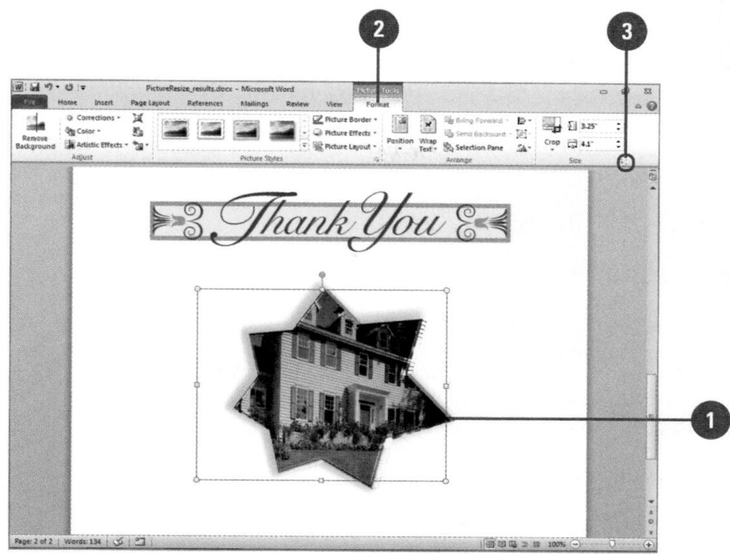

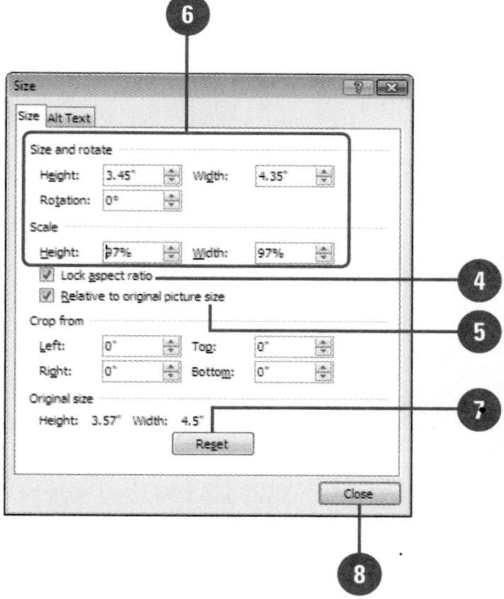

Did You Know?

Resizing bitmaps can cause distortion. Bitmap images are made up of dots, and do not lend themselves as easily to resizing because the dots can't expand and contract, which can lead to distortion. To avoid distortion, resize bitmaps proportionally and try to resize smaller instead of larger.

Compressing a Picture

Office allows you to compress pictures in order to minimize the file size of the image. In doing so, however, you may lose some visual quality, depending on the compression setting (**New!**). You can pick the resolution that you want for the pictures in a document based on where or how they'll be viewed (for example, on the Web or printed). You can also set other options, such as Delete cropped areas of picture, to get the best balance between picture quality and file size or automatically compress pictures when you save your document.

Compress a Picture

1. Click to select the pictures you want to compress.
2. Click the **Format** tab under Picture Tools.
3. Click the **Compress Pictures** button.
4. Select the **Apply only to this picture** check box to apply compression setting to only the selected picture. Otherwise, clear the check box to compress all pictures in your document.
5. Select or clear the **Delete cropped areas of pictures** check box to reduce file.
6. Click the **Print, Screen, E-mail**, or **Document** (**New!**) option to specify a target output.
7. Click **OK**.

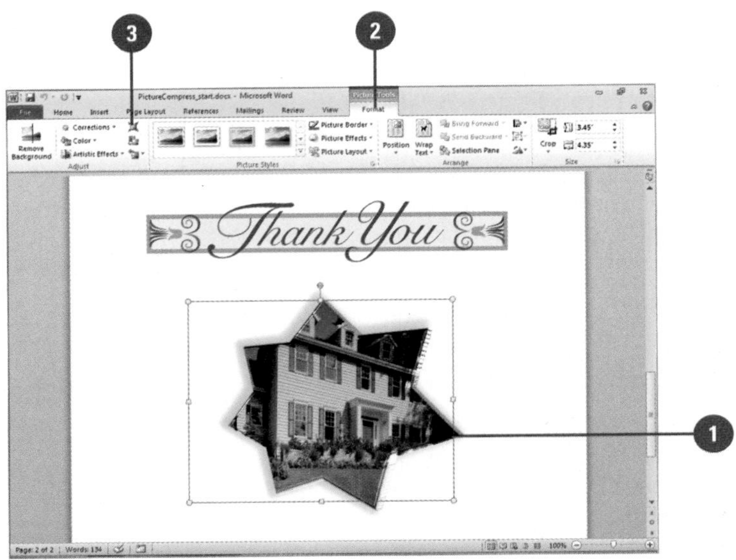

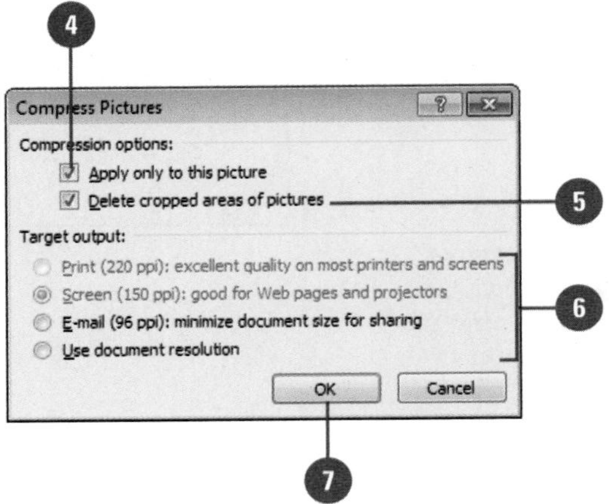

Correcting a Picture

Once you have inserted a picture, you can control the image's colors, brightness, and contrast using Picture tools. The brightness and contrast controls let you make simple adjustments to the tonal range of a picture. The brightness and contrast controls change a picture by an overall lightening or darkening of the image pixels. In addition, you can sharpen and soften pictures by a specified percentage (**New!**). You can experiment with the settings to get the look you want. If you don't like the look, you can use the Reset Picture button to return the picture back to its original starting point.

Change Brightness and Contrast or Sharpen and Soften

1. Click the picture you want to change.
2. Click the **Format** tab under Picture Tools.
3. Click the **Corrections** button, and then do one of the following:
   - **Brightness and Contrast.** Click a brightness and contrast option.

     A positive brightness lightens the object colors by adding more white, while a negative brightness darkens the object colors by adding more black. A positive contrast increases intensity, resulting in less gray, while a negative contrast to decrease intensity, resulting in more gray.
   - **Sharpen and Soften.** Click a sharpen and soften option.
4. To set custom correction percentages, click the **Corrections** button, click **Picture Corrections Options**, specify the options you want, and then click **Close**.

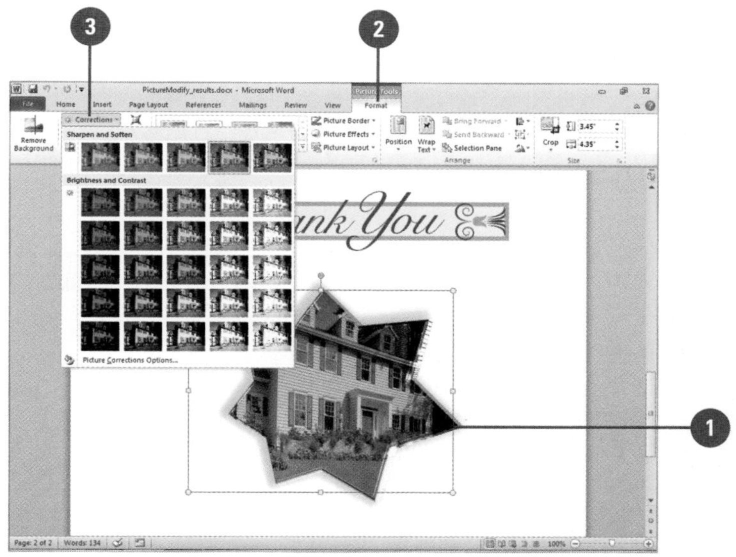

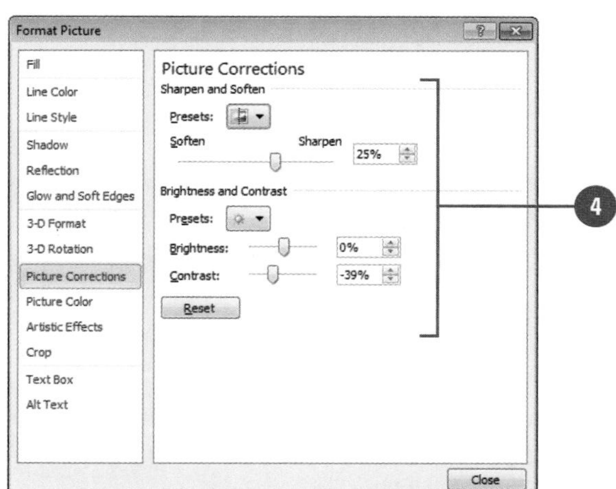

Recoloring a Picture

You can recolor clip art and other objects to match the color scheme of your document. For example, if you use a flower clip art as your business logo, you can change shades of pink in the spring to shades of orange in the autumn. The Color Picture Quick Style gallery (**New!**) provides a variety of different recolor formatting combinations. To quickly see if you like a Color Picture Quick Style, point to a thumbnail in the gallery to display a live preview of it in the selected shape. If you like it, you can apply it. You can also use a transparent background in your picture to avoid conflict between its background color and your document's background. With a transparent background, the picture takes on the same background as your document.

Recolor a Picture

1. Click the picture whose color you want to change.
2. Click the **Format** tab under Picture Tools.
3. Click the **Color** button.
4. Click one of the Color options.
   - **Recolor.** Click an option to apply a color type:

     No Recolor. Click this option to remove a previous recolor.

     Grayscale. Converts colors into whites, blacks and shades of gray between black and white.

     Sepia. Converts colors into very light gold and yellow colors like a picture from the old west.

     Washout. Converts colors into whites and very light colors.

     Black and White. Converts colors into only white and black.
   - **Color Saturation** or **Color Tone.** Click an option to apply a color saturation or tone based on the recolor selection.
   - **More Variations.** Point to this option to select a specific color.
   - **Picture Color Options.** Click this option to set custom recolor options by percentage.

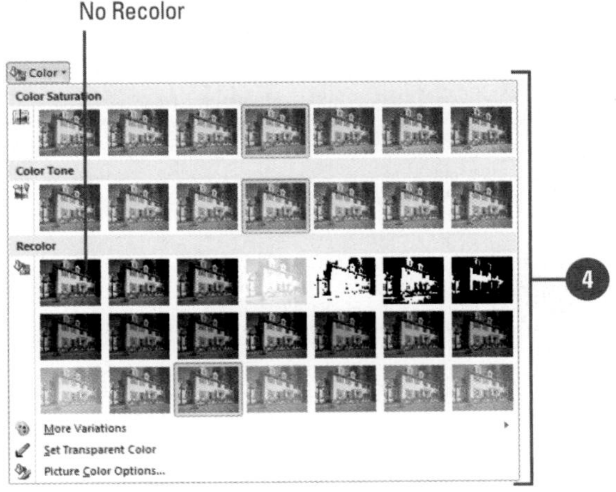

Set a Transparent Background

1. Click the picture you want to change.
2. Click the **Format** tab under Picture Tools.
3. Click the **Color** button, and then click **Set Transparent Color.**
4. Move the pointer over the object until the pointer changes shape.
5. Click the color you want to set as transparent.
6. Move the pointer over the picture where you want to apply the transparent color, and then click to apply it.
7. When you're done, click outside the image.

Did You Know?

Why is the Set Transparent Color command dimmed? Setting a color as transparent works only with bitmaps. If you are working with an object that is not a bitmap, you will not be able to use this feature.

You can't modify some pictures in Office. If the picture is a bitmap (.BMP, .JPG, .GIF, or .PNG), you need to edit its colors in an image editing program, such as Adobe Photoshop, Microsoft Paint, or Paint Shop Pro.

You can reset a picture back to its original state. Click the picture you want to reset, click the Format tab under Picture Tools, and then click the Reset Picture button.

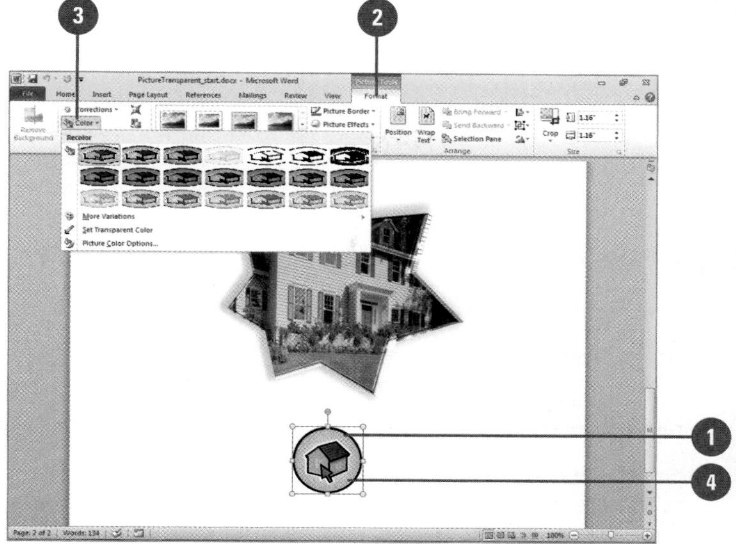

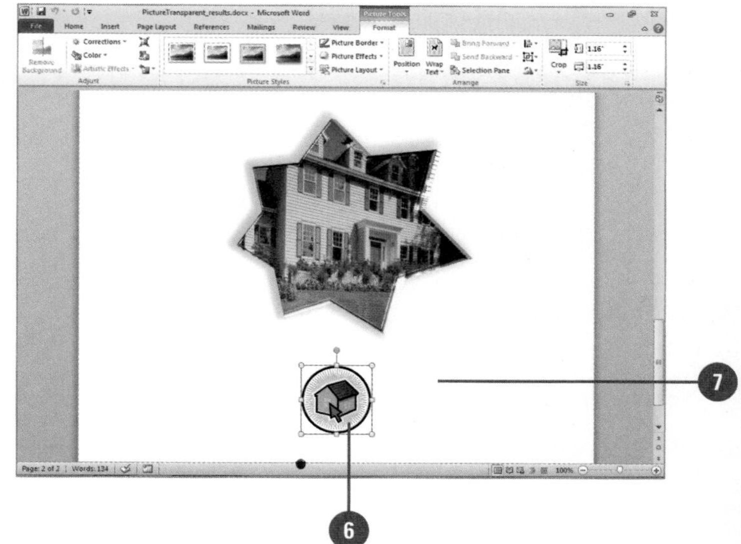

Cropping and Rotating a Picture

You can crop clip art to isolate just one portion of the picture. Because clip art uses vector image technology, you can crop even the smallest part of it and then enlarge it, and the clip art will still be recognizable. You can also crop bitmapped pictures, but if you enlarge the area you cropped, you lose picture detail. Use the Crop button to crop an image by hand. In addition, you can crop a picture while maintaining a selected resize aspect ratio (**New!**) or crop a picture based on a fill or fit (**New!**). You can also rotate a picture by increments or freehand.

Crop a Picture Quickly

1. Click the picture you want to crop.
2. Click the **Format** tab under Picture Tools.
3. Click the **Crop** button.
4. Drag the sizing handles until the borders surround the area you want to crop.
5. Click outside the image when you are finished.

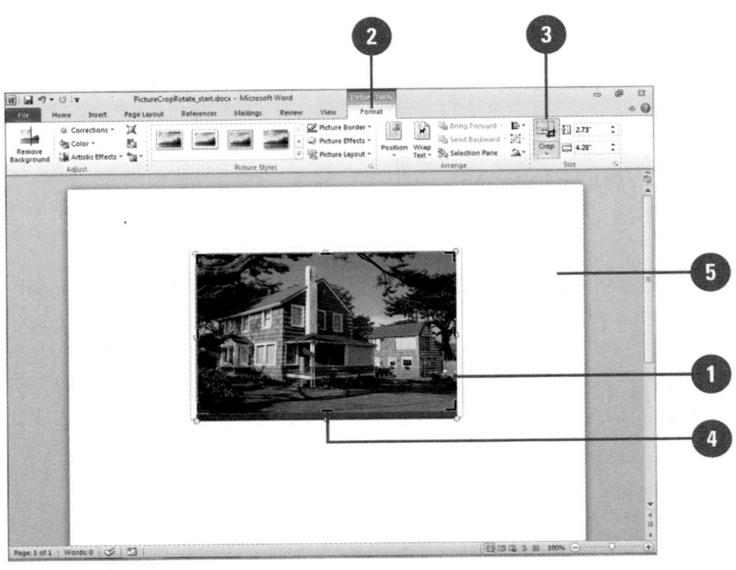

Crop a Picture with an Aspect Ratio

1. Click the picture you want to crop.
2. Click the **Format** tab under Picture Tools.
3. Click the **Crop** button arrow, point to **Aspect Ratio**, and then select an aspect ratio.
4. Drag the sizing handles until the borders surround the area you want to crop.
5. Click outside the image when you are finished.

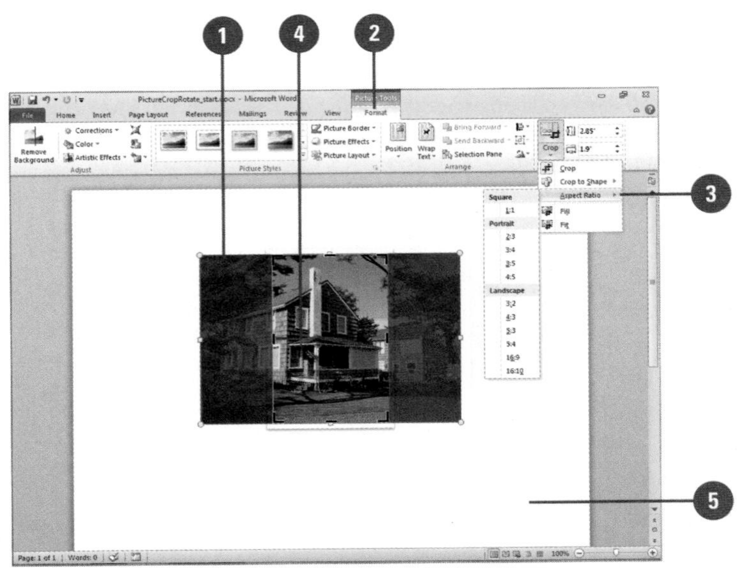

Crop a Picture with a Fill or Fit

1. Click the picture you want to crop.
2. Click the **Format** tab under Picture Tools.
3. Click the **Crop** button arrow, and then select an option:
   - **Fill.** Resizes the picture so the entire picture area is filled while maintaining the aspect ratio. Any area outside of the picture area is cropped.
   - **Fit.** Resizes the picture so the entire picture displays inside the picture area while maintaining the aspect ratio.
4. Drag the sizing handles until the borders surround the area you want to crop.
5. Click outside the image when you are finished.

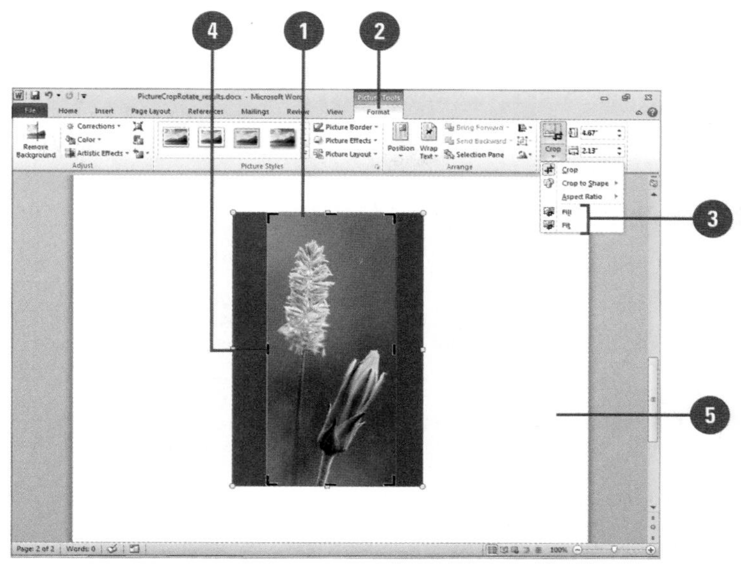

Rotate a Picture

1. Click the object you want to rotate.
2. Position the pointer (which changes to the Free Rotate pointer) over the green rotate lever at the top of the object, and then drag to rotate the object.
3. Click outside the object to set the rotation.

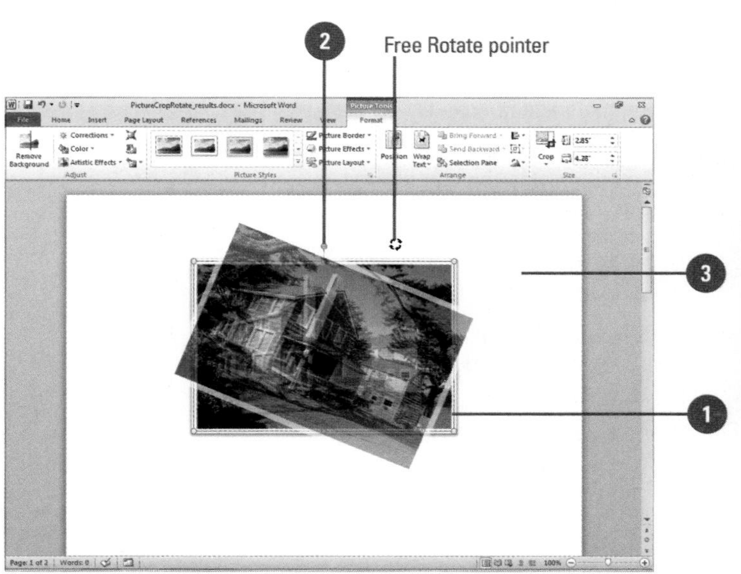

Did You Know?

You can rotate or flip a picture. Select the picture, click the Format tab, click the Rotate button, and then click Rotate Right 90, Rotate Left 90, Flip Vertical, Flip Horizontal, or click More Rotation Options.

Removing a Picture Background

Sometimes you want to use an element from a picture instead of the entire picture. With the Remove Background command (**New!**), you can specify the element you want in a picture, and then remove the background. You can use automatic background removal or you can manually draw lines to specify which parts of the picture background you want to keep and which to remove.

Remove a Picture Background

1. Click the picture you want to change.
2. Click the **Format** tab under Picture Tools.
3. Click the **Remove Background** button.
4. Drag the handles on the marquee lines to specify the part of the picture you want to keep. The area outside the marquee gets removed.
5. To manually specify which areas to keep and which areas to remove, do the following:
   - **Mark Areas to Keep.** Click the button, and then draw lines to specify which parts of the picture you do not want automatically removed.
   - **Mark Areas to Remove.** Click the button, and then draw lines to specify which parts of the picture you do want removed in addition to those automatically marked.
   - **Delete Mark.** Click the button, and then click marked lines to remove them.
6. Click the **Keep Changes** button to close and keep the removal or click the **Discard All Changes** button to close and cancel the automatic removal.

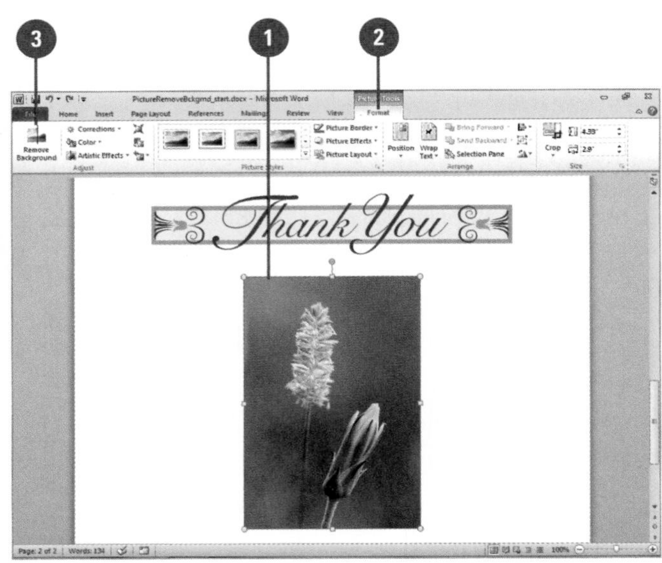

Creating WordArt Text

The WordArt feature lets you create stylized text to draw attention to your most important words. Most users apply WordArt to a word or a short phrase, such as *Home For Sale*. You should apply WordArt to a document sparingly. Its visual appeal and unique look requires uncluttered space. When you use WordArt, you can choose from a variety of text styles that come with the WordArt Quick Style gallery, or you can create your own using tools in the WordArt Styles group. To quickly see if you like a WordArt Quick Style, point to a thumbnail in the gallery to display a live preview of it in the selected text. If you like it, you can apply it. You can also use the free angle handle (pink diamond) inside the selected text box to adjust your WordArt text angle.

Insert WordArt Text

1. Click the **Insert** tab.
2. Click the **WordArt** button, and then click one of the WordArt styles.

   A WordArt text box appears on the document with selected placeholder text.
3. Type the text you want WordArt to use.
   - Drag a resize handle as needed to increase or decrease the size of the WordArt text box.
4. If applicable, use the Font and Paragraph options on the Home tab to modify the text you entered.
5. To edit WordArt text, click to place the insertion point where you want to edit, and then edit the text.

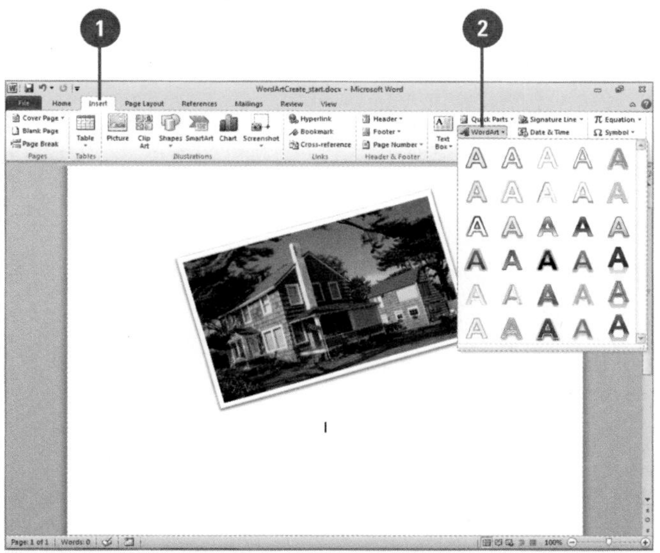

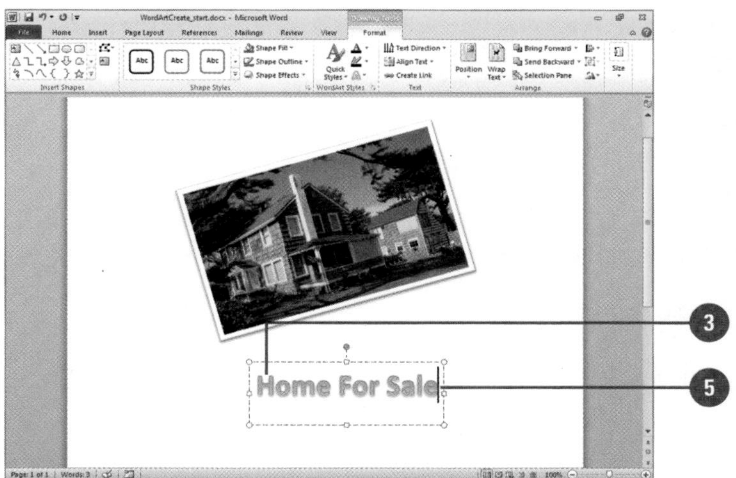

Did You Know?

You can convert text in a text box to WordArt. Select the text box, click the Format tab under Drawing Tools, and then click the WordArt text style you want from the Ribbon.

You can remove WordArt text. Select the WordArt text you want to remove, click the Format tab, click the Quick Styles button, and then click Clear WordArt.

Formatting WordArt Text

In addition to applying one of the preformatted WordArt styles, you can also create your own style by shaping your text into a variety of shapes, curves, styles, and color patterns. The WordArt Styles group gives you tools for changing the fill and outline of your WordArt text. To quickly see if you like a WordArt Style, point to a thumbnail in the gallery to display a live preview of it in the selected text. If you like it, you can apply it.

Apply a Different WordArt Style to Existing WordArt Text

1. Click the WordArt object whose style you want to change.
2. Click the **Format** tab under WordArt Tools.
3. Click the scroll up or down arrow, or click the **More** list arrow in the WordArt Styles group to see additional styles.

   The current style appears highlighted in the gallery.
4. Point to a style.

   A live preview of the style appears in the current shape text.
5. Click the style you want from the gallery to apply it to the selected shape.

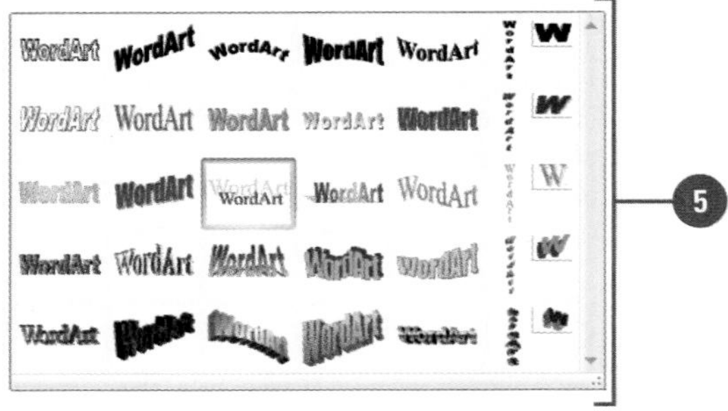

Did You Know?

You can add more formatting to WordArt text. Select the WordArt object, click the Home tab, and then use the formatting button in the Font and Paragraph groups.

You can change the WordArt fill color to match the background. Click the WordArt object, right-click the object, click Format Shape, click the Background option, and then click Close.

Apply a Fill to WordArt Text

1. Click the WordArt object you want to change.
2. Click the **Format** tab under WordArt Tools.
3. Click the **Shape Fill** button arrow, and then click or point to one of the following:
   - **Color** to select a theme or standard color.
   - **No Fill** to remove a fill color.
   - **Picture** to select a picture file.
   - **Gradient** to select No Gradient, one of the shadow types, or More Gradients.
   - **Texture** to select one of the texture types, or More Textures.

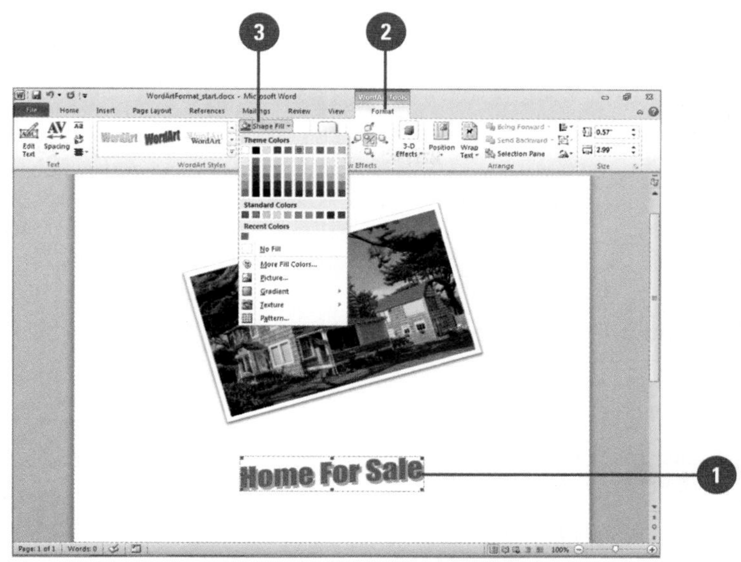

Apply an Outline to WordArt Text

1. Click the WordArt object you want to change.
2. Click the **Format** tab under WordArt Tools.
3. Click the **Shape Outline** button.
4. Click a color, or point to **Weight** or **Dashes**, and then select a style.

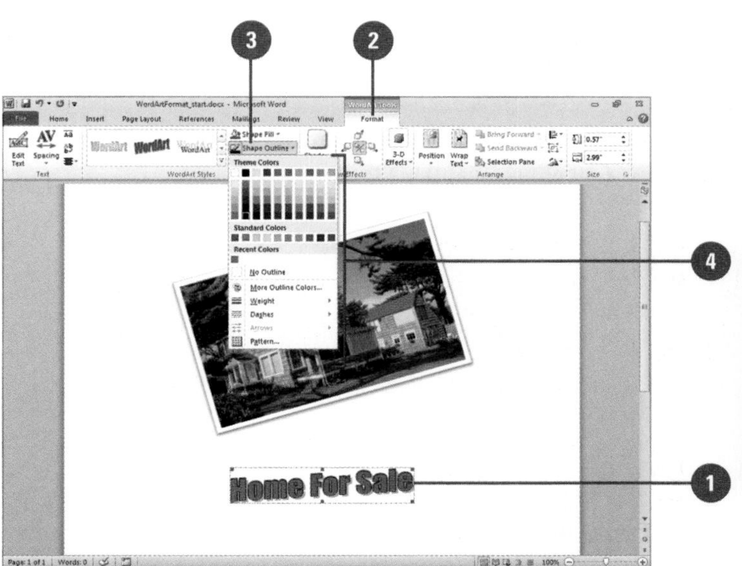

Did You Know?

You can change the shape of WordArt text. Select the WordArt object, click the Format tab under WordArt Tools, click the Change WordArt Shape button, and then select a shape.

Applying WordArt Text Effects

You can change the look of WordArt text by applying effects, such as shadows and 3-D rotations. You can apply effects to a shape by using the Shadow or 3-D Effects gallery for quick results. From the 3-D Effects gallery you can apply a built-in combination of 3-D effects or individual 3-D effects to WordArt text. To quickly see if you like the effect, point to a thumbnail in the Shadow or 3-D Effects gallery to display a live preview of it. If you like it, you can apply it. If you no longer want to apply the effect, you can remove it. Simply, select the WordArt text, and then select the No effect type option on the Shadow Effects or 3-D Effects gallery.

Apply an Effect to WordArt Text

1. Click the WordArt object you want to change.
2. Click the **Format** tab under WordArt Tools.
3. To add a shadow, click the **Shadow Effects** button, and then select a shadow effect.
   - To change the location and length of a shadow, click any of the Nudge Shadow buttons.
   - To remove a shadow, click the **Shadow On/Off** button in the middle of the Nudge Shadow buttons.
4. To add a 3D effect, click the **3-D Effects** button, and then select a 3D effect.
   - To change the location and length of a 3-D effect, click any of the Tilt buttons.
   - To remove a shadow, click the **3-D On/Off** button in the middle of the Tilt buttons.

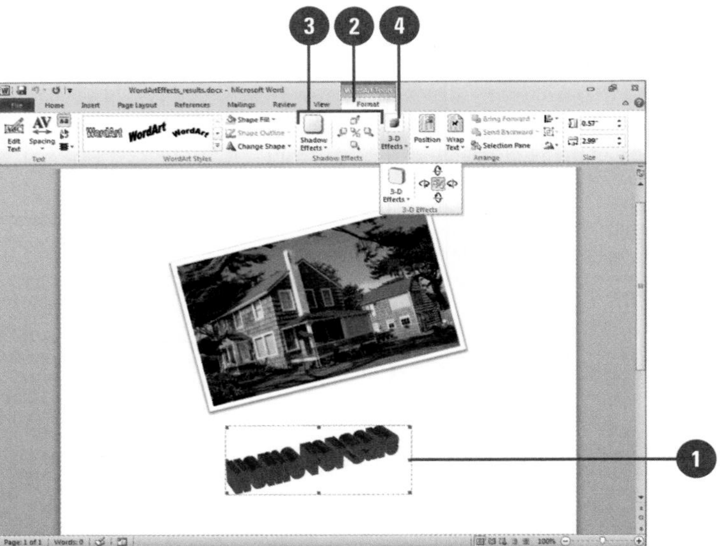

3-D Effects gallery

No 3-D Effect
Parallel
Perspective
Rotate in Perspective
3-D Color
Depth
Direction
Lighting
Surface

Did You Know?

You can change the WordArt text spacing. Select the WordArt object, click the Format tab under WordArt Tools, click the Spacing button, and then select a spacing option.

Modifying WordArt Text Position

You can apply a number of text effects to your WordArt objects that determine letter height, justification, alignment, and spacing. The effects of some of the adjustments you make are more pronounced for certain WordArt styles than others. Some of these effects make the text unreadable for certain styles, so apply these effects carefully. If the text position is not what you want, you can also use the Rotate button to rotate right or left 90 degrees or flip vertical or horizontal.

Change WordArt Text Direction

1. Click the WordArt object you want to change.
2. Click the **Format** tab under WordArt Tools.
3. To align text, click the **Align Text** button, and then select an option: **Left Align, Center, Right Align, Word Justify, Letter Justify, Letter Justify**, or **Stretch Justify**.
4. To stack text vertically, click the **WordArt Vertical Text** button.
5. Click outside the object to deselect it.

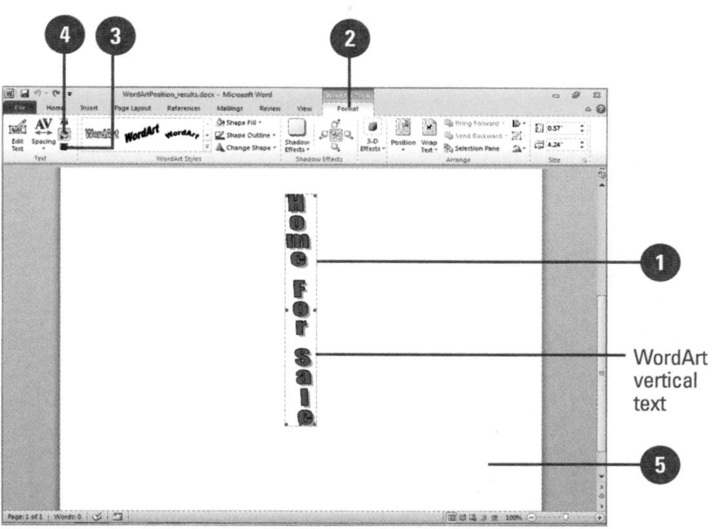

Rotate WordArt Text

1. Click the WordArt object you want to rotate.
2. Click the **Format** tab under WordArt Tools.
3. Click the **Rotate** button, and then select an option: **Rotate Right 90, Rotate Left 90, Flip Vertical**, or **Flip Horizontal**.
4. Click outside the object to deselect it.

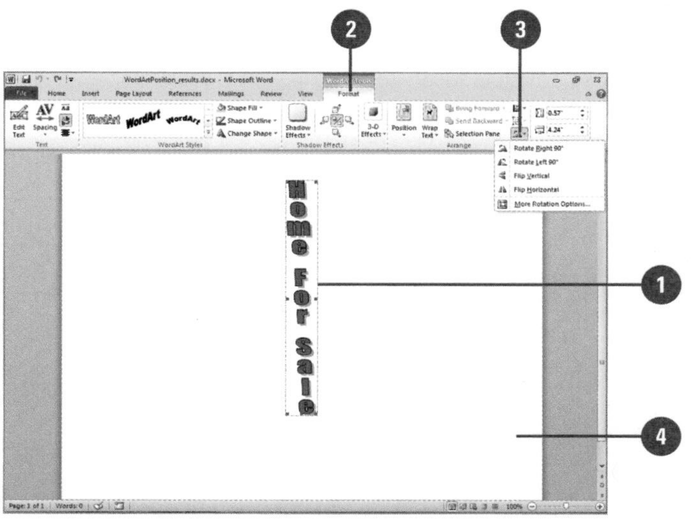

Creating SmartArt Graphics

SmartArt graphics allow you to create diagrams that convey processes or relationships. Office provides a wide variety of built-in SmartArt graphic types, including graphical lists, process, cycle, hierarchy, relationship, matrix, pyramid, picture (**New!**), and Office.com (**New!**). Using built-in SmartArt graphics makes it easy to create and modify charts without having to create them from scratch. To quickly see if you like a SmartArt graphic layout, point to a thumbnail in the gallery to display a live preview of it in the selected shape. If you like it, you can apply it.

Create a SmartArt Graphic

1. Click the **Insert** tab.
2. Click the **SmartArt** button.
3. In the left pane, click a category, such as All, List, Process, Cycle, Hierarchy, Relationship, Matrix, or Pyramid.
4. In the middle pane, click a SmartArt graphic style type.
5. Click **OK**.

   The SmartArt graphic appears in the document.

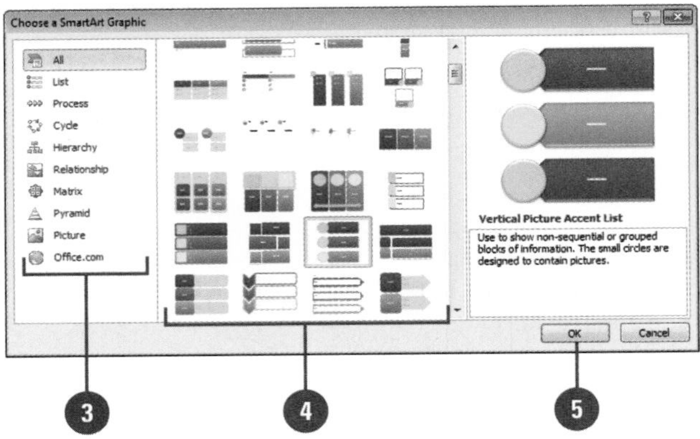

Did You Know?

You can change a SmartArt diagram type. Select the SmartArt graphic, click the Design tab under SmartArt Tools, click the More list arrow for Layouts, click More Layout, select a diagram type, and then click OK.

SmartArt Graphic Purposes

Type	Purpose
List	Show non-sequential information
Process	Show steps in a process or timeline
Cycle	Show a continual process
Hierarchy	Show a decision tree or create an organization chart
Relationship	Illustrate connections
Matrix	Show how parts relate to a whole
Pyramid	Show proportional relationships up and down
Picture	Convert a picture to a SmartArt graphic (**New!**)
Office.com	Show SmartArt graphics from Office.com (**New!**)

6 Click the **Text Pane** button, or click the control with two arrows along the left side of the selection to show the Text pane.

7 Label the shapes by doing one of the following:

- Type text in the [Text] box.

  You can use the arrow keys to move around the Text pane, or use the Promote or Demote buttons to indent.

- At the end of a line, press Enter to insert a line (shape), or select line text, and then press Delete to remove a line (shape).

- Click a shape, and then type text directly into the shape.

8 When you're done, click outside of the SmartArt graphic.

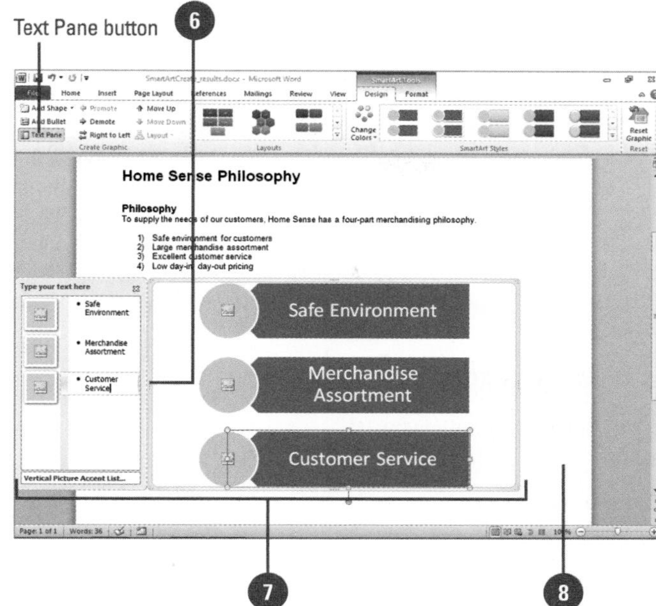

Did You Know?

You cannot drag text into the Text pane. Although you can't drag text into the Text pane, you can copy and paste text.

You can create a blank SmartArt graphic. In the Text pane, press Ctrl+A to select all the placeholder text, and then press Delete.

Using the Text Pane with SmartArt Graphics

After you create a layout for a SmartArt graphic, a Text pane appears next to your selected SmartArt graphic. The bottom of the Text pane displays a description of the SmartArt graphic. The Text pane and SmartArt graphic contain placeholder text. You can change the placeholder text in the Text pane or directly in the SmartArt graphic. The Text pane works like an outline or a bulleted list and the text corresponds directly with the shape text in the SmartArt graphic. As you add and edit content, the SmartArt graphic automatically updates, adding or removing shapes as needed while maintaining the design. If you see a red "x" in the Text pane, it means that the SmartArt graphic contains a fixed number of shapes, such as Counterbalance Arrows (only two).

Show or Hide the Text Pane

1. Click the SmartArt graphic you want to modify.
2. Click the **Design** tab under SmartArt Tools.
3. Do any of the following:
   - **Show**. Click the **Text Pane** button, or click the control with two arrows along the left side of the SmartArt graphic selection to show the Text pane.
   - **Hide.** Click the **Text Pane** button, click the **Close** button on the Text pane, deselect the SmartArt graphic.

   The Text Pane button toggles to show or hide the Text pane.

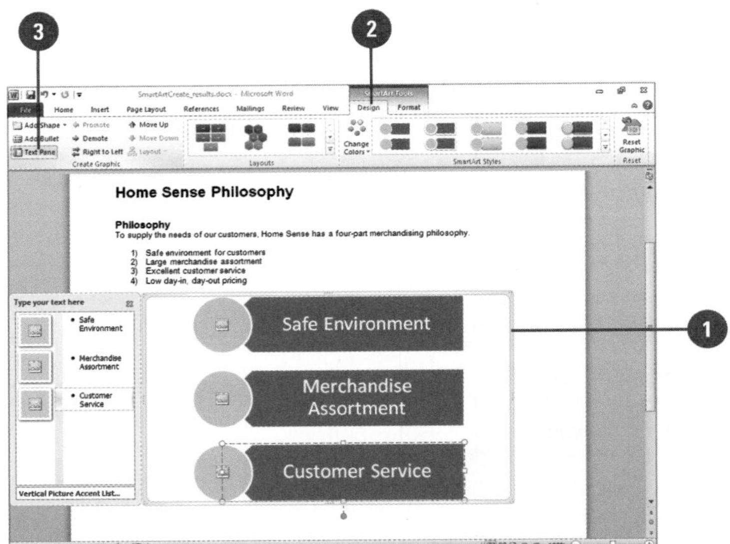

Did You Know?

You can resize the Text pane. To resize the Text pane, point to any edge (pointer changes to double-headed arrow), and then drag to resize it.

You can move the Text pane. To move the Text pane, drag the top of the pane. The Text pane location resets when you exit Excel.

Work with Text in the Text Pane

1. Click the SmartArt graphic you want to modify.
2. Click the **Design** tab under SmartArt Tools.
3. If necessary, click the **Text Pane** button to show the Text pane.
4. Do any of the following tasks:
   - **New line.** At the end of a line, press Enter.
   - **Indent line right.** Press Tab, or click the **Promote** button.
   - **Indent line left.** Press Shift+Tab, or click the **Demote** button.
   - **Delete line.** Select the line text, and then press Delete.

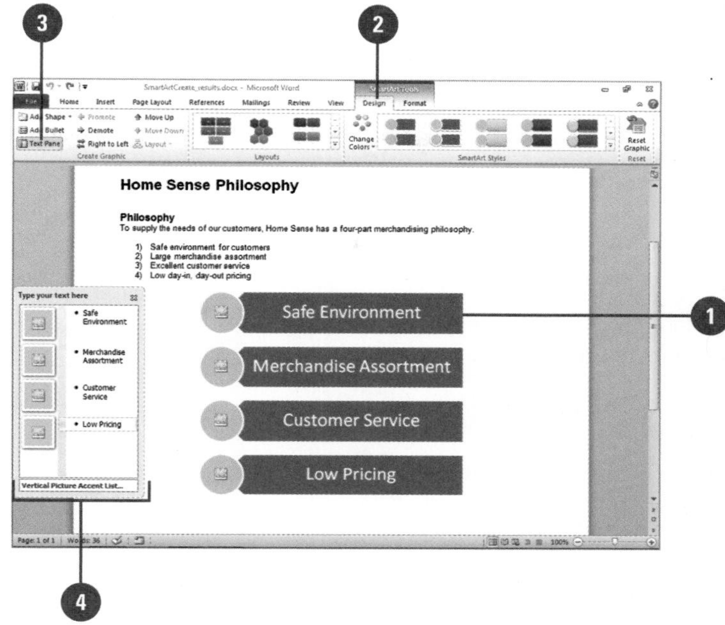

Did You Know?

You can format text in the Text pane. When you apply formatting to text in the Text pane, it doesn't display in the Text pane, but it does display in the SmartArt graphic.

You can remove a shape from a SmartArt graphic. Select the SmartArt graphic, click the shape you want to remove, and then press Delete.

Formatting a SmartArt Graphic

If your current SmartArt graphics don't quite convey the message or look you want, use live preview to quickly preview layouts in the Quick Styles and Layout Styles groups and select the one you want. If you only want to change the color, you can choose different color schemes using theme colors by using the Change Color button. If the flow of a SmartArt graphic is not the direction you want, you can change the orientation.

Apply a Quick Style to a SmartArt Graphic

1. Click the SmartArt graphic you want to modify.
2. Click the **Design** tab under SmartArt Tools.
3. Click the scroll up or down arrow, or click the **More** list arrow in the Quick Styles group to see additional styles.
4. Point to a style.

   A live preview of the style appears in the current shape.
5. Click the layout for the SmartArt graphic you want from the gallery.

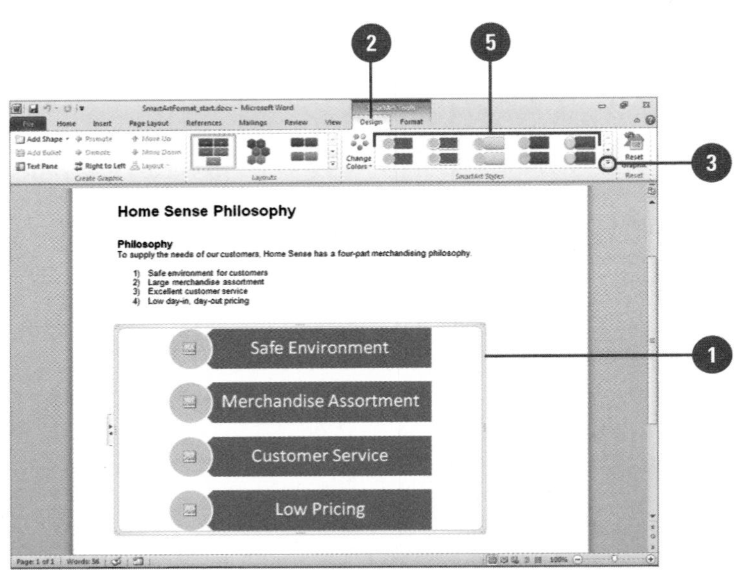

Change a Smart Graphic Orientation

1. Click the SmartArt graphic you want to modify.
2. Click the **Design** tab under SmartArt Tools.
3. Click the **Right to Left** button.

   The button toggles, so you can click it again to switch back.

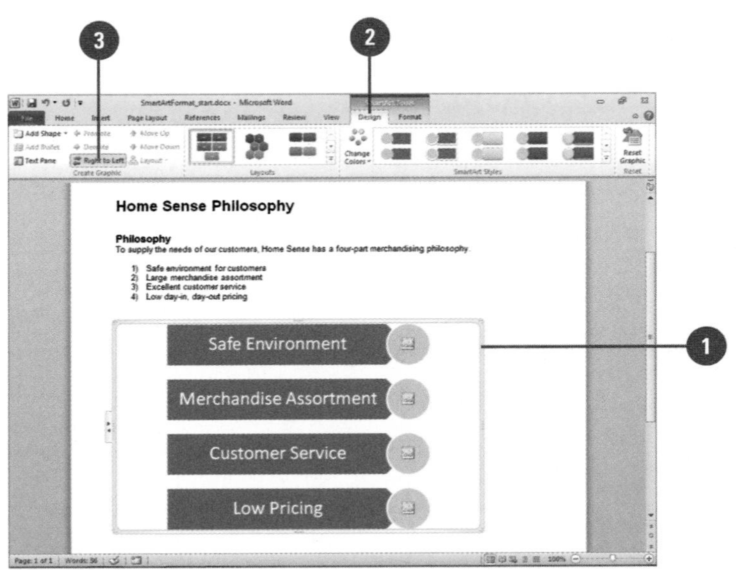

Change a SmartArt Graphic Layout

1. Click the SmartArt graphic you want to modify.
2. Click the **Design** tab under SmartArt Tools.
3. Click the scroll up or down arrow, or click the **More** list arrow in the Layout Styles group to see additional styles.

   The gallery displays layouts designed for bulleted lists.
4. To view the entire list of diagram layouts, click **More Layouts**.
5. Point to a layout.

   A live preview of the style appears in the current shape.
6. Click the layout for the SmartArt graphic you want from the gallery.
7. If you opened the entire list of layouts, click **OK**.

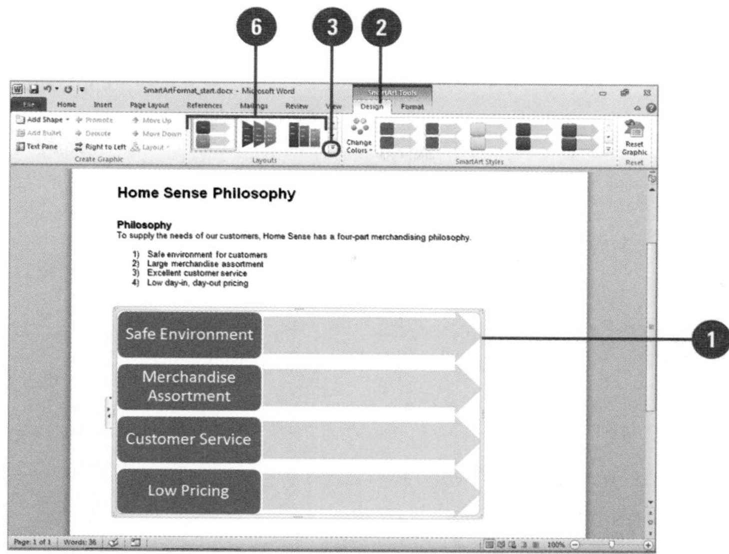

Change a SmartArt Graphic Colors

1. Click the SmartArt graphic you want to modify.
2. Click the **Design** tab under SmartArt Tools.
3. Click the **Change Colors** button.

   The gallery displays the current layout with different theme colors.
4. Point to a style.

   A live preview of the style appears in the current shape.
5. Click the layout for the SmartArt graphic you want from the gallery.

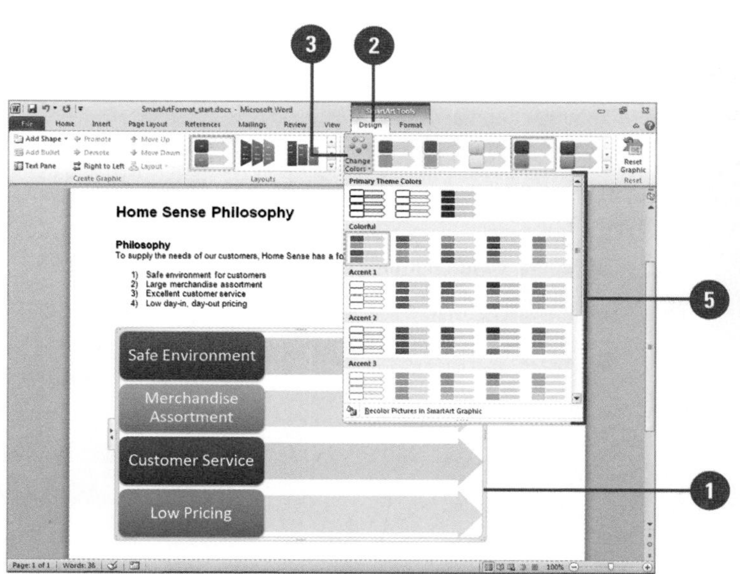

Modifying a SmartArt Graphic

After you create a SmartArt graphic, you can add, remove, change, or rearrange shapes to create a custom look. For shapes within a SmartArt graphic, you can change the shape from the Shape gallery or use familiar commands—such as Bring to Front, Send to Back, Align, Group, and Rotate—to create your own custom SmartArt graphic. If you no longer want a shape you've added, simply select it, and then press Delete to remove it.

Add a Shape to a SmartArt Graphic

1. Select the shape in the SmartArt graphic you want to modify.
2. Click the **Design** tab under SmartArt Tools.
3. Click the **Add Shape** button to insert a shape at the end, or click the **Add Shape** button arrow, and then select the position where you want to insert a shape.

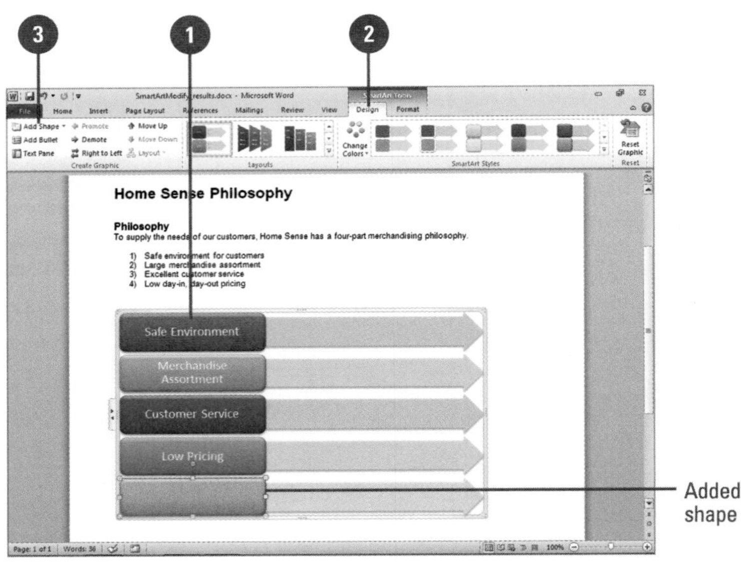

Change Shapes in a SmartArt Graphic

1. Select the shapes in the SmartArt graphic you want to modify.
2. Click the **Format** tab under SmartArt Tools.
3. Click the **Change Shape** button, and then click a shape.
4. To change the size of the selected shape, click the **Larger** or **Smaller** button.

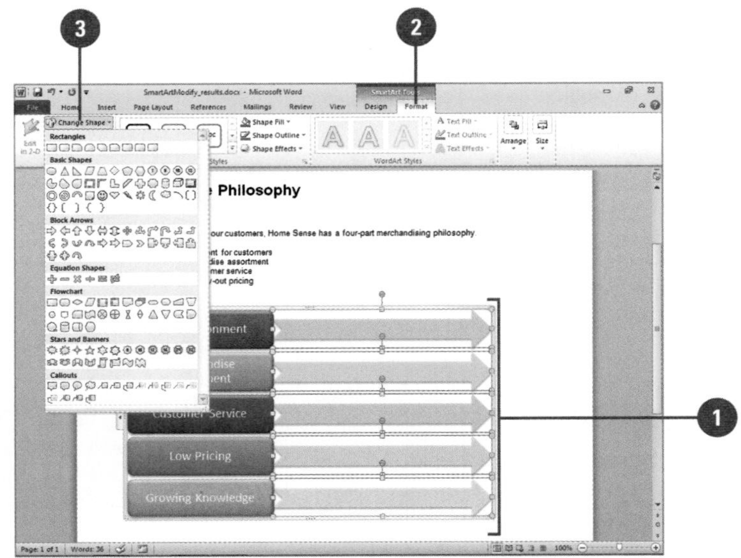

Format Shapes in a SmartArt Graphic

1. Select the shapes in the SmartArt graphic you want to modify.
2. Click the **Format** tab under SmartArt Tools.
3. In the Shape Styles section, use any of the following:
   - **Shape Style.** Click the **More** list arrow, and then select a style.
   - **Shape Fill.** Click the **Shape Fill** button, and then select a fill, such as a color, picture, gradient, or texture.
   - **Shape Outline.** Click the **Shape Outline** button, and then select an outline, such as color, weight, dashes, or arrow.
   - **Shape Effects.** Click the **Shape Effects** button, and then select an effect, such as Shadow, Reflection, Glow, Soft Edges, Bevel, or 3-D Rotation.

Did You Know?

You can reset a SmartArt graphic back to its original state. Select the SmartArt graphic, click the Design tab under SmartArt Tools, and then click the Reset Graphic button.

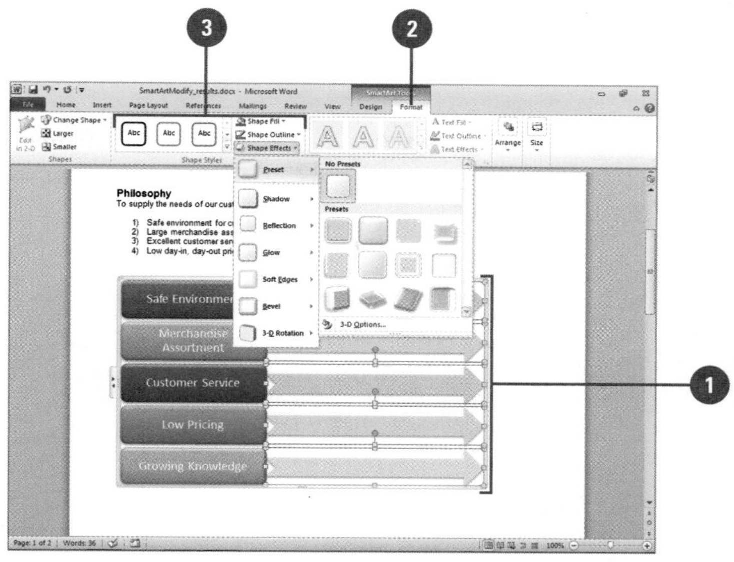

Shape Styles gallery

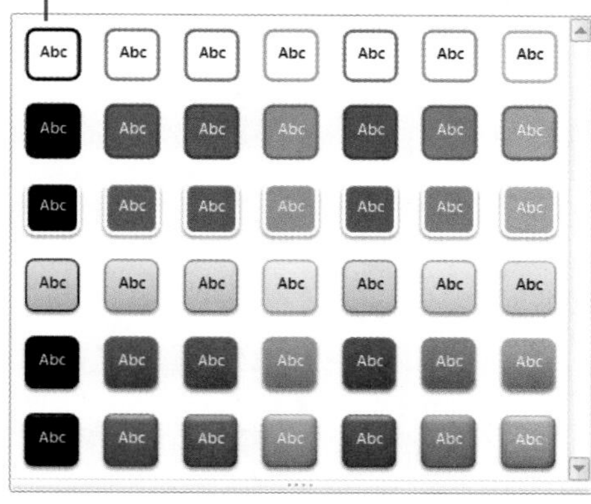

Adding Pictures to a SmartArt Graphic

With SmartArt graphic layouts (**New!**), you can insert pictures in the SmartArt shapes. In addition to the pictures, you can also add descriptive text using the Text pane or shape itself. The process is very simple. Insert a SmartArt picture layout, insert pictures, and then add descriptive text. If you already have pictures in your document, you can convert them to a SmartArt graphic.

Add a SmartArt Graphic to a Picture

1. Use either of the following to add pictures to a SmartArt graphic:
   - **Create New.** Click the **Insert** tab, click the **SmartArt** button, click **Picture**, click a layout, and then click **OK**.
   - **Convert Picture.** Select a picture, click the **Format** tab under Picture Tools, click the **Picture Layout** button, and then select a layout.
2. To add a shape, click the **Design** tab under SmartArt Tools, click the **Add Shape** button arrow, and then select the type of shape you want to add.
3. To add a picture, double-click a graphic placeholder, select a picture file, and then click **Insert**.
4. Label the shapes by doing one of the following:
   - Type text in the [Text] box.
   - Click a shape, and then type text directly into the shape.

Did You Know?

Convert a SmartArt graphic to shapes. Select the SmartArt graphic, click the Design tab under SmartArt Tools, and then click the Convert To Shapes button (**New!**).

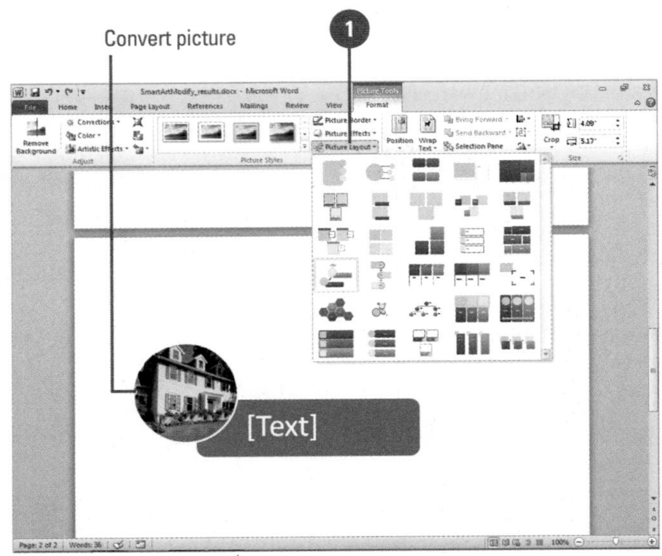

Creating an Organization Chart

An organization chart shows the reporting relationships between individuals in an organization. For example, you can show the relationship between a manager and employees within a company. You can create an organization chart using a SmartArt graphic or using Microsoft Organization Chart. A SmartArt graphic organization chart makes it easy to add shapes using the graphic portion or the Text pane.

Create an Organization Chart Using a SmartArt Graphic

1. Click the **Insert** tab.
2. Click the **SmartArt** button.
3. In the left pane, click **Hierarchy**.
4. In the middle pane, click a SmartArt organization chart type.
5. Click **OK**.

   The SmartArt graphic appears with a Text pane to insert text.
6. Label the shapes by doing one of the following:
   - Type text in the [Text] box.

     You can use the arrow keys to move around the Text pane.
   - Click a shape, and then type text directly into the shape.
7. To add shapes from the Text pane, place the insertion point at the beginning of the text where you want to add a shape, type the text you want, press Enter, and then to indent the new shape, press Tab or to promote, press Shift+Tab.

   You can also click the **Add Shape** button arrow on the **Design** tab under SmartArt Tools, and then select the type of shape you want to add.
8. When you're done, click outside of the SmartArt graphic.

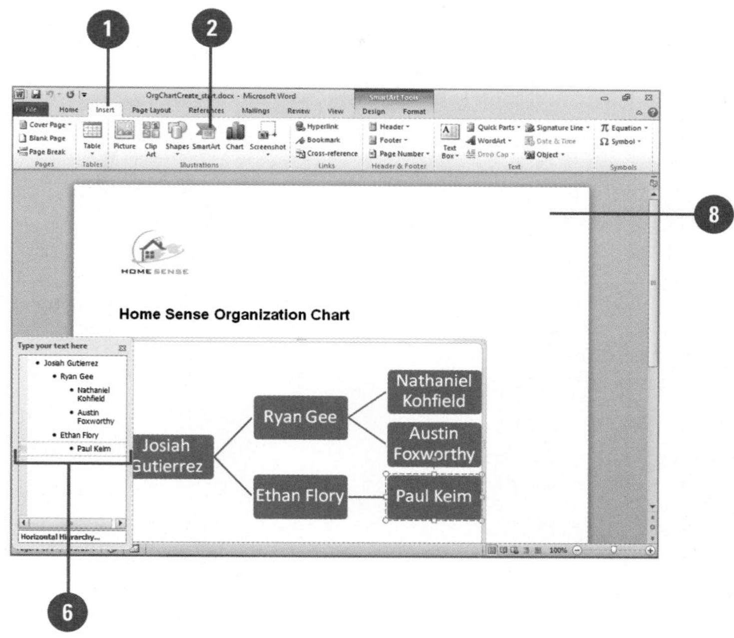

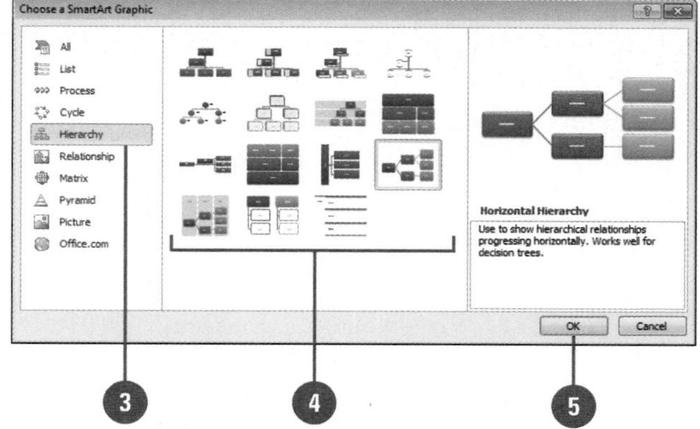

Modifying an Organization Chart

Like any SmartArt graphic, you can add special effects—such as soft edges, glows, or 3-D effects, and animation—to an organization chart. If your organization chart doesn't quite look the way you want, live preview can help you preview layouts in the Quick Styles and Layout Styles groups and select the one you want. If you only want to change the color, you can choose different color schemes using theme colors by using the Change Color button.

Change the Layout or Apply a Quick Style to an Organization Chart

1. Click the SmartArt graphic you want to modify.
2. Click the **Design** tab under SmartArt Tools.
3. Click the scroll up or down arrow, or click the **More** list arrow in the Layouts group or Quick Styles group to see additional styles.

   The gallery displays different layouts or the current layout with different theme colors.
4. Point to a style.

   A live preview of the style appears in the current shape.
5. Click the layout or style for the SmartArt graphic you want from the gallery.

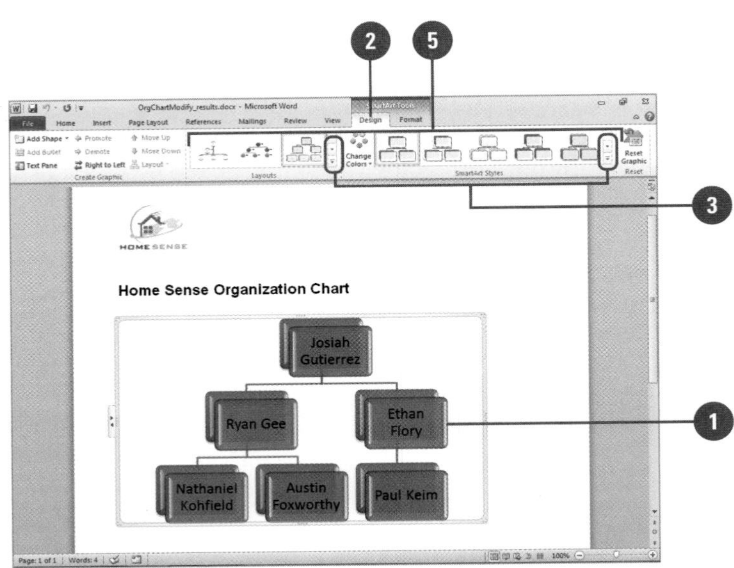

Did You Know?

You can change organization chart lines to dotted lines. Right-click the line you want to modify, click Format Object, click Line Style, click Dash type, click a style, and then click Close.

You can change the colors of an organization chart. Click the SmartArt graphic you want to modify, click the Design tab under SmartArt Tools, click the Change Colors button, and then click the color theme you want.

Adding Tables and Charts to Documents

6

Introduction

There are times when typing a paragraph will not do your text justice. Creating a bulleted or numbered list might better show your information. Another way to organize items in a document is with a table. A **table** is an object that is inserted into the Word document that displays text in rows and columns. You can set up your table with existing text, or create the table, even draw it out, and enter in new text. Once created, you can adjust the cells (where the text is contained in the rows and columns). You can also adjust the table to insert or delete rows, columns or individual cells, change the alignment of text, sort the text, or even apply a border or shading to the table.

Instead of adding a table of data, you can also insert a chart. Charts add visual interest and useful information represented by lines, bars, pie slices, or other markers. When you insert and create a chart in a document, the chart is an embedded object from Microsoft Excel 2010. Word uses Microsoft Excel to embed and display the information in a chart instead of Microsoft Graph. You can resize or move the embedded chart just as you would any graphic object. Your chart is what your reader sees, so make sure to take advantage of the pre-built chart layouts and styles to make the chart appealing and visually informative. There are a wide variety of chart types, available in 2-D and 3-D formats, from which to choose. For each chart type, you can select a predefined chart layout and style to apply the formatting you want.

After you finish creating a chart, you can save it as a chart template. A chart template file saves all the customization you made to a chart for use in other documents. You can save any chart in a document as a chart template file and use it to form the basis of your next document chart, which is useful for standard company financial reporting.

What You'll Do

Creating a Table

A **table** organizes information neatly into rows and columns. The intersection of a row and a column is called a **cell**. You can insert tables by specifying a size, or drawing rows and columns to create a custom table, or you can create a table from existing text separated by paragraphs, tabs, or commas. In addition, you can create **nested tables** (a table created within a table cell), **floating tables** (tables with text wrapped around them), or **side-by-side tables** (separate but adjacent tables). If you decide not to use a table, you can convert it to text.

Create a Table from Existing Text

1. Select the text for the table.
2. Click the **Insert** tab.
3. Click the **Table** button, and then click **Convert Text to Table**.
4. Enter the number of columns.
5. Select an AutoFit column width option.
6. Click a symbol to separate text into cells.
7. Click **OK**.

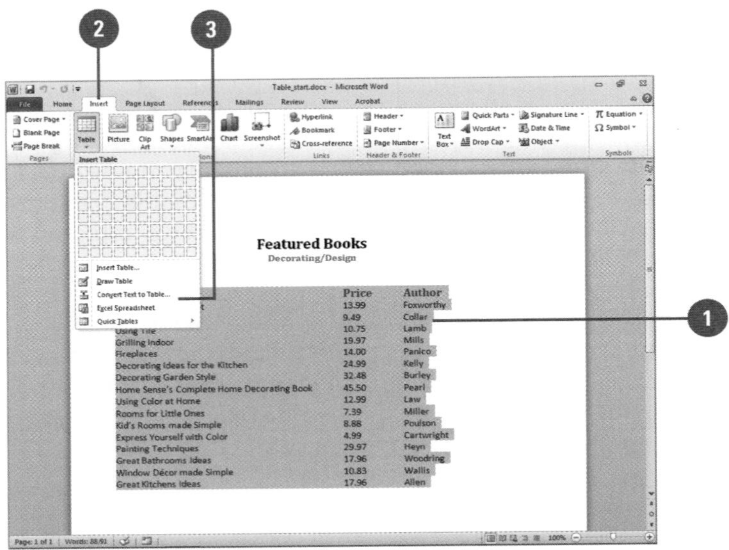

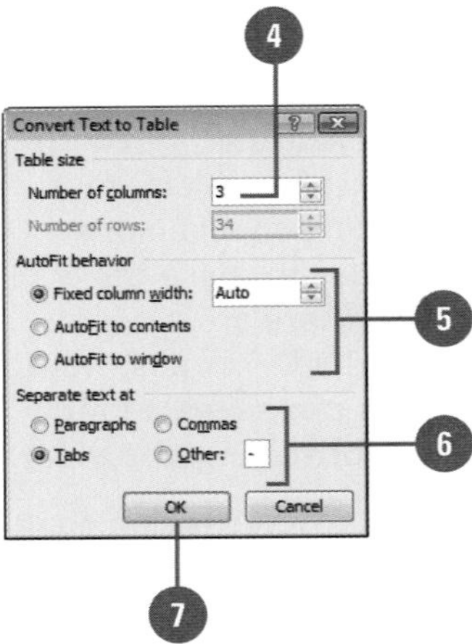

Did You Know?

You can convert a table back to text. Select the table, click the Layout tab under Table Tools, click the Convert To Text button, select the Separate text with option (typically Tabs), and then click OK.

You can insert a Quick Table. If you need a calendar, or a specific table layout, such as double table, matrix, tabular list, you can use the Quick Tables command to select the one you want. The tables come with predefined data or information, which you can delete.

Create a New Table Quickly

1. Click to place the insertion point where you want to insert a table.
2. Click the **Insert** tab.
3. Click the **Table** button, and then drag to select the number of rows and columns you want, or click **Insert Table**, enter the number of columns and rows you want, and then click **OK**.
4. Release the mouse button to insert a blank grid in the document.
5. When you're done, click outside of the table.

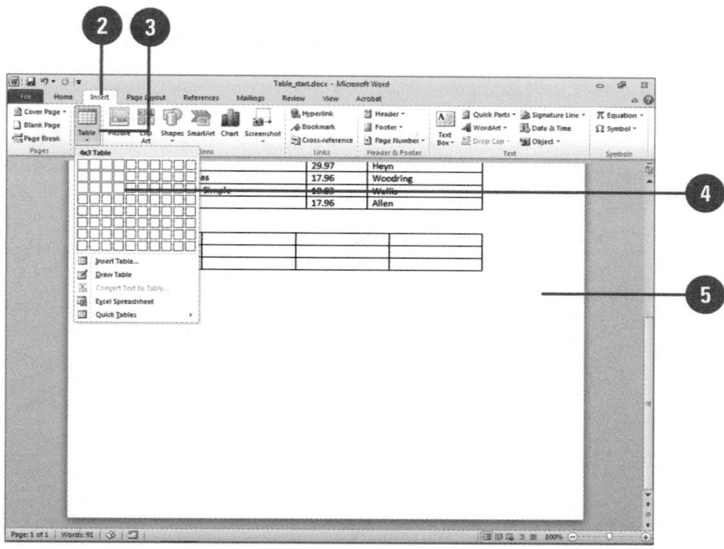

Draw a Custom Table

1. Click the **Insert** tab.
2. Click the **Table** button, and then click **Draw Table**.
3. Draw the table.
   - A rectangle creates individual cells or the table boundaries.
   - Horizontal lines create rows.
   - Vertical lines create columns.
   - Diagonal lines split cells.
4. If necessary, press and hold Shift, and then click one or more lines to erase them.
5. When you're done, click outside of the table.

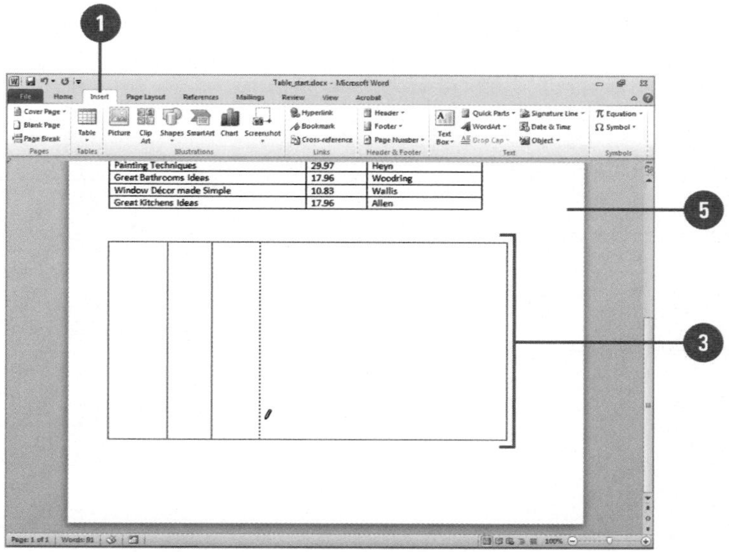

Entering Text in a Table

Once you create your table, you enter text into cells just as you would in a paragraph, except pressing Tab moves you from cell to cell. As you type in a cell, text wraps to the next line, and the height of a row expands as you enter text that extends beyond the column width. The first row in the table is good for column headings, whereas the left-most column is good for row labels. Before you can modify a table, you need to know how to select the rows and columns of a table.

Enter Text and Move Around a Table

1. The insertion point shows where text that you type will appear in a table. After you type text in a cell:
   - Press Enter to start a new paragraph within that cell.
   - Press Tab to move the insertion point to the next cell to the right (or to the first cell in the next row).
   - Press the arrow keys or click in a cell to move the insertion point to a new location.

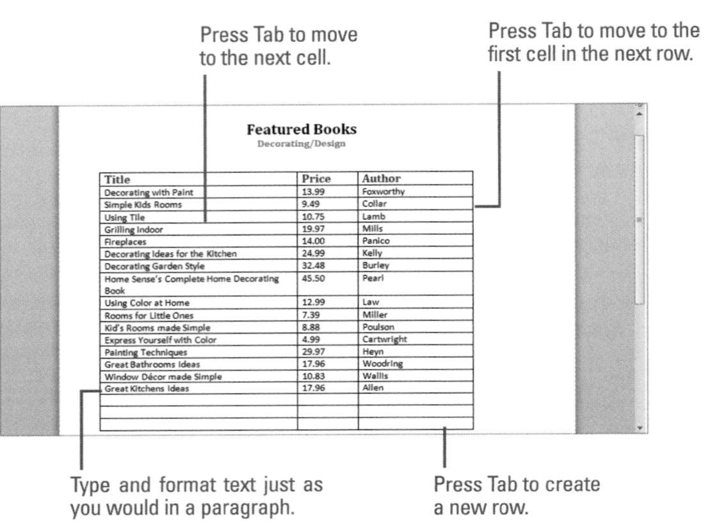

Featured Books

Decorating/Design

Title	Price	Author
Decorating with Paint	13.99	Foxworthy
Simple Kids Rooms	9.49	Collar
Using Tile	10.75	Lamb
Grilling Indoor	19.97	Mills
Fireplaces	14.00	Panico
Decorating Ideas for the Kitchen	24.99	Kelly
Decorating Garden Style	32.48	Burley
Home Sense's Complete Home Decorating Book	45.50	Pearl
Using Color at Home	12.99	Law
Rooms for Little Ones	7.39	Miller
Kid's Rooms made Simple	8.88	Poulson
Express Yourself with Color	4.99	Cartwright
Painting Techniques	29.97	Heyn
Great Bathrooms Ideas	17.96	Woodring
Window Décor made Simple	10.83	Wallis
Great Kitchens Ideas	17.96	Allen

Select Table Elements

Refer to this table for methods of selecting table elements, including:

- The entire table
- One or more rows and columns
- One or more cells

Selecting Table Elements

To Select	Do This
The entire table	Click ⊞ next to the table, or click anywhere in the table, click the Layout tab under Table Tools, click the Select button, and then click Select Table.
One or more rows	Click in the left margin next to the first row you want to select, and then drag to select the rows you want.
One or more columns	Click just above the first column you want to select, and then drag with ⬇ to select the columns you want, or click the Layout tab under Table Tools, click the Select button and then click Select Column or Select Row.
A single cell	Drag a cell or click the cell with ⬈.
More than one cell	Drag with ⬈ to select a group of cells.

Did You Know?

You can delete contents within a cell. Select the cells whose contents you want to delete, and then press Backspace or Delete.

Sorting Table Contents or Lists

After you enter contents in a table or create a bulleted or numbered list, you can reorganize the information by sorting the information. For example, you might want to sort information in a client list alphabetically by last name or numerically by their last invoice date. **Ascending order** lists information from A to Z, earliest to latest, or lowest to highest. **Descending order** lists information from Z to A, latest to earliest, or highest to lowest. You can sort a table columns based on one or more adjacent columns. A sort, for example, might be the telephone directory numerically by area code and then alphabetically by last name.

Sort Table Contents or Lists

1. Select the table column, adjacent columns, or list you want to sort.
2. Click the **Home** tab or the **Layout** tab under Table Tools.
3. Click the **Sort** button.
4. If necessary, click the **Sort by** list arrow, and then select a column name.
5. Click the **Type** list arrow, and then click table cell content type.
6. Click the **Ascending** or **Descending** option.
7. If necessary, click the second **Sort by** list arrow, select another column name, and then select the related sorting options you want.
8. Click the **Header row** or **No header row** option as it applies to the table.
9. Click **OK**.

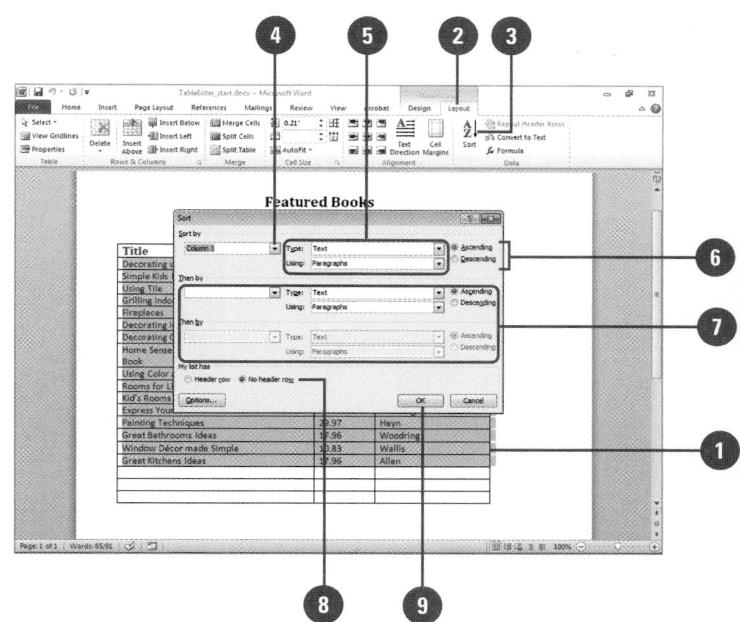

Modifying a Table

As you begin to work on a table, you might need to modify its structure by adding more rows, columns, or cells to accommodate new text, graphics, or other tables. The table realigns as needed to accommodate the new structure. When you insert rows, columns, or cells, the existing rows shift down, the existing columns shift right, and you choose what direction the existing cells shift. Similarly, when you delete unneeded rows, columns, or cells from a table, the table realigns itself.

Insert Additional Rows or Columns

1. Select the row above which you want the new rows to appear, or select the column to the left of which you want the new columns to appear.
2. Drag to select the number of rows or columns you want to insert.
3. Click the **Layout** tab under Table Tools.
4. Click the Row & Column buttons you want:
   - **Insert Above.**
   - **Insert Below.**
   - **Insert Left.**
   - **Insert Right.**

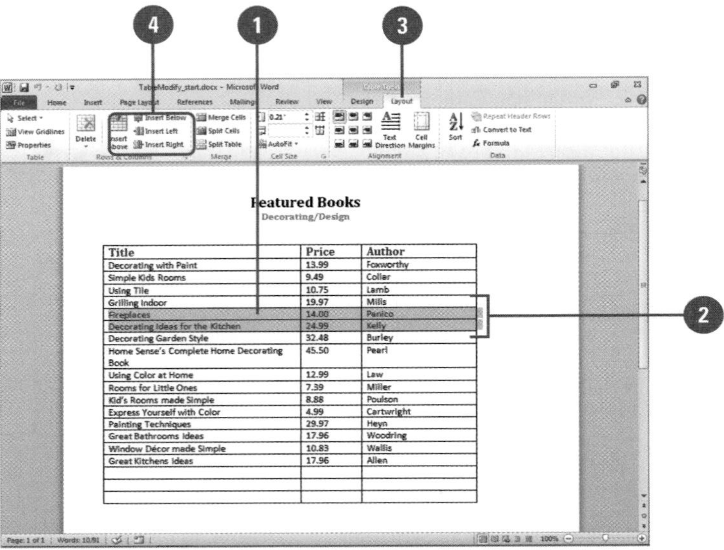

Did You Know?

You can show or hide gridlines in a table. Select the table you want to change, click the Layout tab under Table Tools, and then click View Gridlines to toggle it on and off.

You can resize a table. Drag a corner or middle resize handle to resize the table manually.

Delete Table, Rows, Columns, or Cells

1. Select the rows, columns, or cells you want to delete.
2. Click the **Layout** tab under Table Tools.
3. Click the **Delete** button, and then click the delete option you want:
   - **Delete Cells**. Select the direction in which you want the remaining cells to shift to fill the space, and then click OK.
   - **Delete Columns**.
   - **Delete Rows**.
   - **Delete Table**.

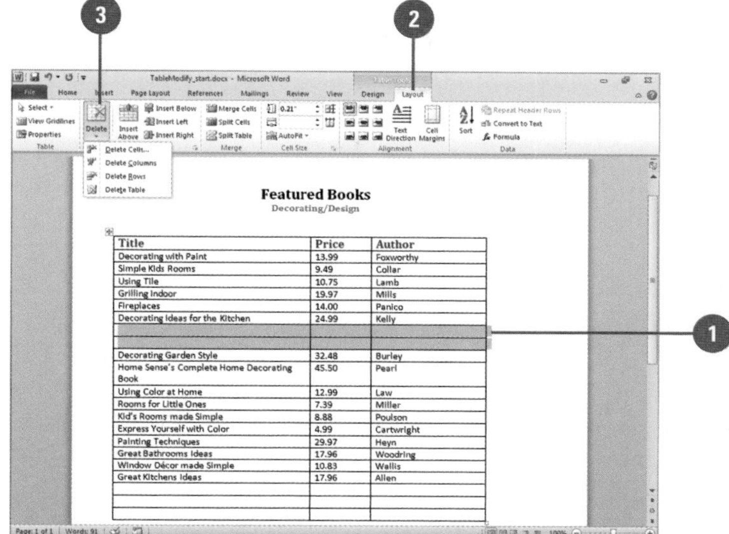

Did You Know?

You can set column widths to fit text. Word can set the column widths to fit the cells' contents or to fill the space between the document's margins. Click in the table, click the Layout tab under Table Tools, click the AutoFit button in the Cell Size group, and then click AutoFit To Contents or AutoFit To Window.

You can evenly distribute columns and rows. Select the columns or rows you want to distribute evenly in a table, click the Layout tab under Table Tools, and then click the Distribute Vertically or Distribute Horizontally button in the Cells Size group.

Adjusting Table Cells

Often there is more to modifying a table than adding or deleting rows or columns; you need to make cells just the right size to accommodate the text you are entering in the table. For example, a title in the first row of a table might be longer than the first cell in that row. To spread the title across the top of the table, you can merge (combine) the cells to form one long cell. Sometimes, to indicate a division in a topic, you need to split (or divide) a cell into two. You can also split one table into two at any row. Moreover, you can modify the width of any column and height of any row to better present your data.

Merge and Split Table Cells and Tables

- To merge two or more cells into a single cell, select the cells you want to merge, click the **Layout** tab under Table Tools, and then click the **Merge Cells** button.
- To split a cell into multiple cells, click the cell you want to split, click the **Layout** tab under Table Tools, and then click the **Split Cells** button. Enter the number of rows or columns (or both) you want to split the selected cell into, clear the **Merge cells before split** check box, and then click **OK**.
- To split a table into two tables separated by a paragraph, click in the row that you want as the top row in the second table, click the **Layout** tab under Table Tools, and then click the **Split Table** button.
- To merge two tables into one, delete the paragraph between them.

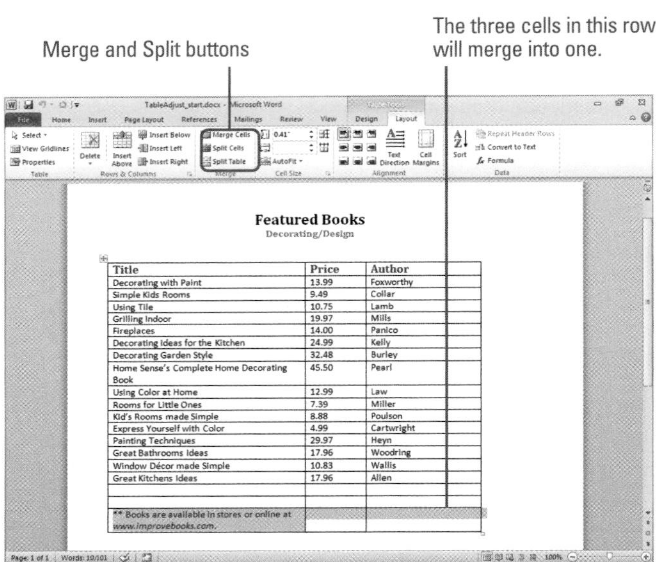

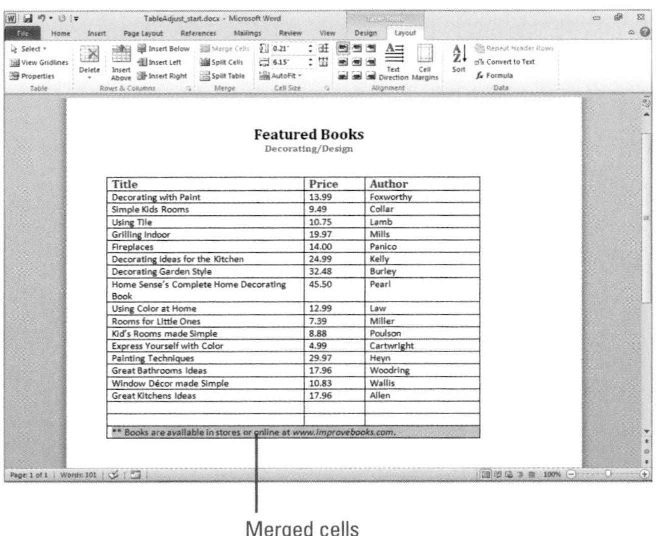

Did You Know?

You can quickly adjust columns and rows. Position the pointer over the boundary of the column or row you want to adjust until it becomes a resize pointer. Drag the boundary to a new location.

Adjust Column Widths and Row Heights

1. Select the columns or rows you want to change.
2. Click the **Layout** tab under Table Tools.
3. Change the Height and Width boxes in the Cell Size group:
   - **Height.** To change the row height, enter a height in the Height box and then press Enter, or use the Up and Down arrows.
   - **Width.** To change the column width, enter a width in the Width box and then press Enter, or use the Up and Down arrows.

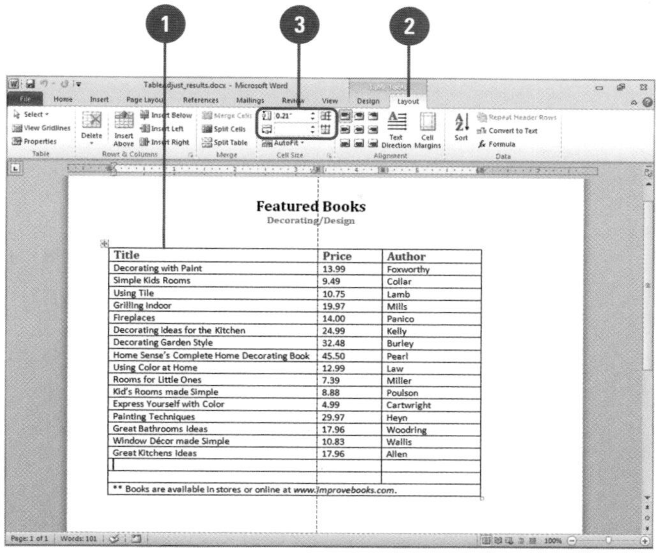

Change Table Properties

1. Click in the table you want to change.
2. Click the **Layout** tab under Table Tools.
3. Click the **Properties** button.
4. On the Table tab, click an alignment option, and then specify an indent from the left (when you select the Left alignment option).
5. Click a text wrapping option.
6. Click **OK**.

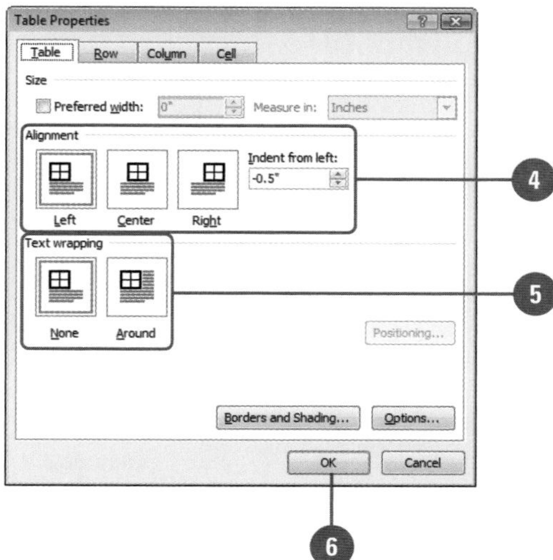

Aligning Table Cells

Tables distinguish text from paragraphs. In turn, formatting, alignment, and text direction distinguish text in table cells. You can customize your table by realigning the cells' contents both horizontally and vertically, changing the direction of text within selected cells, such as the column headings, and resizing the entire table. You can also modify the appearance and size of the cells and the table.

Change Text Direction Within Cells

1. Select the cells you want to change.
2. Click the **Layout** tab under Table Tools.
3. Click the **Text Direction** button until the text is the direction you want.

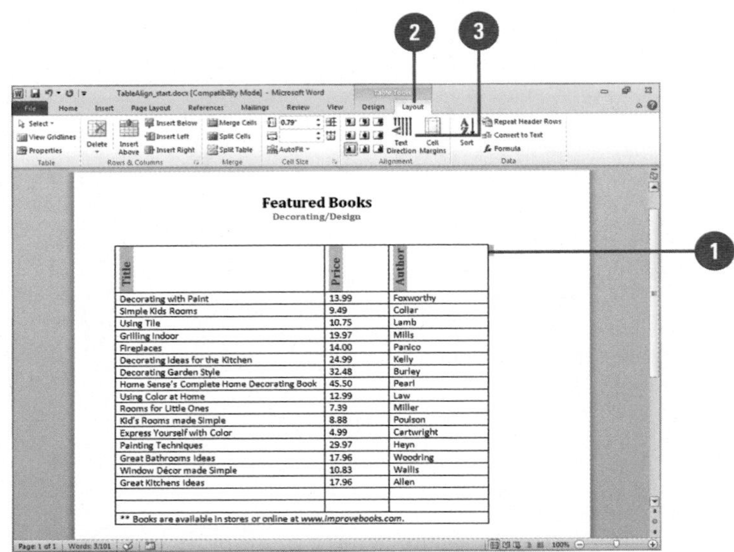

Align Text Within Cells

1. Select the cells, rows, or columns you want to align.
2. Click the **Layout** tab under Table Tools.
3. To align text in a cell, row or column, click one of the alignment buttons in the Alignment group.
4. To evenly distribute the height and width of the selected row and columns, select the row or column, and then click **Distribute Rows** or **Distribute Columns**.

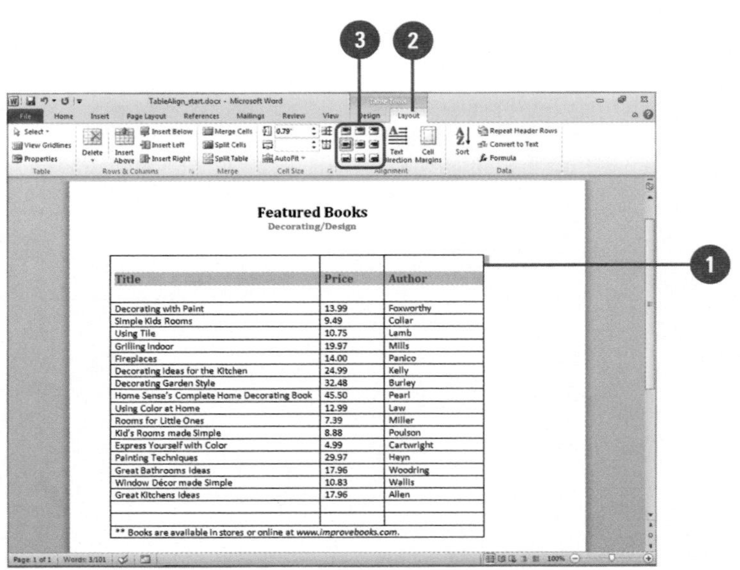

Change Cells Margins

1. Select a cell in the table you want to change.
2. Click the **Layout** tab under Table Tools.
3. Click the **Cell Margins** button.
4. Specify cell margin sizes you want for the table.
5. Click **OK**.

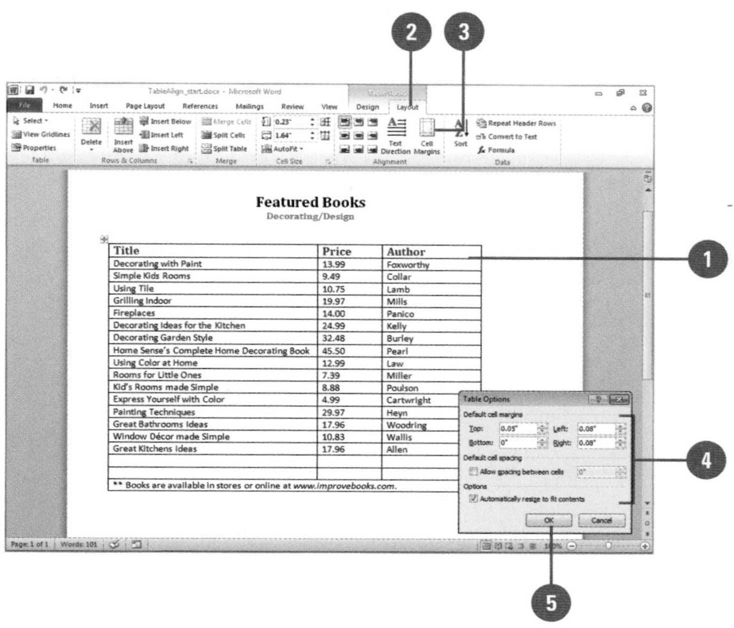

Did You Know?

You can create nested tables. Select the table or cells, click the Home tab, click the Cut or Copy button, right-click the table cell, and then click Paste As Nested Table.

Change Cell Sizes

1. Select the cells in the table you want to change.
2. Click the **Layout** tab under Table Tools.
3. Click the **Up** and **Down** arrows for the **Table Row Height** and **Table Column Width**.
4. To automatically adjust the column width based on the size of the text, click the **AutoFit** button, and then click **AutoFit Contents**, **AutoFit Window**, or **Fixed Column Width**.

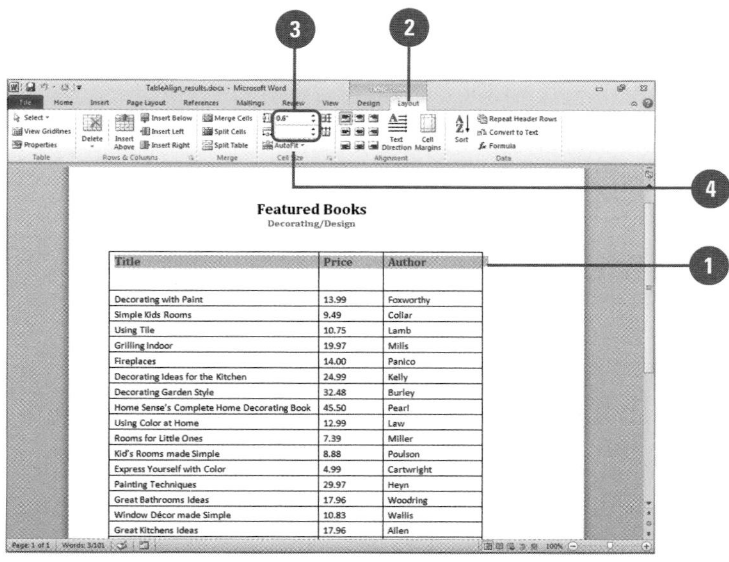

Adding a Quick Style to a Table

Instead of changing individual attributes of a table, such as shape, border, and effects, you can quickly add them all at once with the Table Quick Style gallery. The Table Quick Style gallery provides a variety of different formatting combinations. To quickly see if you like a Table Quick Style, point to a thumbnail in the gallery to display a live preview of it in the selected shape. If you like the style, you can apply it. In addition to applying one of the preformatted tables from the Table Quick Style gallery, you can also create your own style by shaping your text into a variety of shapes, curves, styles, and color patterns.

Add a Quick Style to a Table

1. Click the table you want to change, or select the cells you want to modify.
2. Click the **Design** tab under Table Tools.
3. Click the scroll up or down arrow, or click the **More** list arrow in the Table Styles group to see additional styles.

   The current style appears highlighted in the gallery.

   TIMESAVER *Click the gallery title bar arrow to narrow down the list of styles: All, Document Matching, Light, Medium, or Dark.*
4. Point to a style.

   A live preview of the style appears in the current shape.
5. Click the style you want from the gallery to apply it to the selected table.

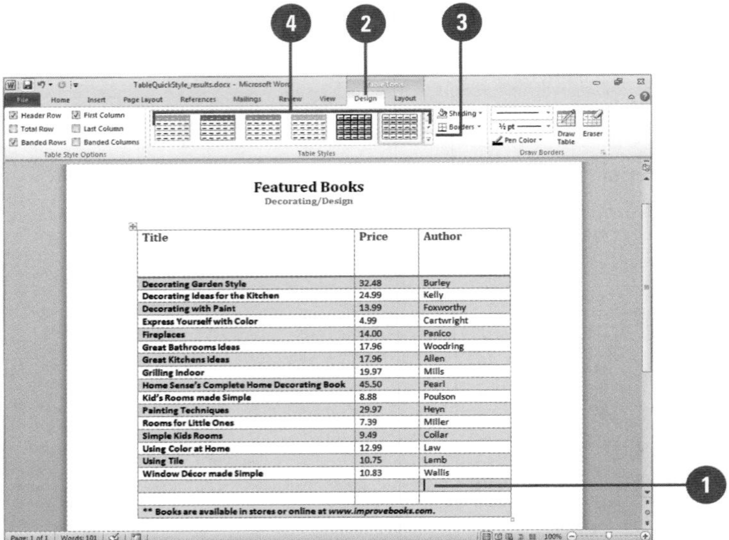

Did You Know?

You can clear table formatting. Select the table you want to change, click the Design tab under Table Tools, click the More list arrow in the Table Styles group, and then click Clear Table.

Apply a Fill to a Table

1. Click the table you want to change, or select the cells you want to modify.
2. Click the **Design** tab under Table Tools.
3. Click the **Shading** button, and then click or point to one of the following:
   - **Color** to select a theme or standard color.
   - **No Color** to remove a color fill.
   - **More Colors** to select a standard or custom color (using the RGB or HSL model).

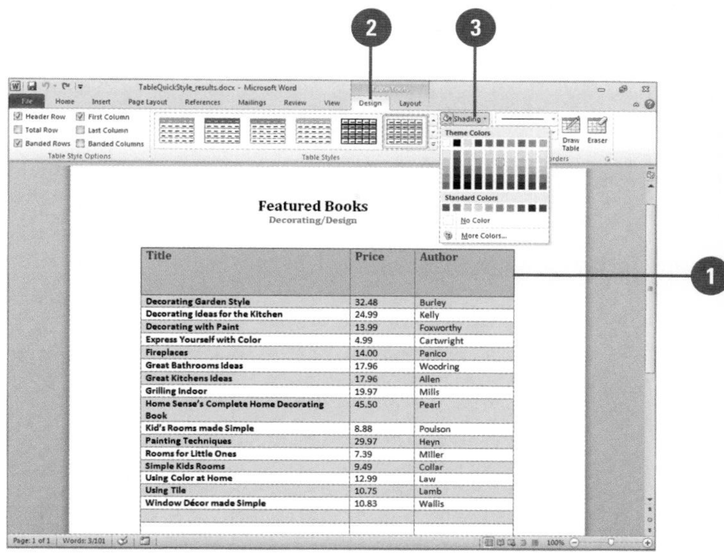

Apply an Outline to a Table

1. Click the table you want to change, or select the cells you want to modify.
2. Click the **Design** tab under Table Tools.
3. Use the **Line Width**, **Line Style**, and **Pen Color** buttons to select the border attributes you want.
4. Click the **Border** button.
5. Click a border option, such as No Border, All Borders, Outside Borders, Inside Horizontal Border, Inside Vertical Border, Diagonal Down Border, or Diagonal Up Border.

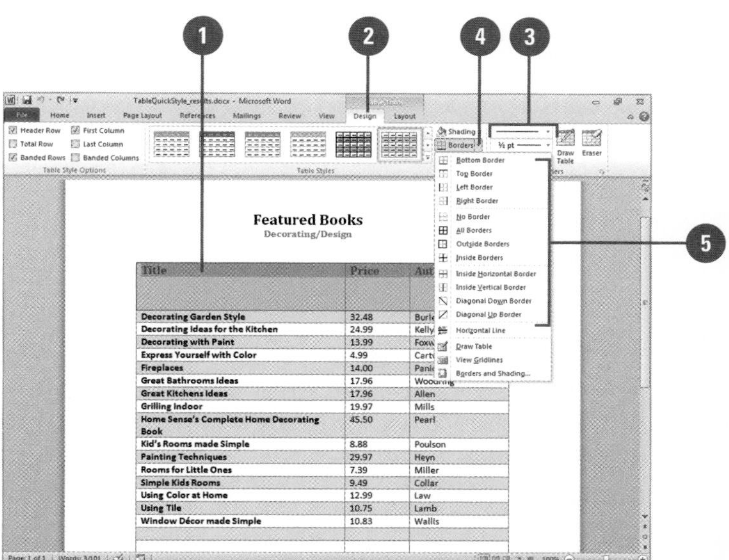

Changing Table Style Options

When you create a table, you typically include a header row or first column to create horizontal or vertical headings for your table information. You can use Quick Style options, such as a header or total row, first or last column, or banded rows and columns, to show or hide a special row and column formatting. The Total Row option displays a row at the end of the table for column totals. The Banded Row or Banded Column option formats even rows or columns differently from odd rows or columns to make a table easier to view.

Change Table Columns Options

1. Click the table you want to change.
2. Click the **Design** tab under Table Tools.
3. Select any of the following row and column check box options:
   - **First Column** to format the first column of the table as special.
   - **Last Column** to format the last column of the table as special.
   - **Banded Columns** to format even columns differently than odd columns.

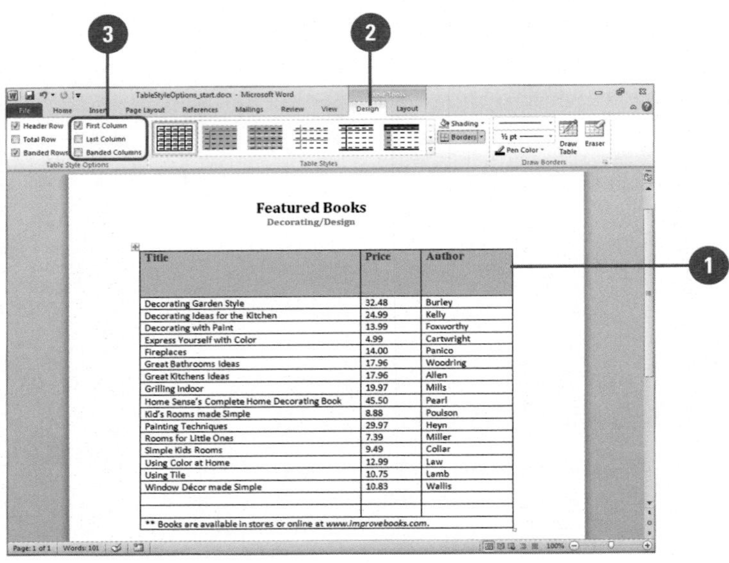

Change Table Rows Options

1. Click the table you want to change.
2. Click the **Design** tab under Table Tools.
3. Select any of the following row and column check box options:
   - **Header Row** to format the top row of the table as special.
   - **Total Row** to format the bottom row of the table for column totals.
   - **Banded Rows** to format even rows differently than odd rows.

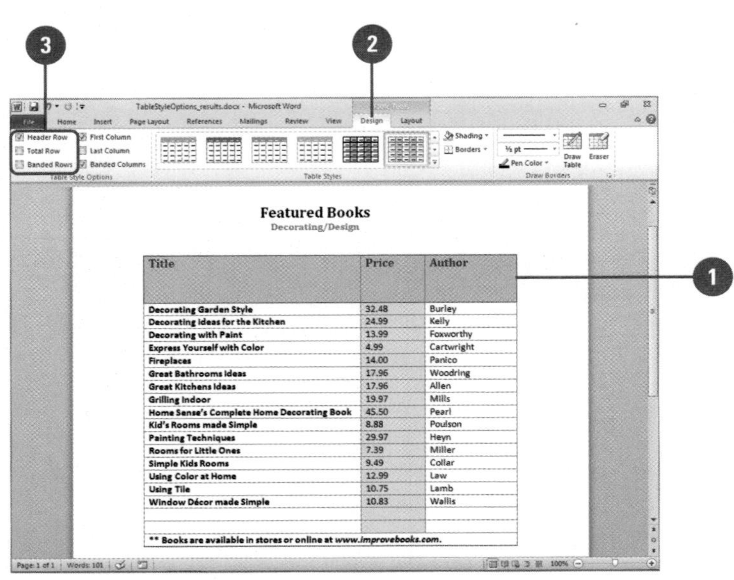

Summing Table Rows and Columns

The fastest way to total the rows or columns of a table is by clicking the Formulas button on the Layout tab under Table Tools. The disadvantage of using this method is that if you subsequently edit the values in the rows and columns of the table, the sums will not automatically update. You would need to remember to click Formula again for each row and column that was updated. To ensure sum totals are automatically calculated anytime the data in a table changes, use the equation functions of Word.

Add the Contents of Rows and Columns

1. Click the cell in which you want the sum to appear.
2. Click the **Layout** tab under Table Tools.
3. Click the **Formula** button. If Word proposes a formula that you do not want to use, delete it from the Formula box.
    - If the cell you selected is at the bottom of a column of numbers, Microsoft Word proposes the formula =SUM(ABOVE).
    - If the cell you selected is at the right end of a row of numbers, Word proposes the formula =SUM(LEFT).
4. Click **OK**.

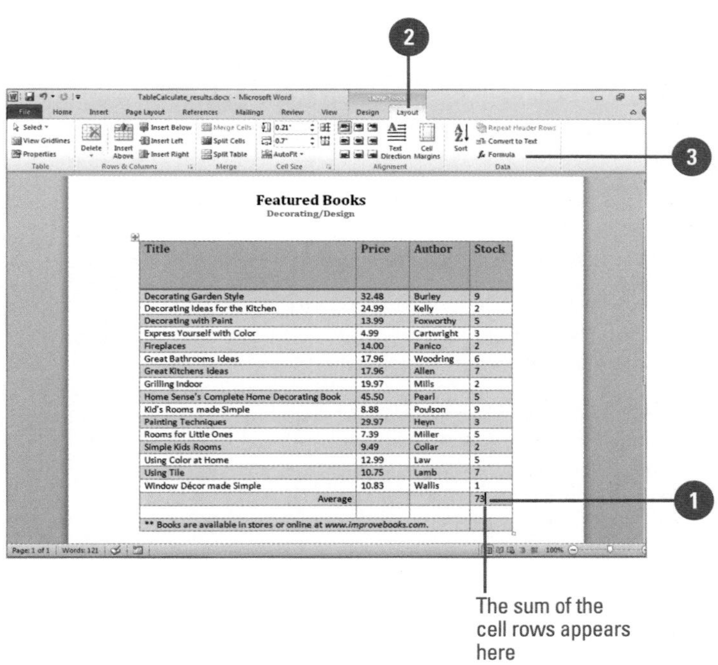

Featured Books
Decorating/Design

Title	Price	Author	Stock
Decorating Garden Style	32.48	Burley	9
Decorating Ideas for the Kitchen	24.99	Kelly	2
Decorating with Paint	13.99	Foxworthy	5
Express Yourself with Color	4.99	Cartwright	3
Fireplaces	14.00	Panico	2
Great Bathrooms Ideas	17.96	Woodring	6
Great Kitchens Ideas	17.96	Allen	7
Grilling Indoor	19.97	Mills	2
Home Sense's Complete Home Decorating Book	45.50	Pearl	5
Kid's Rooms made Simple	8.88	Poulson	9
Painting Techniques	29.97	Heyn	3
Rooms for Little Ones	7.39	Miller	5
Simple Kids Rooms	9.49	Collar	2
Using Color at Home	12.99	Law	5
Using Tile	10.75	Lamb	7
Window Décor made Simple	10.83	Wallis	1
Average			73
** Books are available in stores or online at *www.improvebooks.com*.			

The sum of the cell rows appears here

Word provides the sum formula

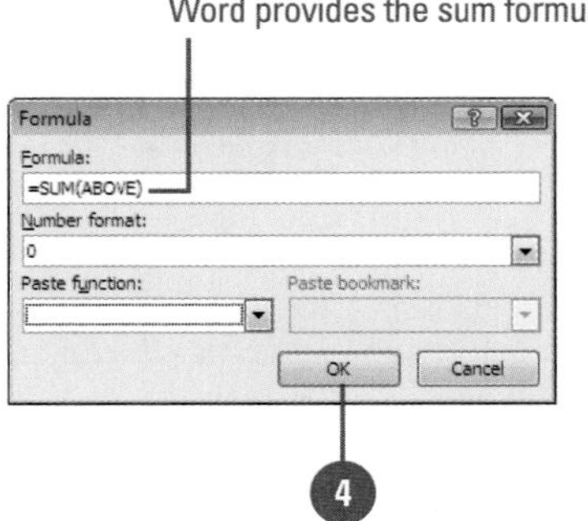

Calculating a Value in a Table

Sometimes the simple equations proposed by Word do not adequately cover what you are trying to calculate in the table. When that is the case, you need to create a custom equation to do the work. The Formula dialog box gives you a choice of 18 paste functions to help you create your formula. Should you need help, you can activate Help to see examples of how to use each paste function, or for more complex formulas, try Microsoft's Online Community to look for advice from other users.

Calculate a Value

1. Click the cell in which you want the result to appear.
2. Click the **Layout** tab under Table Tools.
3. Click the **Formula** button. If Word proposes a formula that you do not want to use, delete it from the Formula box.
4. Click the **Paste Function** list arrow, and then select a function.
5. To reference the contents of a table cell, type the cell references in the parentheses in the formula. For instance, to average the values in cells a1 through a4, the formula would read =Average(a1,a4). If you are doing the average of a row in the last column of the row, simplify this to =Average(left).
6. In the Number format box, enter a format for the numbers. For example, to display the numbers as a decimal percentage, click 0.00%. For now, enter 0 to display the average as the nearest whole number. To display a true average, enter 0.00 in the Number Format box.
7. Click **OK**.

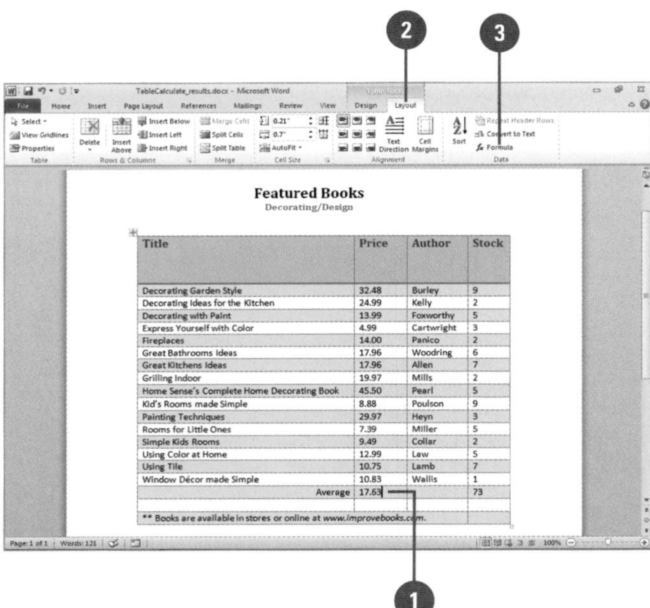

Featured Books

Decorating/Design

Title	Price	Author	Stock
Decorating Garden Style	32.48	Burley	9
Decorating Ideas for the Kitchen	24.99	Kelly	2
Decorating with Paint	13.99	Foxworthy	5
Express Yourself with Color	4.99	Cartwright	3
Fireplaces	14.00	Panico	2
Great Bathrooms Ideas	17.96	Woodring	6
Great Kitchens Ideas	17.96	Allen	7
Grilling Indoor	19.97	Mills	2
Home Sense's Complete Home Decorating Book	45.50	Pearl	5
Kid's Rooms made Simple	8.88	Poulson	9
Painting Techniques	29.97	Heyn	3
Rooms for Little Ones	7.39	Miller	5
Simple Kids Rooms	9.49	Collar	2
Using Color at Home	12.99	Law	5
Using Tile	10.75	Lamb	7
Window Décor made Simple	10.83	Wallis	1
Average	17.63		73

** Books are available in stores or online at www.improvebooks.com.

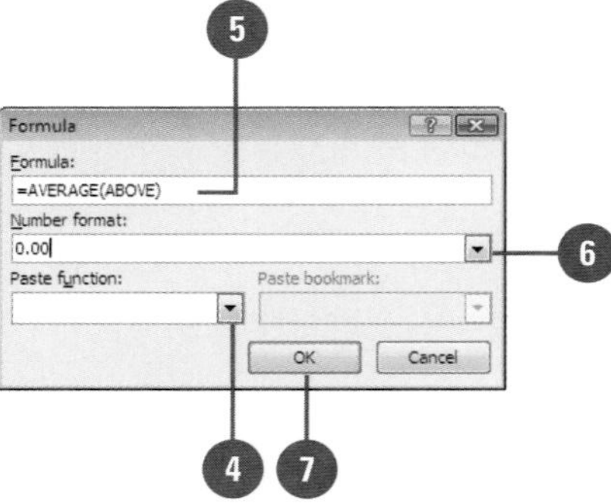

Inserting and Creating a Chart

A **chart** provides a visual, graphical representation of numerical data. Charts add visual interest and useful information represented by lines, bars, pie slices, or other markers. A group of data values from a worksheet row or column of data makes up a **data series**. Each data series has a unique color or pattern on the chart. Titles on the chart, horizontal (x-axis), and vertical (y-axis) identify the data. Gridlines are horizontal and vertical lines to help the reader determine data values in a chart. When you insert and create a chart in a document, the chart is an **embedded object** from Microsoft Excel 2010. You can then resize or move it just as you would any graphic object.

Insert and Create a Chart

1. Click to place the insertion point where you want to insert a Chart.
2. Click the **Insert** tab.
3. Click the **Insert Chart** button.
4. Click a category in the left pane.
5. Click the chart type you want.
6. Click **OK**.

   A Microsoft Excel worksheet opens and tiles next to your Word document, displaying a sample chart.

7. To create a chart, change the sample data in the Excel worksheet. You can enter, paste, or import data.
8. To close the worksheet and view the chart, click the **Close** button on the Excel worksheet and return to Word.

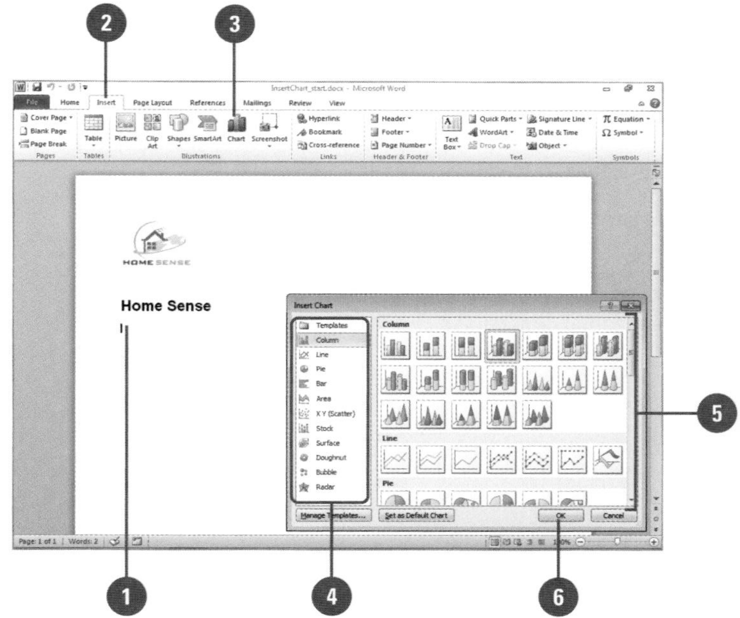

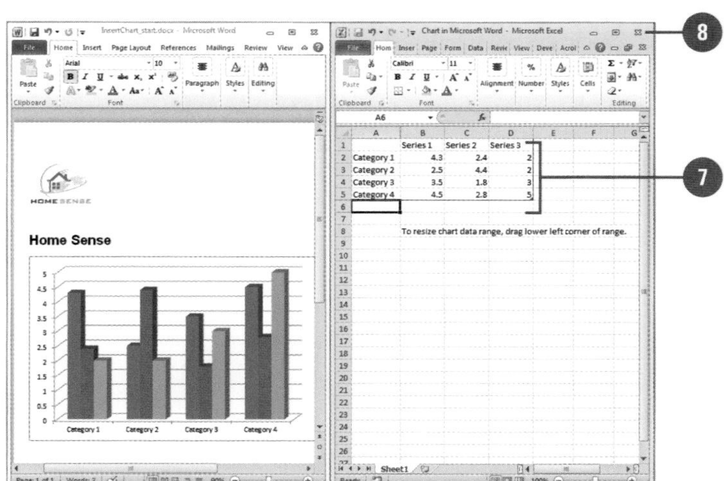

Did You Know?

Word uses Microsoft Excel 2010 to embed a chart. Office programs (including Word) use Microsoft Excel to embed and display a chart instead of Microsoft Graph.

Working with Chart Data

You can enter chart data in the Excel worksheet either by typing it or by inserting it from a different source. The worksheet is designed to make data entry easy, so direct typing is best when you're entering brief, simple data. For more complex or longer data, and when you're concerned about accuracy, insert and link your data to the chart. When you first insert a chart, the worksheet contains sample labels and numbers.

Open and View Chart Data

1. Click the chart you want to modify.

   A chart consists of the following elements.

   - **Data markers**. A graphical representation of a data point in a single cell in the datasheet. Typical data markers include bars, dots, or pie slices.
   - **Legend**. A pattern or color that identifies each data series.
   - **X-axis**. A reference line for the horizontal data values.
   - **Y-axis**. A reference line for the vertical data values.
   - **Tick marks**. Marks that identify data increments.

2. Click the **Design** tab under Chart Tools.
3. Click the **Edit Data** button.

   A Microsoft Excel worksheet opens and tiles next to your Word document.

4. To close the worksheet and view the chart, click the **Close** button on the Excel worksheet and return to Word.

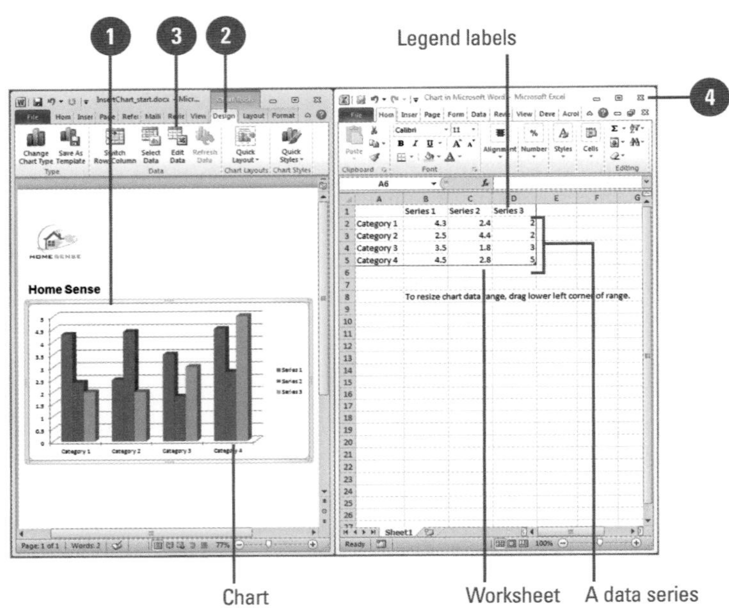

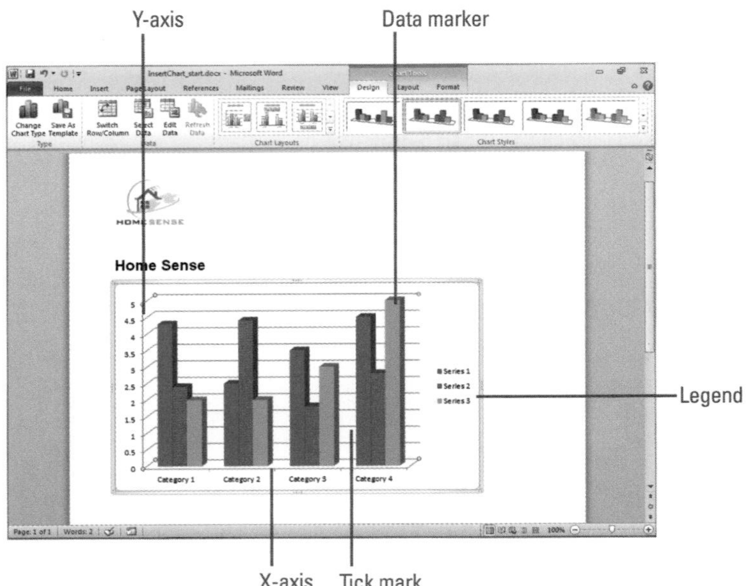

Enter Data in the Worksheet

1. Click the chart you want to modify, and then click the **Edit Data** button on the Design tab under Chart Tools.
2. To delete the sample data, click the upper-left heading button to select all the cells, and then press Delete.
3. Use one of the following to select a cell, row, column, or datasheet.
   - To select a cell, click it.
   - To select an entire row or column, click the row heading or column heading button.
   - To select a range of cells, drag the pointer over the cells you want to select, or click the upper-left cell of the range, press and hold Shift, and then click the lower-right cell. When you select a range of cells, the active cell is white, and all other selected cells are outlined in black.
4. Type the data you want to enter in the cell.
5. Press Enter to move the insertion point down one row or press Tab to move the insertion point right to the next cell.
6. If necessary, select the data you want for the chart, click the Design tab, click the **Resize Table** button, and then click **OK**.
7. To close the worksheet and view the chart, click the **Close** button on the Excel worksheet and return to Word.

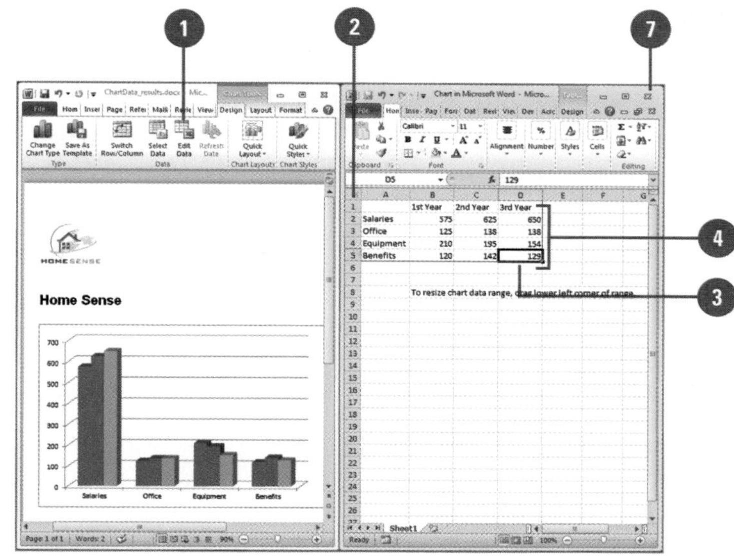

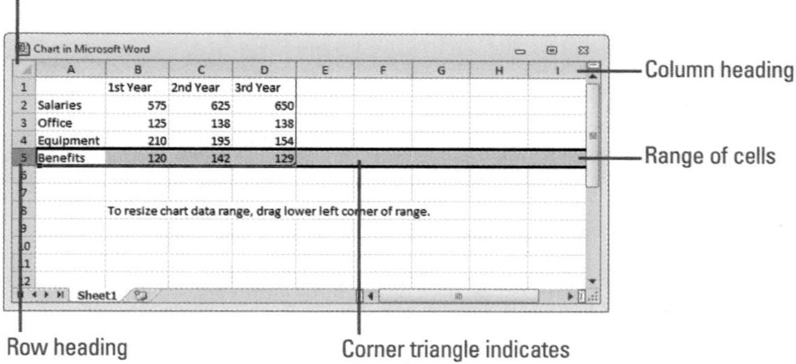

Changing a Chart Type

Your chart is what your reader sees, so make sure to take advantage of the pre-built chart layouts and styles to make the chart appealing and visually informative. Start by choosing the chart type that is best suited for presenting your data. There are a wide variety of chart types, available in 2-D and 3-D formats, from which to choose. For each chart type, you can select a predefined chart layout and style to apply the formatting you want. If you want to format your chart beyond the provided formats, you can customize a chart. Save your customized settings so that you can apply that chart formatting to any chart you create. You can change the chart type for the entire chart, or you can change the chart type for a selected data series to create a combination chart.

Change a Chart Type for an Entire Chart

1. Select the chart you want to change.
2. Click the **Design** tab under Chart Tools.
3. Click the **Change Chart Type** button.
4. Click the chart type you want.
5. Click **OK**.

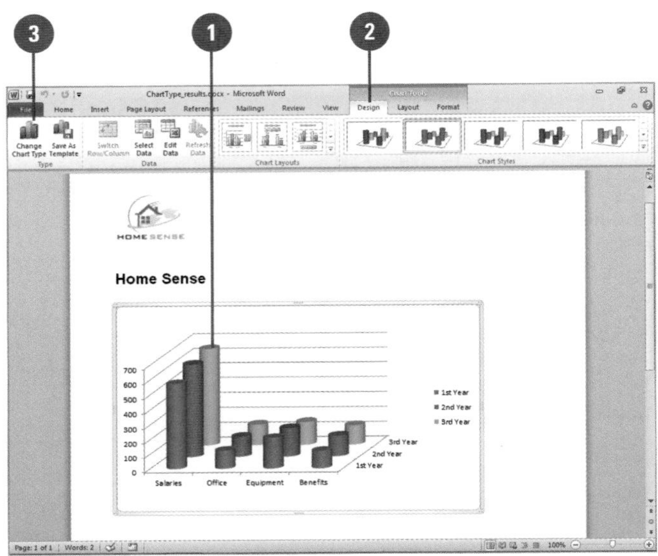

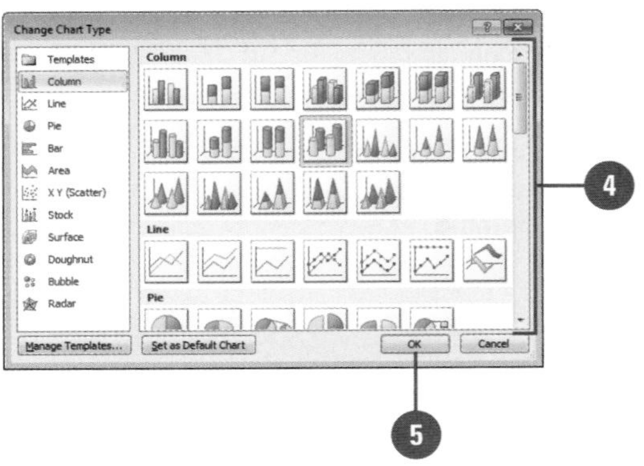

Did You Know?

You can reset chart formatting. Click the chart you want to reset, click the Format tab under Chart Tools, and then click the Reset To Match Style button.

You can delete a chart. Click the chart object, and then press Delete.

Changing a Chart Layout and Style

Office's pre-built chart layouts and styles can make your chart more appealing and visually informative. Start by choosing the chart type that is best suited for presenting your data. There are a wide variety of chart types, available in 2-D and 3-D formats, from which to choose. For each chart type, you can select a predefined chart layout and style to apply the formatting you want. If you want to format your chart beyond the provided formats, you can customize a chart. Save your customized settings so that you can apply that chart formatting to any chart you create.

Change a Chart Layout or Style

1. Select the chart you want to change.
2. Click the **Design** tab under Chart Tools.
3. To change the chart layout, click the scroll up or down arrow, or click the **More** list arrow in the Chart Layouts group, and then click the layout you want.
4. To change the chart style, click the scroll up or down arrow, or click the **More** list arrow in the Chart Styles group, and then click the chart style you want.

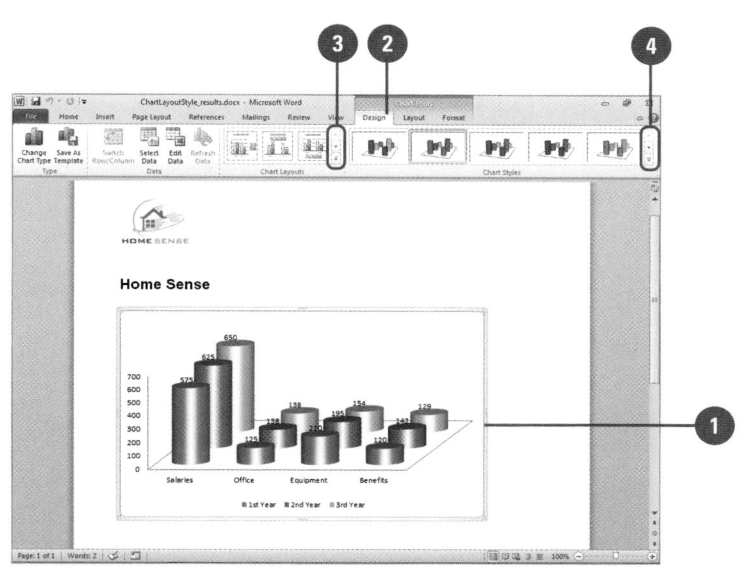

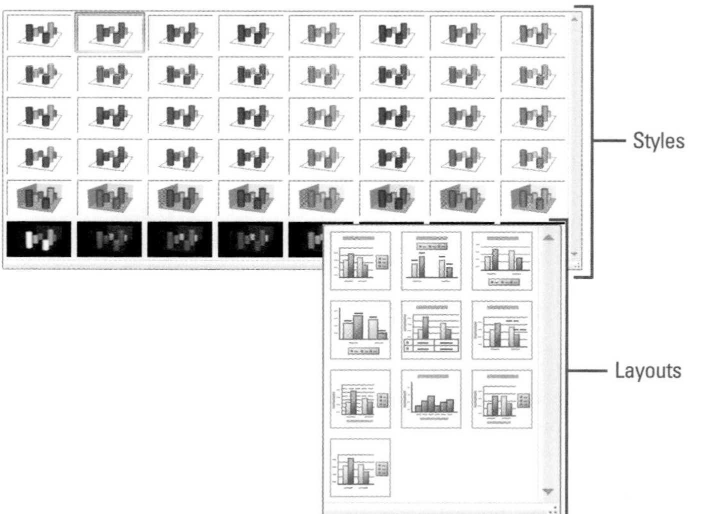

Did You Know?

You can record macros with chart elements. When you use the macro recorder with charts, it now records formatting changes to charts and other objects (**New!**).

Changing Chart Titles

The layout of a chart typically comes with a chart title, axis titles, and a legend. However, you can also include other elements, such as data labels, and a data table. You can show, hide, or change the positions of these elements to achieve the look you want. The chart title typically appears at the top of the chart. However, you can change the title position to appear as an overlap text object on top of the chart. When you position the chart title as an overlay, the chart is resized to the maximum allowable size. In the same way, you can also reposition horizontal and vertical axis titles to achieve the best fit in a chart. If you want a more custom look, you can set individual options using the Format dialog box.

Change Chart Title

1. Select the chart you want to modify.
2. Click the **Layout** tab under Chart Tools.
3. Click the **Chart Titles** button, and then click one of the following:
   - **None** to hide the chart title.
   - **Centered Overlay Title** to insert a title on the chart without resizing it.
   - **Above Chart** to position the chart title at the top of the chart and resize it.
   - **More Title Options** to set custom chart title options.
4. Double-click the text box to place the insertion point, and then modify the text.

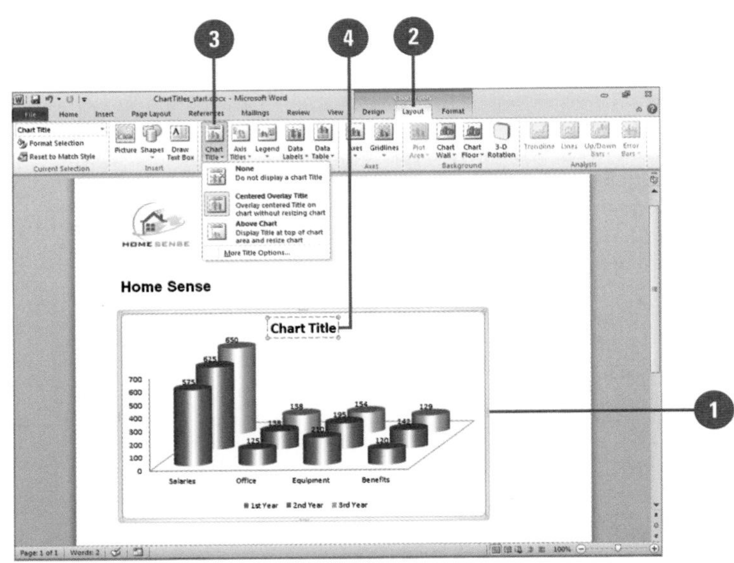

Did You Know?

You can link a chart or axis title to a worksheet cell. On the chart, click the chart or axis title you want to link, click in the formula bar, type equal sign (=), select the worksheet cell that contains the data or text you want to display in the chart, and then press Enter.

Changing Chart Labels

A **legend** is a set of text labels that helps the reader connect the colors and patterns in a chart with the data they represent. Legend text is derived from the data series plotted within a chart. You can rename an item within a legend by changing the text in the data series. If the legend chart location doesn't work with the chart type, you can reposition the legend at the right, left, top or bottom of the chart or overlay the legend on top of the chart on the right or left side. **Data labels** show data values in the chart to make it easier for the reader to see, while a Data table shows the data values in an associated table next to the chart. If you want a customized look, you can set individual options using the Format dialog box. In addition, you can change the label display for axes and show or hide major or minor gridlines.

Change the Chart Legend, Data Labels, and Axis Titles

1. Select the chart you want to modify.
2. Click the **Layout** tab under Chart Tools.
3. Click any of the following label buttons:
   - **Chart Title.** Click to add, remove, or position a chart title.
   - **Axis Titles.** Click to add or remove an axis title on the chart.
   - **Legend.** Click to select a legend position on the chart.
   - **Data Labels.** Click to show or hide data labels on the chart for each data series.
   - **Data Table.** Click to show or hide a table next to the chart with the chart data.
   - **Axes.** Click to show, hide, or position axis labels or tick marks.
   - **Gridlines.** Click to show or hide major or minor gridlines.

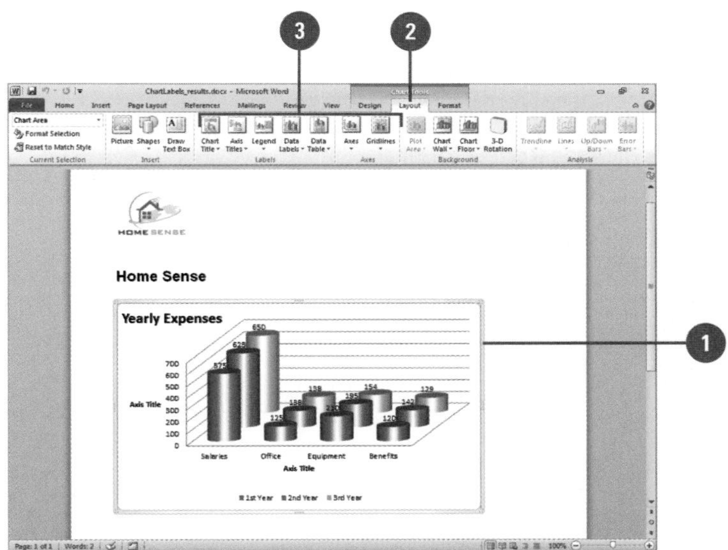

Formatting Line and Bar Charts

If you're using a line or bar chart, you can add trendlines, series lines, drop lines, high-low lines, up/down bars, or error bars with different options to make the chart easier to read. **Trendlines** are graphical representations of trends in data that you can use to analyze problems of prediction. For example, you can add a trendline to forecast a trend toward rising revenue. **Series lines** connect data series in 2-D stacked bar and column charts. **Drop lines** extend a data point to a category in a line or area chart, which makes it easy to see where data markers begin and end. **High-low lines** display the highest to the lowest value in each category in 2-D charts. Stock charts are examples of high-low lines and up/down bars. **Error bars** show potential error amounts graphically relative to each data marker in a data series. Error bars are usually used in statistical or scientific data.

Format Line and Bar Charts

1. Select the line or bar chart you want to modify.
2. Click the **Layout** tab under Chart Tools.
3. In the Analysis group, click any of the following:
   - **Trendline** to remove or add different types of trendlines: Linear, Exponential, Linear Forecast, and Two Period Moving Average.
   - **Lines** to hide Drop Lines, High-Low Lines or Series Lines, or show series lines on a 2-D stacked Bar/Column Pie or Pie or Bar of Pie chart.
   - **Up/Down Bars** to hide Up/Down Bars, or show Up/Down Bars on a line chart.
   - **Error Bars** to hide error bars or show error bars with using Standard Error, Percentage, or Standard Deviation.

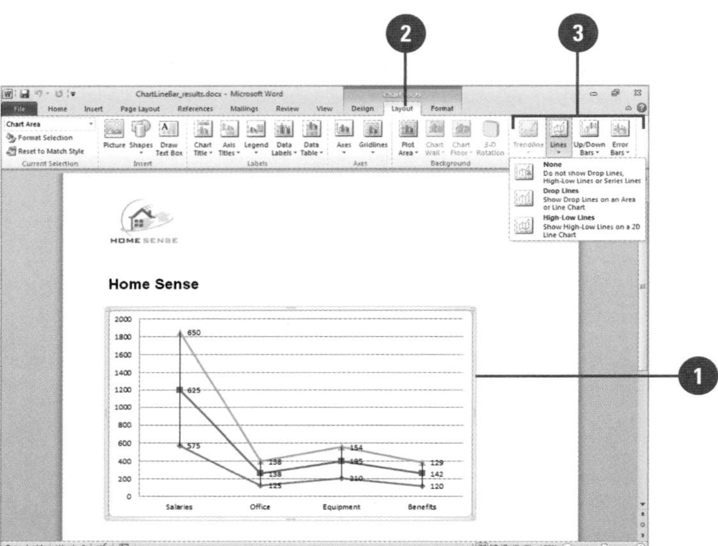

Editing Chart Data

You can edit chart data in a worksheet one cell at a time, or you can manipulate a range of data. If you're not sure what data to change to get the results you want, use the Edit Data Source dialog box to help you. In previous versions, you were limited to 32,000 data points in a data series for 2-D charts. Now you can have as much as your memory to store (**New!**). You can work with data ranges by series, either Legend or Horizontal. The Legend series is the data range displayed on the axis with the legend, while the Horizontal series is the data range displayed on the other axis. Use the Collapse Dialog button to temporarily minimize the dialog to select the data range you want. After you select your data, click the Expand Dialog button to return back to the dialog box.

Edit the Data Source

1. Click the chart you want to modify.
2. Click the **Design** tab under Chart Tools.
3. Click the **Select Data** button on the Design tab under Chart Tools.
4. In the Select Data Source dialog box, use any of the following:
   - **Chart data range.** Displays the data range of the plotted chart.
   - **Switch Row/Column.** Click to switch plotting the data series from rows or columns.
   - **Add.** Click to add a new Legend data series to the chart.
   - **Edit.** Click to make changes to a Legend or Horizontal series.
   - **Remove.** Click to remove the selected Legend data series.
   - **Move Up and Move Down.** Click to move a Legend data series up or down in the list.
   - **Hidden and Empty Cells.** Click to plot hidden data and determine what to do with empty cells.
5. Click **OK.**

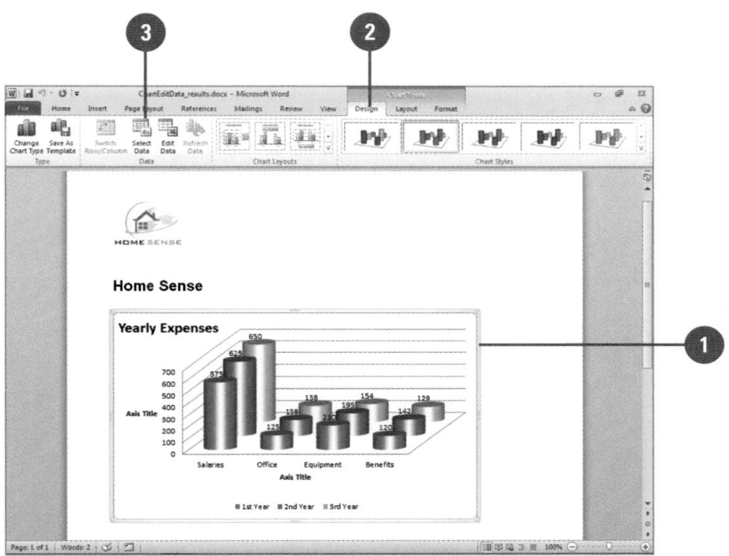

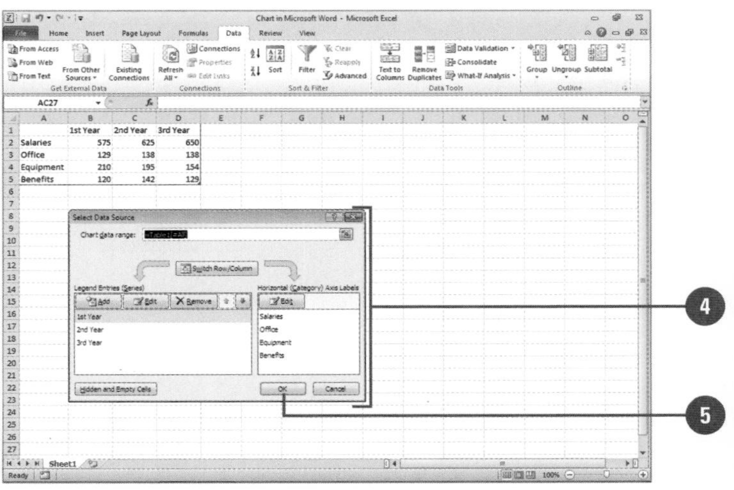

Saving a Chart Template

A chart template file (.crtx) saves all the customization you made to a chart for use in other documents. You can save any chart in a document as a chart template file and use it to form the basis of your next document chart, which is useful for standard company financial reporting. Although you can store your template anywhere you want, you may find it handy to store it in the Templates/Charts folder that Microsoft Office uses to store its templates. If you store your design templates in the Templates/Charts folder, those templates appear as options when you insert or change a chart type using My Templates. When you create a new chart or want to change the chart type of an existing chart, you can apply a chart template instead of re-creating it.

Create a Custom Chart Template

1. Click the chart you want to save as a template.
2. Click the **Design** tab under Chart Tools.
3. Click the **Save As Template** button.
4. Make sure the Charts folder appears in the Save in box.

   Microsoft Office templates are typically stored in the following location:

   Windows 7 or Vista. C:/Users/*your name*/AppData/Microsoft /Roaming/Templates/Charts

   Windows XP. C:/Documents and Settings/*your name*/Application Data/Microsoft/Templates/Charts
5. Type a name for the chart template.
6. Click **Save**.

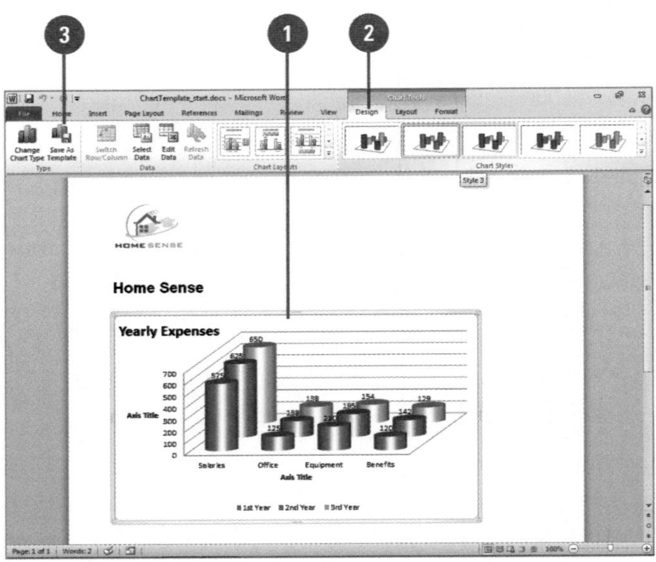

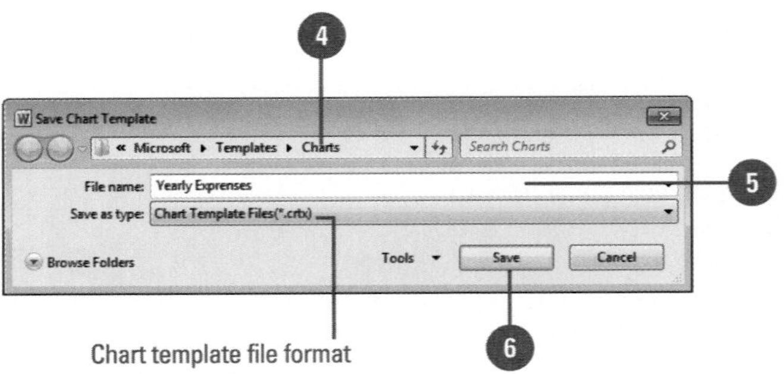

Chart template file format

Creating Desktop Publishing Documents

7

Introduction

When you want to add objects to a document, you can use Microsoft Word as a drawing package. Word provides a wide range of predesigned shapes, line options or freeform tools that allow you to draw, size, and format your own shapes and forms.

You can add several types of drawing objects to your documents—shapes, text boxes, lines, and freeforms. **Shapes** are preset objects, such as stars, circles, or ovals. **Text boxes** are objects with text, a shape without a border. **Lines** are simply the straight or curved lines (arcs) that can connect two points or are used as arrows. **Freeforms** are irregular curves or polygons that you can create as a freehand drawing.

Once you create a drawing object, you can move, resize, nudge, copy or delete it on your documents. You can also change its style by adding color, creating a fill pattern, rotating it, and applying a shadow or 3-D effect. Take a simple shape and by the time you are done adding various effects, it could become an attractive piece of graphic art for your document. If you'd like to use it later, you can save it to the Clip Organizer.

Object placement on your documents is a key factor to successfully communicating your message. To save time and effort, multiple objects should be grouped if they are to be considered one larger object. Grouping helps you make changes later on, or copy your objects to another document. Word has the ability to line up your objects with precision—rulers and grids are part of the alignment process to help you. By grouping and aligning, you are assured that your drawing objects will be accurately placed.

What You'll Do

Add Desktop Publishing Effects

Add a Watermark

Add Page Backgrounds

Arrange Text in Columns

Wrap Text Around an Object

Work with Text Boxes

Draw and Resize Shapes

Add Text to a Shape

Create and Edit Freeforms

Add a Quick Style to a Shape

Add Formatting to Shape Text

Apply Colors Fill

Apply Picture, Texture, and Gradient Fills

Apply Shape Effects

Distribute Objects and Align to Grids

Change Stacking Order

Rotate and Flip Objects

Group and Ungroup Objects

Adding Desktop Publishing Effects

A few simple elements—drop caps, borders, and shading—make your newsletters and brochures look like a professional produced them. A **drop cap** is the enlarged first letter of a paragraph that provides instant style to a document. Instead of using a desktop publishing program to create a drop cap effect, you can quickly achieve the same thing in Word. You can change the drop cap position, font, and height, and then enter the distance between the drop cap and paragraph.

Add a Drop Cap

1. Click the **Print Layout View** button.
2. Click the **Insert** tab.
3. Click the paragraph where you want the drop cap.
4. Click the **Drop Cap** button, and then select the drop cap style you want.

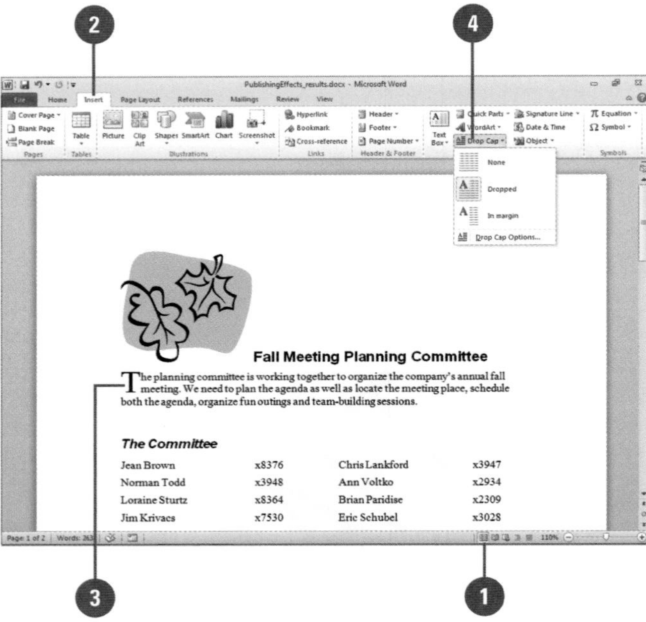

Customize a Drop Cap

1. Click the **Print Layout View** button.
2. Click the **Insert** tab.
3. Click the paragraph with the drop cap.
4. Click the **Drop Cap** button, and then click **Drop Cap Options**.
5. Click a drop cap position.
6. Change the drop cap font and height, and then enter the distance between the drop cap and text.
7. Click **OK**.

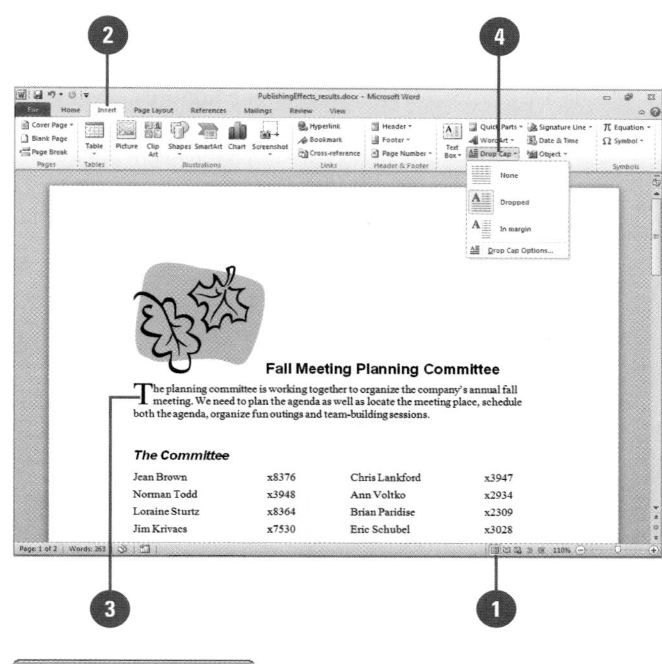

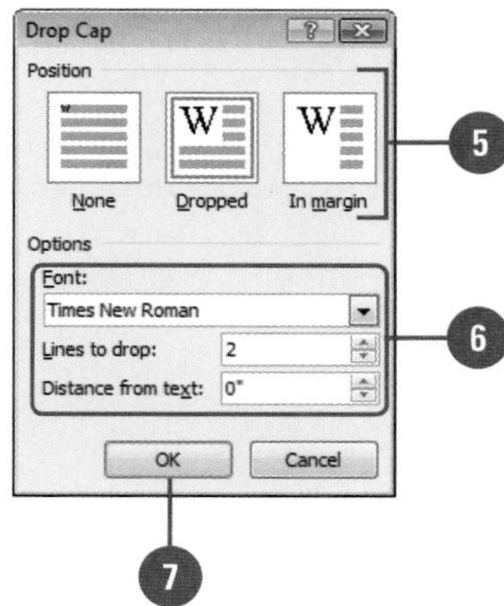

Adding a Watermark

A **watermark** is a background effect—some text or a graphic, that prints in a light shade behind your text on your document. You can use a washed out version of your company logo, or you can add text such as SAMPLE, DRAFT, PROPOSAL, or CONFIDENTIAL. If you can't find the watermark you need, check out Office.com (**New!**). If you decide to change your watermark, it's as easy as typing in some new text.

Add or Remove a Watermark

1. Click the **Print Layout View** button.
2. Click the **Page Layout** tab.
3. Click the **Watermark** button.
4. Do one of the following:
   - **Add.** Click the border you want to add.
   - **Add from Office.com.** Click **More Watermarks from Office.com** (**New!**).
   - **Remove.** Click **Remove Page Border**.

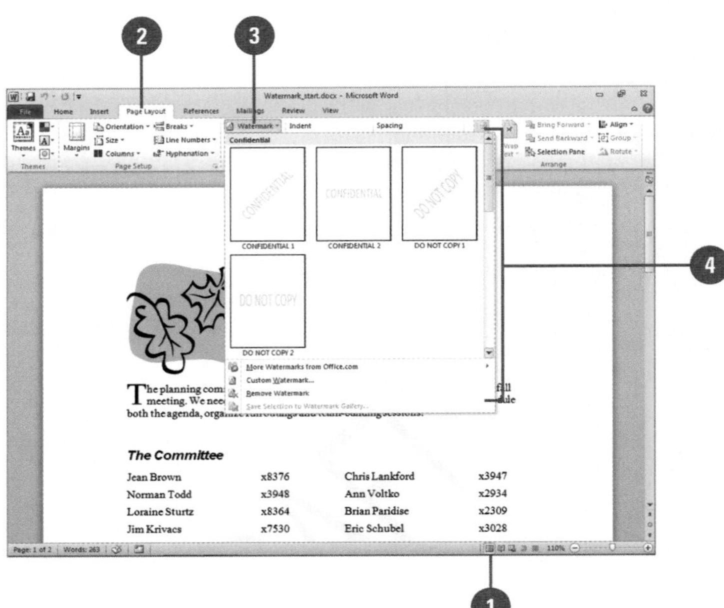

Did You Know?

You can save a selection to the Watermark gallery. Select the image you want to add to the Watermark gallery, click the Page Layout tab, click the Watermark button, and then click Save Selection To Watermark Gallery. In the Create New Building Block dialog box, enter a name, select a category, enter a description, specify a Save in document, specify an option where you insert the content, and then click OK.

Customize or Remove a Watermark

1. Click the **Print Layout View** button.
2. Click the **Page Layout** tab.
3. Click the **Watermark** button, and then click **Custom Watermark**.
4. To remove a watermark, click the **No watermark** option.
5. To insert a picture as a watermark, click the **Picture watermark** option, click **Select Picture**, select a picture, and then click **OK**.
6. To customize watermark text, click the **Text watermark** option, and then select the settings you want.
7. Click **OK**.

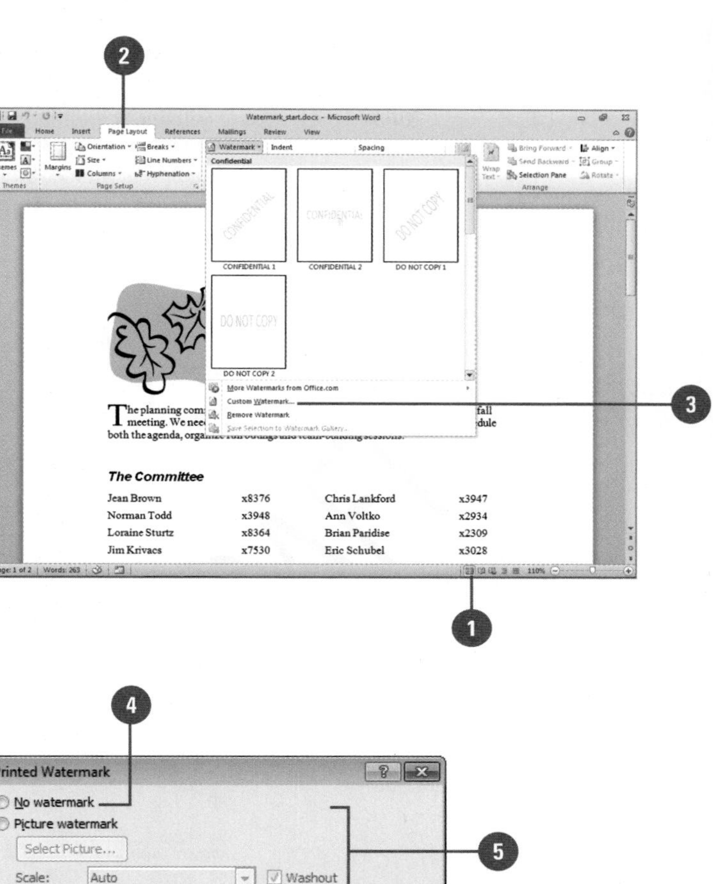

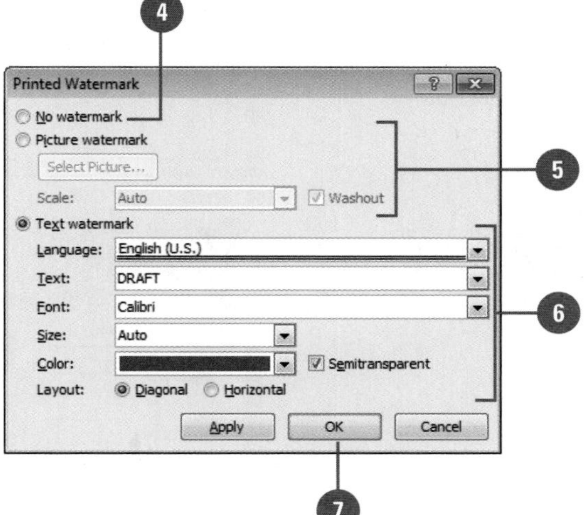

Adding Page Backgrounds

Borders are lines or graphics that appear around a page, paragraph, selected text, or table cells. With borders, you can change the line style, width, and colors, and you can add shadows and 3D effects. In addition to a page border, you can also change the page color. If you apply a theme color as the page color, it changes if you change the document theme. **Shading** is a color that fills the background of selected text, paragraphs, or table cells. For more attractive pages, add clips or columns.

Add Borders and Shading

1. Select the text you want to have a border.
2. Click the **Page Layout** tab.
3. Click the **Page Borders** button.
4. Click the **Borders** tab.
5. Do one of the following:
   - Click a box setting to modify all border edges.
   - Click the edge in the diagram to modify individual border edges.
6. Click a border style, color, and width.
7. Click the **Shading** tab.
8. Click the **Fill** list arrow, and then click a fill color.
9. Click **OK**.

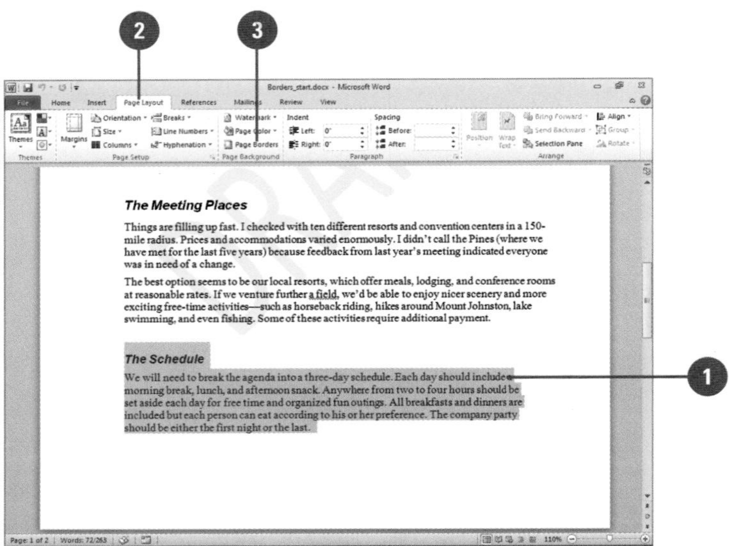

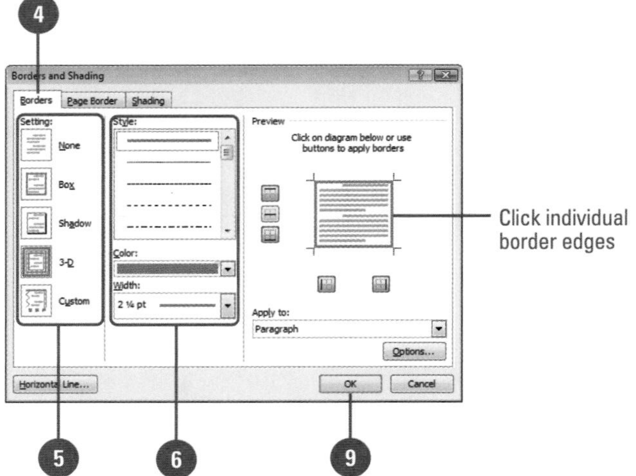

Add or Remove a Page Border

1. Click the page you want to have a border.
2. Click the **Page Layout** tab.
3. Click the **Page Borders** button.
4. Click the **Page Border** tab.
5. Click a box setting.
6. Click a line style, or click the Art list arrow, and then select a line or art style.
7. Click a **Width** list arrow, and then select a width.
8. Click the **Apply to** list arrow, and then select the pages you want to have borders.
9. Click **OK**.

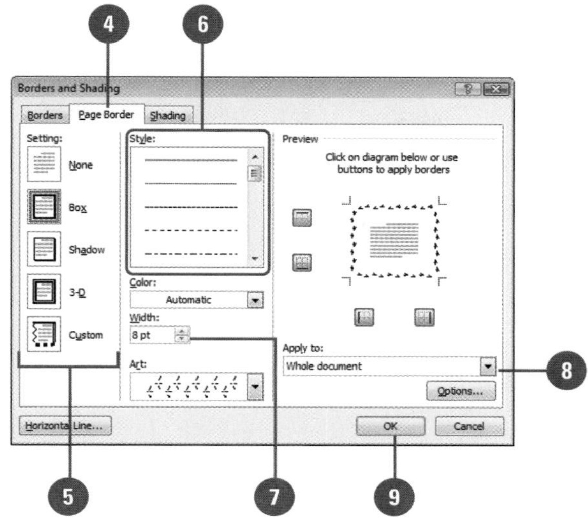

Add Page Color

1. Click the page you want to have a border.
2. Click the **Page Layout** tab.
3. Click the **Page Color** button.
4. Do one of the following:
   - **Add.** Click the color you want to add.
   - **Remove.** Click **No Color**.

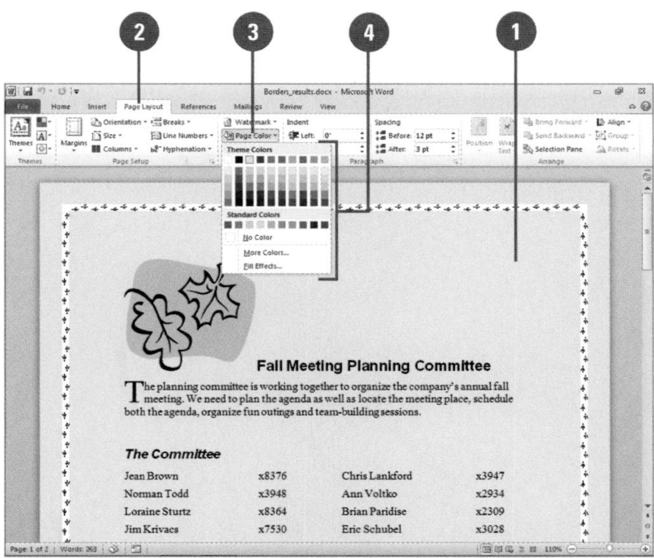

Arranging Text in Columns

Newspaper-style columns can give newsletters and brochures a more polished look. You can format an entire document, selected text, or individual sections into columns. You can create one, two, or three columns of equal size. You can also create two columns and have one column wider than the other. Word fills one column with text before the other, unless you insert a column break. **Column breaks** are used in two-column layouts to move the text after the insertion point to the top of the following column. You can also display a vertical line between the columns. To view the columns side by side, switch to print layout view.

Create Columns

1. Click the **Page Layout** tab.
2. Select the text you want to arrange in columns.
3. Click the **Columns** button.
4. Select the number of columns you want.

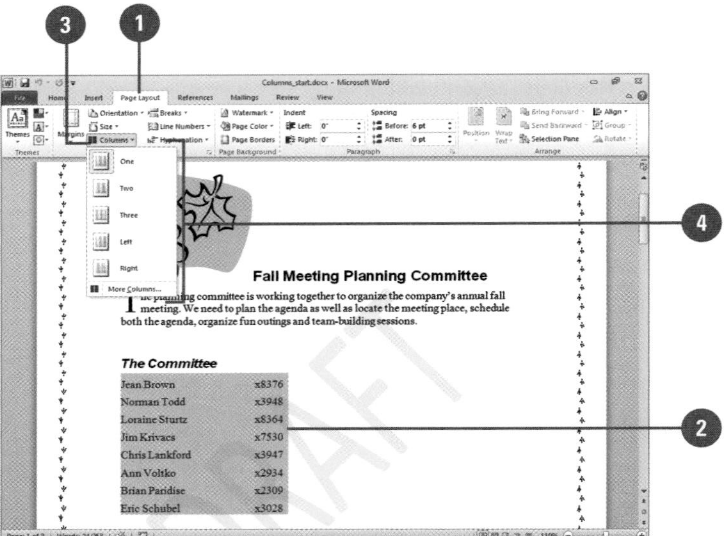

Did You Know?

You can remove columns quickly. Select the columns, click the Columns button on the Page Layout tab, and then click the first column.

You can align text in a column. Click the Align Left, Center, Align Right, or Justify button on the Home tab to align paragraphs in columns.

Modify Columns

1. Click the **Page Layout** tab, and then click in the columns you want to modify.
2. Click the **Columns** button, and then click **More Columns**.
3. Click a column preset format.
4. If necessary, enter the number of columns you want.
5. Enter the width and spacing you want for each column.
6. To place a vertical line between columns, select the **Line between** check box.
7. Click **OK**.

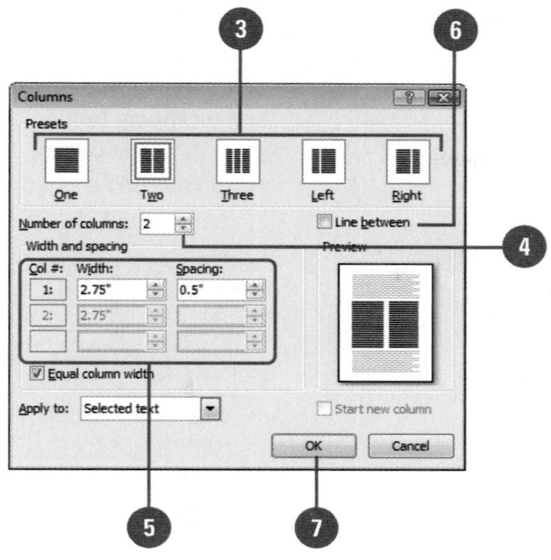

Insert a Column Break

1. Click where you want to insert a column break.
2. Click the **Page Layout** tab.
3. Click the **Break** button, and then click **Column**.
4. To delete a column break, click the column break dotted line in Draft view or select lines above and below the break, and then press the Delete key.

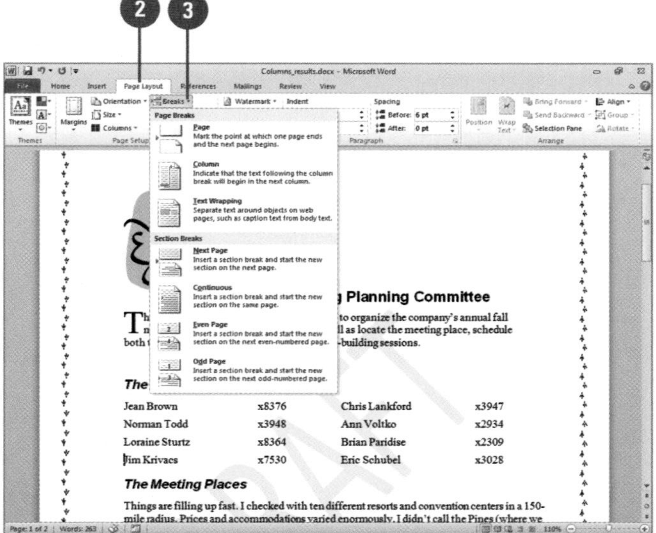

Wrapping Text Around an Object

When integrating pictures, charts, tables, or other graphics with your text, you need to wrap the text around the object regardless of where it is placed on the page. Rather than having to constantly reset margins and make other tedious adjustments, Word simplifies this task with the text wrapping feature. Unless your object or table is large enough to span the entire page, your layout will look more professional if you wrap your text around it instead of leaving excessive white space.

Change the Text Position Around an Object or Picture

1. Select the picture or object.
2. Click the **Page Layout** tab.
3. Click the **Position** button, and then click the text wrapping option you want.
4. To customize text position, click the **Position** button, click **More Layout Options**, specify the options you want, and then click **OK**.

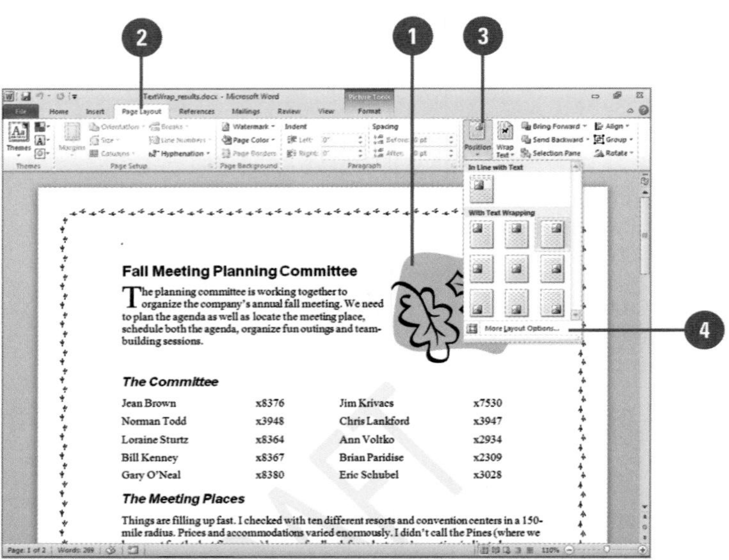

Wrap Text Around an Object or Picture

1. Select the picture or object.
2. Click the **Page Layout** tab.
3. To change text position, click the **Position** button, select a position or click **More Layout Options**, specify the options you want, and then click **OK**.
4. Click the **Wrap Text** button, and then click the text wrapping option you want.

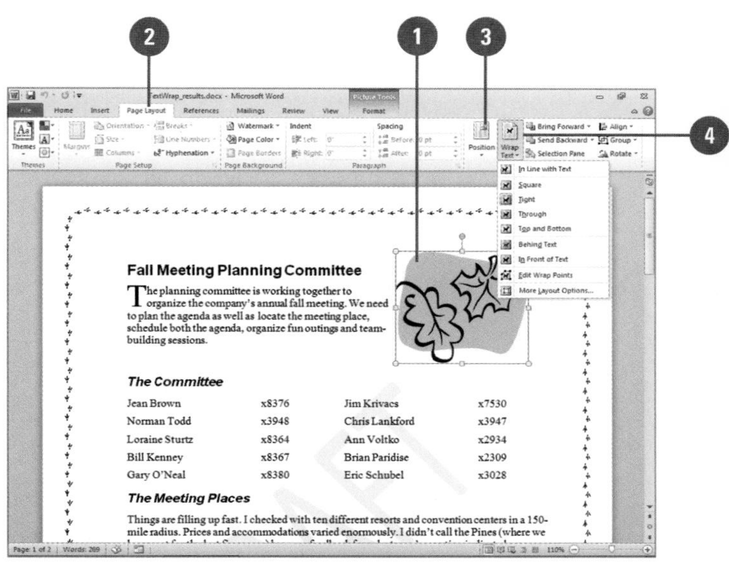

Wrap Text Tightly Around an Object or Picture

1. Select the picture or object.
2. Click the **Page Layout** tab.
3. To change text position, click the **Position** button, select a position or click **More Layout Options**, specify the options you want, and then click **OK**.
4. Click the **Wrap Text** button, and then click **Tight**.
5. Click the **Wrap Text** button, and then click **Edit Wrap Points**.
6. Drag edit points around the object or picture to tighten text around it.
7. Click a blank area of the document to deselect the object or picture.

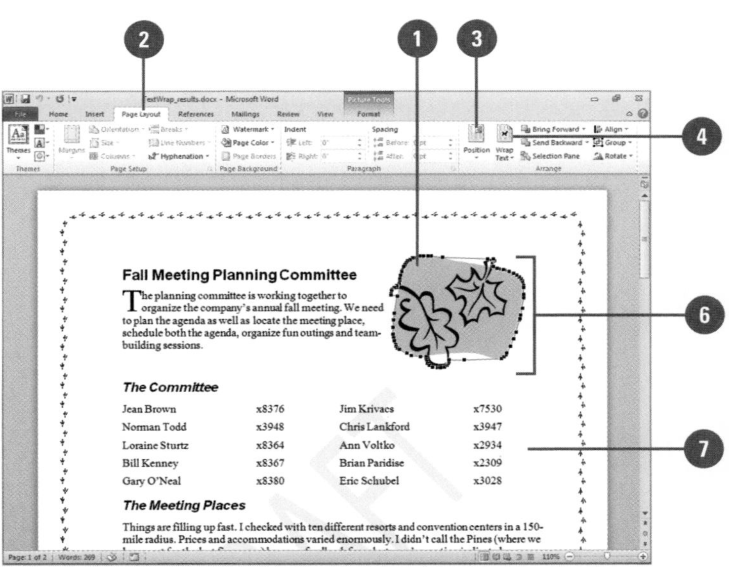

Working with Text Boxes

In addition to normal text on a page, you can also create independent text boxes to hold other types of information—such as titles, heading, pull quotes, and side bars—similar to those found on a desktop publishing page. You can insert a text box with predefined information or you can create a blank text box. If you can't find the predefined text box you need, check out Office.com (**New!**). You can even link two or more text boxes together to have text flow to different parts of a document. If you no longer need the text boxes to link, you can quickly break the link.

Insert a Text Box Pull Quote or Side Bar

1. Click where you want to insert a text box.
2. Click the **Insert** tab.
3. Click the **Text Box** button.
4. Click the predefined text box you want to insert.
   - Add from Office.com. Click **More Text Boxes from Office.com** (**New!**).

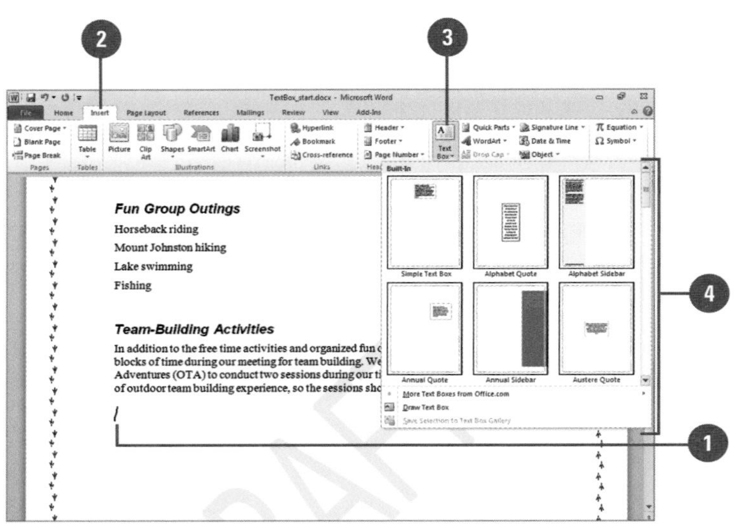

Create a Text Box from Existing Text

1. Select the text you want to place in a text box.
2. Click the **Insert** tab.
3. Click the **Text Box** button.
4. Click **Draw Text Box**.

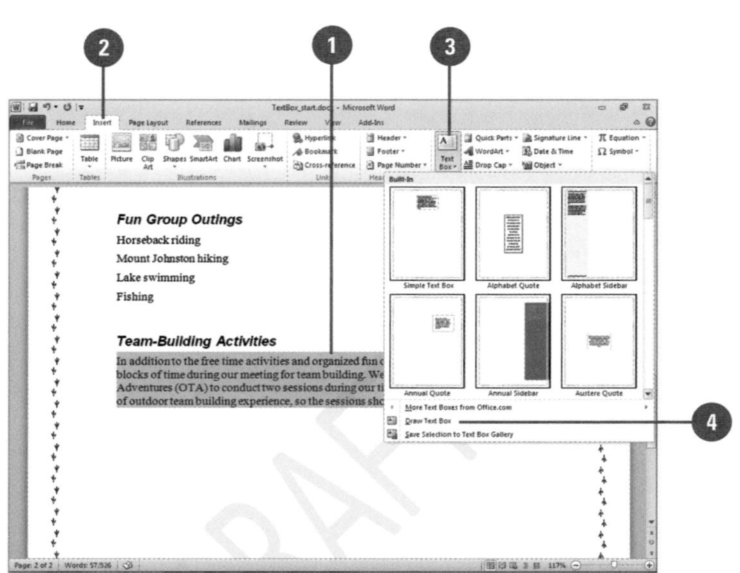

Did You Know?

You can change text direction in a text box. Select the text box you want to modify, click the Text Direction button on the Format tab under Drawing Tools.

Create a Text Box

1. Click the **Insert** tab.
2. Click the **Text Box** button.
3. Point to where you want to place the text box, and then drag to create a text box the size you want.
4. If necessary, click the text box to select it.
5. Type the text you want.
6. To resize the text box, drag a size handle.

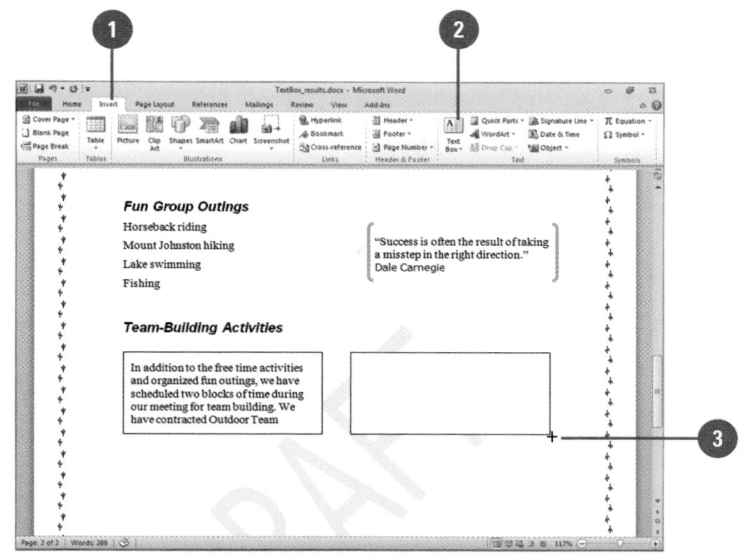

Link Text Boxes

1. Select the source text box.
2. Click the **Format** tab under Drawing Tools.
3. Click the **Create Link** button.
4. Point to the destination text box (the pointer changes to a pitcher), and then click to link the text boxes.

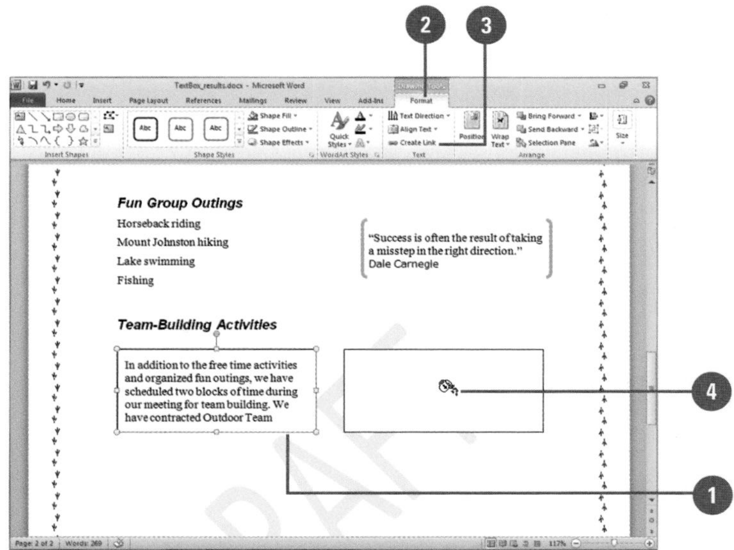

Did You Know?

You can break a link. Select the text box with the link you want to break, click the Break Link button on the Format tab under Drawing Tools, and then click the destination text box to break the link.

Drawing and Resizing Shapes

Word supplies ready-made shapes, ranging from hearts to lightning bolts to stars. The ready-made shapes are available directly on the Shapes gallery on the Insert and Format tabs. Once you have placed a shape on a document, you can resize it using the sizing handles. Many shapes have an **adjustment handle**, a small yellow or pink diamond located near a resize handle that you can drag to alter the shape. For precision when resizing, use the Size Dialog Box Launcher to specify the new size of the shape.

Draw a Shape

1. Click the **Insert** tab.
2. Click the **Shapes** button.
3. Click the shape you want to draw.
4. Drag the pointer on the document where you want to place the shape until the drawing object is the shape and size that you want.

   The shape you draw uses the line and fill color defined by the document's theme.

   TIMESAVER *To draw a proportional shape, hold down Shift as you drag the pointer.*

Did You Know?

You can quickly delete a shape. Click the shape to select it, and then press Delete.

You can draw a perfect circle or square. To draw a perfect circle or square, click the Oval or Rectangle button on the Shapes gallery, and then press and hold Shift as you drag.

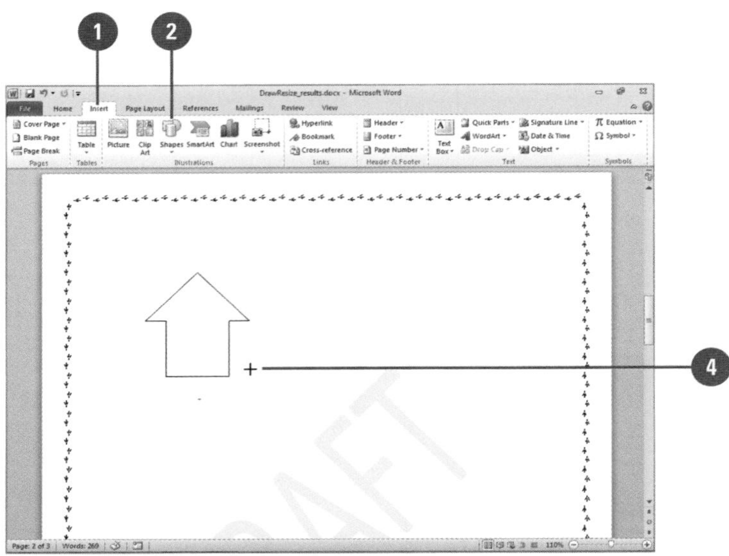

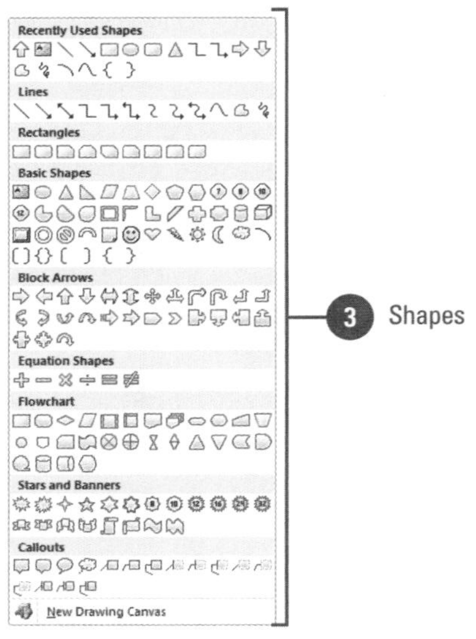

Resize a Shape

1. Select the shape you want to resize.
2. Drag one of the sizing handles.
   - To resize the object in the vertical or horizontal direction, drag a sizing handle on the side of the selection box.
   - To resize the object in both the vertical and horizontal directions, drag a sizing handle on the corner of the selection box.
   - To resize the object with precise measurements, click the **Format** tab under Drawing Tools, and then specify exact height and width settings in the Size group.

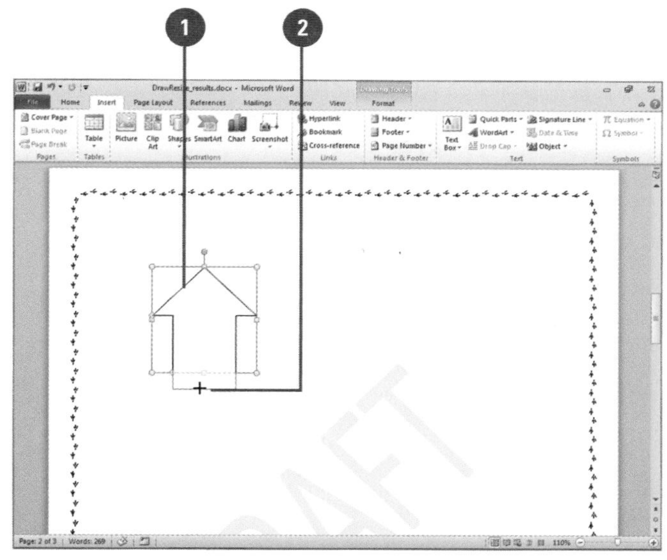

Adjust a Shape

1. Select the shape you want to adjust.
2. Click one of the adjustment handles (small yellow diamonds), and then drag the handle to alter the form of the shape.

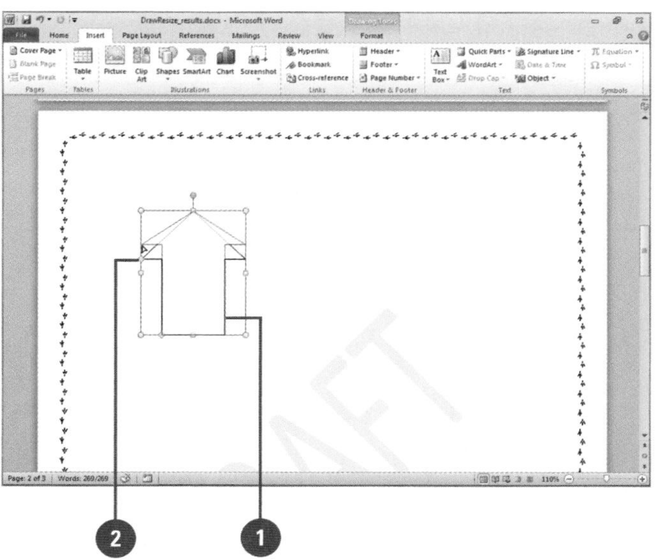

Did You Know?

You can replace a shape. Replace one shape with another, while retaining the size, color, and orientation of the shape. Click the shape you want to replace, click the Format tab, click the Edit Shape button, point to Change Shape, and then click the new shape you want.

Adding Text to a Shape

You can add text to a shape in the same way you add text to a text box. Simply, select the shape object, and then start typing. Shapes range from rectangles and circles to arrows and stars. When you place text in a shape, the text becomes part of the object. If you rotate or flip the shape, the text rotates or flips too. You can use tools, such as an alignment button or Font Style, on the Mini-toolbar and Home tab to format the text in a shape like the text in a text box.

Add Text to a Shape

1. Select the shape in which you want to add text.
2. Right-click the shape, and then click **Add Text**.
3. Type the text you want.
4. To edit the text in a shape, click the text to place the insertion point, and then edit the text.

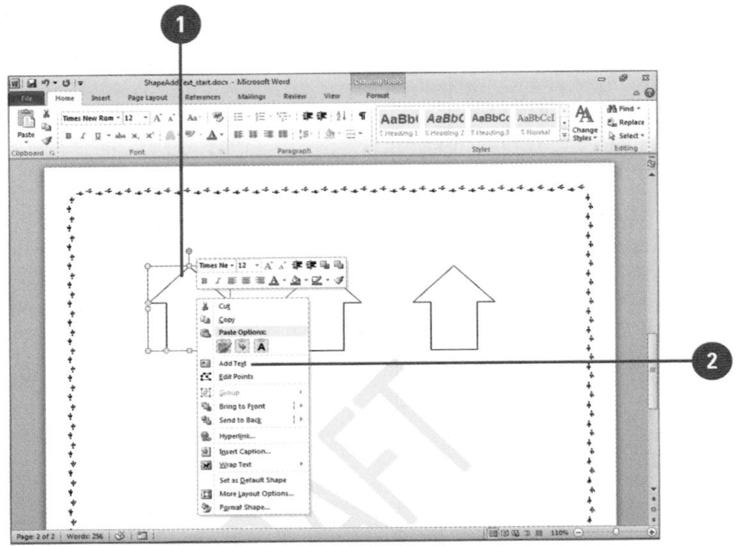

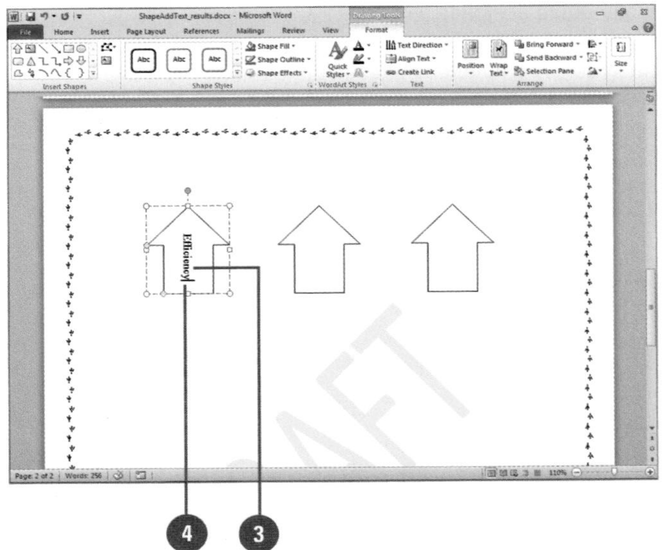

Did You Know?

You can copy and move shapes. To copy a shape, select the shape, click the Copy button on the Home tab, and then click the Paste button. To move a shape, position the cursor (which changes to a 4-headed arrow), and then drag it to a new location.

You can align text in a shape. Select the shapes with the text you want to change, click the Format tab under Drawing Tools, click the Align Text button, and then select an alignment option: Top, Middle, or Bottom.

Creating and Editing Freeforms

When you need to create a customized shape, use the freeform tools. Choose a freeform tool from the Lines category in the list of shapes. Freeforms are like the drawings you make with a pen and paper, except that you use a mouse for your pen and a document for your paper. A freeform shape can either be an open curve or a closed curve. You can edit a freeform by using the Edit Points command to alter the vertices that create the shape.

Draw a Freeform Polygon

1. Click the **Insert** tab.
2. Click the **Shapes** button and then click the **Freeform** shape in the Shapes gallery under Lines.
3. Click the document where you want to place the first vertex of the polygon.
4. Move the pointer, and then click to place the second point of the polygon. A line joins the two points.
   - To draw a line with curves, drag a line instead of clicking in steps 3 and 4.
5. Continue moving the mouse pointer and clicking to create additional sides of your polygon.
6. Finish the polygon. For a closed polygon, click near the starting point. For an open polygon, double-click the last point in the polygon.

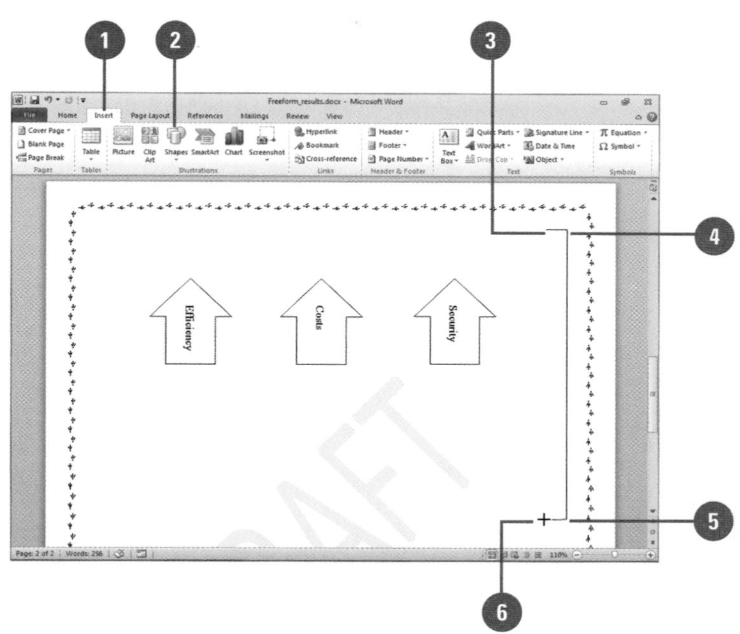

Did You Know?

You can convert a shape to a freeform. Select the shape, click the Edit Shape button, and then click Convert To Freeform.

You can switch between a closed curve and an open curve. Right-click the freeform drawing, and then click Close Path or Open Path.

For Your Information

Modifying a Freeform

Each vertex indicated by a black dot (a corner in an irregular polygon and a bend in a curve) has two attributes: its position, and the angle at which the curve enters and leaves it. You can move the position of each vertex and control the corner or bend angles. You can also add or delete vertices as you like. When you delete a vertex, Word recalculates the freeform and smooths it among the remaining points. Similarly, if you add a new vertex, Word adds a corner or bend in your freeform. To edit a freeform, click the freeform object, click the Format tab under Drawing Tools, click the Edit Shape button, click Edit Points, modify any of the points (move or delete), and then click outside to set the new shape.

Adding a Quick Style to a Shape

Instead of changing individual attributes of a shape—such as shape fill, shape outline, and shape effects—you can quickly add them all at once with the Shape Quick Style gallery. The Shape Quick Style gallery provides a variety of different formatting combinations. To quickly see if you like a Shape Quick Style, point to a thumbnail in the gallery to display a live preview of it in the selected shape. If you like it, you can apply it.

Add a Quick Style to a Shape

1. Select the shapes you want to modify.
2. Click the **Format** tab under Drawing Tools.
3. Click the scroll up or down arrow, or click the **More** list arrow in the Shapes Styles group to see additional styles.

   The current style appears highlighted in the gallery.
4. Point to a style.

   A live preview of the style appears in the current shape.
5. Click the style you want from the gallery to apply it to the selected shape.

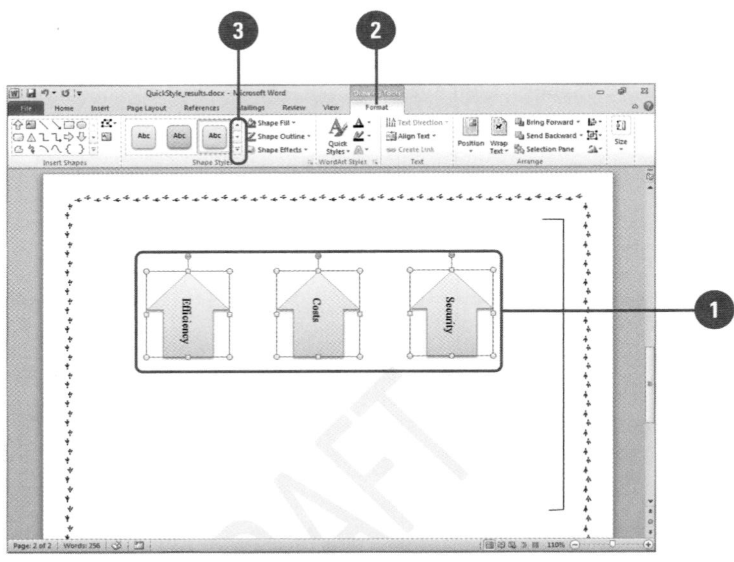

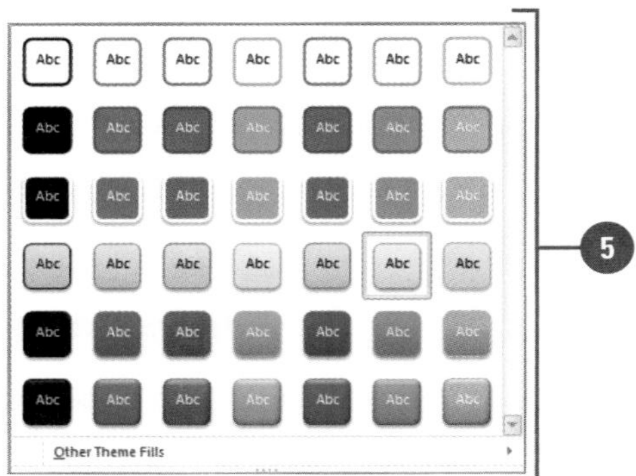

Did You Know?

You can add a Quick Style to a text box. A shape is a text box without a fill and outline (border), so you can apply a Quick Style to a text box using the same steps.

Adding Formatting to Shape Text

You can format text in a shape the same way you format text on a document page. You can change several font attributes—such as bold, italic, underline, font color and gradient (**New!**), outline (**New!**), shadow (**New!**), reflection (**New!**), glow (**New!**), 3-D (**New!**), or highlight—to enhance data to catch the reader's attention. The main formats you apply to text are available on the Home tab in the Font group or in the Font dialog box. Some of the additional formats available include strikethrough, subscript, superscript, small caps, all caps, underline style, and hidden.

Add a Style to Shape Text

1. Select the shapes with the text you want to modify.
2. Click the **Home** tab.
3. To change fonts, click the **Font** list arrow or click the **Font Size** list arrow.
4. Point to a font style or size.

   A live preview of the style or size appears in the current shape.
5. Click the style or size you want to apply it to the selected shape.
6. To apply other formatting, click one or more of the formatting buttons on the Ribbon: **Bold, Italic, Underline, Strikethrough, Subscript, Superscript, Text Effects, Text Highlight Color**, or **Font Color**.
   - **Underline Styles.** Click the **Underline** button arrow, and then select a style.
   - **Gradient Text.** Click the **Font Color** button, point to **Gradient**, and then select a style (**New!**). To create a custom gradient, click **More Gradients**.
7. To use the Font dialog box to change font attributes, click the **Font Dialog Box Launcher**, specify the changes you want, and then click **OK**.

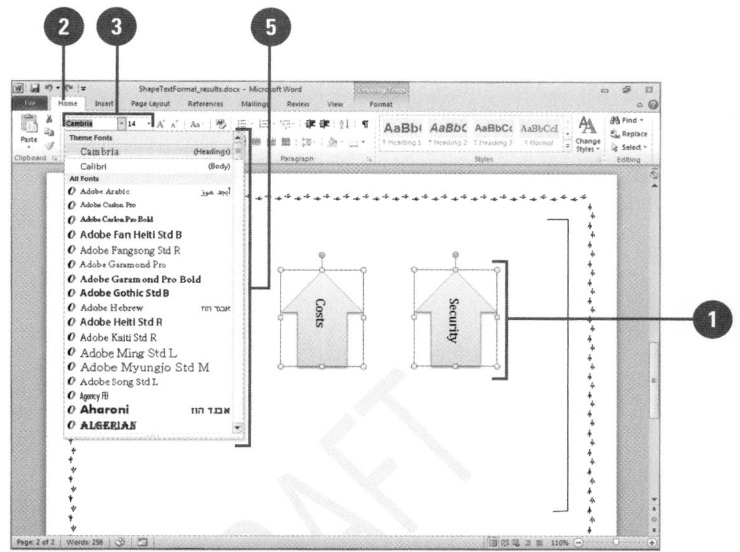

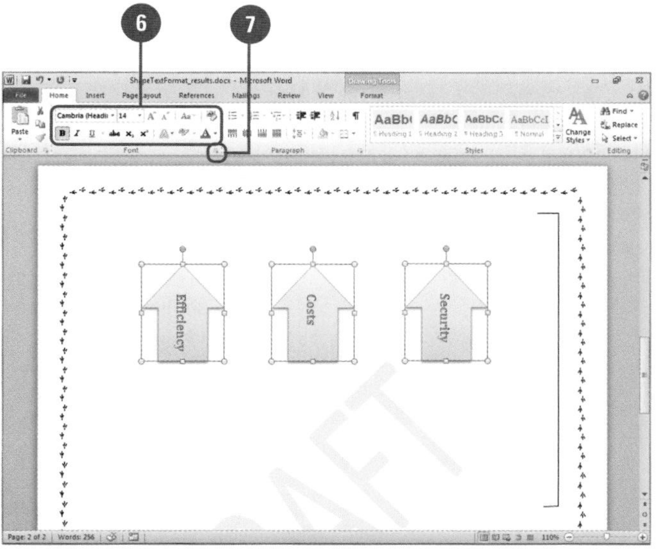

Applying Color Fills

When you create a closed drawing object such as a square, it applies the Shape Fill color to the inside of the shape, and the Shape Outline color to the edge of the shape. A line drawing object uses the Shape Outline color. You can set the Shape Fill to be a solid, gradient, texture or picture, and the Shape Outline can be a solid or gradient. If you want to make multiple changes to a shape at the same time, the Format Shape dialog box allows you to do everything in one place. If the solid color appears too dark, you can make the color fill more transparent. If you no longer want to apply a shape fill to an object, you can remove it.

Apply a Color Fill to a Shape

1. Select the shape you want to modify.
2. Click the **Format** tab under Drawing Tools.
3. Click the **Shape Fill** button.
4. Select the fill color option you want.
5. To remove a color fill, click the **Shape Fill** button, and then click **No Fill**.

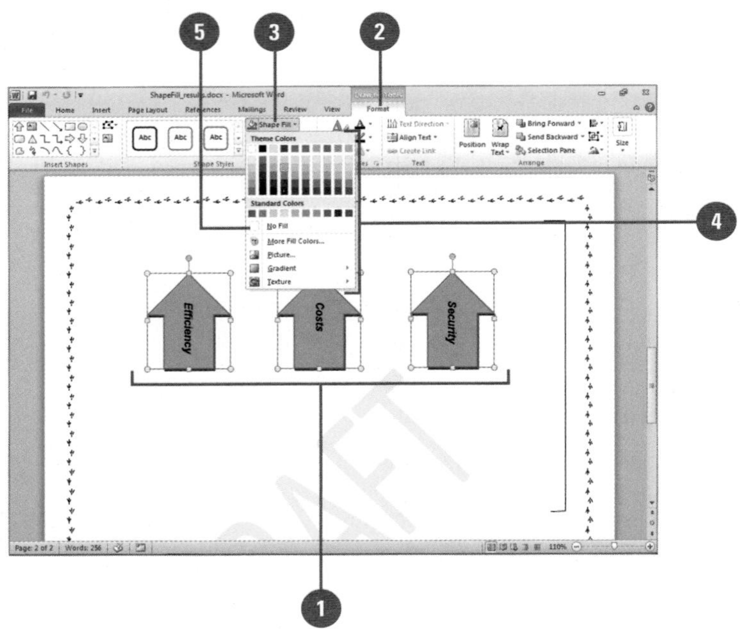

Did You Know?

You can set the color and line style for an object as the default. Right-click the object, and then click Set as Default Shape. Any new objects you create will use the same styles.

You can use the document background as the fill for a shape. Right-click the object, click Format Shape, click Fill in the left pane, click the Background option, and then click Close.

You can undo changes made in the Format Shape dialog box. Since changes made in the Shape Format dialog box are instantly applied, it's not possible to Cancel the dialog box. To remove changes, click the Undo button on the Quick Access Toolbar.

For Your Information

Formatting a SmartArt Shape

In the same way you can apply shape fills, outlines, and effects to a shape, you can also apply them to shapes in a SmartArt graphic. You can modify all or part of the SmartArt graphic by using the Shape Fill, Shape Outline, and Shape Effects buttons. Shape Fill can be set to be a solid, gradient, texture or picture, or set the Shape Outline to be a solid or gradient. In addition, you can change the look of a SmartArt graphic by applying effects, such as glow and soft edges. If a shape in a SmartArt graphic contains text, you can use WordArt style galleries to modify shape text.

Apply a Shape Color Fill with a Transparency

1. Select the shape you want to modify.
2. Click the **Format** tab under Drawing Tools.
3. Click the **Shape Styles Dialog Box Launcher**.
4. Click the **Solid fill** or **Gradient fill** option.
5. Click the **Color** list arrow, and then select the fill color you want.
6. Drag the **Transparency** slider or enter a number from 0 (fully opaque) to 100 (fully transparent).

   All your changes are instantly applied to the shape.
7. Click **Close**.

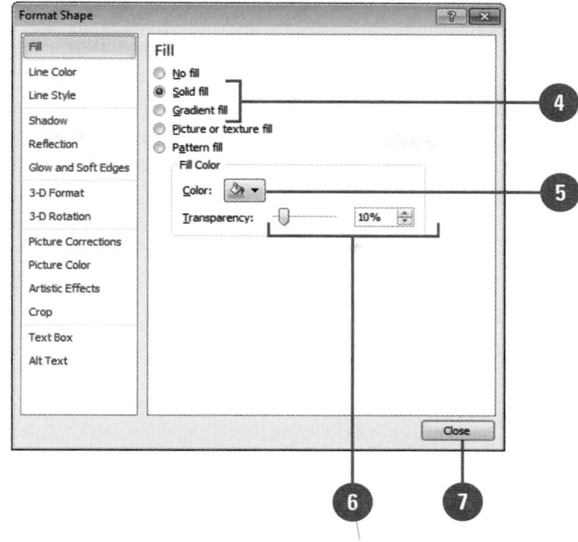

Apply a Color Outline to a Shape

1. Select the shape you want to modify.
2. Click the **Format** tab under Drawing Tools.
3. Click the **Shape Outline** button.
4. Select the outline color you want.
5. To remove an outline color, click the **Shape Outline** button, and then click **No Outline**.

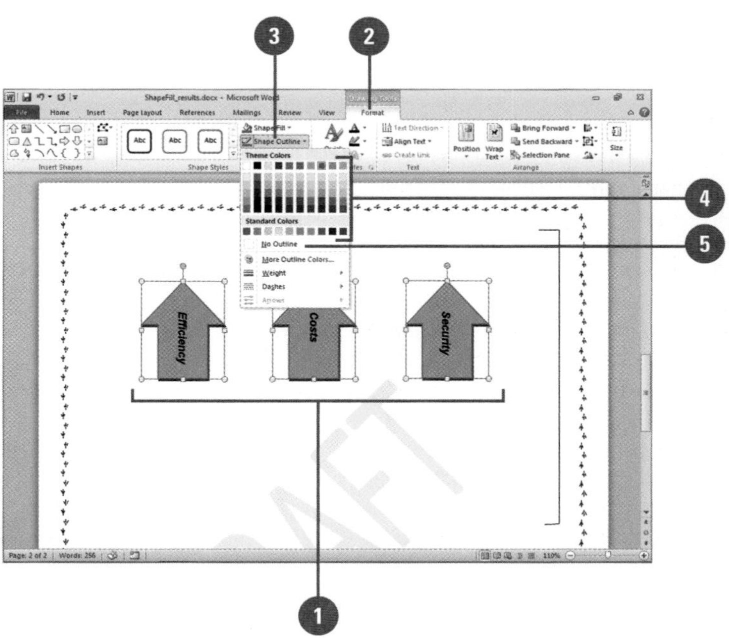

Applying Picture or Texture Fills

Applying a shape fill to a drawing object can add emphasis or create a point of interest in your document. You can insert a picture or clip art or texture into a shape. You can insert a picture from a file or clip art from the Clip Art task pane, or paste one in from the Clipboard. Stretch a picture or texture to fit across the selected shape or repeatedly tile it horizontally and vertically to fill the shape. When you stretch an image, you can also set offsets, which determine how much to scale an image to fit a shape relative to the edges. A positive offset number moves the image edge toward the center of the shape, while a negative offset number moves the image edge away from the shape. If the image appears too dark, you can make the picture more transparent.

Apply a Picture or Texture Fill to a Shape

1. Select the shape you want to modify.
2. Click the **Format** tab under Drawing Tools.
3. Click the **Shape Fill** button.
   - Click **Picture**, locate and select a picture file you want, and then click **Insert**.
   - Point to **Texture**, and then select a texture.

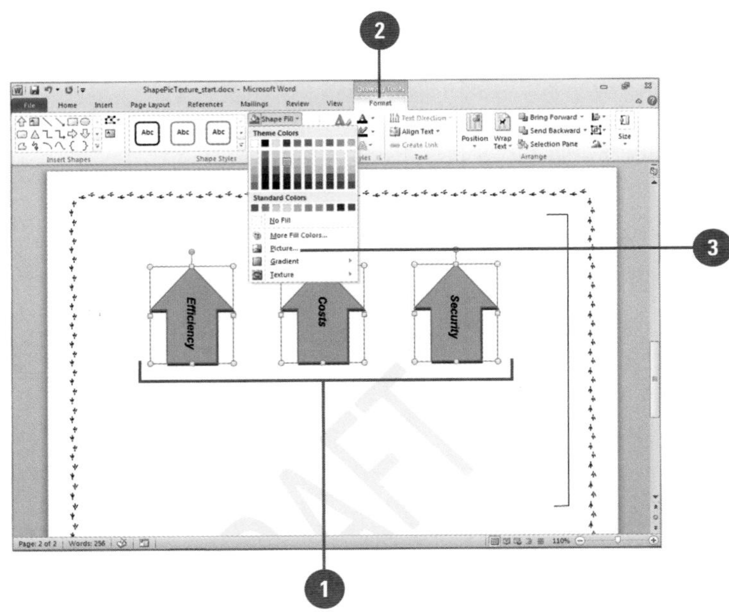

Use to select a picture

Did You Know?

You can apply a custom picture fill. Right-click the object you want to modify, click Format Shape, click Fill, click the Picture or Texture Fill option, click File, Clipboard, or Clip Art to select a picture, select the tile, stretch, and transparency options you want, and then click Close.

You can apply a custom texture fill. Right-click the object you want to modify, click Format Shape, click Fill, click the Picture or Texture Fill option, click the Texture button, select a texture, select the offset, scale, alignment, mirror and transparency options you want, and then click Close.

Applying Gradient Fills

Gradients are made up of two or more colors that gradually fade into each other. They can be used to give depth to a shape or create realistic shadows. Apply a gradient fill to a shape by using a gallery or presets for quick results, or by using the Format dialog box for custom results. A gradient is made up of several gradient stops, which are used to create non-linear gradients. Gradient stops consist of a position, a color, brightness (**New!**), and a transparency percentage.

Apply a Gradient Fill to a Shape

1. Select the shape you want to modify.
2. Click the **Format** tab under Drawing Tools.
3. Click the **Shape Fill** button.
4. Point to **Gradient**, and then select a gradient from the gallery.

   Four gradient modes are available: linear (parallel bands), radial (radiate from center), rectangle (radiate from corners), and path (radiate along path).

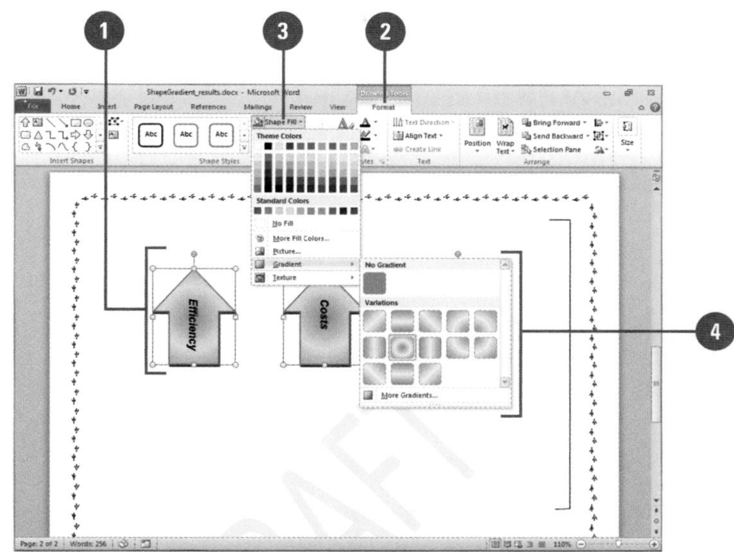

Apply a Custom Gradient Fill

1. Select the shape you want to modify.
2. Click the **Format** tab under Drawing Tools.
3. Click the **Shape Fill** button, point to **Gradient**, and then click **More Gradients**.
4. Click the **Preset colors** list arrow, and then select a gradient preset.
5. Select a type, direction, or angle. Select a gradient stop, and then change color, position, brightness (**New!**), or transparency.
6. Click **Close**.

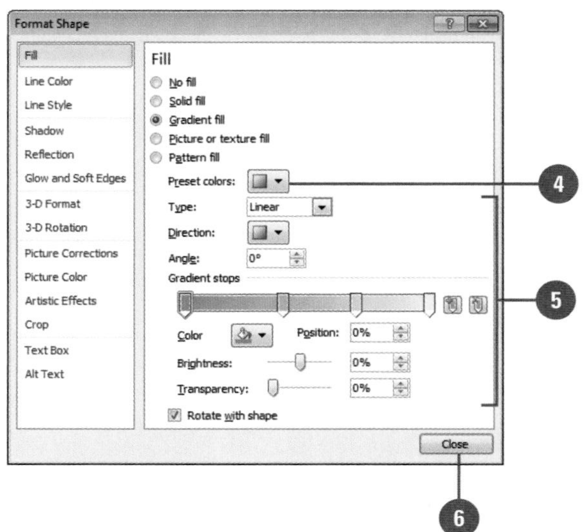

Applying Shape Effects

You can change the look of a shape by applying shape effects, like shadows, reflections (**New!**), glows (**New!**), bevels (**New!**), and 3-D rotations. You can apply effects to a shape by using the Shape Effects gallery for quick results. From the Shape Effects gallery you can apply a built-in combination of 3-D effects or individual 3-D effects to a shape. To quickly see if you like the effect, point to a thumbnail in the Shape Effects gallery to display a live preview of it. If you like it, you can apply it. If you no longer want to apply the effect, you can remove it. Simply, select the shape, and then select the No effect type option on the Shape Effects gallery.

Add or Remove Preset Effects to a Shape

1. Select the shape you want to modify.
2. Click the **Format** tab under Drawing Tools.
3. Click the **Shape Effects** button, point to **Shadow**, **Reflection**, **Glow**, or **Soft Edges**, and then select an effect.
   - **Preset.** Select a preset.
   - **Remove.** Select the No effect type option, such as No Shadow, No Reflection, No Glow, or No Soft Edges.
   - **Options.** Click the Options command for the effect type, such as Shadow Options, Reflection Options, Glow Options, or Soft Edges Options.

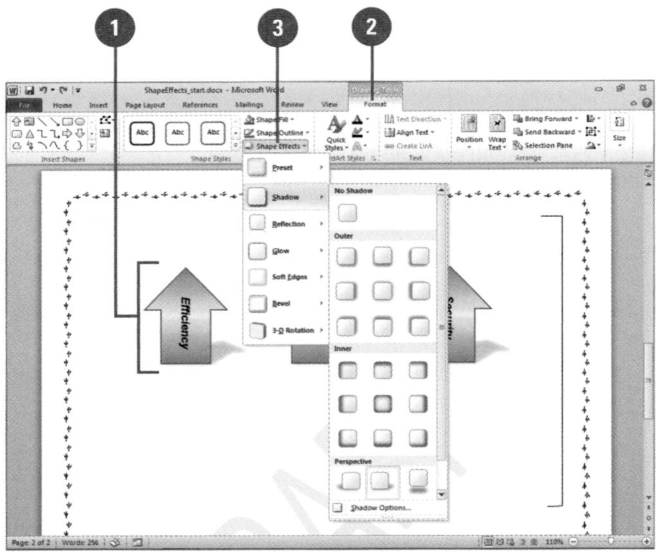

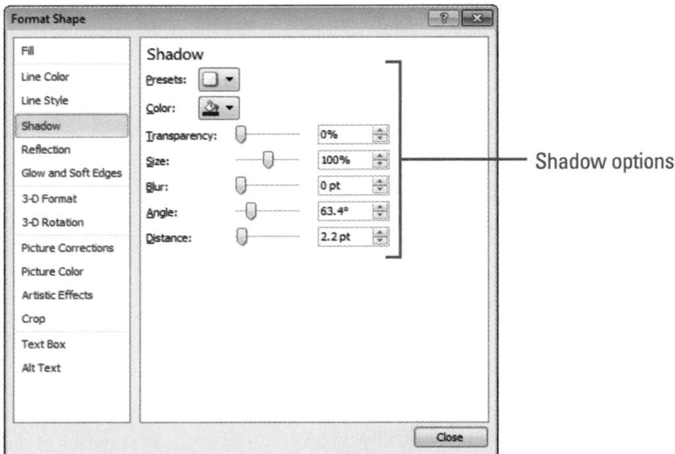

Add a Preset 3-D Effect to a Shape

1. Select the shape you want to modify.
2. Click the **Format** tab under Drawing Tools.
3. To add or remove a 3D effect, click the **Shape Effects**, point to **Preset**, **Bevel**, or **3-D Rotation**, and then select a 3D effect.
   - **Preset.** Select a preset.
   - **Remove.** Select the No Presets option.
4. To change individual 3-D bevel effects, click the **Shape Effects**, point to **Preset** or **Bevel**, click **3-D Options**, select any of the following 3D effect options, and then click **Close**.
   - **Bevel.** Change the bevel top and bottom effects and the width and height for the shape in points.
   - **Depth.** Change the depth color and perspective for the shape in points.
   - **Contour.** Change the contour color and size for the shape in points.
   - **Surface Material.** Change the surface material of the shape.
   - **Surface Lighting.** Change the angle of the lighting source.
5. To change individual 3-D rotation effects, click the **Shape Effects**, point to **3D Rotation**, click **3-D Rotation Options**, select the 3D effect options you want, and then click **Close**.

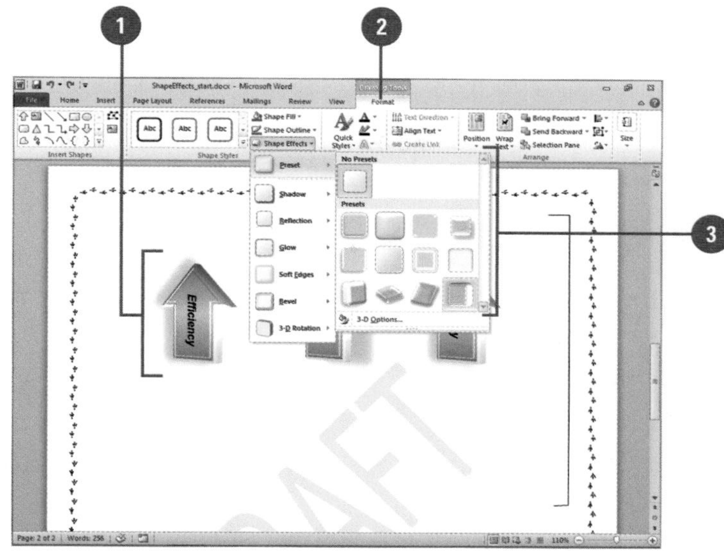

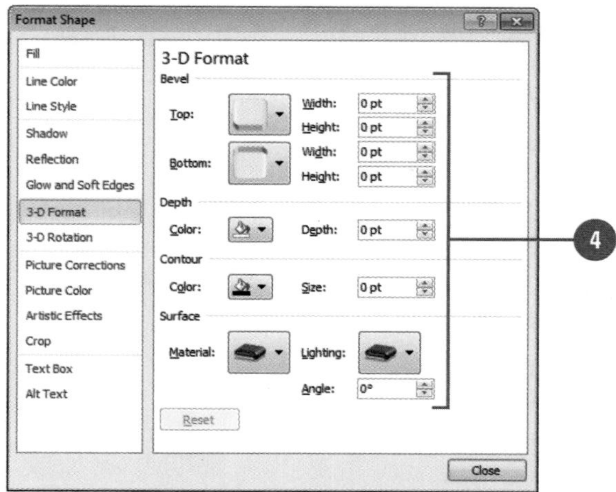

Aligning and Distributing Objects

In addition to using grids and guides to align objects to a specific point, you can align a group of objects to each other. The Align commands make it easy to align two or more objects relative to each other vertically to the left, center, or right, or horizontally from the top, middle, or bottom. To evenly align several objects to each other across the document, either horizontally or vertically, select them and then choose a distribution option. Before you select an align command, specify how you want Word to align the objects. You can align the objects in relation to the document or to the selected objects.

Distribute Objects

1. Select the objects you want to distribute.
2. Click the **Format** tab under Drawing Tools.
3. Click the **Align** button.
4. On the Align menu, click the alignment method you want:
   - Click **Align to Page** if you want the objects to align relative to the document page.
   - Click **Align to Margin** if you want the objects to align relative to the document margin.
5. On the Align submenu, click the distribution command you want:
   - Click **Distribute Horizontally** to evenly distribute the objects horizontally.
   - Click **Distribute Vertically** to evenly distribute the objects vertically.

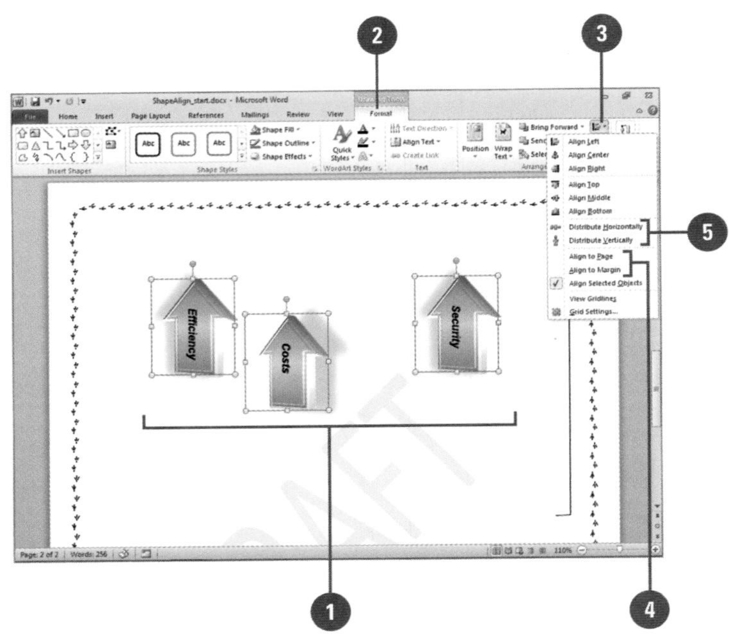

Align Objects with Other Objects

1. Select the objects you want to align.
2. Click the **Format** tab under Drawing Tools.
3. Click the **Align** button.
4. On the Align menu, click the alignment method you want:
   - Click **Align to Page** if you want the objects to align relative to the document page.
   - Click **Align to Margin** if you want the objects to align relative to the document margin.
5. On the Align menu, click the alignment command you want:
   - Click **Align Left** to line up the objects with the left edge of the selection or document.
   - Click **Align Center** to line up the objects with the center of the selection or document.
   - Click **Align Right** to line up the objects with the right edge of the selection or document.
   - Click **Align Top** to line up the objects with the top edge of the selection or document.
   - Click **Align Middle** to line up the objects vertically with the middle of the selection or document.
   - Click **Align Bottom** to line up the objects with the bottom of the selection or document.

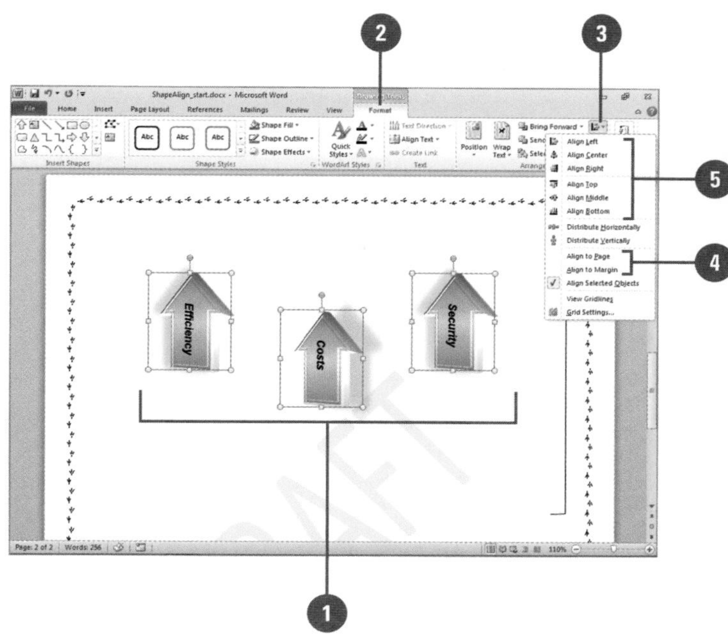

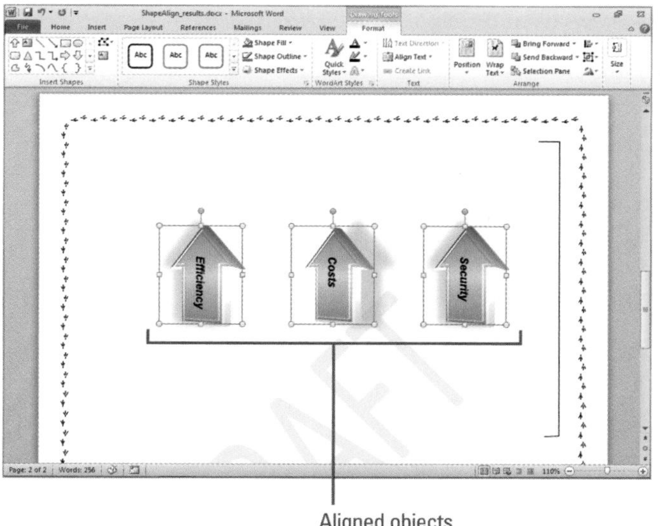

Aligned objects

Aligning Objects to Grids

Word uses a grid to align an individual object or a group of objects to a vertical or horizontal line. Turning on the visible grid option makes it easier to create, modify, and align a shape. Within the Drawing Grid dialog box, you can select from a variety of options, such as snapping objects to the grid or to other objects and displaying drawing guides on-screen.

Turn On or Turn Off the Visible Grid

1. Select the objects you want to arrange.
2. Click the **Format** tab under Drawing Tools.
3. Click the **Align** button, and then click **Grid Settings**.
4. Select or clear the **Display gridlines on screen** check box.
5. Select or clear the **Vertical every** check box, and then enter a value for the vertical and horizontal gridlines, if you turn it on.
6. Click **OK**.

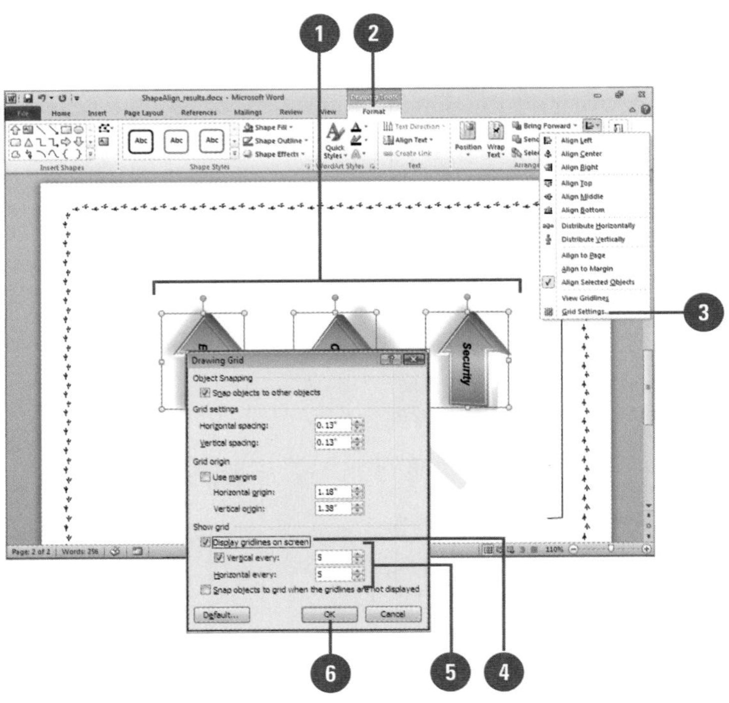

Set Objects to Snap into Place

1. Select the objects you want to arrange.
2. Click the **Format** tab under Drawing Tools.
3. Click the **Align** button, and then click **Grid Settings**.
4. Select the **Snap objects to other objects** check box.
5. Select the **Snap objects to grid when the gridlines are not displayed** check box.
6. Click **OK**.

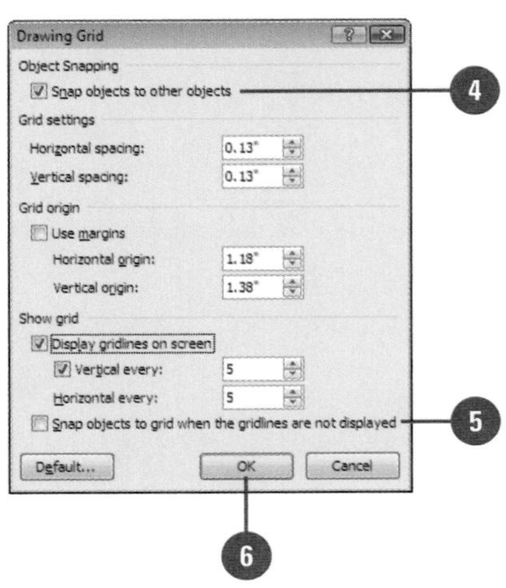

Show or Hide the Gridlines

1. Select the objects you want to arrange.
2. Click the **Format** tab under Drawing Tools.
3. Click the **Align** button, and then click **View Gridlines**.

Gridlines

Align an Object to a Grid

1. If you want, display gridlines on the screen (horizontal and vertical).
2. Drag the object's center or edge near the guide. Word aligns the center or edge to the guide.

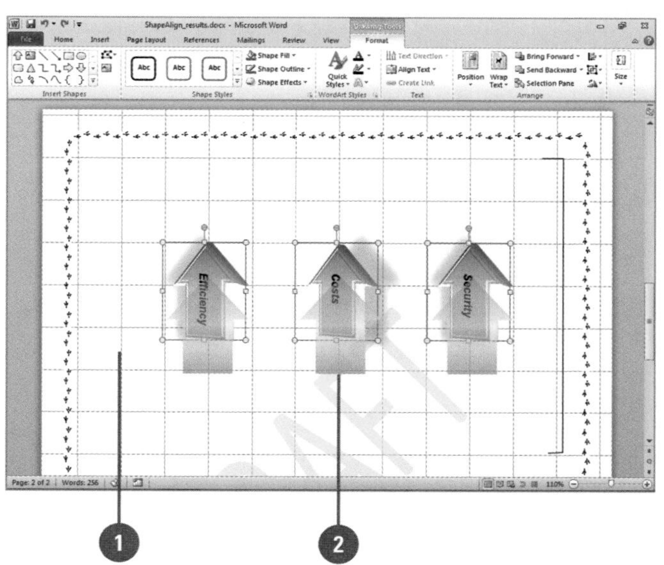

Did You Know?

You can use the keyboard to override grid settings. To temporarily override settings for the grids and guides, press and hold the Alt key as you drag an object.

Changing Stacking Order

Multiple objects on a document appear in a stacking order, like layers of transparencies. Stacking is the placement of objects one on top of another. In other words, the first object that you draw is on the bottom and the last object that you draw is on top. You can change the order of this stack of objects by using the Bring to Front, Send to Back, Bring Forward, and Send Backward commands on the Format tab under Drawing Tools.

Arrange a Stack of Objects

1. Select the objects you want to arrange.
2. Click the **Format** tab under Drawing Tools.
3. Click the stacking option you want.
   - Click the **Bring to Front** button arrow, and then click **Bring to Front, Bring Forward**, or **Bring in Front of Text** to move a drawing to the top of the stack or up one location in the stack.
   - Click the **Send to Back** button arrow, and then click **Send to Back, Send Backward, or Send Behind Text** to move a drawing to the bottom of the stack or back one location in the stack.

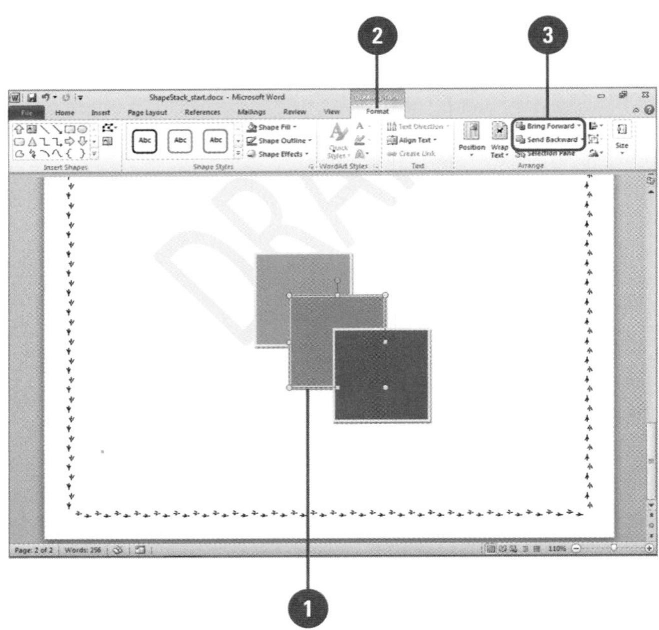

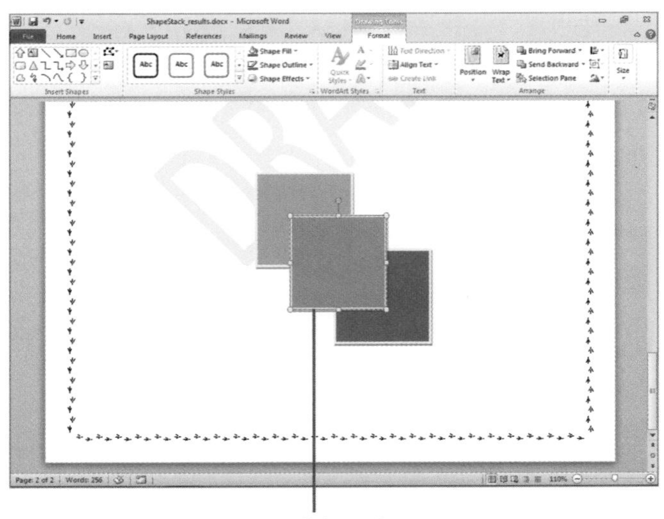

Bring to front

Did You Know?

You can view a hidden object in a stack. Press the Tab key or Shift+Tab to cycle forward or backward through the objects until you select the object you want.

You can connect two shapes. Click the Insert tab, click the Shapes button or list arrow, click a connector (located in the Lines category), position the pointer over an object handle (turns red), drag the connector to the object handle (turns red) on another object. An attached connector point appears as red circles, while an unattached connector point appears as light blue.

Rotating and Flipping Objects

After you create an object, you can change its orientation on the document by rotating or flipping it. Rotating turns an object 90 degrees to the right or left; flipping turns an object 180 degrees horizontally or vertically. For a more freeform rotation, which you cannot achieve in 90 or 180 degree increments, drag the green rotate lever at the top of an object. You can also rotate and flip any type of picture–including bitmaps–in a document. This is useful when you want to change the orientation of an image, such as changing the direction of an arrow.

Rotate an Object to any Angle

1. Select the object you want to rotate.
2. Position the pointer (which changes to the Free Rotate pointer) over the green rotate lever at the top of the object, and then drag to rotate the object.
3. Click outside the object to set the rotation.

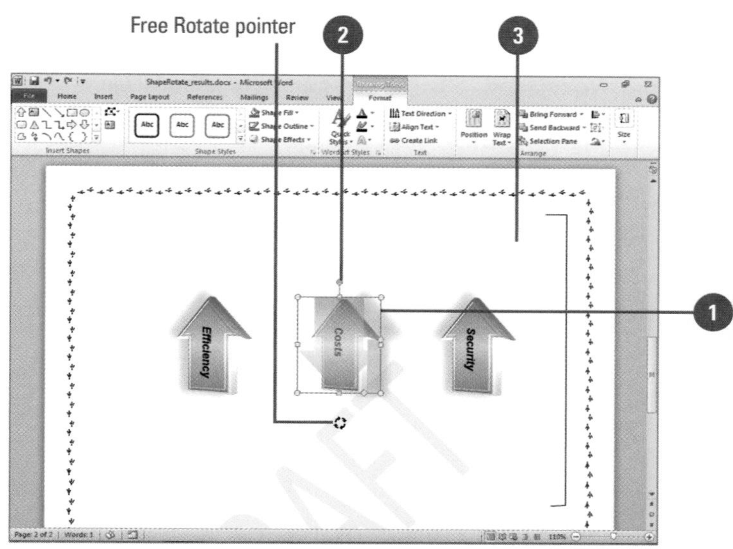

Rotate or Flip an Object Using Preset Increments

1. Select the object you want to rotate or flip.
2. Click the **Format** tab under Drawing Tools.
3. Click the **Rotate** button, and then click the option you want.
   - Rotate. Click **Rotate Right 90°** or **Rotate Left 90°**.
   - Flip. Click **Flip Vertical** or **Flip Horizontal**.

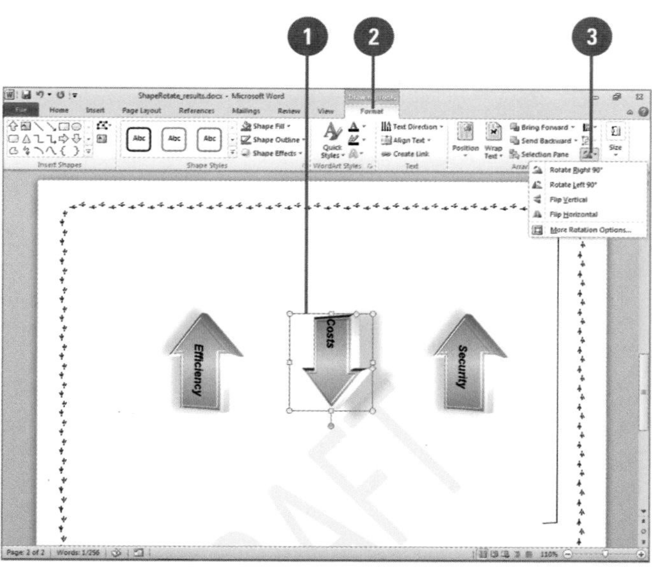

Grouping and Ungrouping Objects

Objects can be grouped, ungrouped, and regrouped to make editing and moving them easier. Rather than moving several objects one at a time, you can group the objects and move them all together. Grouped objects appear as one object, but each object in the group maintains its individual attributes. You can change an individual object within a group without ungrouping. This is useful when you need to make only a small change to a group, such as changing the color of a single shape in the group. You can also format specific shapes, drawings, or pictures within a group without ungrouping. Simply select the object within the group, change the object or edit text within the object, and then deselect the object. However, if you need to move an object in a group, you need to first ungroup the objects, move it, and then group the objects together again.

Group Objects Together

1. Select the shapes you want to group together.
2. Click the **Format** tab under Drawing Tools.
3. Click the **Group** button, and then click **Group**.

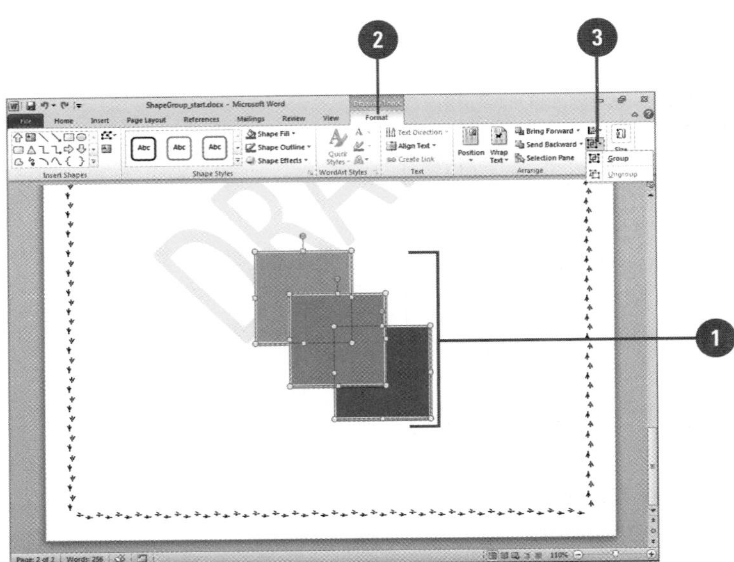

Did You Know?

You can use the Tab key to select objects in order. Move between the drawing objects on your document (even those hidden behind other objects) by pressing the Tab key.

You can use the shortcut menu to select Group related commands. Right-click the objects you want to group, point to Group, and then make your selections.

You can no longer ungroup tables. Due to the increased table size and theme functionality, tables can no longer be ungrouped.

Ungroup Objects

1. Select the grouped object you want to ungroup.
2. Click the **Format** tab under Drawing Tools.
3. Click the **Group** button, and then click **Ungroup**.

Did You Know?

You can troubleshoot the arrangement of objects. If you have trouble selecting an object because another object is in the way, you can use the Selection pane to help you select it.

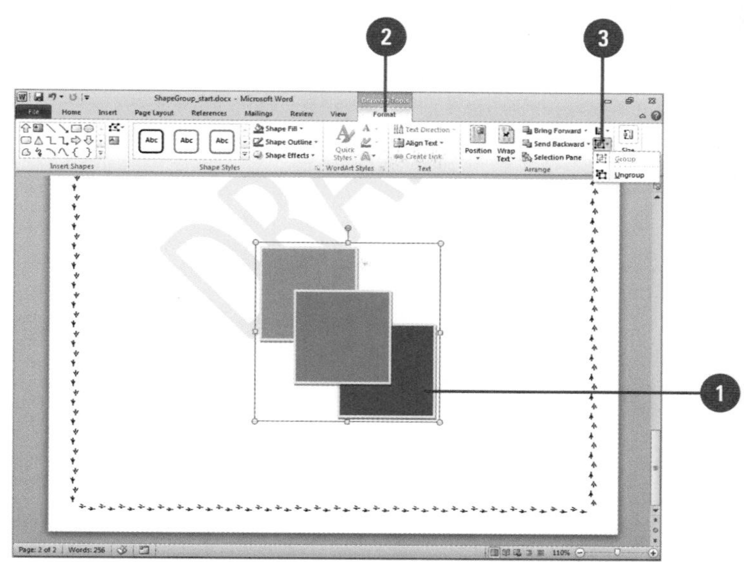

Working with Long Documents

8

Introduction

When working with long documents, the ability to split up the tasks can be crucial to meeting a deadline. Microsoft Word can do just that. By creating a master document in an Outline format, you can simply select the sections of the master that will be sectioned off as a subdocument. Word creates a number of subdocuments off the master, based on how you decide to group them. Once the subdocuments are created, they become separate files that others can open, develop, save and re-insert into the master.

Using master documents and subdocuments by many individuals could be a formatting nightmare. Word has an automatic formatting tool to help you create an overall format for your long document. In order to help your readers process your document, headers and footers, along with a cross reference, are a great way to keep them focused on the material at hand.

Once your long document is created and will be bound in some fashion, it's important to make sure that you have enough white space around the margins so that text won't get cut off during the binding process. And, as you navigate through the document, be sure to check for any special items that might require your attention. You can use the Go To function or Navigation pane to quickly move from object to object, section to section, or page to page, to name a few. The Select Browse Object button is also a way to navigate through your long document. Browse by comments, graphics, tables or footnotes. The availability for Word to seek out these objects and for you to review them is crucial to your long document being a success.

Other documents items, such as a Table of Contents and an Index can all be done very easily in Word. When you need to know that final word count, you can find it quickly through the References tab.

What You'll Do

Creating an Outline

Outlines are useful for organizing information, such as topics in an essay. An outline typically consists of main headings and subheadings. You can create an outline from scratch in Outline view or change a bulleted or numbered list into an outline using the bullets and numbering commands on the Home tab. In Outline view, you can use buttons in the Outlining Tools group or drag the mouse pointer to move headings and subheadings to different locations or levels.

Create an Outline in Outline View

1. In a new document, click the **Outline View** button.
2. Type a heading, and then press Enter.
3. Type another heading or press Tab to add a subheading under the heading.
4. To change a heading or subheading to a different level and apply the corresponding heading style, place the insertion point in the heading, and then click the **Promote** or **Demote** button until the heading is at the level you want, or click the **Promote to Heading** or **Promote to Body** button.
5. To move a heading or subheading to a different location, place the insertion point in the heading, and then click the **Move Up** or **Move Down** button until the heading is moved where you want it to go.
6. When you're done, click the **Close Outline View** button.

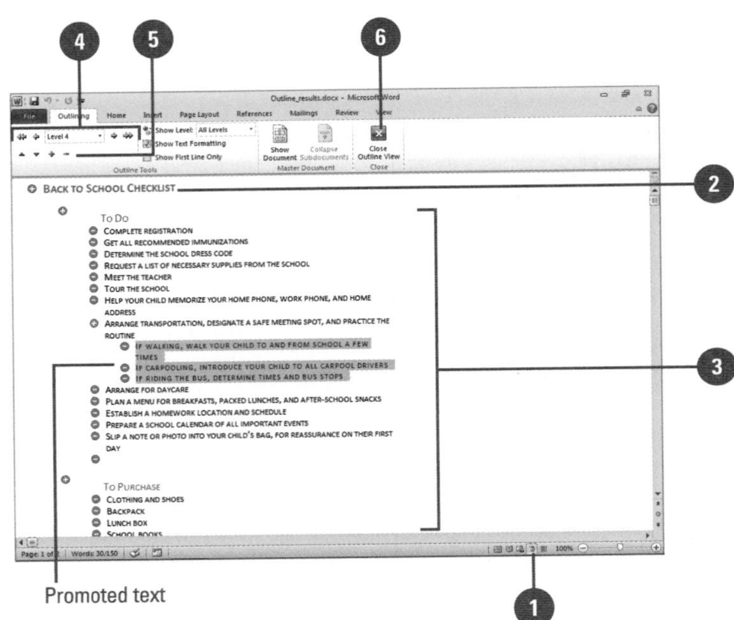

Change the Outline Display in Outline View

1. Open the document with the outline, and then click the **Outline View** button.

2. Use the Outlining Tools to change the display in Outline view.

   - **Show Level.** Click the list arrow, and then select the level you want to display.
   - **Show Text Formatting.** Select or clear to show or hide text formatting.
   - **Show First Line Only.** Select to show the first line only.

3. When you're done, click the **Close Outline View** button.

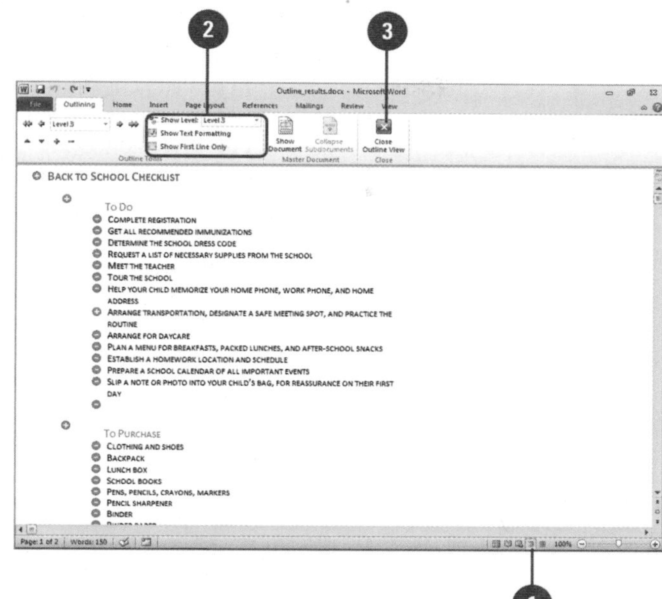

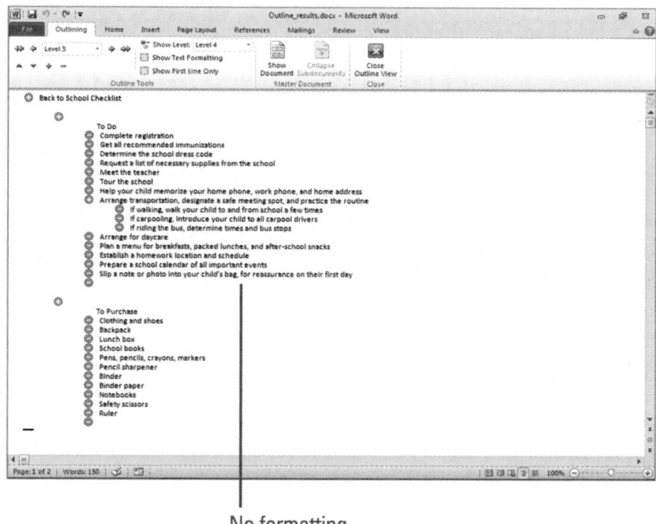

Creating a Multiple-Author Document

When several people are going to collaborate on a document by dividing the workload by section or heading, you can create a master document so that everyone can work concurrent with one another instead of passing one file around. The process of creating a master document begins with an outline. When the outline is complete, individual headings or sections can have subdocuments assigned to them. These subdocuments can be distributed to the collaborators and completed separately. When ready, they can then be combined back into the master document so that all the information is contained in a single file. After you have created a master document, those sections that you have designated as subdocuments can be created and saved as separate files. These files can then be reinserted into the master document as they are completed.

Create a Master Document

1. In a new document, click the **Outline View** button.
2. Enter headings to outline the presentation of topics in the master document, pressing Enter after each entry.
3. Select a heading, and then click one of the buttons in Outline view to assign a heading style (Heading 1 through Heading 9).
   - Click the **Promote** or **Demote** button to increase or decrease the heading level of the headlines and body text.
4. Select the heading that you want to make into a subdocument.
5. Click the **Show Document** button.
6. Click the **Create Subdocument** button.
7. Click the **File** tab, and then click **Save As**.
8. Select the location, type a name, and then click **Save**.
9. When you're done, click the **Close Outline View** button.

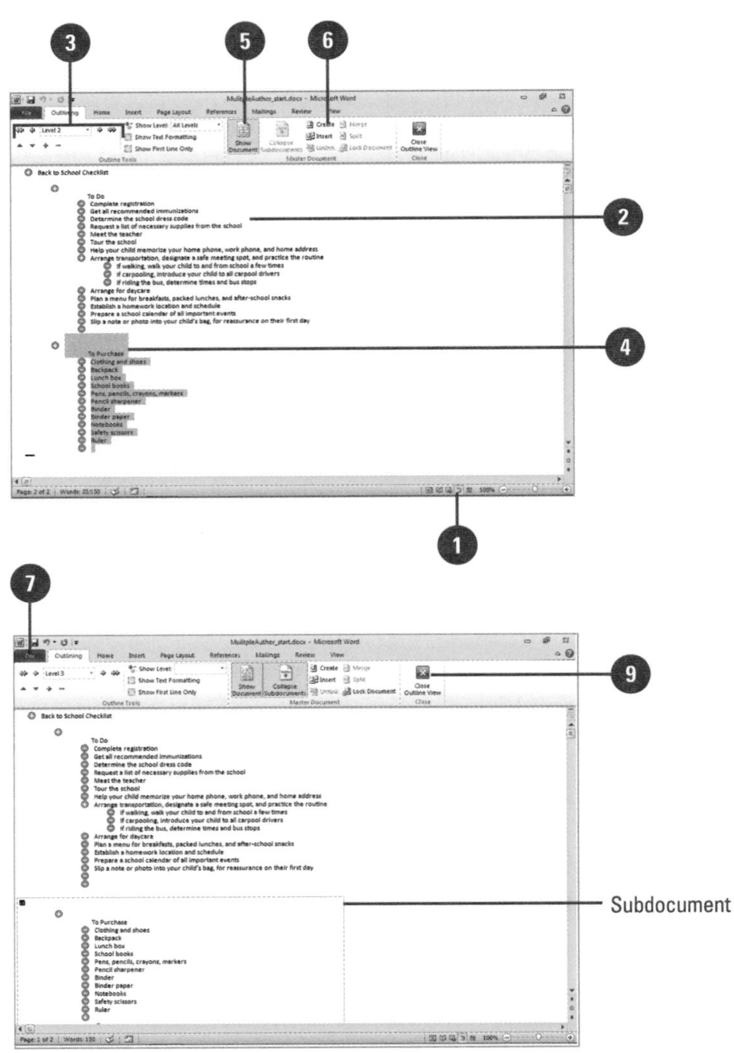

Insert a Subdocument

1. Open the Master document in which you want to add a subdocument.
2. Click the **Show Document** button.
3. If the subdocuments are collapsed, click the **Expand Subdocument** button.
4. Position the insertion point where you want the subdocument inserted.
5. Click the **Insert Subdocument** button.
6. Locate and select the subdocument file you want to insert, and then click **Open**.
7. To open the subdocument, double-click the subdocument or Ctrl+click the subdocument link. Close the subdocument to return to the master document.
8. When you're done, click the **Close Outline View** button, and then click **Yes** to save, if necessary.

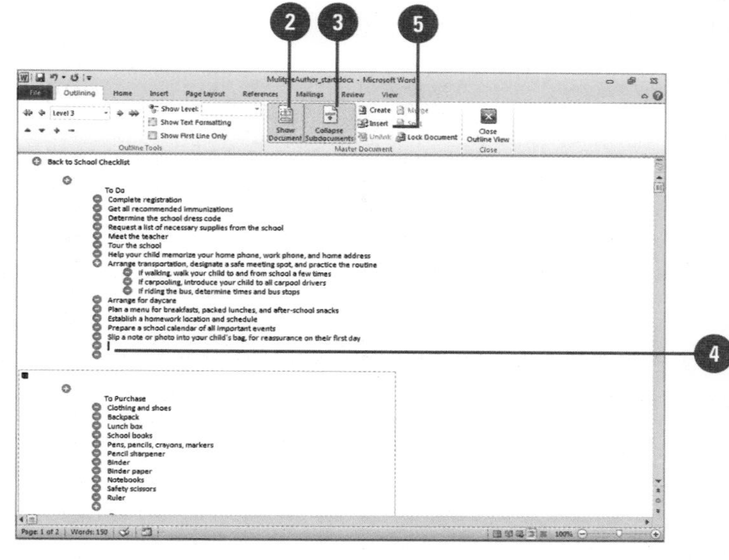

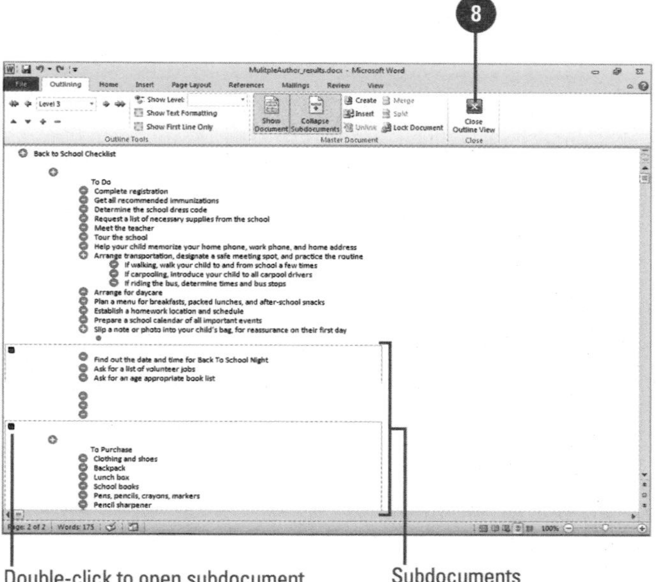

Did You Know?

You can collapse, or hide, all of your subdocuments. To hide (collapse) the subdocuments in a master document, click the Collapse Subdocuments button in Outline view. All subdocuments are collapsed. To show (expand) the subdocuments, click the Expand Subdocuments button.

You can lock and unlock a master document. Click the Show Documents button in Outline view, select text in the master document, and then click Lock Document. To unlock, click Expand Subdocuments button to remove the lock on the files.

Creating Documents Using Automatic Formatting

Word can automatically perform some formatting functions for you as you type a document. For example, you can change straight quotation marks to smart (curly) quotes, hyphens to en-dashes or em-dashes, an asterisk before and after text to bold text, or an underscore before and after text to italic text. You can also type a number and text or a bullet and text to start a numbered or bulleted list. If you had AutoFormat disabled when you created the document, you still have the option of using the feature to find and correct errors in formatting.

Set Up Automatic Formatting As You Type

1. Click the **File** tab, and then click **Options**.
2. In the left pane, click **Proofing**, and then click **AutoCorrect Options**.
3. Click the **AutoFormat As You Type** tab.
4. Select or clear the AutoFormat check boxes you want to use.
5. Click **OK**.

   Your choices take effect, but they only apply to text you will be entering subsequently. In this case, AutoFormat does not correct errors retroactively.

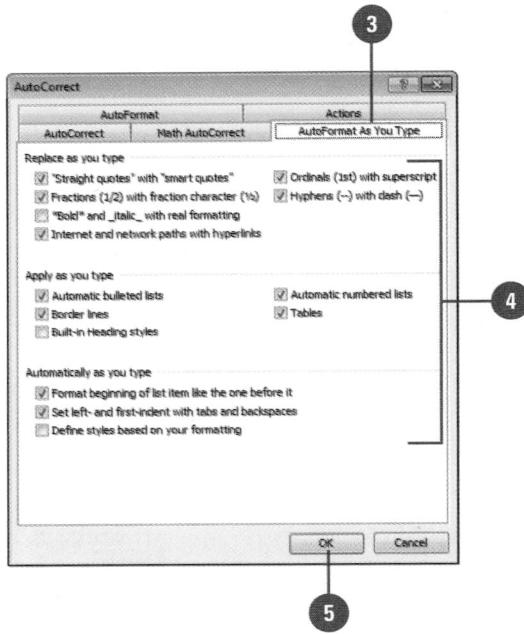

Change Document Formatting with AutoFormat

1. Click the **AutoFormat** button on the Quick Access Toolbar.
   - The AutoFormat button is not on the Quick Access Toolbar by default. Use the Customize pane in Word Options to add the button.
2. Click **Options**.
3. Click the **AutoFormat** tab to select the formatting options you want.
4. Click the other tabs to make any additional changes to your document.
5. Click **OK**.
6. Click the **AutoFormat now** option to have Word automatically format the document, or click the **AutoFormat and review each change** option to review, and then accept or reject each change.
7. Click **OK**.

   If you chose the AutoFormat and review each change option, then continue.
8. Click **Review Changes** to look at changes individually.
9. Click **Style Gallery** if you want to preview your document, and then click **OK**.
10. Use the Accept and Reject buttons to accept or reject the review changes.
11. Click **Close** or **Cancel**.

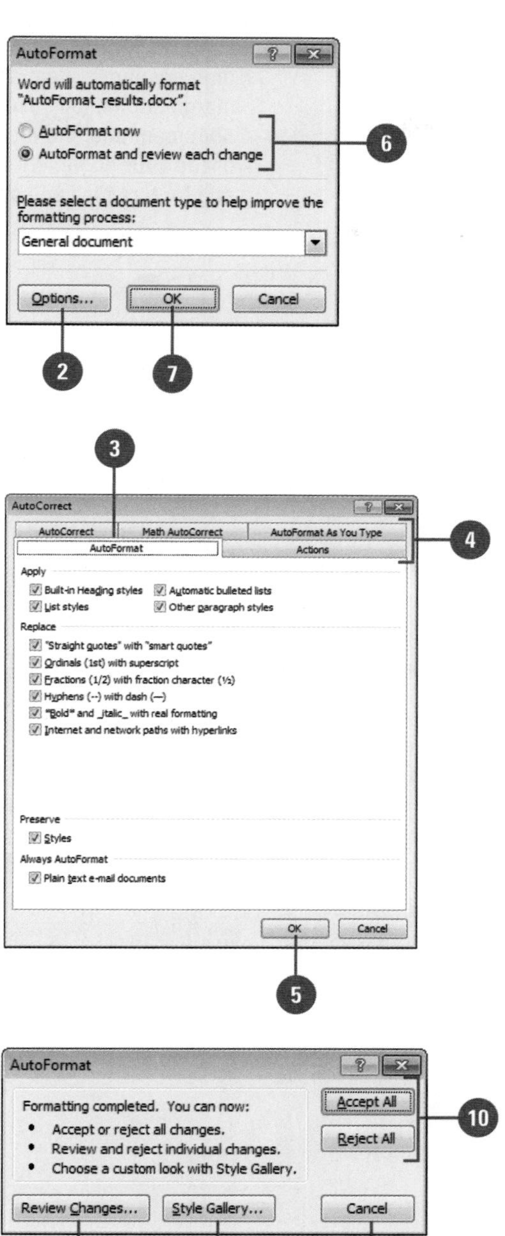

Creating Headers and Footers

Most books, including this one, use headers and footers to help you keep track of where you are. A **header** is text printed in the top margin of every page within a document. **Footer** text is printed in the bottom margin. Commonly used headers and footers contain your name, the document title, the filename, the print date, and page numbers. If you divide your document into sections, you can create different headers and footers for each section.

Create and Edit Headers and Footers

1. Click the **Insert** tab.
2. Click the **Header** or **Footer** button.
3. Click a built-in header or footer, or click **Edit Header** or **Edit Footer** to modify an existing one.

   TIMESAVER *Double-click a header or footer to edit it.*

   The Design tab under Header & Footer Tools displays on the Ribbon.
4. If necessary, click the **Go to Header** or **Go to Footer** button to display the header or footer text area.
5. Click the header or footer box, and then type the text you want. Edit and format header or footer text as usual.
6. To insert common items in a header or footer, click a button (**Date & Time, Quick Parts, Picture,** or **Clip Art**) in the Insert group.
7. When you're done, click the **Close Header and Footer** button.

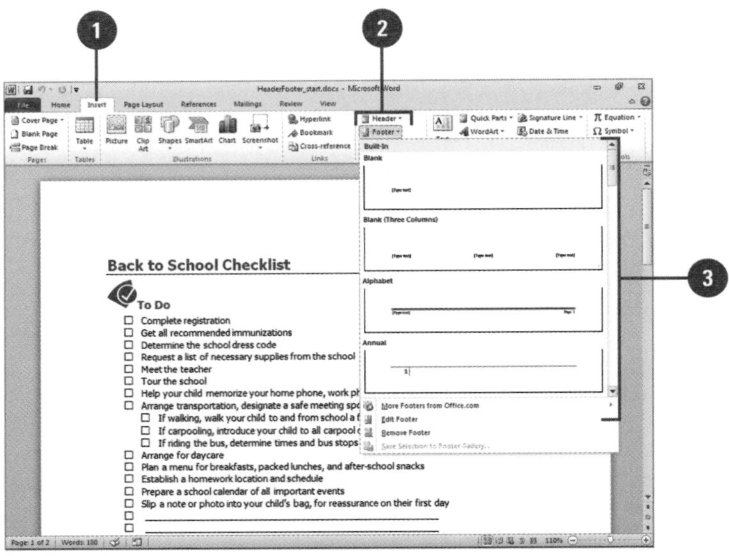

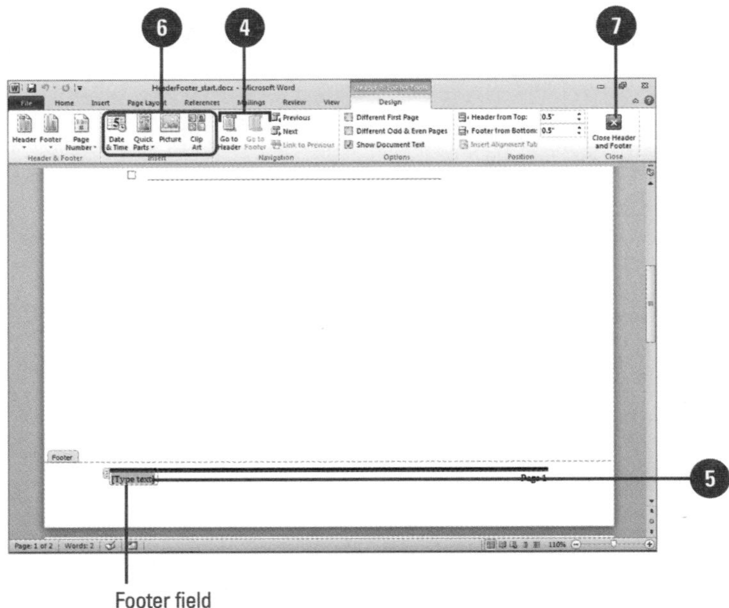

Did You Know?

You can quickly remove a header or footer. Click the Insert tab, click the Header or Footer button, and then click Remove Header or Remove Footer.

Create Different Headers and Footers for Different Pages

1. Click the **Insert** tab.
2. Click the **Header** or **Footer** button.
3. Click a built-in header or footer, or click **Edit Header** or **Edit Footer** to modify an existing one.

   The Design tab under Header & Footer Tools displays on the Ribbon.
4. To create different headers or footers for odd and even pages, click to select the **Different Odd & Even Pages** check box.

   To create a unique header or footer for the document's first page, click to select the **Different First Page** check box.

   To show document text, select the **Show Document Text** check box.
5. When you're done, click the **Close Header and Footer** button.

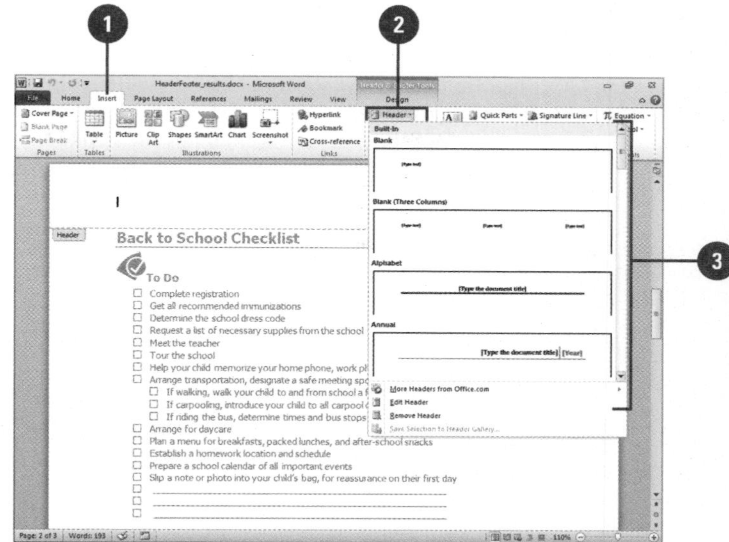

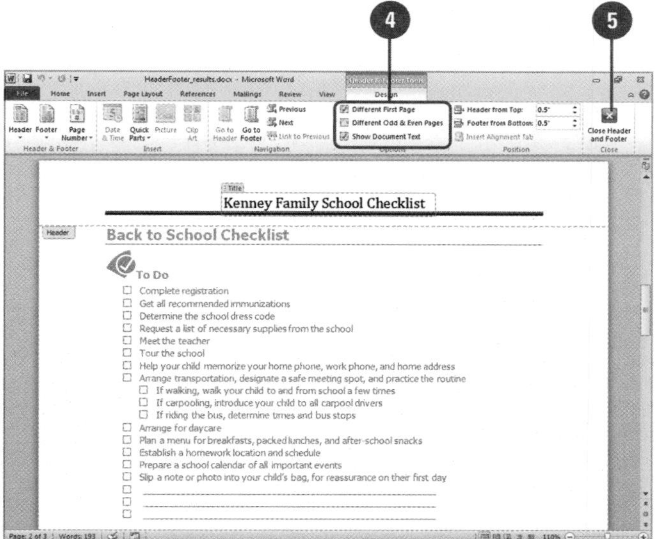

Did You Know?

You can change header and footer position. Double-click the header or footer you want to change, and then adjust the Header from Top or Footers from Bottom settings on the Ribbon.

There are default tab stops used to align header and footer text. Typically, headers and footers have two default tab stops. The first, in the middle, centers text. The second, on the far right, aligns text on the right margin. To left align text, don't press Tab. You can add and move the tab stops as needed. In addition, you can use the alignment buttons on the Home tab.

Inserting Page Numbers and the Date and Time

Page numbers help you keep your document in order or find a topic from the table of contents. Number the entire document consecutively or each section independently; pick a numbering scheme, such as roman numerals or letters. When you insert page numbers, you can select the position and alignment of the numbers on the page. The date and time field ensures you know which printout is the latest. Word uses your computer's internal calendar and clock as its source. You can insert the date and time for any installed language. Add page numbers and the date in a footer to conveniently keep track of your work.

Insert and Format Page Numbers

1. Click the **Insert** tab.
2. Click the **Page Number** button.
3. Point to the position you want (**Top of Page**, **Bottom of Page**, **Page Margins**, or **Current Position**), and then select a position.
4. Click the **Page Number** button, and then click **Format Page Numbers**.
5. Click the **Number format** list arrow, and then select a numbering scheme.
6. Select the starting number.
7. Click **OK**.

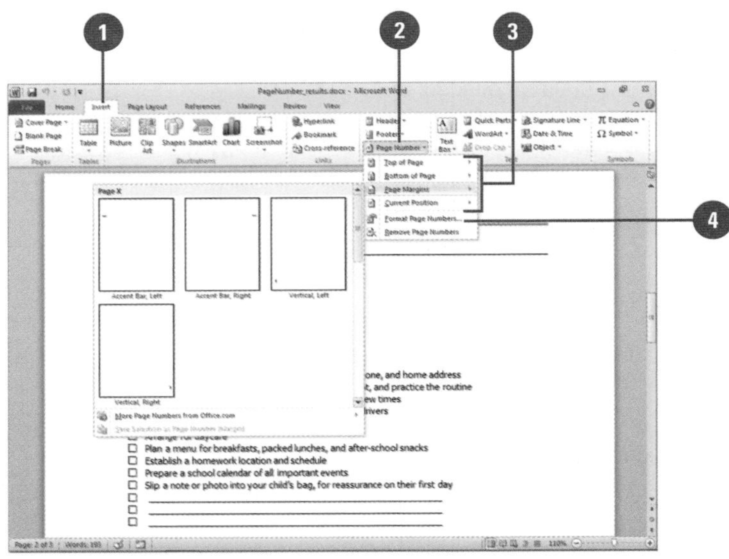

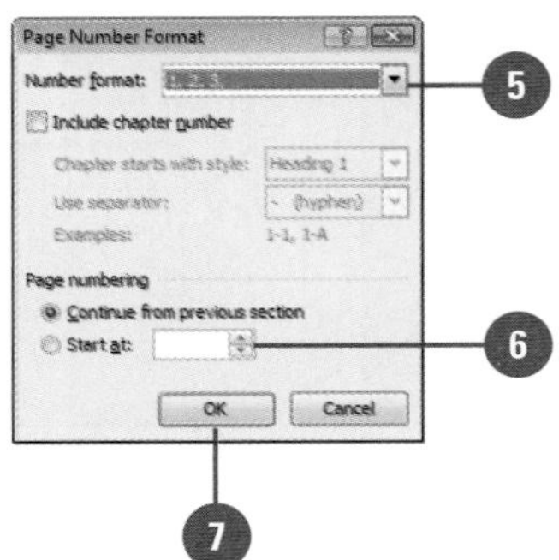

Did You Know?

You can quickly remove page numbers. Click the Insert tab, click the Page Number button, and then click Remove Page Numbers.

Insert the Date or Time

1. To insert the date or time on a single page, display the page, and then click the **Insert** tab.

   - To place the date or time on every page, display or insert a header or footer.

   The Design tab under Header & Footer Tools displays on the Ribbon.

2. Click to place the insertion point where you want to insert the date or time.
3. Click the **Date & Time** button.
4. If necessary, click the **Language** list arrow, and then select a language.
5. To have the date or time automatically update, select the **Update automatically** check box.
6. Click the date and time format you want.
7. To set the current date and time (based on your computer clock) as the default, click **Set as Default**, and then click **Yes**.
8. Click **OK**.

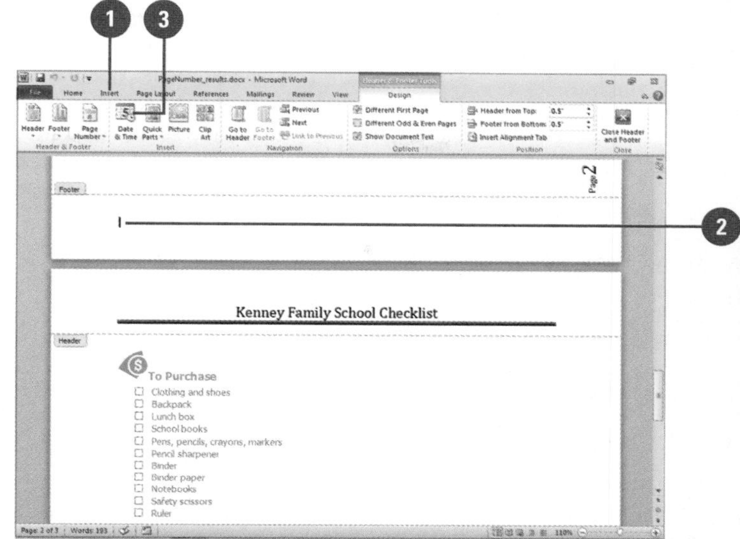

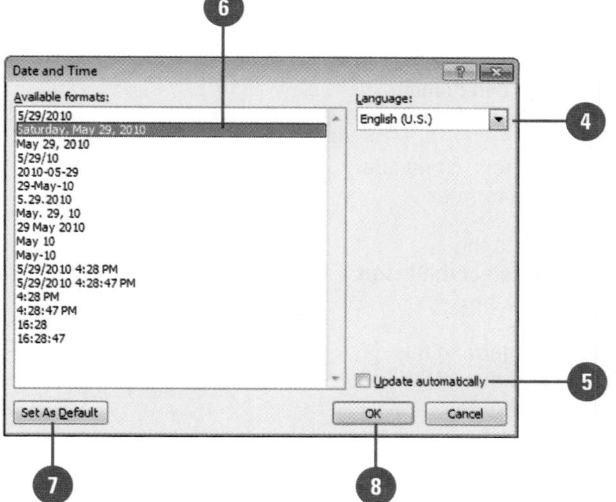

Inserting Cross References

Cross references direct the reader to related information located elsewhere in the document. Cross references can refer to figures or illustrations, sidebars, section headings, even individually marked paragraphs. Without distracting the reader of the document, cross references can be an easy tool to help navigate through a larger document. You can cross-reference only items in the same document. To cross-reference an item in another document, you need to first combine the documents into a master document.

Create a Cross Reference

1. Select the text that starts the cross reference in the document.
2. Click the **References** tab.
3. Click the **Cross-Reference** button.
4. Click the **Reference type** list arrow, and then select the type of item to which you will refer (heading, footnote, bookmark, etc.).
5. Click the **Insert reference to** list arrow, and then select the type of data (page, paragraph number, etc.) that you will be referencing.
6. Click the specific item, by number, to which you want to refer.
7. To let users move to the referenced item, select the **Insert as hyperlink** check box.
8. To include data regarding the relative position of the referenced item, select the **Include above/below** check box.
9. Click **Insert**.
10. Repeat the steps for each additional cross reference that you want to insert into the document, and then click either **Close** or **Cancel**.

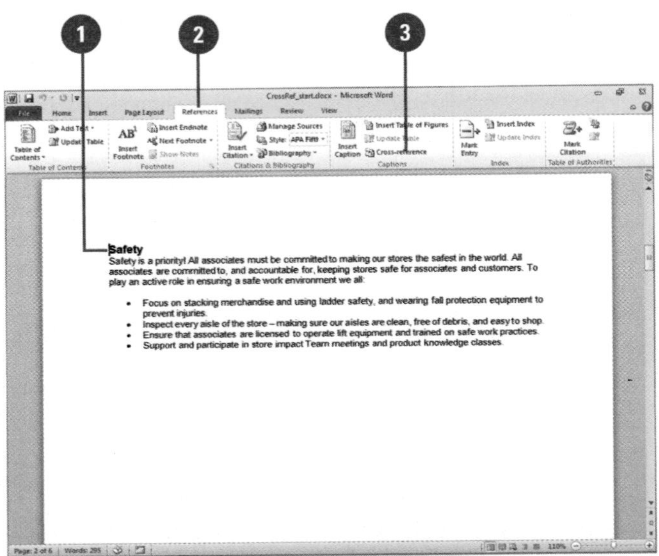

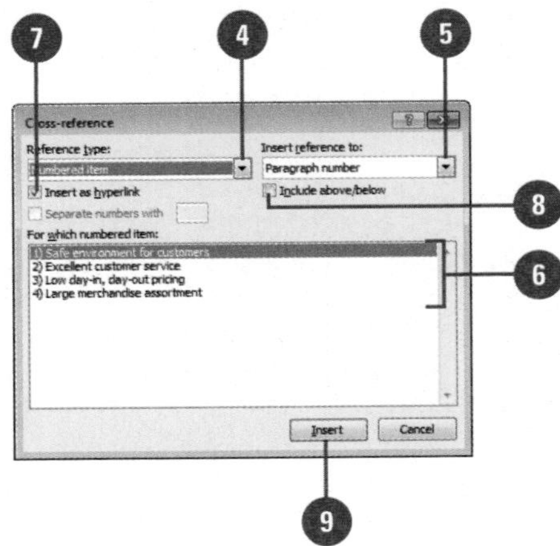

Preparing for a Bound Document

If your finished document will be bound in some fashion, especially if you will use a form of binding such as is found in books, you must allow additional margin space for the binding process; otherwise some of your text can be in the binding fold and therefore unreadable. If you open a book, the crease between the two facing pages is referred to as the gutter. You must take care to ensure that nothing except white space is in the gutter.

Change the Gutter Margin Setting

1. Click the **Page Layout** tab.
2. Click the **Page Setup Dialog Box Launcher**.
3. If necessary, click the **Margins** tab.
4. Enter a value for the gutter margin.
5. Click the **Gutter Position** list arrow, and then click **Left** or **Top** depending on the orientation of your intended binding (Left would be for a normal book, Top would be for a book that flips open from top to bottom).
6. Click **OK**.

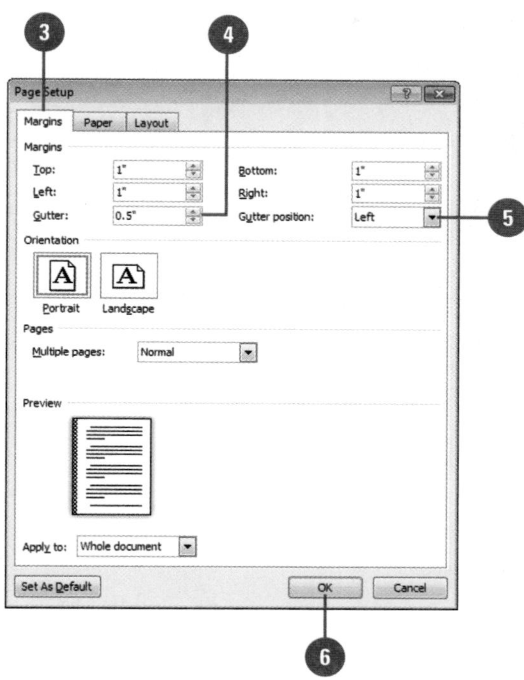

Did You Know?

You can set aside a gutter for printing. The size of the gutter you should use varies greatly depending on the binding process that will be used. Check with your printer before finalizing this setting to ensure that you allow the correct amount of space.

You can use a gutter even if you are printing on both sides. Remember that, if you are using double-sided printing, the gutter will be to the left on odd-numbered pages and to the right on even-numbered pages.

Finding Topics in a Long Document

Instead of searching through pages of text in your document for that certain paragraph, bookmark, tables, footnote or endnote, caption, or other object, you can navigate a lengthy document using the Find and Replace dialog box or the Navigation pane (**New!**). Providing that you have set up your long document with headings, bookmarks, captions, object numbers and the like, you will be able to use those as "clues" in which to locate the specific items you are looking for.

Move to Pages or Document Items Using Go To

1. Click the **Home** tab.
2. Click the **Find** button arrow, and then click **Go To**.
3. Click the type of item to which you want to move to (page, table, etc.).
4. Use one of the following methods:
   - **Specific item.** Type the name or number of the item in the Enter box, and then click **Go To**.
   - **Next or previous item of the same type.** Empty the Enter box, and then click **Next** or **Previous**.
5. Click **Close**.

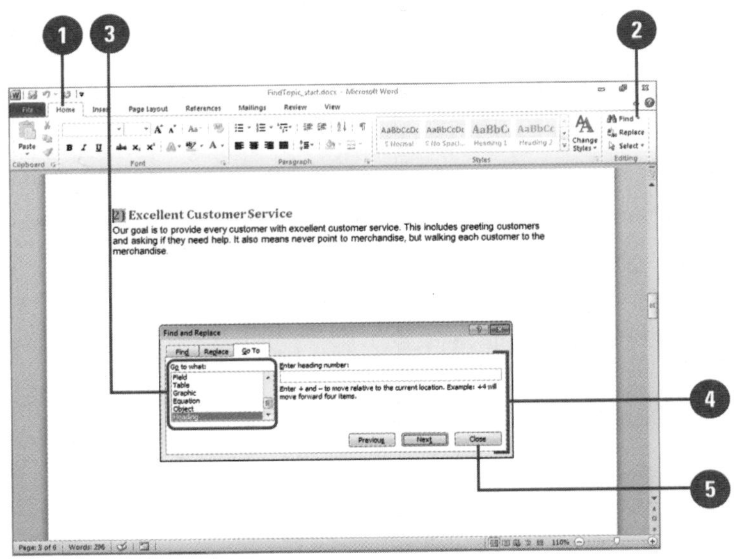

Move to Pages or Document Items Using Navigation Pane

1. Click the **Home** tab.
2. Click the **Find** button.
3. Click the **Browse Headings** or **Browse Pages** tab.
4. Click a heading name or thumbnail of a page to display it.
5. To close the Navigation pane, click the **Close** button on the pane.

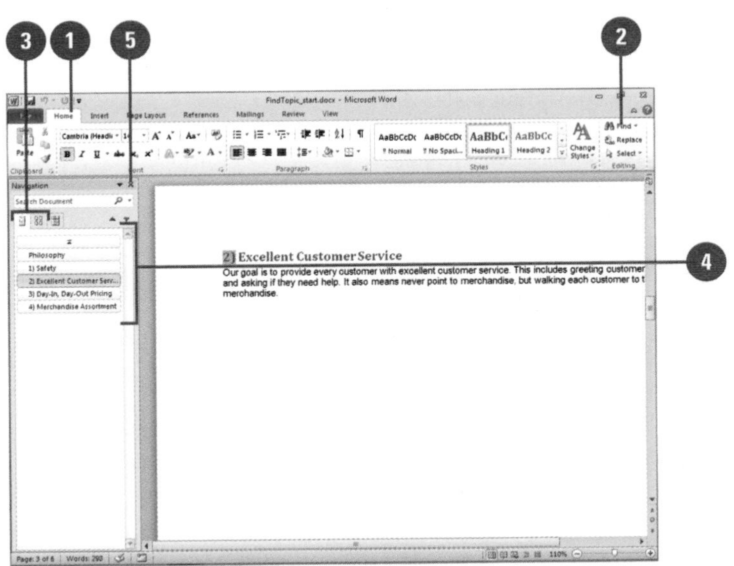

Navigating a Long Document

Word also includes a very unobtrusive, but powerful tool on the vertical scroll bar, the Select Browse Object button. Now that you might be working with a large document and need to navigate through pages of text, multiple graphics and tables, numerous footnotes, reviewer comments and the like, the Select Browse Object button becomes a useful tool. You can navigate through pages easily, instead of relying on all the various commands that are available to locate similar elements of your long document.

Select a Browse Object

1. Click the **Select Browse Object** button on the vertical scroll bar.
2. Click the icon that represents the browse command you want to activate:
   - **By Field**. Click to browse by field.
   - **By Endnote**. Click to browse by endnote.
   - **By Footnote**. Click to browse by footnote.
   - **By Comment**. Click to browse by comment.
   - **By Section**. Click to browse by section.
   - **By Page**. Click to browse by page.
   - **Go To**. Click to go to a specific item.
   - **Find**. Click to find an item.
   - **By Edits**. Click to browse by edits.
   - **By Heading**. Click to browse by heading.
   - **By Graphic**. Click to browse by graphic.
   - **By Table**. Click to browse by table.

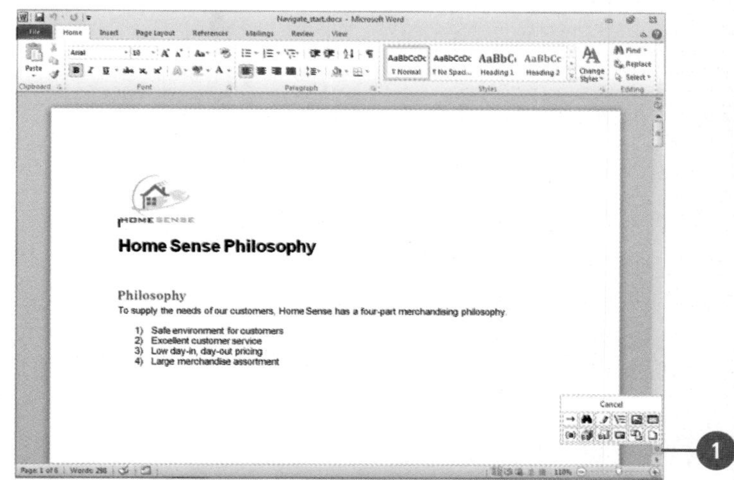

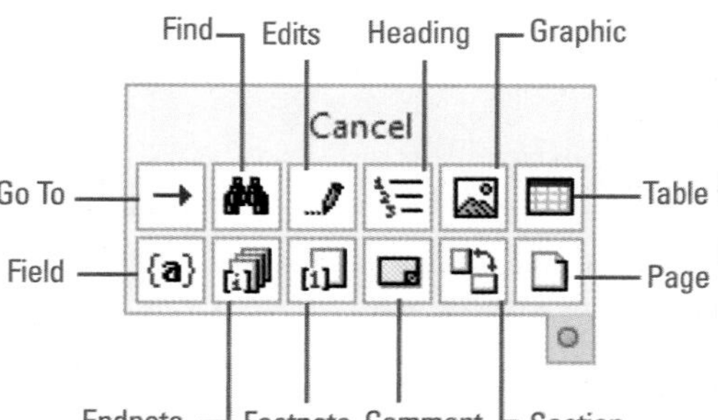

Inserting a Table of Contents

A **table of contents** provides an outline of main topics and page locations. Word builds a table of contents based on the styles in a document that you choose. By default, Heading 1 is the first-level entry, Heading 2 the second level, and so on. In a printed table of contents, a **leader**, a line whose style you select, connects an entry to its page number. In Web documents, entries become hyperlinks. Hide nonprinting characters before creating a table of contents so text doesn't shift to other pages as you print.

Insert a Table of Contents

1. Position the insertion point where you want the table of contents.
2. Click the **References** tab.
3. Click the **Table of Contents** button.
4. Do one of the following:
   - **Add.** Click a Table of Contents style from the gallery.
   - **Remove.** Click **Remove Table of Contents**.
   - **Customize.** Click **Insert Table of Contents**, click the **Table of Contents** tab, select the format, levels, and options you want, and then click **OK**.

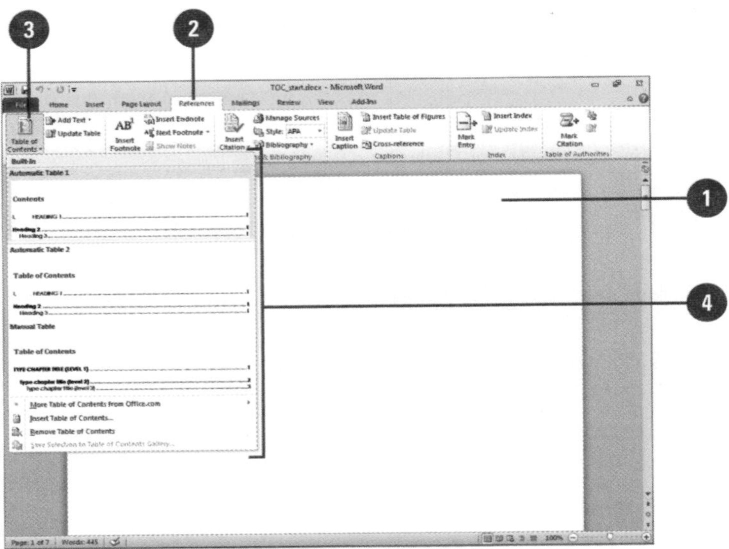

Use to customize a Table of Contents

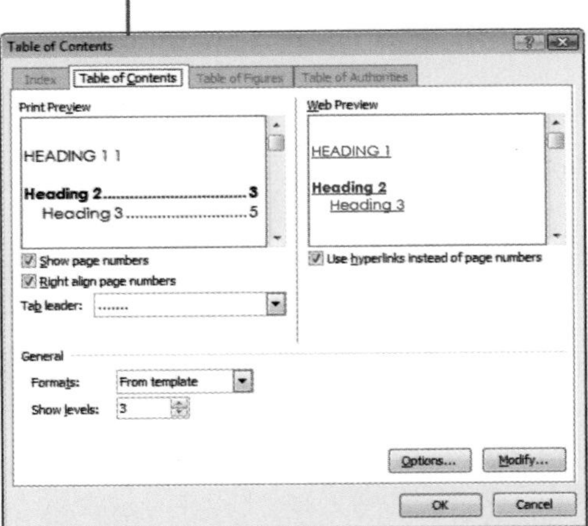

Did You Know?

You can update the table of contents. As you continue to add information to a document, you can quickly update the table of contents. Click the References tab, click Update Table, and then click Update Page Numbers or Update Entire Table. You can also click Update Table on the tab when you select the table of contents.

You can add a specific paragraph to the table of contents. Select the paragraph you want to add, click the References tab, and then click the Add Text button.

Create a Table of Contents Manually

1. Select the text you want to include in your table of contents.
2. Click the **References** tab.
3. Mark entries using heading styles or individual text.
   - **Heading styles.** Click the heading style you want in the Styles group on the Home tab.
   - **Individual text.** Click the **Add Text** button, and then click the table of contents level you want: **Level 1**, **Level 2**, or **Level 3**.
4. To mark additional entries, select the text, use the options in Step 3.
5. Click the place where you want to insert the table of contents.
6. Click the **Table of Contents** button, and then click **Insert Table of Contents**.
7. Click **Options**.
8. Select the **Styles** check box.
9. Specify the TOC levels you want to use.
10. Click **OK**.
11. Select the formatting options you want.
12. Click **OK**.

Did You Know?

You can delete a table of contents. Click the References tab, click Table of Contents, and then click Remove Table of Contents.

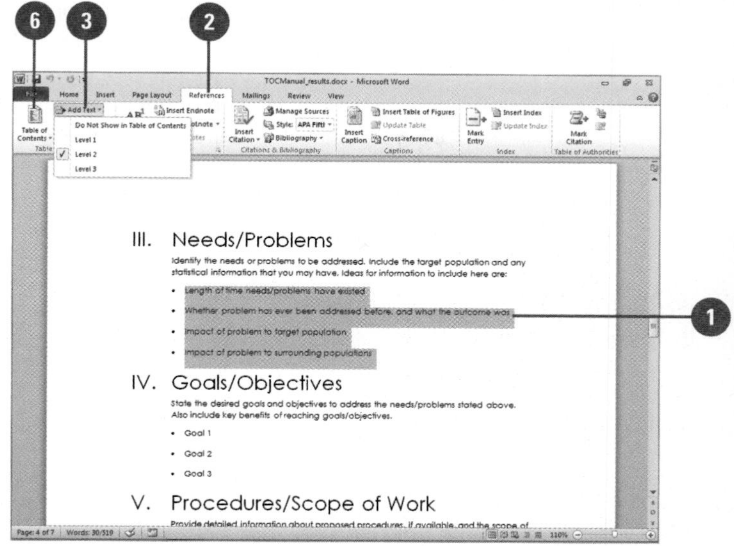

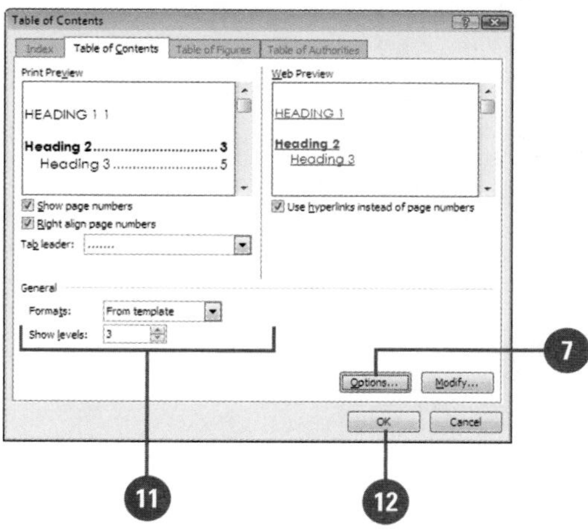

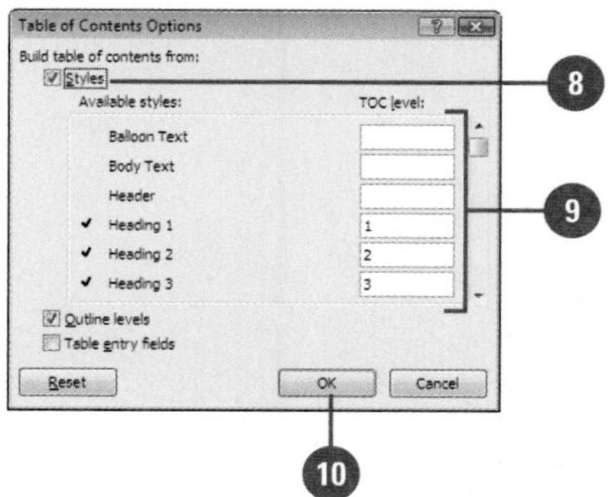

Creating an Index

An index appears at the end of a document and alphabetically lists the main topics, names, and items used in a long document. Each index listing is called an entry. You can create an index entry for a word, phrase, or symbol for a topic. In an index, a cross-reference indicates another index entry that is related to the current entry. There are several ways to create an index. Begin by marking index entries. Some index entries will refer to blocks of text that span multiple pages within a document.

Create an Index

1. Click the **References** tab.
2. To use existing text as an index entry, select the text. To enter your text as an index entry, click at the point where you want the index entry inserted.
3. Click the **Mark Entry** button or press Alt+Shift+X.
4. Type or edit the entry. The entry can be customized by creating a sub-entry or a cross-reference to another entry.
5. To format the text for the index, right-click it in the Main Entry or Sub-entry box, click **Font**, select your formatting options, and then click **OK**.
6. To select a format for the page numbers that will appear in the index, select the **Bold** or **Italic** check boxes.
7. To mark the index entry, click **Mark** or **Mark All** for all similar text.

   Repeat steps 2-7 for additional index entries, and then click **Close**.
8. Go to the page where you want to display your Index.
9. Click the **Insert Index** button.
10. Click the **Index** tab, and then select any options you want.
11. Click **OK**.

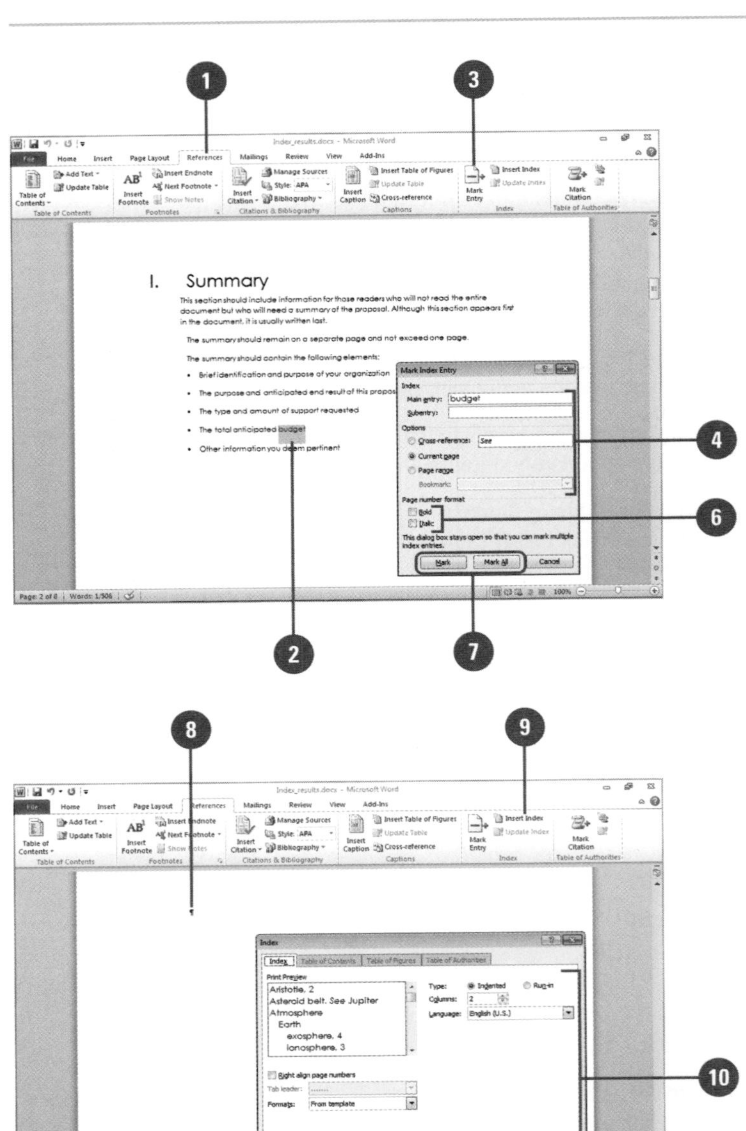

Create Multiple Page Index Entries

1. Click the **Insert** tab.
2. Select the text in which you want the index entry to refer.
3. Click the **Bookmark** button.
4. Enter a name, and then click **Add**.
5. Click after the end of the text in the document that you just marked with a bookmark.
6. Click the **References** tab.
7. Click the **Mark Entry** button or press Alt+Shift+X.
8. Enter the index entry for the marked text.
9. To format the text for the index, right-click the Main Entry or Sub-entry box, click **Font**, select your formatting options, and then click **OK**.
10. To select a format for the page numbers that will appear in the index, select the **Bold** or **Italic** check boxes.
11. Click the **Page Range** option.
12. Select the bookmark name you entered in Step 4.
13. Click **Mark**.
14. Repeat steps 2-13 for additional index entries, and then click **Close** or **Cancel**.

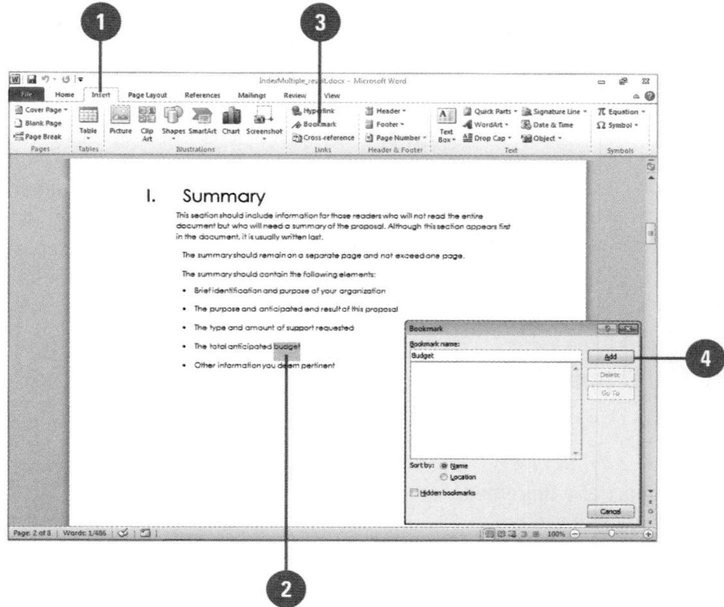

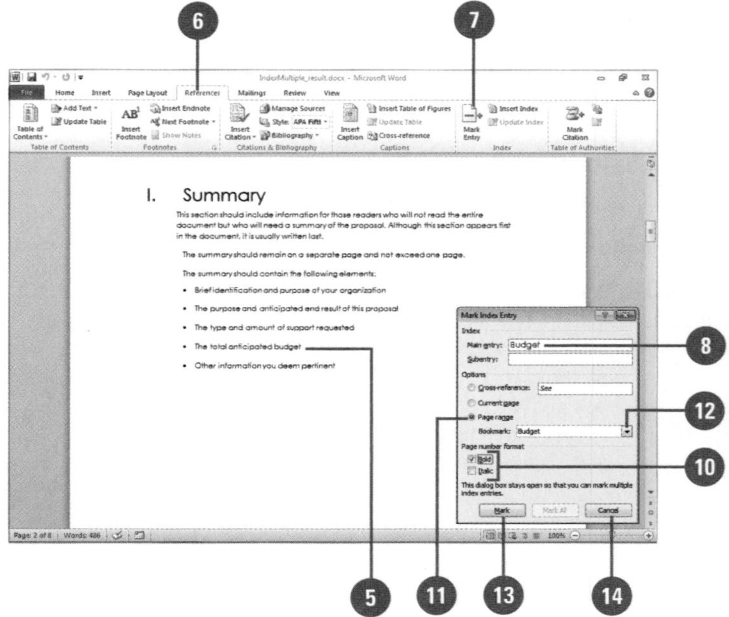

Determining Word Count Statistics

Producing lengthy documents for business, school or as contract work can often be regulated by the word count. Legal briefs may charge by the line or word, or school papers might need to be a certain length in word count. Either way, if you need to determine your word count, there is an easier way than counting each word manually. You can quickly determine the number of words in your document by viewing the Status bar. It appears in the lower-left corner next to the number of pages in your document. You can also use the Word Count button on the Review tab to find out word count statistics, including number of pages, characters, paragraphs, and lines. You have the choice whether to include or exclude text boxes, footnotes, and endnotes in the word count statistics.

Find Out Document Word Count Statistics

1. If you want to find out statistics for only part of a document, select the text you want to count.
2. Click the **Review** tab.
3. Click the **Word Count** button.
4. Select or clear the **Include textboxes, footnotes and endnotes** check box.
5. Click **Close**.

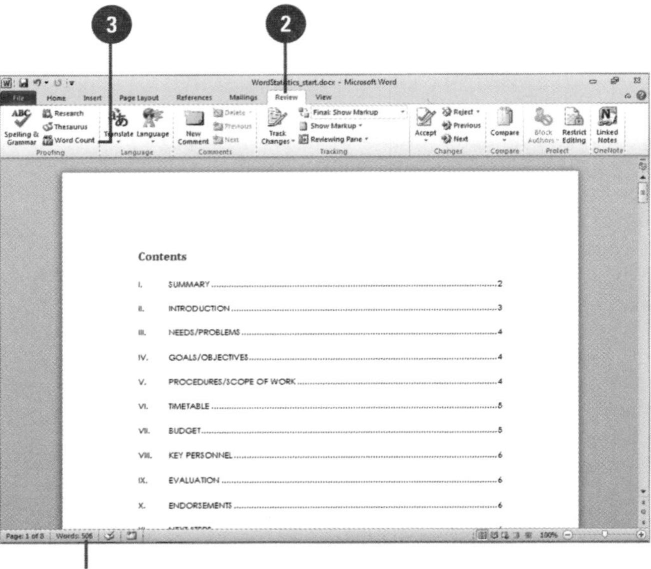

Word count

Word Count

Statistics:

Pages	8
Words	506
Characters (no spaces)	2,635
Characters (with spaces)	3,085
Paragraphs	75
Lines	120

Include textboxes, footnotes and endnotes

Close

4 5

Did You Know?

You can count words in a text box. Select the text in the text box. The Status bar displays the number of words. To count the words in multiple text boxes, press and hold Ctrl while you select the text in each text box.

Adding a Cover Page

A cover page provides an introduction to a report, or an important memo you want to circulate to others. Word makes it easy to add a cover page to any document. You can quickly select one from a gallery of styles that fit your document. If you can't find the cover page you need, check out Office.com (**New!**). Each cover page includes text boxes sample text, which you can change, and defined fields, such as a title and author's name, that automatically get filled in with information from document properties.

Insert a Cover Page

1. Click the **Insert** tab.
2. Click the **Cover Page** button to display a gallery of cover pages.
3. Click the cover page you want.
   - **Add from Office.com.** Click **More Cover Pages from Office.com** (**New!**).

   Word inserts a cover at the beginning of your document.
4. To remove a cover page, click the **Cover Page** button, and then click **Remove Current Cover Page**.

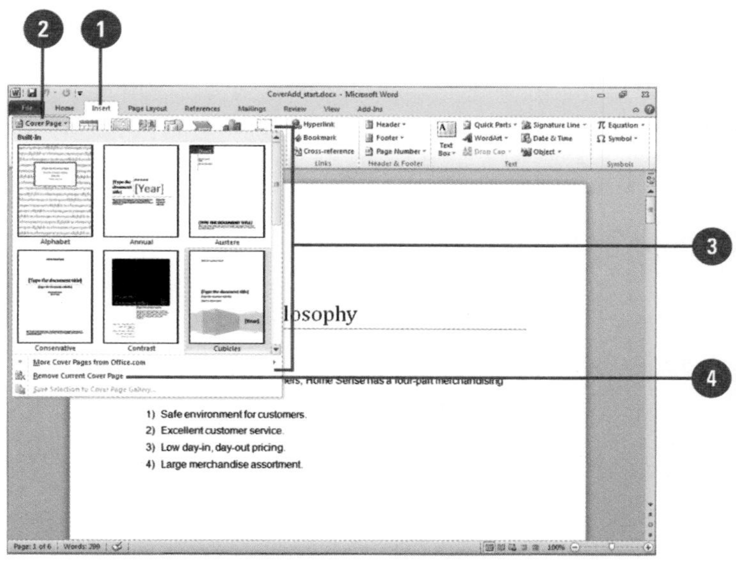

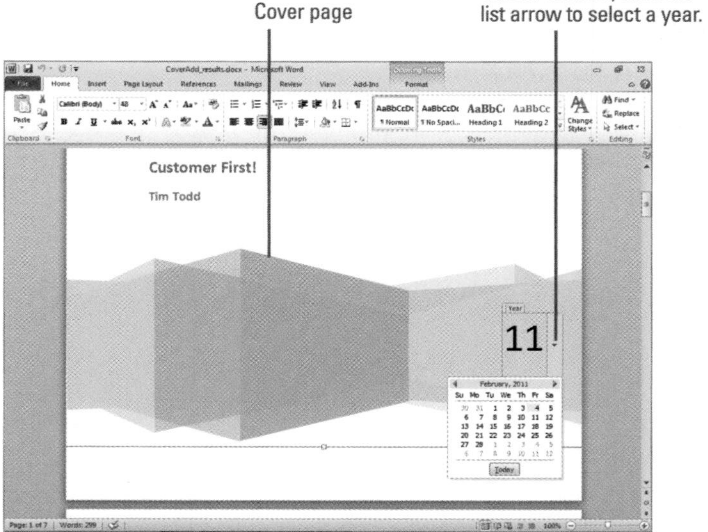

Did You Know?

You can add a custom cover page to the Cover Page gallery. Create the cover page you want to add, select it, click the Insert tab, click the Cover Page button, click Save Selection To Cover Page Gallery, enter a name, select the Cover Pages gallery if necessary, select a category, enter a description, leave remaining options, and then click OK.

Working with Technical Documents

9

Introduction

Microsoft Word has many additional features that help you develop a more technical document. Research papers, business proposals and the like, all require more than just a document with some graphics or special text formatting.

You can find research material and incorporate it into your work quickly and easily. You can access informational services and insert the material right into your document without leaving Word. Material such as dictionaries, thesauruses, research sites, language translations, stock quotes, and company information are all at your finger tips.

With all of this research, it might be necessary to create footnotes or endnotes to reference your sources. You can format the notes to be similar in text to your document, or have an entirely different look. When working with a lot of text, you can create a bookmark to help you jump to various topics in your document.

Creating captions for your graphics is easy with Word. Once you've created captions, you can create a Table of Figures—similar to a Table of Contents, but this item keeps track of your graphics. You can format text in your document to have number lines. This is helpful if you need to locate a specific section of text—such as a legal briefing—in a long document. You can also create an outline in Word to help organize your document.

Some more technical features such as summing up the values in your tables and calculating values, are done with the help of Word's Formula feature. You can also document an equation for that scientific or mathematical paper.

What You'll Do

Insert Building Blocks Using Quick Parts

Insert and Create AutoText

Insert Research Material

Create Footnotes or Endnotes

Modify Footnotes or Endnotes

Format Footnotes or Endnotes

Create a Bibliography

Create a Bookmark

Create Captions

Create a Table of Figures

Number Lines

Create an Equation

Insert Symbols

Inserting Building Blocks Using Quick Parts

A **Quick Part** is a defined field or set of fields that contains information you can use throughout a document. Word calls these building blocks. Instead of typing the company name, address and phone number every time you need it in a document, you can insert a text box field with the information. Word provides a variety of defined Quick Parts—including Author, Company, Company Address, Company E-mail, Manager and Status—you can quickly insert in a document. The Quick Part fields insert information you provide in Document Properties or a placeholder, which you can fill in the first time. If a predefined field doesn't meet your needs, you can create your own or get more on Office.com. If you need to modify a Quick Part, you can use the building block organizer, which stores your custom Quick Parts and those provided by Word. Word uses Quick Parts as part of the program to build page covers, headers and footers, pull quotes, and side bar to name a few.

Insert a Quick Part Building Block

1. Click where you want to insert a text box.
2. Click the **Insert** tab.
3. Click the **Quick Parts** button.
4. Point to **Document Property**, and then click the predefined Quick Part you want to insert.
5. Modify the predefined Quick Part; click the list arrow (if available) to define it.

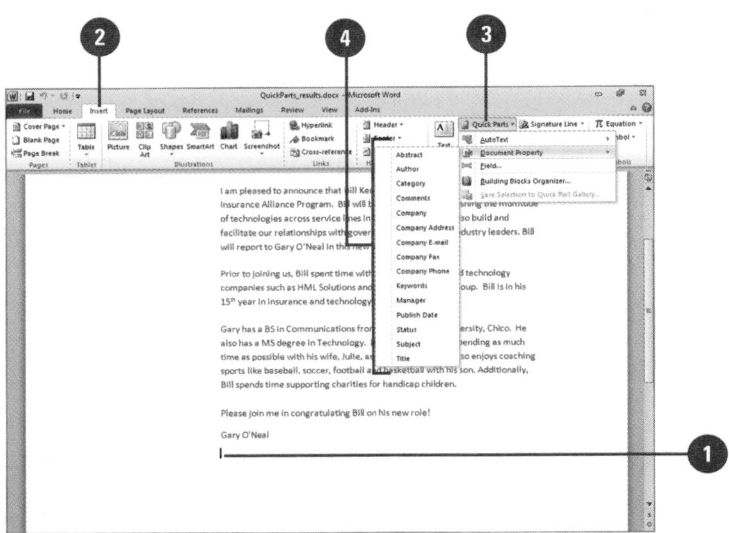

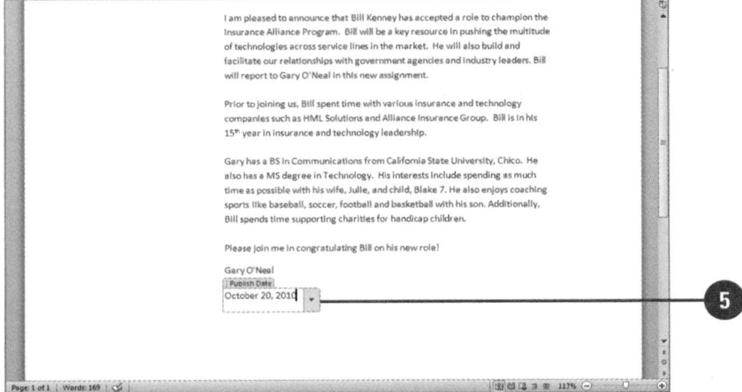

Did You Know?

You can create your own Quick Part. Select the text box you want to use, click the Insert tab, click the Quick Parts button, and then click Save Selection To Quick Parts Gallery.

Create a Quick Part Field

1. Click the **Insert** tab.
2. Click the **Quick Parts** button, and then click **Field**.
3. Click the **Categories** list arrow, and then click a category to narrow down the field names.
4. Click the field name you want to use.
5. Specify field property information.
6. Click the format you want to apply.
7. Click **OK**.

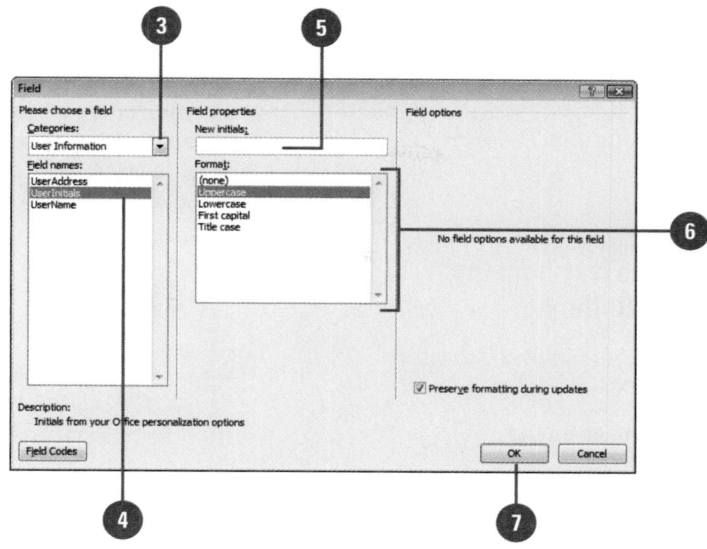

Work with Building Blocks

1. Click the **Insert** tab.
2. Click the **Quick Parts** button, and then click **Building Blocks Organizer**.
3. Select the Quick Part building block you want to modify.
4. Click **Edit Properties**.
5. Specify the properties you want to change, including Name, Gallery, Category, Description, Save in, and Options.
6. Click **OK**.
7. To insert or delete a building block, select it, and then click **Insert** or **Delete**.
8. Click **Close**.

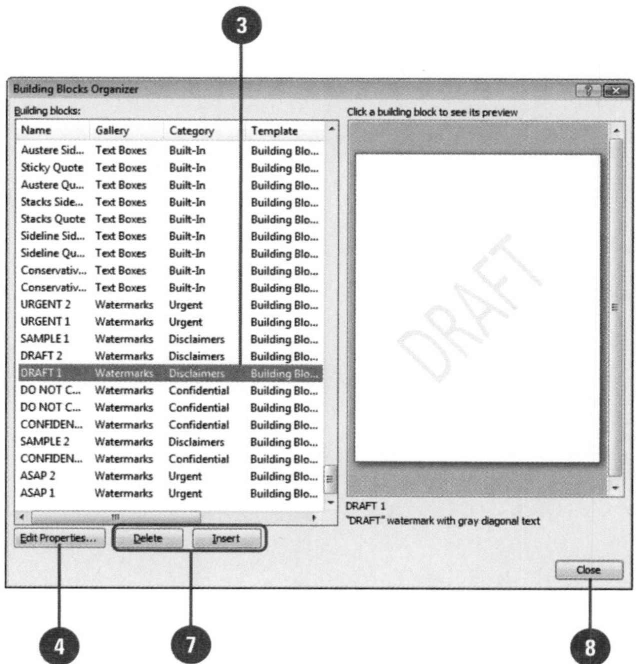

Inserting and Creating AutoText

AutoText stores text and graphics you want to reuse, such as a company logo, boilerplate text, or formatted table. For example, you can use AutoText to quickly insert the text To Whom It May Concern or a graphic of your signature. You can use the AutoText entries that come with Word, or create your own. AutoText is part of Word's building block approach to creating customized documents. Word calls these building blocks. To insert AutoText, you use the Quick Parts button (**New!**) and then AutoText menu.

Insert AutoText from the AutoText Gallery

1. Click where you want to insert AutoText.
2. Click the **Insert** tab.
3. Click the **Quick Parts** button, and then point to **AutoText**.
4. Click the AutoText entry you want from the AutoText gallery.

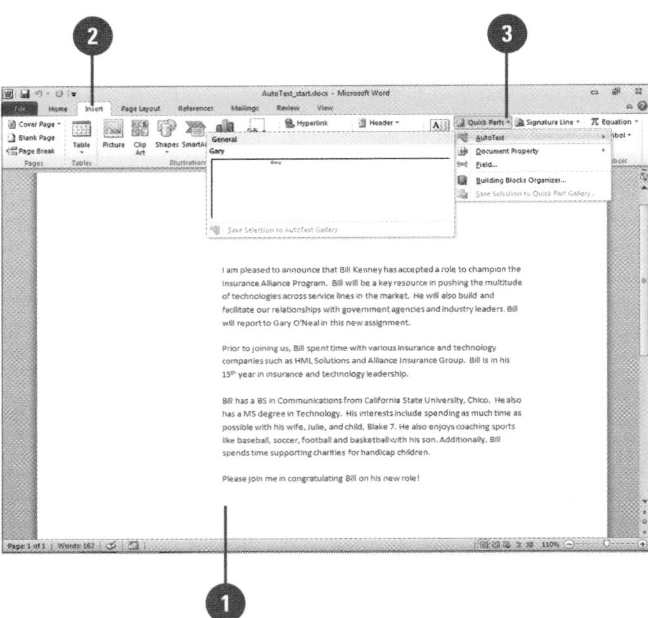

Create AutoText

1. Select the text or graphic in which you want to create an AutoText entry.
2. Click the **Insert** tab.
3. Click the **Quick Parts** button, and then point to **AutoText**.
4. Click **Save Selection to AutoText Gallery**.

   The Create New Building Block dialog box opens.
5. Type an AutoText name, or use the suggested one.
6. Click **OK**.

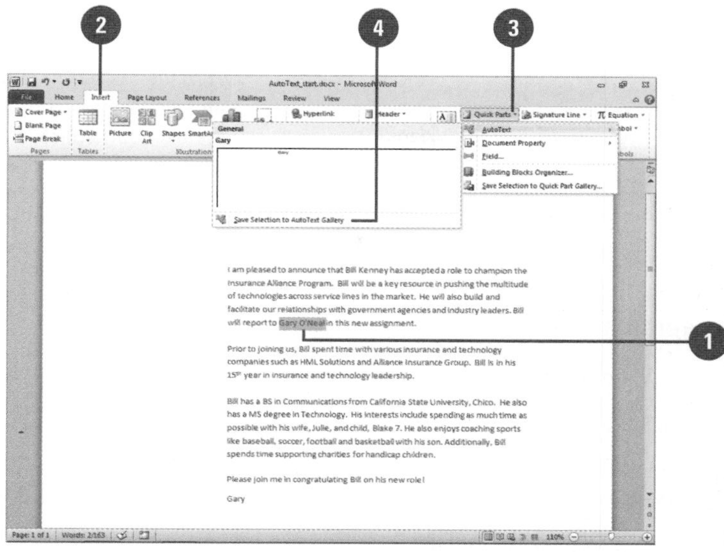

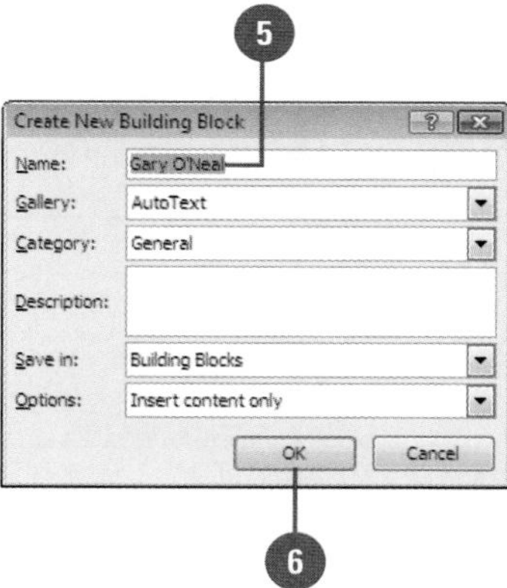

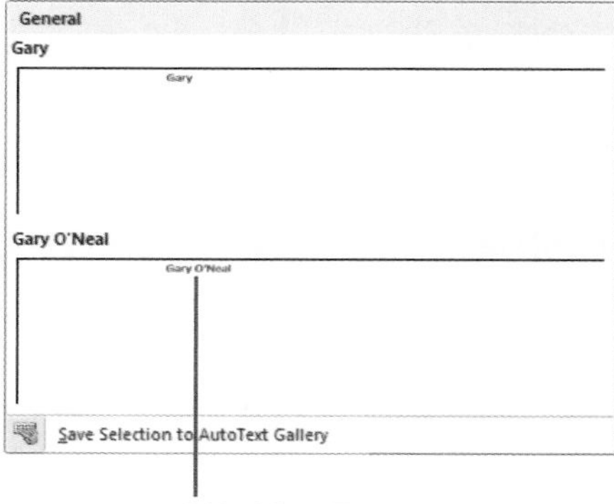

Did You Know?

You can delete an AutoText entry. Click the Insert tab, click the Quick Parts button, point to AutoText, right-click the entry you want to delete, click Organize And Delete, click Delete, click Yes, and then click Close.

Inserting Research Material

With the Research task pane, you can access data sources and insert research material right into your text without leaving Word. The Research task pane can help you access electronic dictionaries, thesauruses, research sites, and proprietary company information. You can select one reference source or search in all reference books. This research pane allows you to find information and quickly and easily incorporate it into your work. If you have a hard time finding research information on a specific topic, you can use the Research Options command to enable and update additional reference books and research Web sites from which to search.

Research a Topic

1. Click the **Review** tab.
2. Click the **Research** button.
3. Type the topic you would like to research.
4. Click the list arrow, and then select a reference source, or click **All Reference Books**.
5. Click the **Start Searching** button (green arrow).
6. Select the information in the task pane that you want to copy.

   To search for more information, click one of the words in the list or click a link to an online site.
7. Select the information you want, and then copy it.

   In the Research task pane, you can point to the item you want, click the list arrow, or right-click selected text, and then click **Copy**.
8. Paste the information into your document.
9. When you're done, click the **Close** button on the task pane.

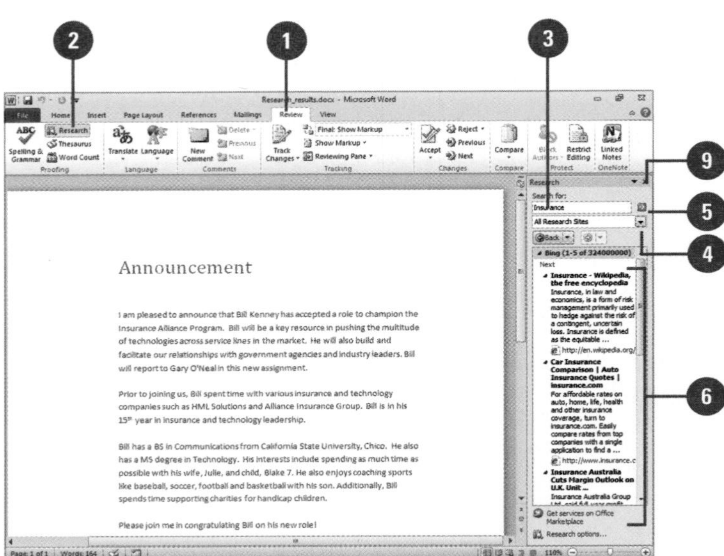

Change Research Options

1. Click the **Review** tab.
2. Click the **Research** button.
3. In the task pane, click **Research Options**.
   - You can also click Research Options in the Privacy Option pane of the Trust Center.
4. Do one or more of the following:
   - **Services.** To activate or remove research services.
   - **Add Services.** To add research services.
   - **Update/Remove.** To update or remove a service provider.
   - **Parental Control.** To turn on parental controls.
5. Click **OK**.
6. When you're done, click the **Close** button on the task pane.

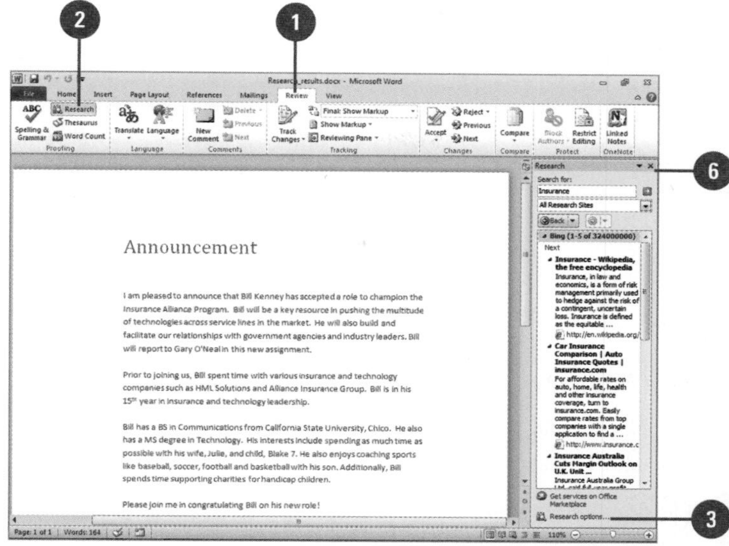

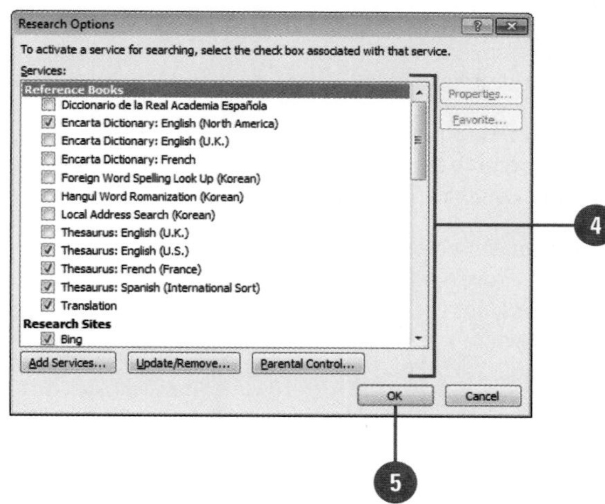

Creating Footnotes or Endnotes

Footnotes are used to provide additional information that is inappropriate for the body of the text, and to document your references for information or quotes presented in the body of the document. Footnotes are appropriate for academic, scientific, and occasionally business purposes. Footnotes appear at the bottom of the page on which the information is cited, and Word automatically inserts a reference mark at the insertion point to associate the information presented with the note at the bottom of the page. Creating and manipulating endnotes is identical to performing the same functions for footnotes. Endnotes differ from footnotes in that they appear at the end of the document or section (in the case of longer documents), not the bottom of the page on which the reference mark appears.

Create a Footnote or Endnote

1. Position the insertion point where you want to insert a footnote.
2. Click the **References** tab.
3. To quickly create a footnote or endnote, click the **Insert Footnote** or **Insert Endnote** button, and then enter footnote or endnote text.
4. To create a customized footnote or endnote, click the **Footnote & Endnote Dialog Box Launcher**.
5. Click the **Footnotes** or **Endnotes** option, click the list arrow next to the option, and then select the location where you want to place the footnote or endnote.
6. Verify that the Number Format option of 1,2,3... is selected.
7. Click **Insert** to insert a reference mark in the text. Word moves the insertion point to the bottom of the page corresponding to the number of the reference mark.
8. Type the text of your footnote or endnote.
9. Click the **Show Notes** button and the **Next Footnote** button to show/hide notes and locate them.
10. Click in the document to continue with your work.

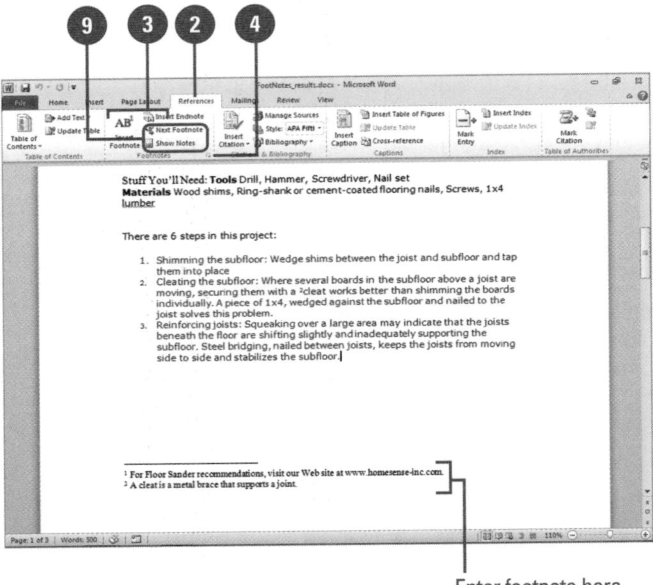

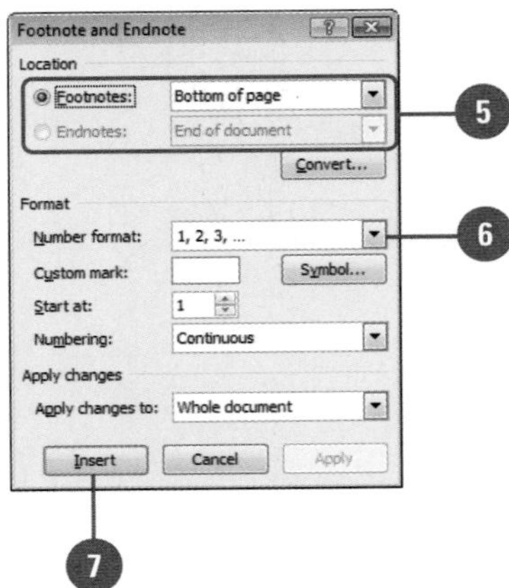

Modifying Footnotes or Endnotes

Editing the actual text of a footnote or endnote is just like editing any text, except that you must first access the note. Use the Show Notes button to display all the notes, click to position your insertion point at the bottom of the page or in the Notes pane, and then edit. As you change other text in a document, Word repositions your notes. When your edits affect sentences with notes, or when you move, copy, or delete notes in your document, Word renumbers the other notes for you. When you move, copy, or delete a note, you work with the note reference mark in the document, not the text in the Notes pane. You can move, copy, or delete a note in the same way you would text in a document.

Edit a Footnote or Endnote

1. To quickly view a footnote or endnote, point to the reference mark to display a ScreenTip with the contents of the note.
2. To go to a note, double-click the reference mark in the document.
   - In Draft view, the Notes pane opens.
3. Click to place the insertion point in the Notes pane or at the bottom of the page where you want to edit the note text, and then edit the note text as if you were editing text in the document.
4. If necessary, click the **Close** button on the Notes pane.
5. To move or copy a note, select the reference mark, click the **Cut** or **Copy** button on the Home tab, click to place the insertion point, and then click the **Paste** button.

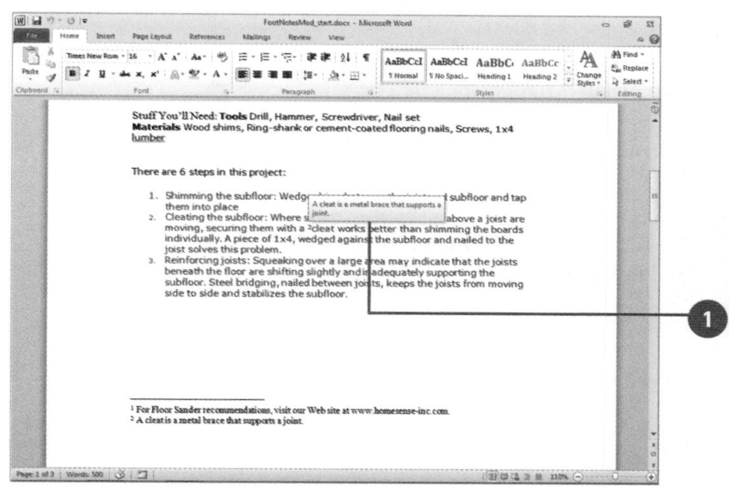

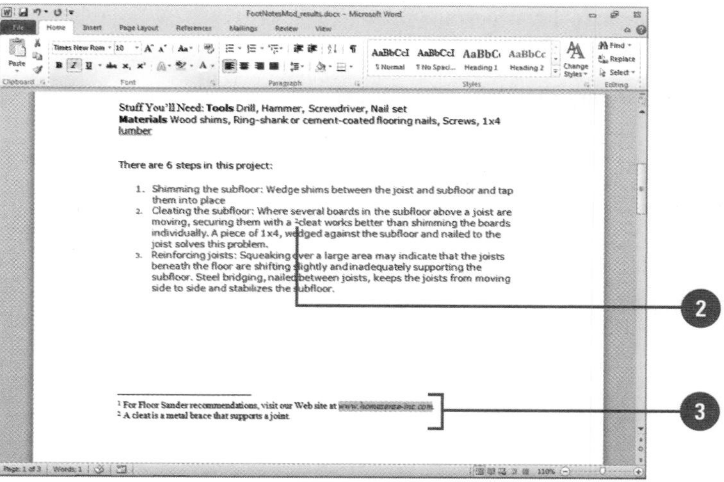

Did You Know?

You can delete a footnote or endnote. Select the reference mark for the footnote or endnote you want to delete, and then press Delete.

Formatting Footnotes or Endnotes

Footnote or endnote reference marks appear as 1,2,3... by default. Word provides you with various options in order to customize the reference marks the way you wish. If you'd like to change your footnotes or endnotes to be a,b,c or Roman numerals i, ii, iii, you can do that through the Insert menu. You can format the location of the footnote or endnote to be at the bottom of the text, or at the bottom of the page. You can also have Word renumber your footnotes or endnotes after each section of your document, and change the font and other formatting for a reference mark. You format a footnote or endnote reference mark in the same way you format any other text in a document.

Change a Footnote or Endnote Format

1. Click to place the insertion point in the section in which you want to change the footnote or endnote format.
2. Click the **References** tab.
3. Click the **Footnote & Endnote Dialog Box Launcher**.
4. Click the **Number Format** list arrow, and then click the format you want.
5. To change the starting point, click the Start at **Up** or **Down** arrows.
6. If necessary, click the **Apply changes to** list arrow, and then click **Whole Document**.
7. Click **Apply**, and then click **Cancel**.

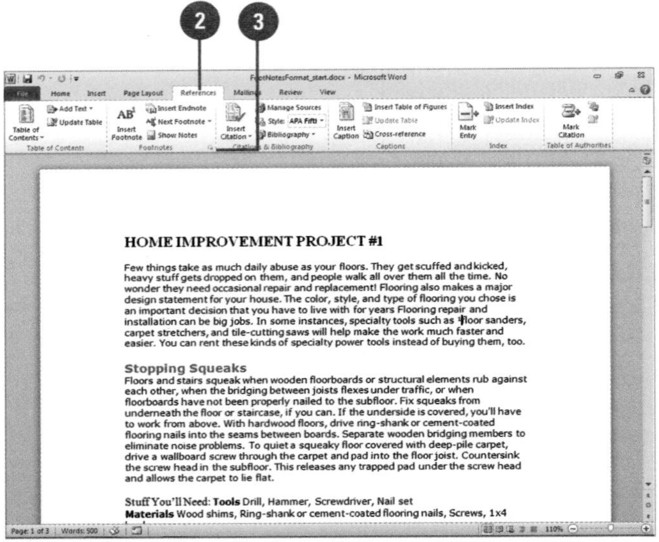

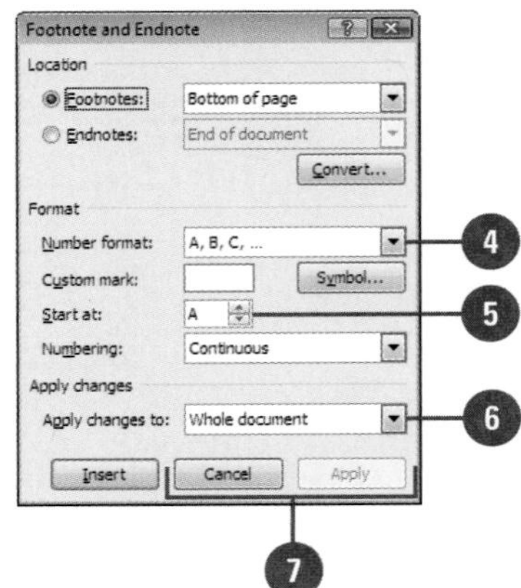

Format Footnotes or Endnotes in a Document

1. In the body text, select the footnote or endnote reference mark.
2. Click the **Home** tab.
3. Use the formatting buttons on the **Home** tab or click the **Font Dialog Box Launcher** to format the reference marks the way you want.

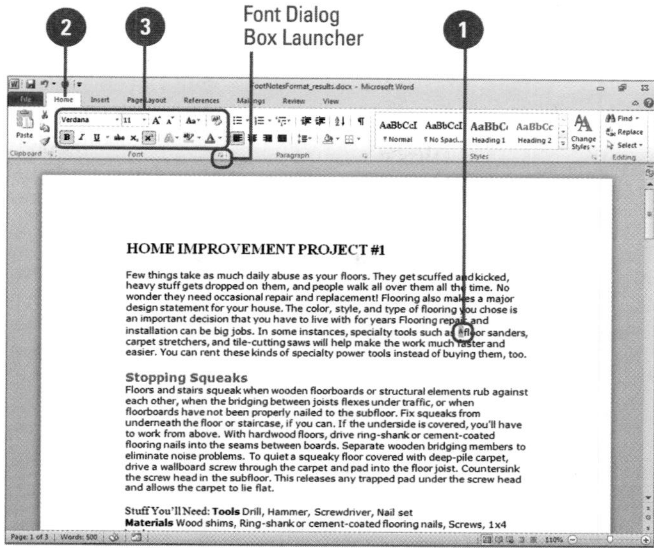

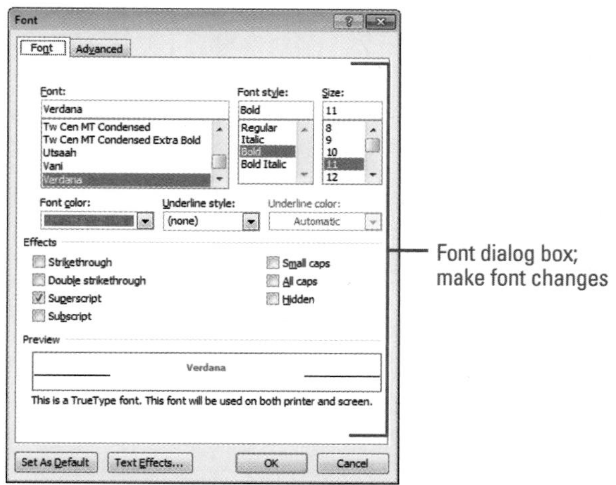

Did You Know?

You can create a footnote or endnote continuation notice when a note is too long. Click the Draft View button on the Status bar, click the References tab, and then click the Show Notes button. If necessary, click the View Footnote Area or View Endnote Area option, and then click OK. In the Notes pane, click the list arrow, click Footnote Continuation Notice or Endnote Continuation Notice, and then type the text you want to use for the notice.

You can convert one or more notes to footnotes or endnotes. Click the Draft View button on the Status bar, and then click the Show Notes button. If necessary, click View Footnote Area or View Endnote Area option, and then click OK. Select the number of the note or notes you want to convert, right-click it, and then click Convert To Footnote or Convert To Endnote. To convert all notes to footnotes or endnotes, click the Footnote & Endnote Dialog Box Launcher, click Convert, click the option you want, click OK, and then click Close.

Creating a Bibliography

A **bibliography** is a list of sources that you cited during the research of a project. A bibliography typically appears at the end of a document and provides information about the source of your research. When you create a bibliography, you can choose a standard style, which is widely accepted by universities and businesses. So, all you need to do is create a citation and enter the source information. If you're not sure what source you want to use, you can insert a placeholder and fill in the source information later. After you finish adding sources to a document, you can use the Manage Source dialog box to choose which ones you want to use before you create the bibliography.

Add a Citation and Source to a Document

1. Click the **References** tab.
2. Click the **Style** list arrow, and then click the style you want.

   If you're not sure, ask your professor or a business associate, or search the Internet.
3. Click to place the insertion point where you want to place the citation.
4. Click the **Insert Citation** button, and then click **Add New Source**.
   - To add new placeholder to fill in the source information later, click **Add new placeholder**, type a placeholder name, and then click **OK**.
5. Click the **Type of Source** list arrow, and then select a source type.
6. Enter the bibliography information for the source.
7. Click **OK**.

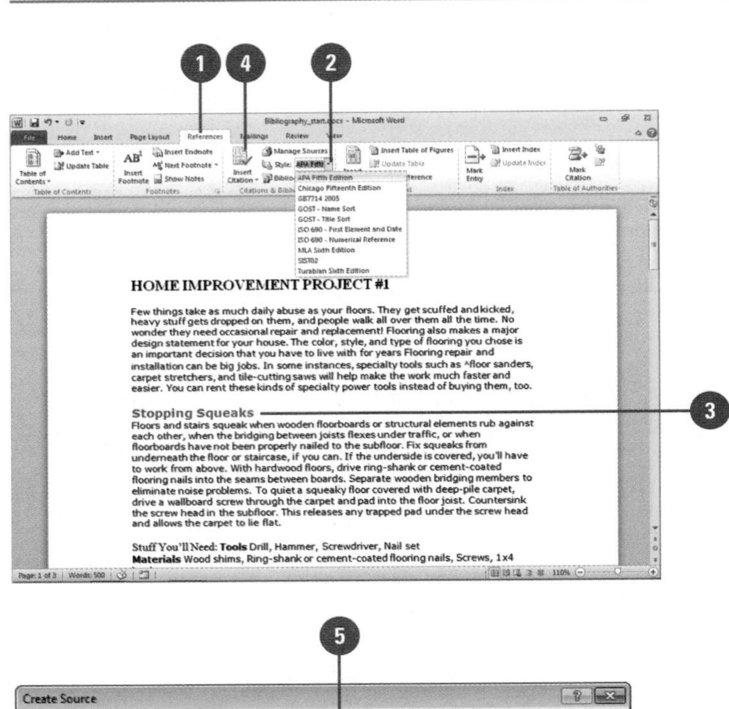

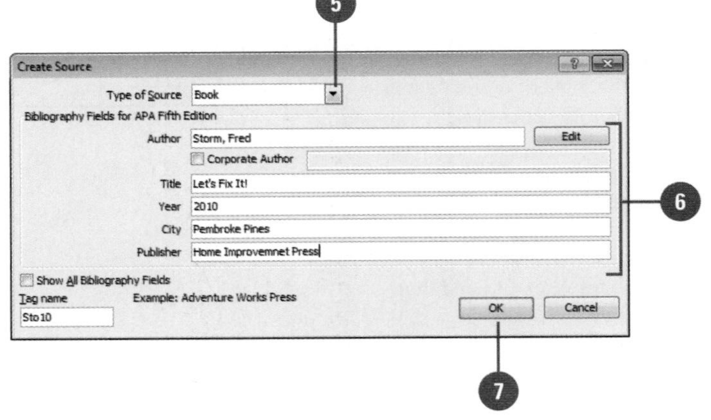

Manage Sources and Placeholders

1. Click the **References** tab.
2. Click the **Manage Sources** button.

   All the sources from previous documents appear in the Master List, and currently cited sources in the Current List.
3. To search for sources, click in the Search box, type search criteria, and then press Enter.
4. To sort source information, click the **Sort** list arrow, and then select a sort type.
5. To edit a placeholder, click the placeholder you want to edit in the Current List, and then click **Edit**.
6. Use the Copy and Delete buttons to move sources around or delete them.
7. Click **Close**.

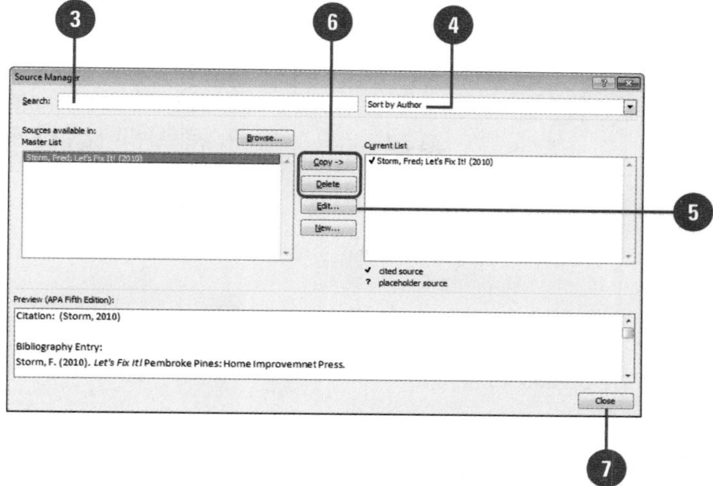

Create a Bibliography

1. Click to place the insertion point where you want to insert a bibliography.
2. Click the **References** tab.
3. Click the **Bibliography** button.
4. Click the bibliography format style you want to insert.
5. To update a bibliography, select the bibliography, click the tab button, and then click **Update Bibliography**.

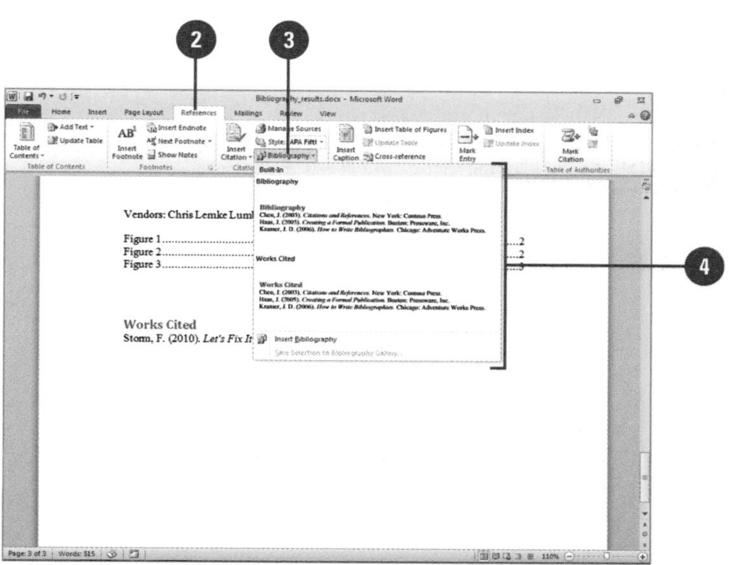

Creating a Bookmark

Instead of scrolling through a long document to find a specific word, phrase, or section, you can use bookmarks. **Bookmarks** are used to mark text so that you, or your reader, can quickly return to it. Using bookmarks as a destination make it easy to navigate through a long document. You can also navigate through documents with bookmarks by selecting a bookmark as a destination in the Go To dialog box.

Create a Bookmark

1. Click in your document where you want to insert a Bookmark.
2. Click the **Insert** tab.
3. Click the **Bookmark** button.
4. Type a one word descriptive name for your Bookmark.
5. Click **Add**.

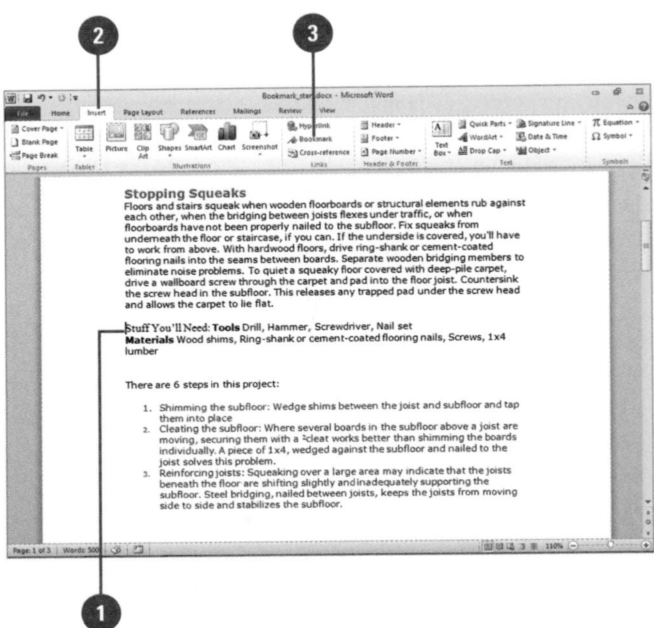

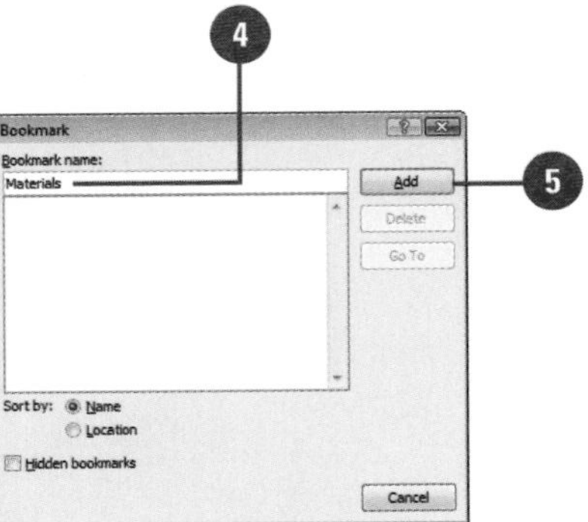

Go to a Bookmark Location

1. Click the **Home** tab.
2. Click the **Find** button arrow, and then click **Go To.**
3. On the Go To tab, click **Bookmark**.
4. Click the **Enter bookmark name** list arrow, and then select the bookmark you want to move to.
5. Click **Go To**.
6. If you want, choose another bookmark.
7. Click **Close**.

Did You Know?

You can go to different locations in Word. Click the Home tab, click the Find button arrow, click Go To, select the Go To What option you want, specify a location, and then click Next or Previous. When you're done, click Close.

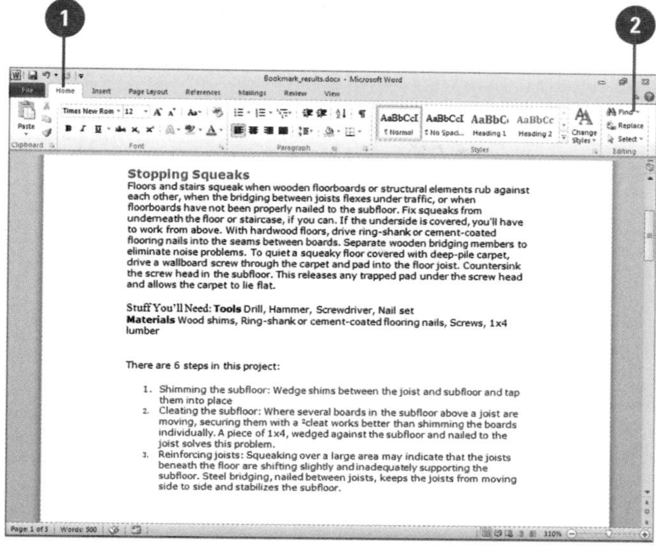

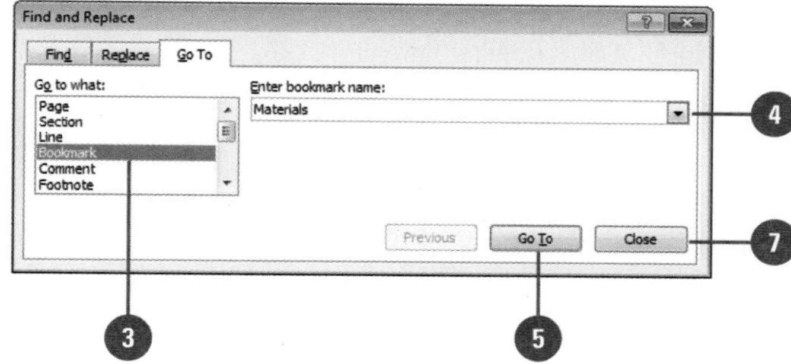

Creating Captions

Captions are helpful not only to associate images with the text that refers to them, but also to provide the reader with amplifying information about the figure, table, chart, or other illustration displayed. You can use preset captions provided, such as Figure, or you can create your own custom caption for your document.

Insert a Caption

1. Select the image that you want to caption.
2. Click the **References** tab.
3. Click the **Insert Caption** button.
4. If you want to use a Label other than the default setting of Figure, which is appropriate for most art, click the **Label** list arrow, and then click **Equation** or **Table**.
5. If you want to use a numbering sequence other than the default setting of 1,2,3..., click **Numbering**, make your selections, and then click **OK**.
6. Click **OK**.

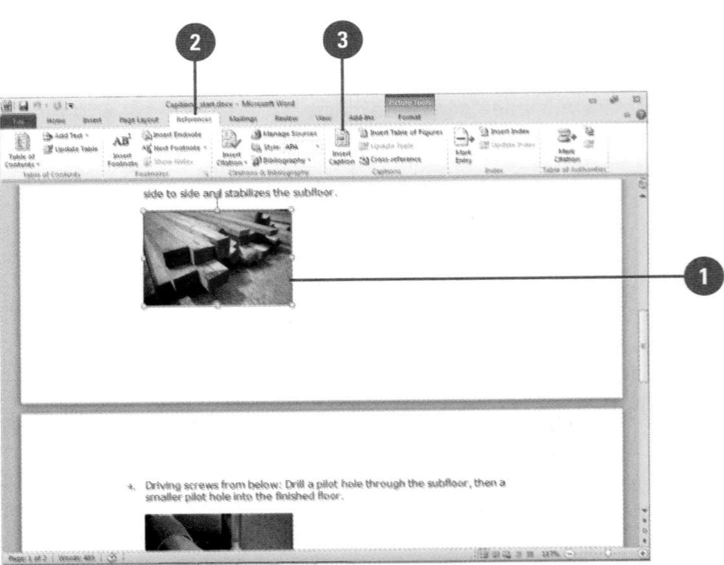

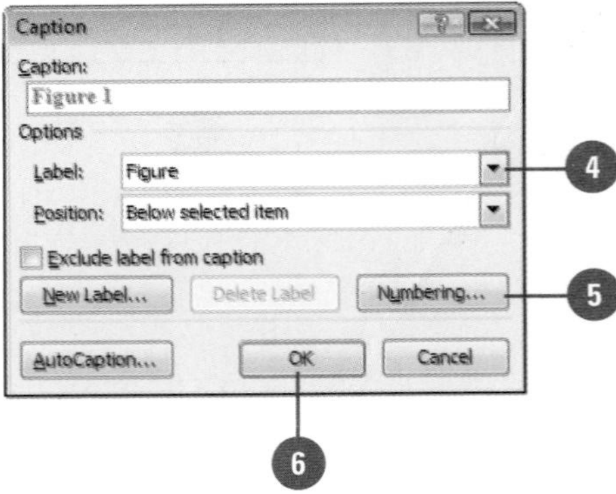

Did You Know?

You can have Word automatically add a caption field. Whenever you insert a particular type of file, such as a bitmapped image, click AutoCaption. In the Add Caption When Inserting list, click the check boxes to select the instances where you want the feature to apply, select the Label, Positioning and Numbering options you want, and then click OK.

You can add custom labels for captions. Click New Label, type the name of the New Label, and then click OK.

Creating a Table of Figures

If you are creating a document in which there are many illustrations (art, photographs, charts, diagrams etc.), it is often helpful to the reader of your document to provide a Table of Figures. A **Table of Figures** is like a Table of Contents except that it deals only with the graphic content of a document, not the written content. To create the Table of Figures, Word looks for text with the Style code that you specify (Figure, Table, etc). You can also add a **tab leader** to make the table easier to read.

Create a Table of Figures

1. Position the insertion point where you want the Table of Figures to appear.
2. Click the **References** tab.
3. Click **Insert Table of Figures** button.
4. Click the **Table of Figures** tab.
5. Click the **Tab leader** list arrow, and then select the tab leader you want to use.
6. Click the **Formats** list arrow, and then select the format you want to use for the Table of Figures.
7. If you want to create a Table of Figures from something other than the default Figure style, or the Table style, click **Options**.
8. Click the **Style** list arrow, select the text formatting that you want Word to search for when building the Table of Figures, and then click **Close**. All figure callouts of the selected style are tagged for inclusion in the Table of Figures.
9. Click **OK**.
10. Click **OK**.

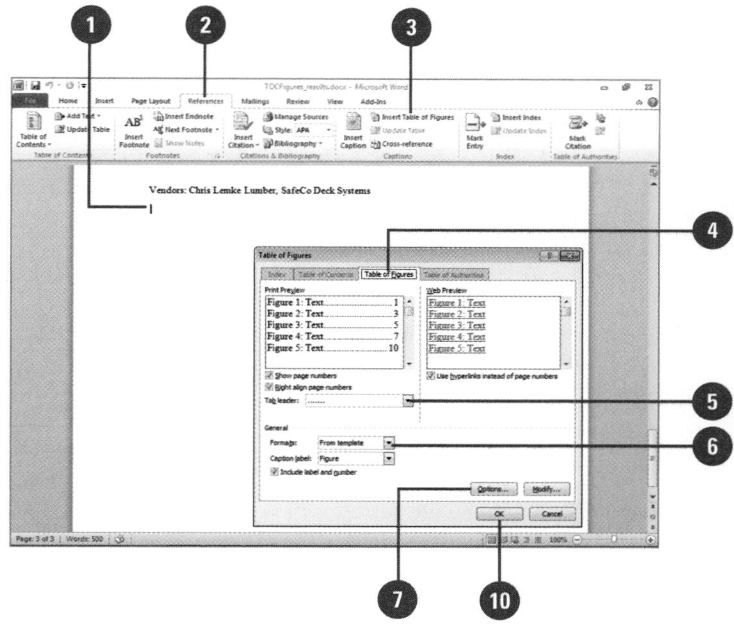

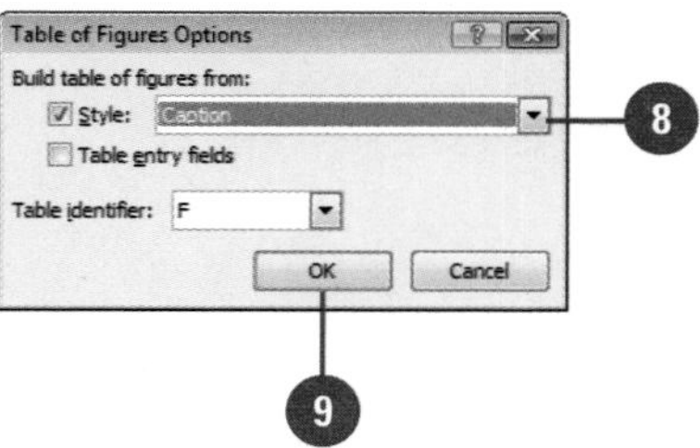

Table of Figures

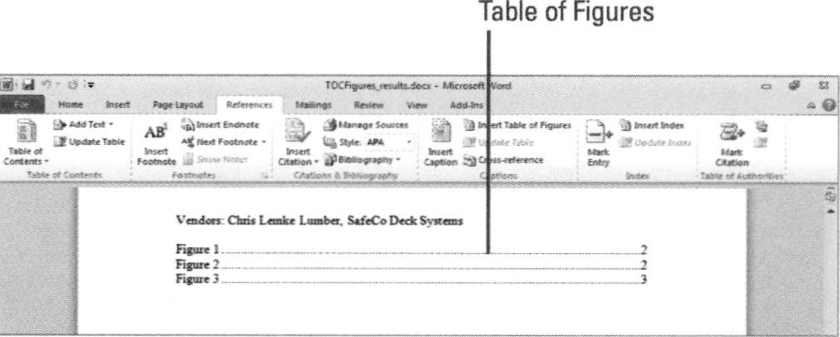

Numbering Lines

Many legal documents use the formatting convention of numbering every line of text to make it easier for multiple parties to refer to very specific text in a longer document in the context of their discussions. Other types of documents that sometimes use this convention are movie and television scripts. You can have Word automatically number each line of text within a document.

Number Each Line in a Document Quickly

1. If you want to show or hide line numbers to only selected text, select the text you want.
2. Click the **Page Layout** tab.
3. Click the **Line Numbers** button, and then click the option you want:
   - **None**. Remove line numbers from the document.
   - **Continuous**. Add line numbers to the document starting from line 1.
   - **Restart Each Page**. Restart line numbers on each page.
   - **Restart Each Section**. Restart line numbers at each section.
   - **Suppress for Current Paragraph**. Remove line numbers from the selected text.

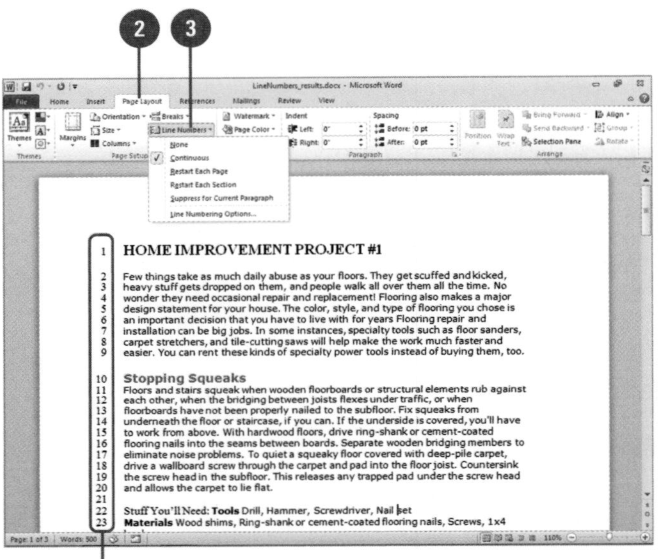

Line numbers

Customize Line Numbering Options

1. If you want to display line numbers to only selected text, select the text you want.
2. Click the **Page Layout** tab.
3. Click the **Line Numbers** button, and then click **Line Numbering Options**.
4. If you're adding line numbers to part of a document, click the **Apply to** list arrow, and then click **Selected text**.
5. Click **Line Numbers**.
6. Click the **Add line numbering** check box.
7. Select the options you want: Start at, From text, Count by, and Numbering.
8. Click **OK**.
9. Click **OK**.

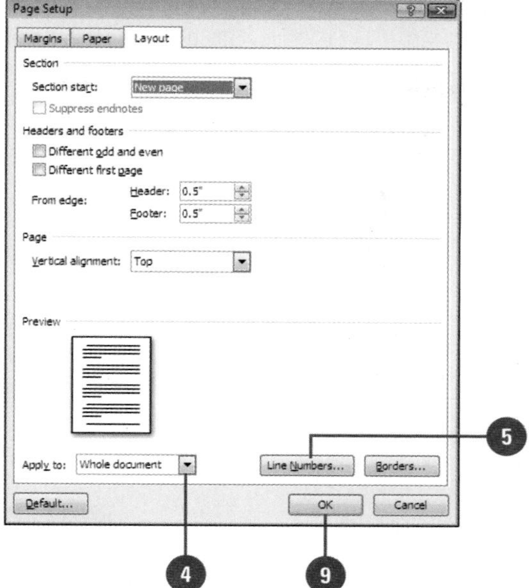

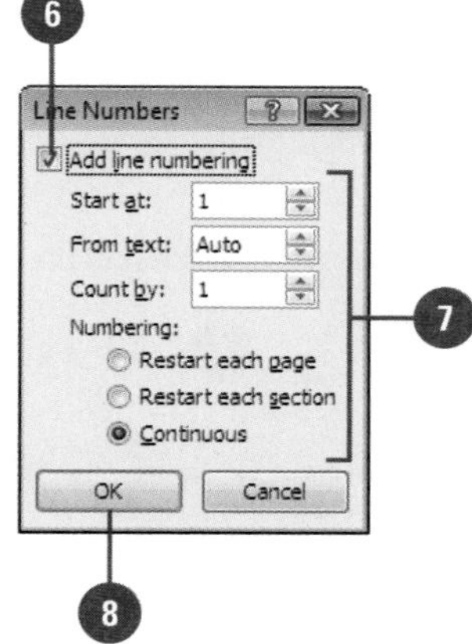

Creating an Equation

If you are creating a scientific or academic paper that involves complex equations, you may need to display them in the text without actually using them in conjunction with a table. The standard keyboard does not have all of the mathematical symbols you might need to create the equation, so you can use the Equations gallery to quickly insert a common equation or the Design tab under Equation Tools to create a custom equation. The Equations gallery is part of Word's building block approach to creating customized documents.

Insert a Common Equation from the Equations Gallery

1. Click where you want to insert an equation.
2. Click the **Insert** tab.
3. Click the **Equation** button arrow.
4. Click a common equation from the Equations gallery.

   The equation appears in the document as a building block.
5. Click to place the insertion point in the equation and then edit it like you would text.
6. To change the equation display, click the **Equations Options** list arrow, and then click the option you want.
   - **Save as New Equation**. Saves the equation as a new building block in the Equations gallery.
   - **Professional**. Displays equation in 2D form.
   - **Linear**. Displays equation in 1D form.
   - **Change to Inline** or **Display.** Changes the equation position to inline with text or display in the middle of the line.
   - **Justification**. Changes alignment: Left, Right, Centered, or Centered as a Group.

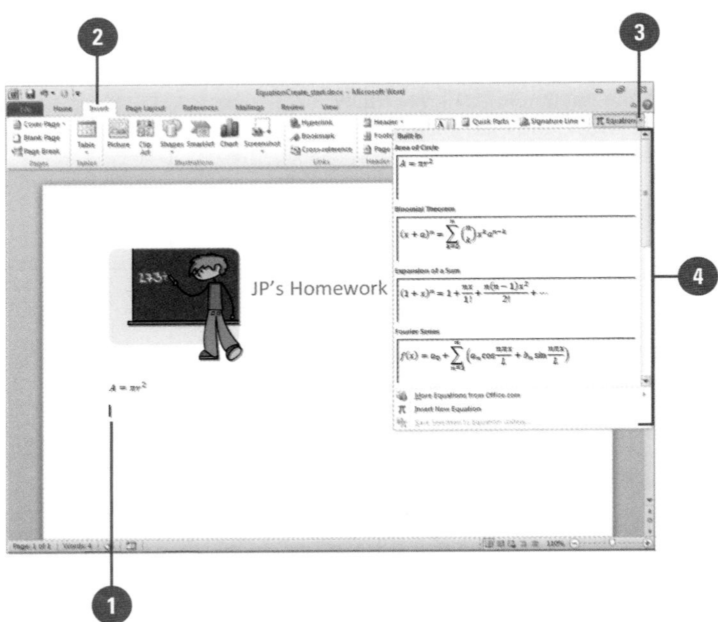

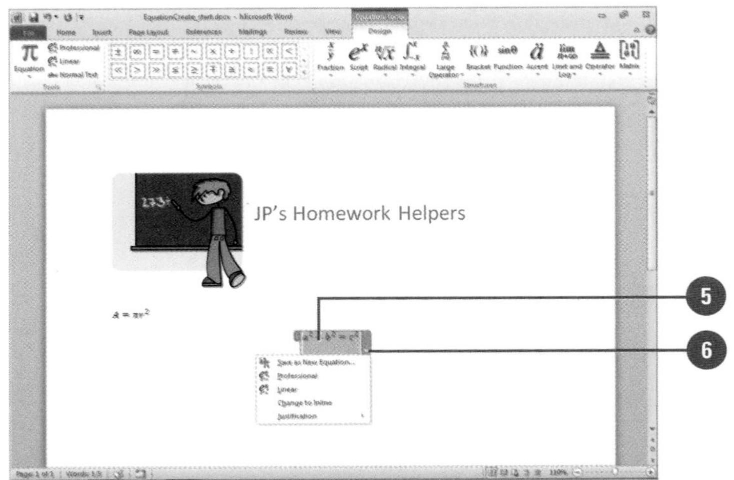

Create an Equation

1. Click where you want to insert an equation.
2. Click the **Insert** tab.
3. Click the **Equation** button arrow, and then click **Insert New Equation**.

   A blank equation building block appears.
4. Click the **Design** tab under Equation Tools.
5. Type any part of the equation, or click any of the buttons in the Structures group you want, and then select the equation segment you want.
6. Select the placeholder you want to insert more of the equation.
7. Click the scroll up or down arrow, or click the **More** list arrow in the Symbols group, and then select the symbol you want to insert.
8. Continue to insert structures and symbols to complete your equation.

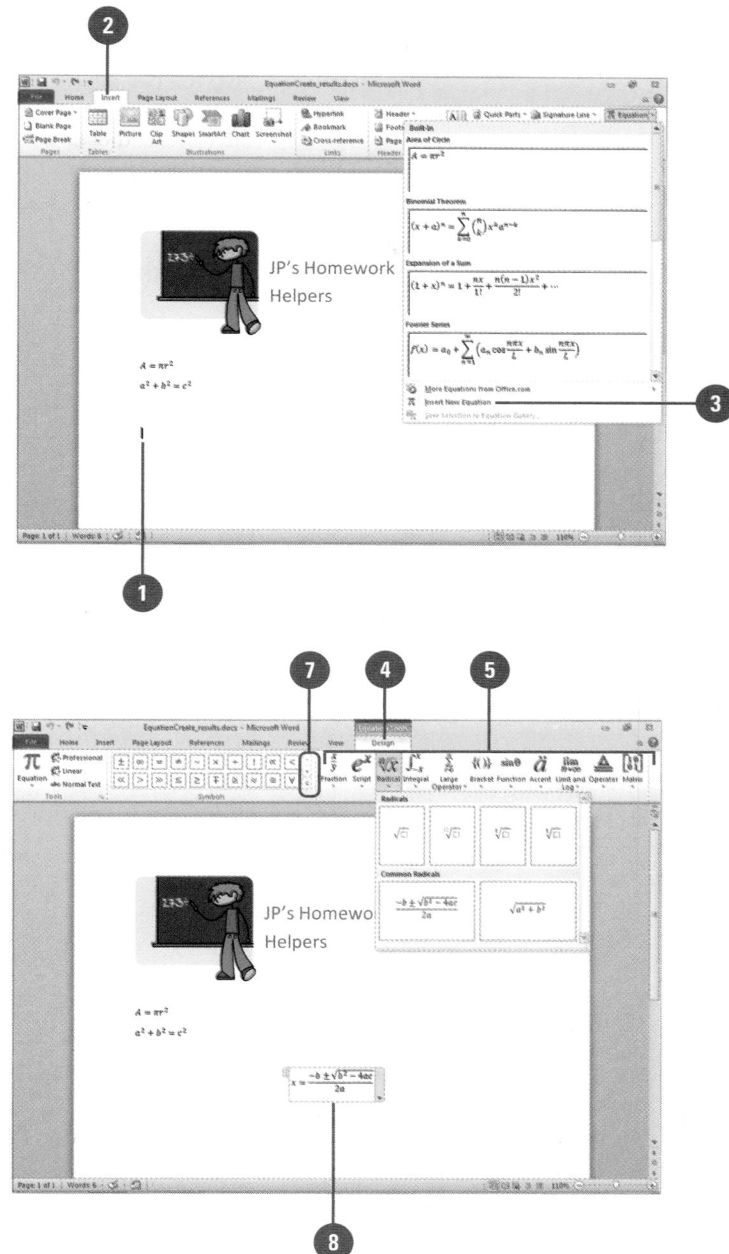

Did You Know?

You can display an equation as regular text. Select an equation, click the Design tab under Equation Tools, click the Linear button, and then click the Normal Text button.

You can change default equation options. Select an equation, click the Design tab under Equation Tools, click the Tools Dialog Box Launcher, specify the options you want, and then click OK.

Inserting Symbols

Word comes with a host of symbols for every need. Insert just the right one to keep from compromising a document's professional appearance with a missing accent or mathematical symbol (å). In the Symbol dialog box, you use the Recently used symbols list to quickly insert a symbol that you want to insert again. If you don't see the symbol you want, use the Font list to look at the available symbols for other fonts installed on your computer.

Insert Recently Used Symbols and Special Characters Quickly

1. Click the document where you want to insert a symbol or character.
2. Click the **Insert** tab.
3. Click the **Symbol** button.
4. Click one of the recently used symbols or special characters from the list to insert it into the document.

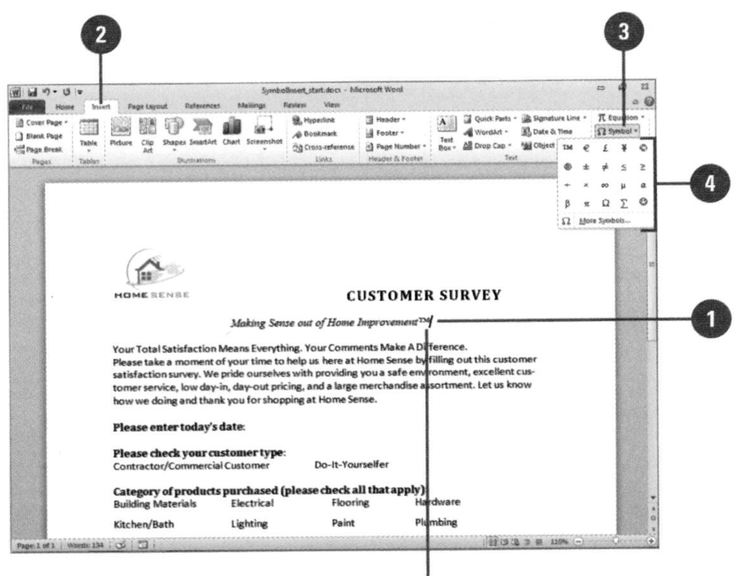

Trademark symbol

Did You Know?

You can insert a symbol using a character code. When the From box displays ASCII (decimal), you can use the number shown in the Character Code box to insert a character or symbol. Place your insertion point where you want the character on the slide, make sure Num Lock is on, hold down the Alt key, and then use the numeric keypad to type 0 (zero) followed by the character code. Then release the Alt key. The code applies to the current code page only, so some characters may not be available this way.

Insert Symbols and Special Characters

1. Click the document where you want to insert a symbol or character.
2. Click the **Insert** tab.
3. Click the **Symbol** button, and then click **More Symbols**.
4. To see other symbols, click the **Font** list arrow, and then click a new font.
5. Click a symbol or character.

   You can use the Recently used symbols list to use a symbol you've already used.
6. Click **Insert**.

Did You Know?

You can assign a shortcut key to insert a symbol within the document. Click the Insert menu, click Symbol, click a symbol, click Shortcut Key, enter the shortcut key information requested, and then click Close.

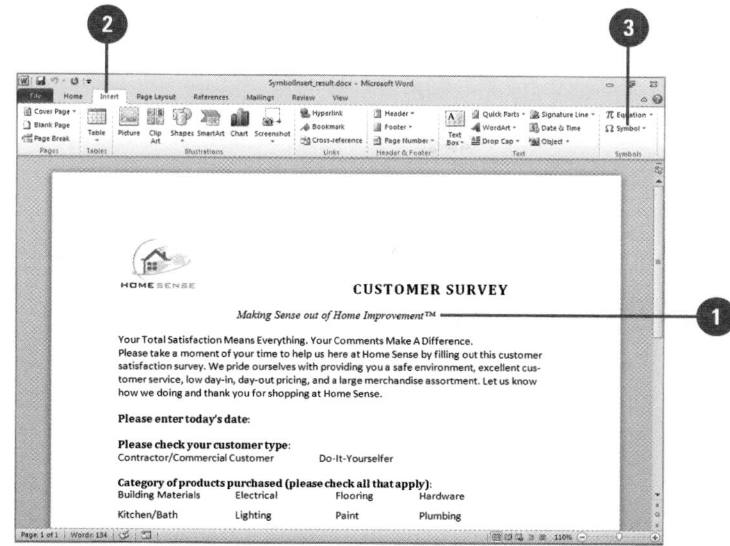

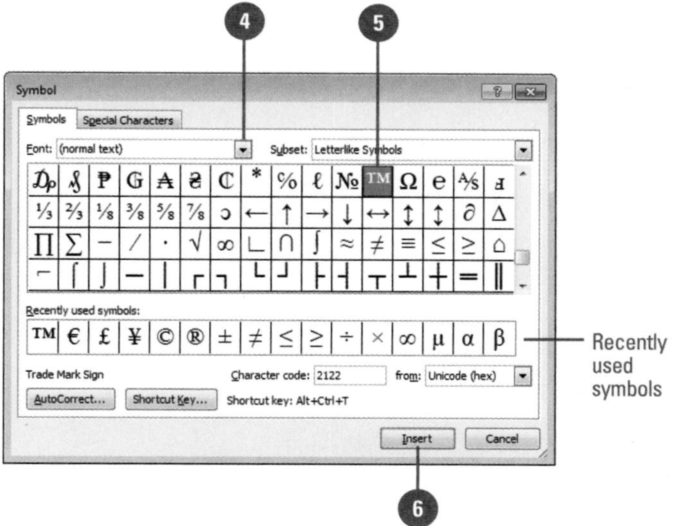

Creating Mail Merge Documents

10

Introduction

Whether you are looking to personalize your annual Christmas letter to friends and family, or prepare a direct-mail marketing piece to 10,000 customers of your business, Word's Mail Merge Wizard is up to the task. To perform a mail merge, you need a **form letter** that contains the text you want to send out, plus **merge fields** for the information that you want to use to personalize each letter, such as the recipient's address, first name in the greeting line, and so forth. These fields can be added manually, or as part of the Mail Merge Wizard process.

You must have a **data document** that contains all of this information in either comma or tab delimited format. Most databases, such as Access or Outlook (contacts), can automatically export into this format. Alternately, you can manually create a data document if you do not have an existing database of contact information that you can use for the merge. Equipped with these two sources, the Mail Merge Wizard can quickly and easily create thousands of personalized letters, address labels, and envelopes, in a fraction of the time it would otherwise take you to do these tasks.

If you prefer a more manual approach to creating a mail merge document, you can perform the process using commands on the Mailings tab. The mail merge process follows the same general steps. First, set up the main document. Second, connect the document to a data source. Third, refine the list of recipients or items. Fourth, add mail merge fields, and fifth, preview and complete the merge. If you need to stop working during the mail merge process, you can save the document and resume it again later. Word saves all information regarding the mail merge and returns you to the place in the task pane where you left off.

What You'll Do

Starting the Mail Merge

Did you ever send the same letter to several people and spend a lot of time changing personal information, such as names and addresses? If so, form letters will save you time. **Mail merge** is the process of combining names and addresses stored in a data file with a main document (usually a form letter) to produce customized documents. There are four main steps to merging. First, select the document you want to use. Second, create a data file with the variable information. Third, create the main document with the boilerplate (unchanging information) and merge fields. Finally, merge the main document with the data source to create a new document with all the merged information. When you start the mail merge, you need to open the letter that you want to mail merge or type one. Don't worry about addressing the letter or adding a greeting line, you can accomplish that with the Mail Merge Wizard.

Start the Mail Merge Wizard

1. Click the **Mailings** tab.
2. Click the **Start Mail Merge** button, and then click **Step by Step Mail Merge Wizard**.

   The Mail Merge task pane opens, displaying Step 1 of 6.
3. Select the type of document you are working on (in this case the Letters option).
4. Click **Next: Starting document** on the task pane to display Step 2 of 6.
5. Click a starting document option (such as Use the current document).
6. Click **Next: Select recipients** on the task pane to display Step 3 of 6.

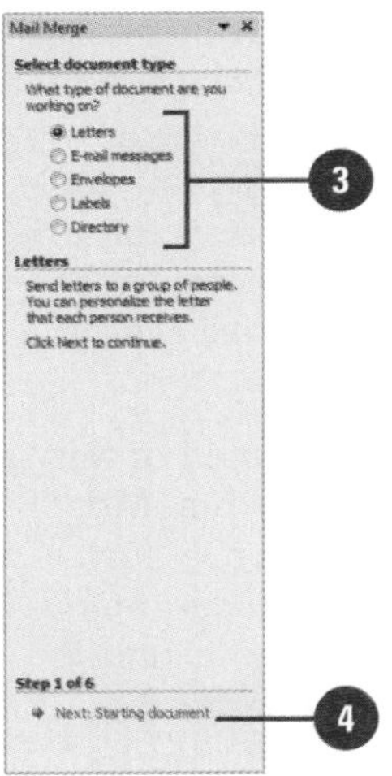

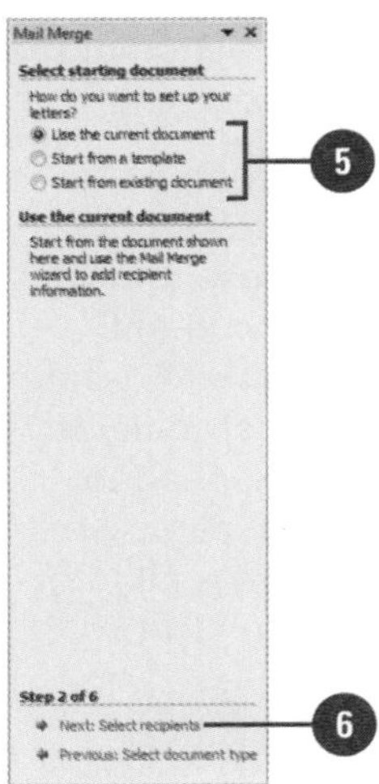

Did You Know?

You can set up the main document manually. Create a new or existing document, click the Mailings tab, click the Start Mail Merge button, select a document type (Letters, E-Mail Messages, etc.), and then select any options, if prompted.

Importing Data from a Database

Now it is time to specify the recipients for your mail merge. To do so, you must identify a **data document** as the source of the recipient information you will use to personalize the mailing. If you have an existing database of information to work with, this is the easiest method. The mail merge works with most standard database and spreadsheet programs including Microsoft Access, Microsoft FoxPro, and Microsoft Excel. Before you can import data into the Mail Merge Wizard from an external database, you must first export it from the database you are using. Follow the instructions for that database to export a file in either comma or tab delimited format, and remember which format you chose. Export the file to the My Data Sources folder.

Import Data from an Existing Database

1. On Step 3 of 6 in the Mail Merge task pane, click the **Use an existing list** option.
2. Click **Browse** on the task pane.
3. Locate and select the database file from which you want to import the recipient data.
4. Click **Open**.
5. If necessary, select a data source, such as a table in an Excel worksheet or Access database, and then click **OK**.

   The Mail Merge Recipient dialog box opens, displaying the data source for the merge.
6. Edit the recipient data (if necessary), and then click **OK**.
7. Click **Next: write your letter** on the task pane to display Step 4 of 6.

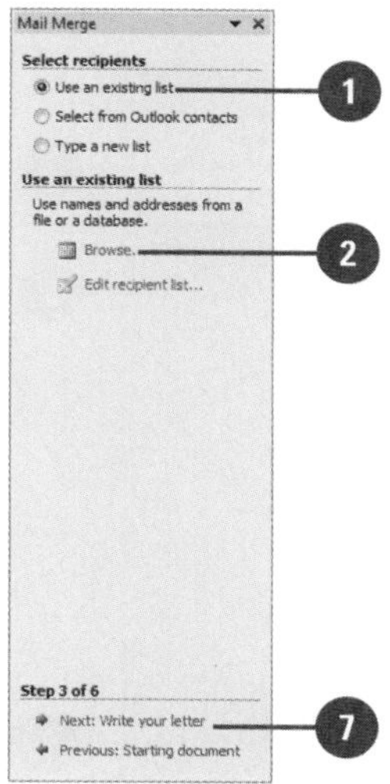

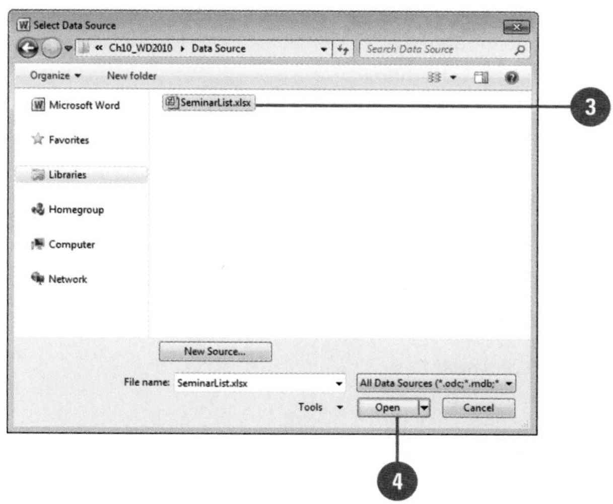

Importing Data from Outlook

If you are already using Outlook to manage your contact database, you can import your Outlook contact records into the Mail Merge Wizard quickly and easily. For example, a contact record for a person or company might contain an address, telephone, e-mail address, and so forth. An item record might contain the part number, description, quantity on hand, and so on. The information in each record is organized by fields. The fields of the database correspond to the merge fields you specify in the Form Letter. Additional fields other than the ones to be used by the merge can exist, and will be ignored by the Mail Merge Wizard. For example, a direct mail piece would use the address field in a record as a merge field and ignore the e-mail address field for that record, whereas an e-mail merge would do exactly the opposite.

Import Data from Outlook

1. On Step 3 of 6 in the Mail Merge task pane, click **Select from Outlook contacts**.
2. Click **Choose Contacts Folder**.
3. If an Outlook profile dialog box opens, select a profile, and then click **OK**.

   The Select Contact List Folder dialog box opens.
4. Select the contacts list you want to use.
5. Click **OK**.

   The Mail Merge Recipients dialog box opens, displaying the data source for the merge.
6. Edit the recipient data (if necessary), and then click **OK**.
7. Click **Next: Write your letter** on the task pane to display Step 4 of 6.

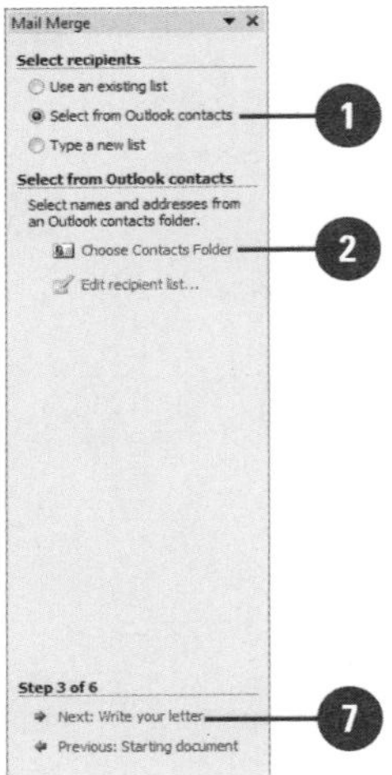

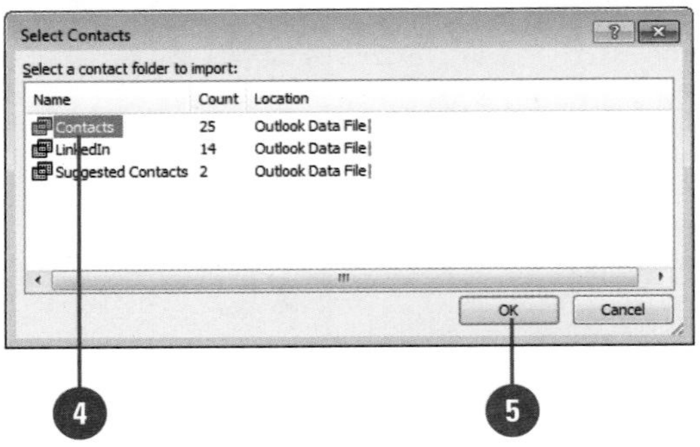

Did You Know?

You can connect the document to a data source manually. In the document, click the Mailings tab, click the Select Recipients button, and then select the data source you want, and any related options, if prompted.

Creating a Data Document

When you are only doing a limited number of pieces in a mail merge, or you cannot input the records into one of the previously mentioned programs for permanent use and then export them to the Mail Merge Wizard to perform the task at hand, you can use the Wizard to create your recipient list. You can also use Word to manually type a data document. The first line of the document should contain the merge field names separated by commas or tabs (choose one format and be consistent throughout the document). For example, FirstName, LastName, Address, City, State, Zip. Note that field names cannot contain spaces. At the end of the field name line, press Enter. Input all of the data for a given record separated by commas on the lines that follow, press Enter after each record entry. When all entries are entered, save the document as a text file and import it as an existing file in Step 3 of 6 in the Mail Merge Wizard.

Create a Data Document

1. On Step 3 of 6 in the Mail Merge task pane, click the **Type a new list** option.
2. Click **Create**.
3. Input your information for the first record, and then click **New Entry**.
4. Continue to input additional records; click **New Entry** after each one until all records have been entered, and then click **OK**.

   The Save Address List dialog box opens, displaying the My Data Sources folder.
5. Enter a name, and then click **Save** to save your work.

   The Mail Merge Recipients dialog box opens, displaying the data source for the merge.
6. Edit the recipient data (if necessary), and then click **OK**.
7. Click **Next: Write your letter** on the task pane to display Step 4 of 6.

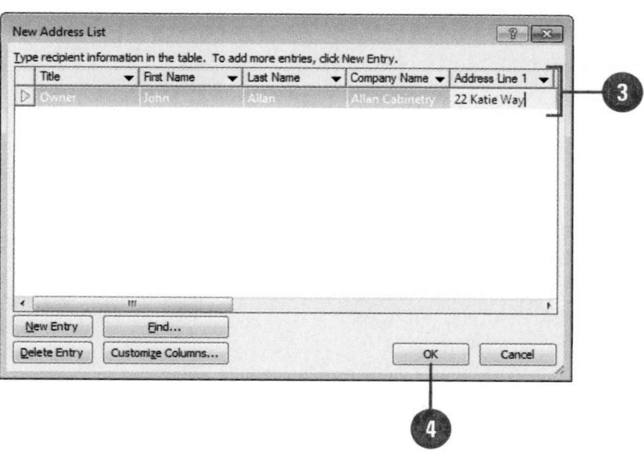

Editing the Data Source

Regardless of the original source of your data, an external database, manually prepared list, Outlook records, or an Address List that you created within the Mail Merge Wizard, periodically you will want to make some changes to the data before completing the merge. The time to do so is in Step 3 of 6 of the Mail Merge Wizard.

Edit a Data Document

1. On Step 3 of 6 in the Mail Merge task pane, click **Edit recipient list.**
2. Select the data source.
3. Click **Edit**, and then make the changes you want to the fields.
4. To add records to the merge, select any existing record, and then click **New Entry**.
5. To remove the selected record from the data document permanently, click **Delete Entry**.
6. Click **OK**.
7. If you want to retain the record in the data document, but exclude it from the merge, clear the check mark next to the record.

   All records begin selected by default and must be manually deselected from the merge.
8. When you're done, click **OK**.
9. Click **Next: Write your letter** on the task pane to display Step 4 of 6.

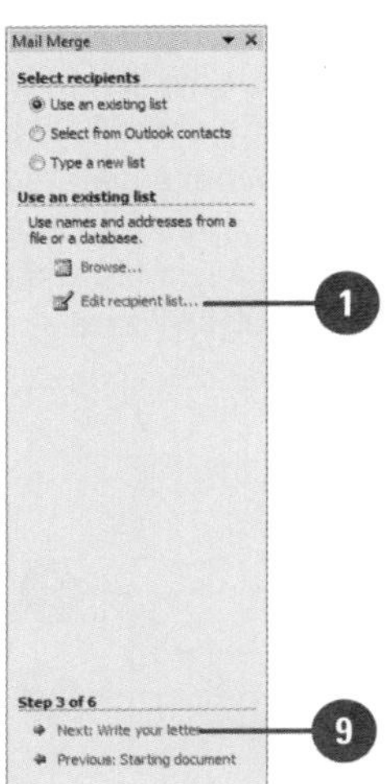

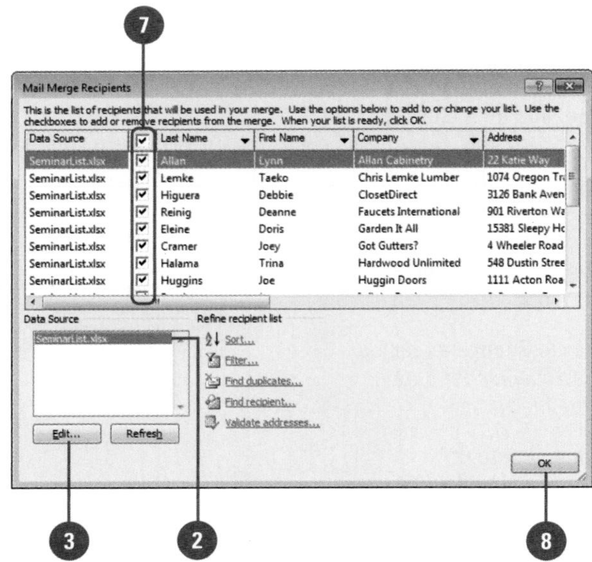

Did You Know?

You can refine the data source manually. In the document, click the Mailings tab, click the Edit Recipient List button, and then make the changes you want, and any related options, if prompted.

Sorting and Filtering Data

When you are working with large numbers of records, it is often helpful to organize those records in a particular order. For example, if you are doing a bulk mailing via the USPS, they require that the pieces of the mailing be sorted in zip code order for you to receive the savings associated with the bulk mail rate. Word can easily accomplish this task for you so the records are merged and printed in zip code order. You can sort and filter records by any of the merge fields in the record.

Sort and Filter Records

1. On Step 3 of 6 in the Mail Merge task pane, click **Edit recipient list**.
2. To sort the data in a column, click the field column heading (not the list arrow inside of it).
3. To filter out data in a field column by a specific criterion or value, click the list arrow in the column heading, and then select a filter option or value.

   TIMESAVER *Click the Filter link in the Mail Merge Recipients dialog box.*
4. To perform advance sorts, where you compare the values of certain fields, click the list arrow for any field, and then click **Advanced.**
5. If you chose an advanced sort, select or enter filter and sort criteria in the Field, Comparison, and Compare to box, and then click **OK**.
6. When you're done, click **OK**.
7. Click **Next: write your letter** on the task pane to display Step 4 of 6.

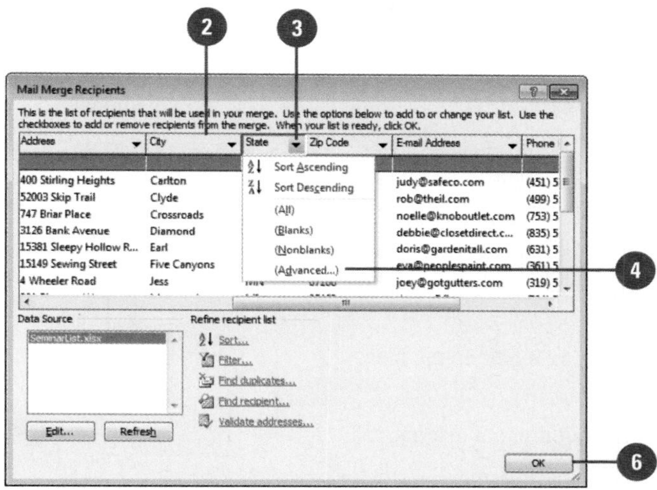

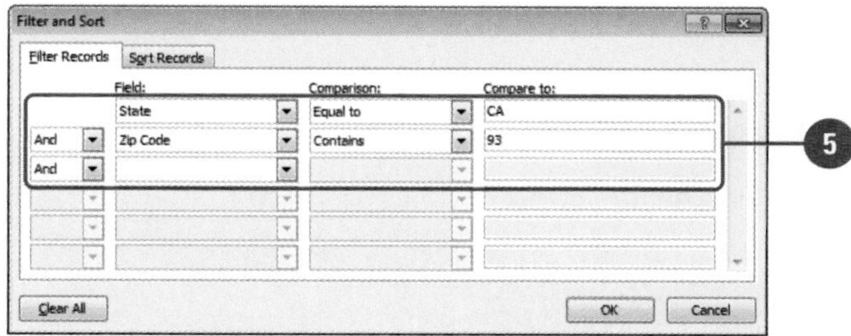

Did You Know?

You can display all the data in a column. In the Mail Merge Recipient dialog box, click the column heading list arrow used for a filter, and then click All.

Creating a Form Letter

The only difference between a normal letter and a **form letter** is the presence of merge fields in the latter. Merge fields can exist anywhere in the document, and correspond to any field in the data document. For example, you can insert the FirstName field periodically in a document to reaffirm to the reader that you are speaking directly to them, and minimize the negative reactions that many people feel when they receive a form letter. The most commonly used fields in a form letter are the address block and the greeting line. Each merge field corresponds to a piece of information in the data source and appears in the main document with the greater than and less than characters around it. For example, the <<Address Block>> merge field corresponds to name and address information in the data source. Word incorporates insert commands for each of these in the Mail Merge Wizard.

Create a Form Letter

1. On Step 4 of 6 in the Mail Merge task pane, position the insertion point in the letter where you want the address block to appear.
2. Click **Address Block** on the task pane.
3. Select the Address Block options you want.
4. Click **OK** to insert the block in the document.
5. Position the insertion point where you want the greeting to appear.
6. Click **Greeting Line**.

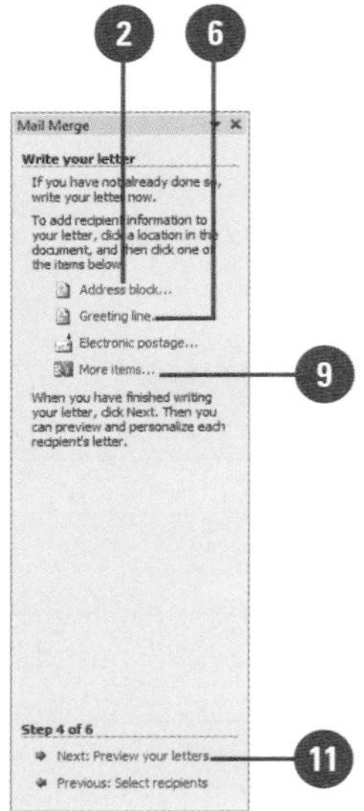

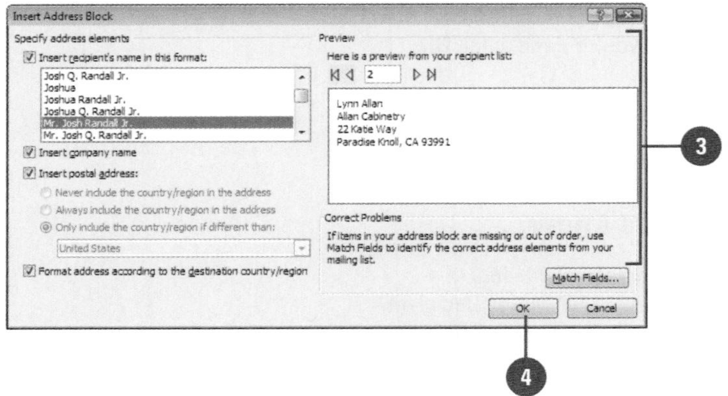

Did You Know?

Word supports international languages in Mail Merge. Mail Merge chooses the correct greeting format based on the gender of the recipient if the language requires it. Mail Merge can also format addresses based on the geographical region of the recipient.

7. Select the format you want for the greeting line.
8. Click **OK** to apply the style to the merge field.
9. If you want to add other merge fields in the body of the form letter, position the insertion point where you want the information, and then click **More Items** on the task pane.
10. Select the merge field you want to place, click **Insert**, and then click **Close**.
11. When you're done, click **Next: Preview your letters** on the task pane to display Step 5 of 6.

Did You Know?

You can edit the style of a field. Right click on the field to bring up a menu of options, and then click Edit.

You can have common words used as field names. Information in a data file is stored in merge fields, labeled with one-word names, such as FirstName, LastName, City, and so on. You can insert merge field names in the main document as blanks or placeholders, for variable information. When you merge the data file and main document, Word fills in the blanks with the correct information.

You should beware of those extra spaces. Don't press the Spacebar after entering data in a field. Extra spaces will appear in the document between the data and the next word or punctuation, leaving ugly gaps or floating punctuation. Add spaces and punctuation to your main document instead.

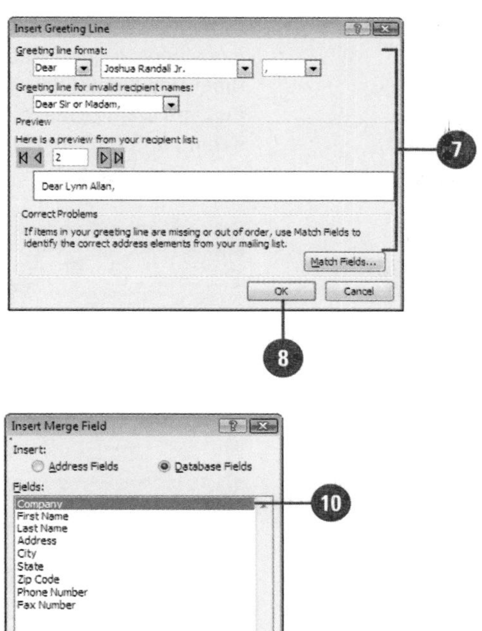

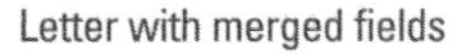
Letter with merged fields

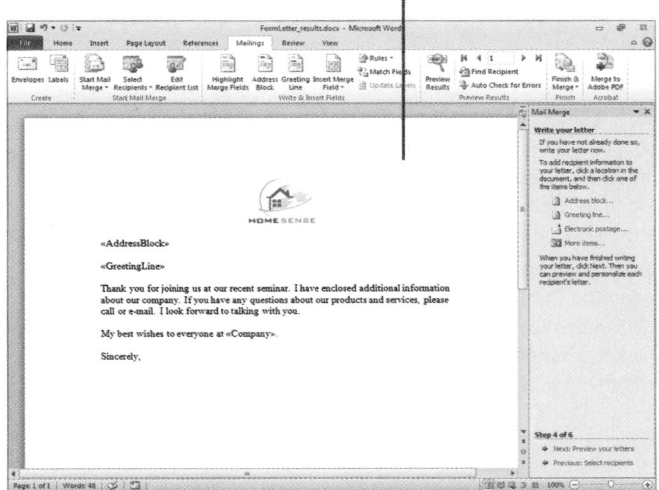

Previewing the Mail Merge

Although Word has automated much of the mail merge process for you, it is always a good idea to review the merged letters before printing them. You might find changes to the body text or even the merge fields that you want to make before the merge is final. The preview process occurs in Step 5 of 6 in the Mail Merge task pane.

Preview the Mail Merge

1. On Step 5 of 6 in the Mail Merge task pane, click the double arrows on the task pane to scroll through the merge letters one at a time.
2. To find a given recipient or group of recipients quickly, click **Find a recipient** on the task pane.
3. If you chose Find, enter search criterion, click the **All fields** option, or **This field** option, and then select a field.
4. Click **Find Next** to proceed to the next matching record.
5. When you're done, click **Close**.
6. Click **Next: Complete the merge** on the task pane to display Step 6 of 6.

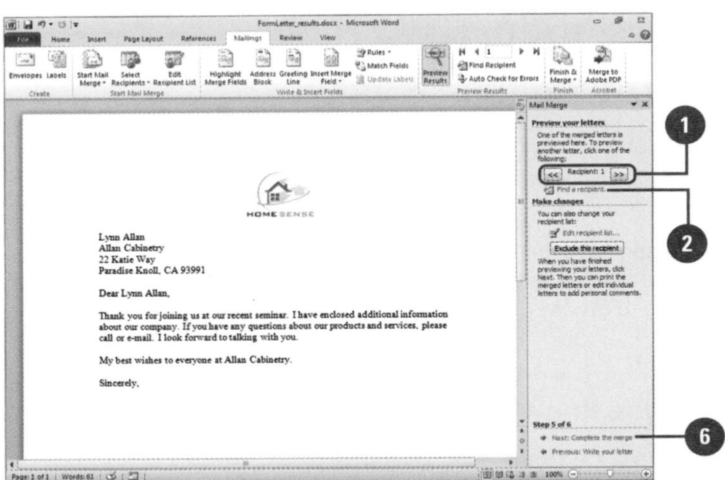

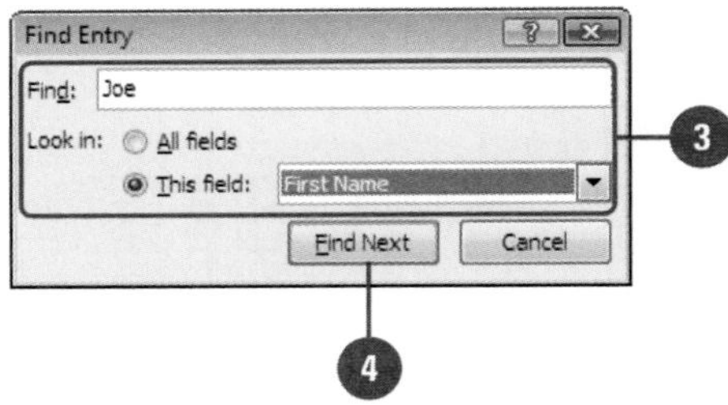

Did You Know?

You can exclude a recipient from the merge. Click the Exclude This Recipient button on the task pane on Step 5 of 6.

You can preview the mail merge results manually. In the document, click the Mailings tab, click the Preview Results button, view the results, and then make the changes you want.

Completing the Mail Merge

After you set up a data document and enter merge fields into the main document, you are ready to merge the document to create a new document with all the merged information. The new document contains individualized copies of the main document for each record in the data source. You can edit the new document to personalize individual copies in the main document, and then print the end result.

Personalize and Print the Mail Merge

1. Proceed to Step 6 of 6 in the Mail Merge task pane.
2. If you want to make additional changes to the letters, click **Edit Individual Letters**.
3. Specify the settings you want to use for the merged records and the selected range of the records are saved to a separate file for editing.
4. Click **OK**.
5. When you're ready to print, click **Print** on the task pane.
6. Click the **All** option to print the entire merge or click another option to print only a selected portion of the merge.
7. Click **OK**.

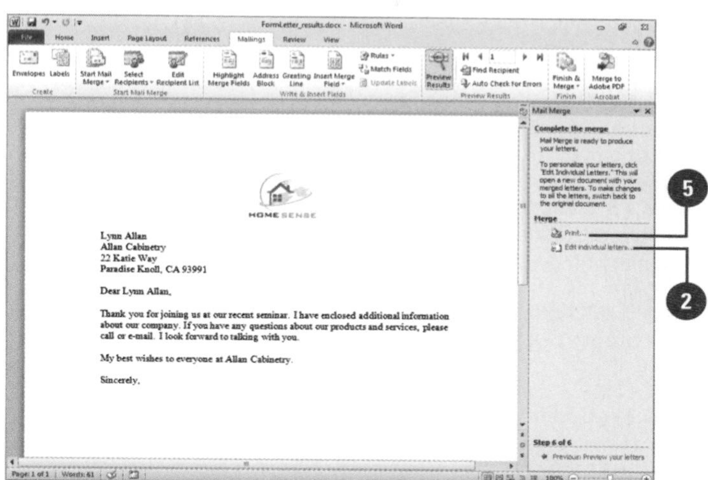

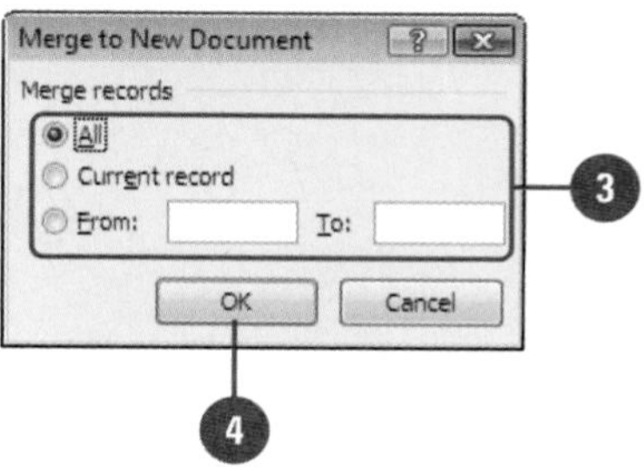

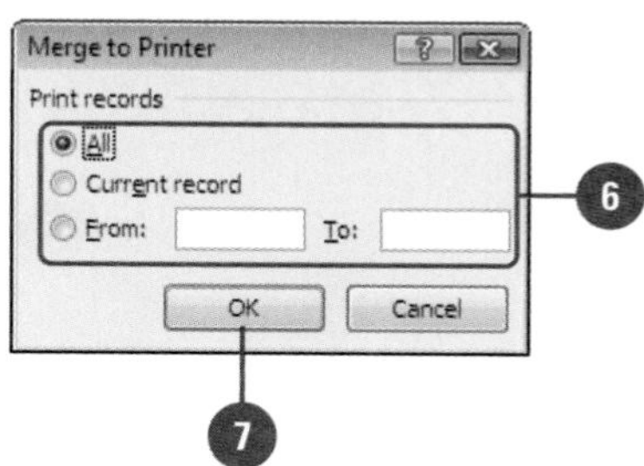

Did You Know?

You can complete the mail merge manually. In the document, click the Mailings tab, click the Find & Merge button, and then click Print Documents or Edit Individual Documents. When you're done, save the main document.

Merging to E-mail

Instead of merging data to create a form letter you can print, you can merge data to an e-mail document. The steps to merge an e-mail document rather than a letter are essentially the same, but there are a few small differences.

Mail Merge to E-mail

1. On Step 1 of 6 in the Mail Merge task pane, click the **E-mail messages** option.
2. Click **Next: Starting document** on the task pane to display Step 2 of 6.
3. Click a starting document option (such as Use The Current Document).
4. Click **Next: Select Recipients** on the task pane to display Step 3 of 6.
5. Click a recipient option (such as Use an existing list or Type a new list).
6. Click **Browse**, double-click a data document, and then click **OK** to select the mail recipients.
7. Click **Next: Write your e-mail message** on the task pane to display Step 4 of 6.

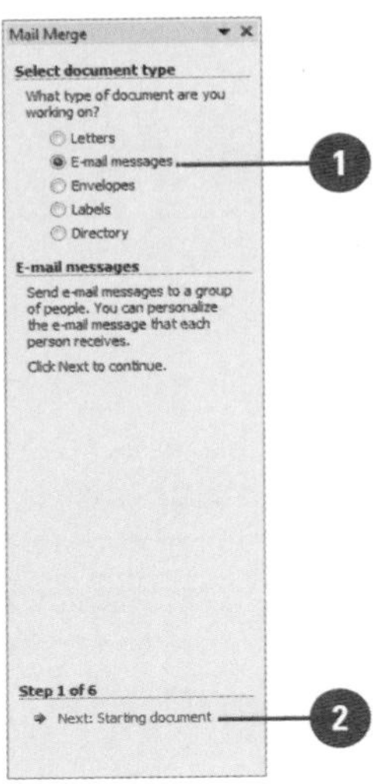

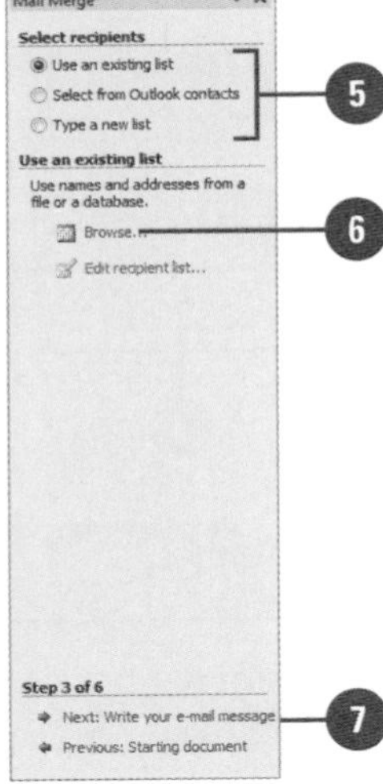

Did You Know?

You can set up the main document for E-mail messages manually. Create a new or existing document, click the Mailings tab, click the Start Mail Merge button, and then click E-mail Messages.

8. Type your e-mail, click a location in the document, click one of the field items on the task pane (such as Address Block or Greeting Line), select the options you want, and then click **OK**.
9. Click **Next: Preview your e-mail message** on the task pane to display Step 5 of 6.
10. Preview the data in the letter, and then make any changes.
11. Click **Next: Complete the merge** on the task pane to display Step 6 of 6.
12. Click **Electronic Mail**.
13. Select the mail format you want to use, normal text, HTML mail, or sending the document as an attachment.
14. Specify the range of records you want to send, and then click **OK.**

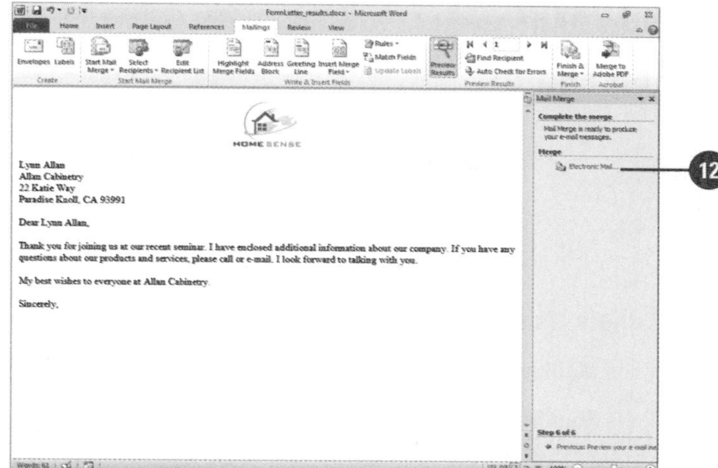

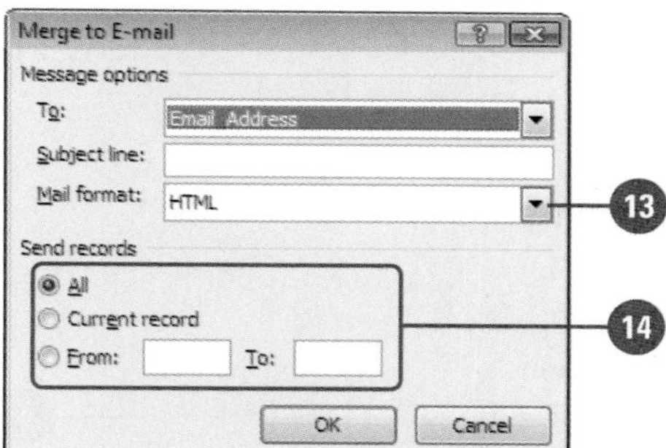

Creating Merged Mailing Labels

You can use a data document to create more than one kind of merge document. For example, you can use a data document to print mailing labels or envelopes to use with your mailing. The process for creating mailing labels is similar to the mail merge process for form letters, except that you insert the merge field into a main document that contains a table with cells in a specific size for labels. During the process for creating mailing labels, you can select brand-name labels in a specific size, such as Avery Standard 1529. After you merge the data into the main document with the labels, you can print the labels on a printer.

Create Labels Using Mail Merge

1. Click the **Mailings** tab.
2. Click the **Start Mail Merge** button, and then click **Step by Step Mail Merge Wizard**.

   The Mail Merge task pane opens, displaying Step 1 of 6.
3. Click the **Labels** option.
4. Click **Next: Starting document** on the task pane to display Step 2 of 6.
5. Click a starting document option button (such as Change Document Layout), and then click **Label Options**.
6. Select the label options you want, and then click **OK**.
7. Click **Next: Select recipients** on the task pane to display Step 3 of 6.

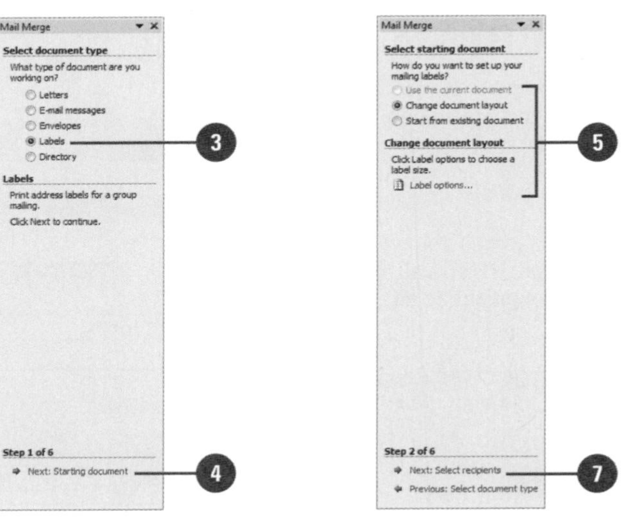

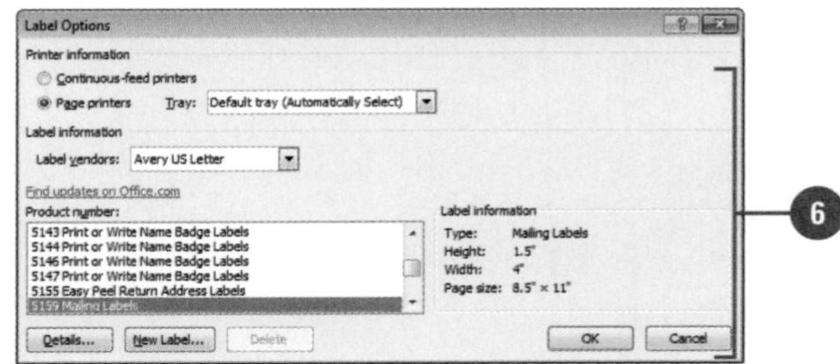

Did You Know?

You can set up the main document for labels manually. Create a new or existing document, click the Mailings tab, click the Start Mail Merge button, click Labels, select the label options you want, and then click OK.

8. Click a recipient option button (such as Use An Existing List or Type A New List), click **Browse**, double-click a data document, select a data source and click **OK**, select the recipients you want, and then click **OK**.
9. Click **Next: Arrange your labels** at the bottom of the task pane. Step 4 of 6 appears on the task pane.
10. Click in the first label of the document, and then click one of the field items on the task pane (such as Address Block or Greeting Line), select the options you want, and then click **OK**.
11. Click **Update all labels**.
12. Click **Next: Preview your labels** at the bottom of the task pane. Step 5 of 6 appears on the task pane.
13. Preview the data in the letter and make any changes, and then click **Next: Complete the merge** at the bottom of the task pane. Step 6 of 6 appears on the task pane.
14. Click **Print**.
15. Click a Print Records option, and then click **OK**.
16. When you're done, click the **Close** button on the task pane, and then save the form letter.

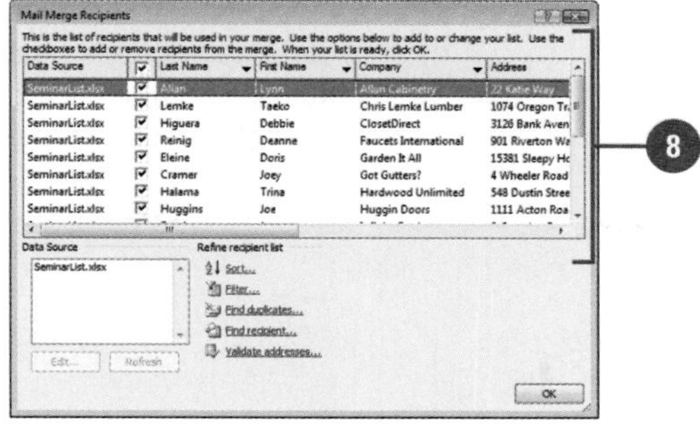

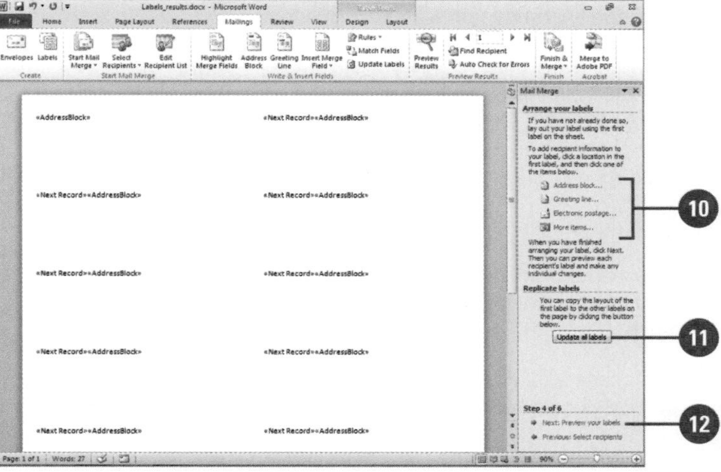

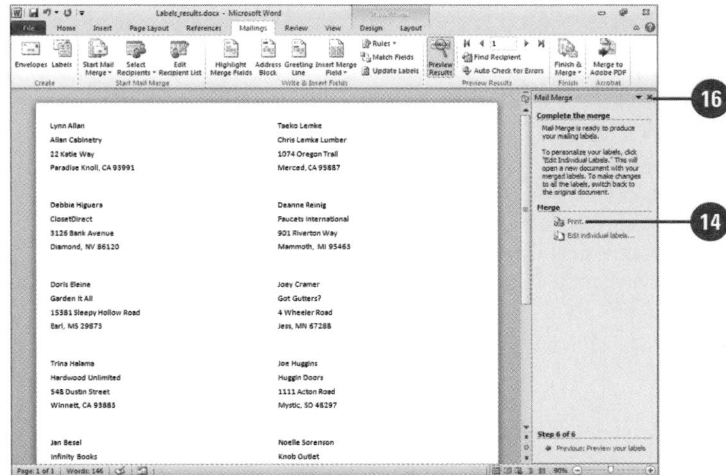

Creating Merged Envelopes

If your printer is set up to accept a batch feed of blank envelopes, you can skip the steps required to create mailing labels, and merge the addresses from the data document directly onto the envelopes. To determine if your printer supports this function, consult the documentation that accompanied your hardware.

Create Envelopes

1. Click the **File** tab, click **New**, click **Blank Document**, and then click **Create**.
2. Click the **Mailings** tab.
3. Click the **Start Mail Merge** button, and then click **Step by Step Mail Merge Wizard**. The Mail Merge task pane opens. Step 1 of 6 appears on the task pane.
4. Click the **Envelopes** option.
5. Click **Next: Starting document** on the task pane to display Step 2 of 6.
6. If necessary, click the **Use the current document** option.
7. Click **Envelope Options**.

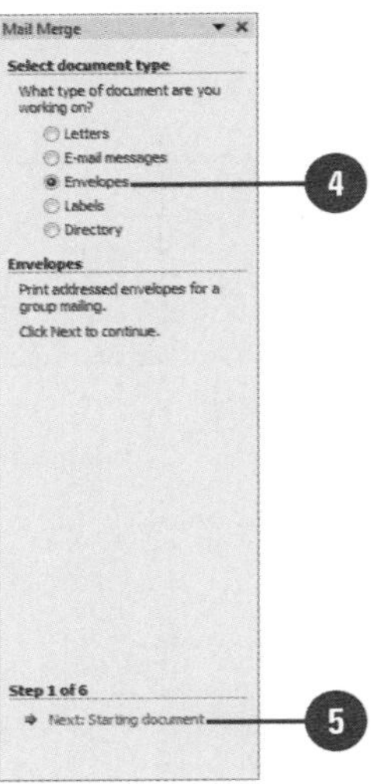

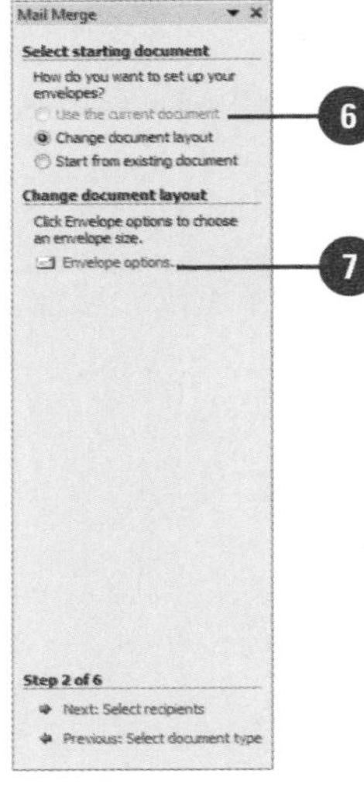

Did You Know?

You can set up the main document for envelopes manually. To create a new or existing document, click the Mailings tab, click the Start Mail Merge button, click Envelopes, select the envelope options you want, and then click OK.

8. Click the **Envelope Options** tab.
9. Select the appropriate envelope size and layout.
10. Click the **Printing Options** tab.
11. Select the printer, feed type, and tray to use for printing.
12. Click **OK**.
13. Click **Next: Select recipients** on the task pane to display Step 3 of 6.
14. If necessary, click the **Use an existing list** option, and then choose the same list you used mail merge to print the letters.
15. Click **Next: Arrange your envelope** on the task pane to display Step 4 of 6.
16. If you want to include a return address on the mailing, type it now, position the insertion point where you want the recipient's mailing address to appear, click **Address Block** on the task pane to insert the merge field, select your options, and then click **OK**.
17. Complete the remaining steps just as you would with creating mailing labels.

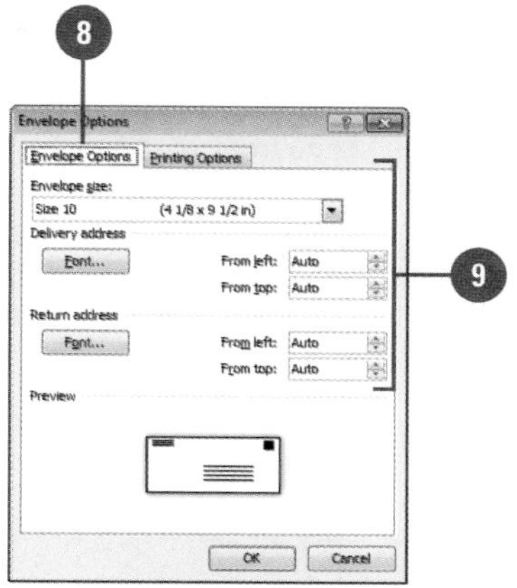

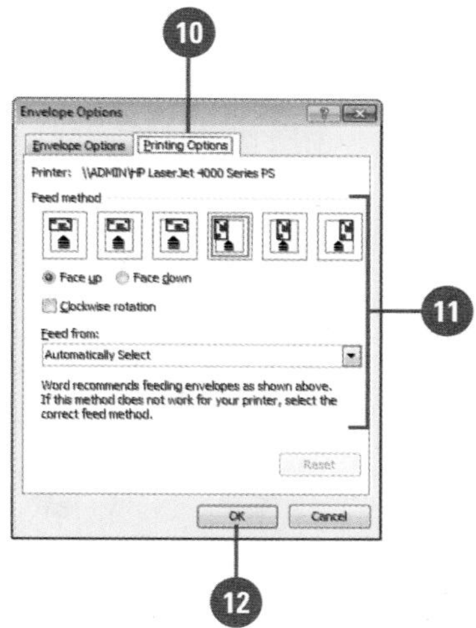

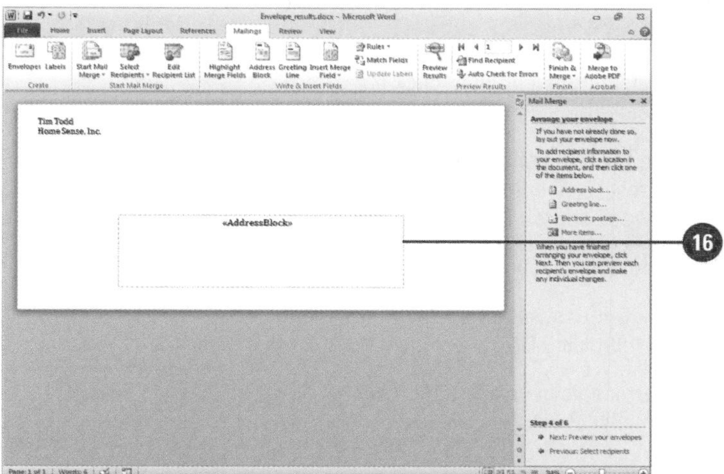

Addressing Envelopes and Labels

When you write a letter, you can use Word to print an address on an envelope or mailing label. Word scans your document to find a delivery address. You can use the one Word finds, enter another one, or select one from your Address Book. You can specify a return address, or you can omit it. Addresses can contain text, graphics, and bar codes. The POSTNET bar code is a machine-readable depiction of a U.S. zip code and delivery address; the FIM-A code identifies the front of a courtesy reply envelope. You can print a single label or multiple labels.

Address and Print Envelopes

1. Click the **Mailings** tab, click the **Envelopes** button, and then click the **Envelopes** tab, if necessary.
2. Type the recipients name and address, or click the **Insert Address** button to search for it.
3. Type your name and address.
4. Click **Options**, select a size, placement, bar code, font, and then click **OK**.
5. Insert an envelope in your printer, and then click **Print**.

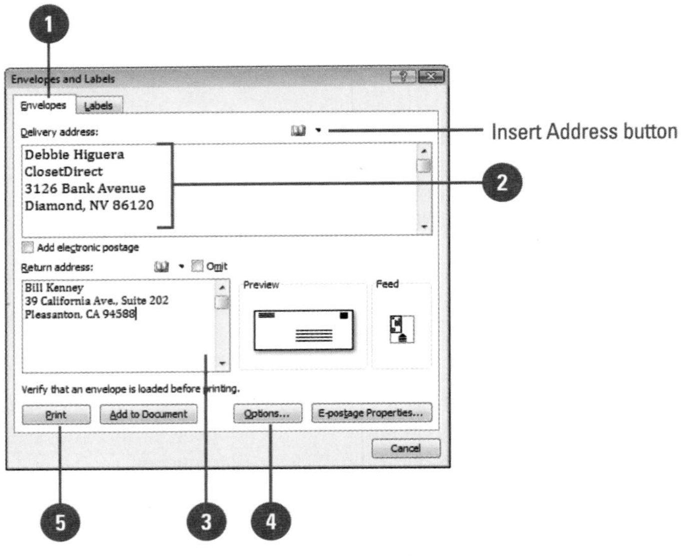

Address and Print Mailing Labels

1. Click the **Mailings** tab, click the **Labels** button, and then click the **Labels** tab.
2. Type the recipients name and address, or the Insert Address button to search for it.
3. Select which labels to print.
4. Click **Options**, select a type or size, and then click **OK**.
5. Insert labels in your printer, and then click **Print**.

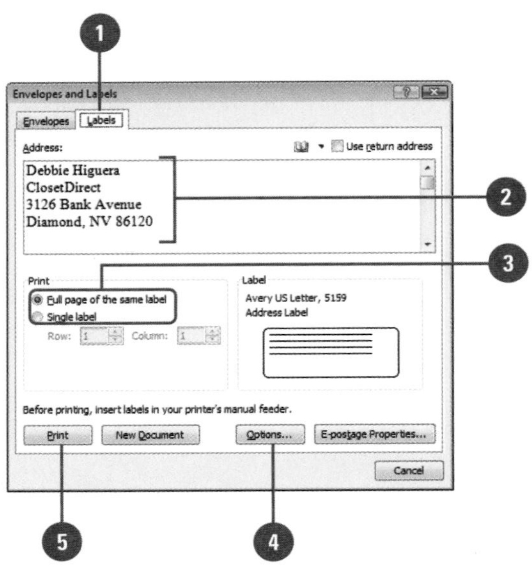

Proofing and Printing Documents

11

Introduction

After finalizing your document, there are some necessary steps you should do prior to printing. You can check for inconsistent formatting in your document. If you have established a certain style, checking your formatting can ensure that your document is formatted correctly.

You can also look up and use synonyms and antonyms to make your document more interesting. Under the Review tab, you can use a Thesaurus, translate a word or document into another language, or even use multiple languages with the Word program. Of course, no document should be printed without first going through the spell checker to check your spelling and grammar usage. You can add personalized names, terms, company information to your spell checker, so that when you are using the spell checker, it won't make unnecessary stops on words that are spelled and used correctly.

If your document is larger, page numbers might be necessary to help your reader follow along. You can insert page numbers for single or double sided printing, and you can even add chapter numbers. When getting ready to print, you might want to preview your document to make sure that your margins are appropriate for your text and printing. If, after previewing your document, you find that some text should be on a different page, you can insert page breaks to end the page early, so that common text stays together on a page. You can also insert a whole new page in your document.

When it's finally time to print, you can print all or part of a document, change your page orientation to print landscape or portrait, print double-sided or specialized documents, and even print document properties.

What You'll Do

Checking for Inconsistent Formatting

By default, Word does not automatically check for inconsistent formatting as you create documents. To instruct Word to mark the document for inconsistent formatting, and also to check documents that you have already prepared for inconsistent formatting, you need to change editing options in the Word Options dialog box. Word will automatically detect any inconsistent format elements and mark them with a blue wavy underline. When you turn on the Keep track of formatting option you can also use the Select Text with Similar formatting command on the shortcut menu that appears if you right-click selected text.

Change Editing Options

1. Click the **File** tab, and then click **Options**.
2. In the left pane, click **Advanced**.
3. Select the **Keep track of formatting** check box.
4. Select the **Mark formatting inconsistencies** check box.
5. Click **OK**.

   The formatting inconsistencies are indicated by a blue wavy underline.

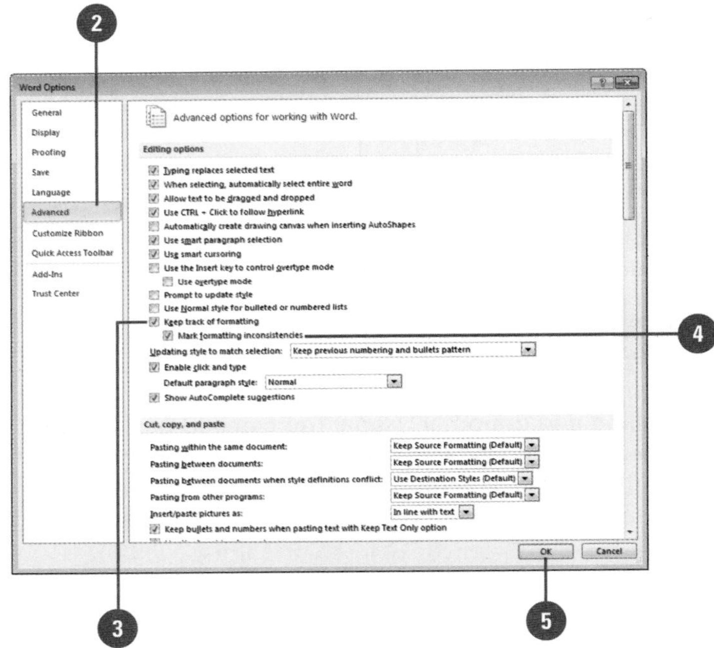

Change Inconsistent Formatting

1. In the document, right-click any wavy, blue line to open a list of Formatting commands.
2. Click the appropriate choice based on the error in the text to make the necessary correction.
   - **Make this text consistent with formatting...**
   - **Ignore Once.**
   - **Ignore Rule.**

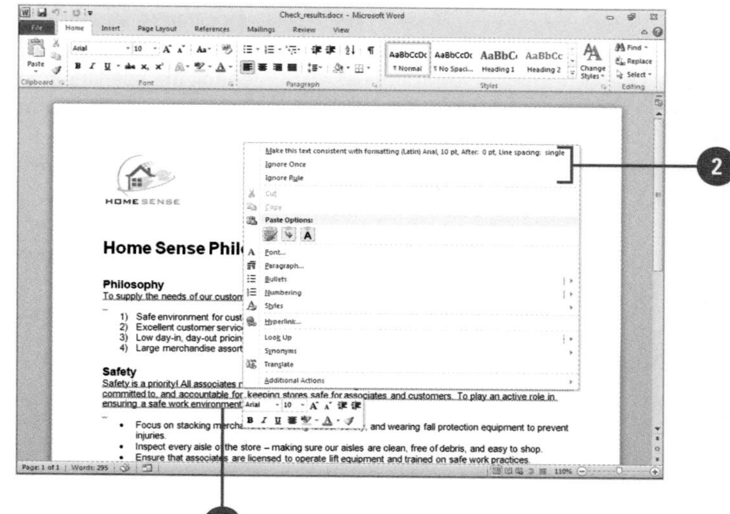

Did You Know?

You can find similar inconsistent formatting quickly. You can also click the Select button on the Home tab, and then click Select Text With Similar Formatting to facilitate global changes of mistakes that have been repeated throughout the document.

Checking Spelling and Grammar

A document's textual inaccuracies can distract the reader, so it's important that your text be error-free. Word provides a spelling checker—common for all Office 2010 programs—so that you can check the spelling in an entire document for words not listed in the dictionary (such as misspellings, names, technical terms, or acronyms) or duplicate words (such as *the the*). You can correct these errors as they arise or after you finish the entire document. You can use the Spelling button on the Review tab to check the entire document using the Spelling dialog box, or you can avoid spelling errors on a document by enabling the AutoCorrect feature to automatically correct words as you type.

Check Spelling All at Once

1. Click the **Review** tab.
2. Click the **Spelling & Grammar** button.
3. If the Spelling dialog box opens, choose an option:
   - Click **Ignore Once** to skip the word, or click **Ignore All** to skip every instance of the word.
   - Click **Add to Dictionary** to add a word to your dictionary, so it doesn't show up as a misspelled word in the future.
   - Click a suggestion, and then click **Change** or **Change All**.
   - Select the correct word, and then click **AutoCorrect** to add it to the AutoCorrect list.
   - If no suggestion is appropriate, click in the document and edit the text yourself. Click **Resume** to continue.
4. Word will prompt you when the spelling check is complete, or you can click **Close** to end the spelling check.

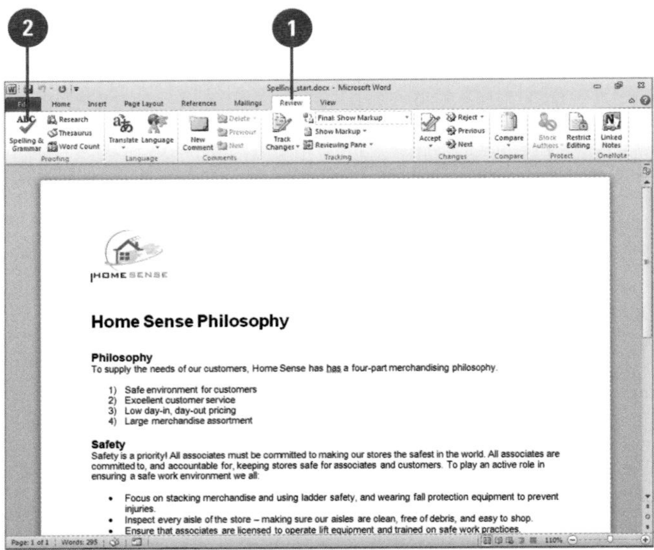

Word not recognized

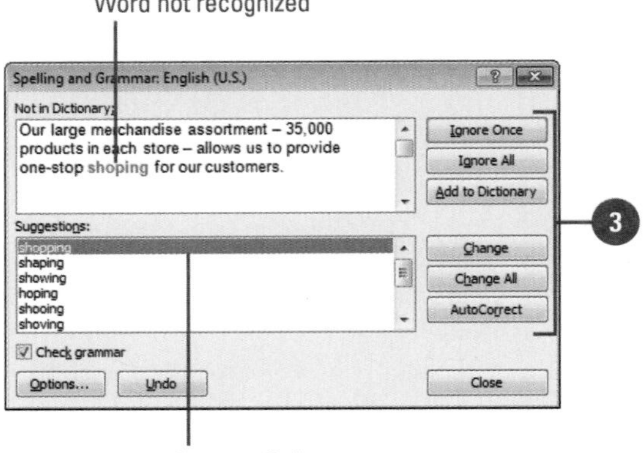

Current dictionary

Correct Spelling and Grammar as you Type

1. Right-click a word with a red or green wavy underline.
2. Click a substitution, or click Ignore (or Grammar) to skip any other instances of the word.

Did You Know?

You can add a familiar word to your dictionary. Right-click the wavy line under the word in question, and then click Add To Dictionary.

You can hyphenate words. Click the Page Layout tab, click the Hyphenation button, and then click Automatic.

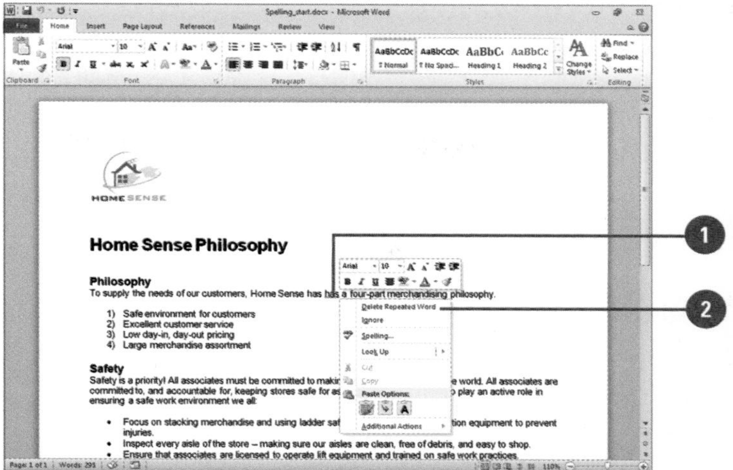

For Your Information

Finding out Document Readability

Word can help you determine the readability of your documents. When you set the readability option and check spelling and grammar, Word displays information and statistics about the reading level of the document, including the Flesch Reading Ease score and the Flesch-Kincaid Grade Level score. The readability scores are based on the average number of syllables per word and words per sentence. To display readability statistics, click the File tab, click Options, click Proofing in the left pane, select the Check Grammar With Spelling check box, select the Show Readability Statistics check box, and then click OK.

Using Custom Dictionaries

Before you can use a custom dictionary, you need to enable it first. You can enable and manage custom dictionaries by using the Custom Dictionaries dialog box. In the dialog box, you can change the language associated with a custom dictionary, create a new custom dictionary, or add or remove an existing custom dictionary. If you need to manage dictionary content, you can also change the default custom dictionary to which the spelling checker adds words, as well as add, delete, or edit words. All the modifications you make to your custom dictionaries are shared with all your Microsoft Office programs, so you only need to make changes once. If you mistakenly type an obscene or embarrassing word, such as *ass* instead of *ask*, the spelling checker will not catch it because both words are spelled correctly. You can avoid this problem by using an exclusion dictionary. When you use a language for the first time, Office automatically creates an exclusion dictionary. This dictionary forces the spelling checker to flag words you don't want to use.

Use a Custom Dictionary

1. Click the **File** tab, and then click **Options**.
2. In the left pane, click **Proofing**.
3. Click **Custom Dictionaries**.
4. Select the check box next to **CUSTOM.DIC (Default)**.
5. Click the **Dictionary language** list arrow, and then select a language for a dictionary.
6. Click the options you want:
   - Click **Edit Word List** to add, delete, or edit words.
   - Click **Change Default** to select a new default dictionary.
   - Click **New** to create a new dictionary.
   - Click **Add** to insert an existing dictionary.
   - Click **Remove** to delete a dictionary.
7. Click **OK** to close the Custom Dictionaries dialog box.
8. Click **OK**.

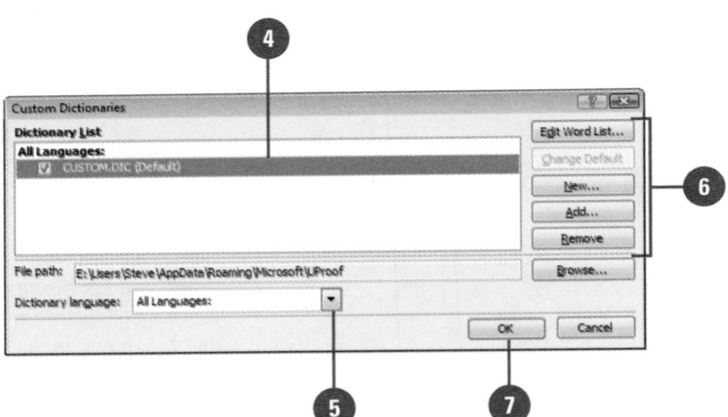

Find and Modify the Exclusion Dictionary

1. In Windows Explorer, go to the folder location where the custom dictionaries are stored.
   - **Windows 7 or Vista.** C:\Users*user name*\AppData\Roaming\Microsoft\UProof
   - **Windows XP.** C:\Documents and Settings*user name*\Application Data\Microsoft\UProof

   TROUBLE? *If you can't find the folder, change folder settings to show hidden files and folders.*

2. Locate the exclusion dictionary for the language you want to change.
   - The file name you want is ExcludeDictionary *Language CodeLanguage LCID*.lex.

     For example, ExcludeDictionary EN0409.lex, where EN is for English.

   Check Word Help for an updated list of LCID (Local Identification Number) numbers for each language.

3. Open the file using Microsoft Notepad or WordPad.
4. Add each word you want the spelling check to flag as misspelled. Type the words in all lowercase and then press Enter after each word.
5. Save and close the file.

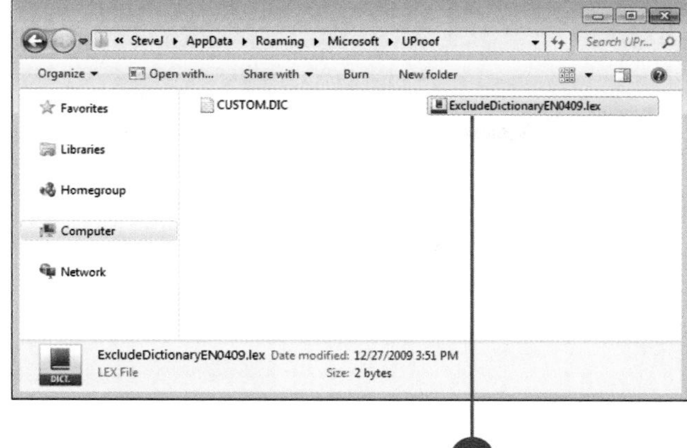

Changing Proofing Options

You can customize the way Microsoft Office spell checks a document by selecting proofing settings in Options. Some spelling options apply to specific Office programs, such as Check spelling as you type, while other options apply to all Microsoft Office programs, such as Ignore Internet and file addresses, and Flag repeated words. If you have ever mistakenly used *their* instead of *there*, you can use contextual spelling to fix it. While you work in a document, you can set options to have the spelling checker search for mistakes in the background.

Change Office Spelling Options

1. Click the **File** tab, and then click **Options**.
2. In the left pane, click **Proofing**.
3. Select or clear the spelling options you want.
   - **Ignore words in UPPERCASE.**
   - **Ignore words that contain numbers.**
   - **Ignore Internet and file addresses.**
   - **Flag repeated words.**
   - **Enforce accented uppercase in French.**
   - **Suggest from main dictionary only**. Select to exclude your custom dictionary.
   - **French modes**. Select an option for working with French.
   - **Spanish modes**. Select an option for working with Spanish (**New!**).
4. Click **OK**.

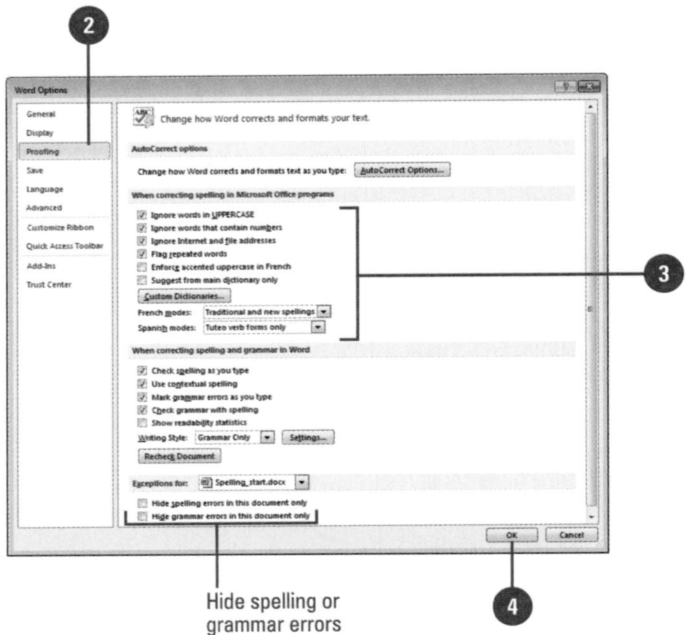

Did You Know?

You can hide spelling or grammar errors for a specific document. Click the File tab, click Options, click Proofing, click the Exceptions For list arrow, select the file you want, select the check boxes to hide spelling or grammar error for this document only, and then click OK.

Change Word Spelling Options

1. Click the **File** tab, and then click **Options**.
2. In the left pane, click **Proofing**.
3. Select or clear the Word spelling options you want.
   - **Check spelling as you type.**
   - **Use contextual spelling.**
   - **Mark grammar errors as you type.**
   - **Check grammar with spelling.**
   - **Show readability statistics.**
   - **Writing Style**. Select to check grammar only or grammar and style.
4. Click **OK**.

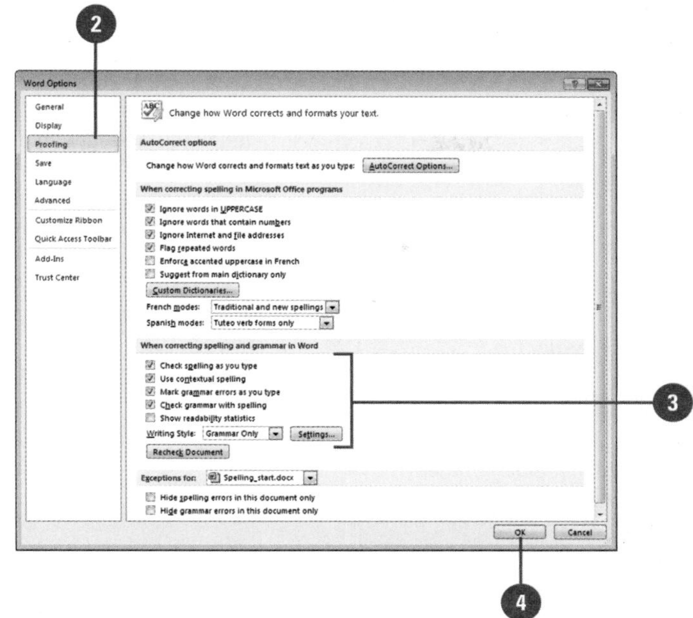

Change Grammar Settings

1. Click the **File** tab, and then click **Options**.
2. In the left pane, click **Proofing**.
3. Click **Settings**.
4. Under Require, click the list arrow, and then select the option you want: **always**, **never**, or **don't check**.
5. Under Grammar, select the check boxes with the grammar and style options you want and clear the ones you don't want.
6. Click **OK**.
7. Click **OK**.

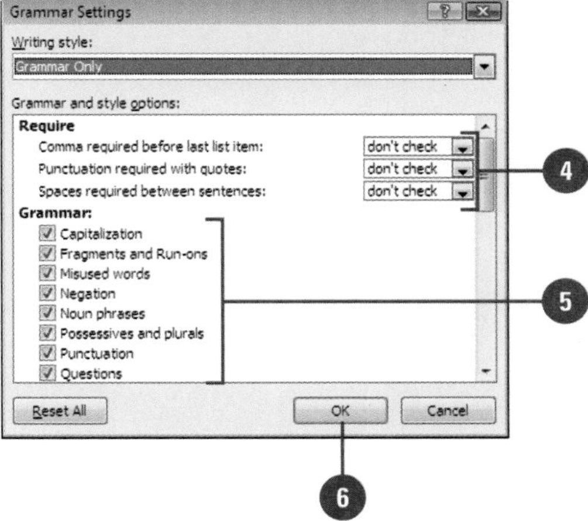

Setting Languages for Proofing

When you're working with more than one language at a time in a document, you can enable a language option to make it easier to switch between languages when typing and editing text. When you select the Detect language automatically option, Word automatically detects the language you are typing and uses the appropriate proofing tool for the language. Along with this option, you can also select the Automatically switch keyboard to match language of surround text option in the Advanced pane of the Word Options dialog box to work more efficiently with multiple languages.

Set a Language for Proofing

1. Click the **Review** tab.
2. Click the **Language** button, and then click **Set Proofing Language**.
3. Review the list of languages above the double line in the Mark selected text as list. Office only detects languages above the double line.
   - **Quickly add a language.** Double-click a language in the Mark selected text as list.
   - **Add/remove a language.** On the Review tab, click the **Language** button, and then click **Language Preferences**.
4. Select or clear the following check boxes:
   - **Do not check spelling or grammar.** Select to not check spelling or grammar for the languages.
   - **Detect language automatically.** Select to automatically detect the language you are typing and enables the proofing tools for the language.
5. To set a language as the default, select the language, and then click **Set As Default**.
6. Click **OK**.

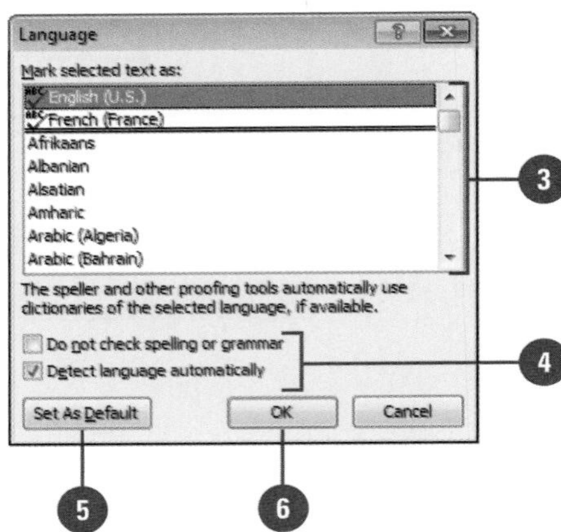

Set an Option to Automatically Switch Keyboard Language

1. Click the **File** tab, and then click **Options**.
2. In the left pane, click **Advanced**.
3. Select the **Automatically switch keyboard to match language of surrounding text** check box.
   - If the option is not available, you need to enable a keyboard layout for a language in the Language pane of the Word Options dialog box.
4. Click **OK**.

See Also

See "Using Multiple Languages" on page 280 for information on enabling a keyboard layout to use with Microsoft Office programs.

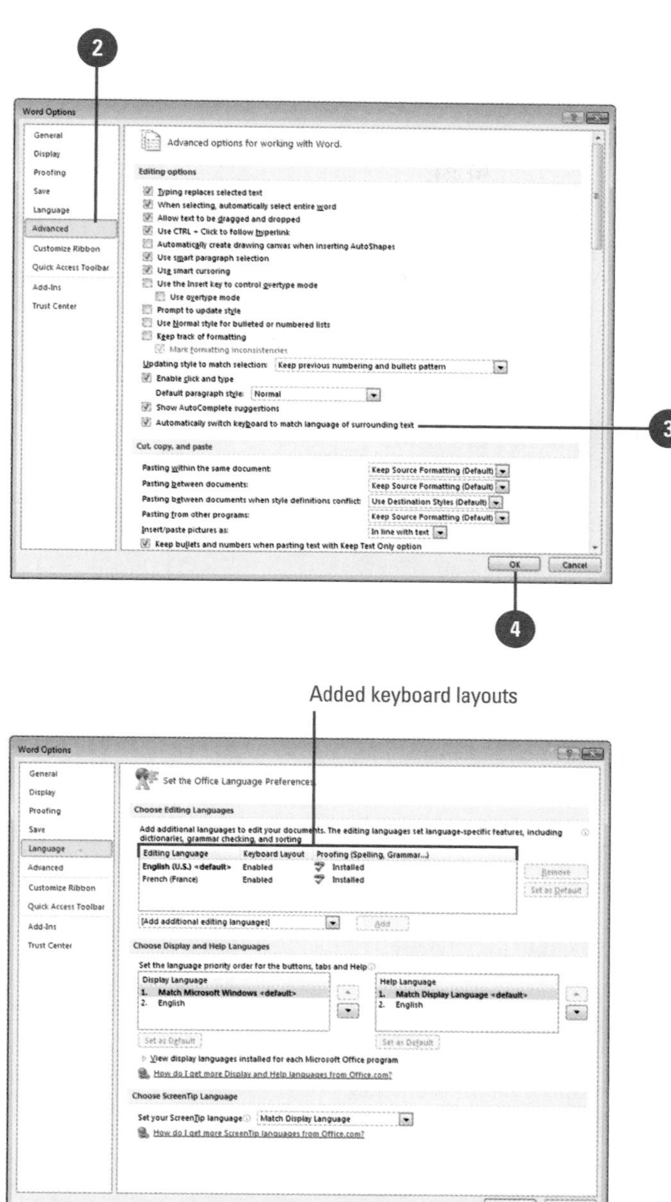

Translating Text to Another Language

If you need to quickly translate a word into another language, you can enable the Mini Translator (**New!**) that translates words when you point to them. The Mini Translator also includes a toolbar, which provides options to copy the translation to the Clipboard or play the word audibly. Before you get started, you need to choose the translation language you want to use. If you don't get the results you want, you can also use the Research task pane to translate text. With the Research task pane, you can translate single words or short phrases into different languages by using bilingual dictionaries and incorporate it into your work. If you need to translate an entire document for basic subject matter understanding, Web-based machine translation services are available using the Translate Document command. A machine translation is helpful for general meaning, but may not preserve the full meaning of the content.

Translate Text Using the Mini Translator

1. Click the **Review** tab.
2. Click the **Translate** button, click **Choose Translation Language,** specify a language for the Mini Translator, and then click **OK**.
3. Click the **Translate** button, and then click the Mini Translator language you set for translation to highlight the icon next to the command.
4. Point to the word you want to display the Mini Translator with the translated word. You can also use the toolbar to perform the following options:
   - **Expand.** Opens the Research pane with more options.
   - **Copy**. Copies the translation to the Clipboard.
   - **Play** and **Stop**. Plays or stops the word audibly.
   - **Help**. Opens Help.
5. To turn off the Mini Translator, click the **Translate** button, and then click the Mini Translator language to clear the highlighted icon next to the command.

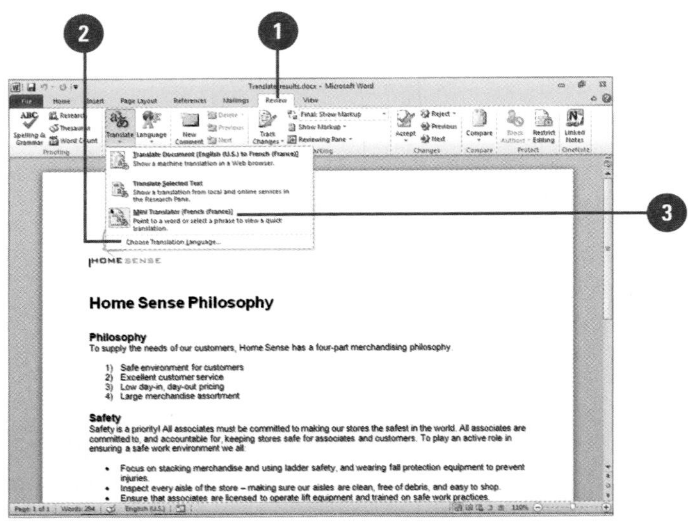

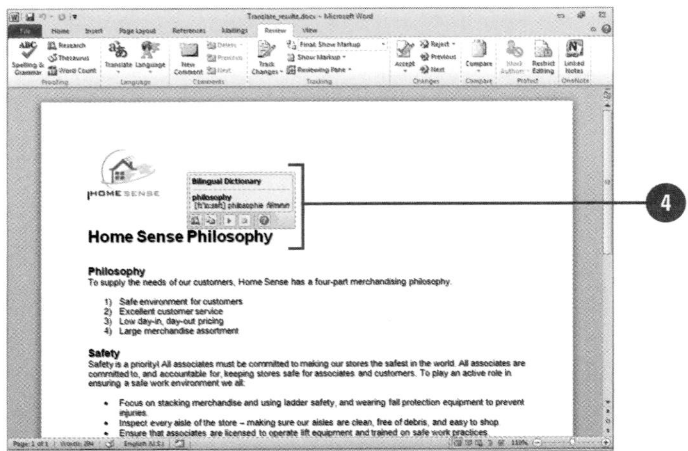

Translate Text Using the Research Pane

1. Select the text you want to translate.
2. Click the **Review** tab.
3. Click the **Translate** button, and then click **Translate Selected Text**.

   If this is the first you have used translation services, click **OK** to install the bilingual dictionaries and enable the service.
4. If necessary, click the list arrow, and then click **Translation**.
5. Click the **From** list arrow, and then select the language of the selected text.
6. Click the **To** list arrow, and then select the language you want to translate into.
7. To customize which resources are used for translation, click **Translation options**, select the look-up options you want, and then click **OK**.
8. Right-click the translated text in the Research task pane that you want to copy, and then click **Copy**.
9. Paste the information into your document.
10. When you're done, click the **Close** button on the task pane.

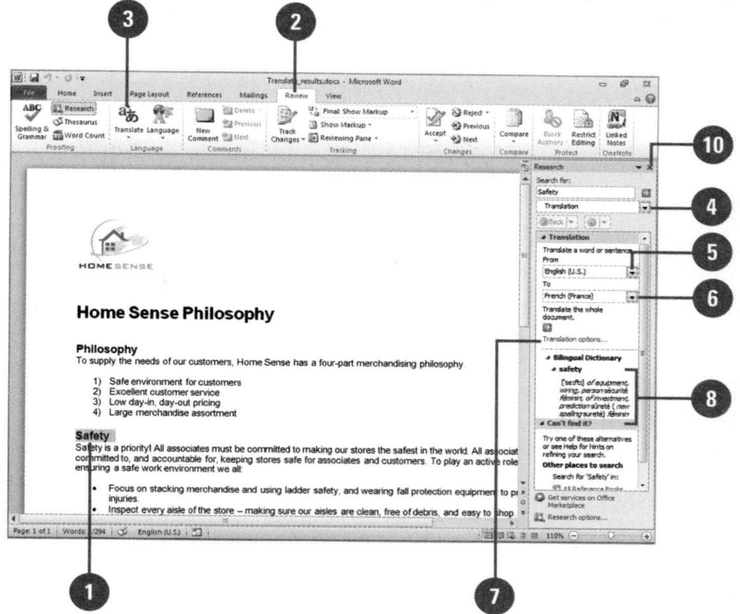

See Also

See "Using Multiple Languages" on page 280 for information on adding languages to use with Microsoft Office programs.

Using Multiple Languages

International Microsoft Office users can change the language that appears on their screens by changing the default language settings. Users around the world can enter, display, and edit text in all supported languages—including European languages, Japanese, Chinese, Korean, Hebrew, and Arabic—to name a few. You'll probably be able to use Office programs in your native language. If the text in your document is written in more than one language, you can automatically detect languages or designate the language of selected text so the spelling checker uses the right dictionary. You can set preferences (**New!**) for editing, display, ScreenTip, and Help languages. If you don't have the keyboard layout or related software installed, you can click links to add or enable them (**New!**).

Add a Language to Office Programs

1. Click the **File** tab, click **Options**, and then click **Language**.
   - You can also click **Start** on the taskbar, point to **All Programs**, click **Microsoft Office**, click **Microsoft Office Tools**, and then click **Microsoft Office 2010 Language Preferences**.
2. Click the **Language** list arrow, and then select the language you want to enable.
3. Click **Add**.
4. To enable the correct keyboard layout for the installed language, click the **Not enabled** link to open the Text Services and Input Language dialog box, where you can select a keyboard layout, and then click **OK**.
5. Set the language priority order for the buttons, tabs, and Help for the Display and Help languages.
6. Set your ScreenTip language to Match Display Language or a specific language.
7. Click **OK**, and then click **Yes** (if necessary) to quit and restart Office.

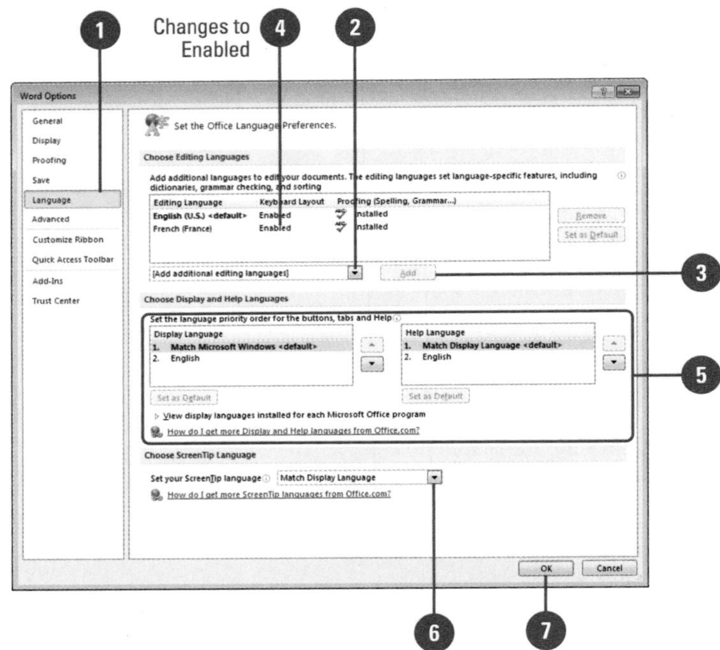

Finding the Right Words

Repeating the same word in a document can reduce a message's effectiveness. Instead, replace some words with synonyms or find antonyms. If you need help finding exactly the right words, use the shortcut menu to look up synonyms quickly or search a Thesaurus for more options. This feature can save you time and improve the quality and readability of your document. You can also install a Thesaurus for another language. Foreign language thesauruses can be accessed under Research Options on the Research task pane.

Use the Thesaurus

1. Select the text you want to translate.
2. Click the **Review** tab.
3. Click the **Thesaurus** button.
4. Click the list arrow, and then select a **Thesaurus**, if necessary.
5. Point to the word in the Research task pane.
6. Click the list arrow, and then click one of the following:
   - **Insert** to replace the word you looked up with the new word.
   - **Copy** to copy the new word and then paste it within the document.
   - **Look Up** to look up the word for other options.
7. When you're done, click the **Close** button on the task pane.

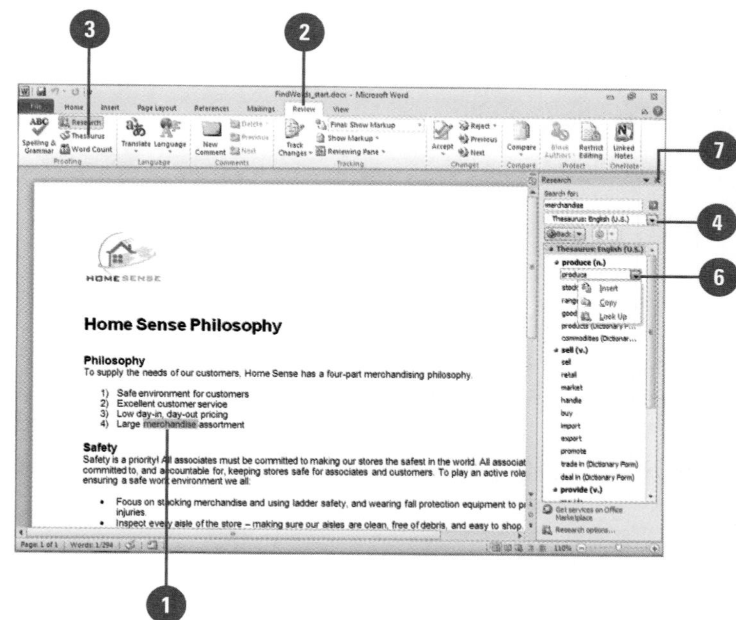

Setting Up Page Margins

Margins are the blank space between the edge of a page and the text. The default setting for Word documents is 1.25 inches on the left and right, and 1 inch on the top and bottom. You can use the mouse pointer to adjust margins visually for the entire document, or you can use the Page Setup dialog box to set precise measurements for an entire document or a specific section. When you shift between portrait and landscape page orientation, the margin settings automatically change. If you need additional margin space for binding pages into a book or binder, you can adjust the left or right gutter settings. Gutters allow for additional margin space so that all of the document text remains visible after binding. Unless this is your purpose, leave the default settings in place.

Adjust Margins Visually

1. Click the **Print Layout** tab.
2. If necessary, click the **View Ruler** button to display it.
3. Select the text where you want to change the margins.
4. Position the pointer over a margin boundary on the horizontal or vertical ruler.
5. Press and hold Alt, and then click a margin boundary to display the measurements of the text and margin areas as you adjust the margins.
6. Drag the left, right, top, or bottom margin boundary to a new position.

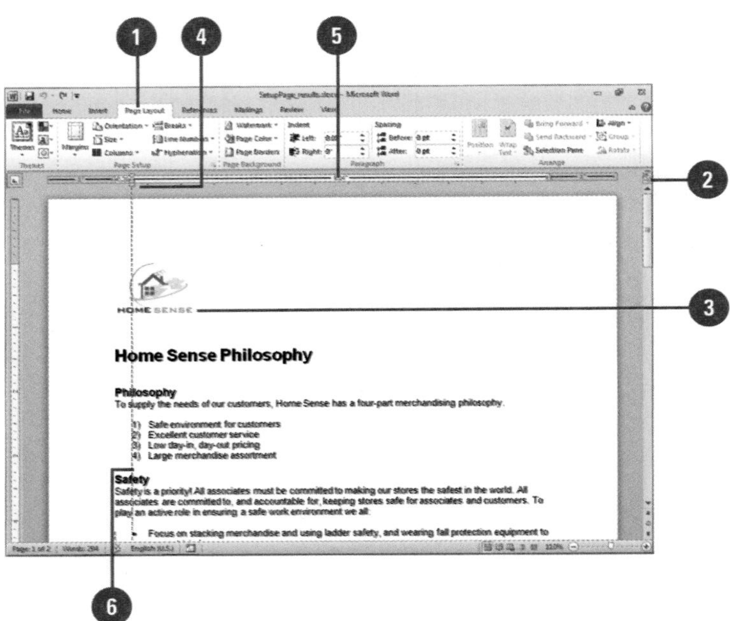

Did You Know?

You can preset gutter measurements. To set the gutters for normal binding, display the Margins tab in the Page Setup dialog box, click the Multiple Pages list arrow, and then click Book Fold.

Select Standard Margins Quickly

1. Click the **Print Layout** tab.
2. Click the **Margins** button, and then click the margin setting you want:
   - **Last Custom Setting.**
   - **Normal.**
   - **Narrow.**
   - **Moderate.**
   - **Wide.**
   - **Mirrored.**
   - **Office 2003 Default.**

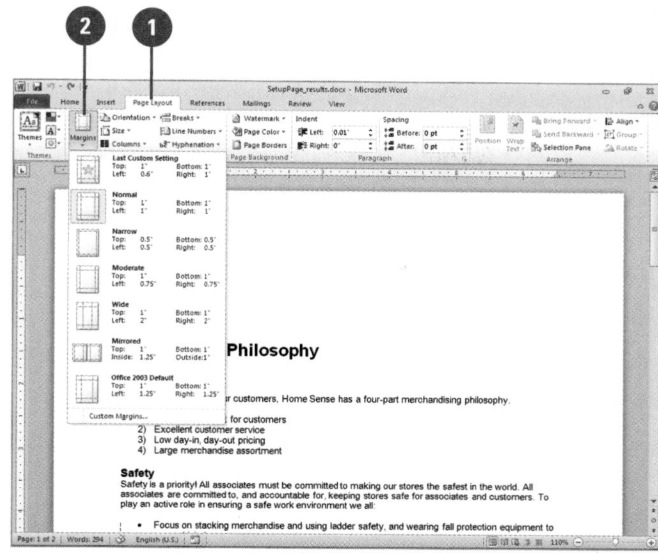

Create Custom Margins Using Page Setup

1. Click the **Print Layout** tab.
2. Click the **Margins** button, and then click **Custom Margins.**

   The Page Setup dialog box opens, displaying the Margins tab.
3. Type new margin measurements (in inches) in the Top, Bottom, Left, or Right boxes, and Gutter boxes.
4. Click the page orientation you want.
5. Click the **Apply to** list arrow, and then click **Selected Text**, **This Point Forward**, or **Whole Document.**
6. To make the new margin settings the default for all new Word documents, click **Set As Default**, and then click **Yes**.
7. Click **OK**.

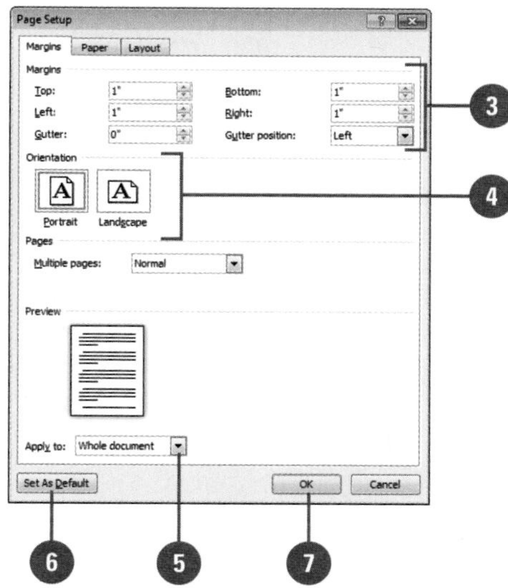

Adjusting Paper Settings

Every document you produce and print might need a different page setup. You can achieve the look you want by printing on a standard paper size (such as letter, legal, or envelope), international standard paper sizes, or any custom size that your printer accepts. The default setting is 8.5 x 11 inches, the most common letter and copy size. You can also print several pages on one sheet. If you want to create a custom paper size, you can input custom settings for special print jobs on odd-sized paper.

Set the Paper Size

1. Click the **Page Layout** tab.
2. Click the **Page Setup Dialog Box Launcher**.
3. Click the **Paper** tab.
4. Click the **Paper size** list arrow, and then select the paper size you want, or specify a custom size.
5. Select the paper source for the first page and other pages.
6. Click the **Apply to** list arrow, and then click **This section**, **This point forward**, or **Whole document**.
7. Verify your selections in the Preview box.
8. To make your changes the default settings for all new documents, click **Set As Default**, and then click **Yes**.
9. Click **OK**.

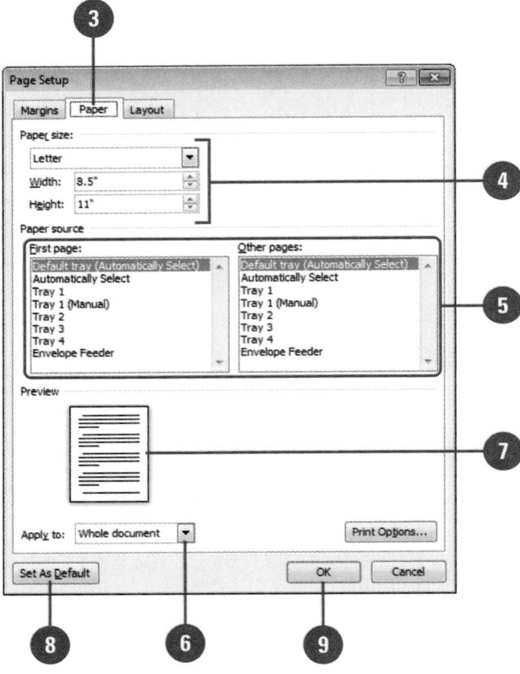

Did You Know?

You can improve printing speed. If printing is slow, you can turn off background printing to speed up the process. In the Page Setup dialog box on the Paper tab, click Print Options, click Advanced in the left pane, clear the Print In Background check box, and then click OK.

Controlling the Way Pages Break

When you're creating a document, sometimes a line of text, known as a widow or orphan, in a paragraph doesn't fit on a page and looks out of place on the next page. A **widow** is the last line of a paragraph printed by itself at the top of a page. An **orphan** is the first line of a paragraph printed by it self at the bottom of a page. You can use the Widow/Orphan Control option to automatically correct the problem. If a widow or orphan occurs, Word adjusts the paragraph to make sure at least two lines appear together on the next page. When two paragraphs need to remain grouped to maintain their impact, regardless of where the normal page break would have occurred, you can keep paragraphs together on a page or in a column. If you need to start a paragraph at the top of a page, you can automatically generate a page break before a paragraph.

Control Pagination

1. Select the paragraph in which you want to control.
2. Click the **Page Layout** tab.
3. Click the **Paragraph Dialog Box Launcher**.
4. Click the **Line and Page Breaks** tab.
5. Choose an option:
   - Select the **Widow/Orphan control** check box to avoid paragraphs ending with a single word on a line or a single line at the top of a page.
   - Select the **Keep with next** check box to group paragraphs together.
   - Select the **Keep lines together** check box to keep paragraph lines together.
   - Select the **Page break before** check box to precede a paragraph with a page break.
6. Click **OK**.

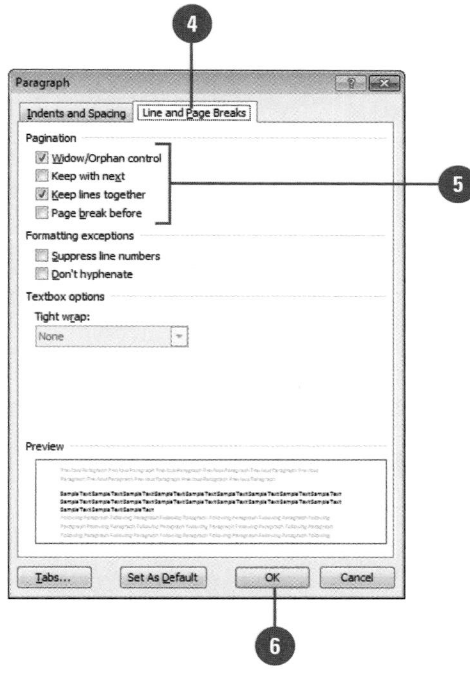

Inserting New Pages and Sections

When you fill a page, Word inserts a page break and starts a new page. As you add or delete text, this **soft page break** moves. A soft page break appears as a dotted gray line in Normal view. To start a new page before the current one is filled, insert a **hard page break** that doesn't shift as you edit text. A hard page break appears as a dotted gray line with the text Page Break centered in Normal view. A **section** is a mini-document within a document that stores margin settings, page orientation, page numbering, and so on. In Page Layout view, you can show or hide the white space on the top and bottom of each page and the gray space between pages.

Insert and Delete a Hard Page Break

1. Click where you want to insert a hard page break.
2. Use one of the following:
   - **Page Break.** Click the **Insert** tab, and then click the **Page Break** button.
   - **Blank Page.** Click the **Insert** tab, and then click the **Blank Page** button.
   - **Page or Section Break.** Click the **Page Layout** button, click **Page Break**, and then click the page break option you want.

   TIMESAVER *Press Ctrl+Enter to insert a page break.*
3. To delete a page break, click the page break in Print Layout view, and then press the Delete key. To move a page break, drag it to a new location.

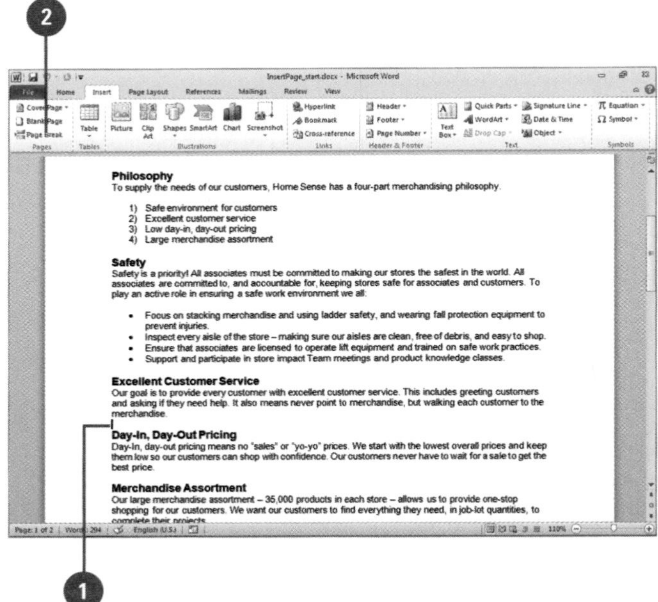

Did You Know?

You can opt to start a new line, but not a new paragraph. Insert a text wrapping break to force text to the next line in the same paragraph—the perfect tool to make a phrase fall on one line. Press Shift+Enter where you want to insert a text wrapping break.

Insert and Delete a Section Break

1. Click where you want to insert a section break.
2. Click the **Page Layout** tab.
3. Click **Page Break** button, and then select the type of section break you want.
   - **Next Page**. Starts the section on a new page.
   - **Continuous**. Starts the section wherever the point is located.
   - **Even Page**. Starts the section on the next even-numbered page.
   - **Odd Page**. Starts the section on the next odd-numbered page.
4. To delete a section break, click the section break in Print Layout view, and then press Delete.

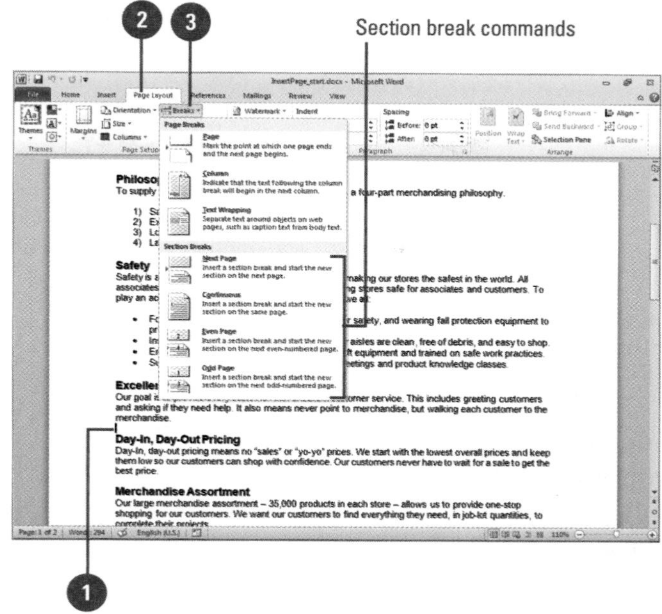

Show or Hide White Space Between Pages

1. Click the **Print Layout View** button.
2. Scroll to the bottom of a page, and then point to the gap between two pages. (The Hide White Space cursor or Show White Space cursor appears.)
3. Click the gap between the pages to show or hide the white space.

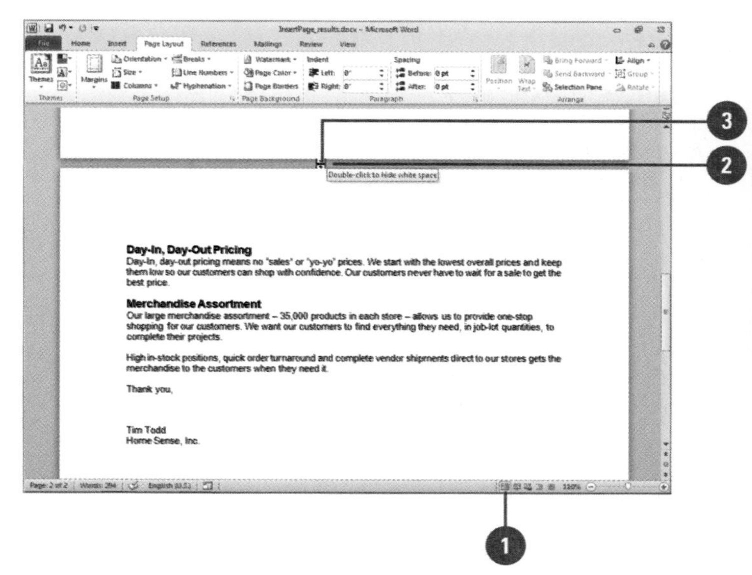

Previewing a Document

Before printing, you should verify that the page looks the way you want. You save time, money, and paper by avoiding duplicate printing. Print Preview shows you the exact placement of your data on each printed page. You can view all or part of your document as it will appear when you print it. Print Preview shows you the pages based on the properties of the selected printer. For example, if the selected printer is setup to print color, Print Preview displays in color. The Print screen (**New!**) on the File tab makes it easy to zoom in and out to view a document more comfortably, switch between pages, preview page breaks, set print options, and print all from the same place.

Preview a Document

1. Click the **File** tab, and then click **Print**.
2. Click the **Zoom to Page** button to toggle the zoom in and out to the page.
3. To adjust the zoom, drag the **Zoom** slider or click the **Zoom In** or **Zoom Out** buttons.
4. To switch pages, click the **Next Page** or **Previous Page** button, or enter a specific page in the Current Page box.
5. If you want to print, click the **Print** button.

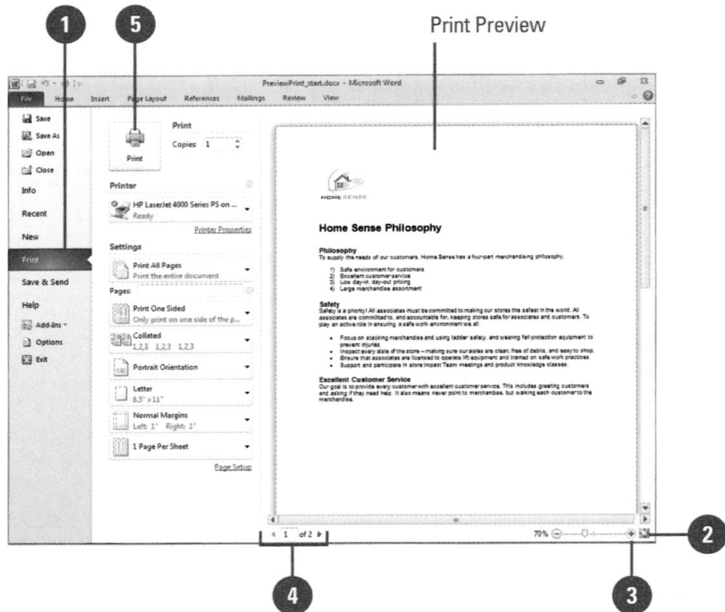

Printing a Document

When you're ready to print your document, you can choose several printing options on the Print screen (**New!**) on the File tab, such as choosing a new printer, selecting the number of pages in the document you want printed and the number of copies, specifying the page size, margins, and orientation, and selecting any scaling or pages to fit on a printed page. You can also use the Page Setup dialog box to control the appearance of pages, such as margins, orientation, paper size and source and the layout of sections, headers and footers, and page alignment. You can quickly print a copy of your document without using the Print screen by clicking the Quick Print button on the Quick Access Toolbar.

Print All or Part of a Document

1. Click the **File** tab, and then click **Print**.

   TIMESAVER *To print without the Print screen, press Ctrl+P, or click the Quick Print button on the Quick Access Toolbar.*

2. Click the **Printer** list arrow, and then click the printer you want to use.
3. To change printer properties, click the **Printer Properties** link, select the options you want, and then click **OK**.
4. Select whether you want to print the entire document or only the pages you specify.
5. Select the other print options you want to use, such as sides to print, collated, orientation, size, margins, or pages per sheet.
6. To change page options, click the **Page Setup** link, select the options you want, and then click **OK**.
7. Click **Print**.

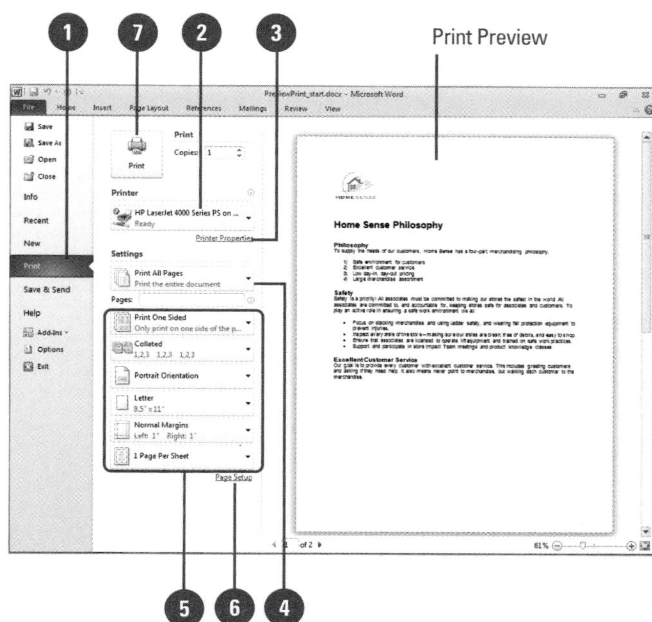

Printing Specialized Documents

Two-sided printing is appropriate for bound reports, pamphlets, brochures and many other types of Word documents. Not all printers support automatic two-sided printing. If your printer does not support two-sided printing, you can use the Manually Print on Both Sides option on the Print screen to help you complete the process. In addition to printing two-side documents, you can also print multiple pages on a page, which is useful for creating handouts for a presentation.

Print a Two-Sided Document

1. Click the **File** tab, and then click **Print**.
2. If necessary, click the **Printer** list arrow, and then click the printer you want to use.
3. Select an option for printing on both sides:
   - **Print on Both Sides (Long edge).** Prints on both sides where pages flip on the long edge.
   - **Print on Both Sides (Short edge).** Prints on both sides where pages flip on the short edge.
   - **Manually Print on Both Sides.** The first side of each alternate page will be printed. Then you will be prompted to reinsert the pages into the printer so that the second side can be printed.
4. Select the other print options you want to use.
5. Click **Print**.

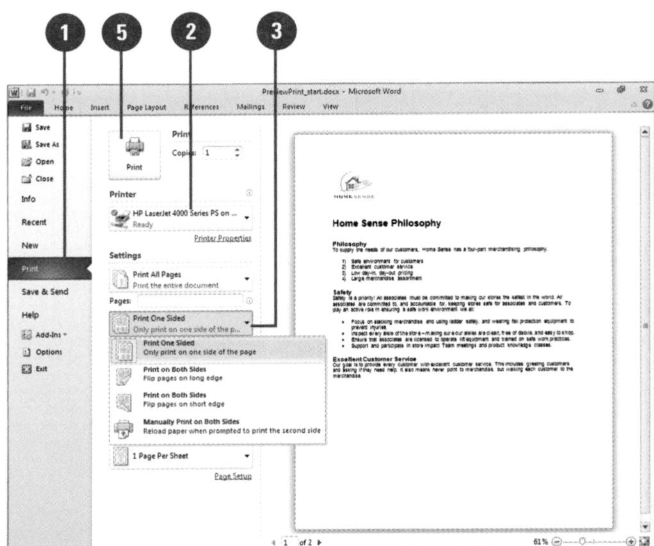

Print Multiple Pages Per Sheet

1. Click the **File** tab, and then click **Print**.
2. If necessary, click the **Printer** list arrow, and then click the printer you want to use.
3. Select an option for printing multiple pages per sheet:
   - **1 Page Per Sheet.**
   - **2 Page Per Sheet.**
   - **4 Page Per Sheet.**
   - **6 Page Per Sheet.**
   - **8 Page Per Sheet.**
   - **16 Page Per Sheet.**
   - **Scale to Paper Size.** Select a paper size for the scaling of the document pages per sheet.
4. Select the other print options you want to use.
5. Click **Print**.

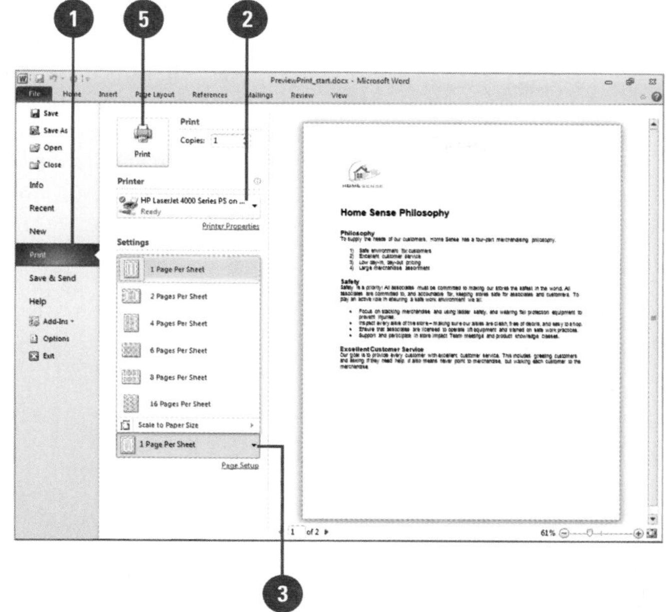

Printing Document Properties

In addition to printing the actual document, you can also print other aspects of a document, such as document properties, document markup, styles, AutoText entries, or shortcut key assignments. If you're working with others who have made a lot of changes to your document, you can use the Print screen on the File tab to select options to print a table of document properties or a list of markup, styles, or AutoText entries. If you want a list of keyboard shortcuts available in Word, you can select the Key assignments options to print out a list.

Print Document Properties

1. Click the **File** tab, and then click **Print**.
2. If necessary, click the **Printer** list arrow, and then click the printer you want to use.
3. Select what you want to print under Document Properties:
   - **Document properties.** Prints a table of properties and values.
   - **List of markup.** Prints a list of markup only from the document.
   - **Styles.** Prints a list of styles used in the document.
   - **AutoText Entries.** Prints a list of AutoText available.
   - **Key assignment.** Prints a list of customized shortcut keys.
   - **Print Markup.** Prints the document with the markup.
4. Select the other print options you want to use.
5. Click **Print**.

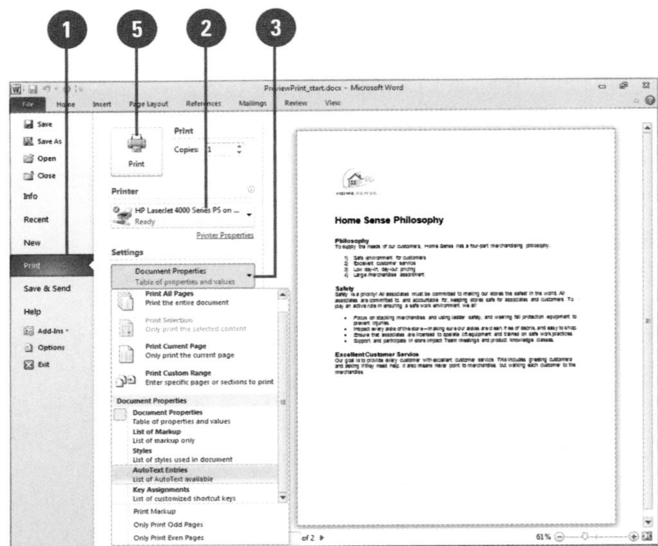

Publishing Documents on the Web

12

Introduction

Web pages are multimedia documents that provide information and contain links to other documents on the Internet, an intranet, a local network, or a hard disk. These links—also called hyperlinks—are highlighted text or graphics that you click to follow a pathway from one Web page to another. Incorporating hyperlinks within your documents adds an element of connectivity to your work. Web pages are based on **Hypertext Markup Language (HTML)**—a simple coding system used to format Web pages. A browser program, such as Microsoft Internet Explorer, interprets these special codes to determine how a certain Web page should be displayed. Different codes mark the size, color, style, and placement of text and graphics as well as which words and graphics should be marked as hyperlinks and to what files they link.

Web technology is available for all your Microsoft Office programs. Word provides you with the tools you need to create and save your documents as a Web page and to publish it on the Web. Word makes it easy to create a Web page without learning HTML. Saving your documents in HTML format means you can use most Web browsers to view them. By saving your documents as Web pages, you can share your data with others via the Internet. You can also preview how your document will look as a Web page in Word or in your browser. Word uses HTML as a companion file format; it recognizes the .html filename extension as accurately as it does those for Word.

What You'll Do

Open a Web Page

Preview a Web Page

Create Hyperlinks

Create a Hyperlink Between Frames

Use and Remove Hyperlinks

Save a Web Page

Change Web Page Options

Transfer Files Over the Web

Create a Blog Posting on the Web

Open an Existing Blog Posting

Manage Blog Accounts

Access Office Information on the Web

Opening a Web Page

After saving a document as a Web page, you can open the Web page, an HTML file. This allows you to quickly and easily switch from HTML to the standard Word format and back again without losing any formatting or functionality. For example, if you create a formatted chart in a Word document, save the document file as a Web page, and then reopen the Web page in Word, the chart will look the same as the original chart in Word. Word preserves the original formatting and functionality of the document. You can also open a Web page from Word in your Web browser.

Open a Document as a Web Page

1. Click the **File** tab, and then click **Open**.
2. Click the **Files of type** list arrow, and then click **All Web Pages**.
3. Click the **Look in** list arrow, and then select the folder where the file is located.
4. Click the Web file you want to open.
5. Click **Open**.

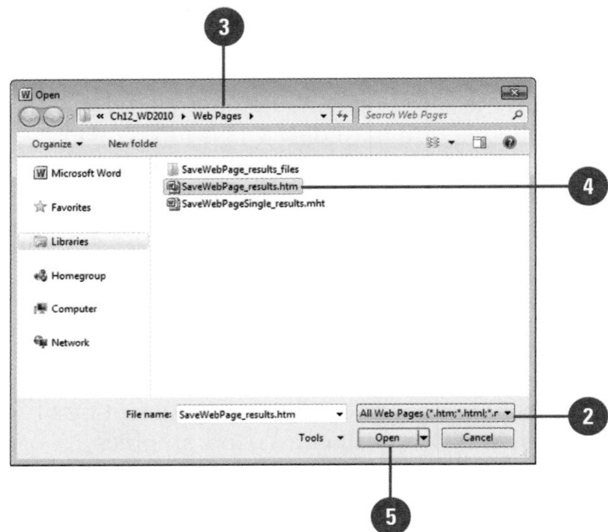

Did You Know?

You can open Web pages in the background while you work. Click the File tab, click Options, click Advanced in the left pane, select the Allow Background Open Of Web Pages check box, and then click OK.

Open a Document as a Web Page in a Browser

1. Click the **File** tab, and then click **Open**.
2. Click the **Files of type** list arrow, and then click **All Web Pages**.
3. Click the **Look in** list arrow, and then select the folder where the file is located.
4. Click the Web file you want to open.
5. Click the **Open** button arrow, and then click **Open in Browser**.
6. If prompted, click **Yes** to the warning alert to view the Web page.

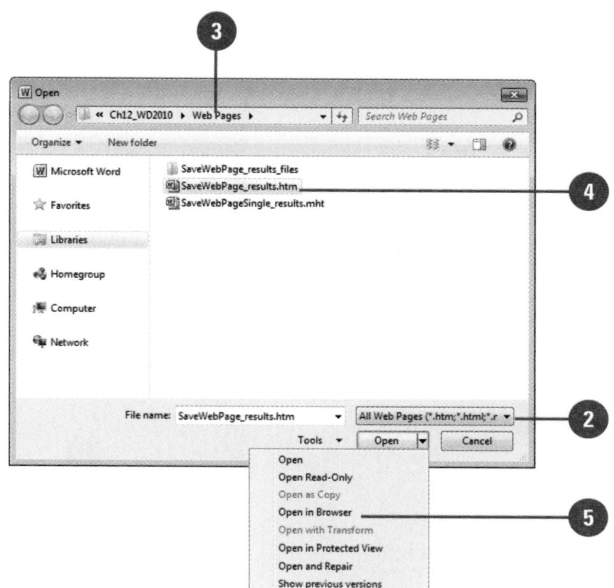

Document web page in a browser

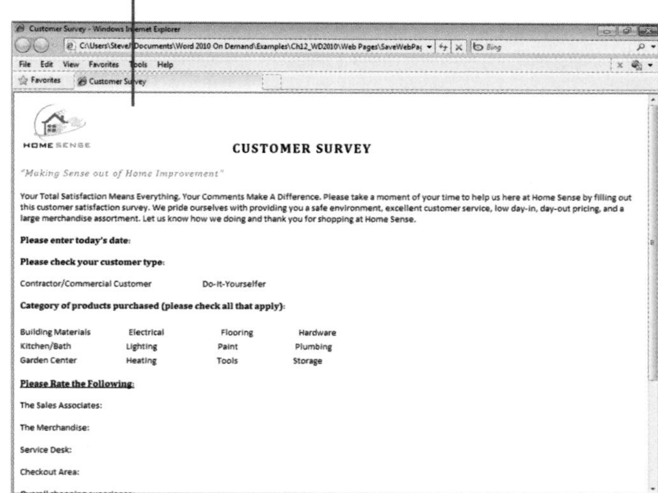

Did You Know?

You can change the appearance of Web pages and Help Viewer window. In the Internet Options dialog box for Windows, click Accessibility on the General tab, select the Ignore Colors Specified On Web pages check box, and then click OK. In the Internet Properties dialog box, click Colors to select text and background colors or Fonts to change text style.

Previewing a Web Page

You can view any document as if it were already on the Web by previewing the Web page. By previewing a file you want to post to the Web, you can see if there are any errors that need to be corrected, formatting that needs to be added, or additions that need to be made. Just as you should always preview a document before you print it, you should preview a Web page before you post it. Previewing the Web page is similar to using the Print Preview feature before you print a document. This view shows you what the page will look like once it's posted on the Internet. You do not have to be connected to the Internet to preview a document as a Web page. Web Layout view shows you how a document will be displayed on the Web. If the document includes formatting or layouts that cannot be achieved in HTML, Word switches to an HTML layout that closely matches the original look.

Preview a Web Page in Word

1. Open the document you want to view as a Web page.
2. Click the **Web Layout View** button.

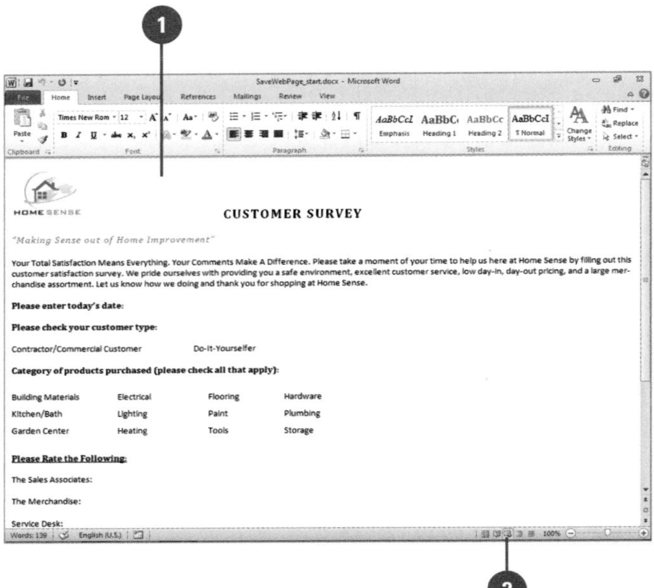

View a Web Page from a Browser

1. Open the document you want to view as a Web page.
2. Click the **Web Page Preview** button on the Quick Access Toolbar.
   - The Web Page Preview button is not on the Quick Access Toolbar by default. Use the Customize pane in Word Options to add the button.

   Your default Web browser starts and displays the Web page.
3. Click the **Close** button to quit your Web browser, and then return to Word.

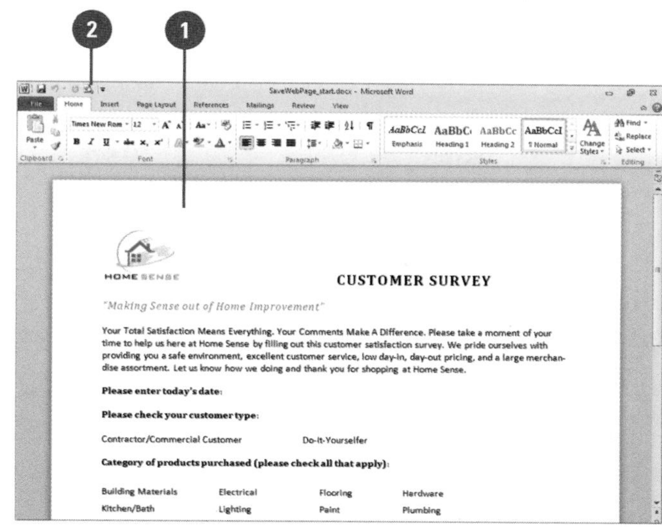

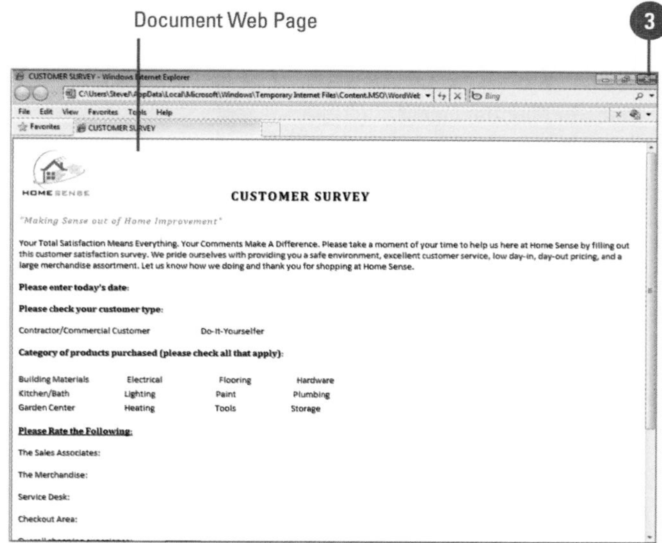

Did You Know?

Web addresses and URLs mean the same thing. Every Web page has a Uniform Resource Locator (URL), or Web address. Each URL contains specific parts that identify where a Web page is located. For example, the URL for Perspection's Web page is: *http://www.perspection.com/index.htm* where "http://" shows the address is on the Web, "www.perspection.com" shows the computer that stores the Web site, and "index.htm" is a Web page on the Web site.

Creating Hyperlinks

With instant access to the Internet, your documents can contain links to specific sites so you and anyone else using your documents can access Web information. You can create a **hyperlink**—a graphic object or colored, underlined text that you click to move (or jump) to a new location (or destination). The destination can be in the same document, another file on your computer or network, or a Web page on your intranet or the Internet. When you point to hyperlinked text or an object, the cursor changes to a pointing hand to indicate it's a hyperlink.

Insert a Hyperlink Within a Document

1. Click where you want to insert the hyperlink, or select the text or object you want to use as the hyperlink.
2. Click the **Insert** tab.
3. Click the **Hyperlink** button.

   TIMESAVER *Press Ctrl+K.*

4. Click **Place in This Document**.
5. Click a destination in the document.
6. Type the text you want to appear as the hyperlink.
7. Click **ScreenTip**.
8. Type the text you want to appear when someone points to the hyperlink.
9. Click **OK**.
10. Click **OK**.

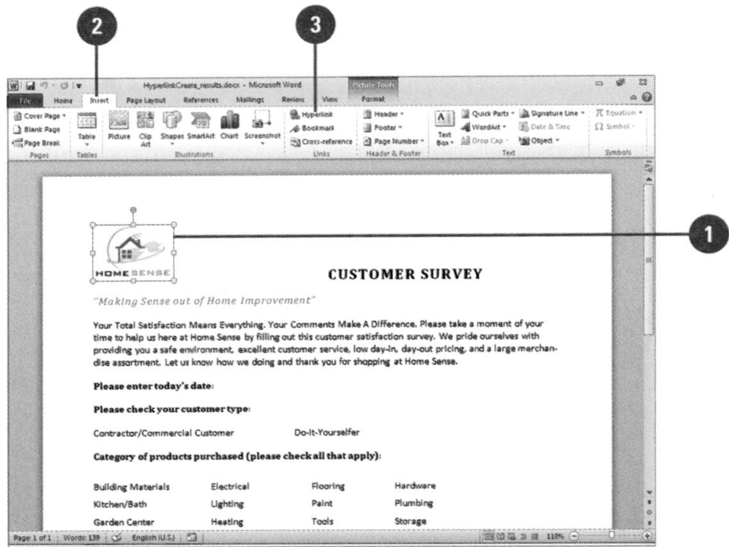

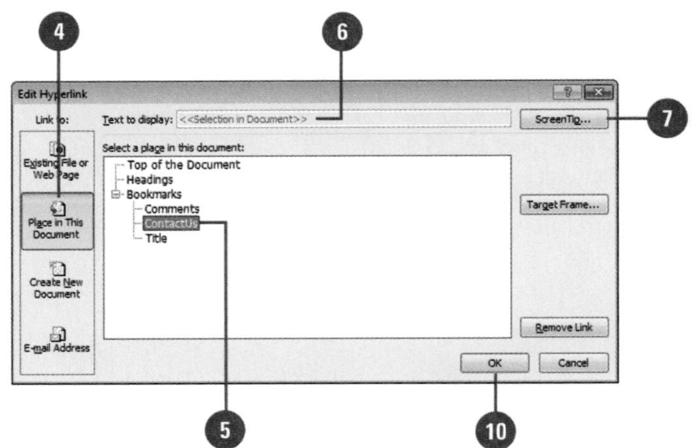

Insert a Hyperlink Between Documents

1. Click where you want to insert the hyperlink, or select the text or object you want to use as the hyperlink.
2. Click the **Insert** tab.
3. Click the **Hyperlink** button.
4. Click **Existing File or Web Page**.
5. Enter the name and path of the destination file or Web page.
   - Or click the **Bookmark** button, select the bookmark, and then click **OK**.
6. Type the text you want to appear as the hyperlink.
7. Click **ScreenTip**.
8. Type the text you want to appear when someone points to the hyperlink.
9. Click **OK**.
10. Click **OK**.

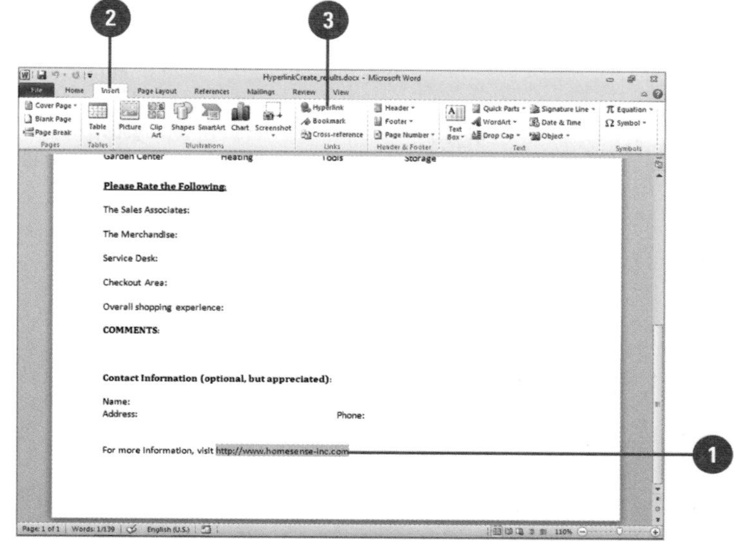

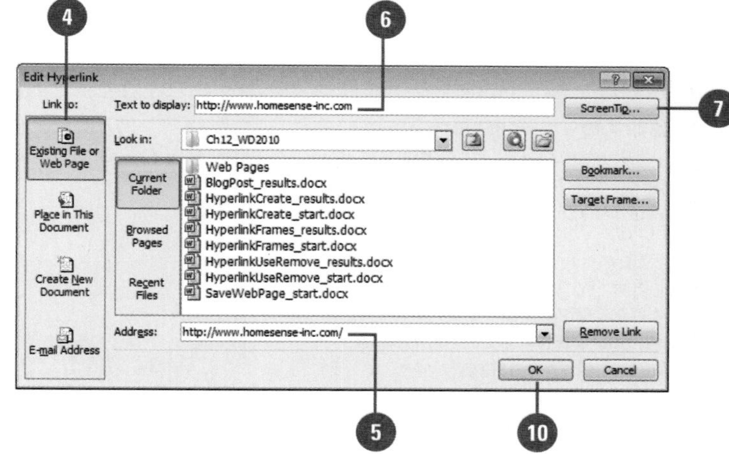

Did You Know?

You can create a hyperlink to send e-mail messages. Click where you want to insert the hyperlink, click the Hyperlink button on the Insert tab, click E-Mail Address, enter the recipient's e-mail address, enter a subject, enter the hyperlink display text, and then click OK.

Creating a Hyperlink Between Frames

If you have a Web page document that contains frames, you can create a hyperlink between frames. A **frame** is a named Web page that appears in a window region on a Web page within a Web browser. You can have multiple frames on a Web page and each frame can have a border and be scrollable and resizeable. You use the Target Frame button in the Insert Hyperlink dialog box to create a hyperlink between frames. If you continually create hyperlinks to the same target frame, you can set a default to save time in the future.

Create a Hyperlink Between Frames

1. Select the text or picture you want to display as the hyperlink.
2. Click the **Insert** tab.
3. Click the **Hyperlink** button.
4. Click **Existing File or Web Page**.
5. Click the **Look in** list arrow, locate and select the file you want to use, or type the address you want to link to.
   - To link to a specific location in a document, click **Bookmark**, select the bookmark you want, and then click **OK**.
6. Click **Target Frame**.
7. Click the frame in the diagram where you want the destination of the hyperlink to display.
8. Click the list arrow, and then select the frame where you want the document to appear.
9. Click **OK**.
10. Click **OK**.

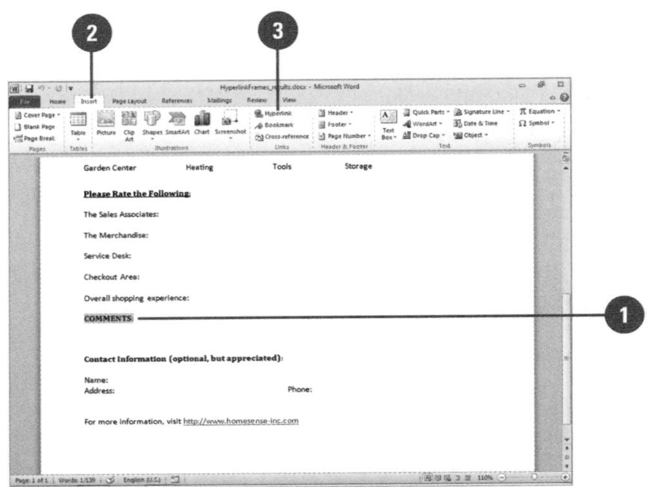

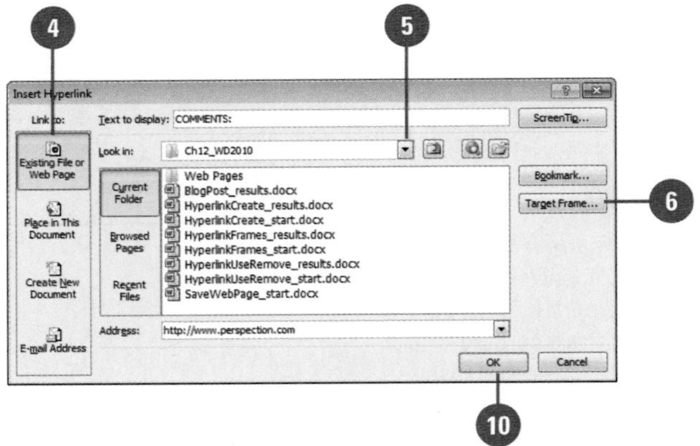

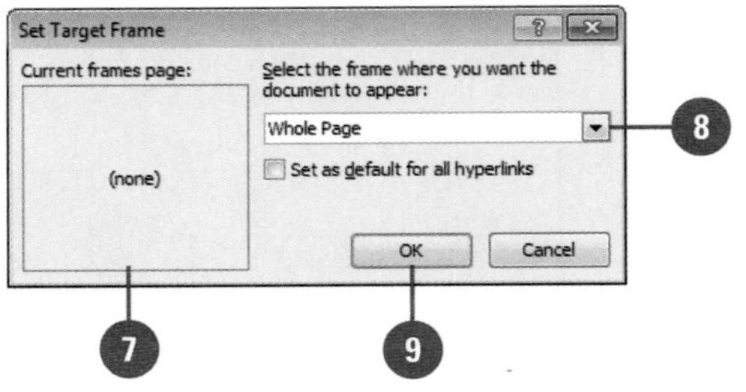

Set the Default Target Frame for All Hyperlinks

1. Open the frames page you want to set as the default.
2. Click the **Insert** tab.
3. Click the **Hyperlink** button.
4. Click **Target Frame**.
5. Click the frame in the program in the diagram where you want the destination of the hyperlink.
6. Select the **Set as default for all hyperlinks** check box.
7. Click **OK**.
8. Click **OK**.

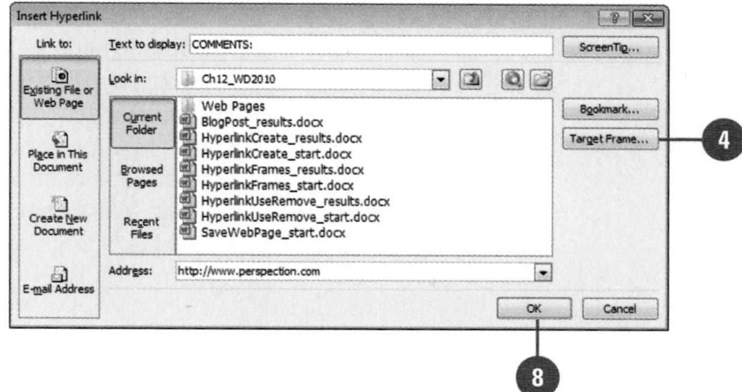

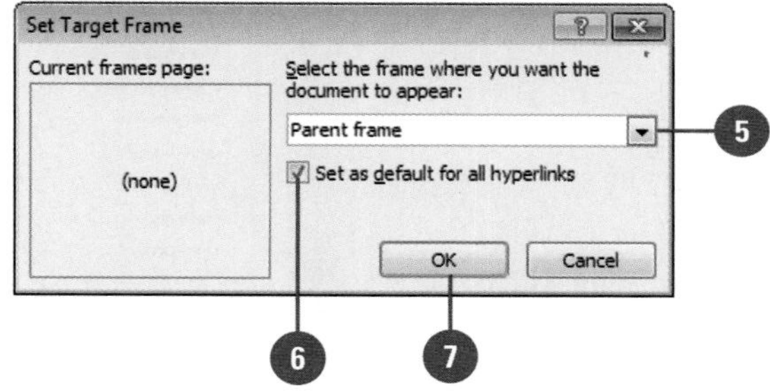

Using and Removing Hyperlinks

Hyperlinks connect you to information in other documents. Rather than duplicating the important information stored in other documents, you can create hyperlinks to the relevant material. When you click a hyperlink for the first time (during a session), the color of the hyperlink changes, indicating that you have accessed the hyperlink. If a link becomes outdated or unnecessary, you can easily revise or remove it. Word also repairs broken links. Whenever you save a document with hyperlinks, Word checks the links and repairs any that aren't working. For example, if a file was moved, Word updates the location.

Use a Hyperlink

1. Position the mouse pointer over any hyperlink.
2. Press and hold Ctrl (which changes to a hand pointer), and then click the hyperlink.

   Depending on the type of hyperlink, the screen:

   - Jumps to a new location within the same document.
   - Jumps to a location on an intranet or Internet Web site.
   - Opens a new file and the program in which it was created.
   - Opens Outlook and displays a new e-mail message.

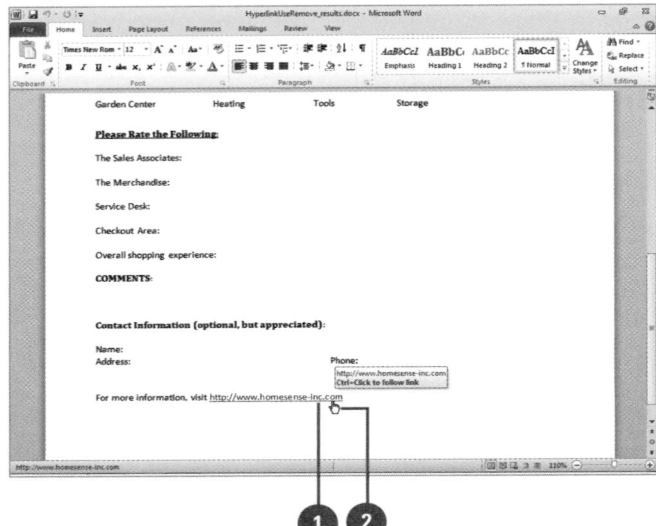

Did You Know?

You can edit a hyperlink. Right-click the hyperlink, and then click Edit Hyperlink. Make the changes you want, and then click OK.

You can copy or move a hyperlink. Right-click the hyperlink you want to copy or move, click Copy or Cut. Right-click the cell you want to copy or move the hyperlink to, and then click Paste.

Remove a Hyperlink

1. Right-click the cell containing the hyperlink you want to remove.
2. Click **Remove Hyperlink** to remove the hyperlink and keep the text.

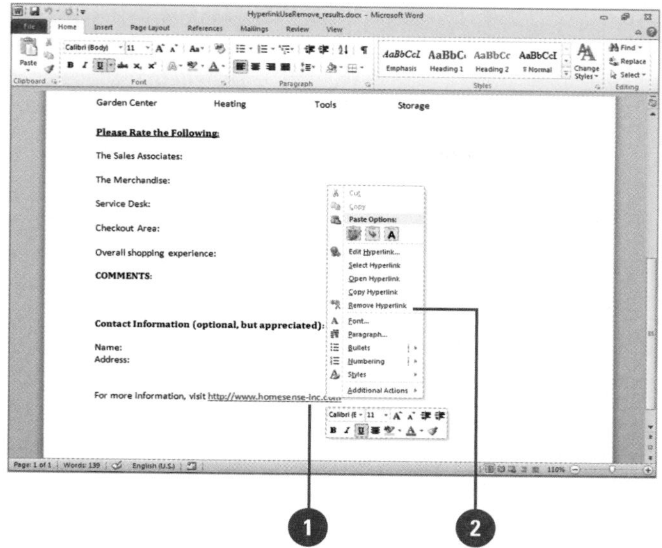

Did You Know?

You can select a hyperlink without activating the link. Click the cell that contains the hyperlink, hold down the mouse button until the pointer becomes a cross, and then release the mouse. If the hyperlink is a graphic, hold down Ctrl, and then click the graphic.

You can create a custom ScreenTip for a hyperlink. Select the hyperlink you want to customize, click the Insert tab, click the Hyperlink button, click ScreenTip, type the ScreenTip text you want, and then click OK twice.

Saving a Web Page

You can place an existing Office document on the Internet for others to use. In order for any document to be placed on the Web, it must be in HTML (Hypertext Markup Language) format—a simple coding system that specifies the formats a Web browser uses to display the document. This format enables you to post, or submit information and data on a Web site for others. You don't need any HTML knowledge to save a document as a Web page. When you save a document as a Web page, you can save it using the Web Page or Single File Web Page format. The Web Page format saves the document as an HTML file and a folder that stores supporting files, such as a file for each graphic, document, and so on. Word selects the appropriate graphic format for you based on the image's content. A single file Web page saves all the elements of a Web site, including text and graphics, into a single file in the MHTML format, which is supported by Internet Explorer 4.0.1 or later.

Save a Document as a Web Page

1. Click the **File** tab, and then click **Save As**.
2. Click the **Save as type** list arrow, and then click **Web Page.**
3. Click the **Save in** list arrow, and then select a location for your Web page.
4. Type the name for the Web page.
5. To change the title of your Web page, click **Change Title**, type the new title in the Set Page Title box, and then click **OK**.
6. To save a thumbnail preview of the Web page, select the **Save Thumbnail** check box.
7. Click **Save**.
8. If necessary, click **Yes** to keep formatting.

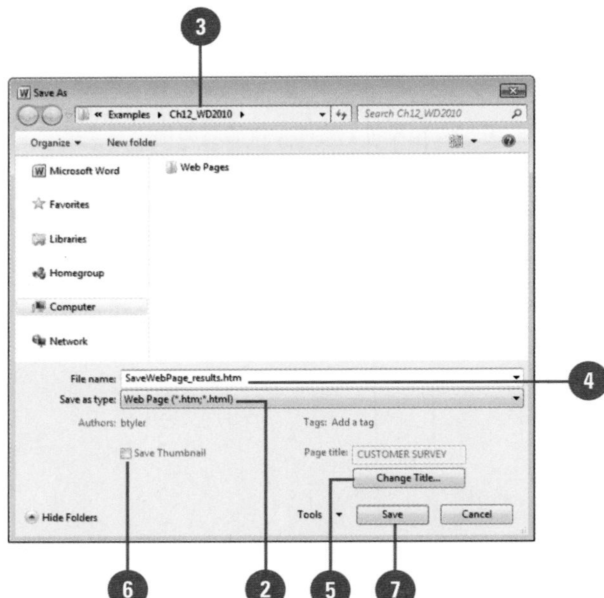

Save a Document as a Single File Web Page

1. Click the **File** tab, and then click **Save As**.
2. Click the **Save as type** list arrow, and then click **Single File Web Page.**
3. Click the **Save in** list arrow, and then select a location for your Web page.
4. Type the name for the Web page.
5. To change the title of your Web page, click **Change Title**, type the new title in the Set Page Title box, and then click **OK**.
6. To save a thumbnail preview of the Web page, select the **Save Thumbnail** check box.
7. Click **Save**.
8. If necessary, click **Yes** to keep formatting.

   The Web page is saved as a single file.

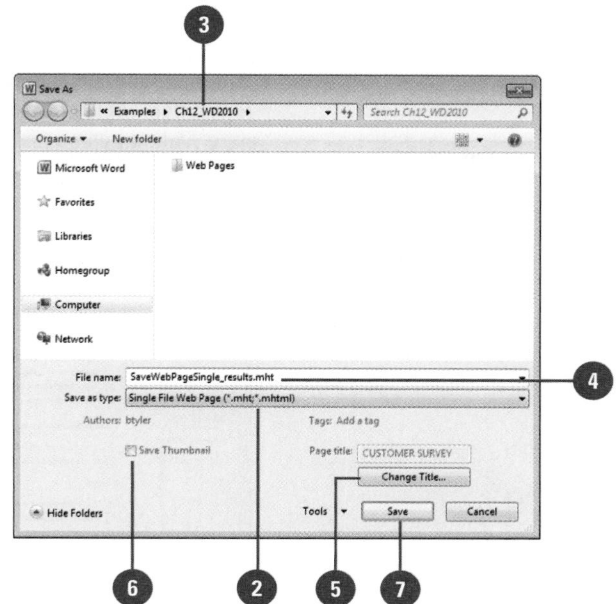

Did You Know?

You can reduce Web page size by filtering HTML in Word. You can save Web pages in filtered HTML to reduce the file size. In Word, click the Office menu, point to Save As, click Other Formats, click the Save As File Type list arrow, click Web Page, Filtered, and then click Save.

Changing Web Page Options

When you save or publish a document as a Web page, you can change the appearance of the Web page by changing Office's Web options. You can set Web options to save any additional hidden data necessary to maintain formulas, allow PNG as a graphic format, rely on CSS for font formatting, reply on VML for displaying graphics in browser, and save new Web pages as Single File Web Pages. Web pages are saved using the appropriate international text encoding so users on any language system are able to view the correct characters.

Change Web Page Options

1. Click the **File** tab, and then click **Options**.
2. In the left pane, click **Advanced**.
3. Click **Web Options**.
4. Click the **Browsers** tab.
5. Click the **Target Browsers** list arrow, and then select the version you want to support.
6. Select or clear the Web page options:
   - **Allow PNG as a graphics format.**
   - **Rely on CSS for font formatting.** Cascading Style Sheets for Web page formatting.
   - **Reply on VML for displaying graphics in browsers.** VML is Vector Markup Language, XML based graphics.
   - **Save new Web pages as Single File Web Pages.**
7. Click the **Files** tab, and then select or clear the file related Web page options:
   - File names and locations.
   - Default editors.
8. Click **OK**.
9. Click **OK**.

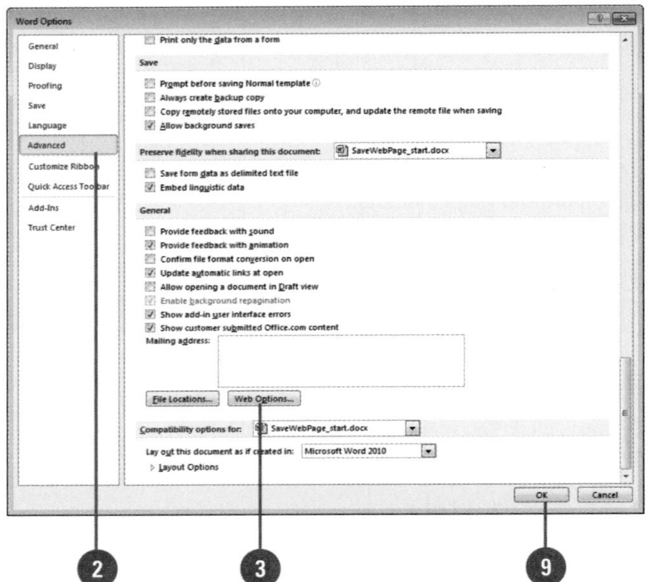

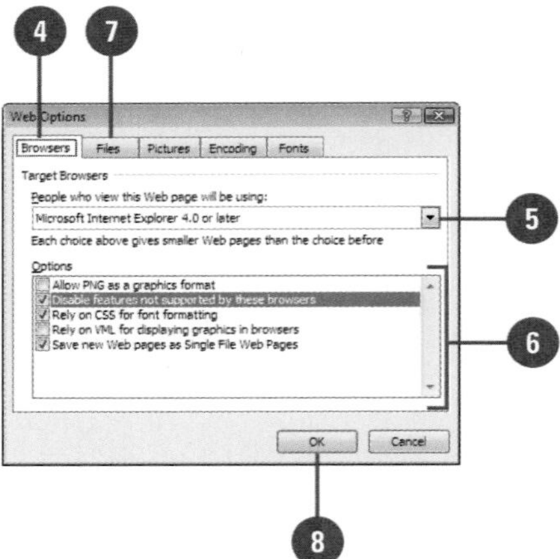

Transferring Files Over the Web

File Transfer Protocol (FTP) is an inexpensive and efficient way to transfer files between your computer and others on the Internet. You can download or receive, from another computer, any kind of file, including text, graphics, sound, and video files. To download a file, you need an ID and password to identify who you are. Anonymous FTP sites are open to anyone; they usually use *anonymous* as an ID and your *e-mail address* as a password. You can also save the FTP site address to revisit the site later.

Add FTP Locations

1. Click the **File** tab, and then click **Open**.
2. Click **Computer** in the left pane.
3. Right-click a blank area, and then click **Add a network location**.
4. Follow the Add Network Location wizard to create a link to an FTP site or other network, and then click **Finish** to complete it.
   - To complete the process, you need the complete address for an FTP site, and a username and password.

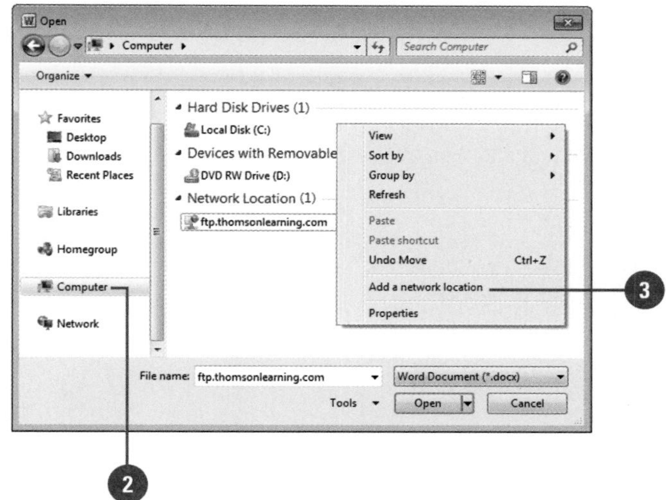

Access an FTP Site

1. Click the **File** tab, and then click **Open**.
2. Click **Computer** in the left pane.
3. Double-click the FTP site to which you want to log in.
4. Enter a password (your E-mail address or personal password), and then select a log on option.
5. Click **Log On**.
6. Select a folder location, and then select a file.
7. Click **Open**.

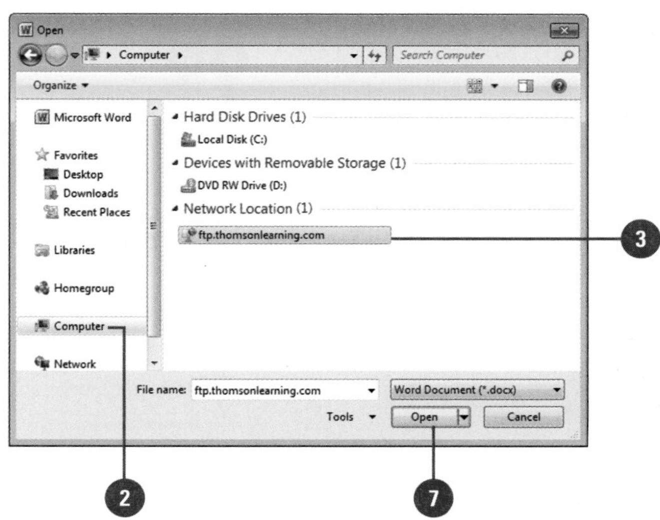

Creating a Blog Posting on the Web

A **blog** is a Web site that provides journal style information on a particular subject, such as news or a diary. Blog is short for Web log. However, you may have heard of other types: vlog (video) or podcasting (audio). A blog combines text, images, and links to other blogs, Web pages, and related topics. In Word, you can create and publish blog postings. Before you can publish a posting, you need to setup an account with a blog service provider and then register it with Word, where you can manage them. Service providers include Windows Live Spaces, Blogger, and Microsoft Windows SharePoint Services with more coming online all the time. Most services are free, so everyone can create an account. Visit Windows Live Space at *http://spaces.live.com* or Blogger at *http://www.blogger.com* and follow the online instructions.

Create a New Blog Posting

1. Click the **File** tab, and then click **New**.
2. Click **Blog post**.
3. Click **Create**.
4. If you have not registered a blog account with Word, click **Register Now** or click **Register Later**.
5. To open your blog on the Web, click the **Home Page** button.
6. To create a new blog posting, select the placeholder title, type a new title, and then type the blog message you want below it.
   - To insert a blog category, click the **Insert Category** button, and then select a category.
   - To insert visuals, click the **Insert** tab, and then use the buttons to insert other content.
7. To post the blog, click the **Publish** button arrow, and then click **Publish** or **Publish as Draft**.
8. When you're done, close and save the posting as a Word document.

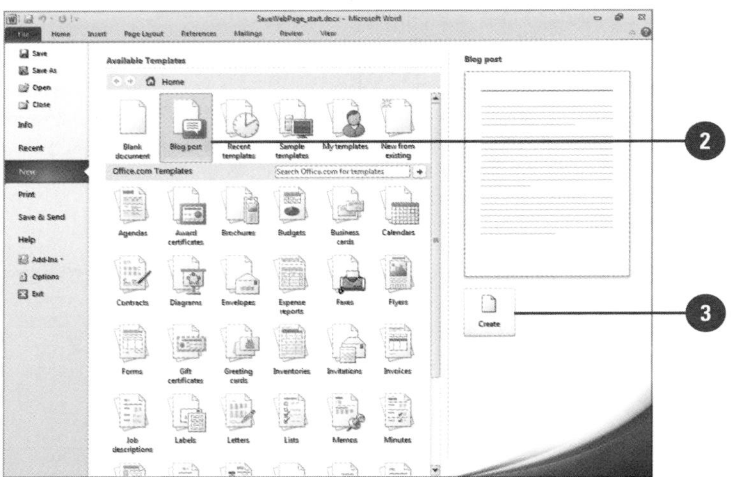

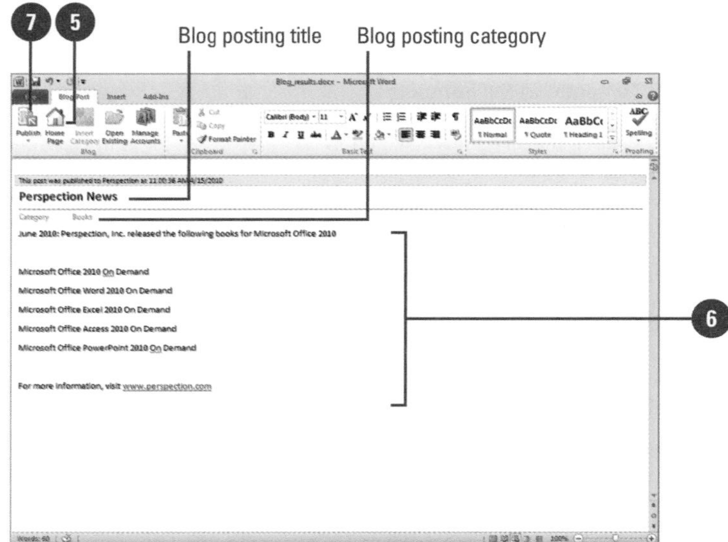

Create a New Blog Posting from an Existing Document

1. Open the document you want to use as a blog posting.
2. Click the **File** tab, and then click **Save & Send**.
3. Click **Publish as Blog Post**.
4. Click the **Publish as Blog Post** button.
5. If you have not registered a blog account with Word, click **Register Now** or click **Register Later**.
6. To open your blog on the Web, click the **Home Page** button.
7. To complete the new blog posting, select the placeholder title, type a new title, and then make any other changes you want.
   - To insert a blog category, click the **Insert Category** button, and then select a category.
   - To insert visuals, click the **Insert** tab, and then use the buttons to insert other content.
8. To post the blog, click the **Publish** button arrow, and then click **Publish** or **Publish as Draft**.
9. When you're done, close and save the posting as a Word document.

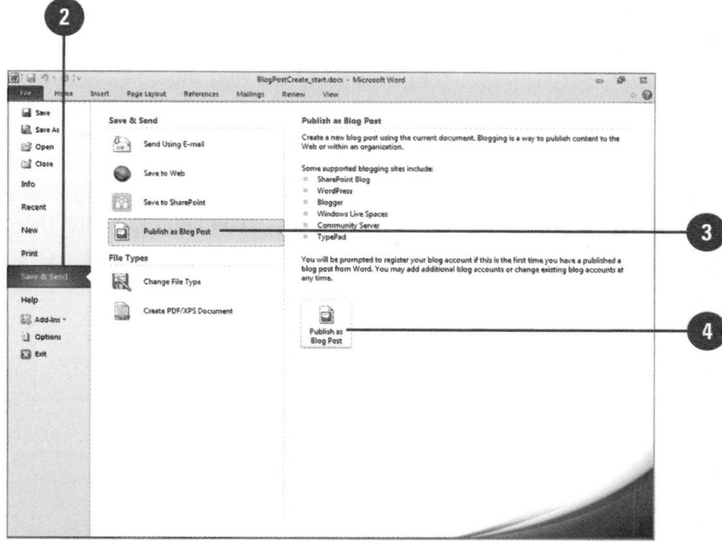

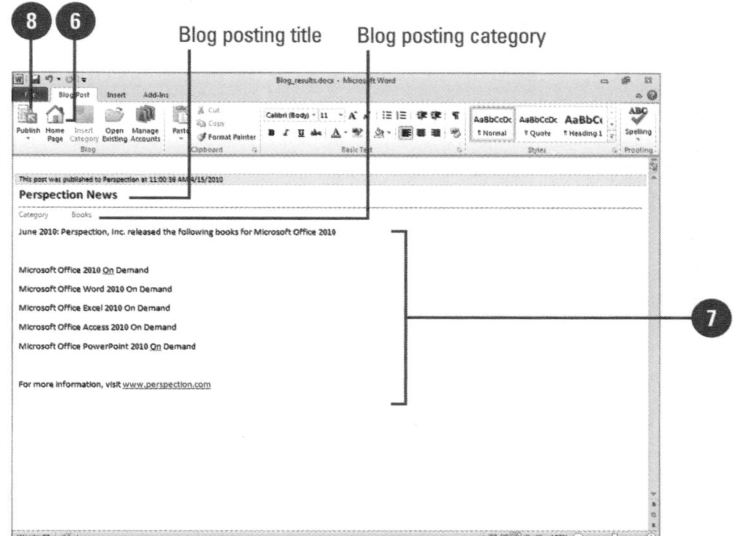

Opening an Existing Blog Posting

If you've already published a blog posting and want to make some changes to it, you can open the existing posting, make the changes you want, and then republish it. In addition to editing the text of a blog posting, you can also insert graphical elements—such as pictures, clip art, shapes, SmartArt, charts, screenshots, WordArt and symbols—using the Insert tab. Instead of using plain text, you can also format blog text by using the common formatting tools—typically found on the Word Home tab—on the Blog Post tab. Before you can open and republish a posting, you need to select the blog service provider and sign in to the account.

Open an Existing Blog Posting and Republish

1. Open the document with the saved posting you want to open.
2. Click the **Open Existing** button, select the blog, and then click **OK**.
3. Select the account with the blog you want to open.
4. Select the blog posting you want open.
5. Click **OK**.
6. Edit the blog posting text and insert any additional visuals you want.
   - To insert visuals, click the **Insert** tab, and then use the buttons to insert other content.
7. Format the blog posting text using tools on the Blog Post tab.
8. When you're done, click the **Publish** button arrow, and then click **Publish** or **Publish as Draft**.
9. When you're done, close and save the posting as a Word document.

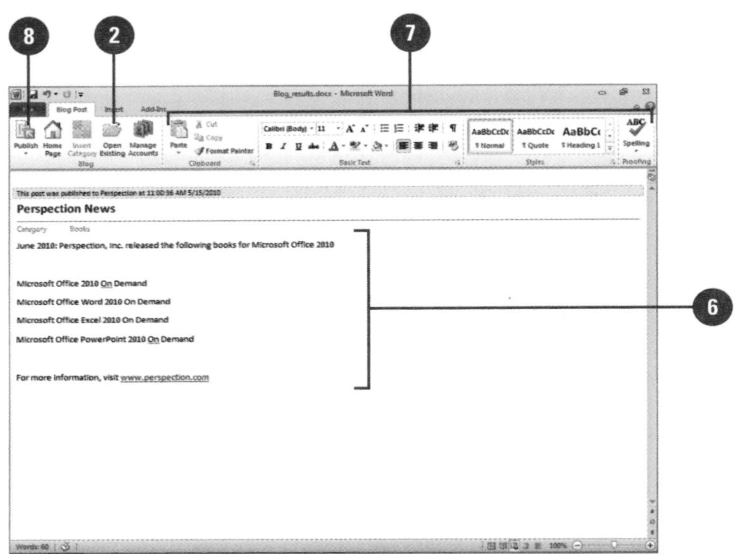

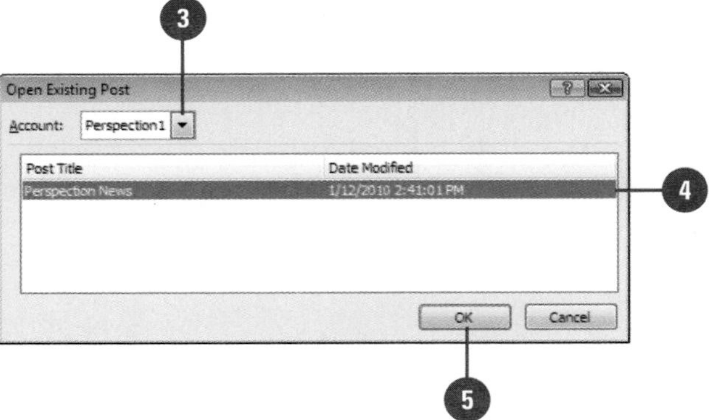

Managing Blog Accounts

Before you can publish a posting, you need to setup an account with a blog service provider and then register it with Word, where you can manage them. If you have more than one blog account, you can register them all with Word and use the Blog Accounts dialog box to manage the accounts. You can register new accounts, change old accounts, set an account as the default, and remove accounts you no longer need. If you need to open your blog account, you can click the Home page button on the Blog Post tab in Word to view your account in a Web browser. Two common sites you can open include Windows Live Space at *http://spaces.live.com* or Blogger at *http://www.blogger.com*.

Manage a Blog Account

1. Open a document with a saved posting or create a new blog posting.
2. To open your blog on the Web, click the **Home Page** button.
3. Click the **Manage Accounts** button.
4. Use any of the following buttons to manage your blog accounts:
   - **New.** Click to register an established blog account with Word.
   - **Change.** Click to change the registration information for the selected account.
   - **Set As Default.** Click to set the selected account as the default.
   - **Remove.** Click to remove the selected account.
5. Click **Close**.

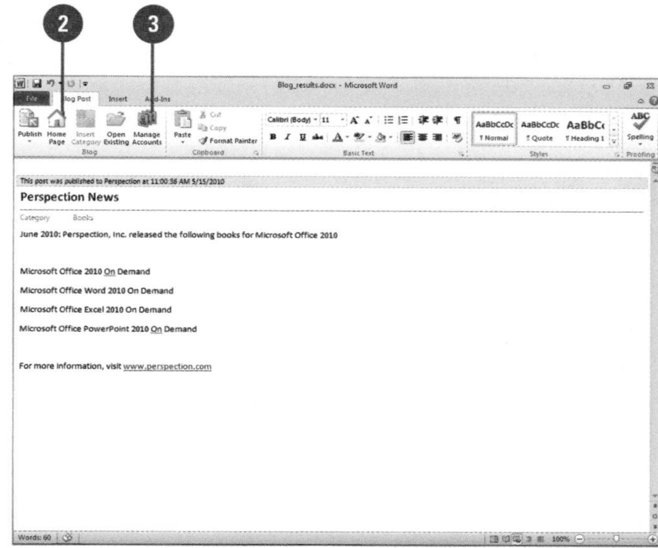

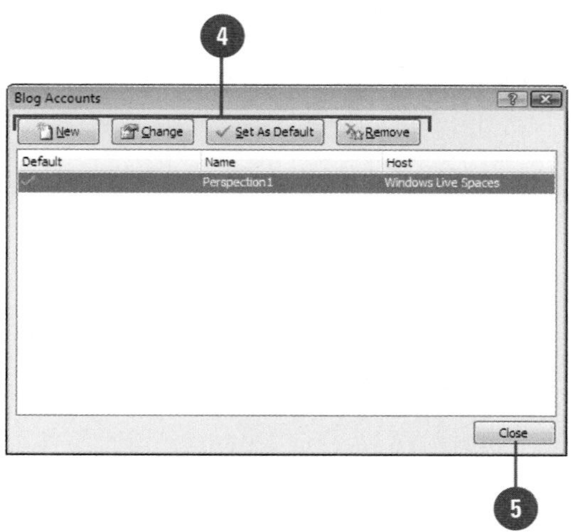

Accessing Office Information on the Web

New information about programs comes out with great frequency. You have access to an abundance of information about Office programs and other programs in the Office Suite from Microsoft. This information is constantly being updated. Answers to frequently asked questions, user forums, and update offers are some of the types of information you can find about Microsoft Office. You can also find out about conferences, books, and other products that help you learn just how much you can do with your Microsoft Office software.

Find Online Office Information

1. Click the **File** tab, and then click **Help**.
2. Click any of the following options to display online information:
   - **Getting Started.** Accesses information to help you get started with the product.
   - **Contact Us.** Accesses the Microsoft Support web site, where you can get assistance.
   - **Check for Updates.** Accesses Windows Update to check for the latest Office updates.

   Your Web browser opens, displaying a Microsoft Office Online Web page.
3. Click a hyperlink of interest.
4. Click the **Close** button to quit the browser and return to the Office program.

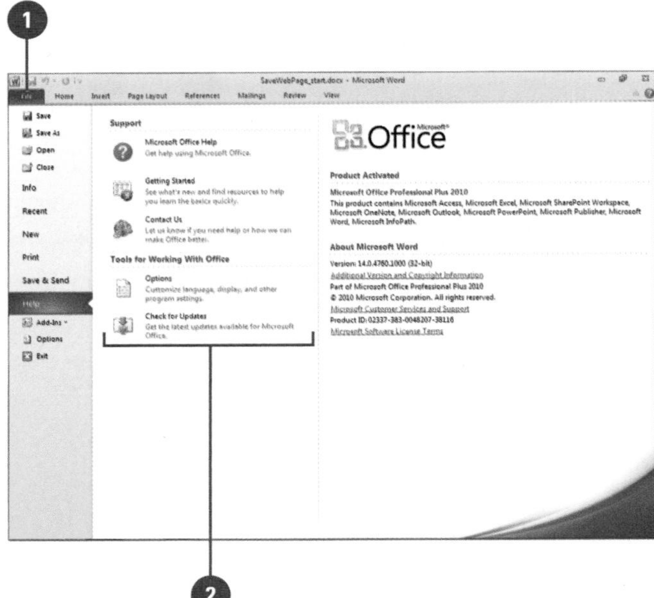

Protecting and Securing Documents

13

Introduction

When you've developed content in your document and want feedback, you can electronically send a document to reviewers so that they can read, revise, and comment on the document without having to print it. Instead of reading handwritten text or sticky notes on your printout, you can get clear and concise feedback.

Adding a password to protect your document is not only a good idea for security purposes, it's an added feature to make sure that changes to your document aren't made by unauthorized people. You can protect all or part of a document. In each case, you'll be asked to supply a password, and then enter it again when you want to work on the file. Not only can you guard who sees your document, you can set rights on who can add changes and comments to your document. If you need to validate the authenticity of a document, you can add an invisible digital signature, an electronic secure stamp of authentication on a document, or a visible signature line. A signature line allows you to create a paperless signature process for documents, such as contracts.

The Trust Center is a place where you set security options and find the latest technology information as it relates to document privacy, safety, and security from Microsoft. The Trust Center allows you to set security and privacy settings and provides links to Microsoft privacy statements, a customer improvement program, and trustworthy computing practices.

What You'll Do

Inspecting Documents

While you work on your document, Word automatically saves and manages personal information and hidden data to enable you to create and develop a document with other people. The personal information and hidden data includes comments, revision marks, versions, ink annotations, document properties, invisible content (**New!**), header and footer information, hidden text, document server properties, and custom XML data. The **Document Inspector** uses inspector modules to find and remove any hidden data and personal information specific to each of these modules that you might not want to share with others. If you remove hidden content from your document, you might not be able to restore it by using the Undo command, so it's important to make a copy of your document before you remove any information.

Inspect a Document

1. Click the **File** tab, click **Save As**, type a name to save a copy of the original, specify a folder location, and then click **Save**.
2. Click the **File** tab, and then click **Info**.
3. Click the **Check for Issues** button, and then click **Inspect Document**.
4. Select the check boxes with the content you want to find and remove:
   - **Comments, Revisions, Versions, and Annotations.** Includes comments, versions, revision marks, and ink annotations.

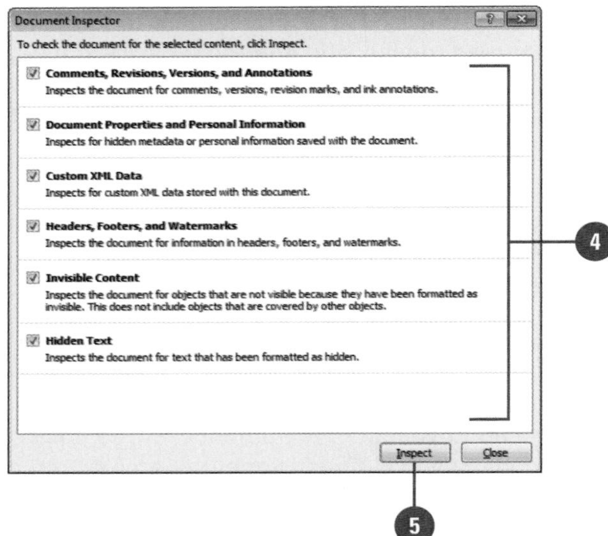

Did You Know?

What is metadata? Metadata is data that describes other data. For example, text in a document is data, while the number of worksheets is metadata.

- **Document Properties and Personal Information.** Includes metadata document properties (Summary, Statistics, and Custom tabs), the file path for publishing Web pages, document server properties, and content type information.
- **Custom XML Data.** Includes any custom XML data.
- **Headers, Footers, and Watermarks.** Includes information in headers, footers, and watermarks.
- **Invisible Content.** Includes objects formatted as invisible. Doesn't include objects covered by other objects. (**New!**)
- **Hidden Text.** Includes information formatted as hidden text.

5. Click **Inspect**.

   A progress meter appears while Word inspects the document.

6. Review the results of the inspection.

7. Click **Remove All** for each inspector module in which you want to remove hidden data and personal information.

   TROUBLE? *Before you click Remove All, be sure you want to remove the information. You might not be able to restore it.*

8. To reinspect the document, click **Reinspect**, and then click **Inspect**.

9. Click **Close**.

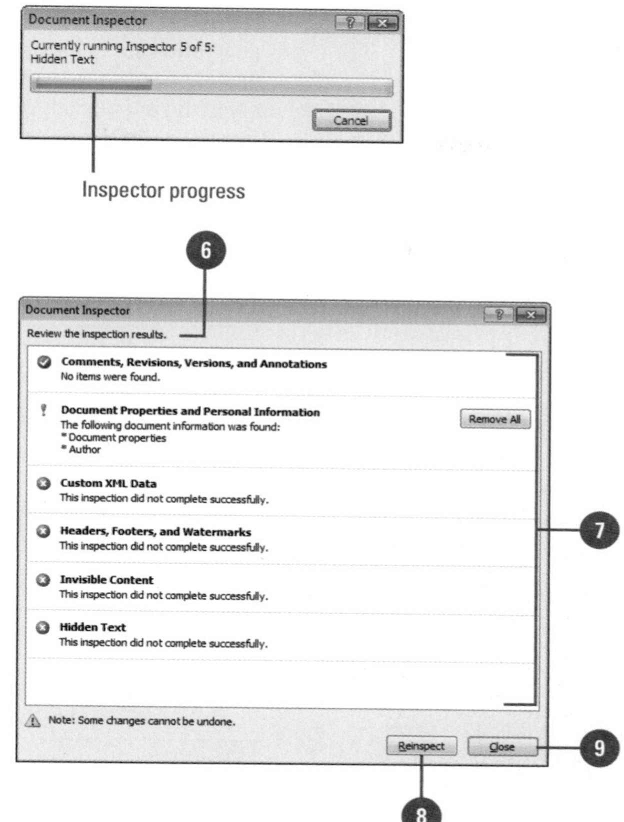

Adding Security Encryption to a Document

File encryption is additional security you can apply to a document. **File encryption** scrambles your password to protect your document from unauthorized people from breaking into the file. You don't have to worry about the encryption, Word handles everything. All you need to do is remember the password. If you forget it, you can't open the file. Password protection takes effect the next time you open the document. To set password protection using file encryption, select the File tab, point to Prepare, select Encrypt Document, enter a password, write it down for safekeeping, and then reenter the password again. Password protection takes effect the next time you open the document.

Apply File Encryption

1. Click the **File** tab, and then click **Info**.
2. Click the **Protect Document** button, and then click **Encrypt with Password**.
3. Type a password.
4. Click **OK**.
5. Retype the password.
6. Click **OK**.

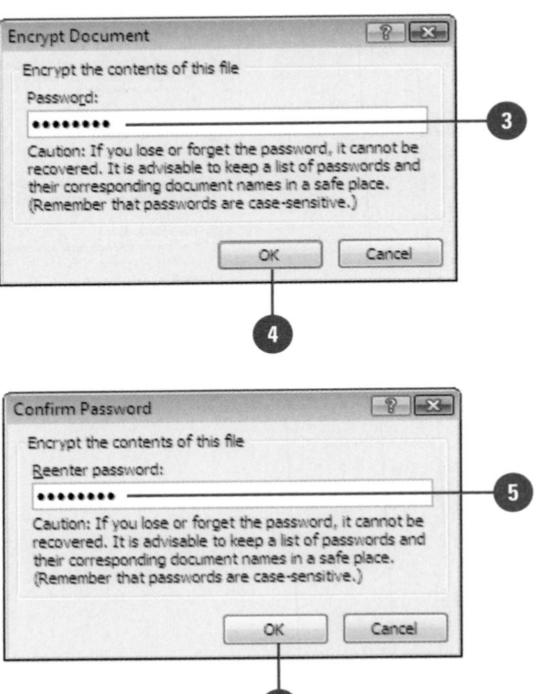

For Your Information

Using a Strong Password

Hackers identify passwords as strong or weak. A strong password is a combination of uppercase and lowercase letters, numbers, and symbols, such as Grea8t!, while a weak one doesn't use different character types, such as Hannah1. Be sure to write down your passwords and place them in a secure location.

Open File with Encryption

1. Click the **File** tab, click **Open**, navigate to a document with the password encryption, and then click **Open**.
2. Type the password.
3. Click **OK**.

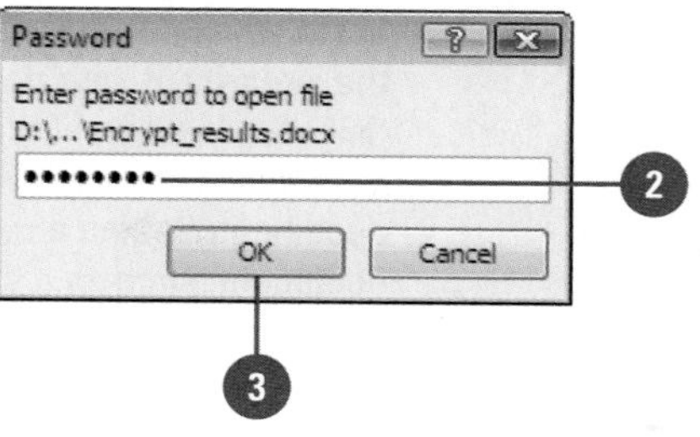

Remove File Encryption

1. Click the **File** tab, click **Open**, navigate to a document with the password encryption, and then click **Open**.
2. Type the password, and then click **OK**.
3. Click the **File** tab, and then click **Info**.
4. Click the **Protect Document** button, and then click **Encrypt with Password**.
5. Delete the file encryption password.
6. Click **OK**.

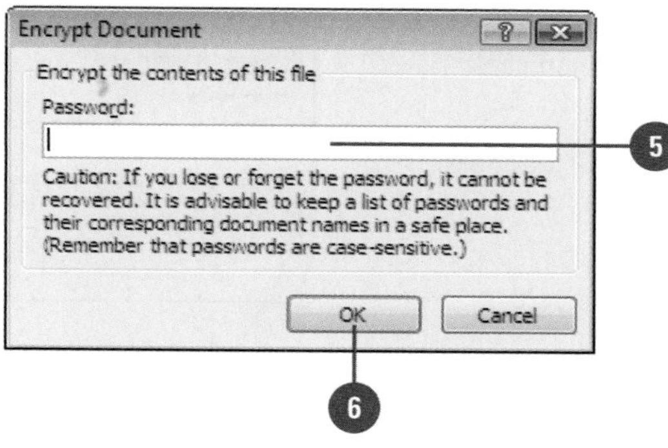

Adding Password Protection to a Document

You can assign a password and other security options so that only those who know the password can open the document, or to protect the integrity of your document as it moves from person to person. At times, you will want the information to be used but not changed; at other times, you will want only specific people to be able to view the document. Setting a document as read-only is useful when you want a document, such as a company-wide bulletin, to be distributed and read, but not changed. Password protection takes effect the next time you open the document.

Add Password Protection to an Office Document

1. Open the document you want to protect.
2. Click the **File** tab, and then click **Save As**.
3. Click **Tools**, and then click **General Options**.
4. Type a password in the Password to open box or the Password to modify box.

   IMPORTANT *It's critical that you remember your password. If you forget your password, Microsoft can't retrieve it.*

5. Select or clear the **Remove automatically created personal information from this file on save** check box.
6. To set macro security options in the Trust center, click **Macro Security**.
7. Click **OK**.
8. Type your password again.
9. Click **OK**.
10. If you entered passwords for Open and Modify, type your password again, and then click **OK**.
11. Click **Save**, and then click **Yes** to replace existing document.

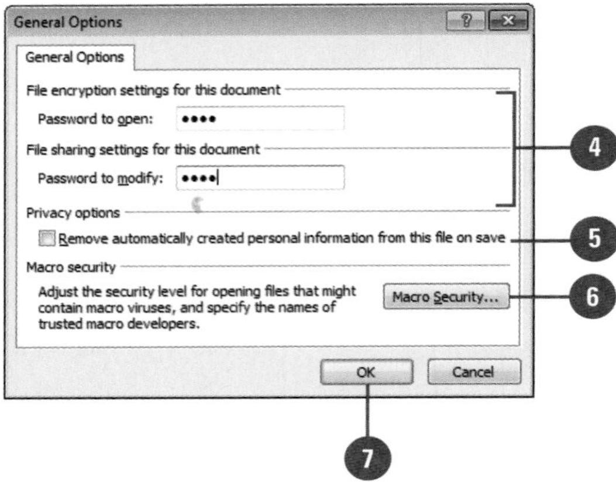

Open a Document with Password Protection

1. Click the **File** tab, click **Open**, navigate to a document with password protection, and then click **Open**.
2. Click **Read Only** if you do not wish to modify the document, or type the password in the Password dialog box.
3. Click **OK**.

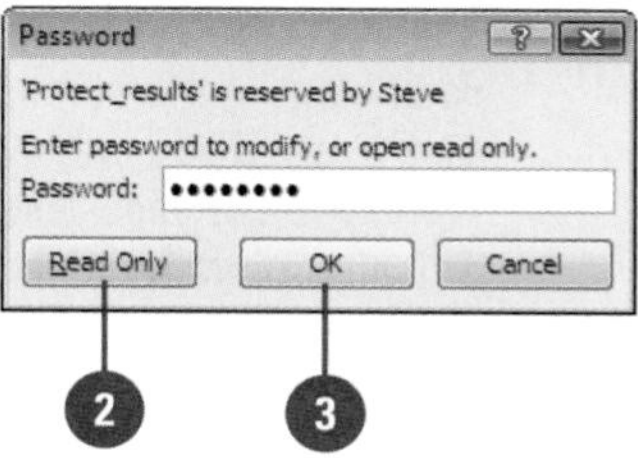

Change or Remove the Password Protection

1. Click the **File** tab, click **Open**, navigate to a document with password protection, and then click **Open**.
2. Type the password in the Password dialog box.
3. Click **OK**.
4. Click the **File** tab, click **Save As**, click **Tools**, and then click **General Options**.
5. Select the contents in the Password to modify box or the Password to open box, and then choose the option you want:
   - **Change password.** Type a new password, click **OK**, and then retype your password.
   - **Delete password.** Press Delete.
6. Click **OK**.
7. Click **Save**, and then click **Yes** to replace existing document.

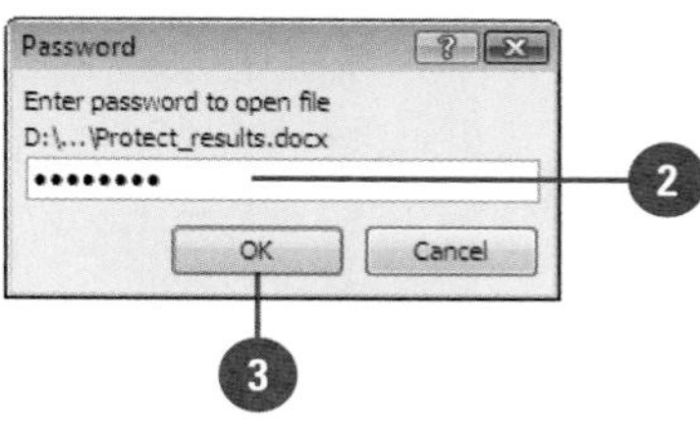

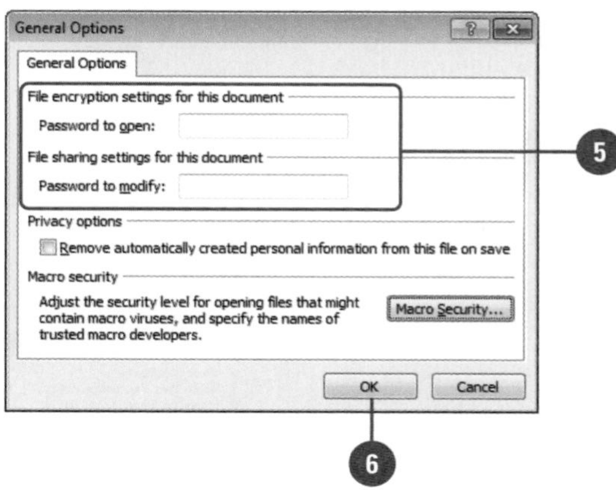

Restricting Formatting and Editing

If you want to protect parts of a document, yet grant permission for specific users to change other parts of the document, you can set restriction and protection options in the Restrict Formatting and Editing task pane. If you only want to prevent users from formatting a document, you can also restrict users from making any formatting changes or limit formatting to a selection of styles.

Restrict Formatting Changes

1. Open the document you want to protect.
2. Click the **Review** tab.
3. Click the **Protect Document** button, and then click **Restrict Formatting and Editing**.
4. Select the **Limit formatting to a selection of styles** check box.
5. Click **Settings**.
6. If necessary, select the **Limit formatting to a selection of styles** check box.
7. Select the check boxes next to the styles you want to allow in the document. To provide a standard minimum amount of restriction, click **Recommended Minimum**.
8. To allow AutoFormat, block theme or color scheme switching, or block Quick Style Set switching, select the check boxes.
9. Click **OK**.
10. If a message alert appears, click **Yes** to remove styles, or click **No** to keep the formatting.
11. Click **Yes, Start Enforcing Protection**.
12. To assign a password, type a password, and then reenter it.
13. Click **OK**.
14. Click the **Close** button on the task pane.

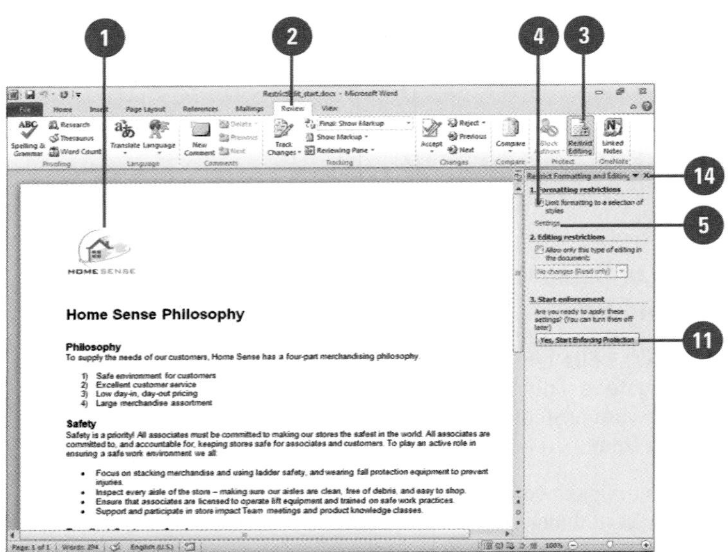

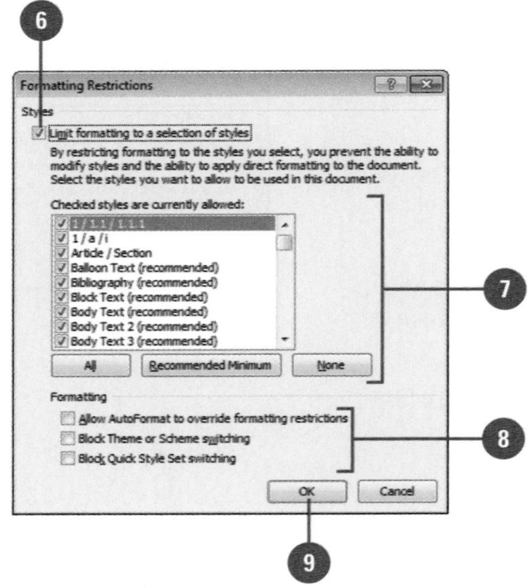

Allow Changes to Part of a Protected Document

1. Open the document you want to protect.
2. Click the **Review** tab.
3. Click the **Protect Document** button, and then click **Restrict Formatting and Editing**.
4. If the document is already protected, click **Stop Protection**.
5. If you assigned a password to help protect the document, type the password.
6. Select the **Allow only this type of editing in the document** check box.
7. Click the list arrow, and then select an editing protection option: **Tracked changes, Comments, Filling in forms, No changes (Read only)**.
8. To add specific user, click **More users**, enter names as shown in the example (separated by semicolons), and then click **OK**.
9. Select the parts of the document you want to be unrestricted, and the check box next to the user you want to be able to edit it.
10. Click **Yes, Start Enforcing Protection**.
11. Click the **Password** option, type a password and reenter it, or click the **User authentication** option, which encrypts the document.
12. Click **OK**.
13. Click the **Close** button on the task pane.

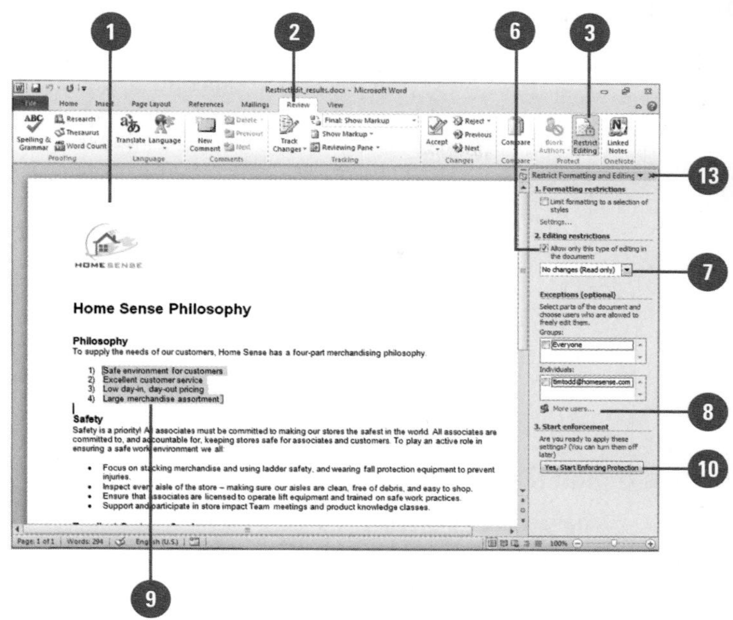

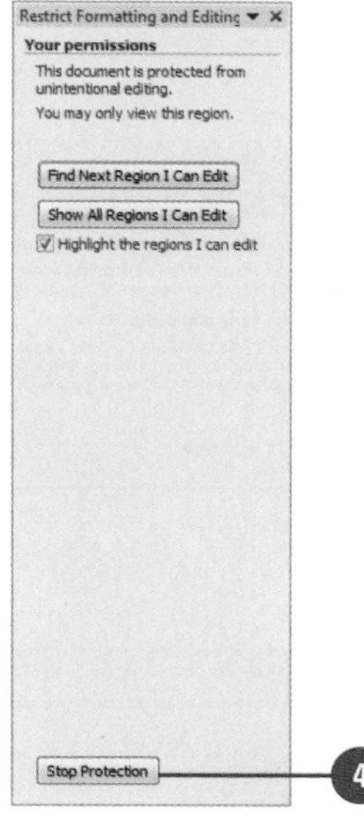

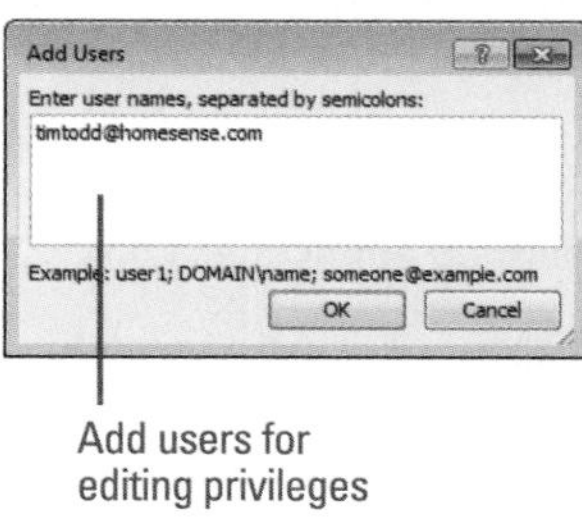

Add users for editing privileges

Adding a Digital Signature

After you've finished a document, you might consider adding an invisible digital signature—an electronic, secure stamp of authentication on a document. Before you can add a digital signature, you need to get a **digital ID**, or **digital certificate**, which provides an electronic way to prove your identity. A digital certificate checks a public key to validate a private key associated with a digital signature. To assure a digital signature is authentic, it must have a valid (non expired or revoked) certificate issued by a reputable certification authority (CA), and the signing person must be from a trusted publisher. If you need a verified authenticate digital certificate, you can obtain one from a trusted Microsoft partner CA. If you don't need a verified digital certificate, you can create one of your own. If someone modifies the file, the digital signature is removed and revoked. If you're not sure if a document is digitally signed, you can use the Signatures task pane to view or remove valid signatures.

Create a Digital ID

1. Click the **File** tab, click **Info**, click the **Protect Document** button, and then click **Add a Digital Signature**.
2. If an alert message appears, click **Signature Services from the Office Marketplace** to open an informational Web site where you can sign up for a digital certificate, or click **OK** to create your own.

   If you don't want to see this dialog box again, select the **Don't show this message again** check box.
3. If necessary, click **OK** and verify your Rights Management account credentials using your .NET password.
4. If you don't have a digital ID, click the option to get an ID from a Microsoft Partner or create your own, and then click **OK**.
5. Enter your name, e-mail address, organization name, and location.
6. Click **Create**.

   You can sign a document, or click **Cancel**.

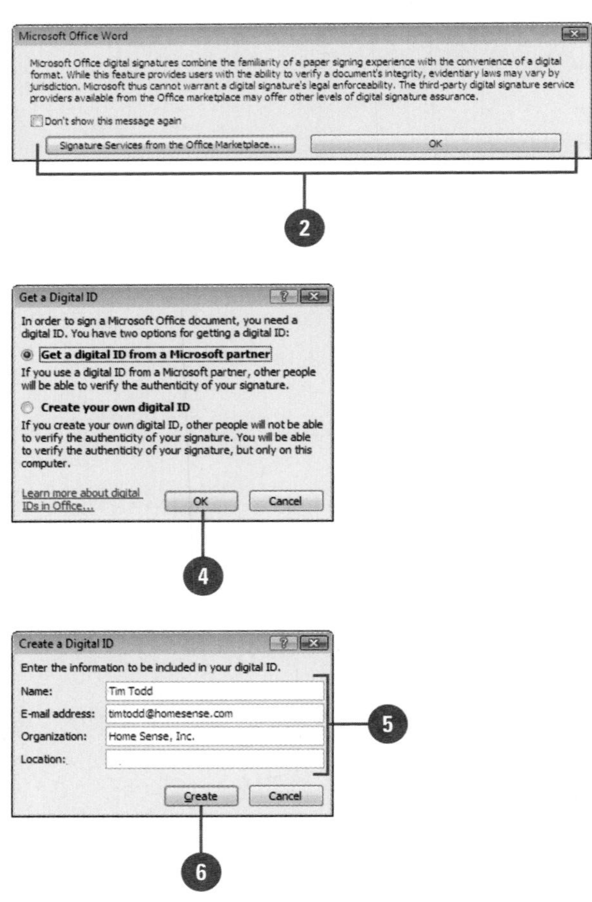

Add a Digital Signature to a Document

1. Click the **File** tab, click **Info**, click the **Protect Document** button, and then click **Add a Digital Signature**.
2. To change the digital signature, click **Change**, select the one you want, and then click **OK**.
3. Enter the purpose for signing this document.
4. Click **Sign**.
5. If necessary, click **OK**.

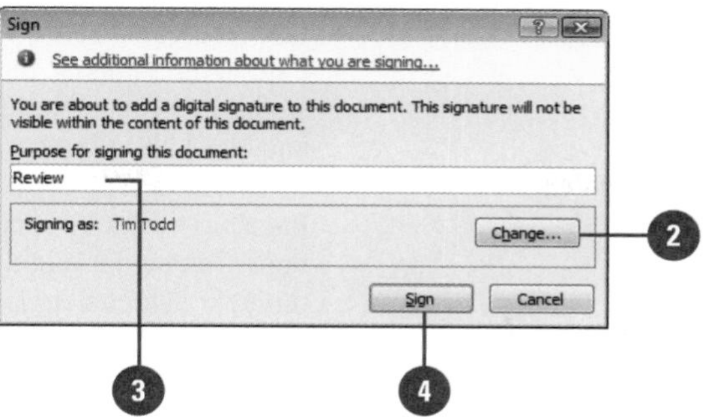

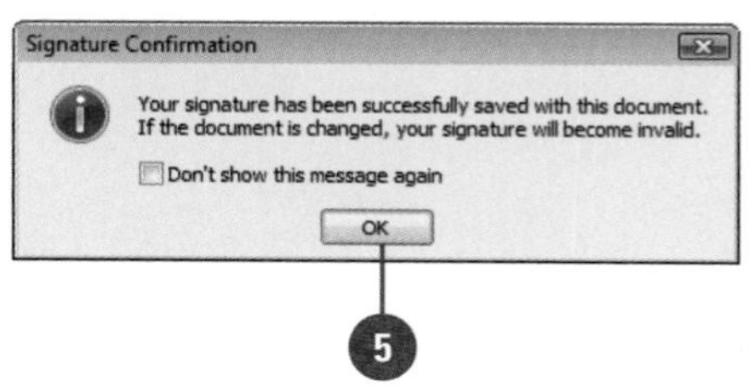

View or Remove Signatures

1. Click the **Signature** icon on the Status bar, or click the **File** tab, click **Info**, and then click the **View Signatures** button.

   The Signatures task pane appears, displaying valid signatures in the document. Invalid signatures are no longer automatically removed.
2. Point to a signature, and then click the list arrow.
3. To see signature details, click **Signature Details**, select a signature, click **View**, click **OK** when you're done, and then click **Close**.
4. To remove a signature, point to a signature, click the list arrow, click **Remove Signature**, click **Yes**, and then if necessary click **OK**.
5. Click the **Close** button on the task pane.

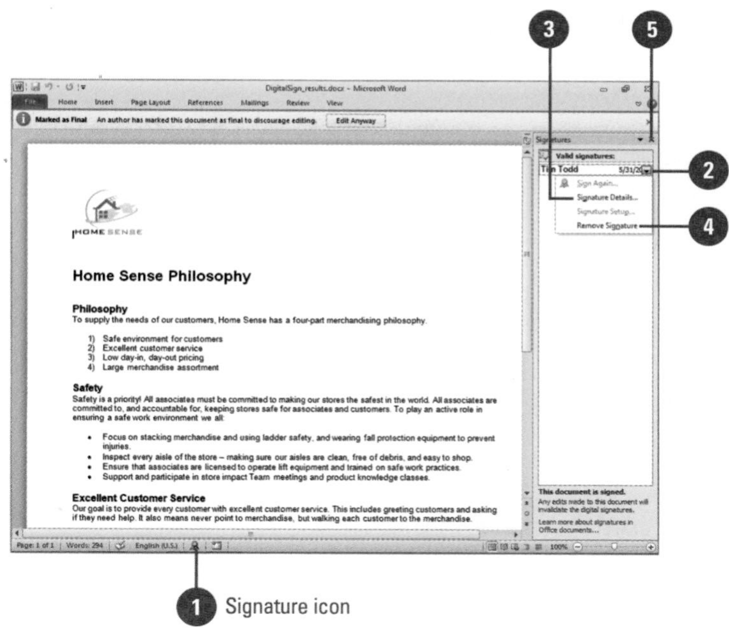

Adding a Signature Line

If you prefer a visible signature line instead of an invisible digital signature, you can insert a visible signature line along with a digital certificate of authenticity. Signature lines allow you to create a paperless signature process for documents, such as contracts. A visible signature line looks like a typical signature line with a name, a date and a line for a signature. When you send a document out with a signature request, the signer sees a signature line and a notification request with instructions. The signer can type—or ink with a Tablet PC—a signature next to the *X*, or select a signature image. To add a signature line and digital signature at the same time, first you insert a signature line into your document, and then you sign it.

Add a Signature Line

1. Click the **Insert** tab.
2. Click to place the insertion point where you want to insert a signature line.
3. Click the **Signature Line** button arrow, and then click **Microsoft Office Signature Line**.
4. If an alert message appears, click **Signature Services from the Office Marketplace** to open an informational Web site where you can sign up for a digital certificate, or click **OK** to create your own.
5. Type information about the person who will be signing on this signature line.
6. If you want, type any instructions for the signer.
7. To show the signature date, select the **Allow the signer to add comments in the Sign dialog** check box.
8. To show the signature date, select the **Show sign data in signature line** check box.
9. Click **OK**.

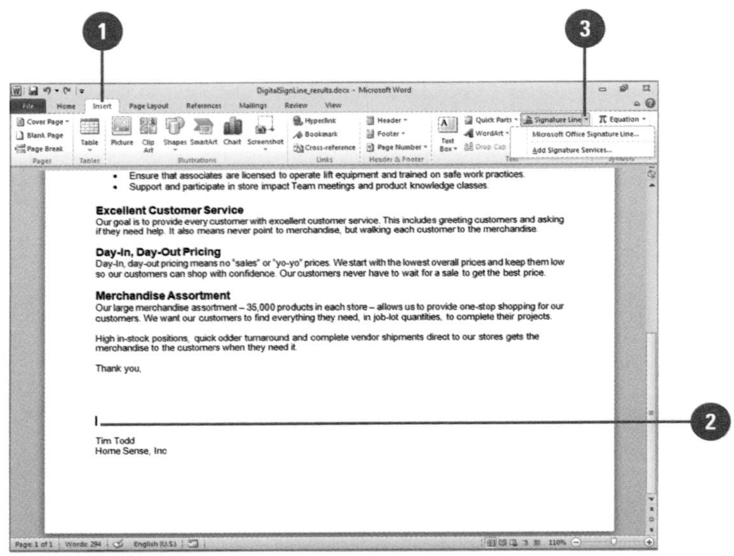

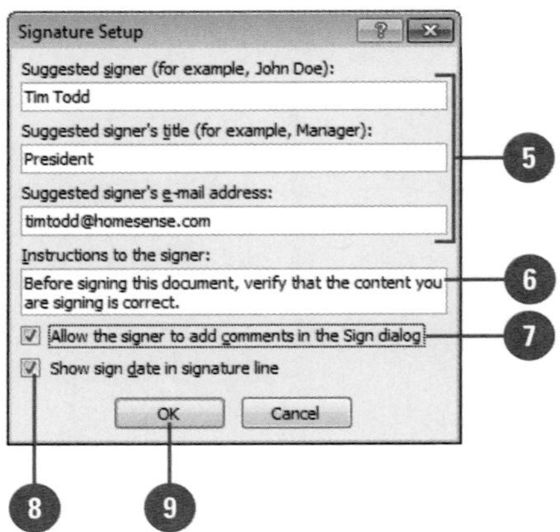

Sign the Signature Line

1. Double-click the signature line that needs a signature.
2. If an alert message appears, click **OK**.
3. To add a printed version of your signature, type your name.

   If you have a Tablet PC, you can sign your name.
4. To select an image of your written signature, click **Select Image**, navigate to the signature image, and then click **Select**.
5. Click **Sign**.
6. To view the signature, click the **Signature** icon on the Status bar, or click the **File** tab, click **Info**, and then click the **View Signatures** button.
7. To make changes to the signature, point to the signature, click the list arrow, and then select the command you want.

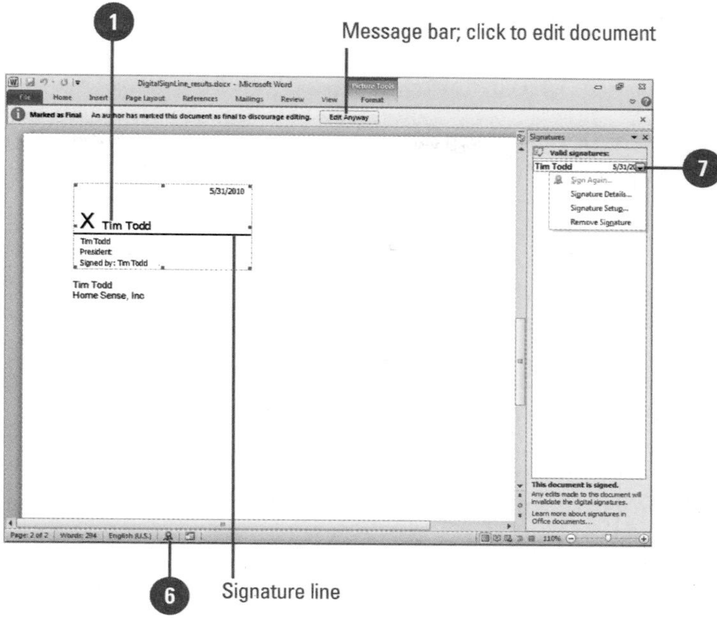

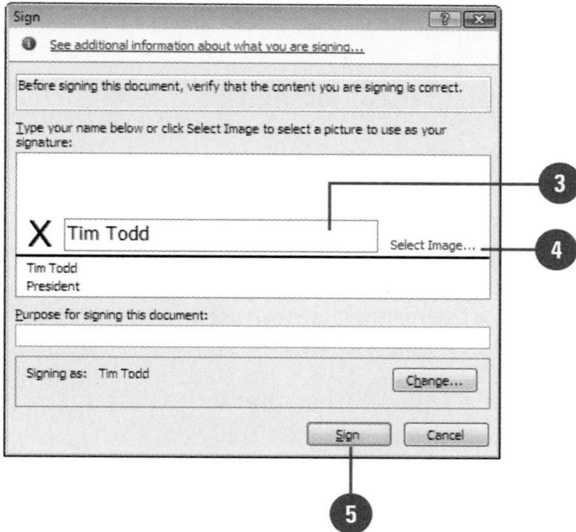

Avoiding Harmful Attacks

Spreading Harmful Viruses

Many viruses and other harmful attacks spread through file downloads, attachments in e-mail messages, and data files that have macros, ActiveX controls, add-ins, or Visual Basic for Applications (VBA) code attached to them. Virus writers capitalize on people's curiosity and willingness to accept files from people they know or work with, in order to transmit malicious files disguised as or attached to benign files. When you start downloading files to your computer, you must be aware of the potential for catching a computer virus, worm, or Trojan Horse. Typically, you can't catch one from just reading a mail message or downloading a file, but you can catch one from installing, opening, or running an infected program or attached code.

Understanding Harmful Attacks

Phishing is a scam that tries to steal your identity by sending deceptive e-mail asking you for bank and credit card information online. Phishers spoof the domain names of banks and other companies in order to deceive consumers into thinking that they are visiting a familiar Web site.

Phishers create a Web address that looks like a familiar Web address but is actually altered. This is known as a **homograph**. The domain name is created using alphabet characters from different languages, not just English. For example, the Web site address "www.microsoft.com" looks legitimate, but what you can't see is that the "i" is a Cyrillic character from the Russian alphabet.

Don't be fooled by spoofed Web sites that looks like the official site. Never respond to requests for personal information via e-mail; most companies have policies that do not ask for your personal information through e-mail. If you get a suspicious e-mail, call the institution to investigate and report it.

Spam is unsolicited e-mail, which is often annoying and time-consuming to get rid of. Spammers harvest e-mail addresses from Web pages and unsolicited e-mail. To avoid spam, use multiple e-mail addresses (one for Web forms and another for private e-mail), opt-out and remove yourself from e-mail lists. See the Microsoft Windows and Microsoft Office Help system for specific details.

Spyware is software that collects personal information without your knowledge or permission. Typically, spyware is downloaded and installed on your computer along with free software, such as freeware, games, or music file-sharing programs. Spyware is often associated with **Adware** software that displays advertisements, such as a pop-up ad. Examples of spyware and unauthorized adware include programs that change your home page or search page without your permission. To avoid spyware and adware, read the fine print in license agreements when you install software, scan your computer for spyware and adware with detection and removal software (such as Ad-aware from Lavasoft), and turn on Pop-up Blocker. See the Microsoft Windows Help system for specific details.

Avoiding Harmful Attacks Using Office

There are a few things you can do within any Office program to keep your system safe from the infiltration of harmful attacks.

1) Make sure you activate macro, ActiveX, add-in, and VBA code detection and notification. You can use the Trust Center to help protect you from attached code attacks. The Trust Center checks for trusted publisher and code locations on your computer and provides security options for add-ins, ActiveX controls, and macros to ensure the best possible protection. The Trust Center displays a security alert in the Message Bar when it detects a potentially harmful attack.

2) Make sure you activate Web site spoofing detection and notification. You can use the Trust Center to help protect you from homograph attacks. The *Check Office documents that are from or link to suspicious Web sites* check box under Privacy Options in the Trust Center is on by default and continually checks for potentially spoofed domain names. The Trust Center displays a security alert in the Message Bar when you have a document open and click a link to a Web site with an address that has a potentially spoofed domain name, or you open a file from a Web site with an address that has a potentially spoofed domain name.

3) Be very careful of file attachments in e-mail you open. As you receive e-mail, don't open or run an attached file unless you know who sent it and what it contains. If you're not sure, you should delete it. The Attachment Manager provides security information to help you understand more about the file you're opening. See the Microsoft Office Help system for specific details.

Avoiding Harmful Attacks Using Windows

There are a few things you can do within Microsoft Windows to keep your system safe from the infiltration of harmful attacks.

1) Make sure Windows Firewall is turned on. Windows Firewall helps block viruses and worms from reaching your computer, but it doesn't detect or disable them if they are already on your computer or come through e-mail. Windows Firewall doesn't block unsolicited e-mail or stop you from opening e-mail with harmful attachments.

2) Make sure Automatic Updates is turned on. Windows Automatic Updates regularly checks the Windows Update Web site for important updates that your computer needs, such as security updates, critical updates, and service packs. Each file that you download using Automatic Update has a digital signature from Microsoft to ensure its authenticity and security.

3) Make sure you are using the most up-to-date antivirus software. New viruses and more virulent strains of existing viruses are discovered every day. Unless you update your virus-checking software, new viruses can easily bypass outdated virus checking software. Companies such as McAfee and Symantec offer shareware virus checking programs available for download directly from their Web sites. These programs monitor your system, checking each time a file is added to your computer to make sure it's not in some way trying to change or damage valuable system files.

4) Be very careful of the sites from which you download files. Major file repository sites, such as FileZ, Download.com, or TuCows, regularly check the files they receive for viruses before posting them to their Web sites. Don't download files from Web sites unless you are certain that the sites check their files for viruses. Internet Options monitors downloads and warns you about potentially harmful files and gives you the option to block them.

Using the Trust Center

The **Trust Center** is a place where you set security options and find the latest technology information as it relates to workbook privacy, safety, and security from Microsoft. The Trust Center allows you to set security and privacy settings—Trusted Publishers, Trusted Locations, Trusted Documents (**New!**), Add-ins, ActiveX Settings, Macro Settings, Protected view (**New!**), Message Bar, External Content, File Block Settings (**New!**) ,and Privacy Options—and provides links to Microsoft privacy statements, a customer improvement program, and trustworthy computing practices.

View the Trust Center

1. Click the **File** tab, and then click **Options**.
2. In the left pane, click **Trust Center**.
3. Click the links in which you want online information at the Microsoft Online Web site.
   - **Show the Microsoft Word privacy statement.** Opens a Microsoft Web site detailing privacy practices.
   - **Office.com privacy statement.** Opens a Microsoft Office Web site detailing privacy practices.
   - **Customer Experience Improvement Program.** Opens the Microsoft Customer Experience Improvement Program (CEIP) Web site.
   - **Microsoft Trustworthy Computing.** Opens a Microsoft Web site detailing security and reliability practices.
4. When you're done, close your Web browser or dialog box, and return to Word.
5. Click **OK**.

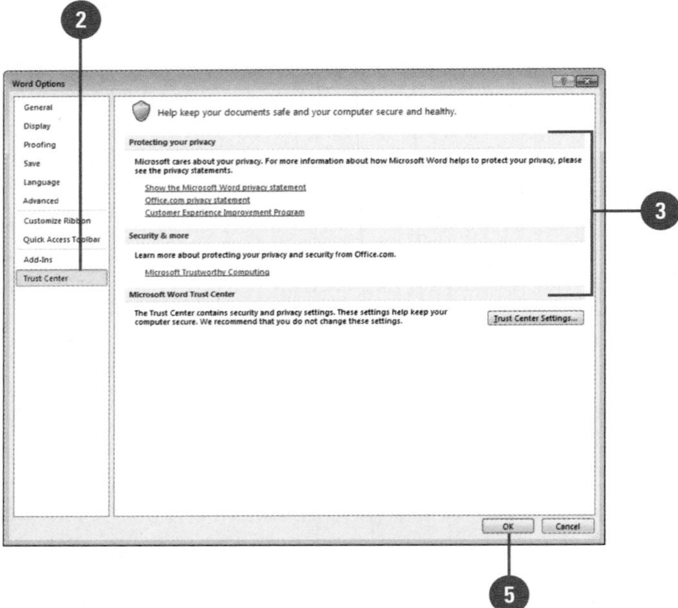

Selecting Trusted Publishers and Locations

The Trust Center security system continually checks for external potentially unsafe content in your documents. Hackers can hide Web beacons in external content—images, linked media, data connections and templates—to gather information about you or cause problems. When the Trust Center detects potentially harmful external content, the Message Bar appears with a security alert and options to enable or block the content. Trusted publishers are reputable developers who create application extensions, such as a macro, ActiveX control, or add-in. The Trust Center uses a set of criteria—valid and current digital signature, and reputable certificate—to make sure publishers' code and source locations are safe and secure. If you are sure that the external content is trustworthy, you can add the content publisher and location to your trusted lists, which allows it to run without being checked by the Trust Center.

Modify Trusted Publishers and Locations

1. Click the **File** tab, and then click **Options**.
2. In the left pane, click **Trust Center**.
3. Click **Trust Center Settings**.
4. In the left pane, click **Trusted Publishers**.
5. Select a publisher, and then use the **View** and **Remove** buttons to make the changes you want.
6. In the left pane, click **Trusted Locations**.
7. Select a location, and then use the **Add new location**, **Remove**, and **Modify** buttons to make the changes you want.
8. Select or clear the **Allow Trusted Locations on my network (not recommended)** check box.
9. Select or clear the **Disable all Trusted Locations** check box.
10. Click **OK**.
11. Click **OK**.

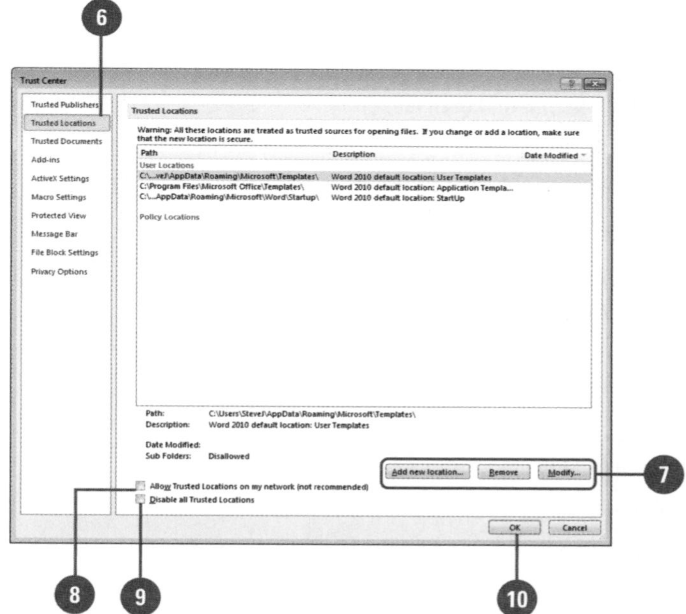

Setting Document Related Security Options

The Trust Center security system allows you to set file-related options to check for potentially unsafe content in your documents (**New!**). In Trusted Documents (**New!**), you can set options to open trusted documents without any security prompts for macros, ActiveX controls and other types of active content in the document. For a trusted document, you won't be prompted the next time you open the document even if new active content was added to the document or changes were made to existing active content. You should only trust documents if you trust the source. Protected view (**New!**) provides a place to open potentially dangerous files, without any security prompts, in a restricted mode to help minimize harm to your computer. If you disable Protected view, you could expose your computer to possible harmful threats. In File Block Settings (**New!**), you can select the Open and Save check boxes to prevent each file type from opening, or just opening in Protected view, and from saving.

Set Options for Trusted Documents

1. Click the **File** tab, and then click **Options**.
2. In the left pane, click **Trust Center**.
3. Click **Trust Center Settings**.
4. In the left pane, click **Trusted Documents**.
5. Select or clear the check boxes you do or don't want.
   - **Allow documents on a network to be trusted.**
   - **Disable Trusted Documents.**
6. To clear all trusted documents so they are no longer trusted, click **Clear**.
7. Click **OK**.
8. Click **OK**.

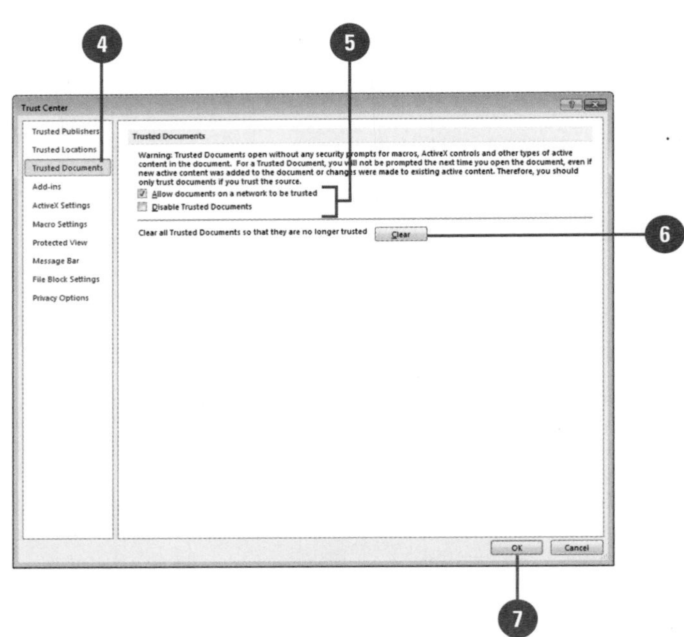

Set Options for Protected View

1. Click the **File** tab, and then click **Options**.
2. In the left pane, click **Trust Center**.
3. Click **Trust Center Settings**.
4. In the left pane, click **Protected View**.
5. Select or clear the check boxes you do or don't want.
   - **Enable Protected View for files originating from the Internet.**
   - **Enable Protected View for files located in potentially unsafe locations.**
   - **Enable Protected View for Outlook attachments.**
6. Click **OK**.
7. Click **OK**.

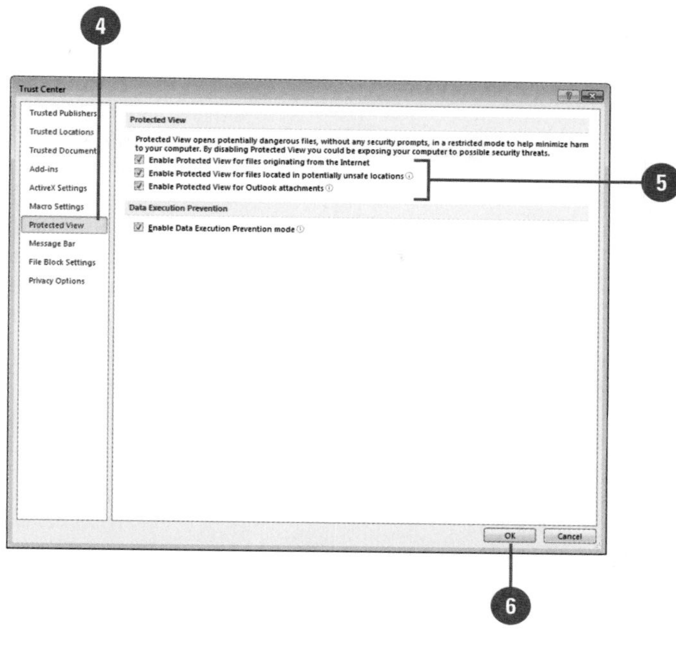

Set Options for File Block Settings

1. Click the **File** tab, and then click **Options**.
2. In the left pane, click **Trust Center**.
3. Click **Trust Center Settings**.
4. In the left pane, click **File Block Settings**.
5. Select the **Open** and **Save** check boxes you want to block for the different file types from opening or saving or clear the ones you don't want.
6. Select the open behavior option you want.
7. Click **OK**.
8. Click **OK**.

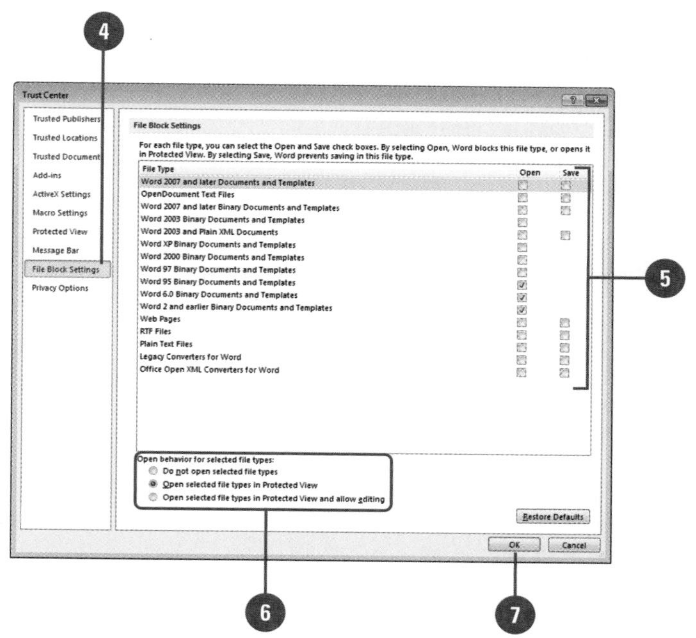

Setting Add-in Security Options

An add-in, such as smart tags, extends functionality to Microsoft Office programs. An add-in can add buttons and custom commands to the Ribbon. When an add-in is installed, it appears on the Add-Ins tab of an Office program and includes a special ScreenTip that identifies the developer. Since add-ins are software code added to Microsoft Office programs, hackers can use them to do malicious harm, such as spreading a virus. The Trust Center uses a set of criteria—valid and current digital signature, reputable certificate and a trusted publisher—to make sure add-ins are safe and secure. If it discovers a potentially unsafe add-in, it disables the code and notifies you in the Message Bar. If the add-in security options are not set to the level you need, you can change them in the Trust Center.

Set Add-in Security Options

1. Click the **File** tab, and then click **Options**.
2. In the left pane, click **Trust Center**.
3. Click **Trust Center Settings**.
4. In the left pane, click **Add-ins**.
5. Select or clear the check boxes you do or don't want.
   - **Require Application Add-ins to be signed by Trusted Publisher.** Select to check for a digital signature on the .dll file.
   - **Disable notification for unsigned add-ins (code will remain disabled).** Only available if the above check box is selected. Select to disable unsigned add-ins without notification.
   - **Disable all Application Add-ins (may impair functionality).** Select to disable all add-ins without any notifications.
6. Click **OK**.
7. Click **OK**.

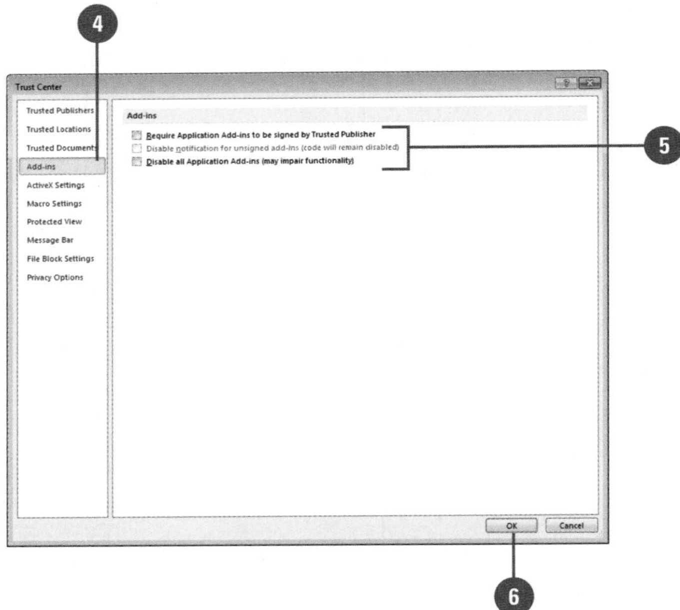

Setting ActiveX Security Options

An ActiveX control provides additional functionality, such as a text box, button, dialog box, or small utility program. ActiveX controls are software code, so hackers can use them to do malicious harm, such as spreading a virus. You can use the Trust Center to prevent ActiveX controls from harming your computer. If the ActiveX security options are not set to the level you want, you can change them in the Trust Center. If you change ActiveX control settings in one Office program, it effects all Microsoft Office programs. The Trust Center uses a set of criteria—checks the kill bit and Safe for Initialization (SFI) settings—to make sure ActiveX controls run safely.

Change ActiveX Security Settings

1. Click the **File** tab, and then click **Options**.
2. In the left pane, click **Trust Center**.
3. Click **Trust Center Settings**.
4. In the left pane, click **ActiveX Settings**.
5. Click the option you want for ActiveX in documents not in a trusted location.
   - Disable all controls without notification.
   - Prompt me before enabling Unsafe for Initialization controls with additional restrictions and Save for Initialization (SFI) controls with minimal restrictions (default).
   - Prompt me before enabling all controls with minimal restrictions.
   - Enable all controls with restrictions and without prompting (not recommended, potentially dangerous controls can run).
6. Click **OK**.
7. Click **OK**.

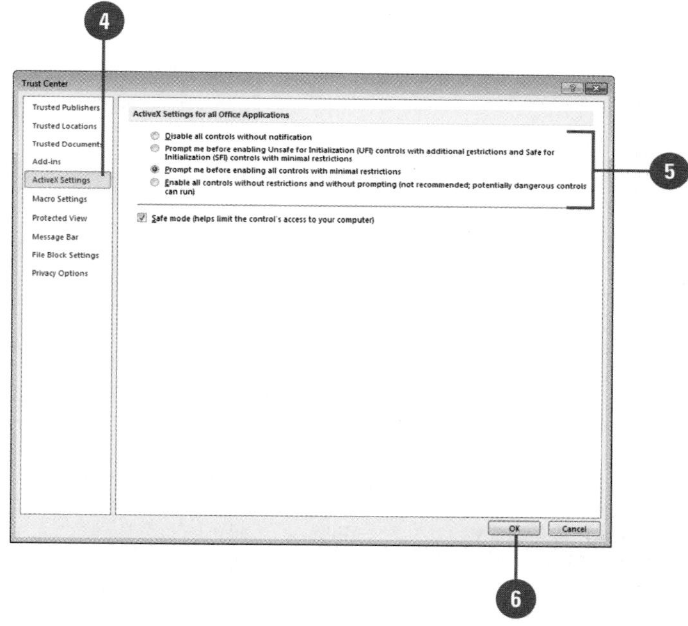

Setting Macro Security Options

A macro allows you to automate frequently used steps or tasks to save time and work more efficiently. Macros are written using VBA (Visual Basic for Applications) code, which opens the door to hackers to do malicious harm, such as spreading a virus. The Trust Center uses a set of criteria—valid and current digital signature, reputable certificate and a trusted publisher—to make sure macros are safe and secure. If the Trust Center discovers a potentially unsafe macro, it disables the code and notifies you in the Message Bar. You can click Options on the Message Bar to enable it or set other security options. If the macro security options are not set to the level you need, you can change them in the Trust Center.

Change Macro Security Settings

1. Click the **File** tab, and then click **Options**.
2. In the left pane, click **Trust Center**.
3. Click **Trust Center Settings**.
4. In the left pane, click **Macro Settings**.
5. Click the option you want for macros in documents not in a trusted location.
   - Disable all macros without notification.
   - Disable all macros with notification (default).
   - Disable all macros except digitally signed macros.
   - Enable all macros (not recommended, potentially dangerous code can run).
6. If you're a developer, select the **Trust access to the VBA project object model** check box.
7. Click **OK**.
8. Click **OK**.

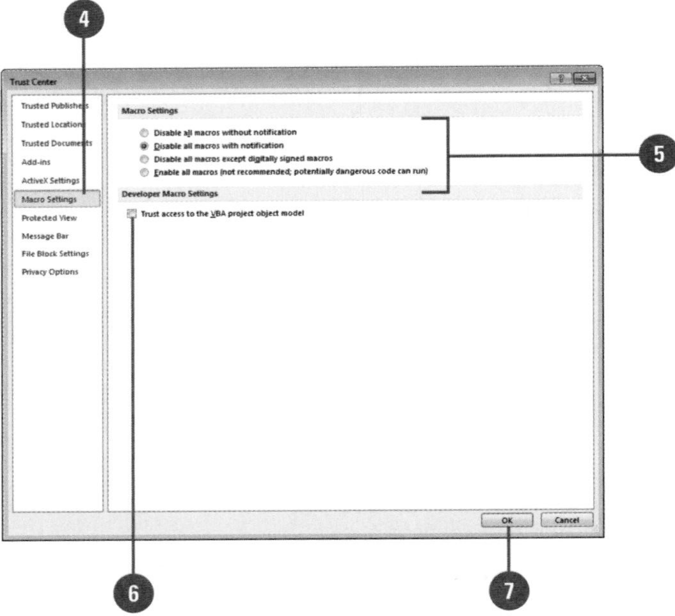

Changing Message Bar Security Options

The Message Bar displays security alerts when Office detects potentially unsafe content in an open document. The Message Bar appears below the Ribbon when a potential problem arises. The Message Bar provides a security warning and options to enable external content or leave it blocked. If you don't want to receive alerts about security issues, you can disable the Message Bar.

Modify Message Bar Security Options

1. Click the **File** tab, and then click **Options**.
2. In the left pane, click **Trust Center**.
3. Click **Trust Center Settings**.
4. In the left pane, click **Message Bar**.
5. Click the option you want for showing the Message bar.
   - Show the Message Bar in all applications when active content, such as ActiveX controls and macros, has been blocked (default).

     This option is not selected if you selected the Disable all macros without notification check box in the Macros pane of the Trust Center.
   - Never show information about blocked content.
6. Click **OK**.
7. Click **OK**.

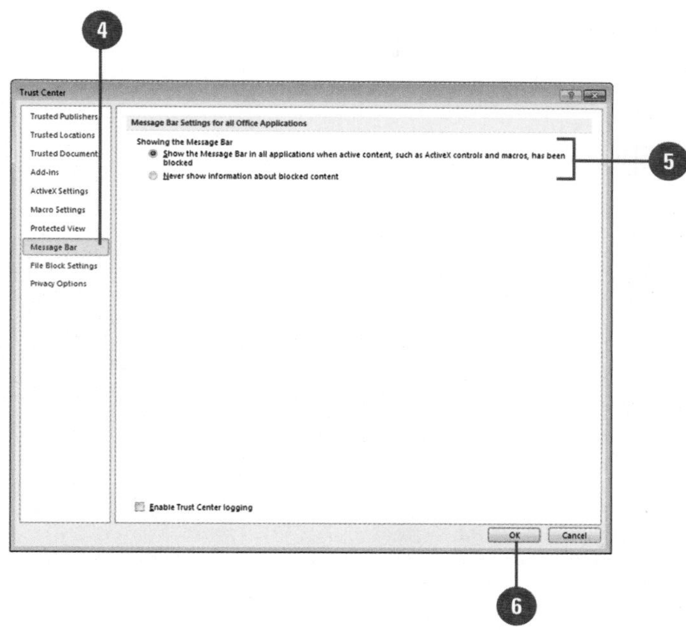

Setting Privacy Options

Privacy options in the Trust Center allow you to set security settings that protect your personal privacy online. For example, the *Check Office documents that are from or link to suspicious Web sites* option checks for spoofed Web sites and protects you from phishing schemes. If your kids are doing research online using the Research task pane, you can set Privacy Options to enable parental controls and a password to block sites with offensive content.

Set Privacy Options

1. Click the **File** tab, and then click **Options**.
2. In the left pane, click **Trust Center**.
3. Click **Trust Center Settings**.
4. In the left pane, click **Privacy Options**.
5. Select or clear the check boxes you do or don't want.
   - **Connect to Office.com for updated content when I'm connected to the Internet.**
   - **Download a file periodically that helps determine system problems.** Select to have Microsoft request error reports, update help, and accept downloads from Office.com.
   - **Automatically detect installed Office applications to improve Office.com search results.** Select to automatically detect applications.
   - **Check Microsoft Office documents that are from or link to suspicious Web sites.** Select to check for spoofed Web sites.
   - **Allow the Research task pane to check for and install new services.**
   - **Allow sending files to improve file validation.**
6. Click **OK**.
7. Click **OK**.

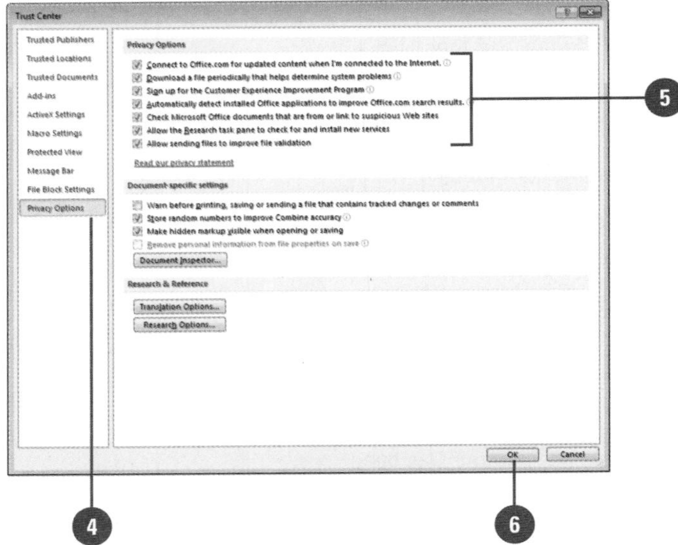

Set Parental Controls for Online Research

1. Click the **File** tab, and then click **Options**.
2. In the left pane, click **Trust Center**.
3. Click **Trust Center Settings**.
4. In the left pane, click **Privacy Options**.
5. Click **Research Options**.
6. Click **Parental Control**.
7. Select the **Turn on content filtering to make services block offensive results** check box.
8. Select the **Allow users to search only the services that can block offensive results** check box, if necessary.
9. Enter a password, so users cannot change these settings.
10. Click **OK**, retype the password, and then click **OK**.
11. Click **OK**.
12. Click **OK**.

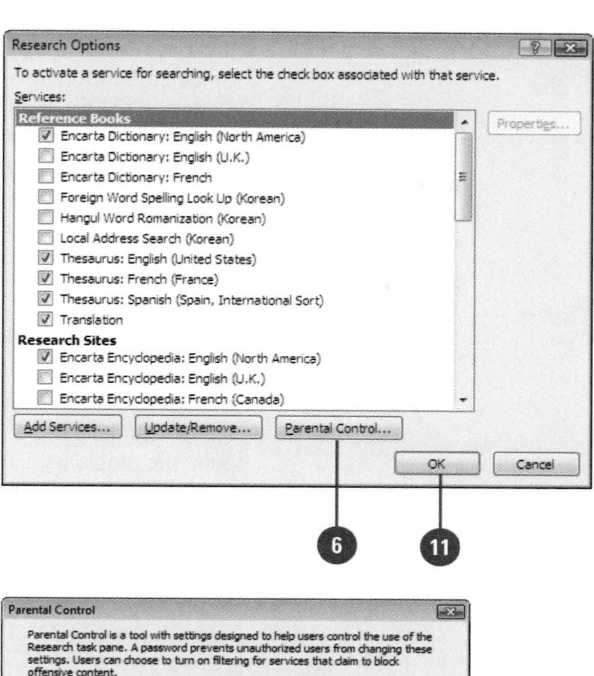

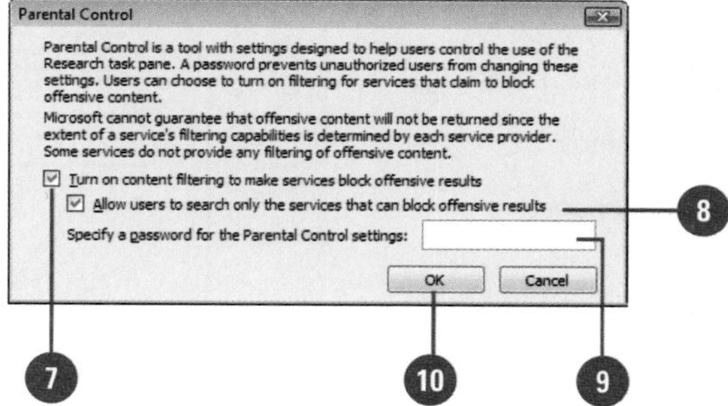

Working with Office Safe Modes

Microsoft Office uses two types of safe modes—Automated and User-Initiated—when it encounters a program problem. When you start an Office 2010 program, it automatically checks for problems, such as an extension not properly loading. If the program is not able to start the next time you try, the programs starts in **Automated Safe mode**, which disables extensions—macros, ActiveX controls, and add-ins—and other possible problem areas. If you're having problems and the Office program doesn't start in Automated Safe mode, you can start the program in **User-Initiated Safe mode**. When you start an Office program in Office Safe mode, not all features are available. For instance, templates can't be saved, AutoCorrect list is not loaded, preferences cannot be saved, and all command-line options are ignored (except /a and /n). Before you can use Office Safe mode, you need to enable it in the Trust Center. When you're in safe mode, you can use the Trust Center to find out the disabled items and enable them one at a time to help you pin point the problem.

Enable Safe Mode

1. Click the **File** tab, and then click **Options**.
2. In the left pane, click **Trust Center**.
3. Click **Trust Center Settings**.
4. In the left pane, click **ActiveX Settings**.
5. Select the **Safe Mode (helps limit the control's access to your computer)** check box.
6. Click **OK**.
7. Click **OK**.

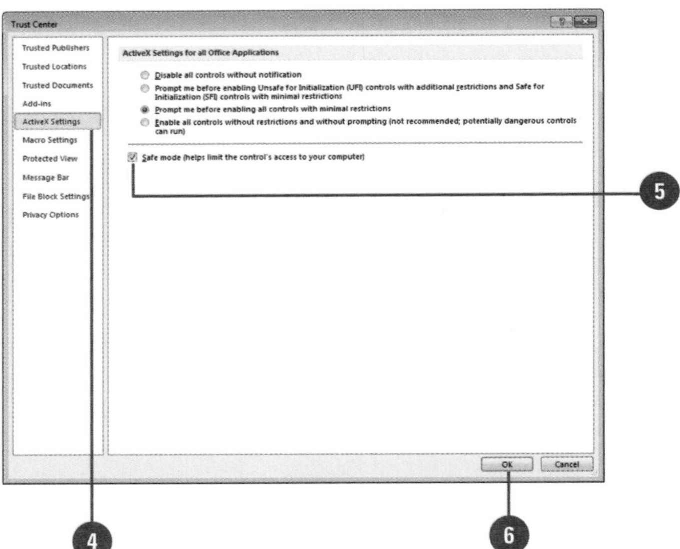

See Also

See "Maintaining and Repairing Office" on page 32 for information on fixing problems with a Microsoft Office program.

Start User-Initiated Safe Mode

1. Click the **Start** button on the taskbar, point to **All Programs**, and then click **Microsoft Office**.
2. Press and hold Ctrl, and then click **Microsoft Word 2010**.

Did You Know?

You can use the Run dialog box to work in Safe mode. At the command prompt, you can use the */safe* parameter at the end of the command-line to start the program.

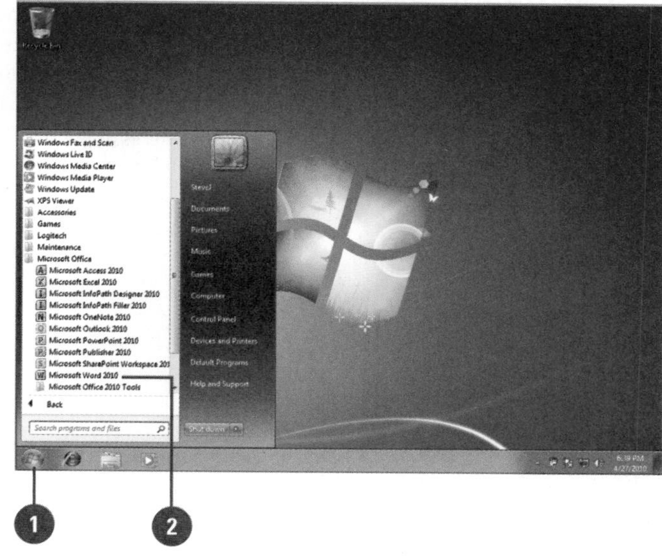

View Disabled Items

1. Click the **File** tab, and then click **Options**.
2. In the left pane, click **Add-Ins**.
3. Click the **Manage** list arrow, and then click **Disabled Items**.
4. Click **Go**.
5. In the dialog box, you can select an item, click **Enable** to activate and reload the add-in, and then click **Close**.
6. Click **OK**.

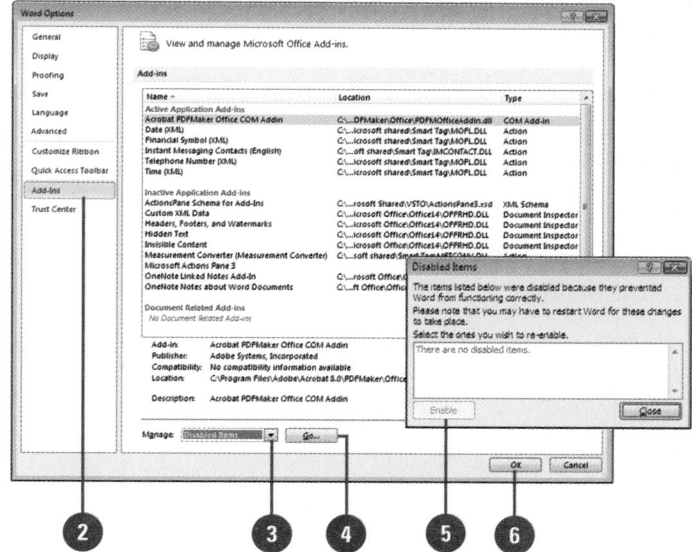

Marking a Document as Read-Only

As a precaution to prevent readers and reviews from making accidental changes, you can use the Mark as Final command to make a Word document read-only. The Mark as Final command disables or turns off typing, editing commands, and proofing marks, and sets the *Status property* field in the Document Information Panel to Final. The Mark as Final command is not a security option; it only prevents changes to the document while it's turned on and it can be turned off by anyone at any time.

Mark a Document as Final

1. Click the **File** tab, click **Info**, click the **Protect Document** button, and then click **Mark as Final**.
2. Click **OK**, and then click **OK** again, if necessary.

   The document is marked as final and then saved.
3. If necessary, click **OK**.

   The Mark as Final icon appears in the Status bar to indicate the document is currently marked as final.

   IMPORTANT *A Word 2010 document marked as final is not read-only when opened in an earlier version of Microsoft Word.*

Did You Know?

You can enable editing for a document marked as final. Click the Edit Anyway button in the Message Bar or click the File tab, click Info, click the Protect Document button, and then click Mark As Final again to toggle off the Mark As Final feature.

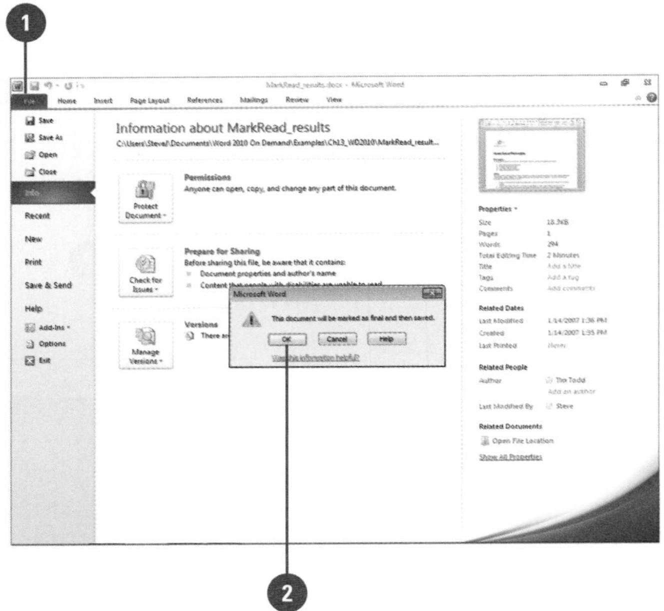

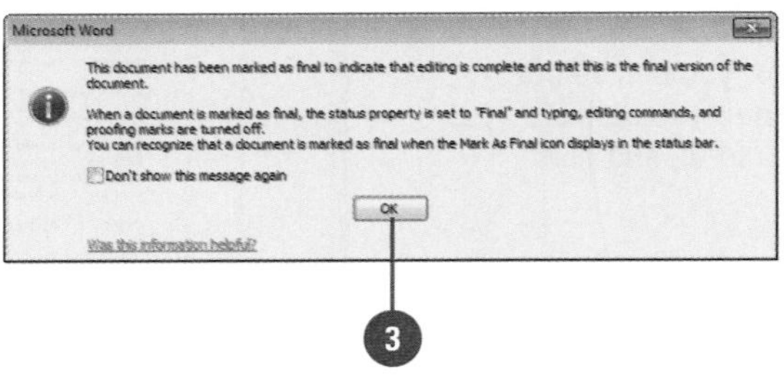

Mark as Final icon

Reviewing and Sharing Documents

14

Introduction

If you work in an office environment with Microsoft Word, or are part of some other group that routinely collaborates in document preparation, learning the basics of document sharing is a must. The greater the number of people that interact with a document before it reaches final form, the more critical it becomes for you to keep track of versions, comments, the source of all editing marks, and adequately manage the process of correcting them.

Because working together on a document may be crucial to the success of its completion, there might be various levels of security that need to be set for your readers. Some may have full access to read and make changes, while others are limited to just reading the document, and still others may only be able to read part of the document because it contains hidden text.

After you finish making changes to a document, you can quickly send it to another person for review using e-mail. Word allows you to send documents out for review as an attachment, either a document, PDF, or XPS document, using e-mail from within the program so that you do not have to open your e-mail program. If you are a member of an online fax service—such as eFax, InterFAX, MyFax, or Send2Fax—you can use Office to send and receive faxes over the Internet directly from within Word.

What You'll Do

Preparing for Comments and Track Changes

When you enter a comment or make a change in a document with track changes, Word includes the name and initials of the person who made the comment or change. You can set or change this information in the Word Options dialog box, which you can access from the Track Changes button on the Review tab. When you work with comments or track changes, you can choose to display them in balloons that show off the right-side of the document or in the Reviewing pane that show vertically or horizontally in a separate pane. After you choose how you want to display comments and track changes, you can use the Show Markup button to show or hide different elements—including Comments, Ink, Insertion and Deletions, Formatting, and Markup Area Highlights—on the screen during your review. If you have multiple people reviewing a document, you can use the Show Markup button to display the reviewers you want to display. Once you choose the elements you want to show, you can use the Display for Review list arrow on the Review tab to choose how to view the proposed changes to a document. You can show the original or final proposed document with or without showing markup.

Set User Information for Comments and Track Changes

1. Click the **Review** tab.
2. Click the **Track Changes** button, and then click **Change User Name**.
   - You can also click the **File** tab, click **Options**, and then click **General** in the left pane.
3. Type your name.
4. Type your initials.
5. Click **OK**.

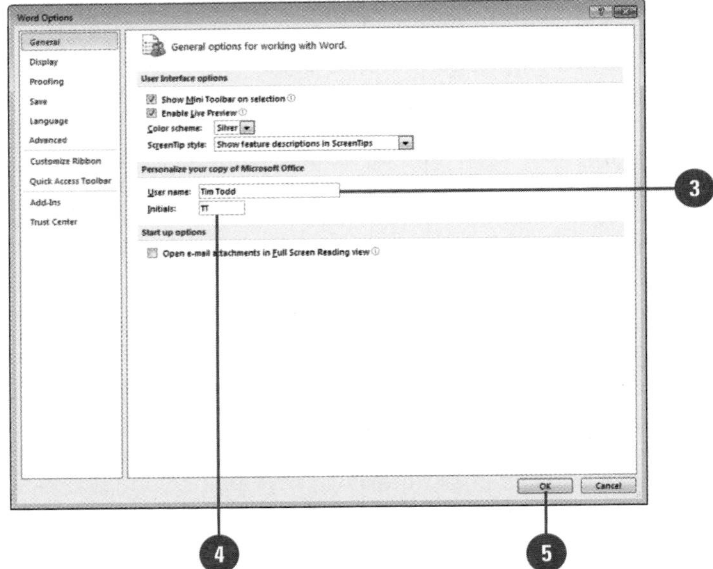

Use Balloons or Reviewing Pane

1. Click the **Review** tab.
2. Click the **Show Markup** button, point to **Balloons**, and then select the option you want:
   - **Show Revisions in Balloons.**
   - **Show All Revisions Inline.** Show changes in the document.
   - **Show Only Comments and Formatting in Balloons.** Hide content changes.
3. Click the **Reviewing Pane** button arrow, and then click **Reviewing Pane Vertical** or **Reviewing Pane Horizontal**.
   - To show or hide the Reviewing pane, click the **Reviewing Pane** button.

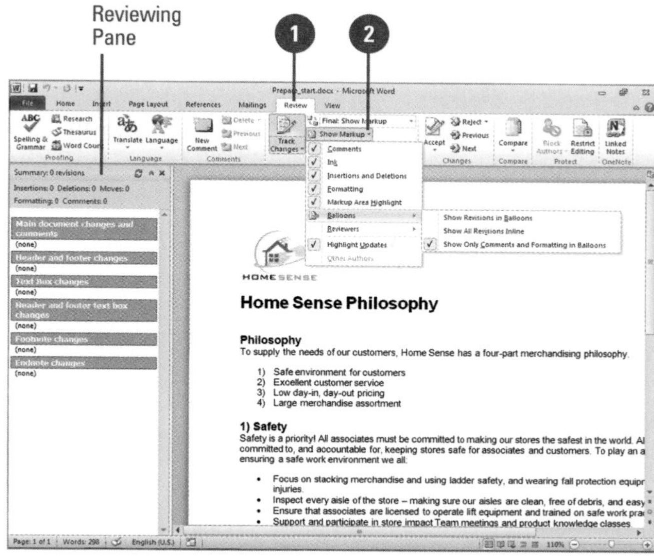

Show or Hide Elements Using Show Markup

1. Click the **Review** tab.
2. Click the **Show Markup** button, and then select the option you want: **Comments, Ink, Insertion and Deletions, Formatting, Markup Area Highlight, Balloons,** or **Reviewers.**
   - For the Reviewers option, you can show individual or All Reviewer's contributions.
3. Click the **Display for Review** list arrow, and then select how to view the proposed changes to the document: **Final Showing Markup, Final, Original Showing Markup,** or **Original.**

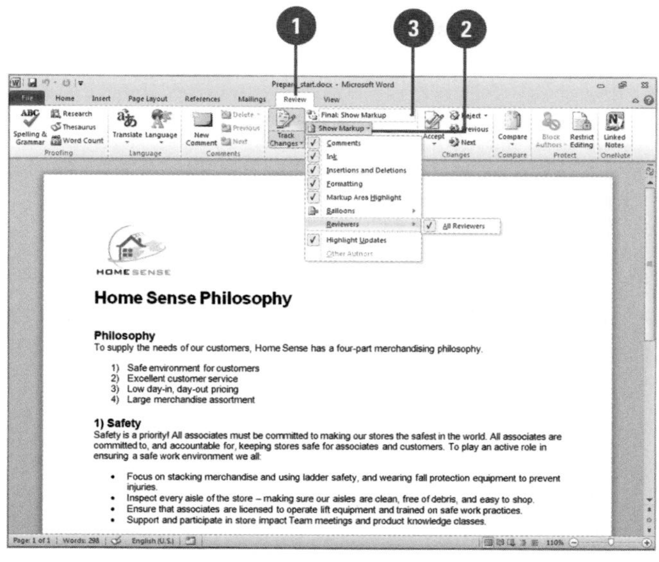

Inserting Comments

Comments are useful when someone who is editing the document has questions pertaining to the document. Perhaps a particular passage needs to be clarified. Maybe the formatting of an item is inconsistent. In Word, you can insert a comment or respond to a comment as you review a document and provide feedback. When you insert a comment in Print Layout view, it opens a balloon or the Reviewing pane where you can enter a comment. If you use a Tablet PC, you can also insert a voice comment or a handwritten comment.

Insert a Comment

1. Position the insertion pointer where you want to insert a comment.
2. Click the **Review** tab.
3. Click the **New Comment** button.
4. Type your comment in the balloon, and then click outside the balloon to save it.

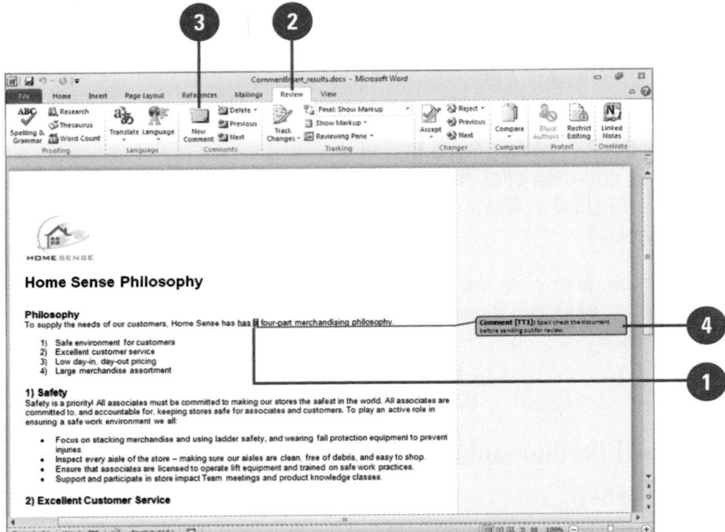

Did You Know?

You can insert a voice comment. On a Tablet PC, add the Insert Voice button command to the Quick Access Toolbar using the Customize pane in Word Options. Click the Insert Voice button, click the Start button and record the voice comment. When you're done, press the Stop button and close the dialog box. If necessary, click Yes to update the sound object.

Respond to a Comment

1. Click the balloon of the comment in which you want to respond.
2. Click the **Review** tab.
3. Click the **New Comment** button.
4. Type your response in the new comment balloon, and then click outside the balloon to save it.

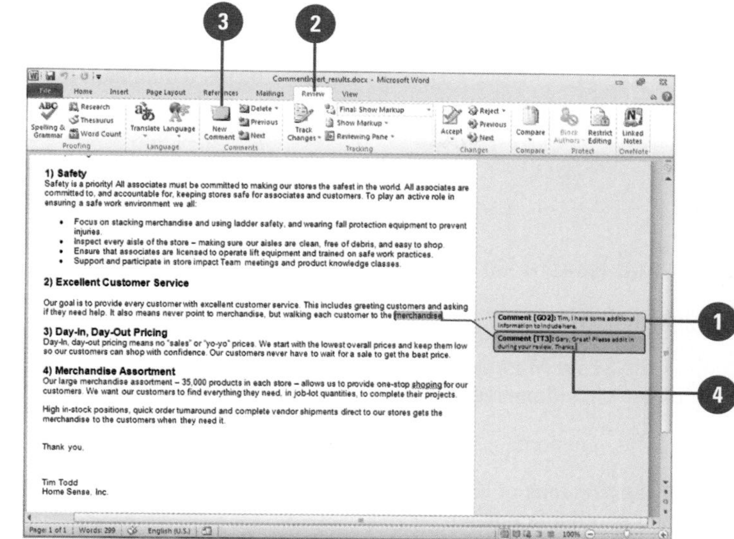

Did You Know?

You can insert a handwritten comment. On a Tablet PC, click the Review tab, click the New Comment button, and then write the comment in the comment balloon. To show ink, click the Show Markup button, and then click Ink.

Reading and Editing Comments

Before you can view, read and edit comments, you need to show them on the screen. The Show Markup button on the Review tab allows you to show or hide comments and tracking information. You can edit the text in a comment the same way you edit text in a document. If you have dealt with a comment or no longer need it, you can delete it. If you prefer to delete comments all at once, you can use the Delete button on the Review tab to delete all comments shown or all comments in the document.

Display and Read a Comment

1. Click the **Review** tab.
2. Click the **Show Markup** button, and then click **Comments**.
3. Read the comment.
4. Click the **Previous** or **Next** button to read another comment.

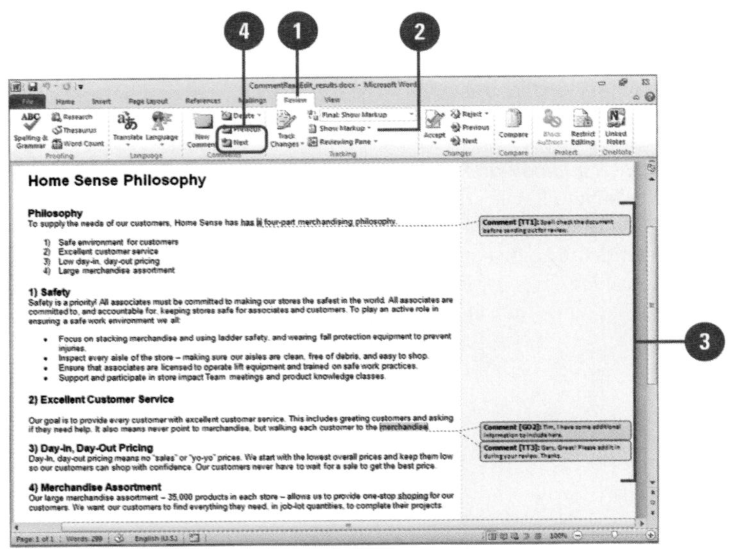

Edit a Comment

1. Click the **Review** tab.
2. Click the **Show Markup** button, and then click **Comments**.
3. Click the text in the comment, make your changes, and then click outside the balloon to save it.

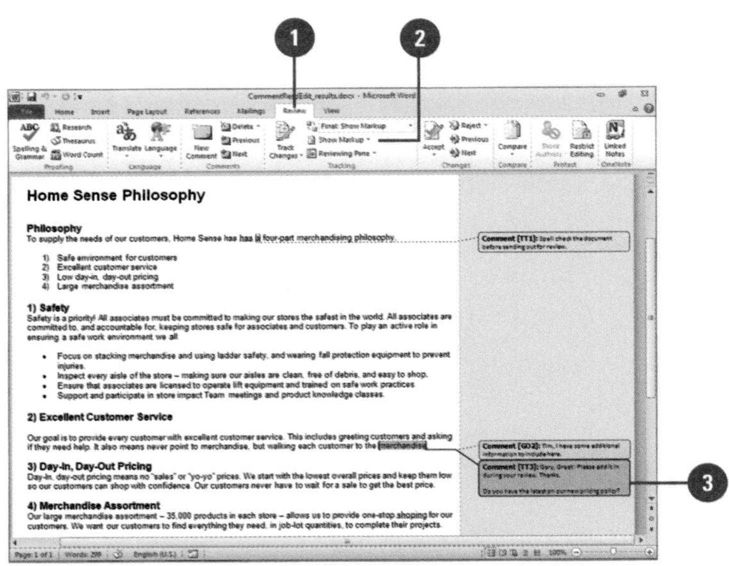

Delete Comments for a Specific Reviewer

1. Click the **Review** tab.
2. Click the **Show Markup** button arrow, and then point to **Reviewers**.
3. Click the name of the reviewer whose comments you want to delete, or click **All Reviewers**.
4. Click the **Delete** button arrow, and then click **Delete All Comments Shown.**

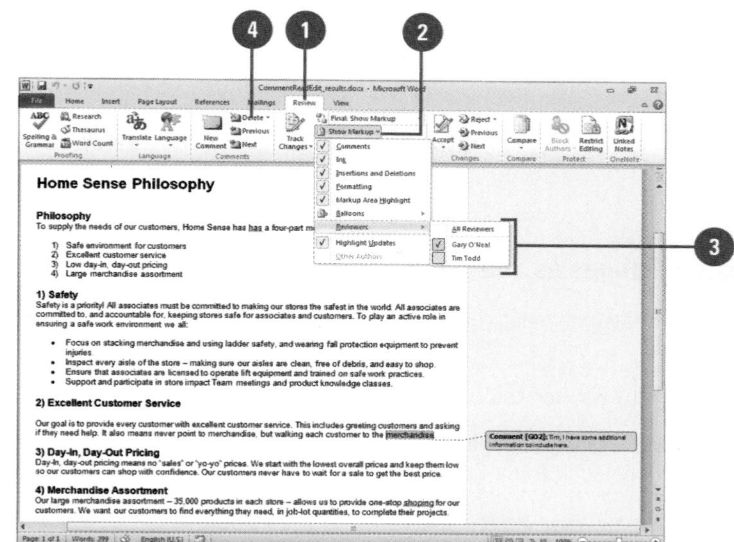

Delete All Comments

1. Click the **Review** tab.
2. Click the **Delete** button arrow, and then click **Delete All Comments in Document**.

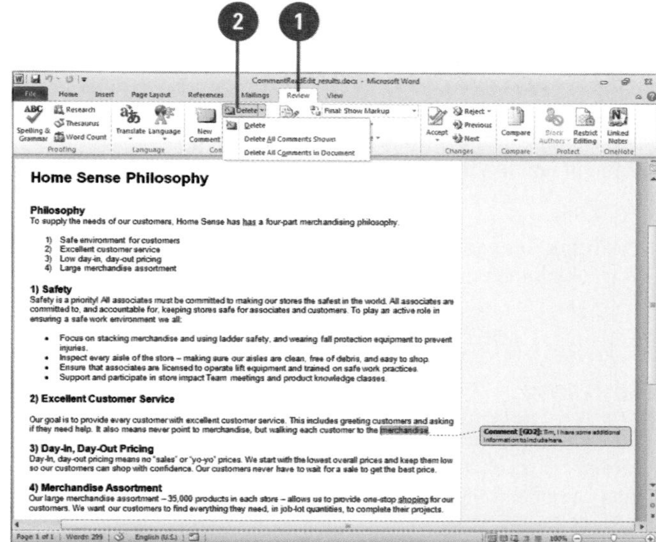

Did You Know?

You can quickly delete a comment. Select the comment, and then click the Delete button on the Review tab, or right-click the comment, and then click Delete Comment.

You can also use the Reviewing Pane to work with comments. Click the Review tab, click the Reviewing Pane button arrow, click Reviewing Pane Vertical or Reviewing Pane Horizontal.

Using Track Changes

Tracking changes in a document allows you to make revisions to a document without losing the original text. Word shows changed text in a different color from the original text and uses revision marks, such as underlines, to distinguish the revised text from the original. You can review changes by using the Review tab, which contains buttons that let you accept and reject changes and comments. If you compare and merge two documents, you can review the changes and accept or reject the results.

Track Changes as You Work

1. Open the document you want to edit.
2. Click the **Review** tab.
3. Click the **Track Changes** button, and then click **Track Changes**.

   TIMESAVER *Click Track Changes on the Status bar or press Ctrl+Shift+E to turn tracking on or off.*

4. Make changes to your document. The changes are reflected using alternate color characters, along with comments in balloons at the side of the screen (if you are in Print Layout view) or displayed in a separate window at the bottom of the screen (if you are in Draft view).
5. Click the **Track Changes** button to turn off track changes.

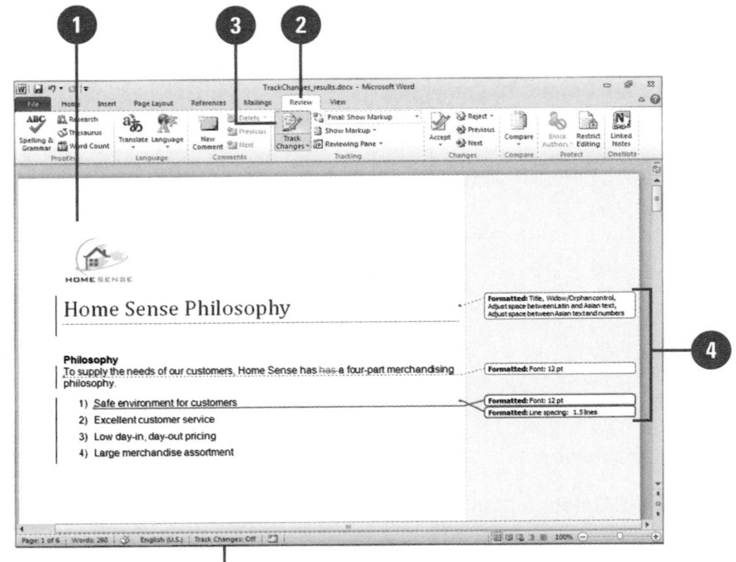

Track Changes turned on

Did You Know?

You can show or hide balloons. Click the Review tab, click the Show Markup button, point to Balloons, and then select Show Revisions In Balloons, Show All Revisions Inline, or Show Only Comments And Formatting in Balloons.

Review Changes

1. Open the document you want to review.
2. Click the **Review** tab.
3. Use the buttons on the Review tab to review changes:
   - Click the **Next** button or the **Previous** button to view changes one at a time.
   - Click the **Accept** button or the **Reject** button to respond to the revisions.
   - Click the **Accept** button arrow, and then click **Accept All Changes in Document** to accept all changes at once.
   - Click the **Reject** button arrow, and then click **Reject All Changes in Document** to reject all changes at once.

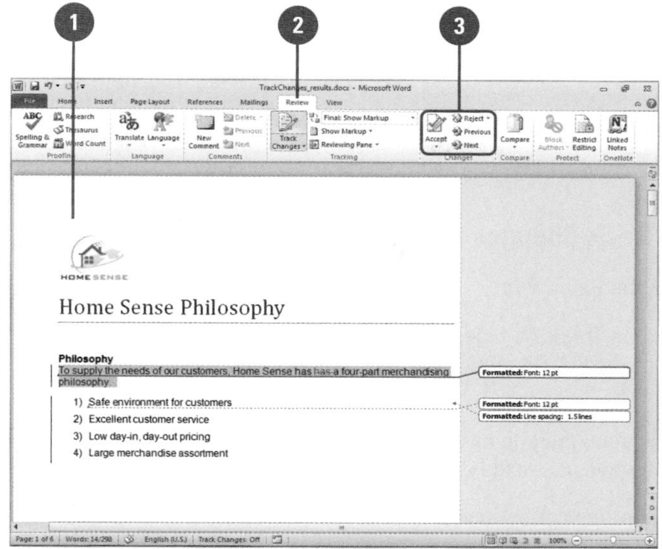

Did You Know?

You can display different versions of reviewing marks. Click the Review tab, click the Display For Review list arrow, and then select an option: Final Showing Markup, Final, Original Showing Markup, or Original.

You can show or hide individual reviewers. Click the Review tab, click the Show Markup button, point to Reviewers, and then click the reviewer you want to show or hide.

You can show or hide the Reviewing pane. The Reviewing pane shows a list of changes in a pane. Click the Review tab, click the Reviewing Pane button, and then click the option you want.

For Your Information

Printing a Document with Track Changes

If you want to review a print out of document changes, Word provides several options for printing documents with track changes. Before you can print a document with track changes and comment showing, you need to switch to Print Layout view and display the tracked changes and comments you want to print. Click the Review tab, click the Show Markup button, and then select the options or reviewers you want to display. Click the Display For Review list arrow, and then select the option you want to display. Click the File tab, click Print, click the Print What list arrow, click Document Showing Markup or List Of Markup, select other print options you want, and then click OK. To change the print layout for track changes, click the Track Changes button arrow, click Change Tracking Options, click the Paper Orientation In Printing list arrow, select the option you want, and then click OK.

Modifying Track Changes Options

You can customize the way track changes marks up a document. When you make insertion, deletion, and formatting changes, you can change the markup text to display the change with a specific color or formatting style, such as bold, italic, underline, double underline, and strikethrough. If you are using balloons in Print and Web Layout views, you can specify a preferred size and location in your document. If you prefer not to use balloons, you can turn the option off.

Modify Track Changes Options

1. Click the **Review** tab.
2. Click the **Track Changes** button, and then click **Change Tracking Options**.
3. Specify the markup options you want when you make changes.
   - **Insertions**. Marks inserted text.
   - **Deletions**. Marks deleted text.
   - **Formatting**. Marks formatting changes.
   - **Changed Lines**. Sets the location of vertical line that marks changed paragraphs.
   - **Comments Color**. Sets the color applied to all comments.
4. Specify the balloons options you want.
   - **Use Balloons (Print and Web Layout)**. Sets display option for balloons.
   - **Preferred width**. Sets balloon width.
   - **Margin**. Sets margin location for balloons.
5. Click **OK**.

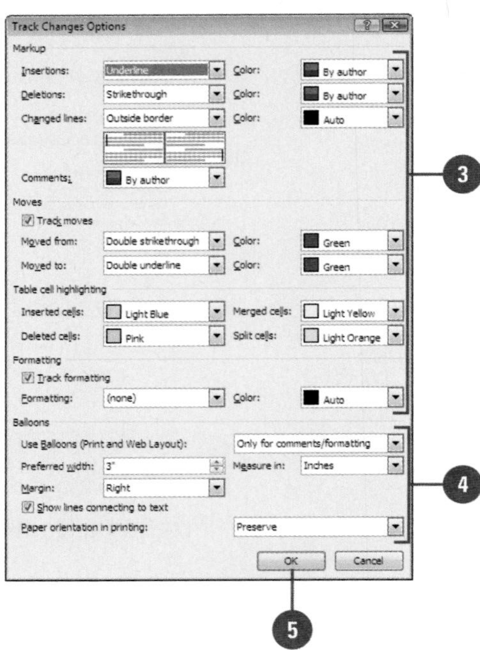

Comparing and Merging Documents

If you want to compare an earlier version of a document with the current version, or if you receive multiple edited versions of the original document back from the recipients, you can compare the documents and merge the changes into one document. The changes can be merged into one document or viewed for comparison. When you compare or merge documents, the text that differs between the two versions will be highlighted in a different color or with track reviewing marks.

Compare and Merge Documents

1. Click the **Review** tab.
2. Click the **Compare** button, and then click **Compare**.

   To merge documents, click the **Compare** button, and then click **Combine**.
3. Click the **Original document** list arrow, and then select the original document you want to use, or click the **Browse** button and double-click it.
4. Click the **Revised document** list arrow, and then select the revised document you want to use, or click the **Browse** button and double-click it.

   If necessary, click **More**.
5. Select and clear the comparison settings you want and don't want.
6. Click a Show changes at option: **Character level** or **Word level**.
7. Click a Show changes in option: **Original document**, **Revised document**, or **New document**.
8. Click **OK**.
9. If necessary, select a keep formatting option, and then click **OK**.
10. To show or hide documents, click the **Compare** button, point to **Show Source Documents**, and then select an option.

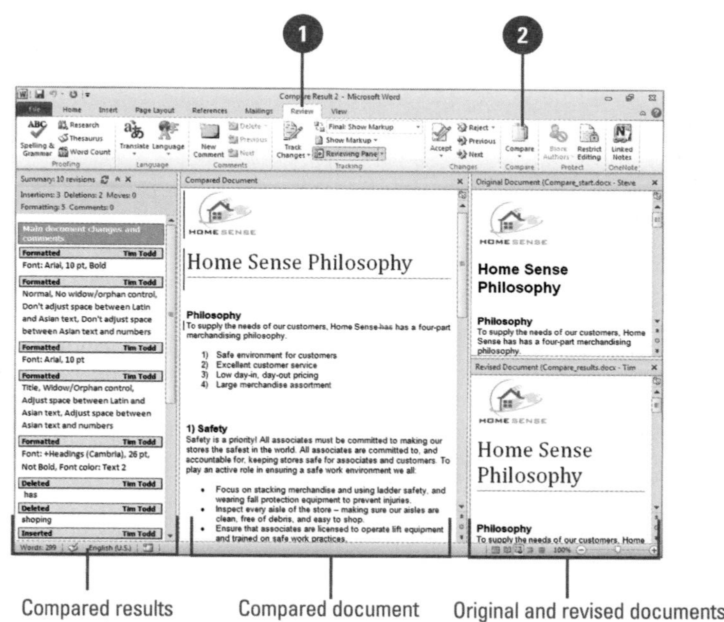

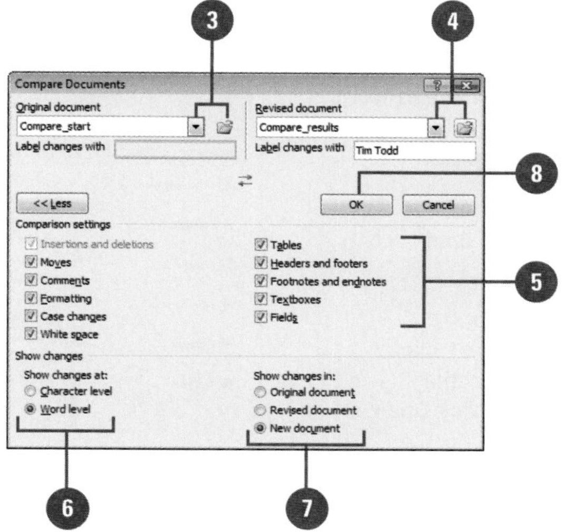

Sharing Templates

To save time, Word allows you to copy features from one template to another. Once you create a style or macro you never have to create it again. You can simply copy it to another template to use it with a whole new set of documents. You can also replace all the styles in a document with those from a different template by attaching the new template to that document. Word uses two types of templates—global and document. All documents have access to the Normal global template, and many documents have document templates attached that provide formatting instructions. You can load templates as needed to serve as global templates. When you load global templates, you can specify whether they are to be available for the current session only or available whenever you start Word. If you want to change the template used by the current document (typically Normal.dotx) to another one, use the Attach button in the Template and Add-Ins dialog box.

Load, Unload, or Attach Templates

1. Open the document with the template you want to use to attach another template, and then click the **Developer** tab.
2. Click the **Document Template** button.
3. Select or clear the check box next to the global template or add-in you want to load or unload.
4. To add or remove a global template or add-in, do one of the following:
   - **Add.** Click **Add**, navigate to the folder that contains the add-in, click the **Files of type** list arrow, select **Word Add-Ins**, click the add-in, and then click **OK**.
   - **Remove.** Select the item you want to remove, and then click Remove.
5. To attach a template to a document (transfer styles), click **Attach**, locate and select the template file, and then click **Open**.
6. Click **OK**.

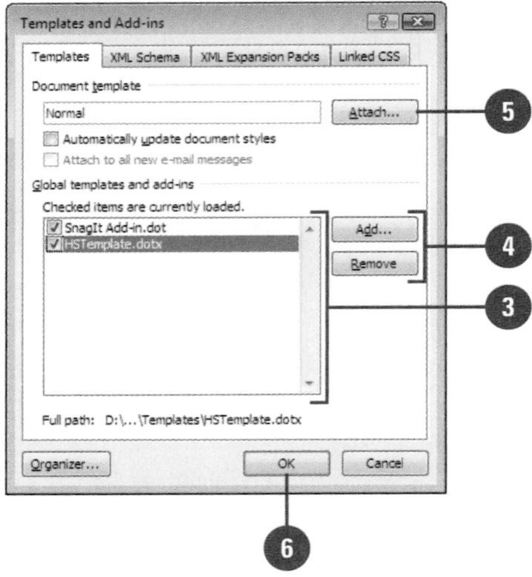

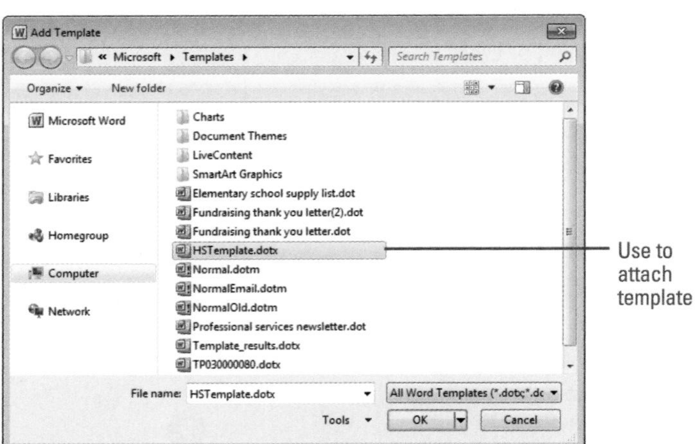

Copy Functionality Between Templates

1. With one template open, click the **Developer** tab.
2. Click the **Document Template** button.
3. Click **Organizer** on the Templates tab.
4. Click a tab on the Organizer dialog box with the part of the template that you want to copy.
5. To copy items either to or from a different template, click **Close File**.
6. Click **Open File**, and then open the template (or file) you want.
7. Click the items you want to copy in either list.
8. Click **Copy**.
9. When you're done, click **Close.**
10. Click **OK**.

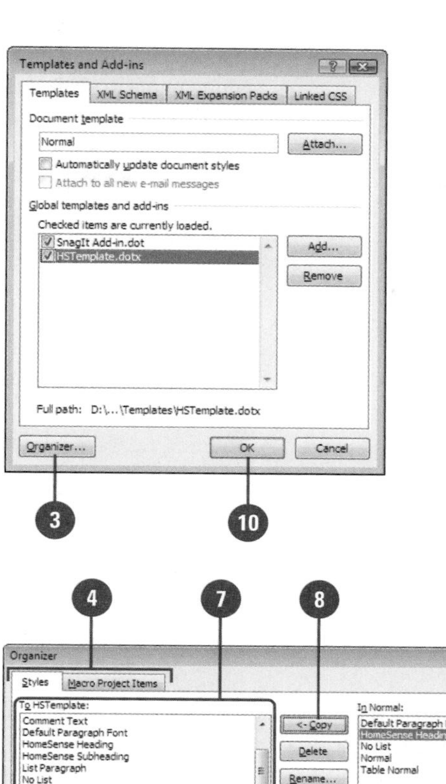

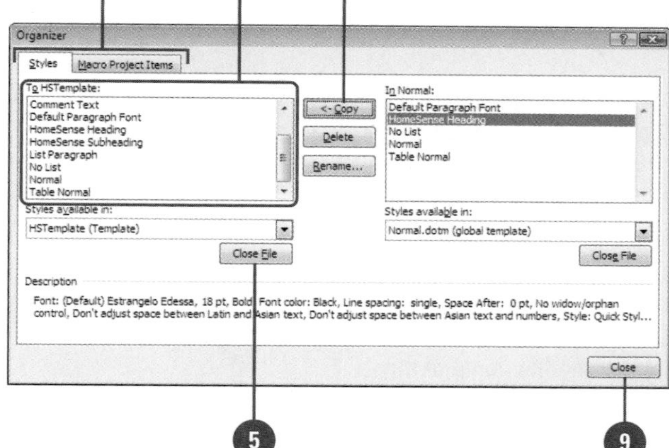

Did You Know?

Templates can be password protected from unwanted changes. If the Copy button is unavailable in the Organizer dialog box, check to see if the template has been password protected against tracked changes, comments, or forms. If so, these settings must be changed before the elements can be copied to the template.

See Also

See "Setting Developer Options" on page 409 for information on showing the Developer tab.

Sending a Document for Review Using E-mail

After you finish making changes to a document, you can quickly send it to another person for review using e-mail. Word allows you to send documents out for review as an attachment—either a document, PDF, or XPS document—or as a link (document in a shared location) using e-mail from within the program so that you do not have to open your e-mail program. An e-mail program, such as Microsoft Outlook, needs to be installed on your computer before you begin. When you send your document out for review, reviewers can add comments and then send it back to you.

Send a Document for Review Using E-mail

1. Click the **File** tab, click **Save & Send**, and then click **Send Using E-mail.**
2. Click the **Send as Attachment** or **Send a Link** button.
3. If the Compatibility Checker appears, click **Continue** or **Cancel** to stop the operation.

   IMPORTANT *To complete the following steps, you need to have an e-mail program installed on your computer and an e-mail account set-up.*

   An e-mail message opens in Microsoft Outlook with your document attached. The subject line contains the file name of the document that you are sending.
4. Enter your recipients and subject line (appears with document name by default).
   - To add recipients from your address book or contacts list, click **To**, click the recipient names, click **To**, **Cc**, or **Bcc** until you're done, and then click **OK**.
5. Enter a message for your reviewer with instructions.
6. Click the **Send** button.

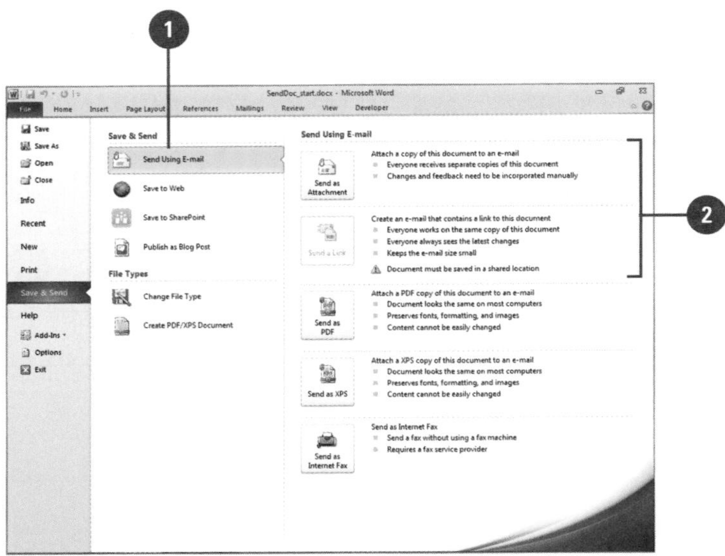

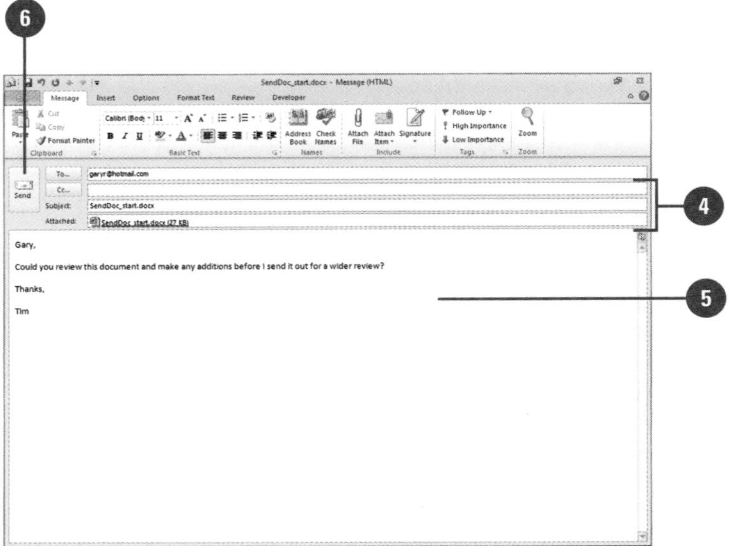

Send a Document as a PDF or XPS Using E-mail

1. Click the **File** tab, click **Save & Send**, and then click **Send Using E-mail**.
2. Click the **Send as PDF** or **Send as XPS** button.
3. If the Compatibility Checker appears, click **Continue** or **Cancel** to stop the operation.

   IMPORTANT *To complete the following steps, you need to have an e-mail program installed on your computer and an e-mail account set-up.*

   An e-mail message opens in Microsoft Outlook with your document attached. The subject line contains the file name of the document that you are sending.
4. Enter your recipients and subject line (appears with document name by default).
   - To add recipients from your address book or contacts list, click **To**, click the recipient names, click **To**, **Cc**, or **Bcc** until you're done, and then click **OK**.
5. Enter a message for your reviewer with instructions.
6. Click the **Send** button.

See Also

See "Creating a PDF Document" on page 376 or "Creating an XPS Document" on page 377 for information on working with PDF and XPS documents.

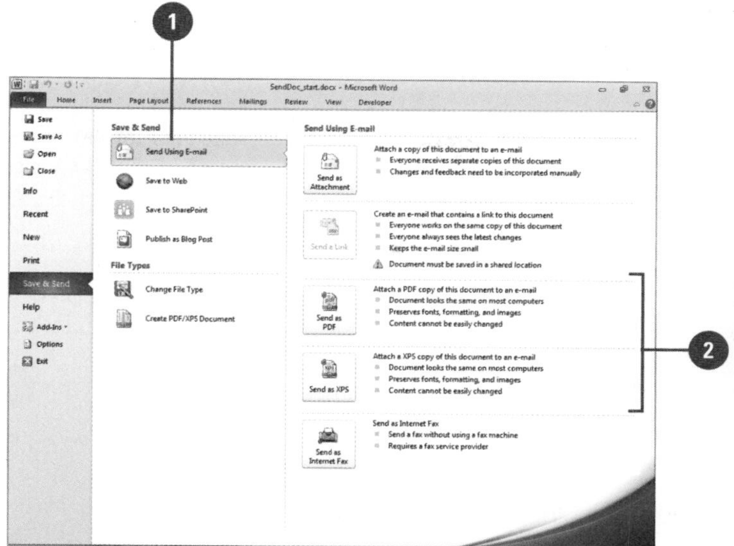

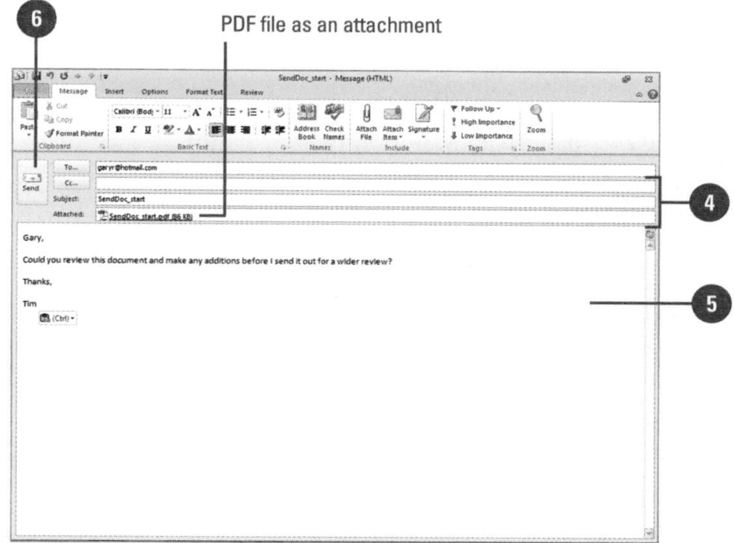

Sending a Document by Internet Fax

If you are a member of an online fax service—such as eFax, InterFAX, MyFax, or Send2Fax—you can use Office to send and receive faxes over the Internet directly from within Word. If you're not a member, a Web site can help you sign up. You also need to have Microsoft Outlook and Word installed to use the fax service and Outlook must be open to send your fax. If Outlook is not open and you send the fax, it will be stored in your Outbox and not sent until you open Outlook again.

Send a Document by Internet Fax

1. Click the **File** tab, click **Save & Send**, and then click **Send Using E-mail**.
2. Click the **Send as Internet Fax** button.
3. If you're not signed up with an Internet Fax service, click **OK** to open a Web page and sign up for one. When you're done, return to Word, and then repeat Step 1.
4. If the Compatibility Checker appears, click **Continue** or **Cancel** to stop the operation.

   An e-mail message opens in Microsoft Outlook with your document attached as a .tif (image) file.
5. Enter a Fax Recipient, Fax Number and Subject (appears with document name by default).
   - You can enter a fax number from your address book. Country codes in your address book must begin with a plus sign (+).
   - To send your fax to multiple recipients, click **Add More**, and then enter fax information.
6. In the Fax Service pane, choose the options you want.
7. Complete the cover sheet in the body of the e-mail message.
8. Click the **Send** button.

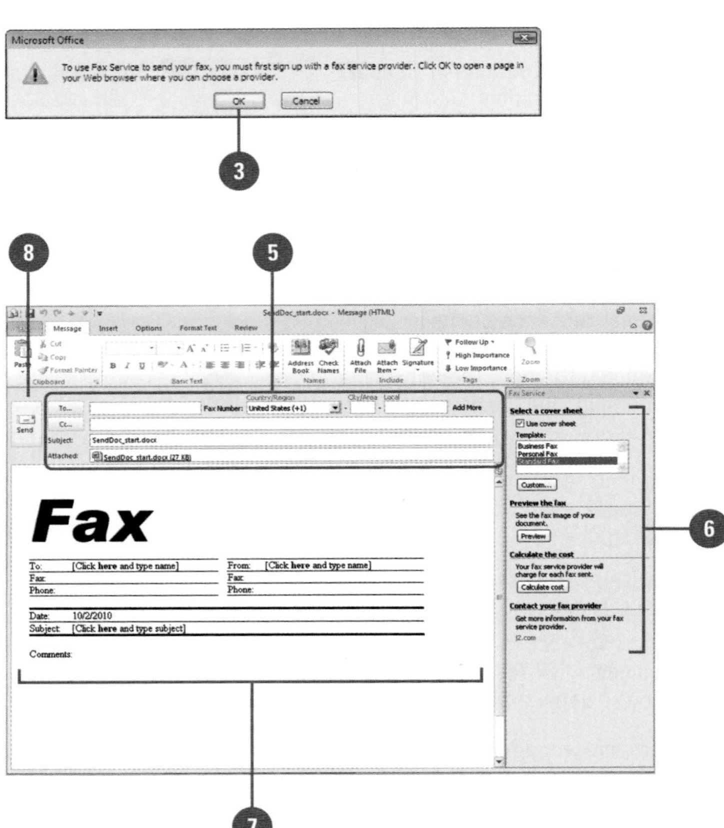

Sharing Information Between Programs

15

Introduction

Microsoft Word has the power and flexibility to share information between programs. You can create, store, and manage information in the program that works best for you, and then move that information to another program. You can also import or export data to and from Word to make your documents be the best they can be.

Completing a successful project in Word is not always a solitary venture; sometimes you may need to share data with others or obtain data from other programs. In many offices, your co-workers (and their computers) are located across the country or around the world. You can merge information from different programs into a single document, and you can link data between programs.

XML (**Extensible Markup Language**) is a universal language that enables you to create documents in which data is stored independently of the format so you can use the data more seamlessly in other forms. You can work with the familiar Office interface and create and save documents as XML, without ever knowing the language. You can also attach a Word XML Schema or XML Schema (created by a developer)—a set of rules that defines the elements and content used in an XML document—and validate the data against it. Word allows you to open, view, modify, and save XML files and data.

You can create one seamless document that includes data from several programs. You can include Excel data, PowerPoint slides, or an Access database into your document. The ability to copy data from Excel and create a chart using Excel to embed and display the information in a chart are all features that help make Word a useful tool when creating more technical documents. Word also allows you to save a document as an XPS or PDF file, which are secure fixed-layout formats you can send to others.

What You'll Do

Sharing Information Between Programs

Office can convert data or text from one format to another using a technology known as **object linking and embedding** (OLE). OLE allows you to move text or data between programs in much the same way as you move them within a program. The familiar cut and paste or drag and drop methods work between programs and documents just as they do within a document. In addition, all Office programs have special ways to move information from one program to another, including importing, exporting, embedding, linking, and hyperlinking.

Importing and Exporting

Importing and exporting information are two sides of the same coin. **Importing** copies a file created with the same or another program into your open file. The information becomes part of your open file, just as if you created it in that format. Some formatting and program-specific information such as formulas may be lost. **Exporting** converts a copy of your open file into the file type of another program. In other words, importing brings information into your open document, while exporting moves information from your open document into another program file.

Embedding

Embedding inserts a copy of a file created in one program into a file created in another program. Unlike imported files, you can edit the information in embedded files with the same commands and toolbar buttons used to create the original file. The original file is called the **source file**, while the file in which it is embedded is called the **destination file**. Any changes you make to an embedded object appear only in the destination file; the source file remains unchanged.

Linking

Linking displays information from one file (the source file) in a file created in another program (the destination file). You can view and edit the linked object from either the source file or the destination file. The changes are stored in the source file but also appear in the destination file. As you work, Office updates the linked object to ensure you always have the most current information. Office keeps track of all the drive, folder, and file name information for a source file. However, if you move or rename the source file, the link between files will break.

Once the link is broken, the information in the destination file becomes embedded rather than linked. In other words, changes to one copy of the file will no longer affect the other.

Embedding and Linking

Term	Definition
Source program	The program that created the original object
Source file	The file that contains the original object
Destination program	The program that created the document into which you are inserting the object
Destination file	The file into which you are inserting the object

Hyperlinking

The newest way to share information between programs is hyperlinks—a term borrowed from Web technology. A **hyperlink** is an object (either colored, underlined text or a graphic) that you click to jump to a different location in the same document or a different document. (See "Creating Hyperlinks" on page 298 and "Using and Removing Hyperlinks" on page 302 for more information about creating and navigating hyperlinks in Microsoft Word documents.)

Deciding Which Method to Use

With all these different methods for sharing information between programs to choose from, sometimes it is hard to decide which method to use. To decide which method is best for your situation, answer the following questions:

1. Do you want the contents of another file displayed in the open document?
   - **No**. Create a hyperlink. See "Creating Hyperlinks" on page 298.
   - **Yes**. Go to question 2.
2. Do you want to edit the content of the file from within the open document?
   - **No**. Embed the file as a picture. See "Embedding and Linking Files" on page 362.
   - **Yes**. Go to question 3.
3. Is the source program (the program used to create the file) available on your computer?
   - **No**. Import the file. See "Exporting and Importing Data" on page 360.
   - **Yes**. Go to question 4.
4. Do you want to use the source program commands to edit the file?
   - **No**. Import the file. See "Exporting and Importing Data" on page 360.
   - **Yes**. Go to question 5.
5. Do you want changes you make to the file to appear in the source file (the original copy of the file)?
   - **No**. Embed the file. See "Embedding and Linking Files" on page 362.
   - **Yes**. Link the file. See "Embedding and Linking Files" on page 362.

Exporting and Importing Data

When you **export** data, you save an open document in a new format so that it can be opened in an entirely different program. When you **import** data, you insert a copy of a file (from the same or another program) into an open document. You can insert into a Word document a bookmarked section of a Word document or a specific range in an Excel worksheet. For example, you might import an Excel worksheet into a Word document to create a one-page report with text and a table. Or you might want to export a document as a Web page or export text as XML data or in the standard Rich Text Format to use in another program.

Import or Export Data Using Copy and Paste

1. Select the text or other element that you want to copy.
2. Click the **Home** tab.
3. Click the **Copy** button.
4. Open the destination file, or click the program's taskbar button if the program is already open.
5. Select the location where you want the data to be copied.
6. Click the **Paste** button or click the **Paste** button arrow, and then point to a paste option icon to display a preview of the data (**New!**).
7. Click the **Paste Options** button, and then click the option you want.
   - You can point to a paste option icon to display a ScreenTip with the function name, and display a preview of the data (**New!**).

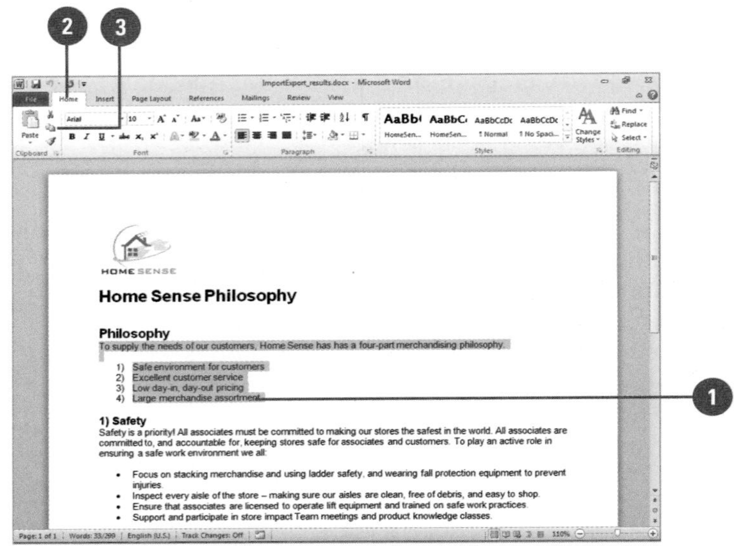

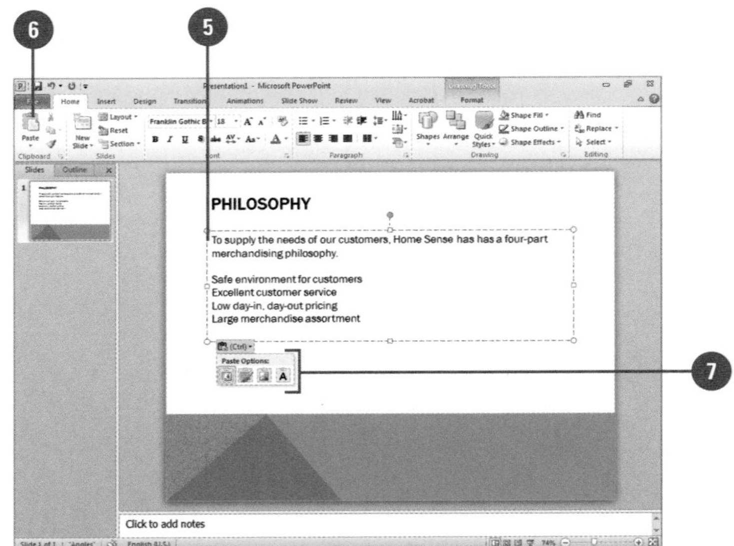

Did You Know?

You can link a file in Word. If you start to import a file into Word, you can link it instead. Click the Insert tab, click the Object button arrow, click Text From File, select the file to link, click the Insert button arrow, and then click Insert As Link.

Export a File to Another Program Format

1. Open the file from which you want to export data.
2. Click the **File** tab, and then click **Save As**.
   - You can also click the **File** tab, click **Save & Send**, click **Change File Type**, select a file type, and then click the **Save As** button.
3. Click the **Save in** list arrow, and then select the folder where you want to save the file.
4. Click the **Save as type** list arrow, and then click the format you want.
5. If you want, change the file name.
6. Click **Save**.

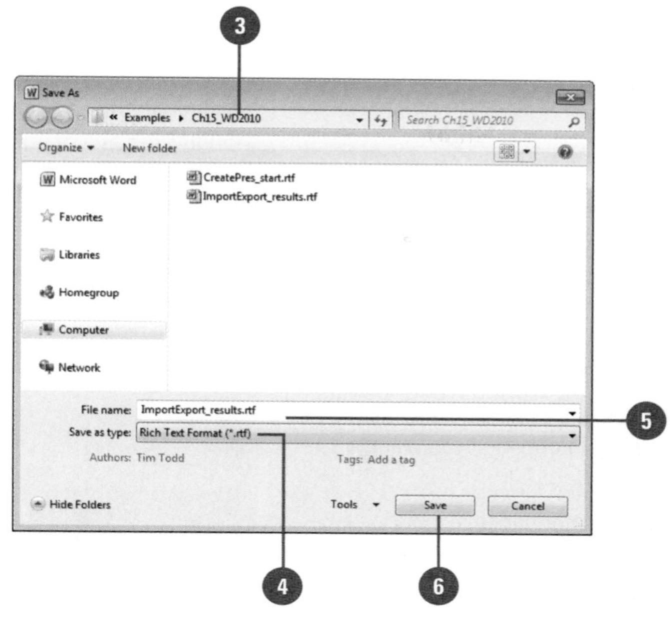

Import a File

1. Click where you want to insert the imported file.
2. Click the **Insert** tab.
3. Click the **Object** button arrow, and then click **Text from File**.
4. Click the **Files of type** list arrow, and then click **Text Files**.
5. Click the **Look in** list arrow, and then select the folder where the text file is located.
6. To import part of a Word document or range from Excel, click **Range**, enter a bookmark name or range, and then click **OK**.
7. Click the text file you want to import.
8. Click **Insert**.

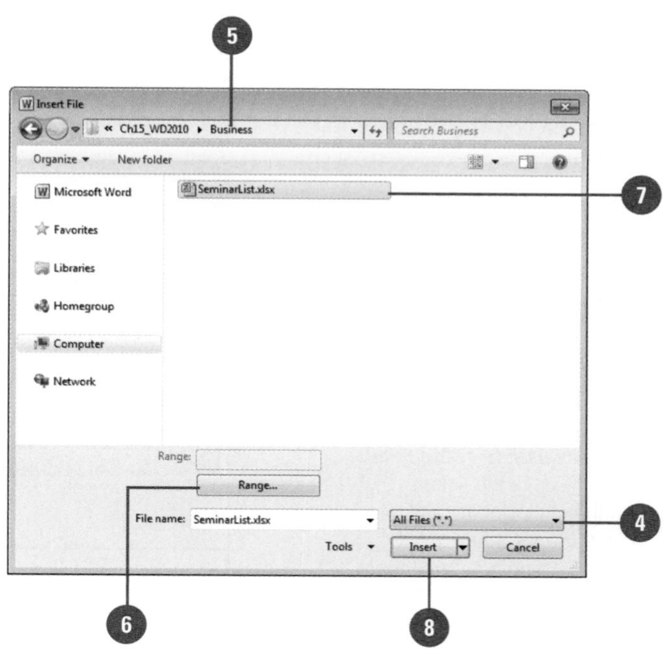

Linking and Embedding Files

Embedding inserts a copy of one document into another. When data is embedded, you can edit it using the menus and toolbars of the program in which it was created (that is, the **source program**). **Linking** displays information stored in one document (the **source file**) into another (the **destination file**). You can edit the linked object from either file, although changes are stored in the source file. For example, you might link an Excel chart or a PowerPoint slide to a Word document so you can update the chart or slide from any of the files. If you break the link between a linked object and its source file, the object becomes embedded. You can use the Object button on the Insert tab to modify a link.

Create a Link to Another File Using Paste Special

1. Open the source file and any files containing information you want to link.
2. Select the information in the source file.
3. Click the **Home** tab.
4. Click the **Copy** button.
5. Click the insertion point in the file containing the link.
6. Click the **Paste** button arrow, and then click **Paste Special**.
7. Click the **Paste Link** option, and then select the object format you want to use.
8. Click **OK**.

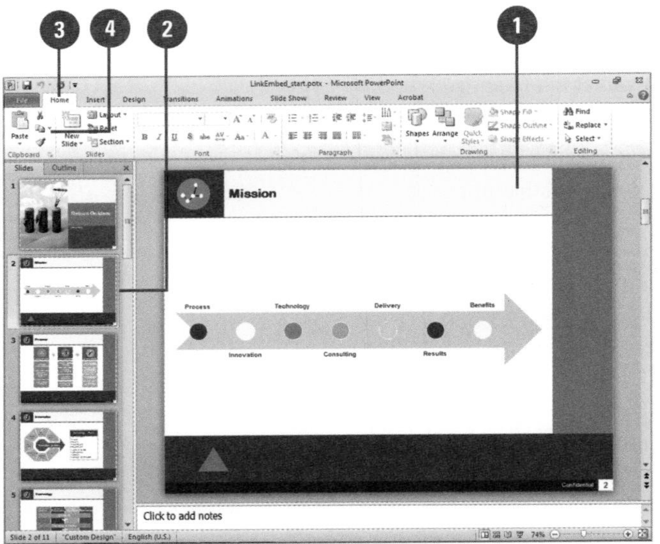

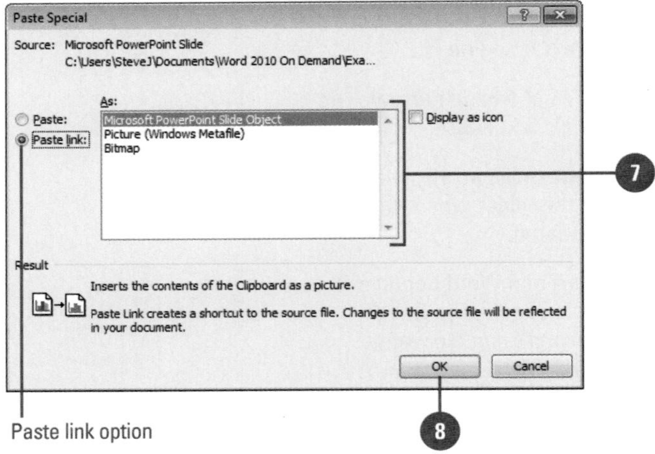

Paste link option

Did You Know?

You can edit an embedded object. Edit an embedded object only if the program that created it is installed.

You can manually update or break an object link. Right-click the linked object, and then click Update Link or point to Linked <Item> Object, click Links, click the link you want to update, and then click Manual Update. To break a link, click Break Link.

Embed a New Object

1. Click the **Insert** tab.
2. Click the **Insert Object** button.
3. Click the **Create New** tab.
4. Click the object type you want to insert.
5. Click **OK**.
6. Follow the necessary steps to insert the object.

   The steps will vary depending on the object type.

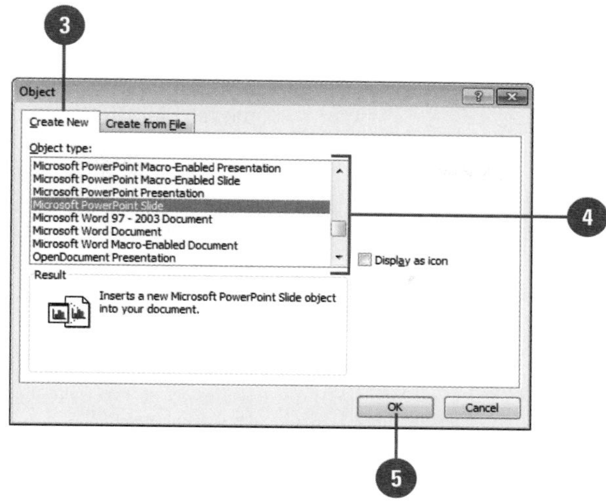

Embed or Link to an Existing Object

1. Click the **Insert** tab.
2. Click the **Insert Object** button.
3. Click the **Create from File** tab.
4. Click **Browse**, locate and select the file that you want to link, and then click **Open**.
5. To create a link to the object, select the **Link to file** check box.
6. Click **OK**.

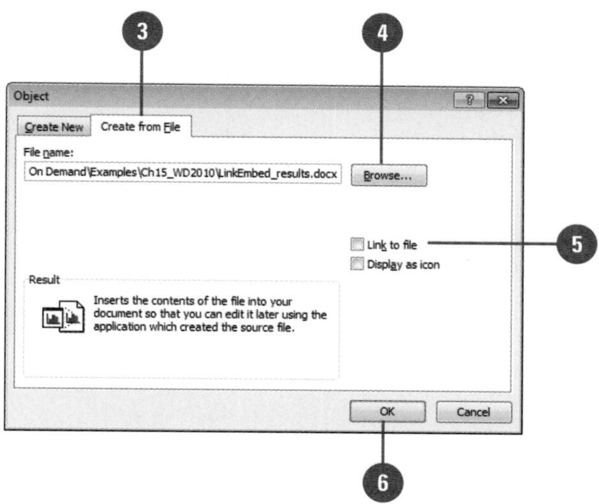

Did You Know?

You can update links each time you open a linked document. When you open a document that contains links, a warning dialog box opens asking you if you want to update all linked information (click Yes) or to keep the existing information (click No).

Creating an XML Document

XML (Extensible Markup Language) is a universal language that enables you to create documents in which data is stored independently of the format so you can use the data more seamlessly in other forms. XML is fully supported in Microsoft Word. XML allows you to work with the familiar Office interface and create and save documents as XML, without ever knowing the XML language. When you work with XML, you can attach a Word XML Schema or XML Schema (created by a developer)—a set of rules that defines the elements and content used in an XML document—and validate the data against it. Word allows you to open, view, modify, and save XML files and data.

Attach or Separate a Schema

1. Click the **Developer** tab.
2. Click the **Schema** button.
3. Click **Add Schema**.
4. Locate and select the XML schema file you want to attach, and then click **Open**.
5. Select or clear a schema to attach or separate it.
6. Select the **Validate document against attached schemas** check box to validate the document.
7. Click **OK**.

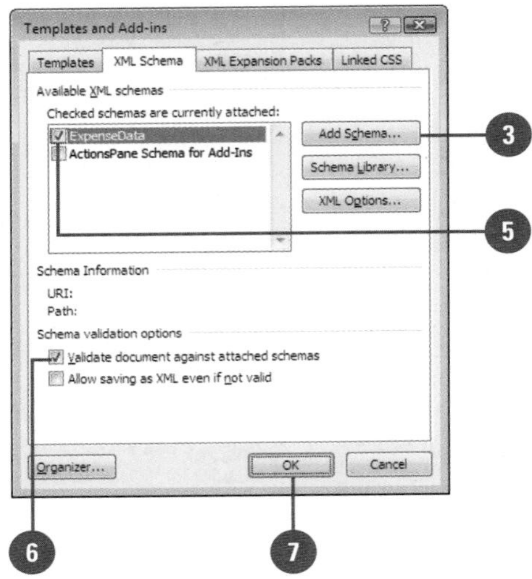

Change XML Options

1. Click the **Developer** tab.
2. Click the **Schema** button.
3. Click **XML Options**.
4. Select or clear the check boxes for the validation options.
5. Select or clear the check boxes for the view options.
6. Click **OK**, and then click **OK** again.

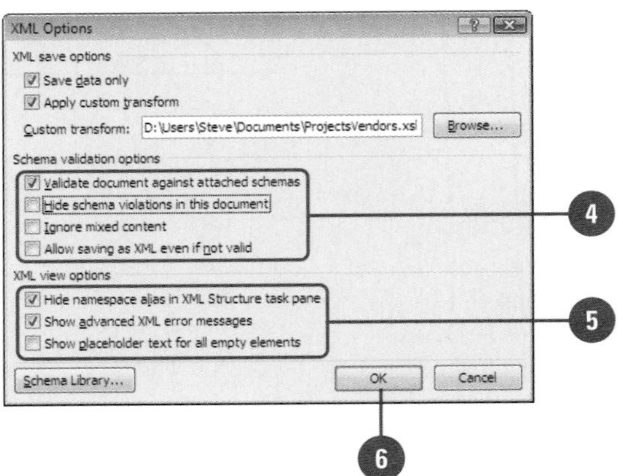

Open, View, and Modify an XML Data File

1. Click the **File** tab, and then click **Open**.
2. Click the **Files of type** list arrow, and then click **XML Files**.
3. Locate the XML file you want to open.
4. Select the XML file.
5. Click **Open**.
6. To show XML tags, select the **Show XML tags in the document** check box.
7. To add an XML tag, select the content you want to tag, and then click an element tag in the XML Structure task pane.
8. As necessary, double-click an XML tag to select its contents, and then use common editing techniques to move, copy, and delete it.
9. When you're done, click the **Close** button on the task pane.

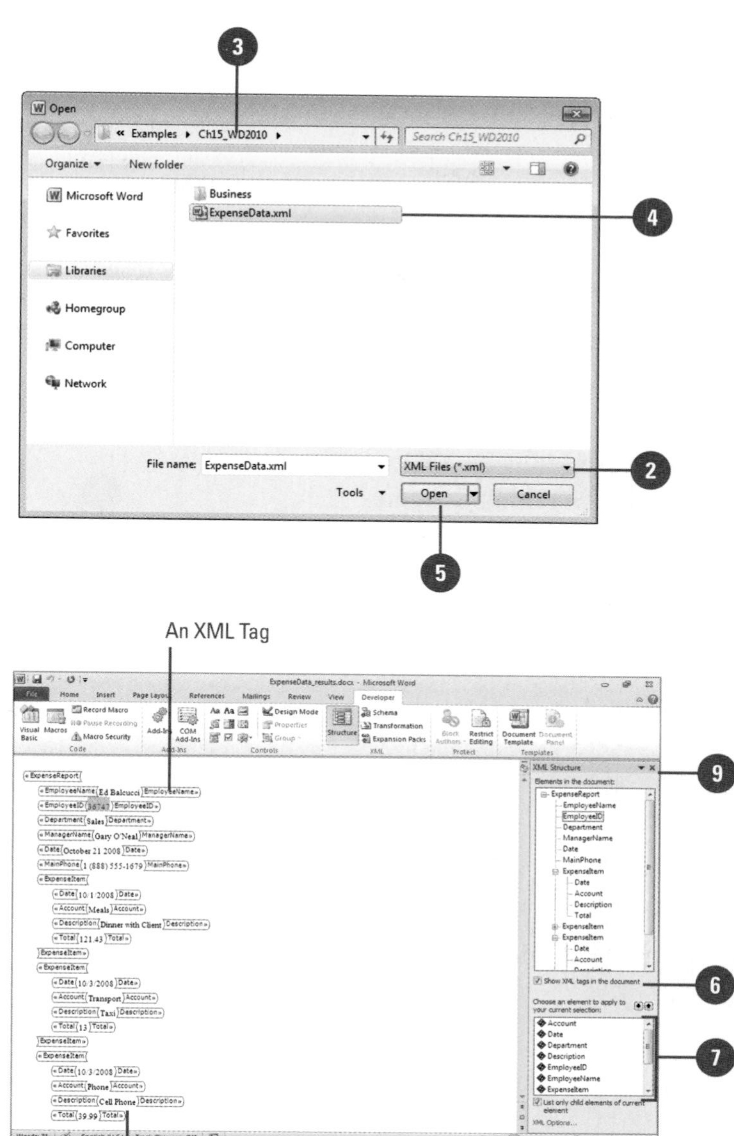

Did You Know?

You can remove an XML tag quickly. Point to the start or end of the tag name, right-click the tag, and then click Remove *Tag Name* tag.

You can locate XML problems quickly. If the structure of the document violates the rules of the schema, a purple wavy line marks the document location.

Working with XML Data

The **Schema Library** is a place to manage XML schemas. When you add a schema to the Schema Library, you create a namespace for any XML document in which the schema is attached. A namespace provides a unique identifier for elements defined by a schema. A namespace can also associate other XML related files, such as an XML Transformations file, to the XML document. An **XML Transformations file (XSLT)** is used to save and transform XML documents into other types of documents, such as HTML or XML, in different views. In the Schema Library, you can add, delete, update, and modify schemas and solutions, which are the files associated with the schema, such as XSLT. For example, you can add friendly names (aliases) to schemas and any files associated with the schema. You can add more than one schema to a single document. Word applies both sets of rules and alerts you of any conflicts.

Associate or Modify an XML Transformation with a Schema

1. Click the **Developer** tab.
2. Click the **Schema Library** button.
3. Click the schema you want to associate a transformation file (XSLT) with.
4. Click the **Use solution with** list arrow, and then click **Word**.
5. Click **Add Solution**.
6. Locate and select the XSLT file, and then click **Open**.
7. Type a name for the XSLT file, and then select the options you want.
8. Click **OK**.
9. Click the **Default solution** list arrow, and then click the default transform you want.
10. To delete a solution or update settings, select the solution, and then click **Delete Solution** or **Solution Settings**.
11. Click **OK**, and then click **OK** again.

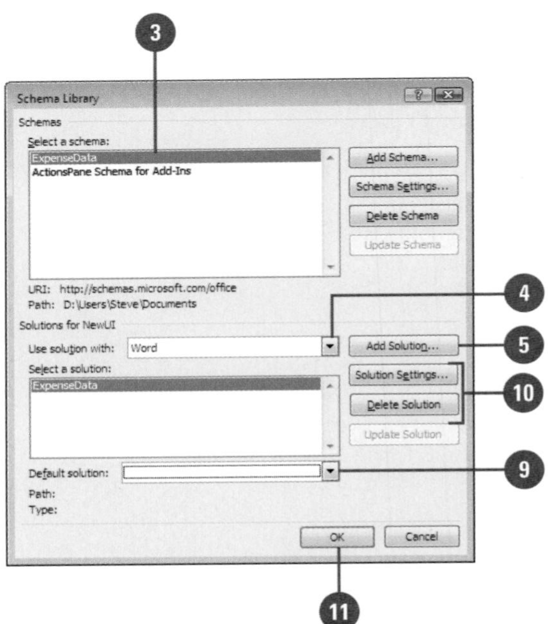

Save an XML Document and Apply a Transformation

1. Open the document you want to save as an XML document.
2. Click the **File** tab, and then click **Save As**.
3. Select a location where you want to save the XML data.
4. Click the **Save as type** list arrow, and then click **Word XML Document** or **Word 2003 XML Document**.
5. For a Word 2003 XML Document, select the **Save data only** check box to save only XML data (disregard Word formatting). To apply a transformation, select the **Apply transform** check box, click **Transform**, select a transformation file (XSLT), and then click **Open**.
6. Type a name for the XML document.
7. Click **Save**.

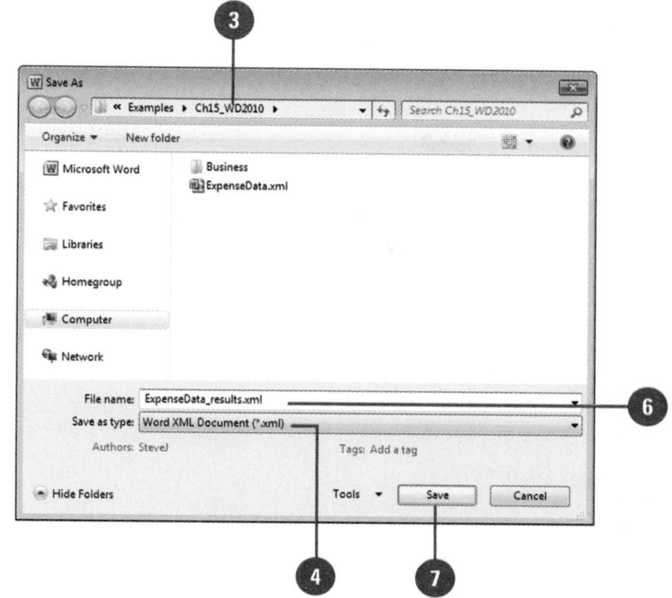

Did You Know?

You can insert XML data. Place the insertion point where you want to insert the data, click the Insert tab, click the Object button arrow, click Text From File, click the Files Of Type list arrow, click XML Files, locate and select the XML file, and then click Insert.

See Also

See "Using Content Controls to Create Form Documents" on page 420 for information on mapping XML data to content controls.

Creating a Word Document with Excel Data

A common pairing of Office programs combines Word and Excel. As you write a sales report, explain a budget, or create a memo showing distribution of sales, you often want to add existing spreadsheet data and charts to your text. Instead of re-creating the Excel data in Word, you can insert all or part of the data or chart into your Word document. You can use the Object button on the Insert tab or copy and paste the information from Excel into Word. The Paste Special command allows you to specify how you want to paste external information into Word. After you insert data or a chart into your word document, you can double-click the embedded Excel object to modify the data or chart.

Insert an Excel Worksheet Range to a Word Document

1. Click in the Word document where you want to copy the Excel range.
2. Click the **Insert** tab.
3. Click the **Object** button arrow, and then click **Text from File**.
4. Click the **Files of type** list arrow, and then click **All Files**.
5. Locate and select the file name of the workbook you want to copy.
6. Click **Range**.
7. Specify the range you want.
8. Click **OK**.
9. Click **Insert**.

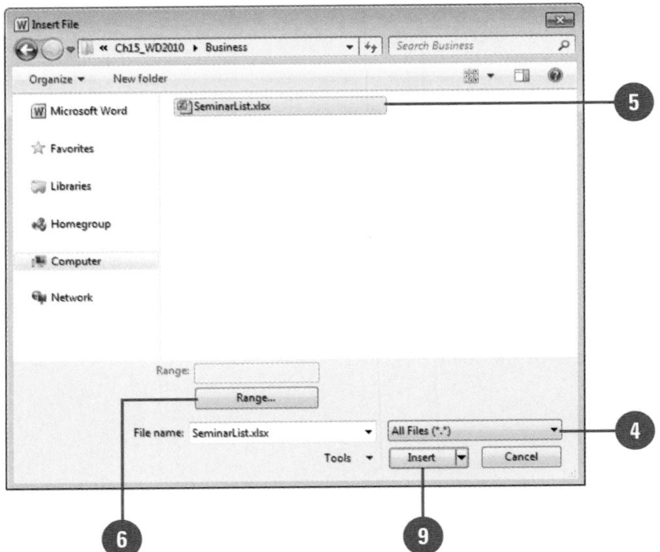

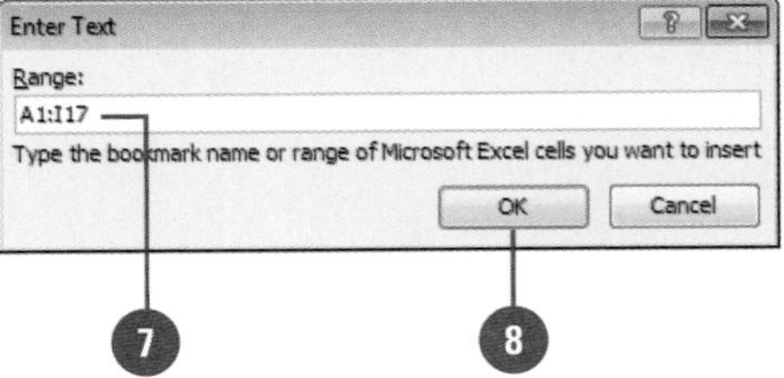

Did You Know?

You can name a range to make it easier to use in Word. If you plan to insert part of an Excel worksheet in a Word document, name the range. This is easier to recall than the specific cell references. Check Help in Microsoft Excel for details.

Copy Data from Excel

1. Open both the Word document and the Excel worksheet that contain the data you want to link or embed an object.
2. Switch to Excel, and then select the entire worksheet, a range of cells, or the chart you want.
3. Click the **Home** tab, and then click the **Copy** button.
4. Switch to the Word document, and then click where you want the information to appear.
5. Click the **Home** tab.
6. Use either of the following methods.
   - Paste. Click the **Paste** button, click the **Paste Options** button, point to a paste option icon to display a ScreenTip with the function name and display a preview of the data (**New!**), and then select an option.
   - Paste Special. Click the **Paste** button arrow, click **Paste Special**, click **Microsoft Excel Worksheet Object**, and then click **OK**.

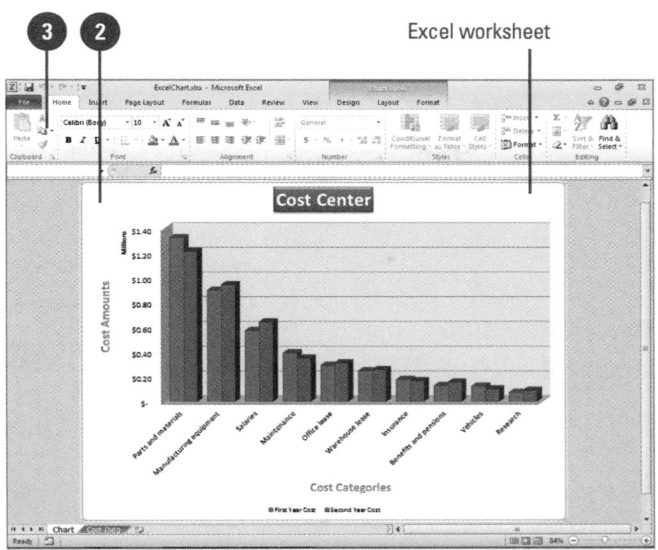

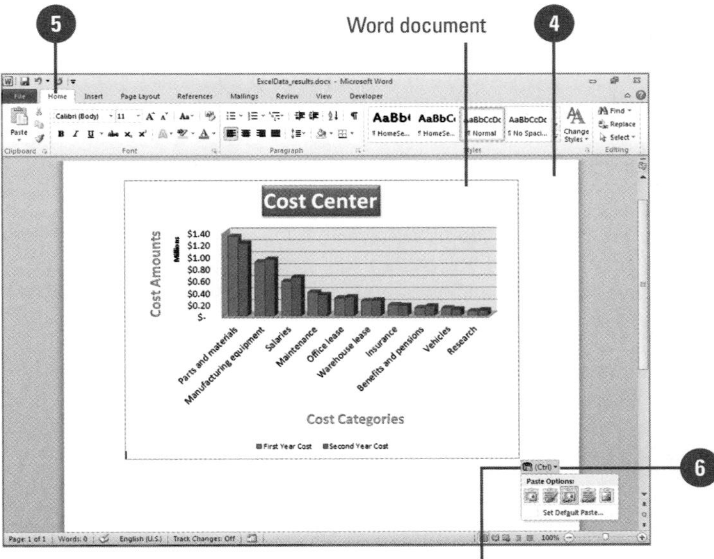

Did You Know?

You can import Excel data as a picture. Data inserted this way becomes a table that you cannot edit. Select the data you want to import, click the Copy button on the Home tab. Click in the Word document where you want to insert the picture, click the Paste button arrow on the Home tab, and then click Picture. Drag the picture to a new location, or drag its resize handles to enlarge or shrink it.

Creating a Presentation with Word Text

PowerPoint presentations are based on outlines, which you can create using either PowerPoint, or the more extensive outlining tools in Word. You can import any Word document into PowerPoint, although only paragraphs tagged with heading styles become part of the slides. Each Heading 1 style in a Word document becomes the title of a separate PowerPoint slide. Heading 2 becomes the first level of indented text, and so on. If a document contains no styles, PowerPoint uses the paragraph indents to determine a slide structure. You can edit the slides using the usual PowerPoint commands. You can also copy any table you created in Word to a PowerPoint slide.

Create PowerPoint Slides from a Word Document

1. Open or create a Word document with heading styles.
2. Click the **Send to Microsoft PowerPoint** button on the Quick Access Toolbar.
   - The Send to Microsoft PowerPoint button is not on the Quick Access Toolbar by default. Use the Customize pane in Word Options to add the button.

   PowerPoint opens; each Heading 1 style text becomes the title of a new slide and Heading 2 style text becomes top-level bullets on a slide, and so forth.
3. Save the presentation, and then edit it by adding slides, changing slide layouts, and applying a design template.

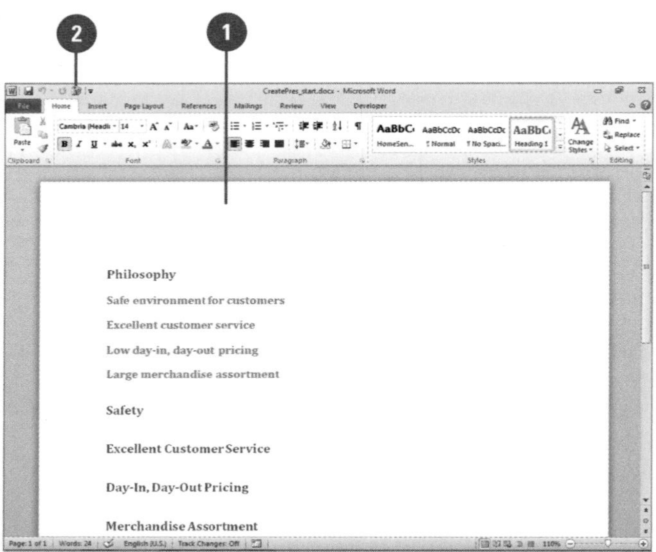

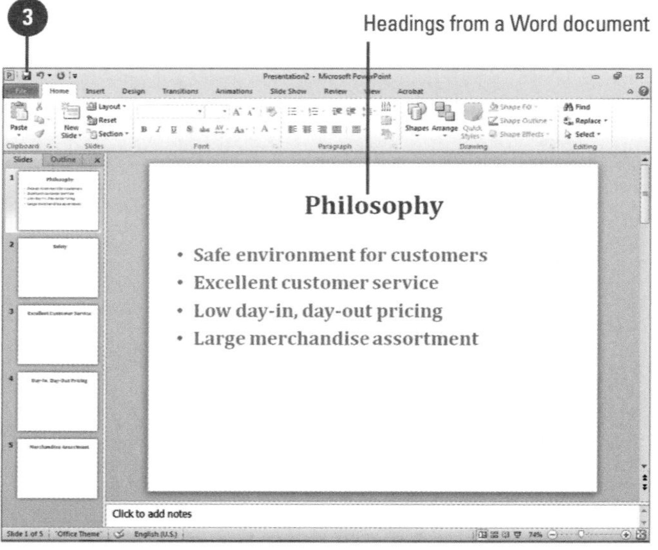

Embed a Word Table in a Slide

1. Click in the Word table you want to use in a slide.
2. Click the table selection box (small black box in the upper-left corner of the table).
3. Click the **Home** tab, and then click the **Copy** button.
4. Click the PowerPoint slide where you want to insert the Word table.
5. Click the **Home** tab, and then click the **Paste** button.
6. Click the **Paste Options** button, and then click the option you want.
   - You can point to a paste option icon to display a ScreenTip with the function name, and display a preview of the data (**New!**).

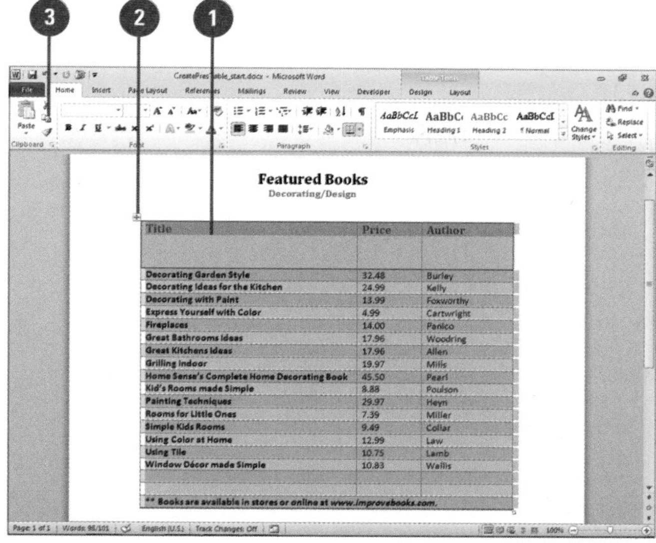

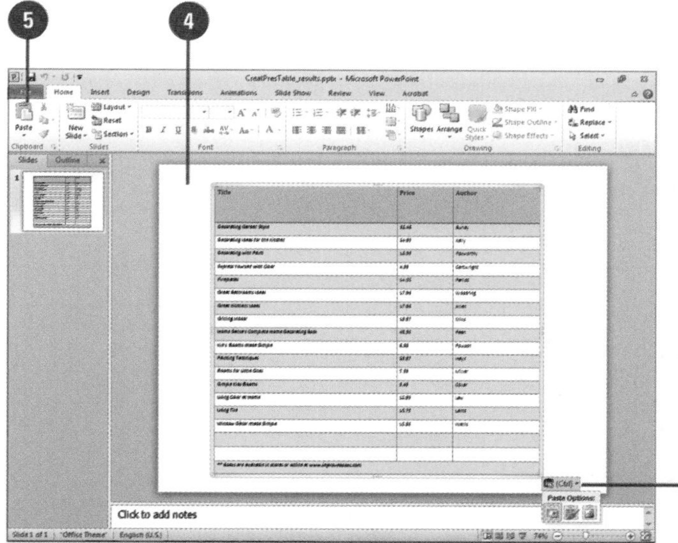

Did You Know?

You can create slides from a Word outline and insert them into an existing PowerPoint presentation. In PowerPoint, display the slide after which you want to insert the new slides. Click the Home tab, click the New Slide button arrow, click Slides From Outline, and then select the Word document you want.

Using an Access Database to Create Word Documents

Access is a great program for storing and categorizing large amounts of information. You can combine, or **merge**, database records with Word documents to create tables or produce form letters and envelopes based on names, addresses, and other Access records. For example, you might create a form letter in Word and personalize it with an Access database of names and addresses. Word uses the Mail Merge task pane to step you through the process. Mail merge is the process of combining names and addresses stored in a data file with a main document (usually a form letter) to produce customized documents.

Insert Access Data into a Word Document

1. In Access, click the table or query in the Navigation pane that you want to insert in a Word document.

   IMPORTANT *The database cannot be in exclusive mode.*

2. Click the **External Data** tab.
3. Click the **Word Merge** button.
4. Click the export options you want to use.
5. Click **OK**.

   If you selected the option for linking to an existing Word document, open the document.

6. In Word, follow the step-by-step instructions in the Mail Merge task pane to create a letter or mailing list using the data from Access.

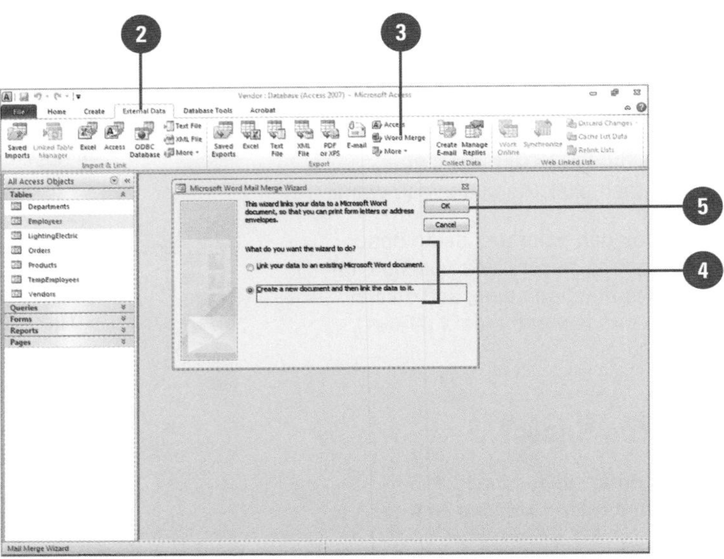

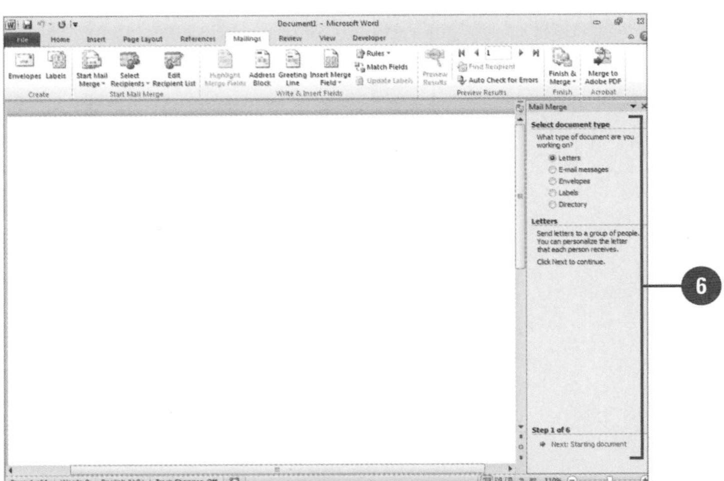

See Also

See "Creating a Form Letter" on page 256 for information on using the Mail Merge task pane.

Create a Word Document from an Access Database

1. In Access, click the table, query, report, or form in the Navigation pane that you want to save as a Word document.
2. Click the **External Data** tab.
3. Click the **Export to Text File** button (for a .txt file) , or click the **More** button, and then click **Word** (for an .rtf file).
4. Click **Browse**, select a location, enter a name, and then click **Save**.
5. Click the export options you want to use.
6. Click **OK**.

   Word opens and displays the document.
7. Edit the document using Word commands and features.

Did You Know?

You can save in Rich Text Format. A Rich Text Format file (.rtf) retains formatting, such as fonts and styles, and can be opened from Word or other word processing or desktop publishing programs.

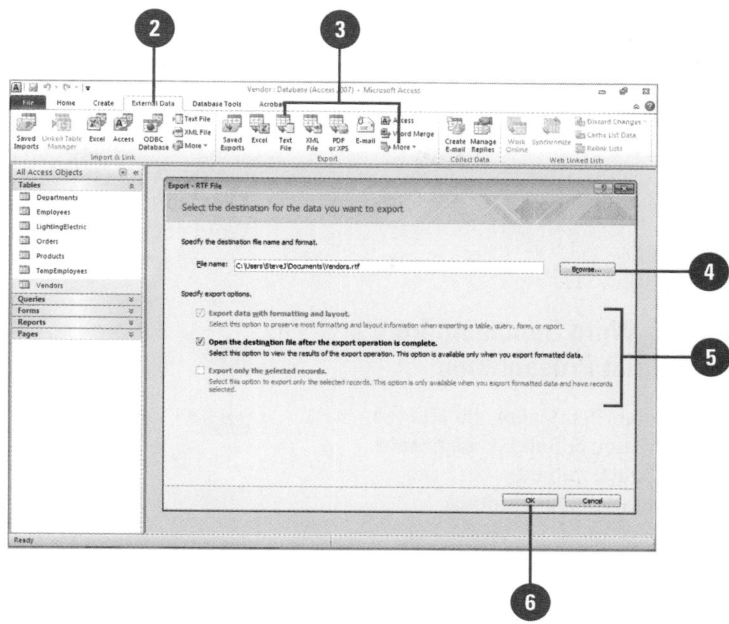

Access data in a Word document

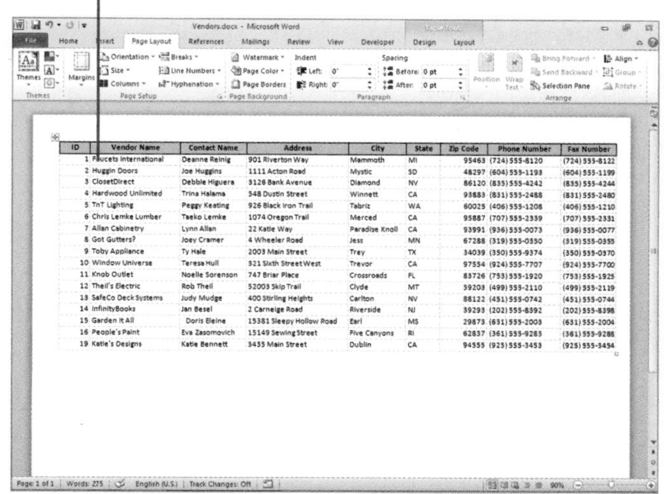

Creating a Word Outline from a Presentation

You can send both your notes and slides to Word so that you can use a full array of word processing tools. This is especially handy when you are developing more detailed materials, such as training presentations and manuals. By default, PowerPoint pastes the presentation into the Word document. If you change the presentation after sending it to Word, the changes you make to the presentation are not reflected in the Word document. If you click the Paste Link option in the Send To Microsoft Word dialog box, however, you create a link between the Word document and the presentation, so that changes you make in one are reflected in the other.

Create a Word Document from a PowerPoint Presentation

1. In PowerPoint, click the **File** tab, click **Save & Send**, click **Create Handouts**, and then click the **Create Handouts** button.
2. Click the page layout option you want for handouts.
3. To create a link to the presentation, click the **Paste Link** option.
4. Click **OK**.

   Word starts, creates a new document, and inserts your presentation slides with the page layout you selected.
5. Print the document in Word, editing and saving it as necessary.
6. When you're done, click the **Close** button to quit Word.

Creating and Opening OneNotes

Microsoft OneNote is a digital notebook program you can use to gather, manage, and share notes and information. In PowerPoint and Word, you can create and open notes directly from the Review tab (**New!**) by using the Linked Notes button. OneNote auto-links notes to the Office document you're viewing, which you can disable or change in the Advanced section of OneNote Options. You can open a OneNote note by clicking the Linked Notes button. The Linked Notes button is not available on the Review tab until you start the program and create an initial account, which is quick and easy.

Create and Open OneNotes

1. Open a document you want to use to create notes.
2. Click the **Review** tab.
3. Click the **Linked Notes** button.
4. On first document use, select a section or page in which to put the notes, and then click **OK**.
5. In OneNote, enter the notes you want for the page.
6. To work with notes in OneNote, click the **Linked Note** icon, and then click an option:
   - **Linked File(s).** Use to select a linked Office document to view.
   - **Delete Link(s) on This Page.** Use to delete links on the current page.
   - **Linked Notes Options.** Select to open OneNote Options.
7. When you're done, click the **Linked Note** icon in OneNote, and then click **Stop Taking Linked Notes**. To restart it, click **Start Taking Linked Notes** on the file tab.
8. To view linked notes, click the **Linked Notes** button to open OneNotes if needed, point to a note, and then click the Office program icon.

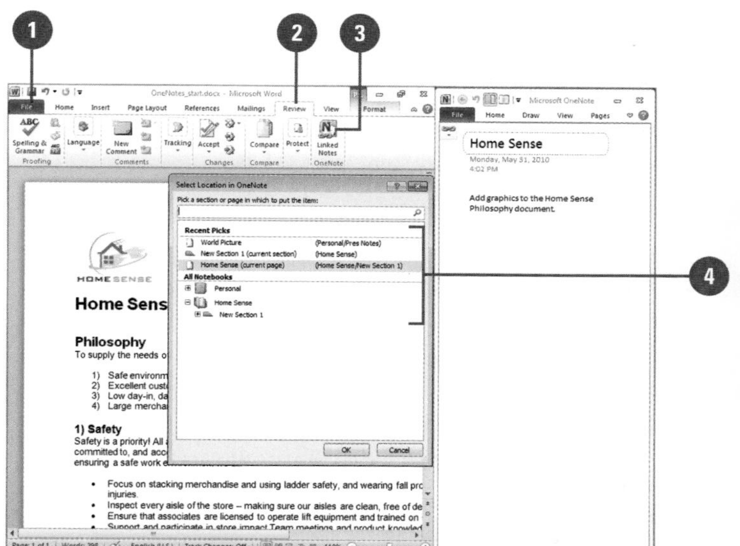

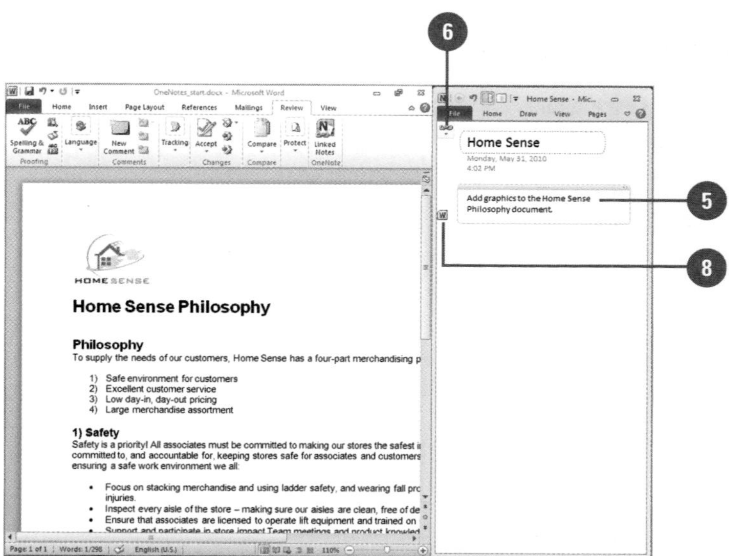

Creating a PDF Document

Portable Document Format (PDF) is a fixed-layout format developed by Adobe Systems that retains the form you intended on a computer monitor or printer. A PDF is useful when you want to create a document primarily intended to be read and printed, not modified. Office allows you to save a document as a PDF file, which you can send to others for review in an e-mail. To view a PDF file, you need to have Acrobat Reader—free downloadable software from Adobe Systems—installed on your computer.

Save a Document as a PDF Document

1. Click the **File** tab, click **Save & Send**, and then click **Create PDF/XPS Document**.
2. Click the **Create PDF/XPS** button.
3. Click the **Save as type** list arrow, and then click **PDF**.
4. Click the **Save in** list arrow, and then click the folder where you want to save the file.
5. Type a PDF file name.
6. To open the file in Adobe Reader after saving, select the **Open file after publishing** check box.
7. Click the **Standard** or **Minimum size** option to specify how you want to optimize the file.
8. Click **Options**.
9. Select the publishing options you want, such as what to publish, range to publish, whether to include non-printing information, or PDF options.
10. Click **OK**.
11. Click **Publish**.
12. If necessary, install Adobe Acrobat Reader and related software as directed.

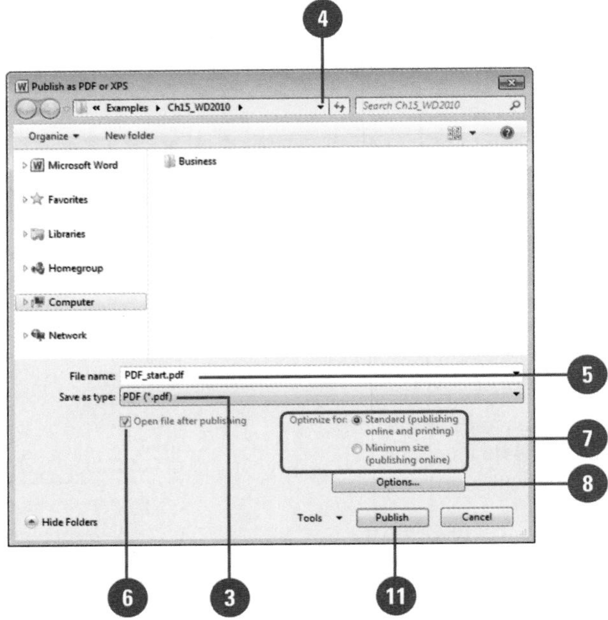

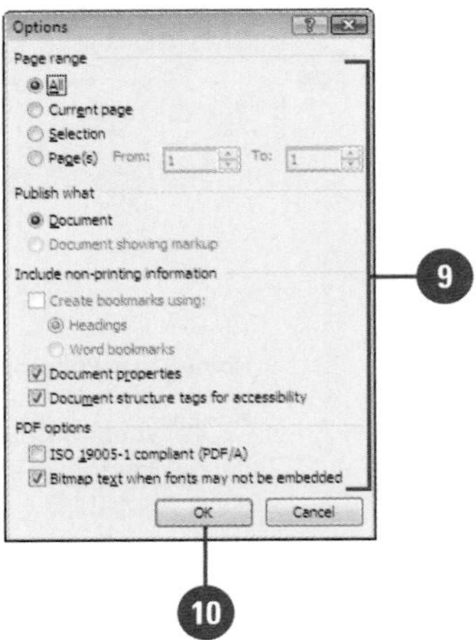

Creating an XPS Document

XML Paper Specification (XPS) is a secure fixed-layout format developed by Microsoft that retains the form you intended on a monitor or printer. An XPS is useful when you want to create a document primarily intended to be read and printed, not modified. Office allows you to save a document as an XPS file, which you can send to others for review in an e-mail. XPS includes support for digital signatures and is compatible with Windows Rights Management for additional protection. The XPS format also preserves live links with documents, making files fully functional. To view an XPS file, you need to have a viewer—free downloadable software from Microsoft Office Online—installed on your computer.

Save a Document as an XPS Document

1. Click the **File** tab, click **Save & Send**, and then click **Create PDF/XPS Document**.
2. Click the **Create PDF/XPS** button.
3. Click the **Save as type** list arrow, and then click **XPS Document.**
4. Click the **Save in** list arrow, and then click the folder where you want to save the file.
5. Type an XPS file name.
6. To open the file in viewer after saving, select the **Open file after publishing** check box.
7. Click the **Standard** or **Minimum size** option to specify how you want to optimize the file.
8. Click **Options**.
9. Select the publishing options you want, such as what to publish, range to publish, whether to include non-printing information, or XPS options.
10. Click **OK**.
11. Click **Publish**.

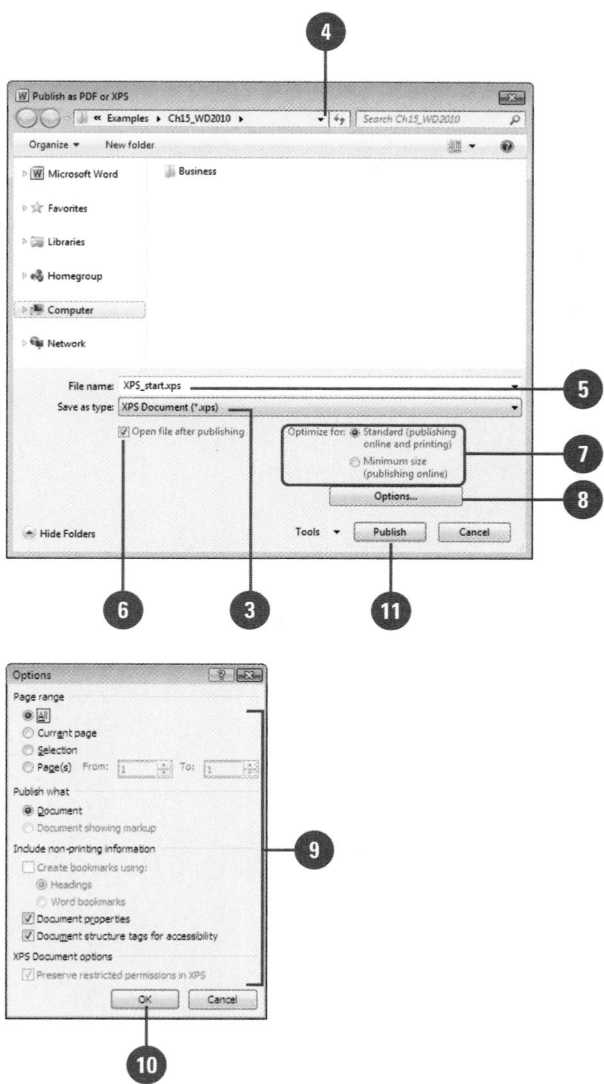

Customizing Word

16

Introduction

Once you've become familiar with Microsoft Word and all its features, you might want to customize the way you work with Word. You can change your view settings so that your Word window looks the way you want it to. Word comes with set defaults—such as showing the vertical ruler, or how many files you've recently opened—which you can change to suit your needs.

Some of the other Word customization features allow you to set a default font and related attributes to use when you are typing text in text boxes. Other defaults might be the color or line style of a shape object that you create. You can change the location of the Ribbon and the configuration of the Quick Access Toolbar to include commands not available on the Ribbon.

When you need to manage all the pictures on your computer, Microsoft Office Picture gives you a flexible way to organize, edit, and share your pictures. With Picture Manager, you can view all the pictures on your computer no matter where you store them. If you need to edit a picture, you can use Picture Manager to remove red eye and to change brightness, contrast, and color. You can also crop, rotate and flip, resize, and compress a picture.

What You'll Do

Setting General Options

You can customize the performance of many Word features including its editing, saving, spelling, viewing, printing and security procedures. Each person uses Word in a different way. Word Options allows you to change general options to personalize what appears in the Word window. When you change these options, Word uses them for all subsequent Word sessions until you change them again.

Change General Options

1. Click the **File** tab, and then click **Options**.
2. In the left pane, click **General**.
3. Select the Top options for working with Word you want:
   - **Show Mini Toolbar on Selection**. Select to show a miniature semi-transparent toolbar that helps you work with selected text.
   - **Enable Live Preview**. Select to show preview changes in a document.
   - **Color Scheme**. Click the list arrow to select a Windows related color scheme.
   - **ScreenTip style**. Click the list arrow to select a screentip option: Show enhanced ScreenTips, Don't show enhanced ScreenTips, or Don't show ScreenTips.
4. Type your name and initials as you want them to appear in Properties, and review comments.
5. Select the **Open e-mail attachments in Full Screen Reading view** check box to use Full Screen Reading view or clear to use Print Layout view.
6. Click **OK**.

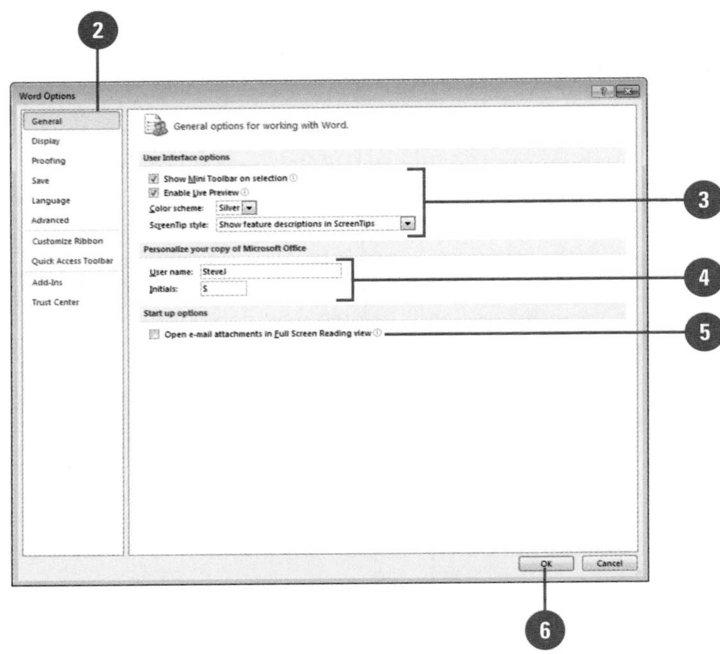

Setting Page Display Options

Sometimes it's hard to determine whether a blank is a tab or space. You can set options on the Display pane in Word Options to show or hide formatting marks. Formatting marks help you see characters that are not visible, such as tabs, spaces, paragraph marks, and hidden text. You can also set page display that show white space between pages in Print Layout view, show highlighted text on the screen and in print, or show tooltip information when you point to a hyperlink or reviewer's comment.

Change Page Display Options

1. Click the **File** tab, and then click **Options**.
2. In the left pane, click **Display**.
3. Select or clear any of the check boxes to change the display options you want.
   - **Show white space between pages in Print Layout view.** Select to display top and bottom margins. (Default on).
   - **Show highlighter marks**. Select to display highlighted text on the screen and in print. (Default on).
   - **Show document tooltips on hover.** Select to display information when you point to a hyperlink or reviewer's comment. (Default on).
4. Select or clear any of the check boxes to display or hide the formatting marks you want.
   - **Tab characters**, **Spaces**, **Paragraph marks**, **Hidden text**, **Optional hyphens**, or **Object anchors.** (Default off).
   - **Show all formatting marks.** (Default off).
5. Click **OK**.

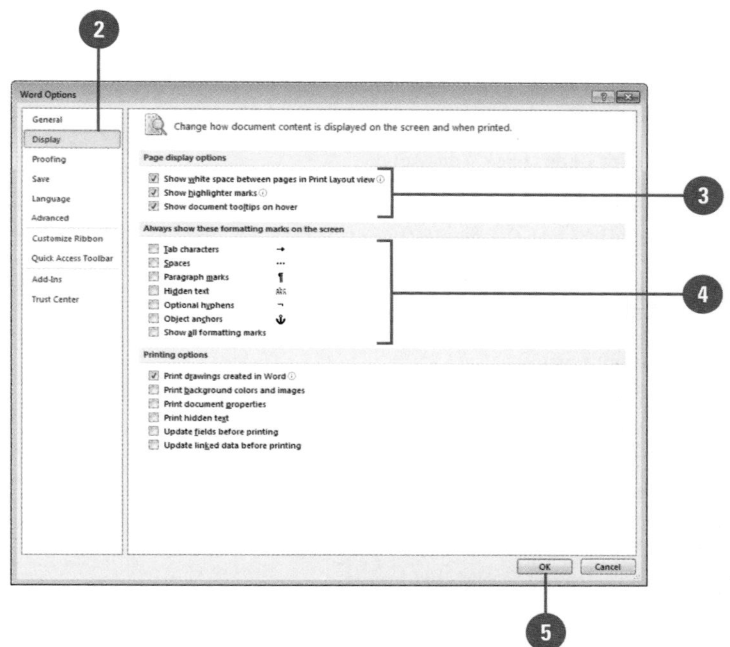

Setting Display Options

Word uses unique characters and formatting to display specialized document elements, such as bookmarks, crop marks, text boundaries and wrapping, and background colors and images. You can set options on the Advanced pane in Word Options to show or hide these elements when you work on a document. In addition, you can also show or hide Word window elements, such as scroll bars, shortcut keys, and the vertical ruler. If you want to change the number of recent documents shown on the File tab or the units of measurement used in a document, you can set the options on the Advanced pane.

Change Display View Options

1. Click the **File** tab, and then click **Options**.
2. In the left pane, click **Advanced**.
3. Select or clear any of the check boxes to change the display view options you want.
   - **Show background colors and images in Print Layout view.** (Default off).
   - **Show text wrapped within the document window.** (Default off).
   - **Show picture placeholders.** Shows empty boxes; speeds up the display. (Default off).
   - **Show drawings and text boxes on screen.** (Default on).
   - **Show text animation.** (Default on).
   - **Show bookmarks.** (Default on).
   - **Show text boundaries.** Shows dotted lines. (Default on).
   - **Show crop marks.** Shows corner of margins. (Default off).
   - **Show field codes instead of their values.** (Default off).
   - **Use draft font in Draft and Outline views.** (Default off).
4. Click **OK**.

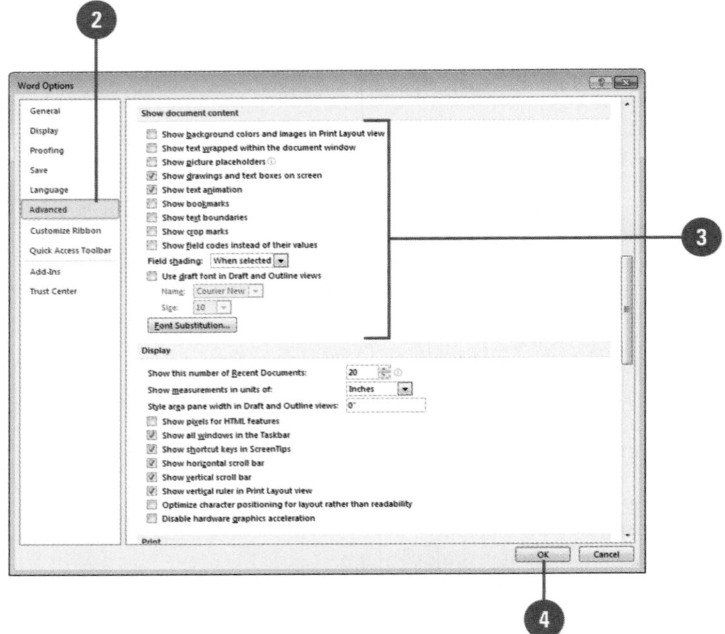

Change Display Options

1. Click the **File** tab, and then click **Options**.
2. In the left pane, click **Advanced**.
3. Select or clear any of the check boxes to change the display options you want.
   - **Show this number of Recent Documents.** Set to 0 to turn off the recent documents display.
   - **Show measurements in units of**. Set ruler units. (Default is Inches).
   - **Style area pane width in Draft and Outline views.** Set the pane width. (Default is 0").
   - **Show pixels for HTML features.** Uses pixels as the unit of measurement for HTML features. (Default on).
   - **Show all windows in the Taskbar.** Select to show each document window on the taskbar. (Default on).
   - **Show shortcut keys in ScreenTips.** (Default on).
   - **Show horizontal scroll bar.** (Default on).
   - **Show vertical scroll bar.** (Default on).
   - **Show vertical ruler in Print Layout view.** (Default on).
   - **Optimize character positioning for layout rather than readability.** Select to optimize for printing. (Default off)
   - **Disable hardware graphics acceleration** (**New!**). Select to disable hardware graphics acceleration. (Default off)
4. Click **OK**.

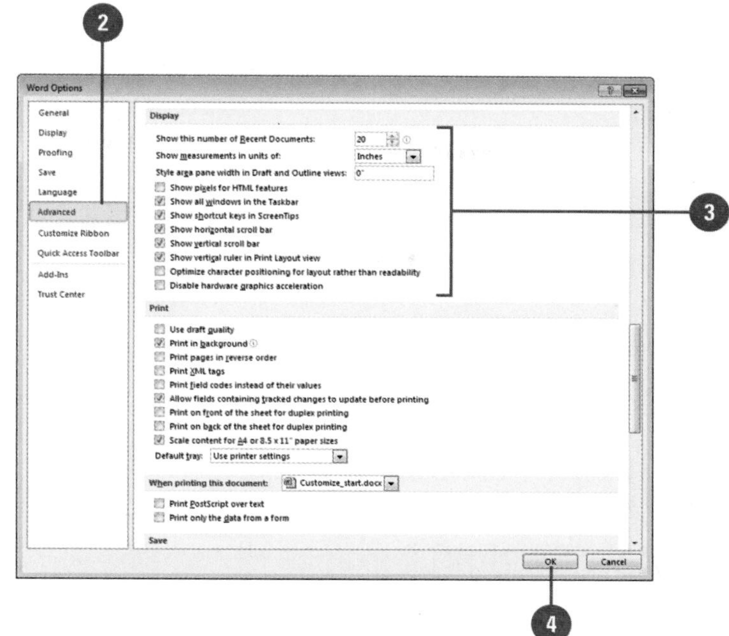

Setting Print Options

If your document contains a lot of graphics, colors, and drawings, it could slow down the printing process. While you're working on the document, you can turn off options to speed up the printing process. When you're ready to print the final version, you can turn the options back on. If you have marked text in the document as hidden, you can turn on the Print hidden text option to print it. You can also set options to print on both sides of a page (known as duplex printing) and select the default paper tray you like to use.

Change Print Display Options

1. Click the **File** tab, and then click **Options**.
2. In the left pane, click **Display**.
3. Select or clear any of the check boxes to change the print display options you want.
   - **Print drawings created in Word.** Clear to speed up the process. (Default on).
   - **Print background colors and images**. Clear to speed up the process. (Default off).
   - **Print document properties.** Select to print document summary information. (Default off).
   - **Print hidden text.** Select to print text marked as hidden without the dotted lines. (Default off).
   - **Update fields before printing.** (Default off).
   - **Update linked data before printing.** (Default on).
4. Click **OK**.

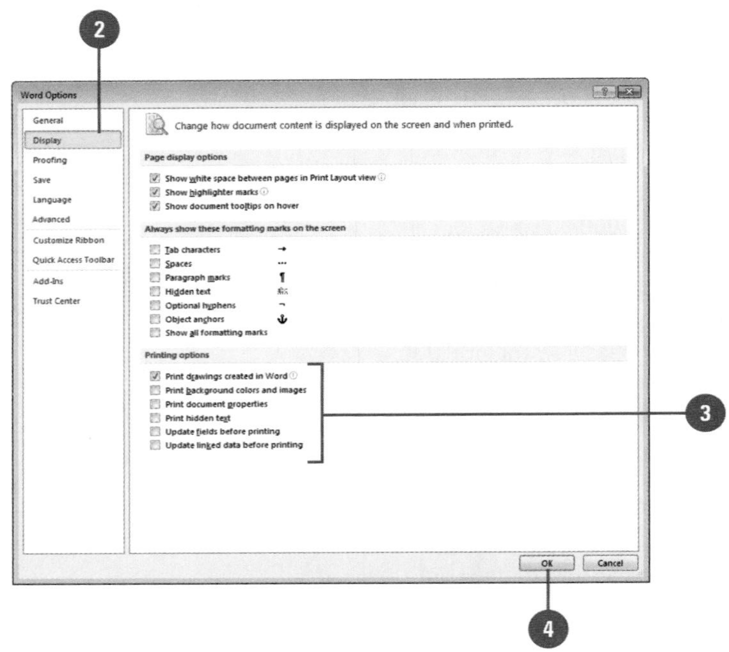

Change Print Options

1. Click the **File** tab, and then click **Options**.
2. In the left pane, click **Advanced**.
3. Select or clear any of the check boxes to change the print options you want.
   - **Use draft quality.** Select for documents with minimal formatting. (Default on).
   - **Print in background**. Set to print while you continue to work. (Default on).
   - **Print pages in reverse order.** (Default off).
   - **Print XML tags.** Select when a Schema is attached to the document. (Default off).
   - **Print field codes instead of their values.** (Default off).
   - **Print on front of the sheet for duplex printing.** Prints in reverse order, so you can flip and print on the back. (Default off).
   - **Print on back of the sheet for duplex printing.** Prints in ascending order so you can print on the front in reverse order. (Default off).
   - **Scale content for A4 or 8.5 x 11" paper sizes.** (Default on).
   - **Default tray.** Select the printer tray you want. (Default is Use printer settings).
4. Click **OK**.

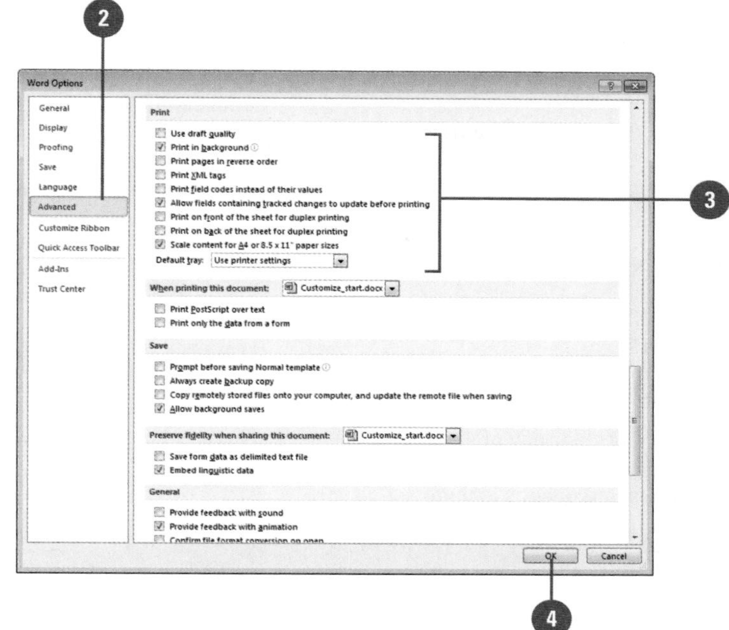

Setting Editing Options

If you spend a lot of time modifying documents, you can set editing options in Word to customize the way you work. You can set options to automatically select entire words, use smart paragraph selection (includes the paragraph mark), allow text to be dragged and dropped, and identify formatting inconsistencies, keep track of formatting, and show AutoComplete suggestions (**New!**). You can also set cutting, copying, and pasting options to specify formatting preferences when you paste text and graphics.

Change Editing Options

1. Click the **File** tab, and then click **Options**.
2. In the left pane, click **Advanced**.
3. Select or clear any of the check boxes to change the options you want, some options include:
   - **Typing replaces selected text.** (Default on).
   - **When selecting, automatically select entire word.** (Default on).
   - **Allow text to be dragged and dropped**. (Default on).
   - **Use CTRL+ Click to follow hyperlink.** (Default on).
   - **Automatically create drawing canvas when inserting AutoShapes.** (Default off).
   - **Use smart paragraph selection.** (Default on).
   - **Use smart cursoring.** (Default on).
   - **Use the Insert key to control overtype mode**. (Default off).
   - **Prompt to update style.** (Default off).
   - **Use Normal style for bulleted or numbered lists.** (Default off).
   - **Enable click and type.** Select a default paragraph style. (Default on and Normal).
   - **Show AutoComplete suggestions (New!).** (Default on).
4. Click **OK**.

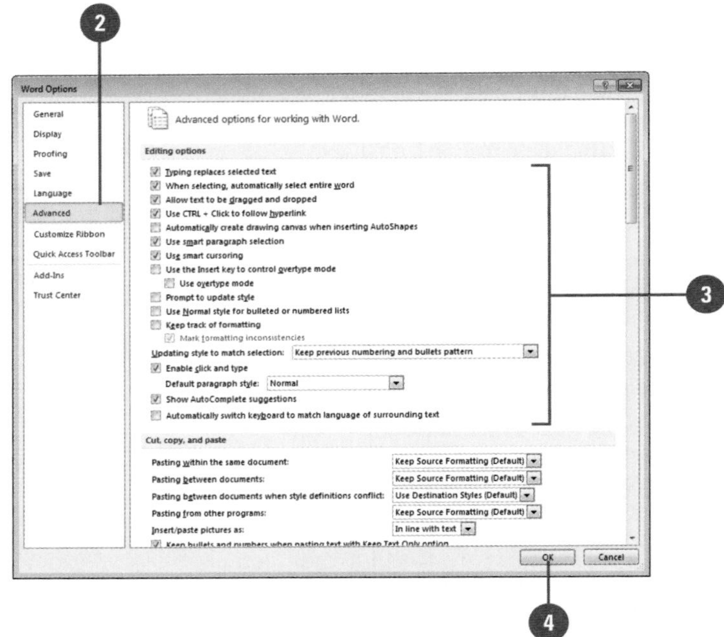

Change Cut, Copy, and Paste Options

1. Click the **File** tab, and then click **Options**.
2. In the left pane, click **Advanced**.
3. Click the list arrow next to any of the following, and then select the option you want:
   - **Pasting within the same document.** (Default: Keep Source Formatting).
   - **Pasting between documents.** (Default: Keep Source Formatting).
   - **Pasting between documents when style definitions conflict.** (Default: Use Destination Styles).
   - **Pasting from other programs.** (Default: Keep Source Formatting).
   - **Insert/paste pictures as.** (Default: In line with text).
4. Select or clear any of the check boxes to change the options you want, some options include:
   - **Keep bullets and numbers when pasting text with Keep Text Only option.** (Default on).
   - **Use the Insert Key for paste.** (Default off).
   - **Show Paste Options button when content is pasted.** (Default on).
   - **Use smart cut and paste.** (Default on).
5. Click **OK**.

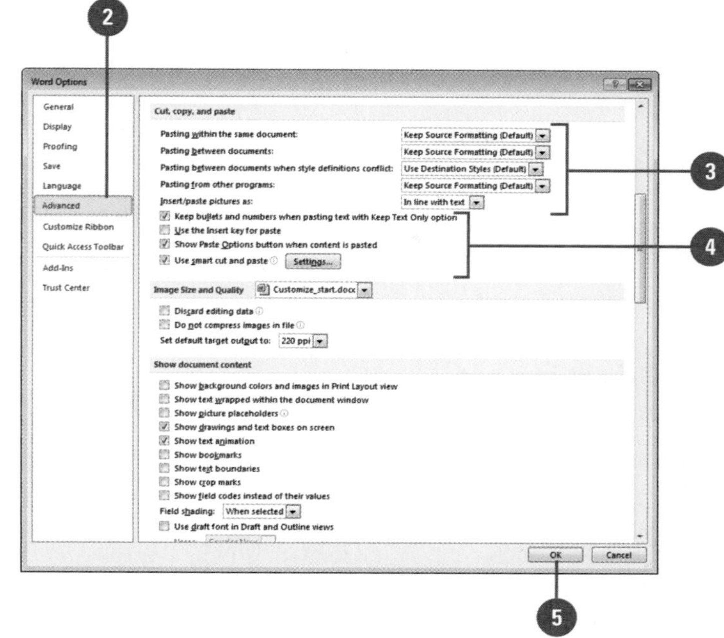

Changing Default Text and Page Settings

When you type text in a document, Word applies a set of default text font and paragraph attributes. Some examples of Word's font default settings include font style, size, and formatting options, such as bold, italic, and underline. You can also include text effects (**New!**), such as text fill, outline, style, shadow, reflection, glow and soft edges, and 3-D. Some paragraph examples include alignment, indents, and spacing. You might find that having your own personalized font style and color, indent, and spacing settings would really make your documents more custom. In the same way, you can also set default page options—such as margins, paper sizes, and layout—for a new document. To find out the current default settings for your document, you can open a new document, and then type some text.

Change Default Text and Character Spacing

1. Click the **Home** tab.
2. Click the **Font Dialog Box Launcher**.
3. Change the font options to what you want to be the default.
4. Click the **Advanced** tab.
5. Change the character spacing options and OpenType Features to what you want to be the default.
6. To specify text effects (**New!**), click **Text Effects**, set the options you want, and then click **Close**.
7. Click **Set As Default**.
8. Click the **This document only?** or **All documents based on the Normal.dotm template?** option.
9. Click **OK**.

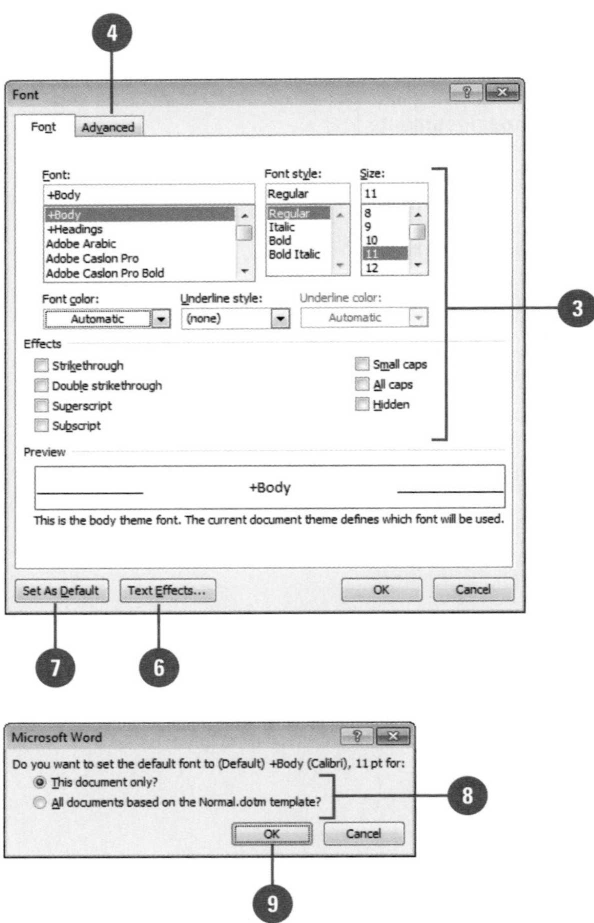

Change Default Paragraph Text

1. Click the **Home** tab.
2. Click the **Paragraph Dialog Box Launcher**.
3. Click the **Indents and Spacing** or **Line and Page Breaks** tab.
4. Change the paragraph options to what you want to be the default.
5. Click **Default**.
6. Click the **This document only?** or **All documents based on the Normal.dotm template?** option, and then click **OK**.

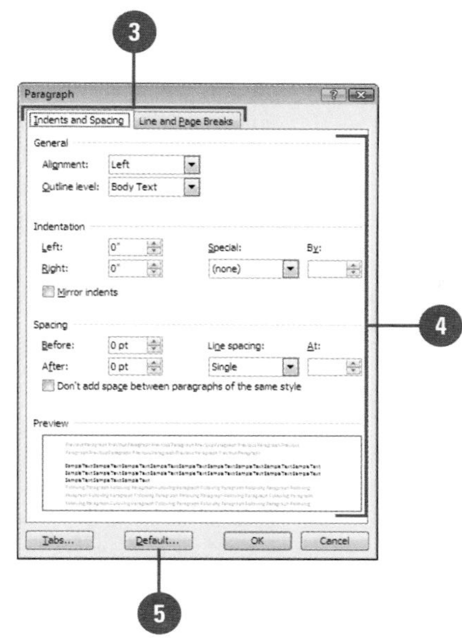

Change Default Page Setup

1. Click the **Page Layout** tab.
2. Click the **Page Setup Dialog Box Launcher**.
3. Click the **Margins**, **Paper**, or **Layout** tab.
4. Change the margin, paper, and layout options to what you want to be the default.
5. Click **Default**, and then click **Yes**.

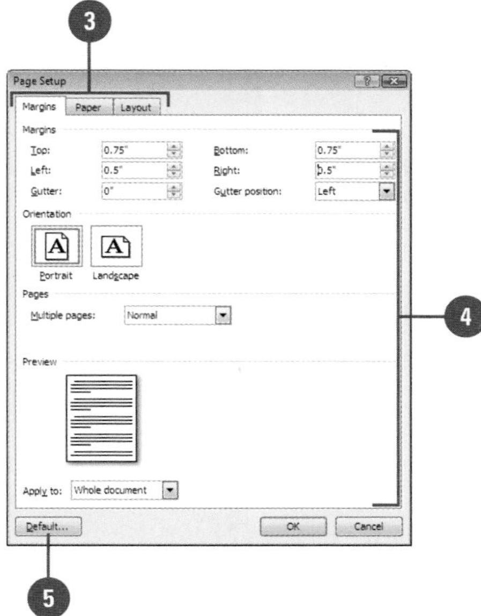

Setting Advanced Save Options

In addition to the standard save options on the Save pane in Word Options, you can also set more advanced save options that allow you to automatically create a backup copy of a document, save form data, and update remotely stored files. If you are using nonstandard fonts to create a document, you can embed the fonts you use so they "travel" (are saved) with your document, Then, if the computer you use to show or print the document does not have all your document fonts installed, the embedded fonts appear in the document and your document quality will not suffer. When you embed fonts, the size of your document increases.

Change Advanced Save Options

1. Click the **File** tab, and then click **Options**.
2. In the left pane, click **Advanced**.
3. Select the save options you want:
   - **Prompt before saving Normal template.** (Default off).
   - **Always create backup copy.** (Default off).
   - **Copy remotely stored files onto your computer, and update the remote file when saving.** (Default off).
   - **Allow background saves.** (Default on).
4. Click the **Preserve fidelity when sharing this document** list arrow, and then select the document you want to specify options.
5. Select the save options you want:
   - **Save form data as delimited text file.** (Default off).
6. Click **OK**.

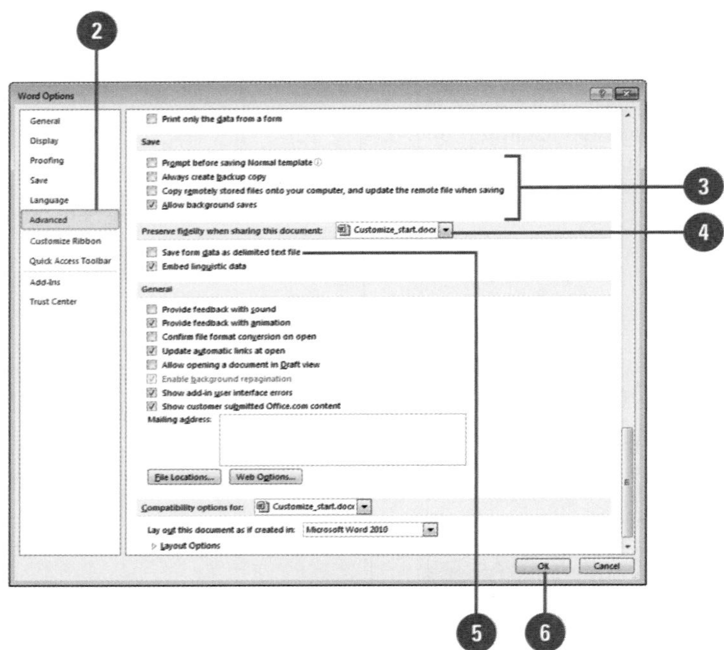

Change Embedding Options

1. Click the **File** tab, and then click **Options**.
2. In the left pane, click **Save**.
3. Click the **Preserve fidelity when sharing this document** list arrow, and then select the document you want to specify options.
4. Select the document embedding options you want:
   - **Embed fonts in the file.** Select to save fonts in a document file. (Default off).
   - **Embed only the characters used in the document.** Select to save only the fonts you actually use in a document. (Default off).
   - **Do not embed common system fonts.** Select to reduce file size when you use Windows and Office fonts. (Default off).
5. In the left pane, click **Advanced**.
6. Select the document embedding options you want:
   - **Embed linguistic data.** Select to save speech and hand-written text. (Default on).
7. Click **OK**.

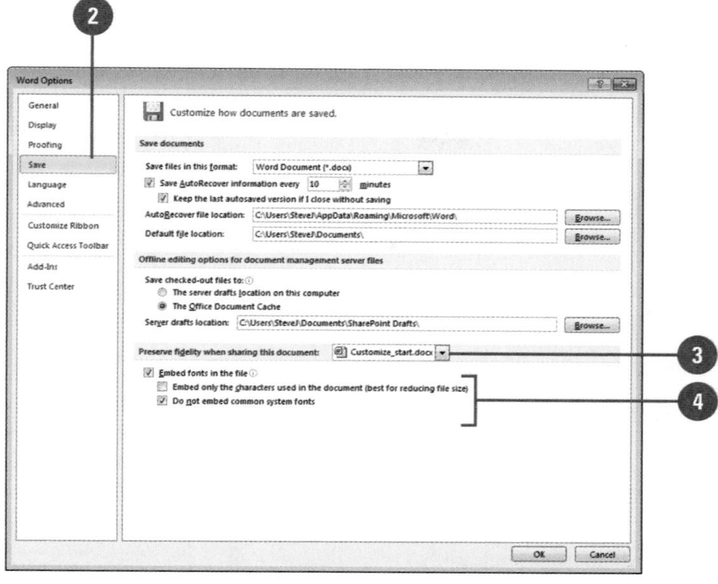

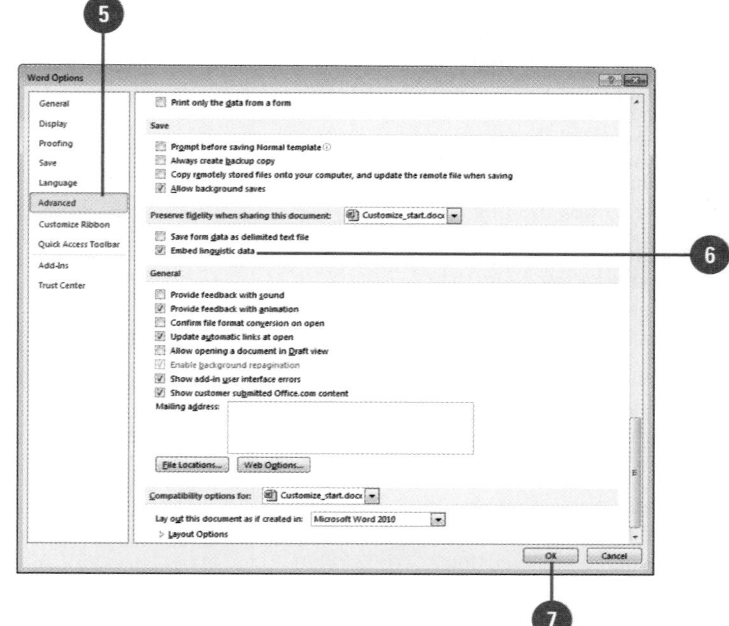

Setting Advanced General Options

In addition to display options, the Advanced pane in Word Options also includes options to provide general user feedback. You can set the feedback options to play sound, show simple animation, show add-in user interface error, or display alerts to update links. You can also set options for default file locations, Web pages, and shared workspaces using the File Locations, Web Options, and Service buttons.

Change Advanced General Options

1. Click the **File** tab, and then click **Options**.
2. In the left pane, click **Advanced**.
3. Select the general options you want:
   - **Provide feedback with sound**. (Default off).
   - **Provide feedback with animation**. (Default on).
   - **Confirm file format conversion on open**. Select to choose a file converter. (Default off).
   - **Update automatic links at open**. (Default on).
   - **Allow opening a document in Draft view**. (Default off).
   - **Enable background repagination**. Select to repaginate documents as needed. (Default on).
   - **Show add-in user interface errors**. Select to display alerts for custom interface problems. (Default off).
   - **Show customer submitted Office.com content**. (New!) Select to show customer content from Office.com. (Default on).
   - **Mailing address**. Enter to use as the default return address for envelopes and letters.
4. Click **OK**.

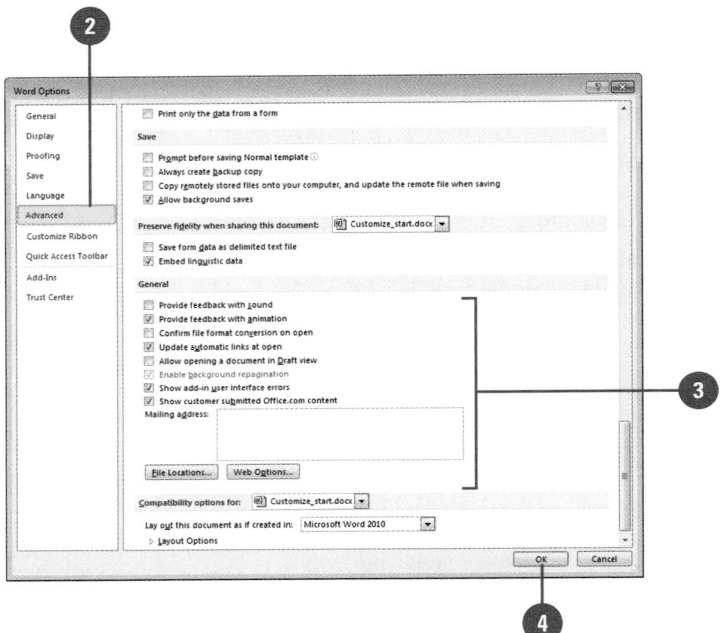

For Your Information

Changing Default File Locations

If you always save documents in a specific folder, you can change the default location where documents are saved. You can change the default file location for documents, clip art pictures, user templates, workgroup templates, AutoRecover files, tools, and startup. Unless you fully understand the internal connects between Word and the clip art, tools, and startup folders, you should not change those default file locations. After you make a change, Word uses the new setting for all subsequent Word sessions until you change the setting again. In the Advanced pane of the Word Options dialog box, click File Locations, select the file type you want to change, click Modify, open the new default folder location, click OK, and then click OK.

Setting Compatibility Options

If you have an older Word or WordPerfect document that doesn't display very well in Word 2010, you can set compatibility options to simulate the layout of an older format to improve the display. Word 2010 provides compatibility for all previous versions of Word going back to Word for Windows 1.0 and WordPerfect 5.x. Compatibility options are available on the Advanced pane in Word Options. After you select the layout version you want to use, you click the arrow to display the long list of compatibility options.

Change Compatibility Options

1. Click the **File** tab, and then click **Options**.
2. In the left pane, click **Advanced**, and then scroll to the bottom of the dialog box.
3. Click the **Compatibility options for** list arrow, and then select the document in which you want to set options.
4. Click the **Layout this document as if created in** list arrow, and then select the version of Word you want.
5. Click the arrow next to Layout Options.
6. Select or clear the layout check box options in the list.
7. Click **OK**.

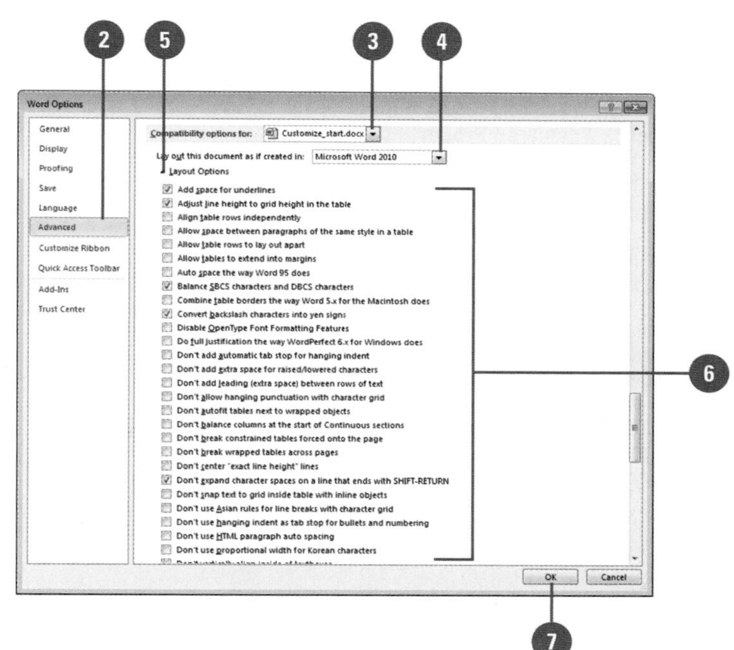

Changing Advanced Document Properties

You can use document properties—also known as metadata—to help you manage and track files. Search tools can use the metadata to find a document based-on your search criteria, such as title, subject, author, category, keywords, or comments. You can create advanced custom properties to associate more specific criteria for search tools to use. If you associate a document property to an item in the document, the document property updates when you change the item.

Customize Advanced Properties

1. Click the **File** tab, and then click **Info**.
2. Click the **Properties** button, and then click **Advanced Properties**.
3. Click the tabs to view and add information:
   - **General**. To find out file location or size.
   - **Summary**. To add title and author information for the document.
   - **Statistics**. To display the number of slides, paragraphs, words and other details about the document.
   - **Contents**. To display document contents.
4. Click the **Custom** tab.
5. Type the name for the custom property or select a name from the list.
6. Select the data type for the property you want to add.
7. Type a value for the property.
8. Click **Add**.
9. Click **OK**.

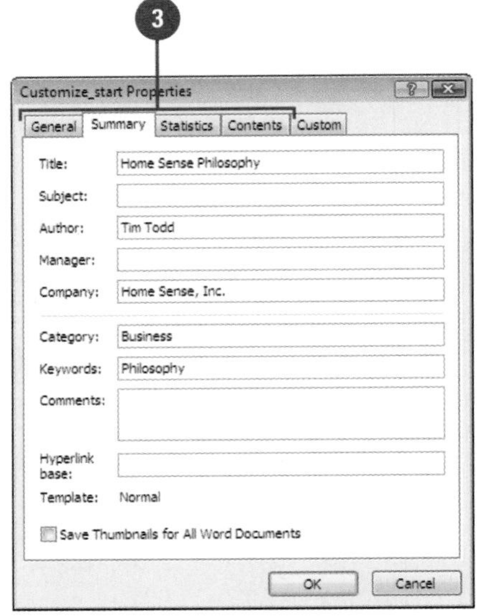

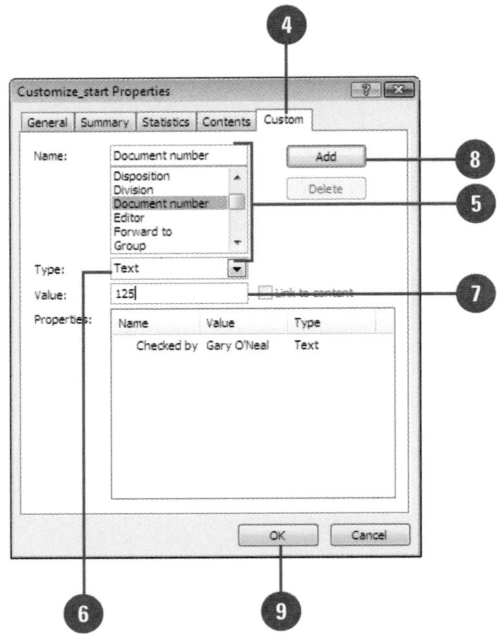

Changing Research Options

When you want to research a topic and use the material in a document, you can use the Research button on the Review tab to find the information you want directly from Word. Once you find it, you can copy and paste it into your document. If you have a hard time finding research information on a specific topic, you can use the Research Options command to enable and update additional reference books and research Web sites from which to search.

Change Research Options

1. Click the **Review** tab.
2. Click the **Research** button.
3. In the task pane, click **Research options**.
4. Do one or more of the following:
    - **Services.** To activate or remove research services.
    - **Add Services.** To add research services.
    - **Update/Remove.** To update or remove a service provider.
    - **Parental Control.** To turn on parental controls.
5. Do one or more of the following:
    - **Properties.** To display properties for the selected service.
    - **Favorite.** To make the selected service your favorite (**New!**).
6. Click **OK**.
7. When you're done, click the **Close** button on the task pane.

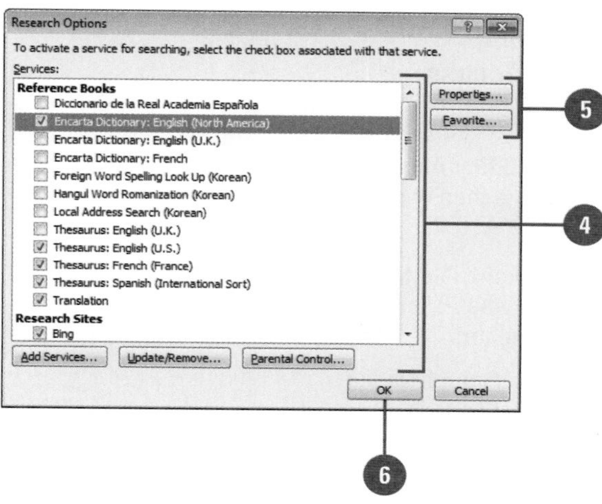

Accessing Commands Not in the Ribbon

If you don't see a command in the Ribbon that was available in an earlier version of Word, you might think Microsoft removed it from the product. To see if a command is available, check out the Customize section in Word Options. The Quick Access Toolbar gives access to commands not in the Ribbon, which you can add to the toolbar. For example, you can add the following commands: Create Microsoft Outlook Task, Replace Fonts, AutoFormat, Set AutoShape Defaults, Send to Microsoft PowerPoint, and Web Page Preview.

Add Commands Not in the Ribbon to the Quick Access Toolbar

1. Click the **Customize Quick Access Toolbar** list arrow, and then click **More Commands**.
   - You can also click the **File** tab, click **Options**, and then click **Quick Access Toolbar**.
2. Click the **Choose command from** list arrow, and then click **Commands Not in the Ribbon**.
3. Click the **Customize Quick Access Toolbar** list arrow, and then click **For all documents** (Default).
4. Click the command you want to add (left column).

   TIMESAVER *Click <Separator>, and then click Add to insert a separator line between buttons.*
5. Click **Add**.
6. Click the **Move Up** and **Move Down** arrow buttons to arrange the commands in the order you want them to appear.
7. To reset the Quick Access Toolbar to its original state, click **Reset**.
8. Click **OK**.

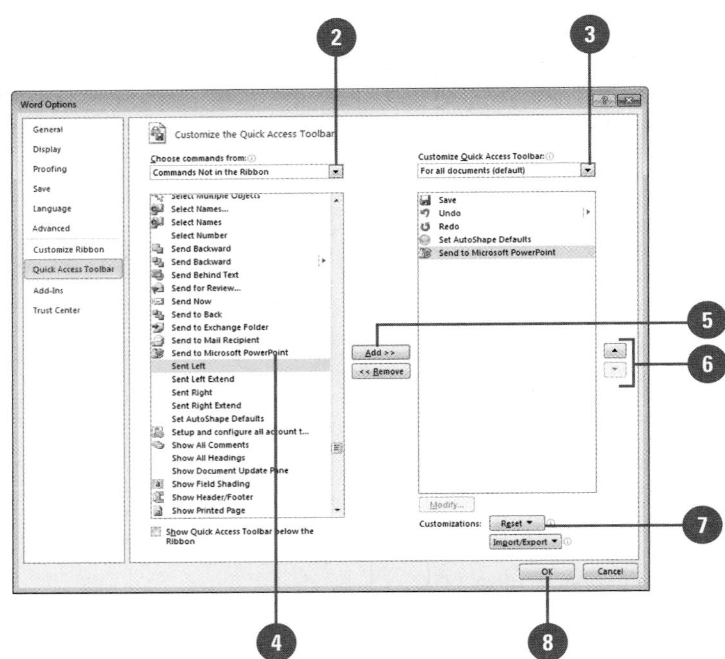

Customizing the Way You Create Objects

When you draw an object, Word applies a set of default object attributes. Examples of object default settings include fill color, shadow, and line style. To find out the current default settings for your document, you can draw an object, or create a text object and check the object's attributes. If you change a default setting, Word will use the new setting for all subsequent Word sessions until you change the setting again.

Customize the Way You Create Shape Objects

1. Create a shape.
2. Change the shape attributes, including fill color or effect, text color, outline color and style; and font type, style, and size.
3. Right-click the shape, and then click **Set as Default Shape**.

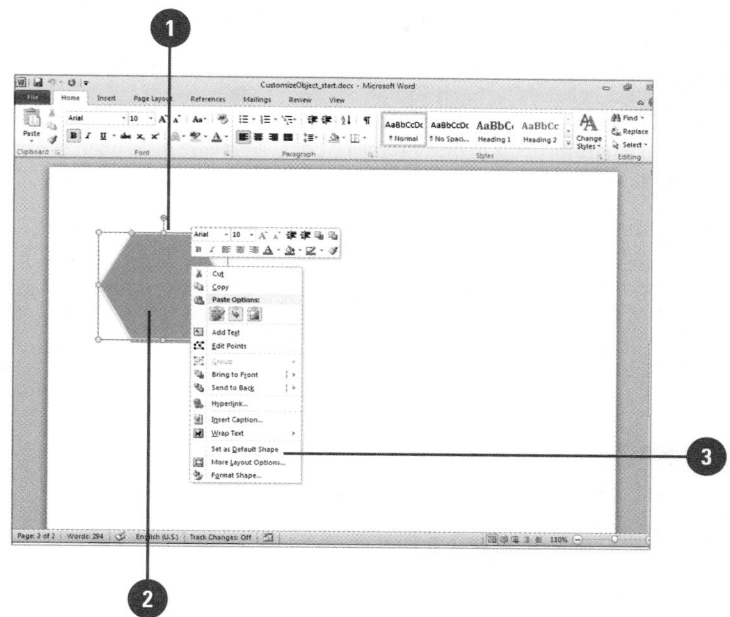

Managing Pictures

With Microsoft Office Picture Manager, you can manage, edit, and share your pictures. You can view all the pictures on your computer and specify which file type you want to open with Picture Manager. If you need to edit a picture, you can use Picture Manager to change brightness, contrast, and color, and to remove red eye. You can also crop, rotate and flip, resize, and compress a picture.

Open Picture Manager and Locate Pictures

1. Click the **Start** button, point to **All Programs**, click **Microsoft Office**, click **Microsoft Office Tools**, and then click **Microsoft Office Picture Manager**.

   The first time you start the program, it asks you to select the file types you want to open with Picture Manager. Select the check boxes with the formats you want, and then click **OK**.

2. If necessary, click **Add Picture Shortcut**.
3. Click **Locate Pictures**.
4. Click the **Look in** list arrow, and then click a drive location.
5. Click **OK**.
6. Use the **View** buttons to view your pictures.
7. When you're done, click the **Close** button.

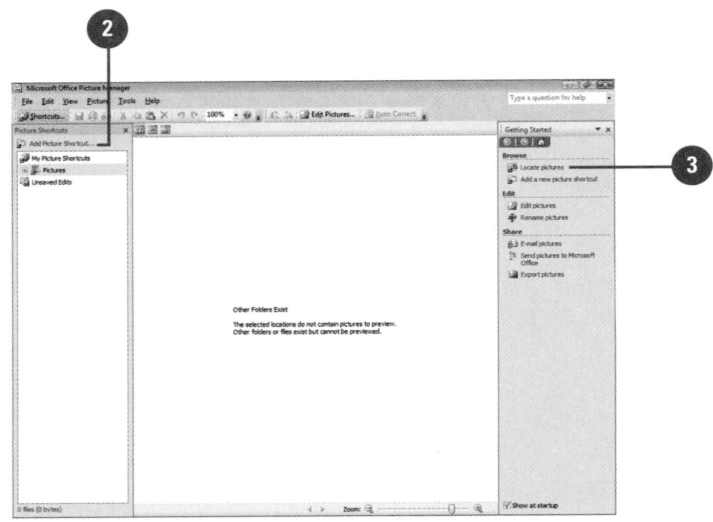

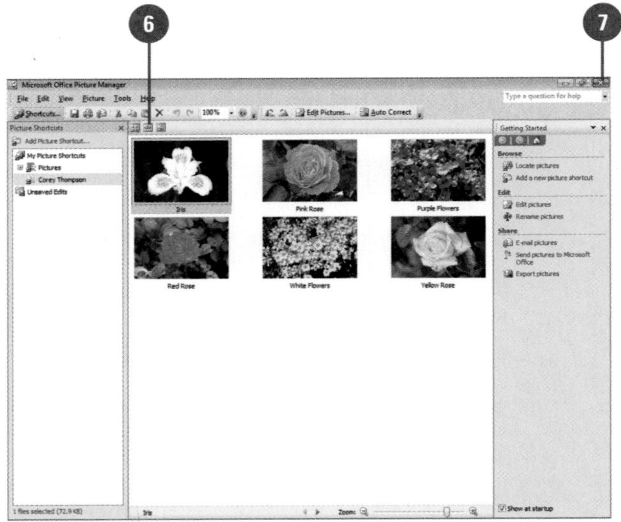

Did You Know?

You can export a folder of files with a new format or size. In Picture Manager, click the File menu, click Export, specify the folder with the pictures you want to change, select an export file format or select a size, and then click OK.

Edit Pictures

1. In Picture Manager, select the picture you want to edit.
2. Click the **Edit Pictures** button on the Standard toolbar.
3. Use the editing tools on the Edit Pictures task pane to modify the picture.
   - Brightness and Contrast
   - Color
   - Crop
   - Rotate and Flip
   - Red Eye Removal
4. Use the sizing tools on the Edit Pictures task pane to change the picture size.
   - Resize
   - Compress Pictures
5. Click the **Save** button on the Standard toolbar.
6. When you're done, click the **Close** button.

Did You Know?

You can discard changes to a picture. If you don't like the changes you make to a picture, click the Edit menu, and then click Discard Changes to restore the picture.

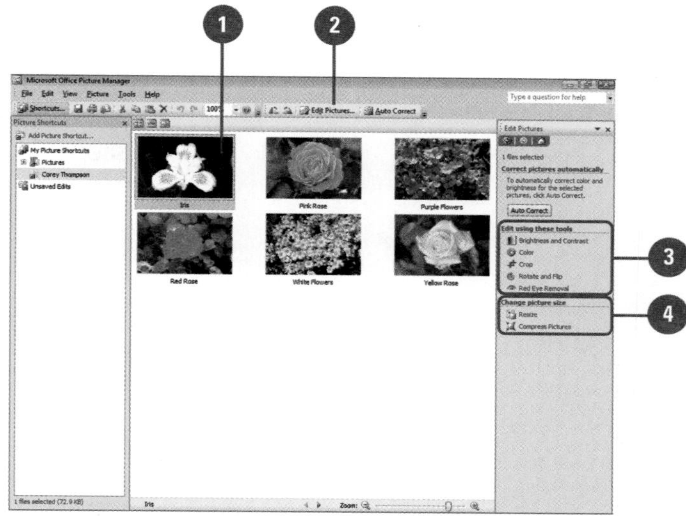

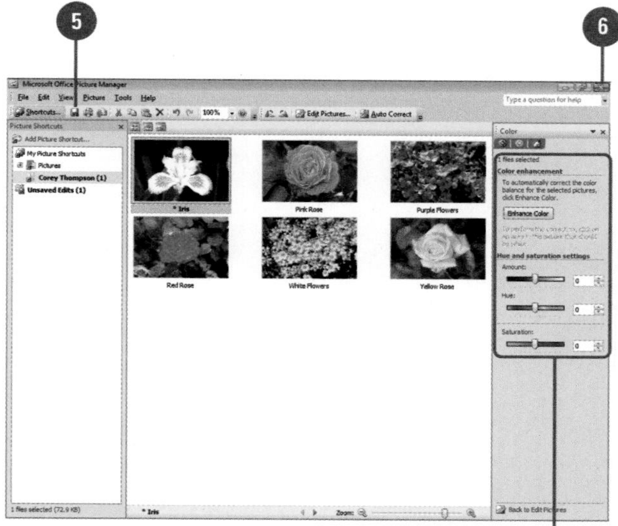

Color enhancing options

Expanding Word Functionality

17

Introduction

An add-in extends the functionality of Word and other Microsoft Office programs. Word includes a variety of add-ins—programs that are included with Word but not essential to its functionality. Before you can use a Word or a third-party add-in, you need to load it first. When you load an add-in, the feature may add a command to a Ribbon tab.

If you want to customize Microsoft Word and create advanced documents, you'll need to learn how to work with the Microsoft Office programming language, **Microsoft Visual Basic for Applications (VBA)**. VBA is powerful and flexible, and you can use it in all major Office applications. To create a VBA application, you have to learn VBA conventions and syntax. Office makes VBA more user-friendly by providing the Visual Basic Editor, an application that includes several tools to help you write error-free VBA applications. The Visual Basic Editor provides extensive online Help to assist you in this task.

A practical way to use VBA is to create macros. Macros can simplify common repetitive tasks that you regularly use in Word. Macros can reside on the Quick Access Toolbar for easy access. If a macro has a problem executing a task, the Visual Basic Editor can help you debug, or fix the error in your macro.

An ActiveX control is a software component that adds functionality to an existing program. An ActiveX control supports a customizable, programmatic interface for you to create your own functionality, such as a form. Word includes several pre-built ActiveX controls—including a label, text box, command button, and check box—to help you create a user interface.

What You'll Do

View and Manage Add-ins

Load and Unload Add-ins

Enhance a Document with VBA

View the Visual Basic Editor

Set Developer Options

Understand How Macros Automate Your Work

Record or Create a Macro

Run and Control a Macro

Add a Digital Signature to a Macro Project

Assign a Macro to a Toolbar

Save and Open a Document with Macros

Use Content Controls to Create Documents

Insert and Use ActiveX Controls

Set ActiveX Control Properties

Add VBA Code to an ActiveX Control

Play a Movie Using an ActiveX Control

Change the Document Information Panel

Viewing and Managing Add-ins

An add-in extends functionality to Word and other Microsoft Office programs. An add-in can add buttons and custom commands to the Ribbon or menu items on the File tab (**New!**). You can get add-ins for Word on the Office.com Web site in the Downloads area, or on third-party vendor Web sites. When you download and install an add-in, it appears on the Add-Ins or other tabs depending on functionality, and includes a special ScreenTip that identifies the developer. You can view and manage add-ins from the Add-Ins pane in Word Options.

View Installed Add-ins

1. Click the **Add-Ins** tab, or click the **File** tab, click **Add-Ins**, point to an add-in menu option, and then select a command (**New!**).

   Add-ins with buttons and controls appear on the Ribbon. To display a ScreenTip, point to a button or control.

2. Click the **File** tab, and then click **Options**.
3. In the left pane, click **Add-Ins**.

   The installed add-ins appear in the list by category.

   - **Active Application Add-ins.** Lists the registered and running add-ins. A selected check box for a COM add-in appears here.
   - **Inactive Application Add-ins.** Lists the installed add-ins, but not currently loaded. A cleared check box for a COM add-in appears here.
   - **Document Related Add-ins.** Lists template files currently open in a document.
   - **Disabled Application Add-ins.** Lists automatically disabled add-ins causing Office programs to crash.

4. Click an add-in to display information about it.
5. Click **OK**.

Manage Installed Add-ins

1. Click the **File** tab, and then click **Options**.
2. In the left pane, click **Add-Ins**.
3. Click the **Manage** list arrow, and then click the add-in list you want to display:
   - **COM Add-ins.** Opens the COM Add-Ins dialog box and lists the Component Object Model (COM) add-ins.
   - **Actions.** Opens the AutoCorrect dialog with the Actions tab and list the installed actions (**New!**).
   - **Word Add-ins.** Opens the Templates and Add-ins dialog box with the Templates tab and lists the currently installed Word add-ins.
   - **Templates.** Opens the Templates and Add-ins dialog box with the Templates tab and lists the currently installed global templates.
   - **XML Schemas.** Opens the Templates and Add-ins dialog box with the XML Schema tab.
   - **XML Expansion Pack.** Opens the Templates and Add-ins dialog box with the XML Expansion Packs tab. XML Expansion Packs provide additional XML functionality.
   - **Disabled Items.** Opens the Disabled Items dialog box and lists the disabled items that prevent Word from working properly. If you want to try and enable an item, select it, click Enable, click Close, and then restart Word.
4. Click **Go**.
5. Click **OK**.

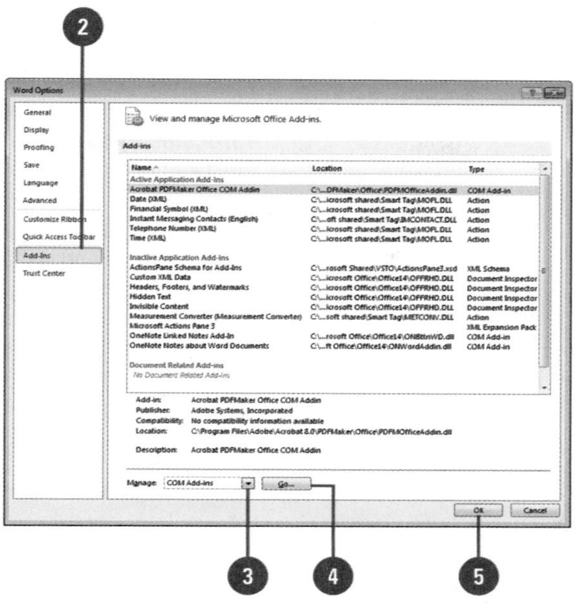

COM Add-Ins dialog box

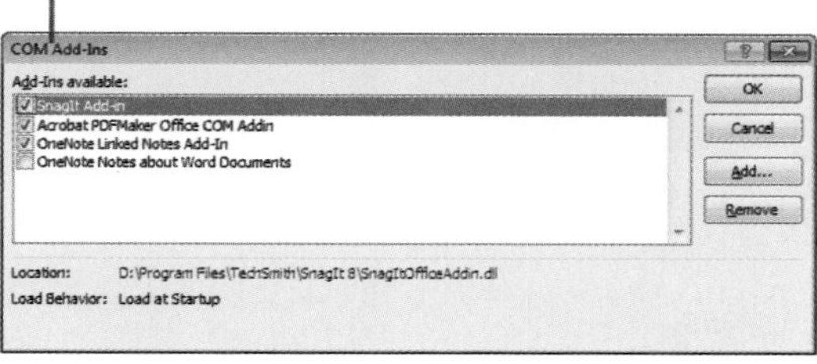

Templates and Add-ins dialog box

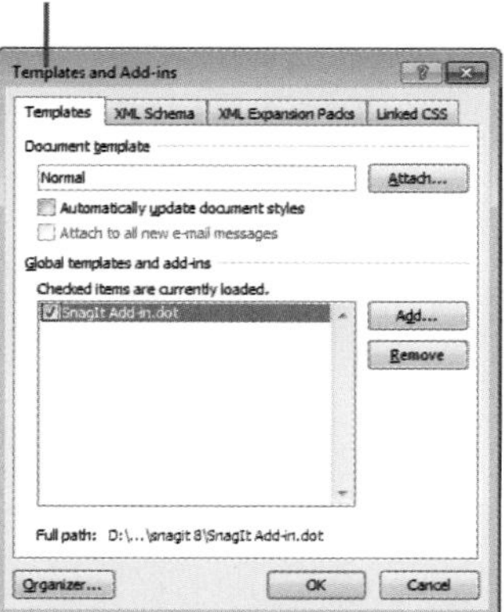

Loading and Unloading Add-ins

Add-ins are additional programs, designed to run seamlessly within Word or Office. There are two main types of add-ins: Word and **Component Object Model (COM)**. Word add-ins are custom controls designed specifically for Word, while COM add-ins are designed to run in one or more Office programs and use the file name extension .dll or .exe. Some add-ins are installed when you run the Setup program, while others can be downloaded from Office.com or purchased from third-party vendors. To load or unload add-ins, Word provides commands you can access from an added button on the Quick Access Toolbar, Developer tab, or the Add-Ins pane in Word Options. When you load an add-in, the feature may add a command to a tab or toolbar. You can load one or more add-ins. If you no longer need an add-in, you should unload it to save memory and reduce the number of commands on a tab. When you unload an add-in, you also may need to restart Word to remove an add-in command from a tab.

Load or Unload a Word Add-in

1. Click the **Developer** tab.
   - To display the Developer tab, use the Customize Ribbon pane in Options.
2. Click the **Add-Ins** or **Document Template** button.
3. Select or clear the check box next to the global template or add-in you want to load or unload.
4. To add or remove a global template or add-in, do one of the following:
   - **Add.** Click **Add**, navigate to the folder that contains the add-in, click the **Files of type** list arrow, select **Word Add-Ins**, click the add-in, and then click **OK**.
   - **Remove.** Select the item you want to remove, and then click **Remove**.
5. Click **OK**.

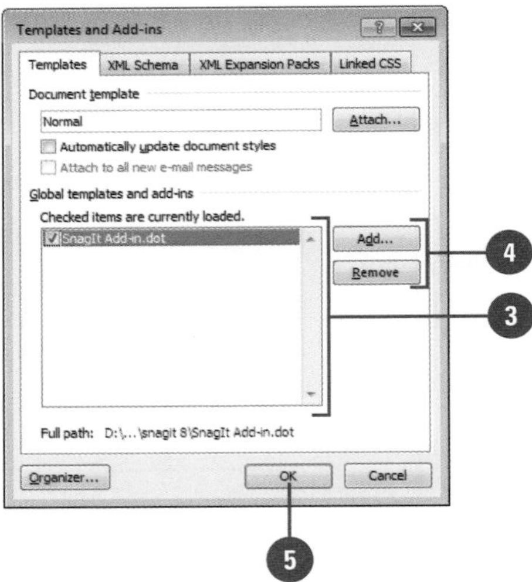

Load or Unload a COM Add-in

1. Click the **Developer** tab.
   - To display the Developer tab, use the Customize Ribbon pane in Options.
2. Click the **COM Add-Ins** button.
3. Select the check box next to the add-in you want to load, or clear the check box you want to unload.

   TROUBLE? *If the add-in is not available in the list, click Add, locate and select the add-in you want, and then click OK.*
4. To remove the selected add-in, click **Remove**.
5. Click **OK**.

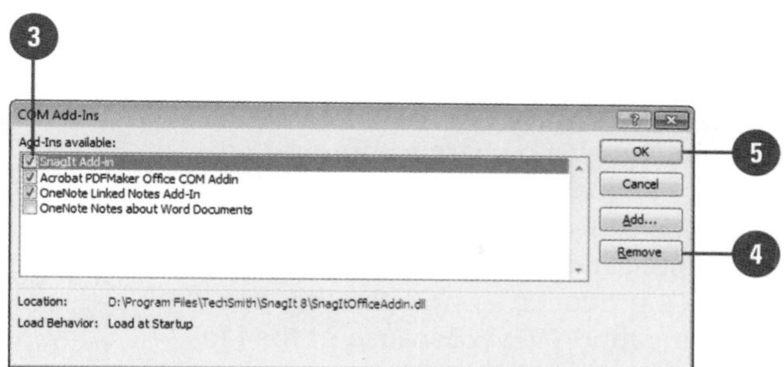

Did You Know?

You can can get more information about COM online. Visit *www.microsoft.com/com.*

You can open an add-in dialog box from Word Options. Click the File tab, click Options, click Add-ins, click the Manage list arrow, click Word Add-ins or COM Add-ins, and then click Go.

See Also

See "Working with Toolbars" on page 6 for information on adding a button to the Quick Access Toolbar.

See "Setting Developer Options" on page 409 for information on displaying the Developer tab.

For Your Information

Dealing with an Add-in Security Alert

When there is a problem with an add-in, Word disables it to protect the program and your data. When a problem does occur, a security alert dialog box appears, displaying information about the problem and options you can choose to fix or ignore it. You can choose an option to help protect you from unknown content (recommended), enable this add-in for this session only, or enable all code published by this publisher. See "Setting Add-in Security Options" on page 332 for more information about setting options that trigger the Add-in security alert.

Enhancing a Document with VBA

Office applications like Word, Access, Excel, PowerPoint, and Visio share a common programming language: Visual Basic for Applications (VBA). With VBA, you can develop applications that combine tools from these Office products, as well as other programs that support VBA. Because of the language's power and flexibility, programmers often prefer to use VBA to customize their Office applications.

Introducing the Structure of VBA

VBA is an object-oriented programming language because, when you develop a VBA application, you manipulate objects. An object can be anything within your document, such as a shape, text box, picture, or table. Even Word itself is considered an object. Objects can have properties that describe the object's characteristics. Text boxes, for example, have the Font property, which describes the font Word uses to display the text. A text box also has properties that indicate whether the text is bold or italic.

Objects also have methods—actions that can be done to the object. Deleting and inserting are examples of methods available with a record object. Closely related to methods are events. An event is a specific action that occurs on or with an object. Clicking a button initiates the Click event for the button object. VBA also refers to an event associated with an object as an event property. The form button, for example, has the Click event property. You can use VBA to either respond to an event or to initiate an event.

Writing VBA Code

A VBA programmer types the statements, or **code**, that make up the VBA program. Those statements follow a set of rules, called **syntax**, that govern how commands are formulated. For example, to change the property of a particular object, the command follows the general form:

```
Object.Property = Expression
```

Where **Object** is the name of a VBA object, **Property** is the name of a property that object has, and **Expression** is a value that will be assigned to the property. The following statement turns on track changes in the active document:

```
ActiveDocument.TrackRevisions = TRUE
```

You can use Office and VBA's online Help to learn about specific object and property names. If you want to apply a method to an object, the syntax is:

```
Object.Method arg1, arg2, ...
```

Where **Object** is the name of a VBA object, **Method** is the name of method that can be applied to that object, and **arg1**, **arg2**, ... are optional **arguments** that provide additional information for the method operation. For example, to clear the Find and Replace formatting, you could use the following method:

```
Selection.Find.ClearFormatting
Selection.Find.Replacement.ClearFormatting
```

Working with Procedures

You don't run VBA commands individually. Instead they are organized into groups of commands called **procedures**. A procedure either performs an action or calculates a value. Procedures that perform actions are called **Sub procedures**. You can run a Sub procedure directly, or Office can run it for you in response to an event, such as clicking a button or opening a form. A Sub procedure initiated by an event is also called an **event procedure**. Office provides event procedure templates to help you easily create procedures for common events. Event procedures are displayed in each object's event properties list.

A procedure that calculates a value is called a **function procedure**. By creating function procedures you can create your own function library, supplementing the Office collection of built-in functions. You can access these functions from within the Expression Builder, making it easy for them to be used over and over again.

Working with Modules

Procedures are collected and organized within **modules**. Modules generally belong to two types: class modules and standard modules. A **class module** is associated with a specific object. In more advanced VBA programs, the class module can be associated with an object created by the user. **Standard modules** are not associated with specific objects, and they can be run from anywhere within a database. This is usually not the case with class modules. Standard modules are listed in the Database window on the Modules Object list.

Building VBA Projects

A collection of modules is further organized into a **project**. Usually a project has the same name as a document. You can create projects that are not tied into any specific document, saving them as Word add-ins that provide extra functionality to Word.

Using the Visual Basic Editor

You create VBA commands, procedures, and modules in Office's **Visual Basic Editor**. This is the same editor used by Word and other Office programs. Thus, you can apply what you learn about creating programs in Word to these other applications.

The Project Explorer

One of the fundamental tools in the Visual Basic Editor is the Project Explorer. The **Project Explorer** presents a hierarchical view of all of the projects and modules currently open in Word, including standard and class modules.

The Modules Window

You write all of your VBA code in the **Modules** window. The Modules window acts as a basic text editor, but it includes several tools to help you write error-free codes. Word also provides hints as you write your code to help you avoid syntax errors.

The Object Browser

There are hundreds of objects available to you. Each object has a myriad of properties, methods, and events. Trying to keep track of all of them is daunting, but the Visual Basic Editor supplies the **Object Browser**, which helps you examine the complete collection of objects, properties, and methods available for a given object.

Viewing the Visual Basic Editor

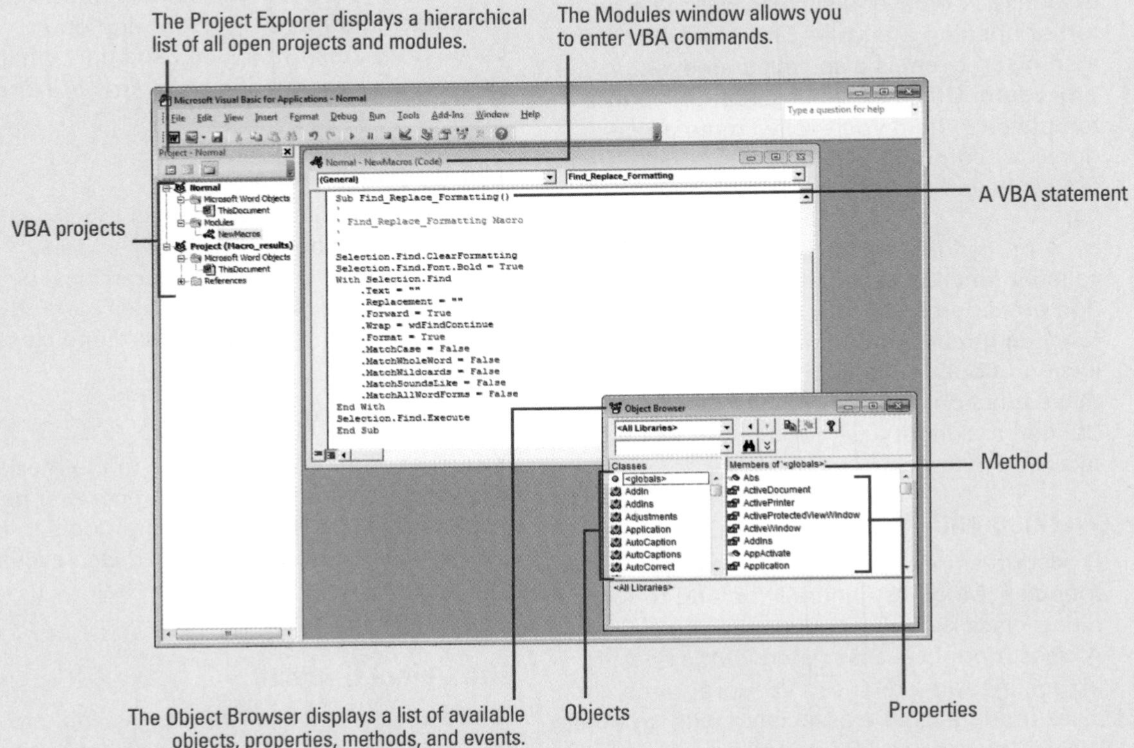

Setting Developer Options

The Developer tab is a specialized Ribbon that you can use to access developer controls, write code, or create macros. You can set an option in the Customize Ribbon pane in Word Options to show or hide the Developer tab. As a developer, you can also set an option to show errors in your user interface customization code.

Set Developer Options

1. Click the **File** tab, and then click **Options**.
2. In the left pane, click **Customize Ribbon**.
3. Select the **Developer** check box to display the Developer tab.
4. In the left pane, click **Advanced**.
5. Select the **Show add-in user interface errors** check box.
6. Click **OK**.

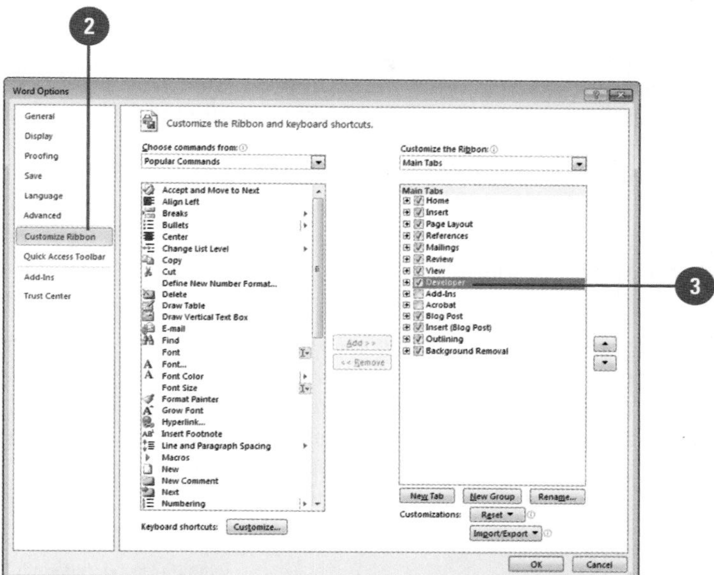

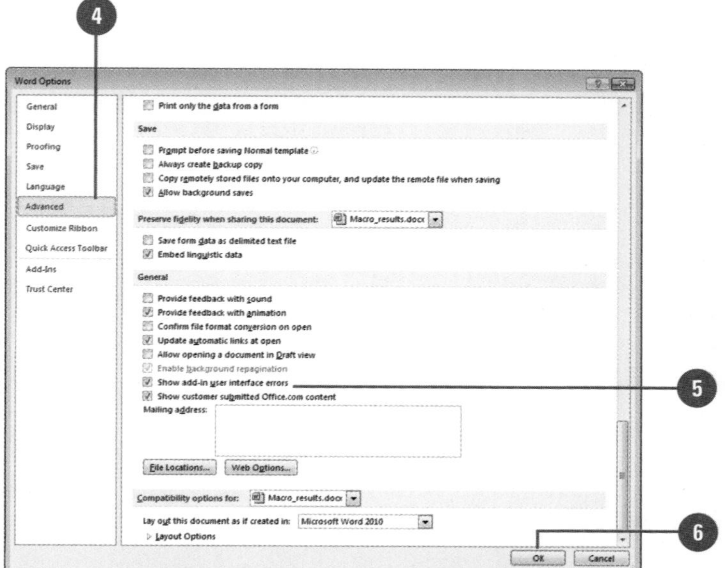

Understanding How Macros Automate Your Work

To complete many tasks in Word, you need to execute a series of commands and actions. To print two copies of a selected text in a document, for example, you need to open the document, select the text, open the Print dialog box, and specify that you want to print two copies. If you often need to complete the same task, you'll find yourself repeatedly taking the same series of steps. It can be tiresome to continually repeat the same commands and actions when you can easily create a mini-program, or macro, that accomplishes all of them with a single command.

Creating a **macro** is easy and requires no programming knowledge on your part. Word simply records the steps you want included in the macro while you use the keyboard and mouse. When you record a macro, Word stores the list of commands with any name you choose. You can store your macros in the current document or in a new document.

Once a macro is created, you can make modifications to it, add comments so other users will understand its purpose, and test it to make sure it runs correctly.

You can run a macro by choosing the Macro command on the View or Developer tab, or by using a shortcut key or clicking a Quick Access Toolbar button you've assigned to it. From the Macro dialog box, you can run, edit, test, or delete any Word macro on your system, or create a new one.

If you have problems with a macro, you can step through the macro one command at a time, known as **debugging**. Once you identify any errors in the macro, you can edit it.

Indicates the document(s) from which you can access the selected macro.

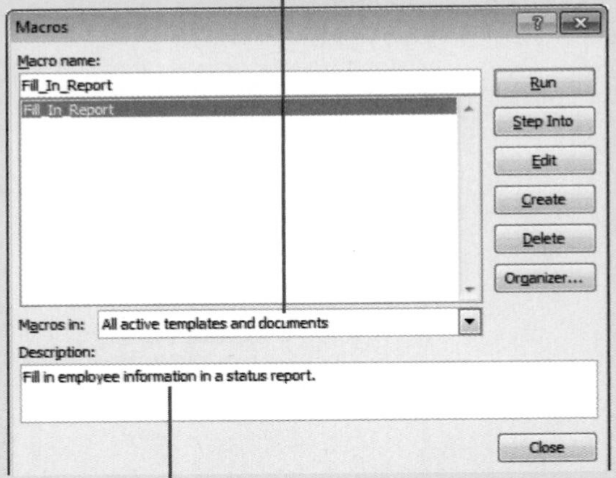

When you create a macro, you can add a description of what the macro does.

Recording a Macro

If you find yourself repeating the same set of steps over and over, you can record a macro. Macros can run several tasks for you at the click of a button. When you turn on the macro recorder, Word records every mouse click and keystroke action you execute until you turn off the recorder. You can even record formatting changes to charts and other objects (**New!**). Then you can "play," or run, the macro whenever you want to repeat that series of actions—but Word will execute them at a much faster rate. The macro recorder doesn't record in real time, so you can take your time to correctly complete each action.

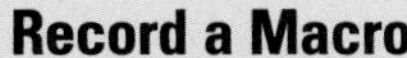

Record a Macro

1. Click the **Developer** or **View** tab.
2. Click the **Record Macro** button.
   - If you use the View tab, click **View Macros** on the menu.

   TIMESAVER *To quickly start or stop a macro recording, click the Record icon or Stop Record icon on the Status bar (left side).*
3. Type a name for the macro.
4. Assign a shortcut key to use a keystroke combination or assign a button to run the macro.
5. Click the **Store macro in** list arrow, and then select a location.
   - **All Documents**. The macro is available whenever you use Word.
   - **Documents Based On**. The macro is available in documents based on this document.
   - **This Document**. The macro is available only in this document.
6. If you want, type a description.
7. Click **OK**.
8. Execute the commands or actions you want to complete the task.
9. Click the **Stop Recording** button.

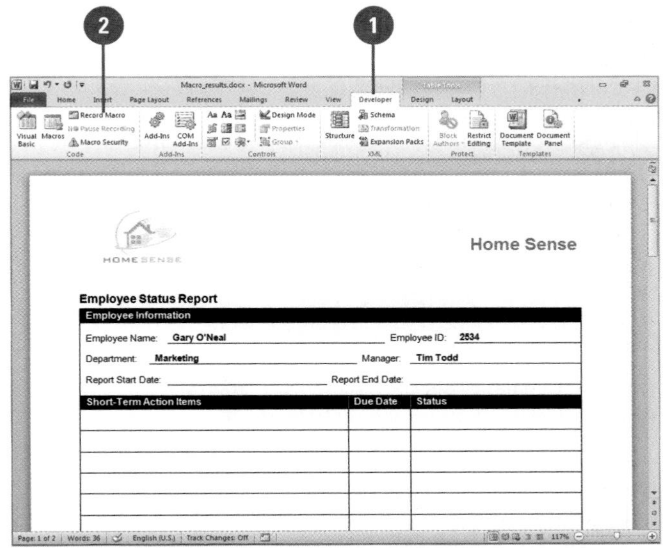

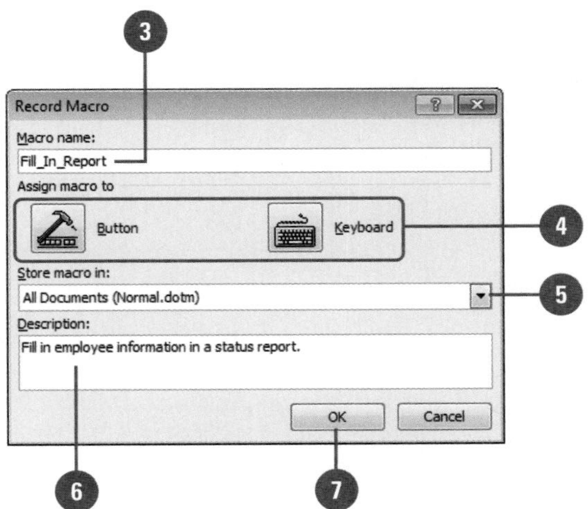

Creating a Macro

If you find yourself repeating the same set of steps over and over, or if you need to add new functionality to Word, you could create a macro. If you find it difficult to record a macro, you can create one using a programming language called Microsoft Visual Basic for Applications (VBA). With VBA, you create a macro by writing a script to replay the actions you want. The macros for a particular document are stored in a macro module, which is a collection of Visual Basic codes.

Create a Macro

1. Click the **Developer** or **View** tab.
2. Click the **Macros** button.
   - If you use the View tab, click **View Macros** on the menu.
3. Type a name for the macro.
4. Click the **Macros in** list arrow, and then click **All active templates and documents** or the document to which you want the macro stored.
5. Click **Create**.

   The Microsoft Visual Basic window opens.
6. Click the Module window (if necessary), and then type new Visual Basic commands, or edit existing ones.

   To run the macro, press F5.
7. When you're done, click the **Save** button, click the **File** menu, and then click **Close and Return to Microsoft Word**.

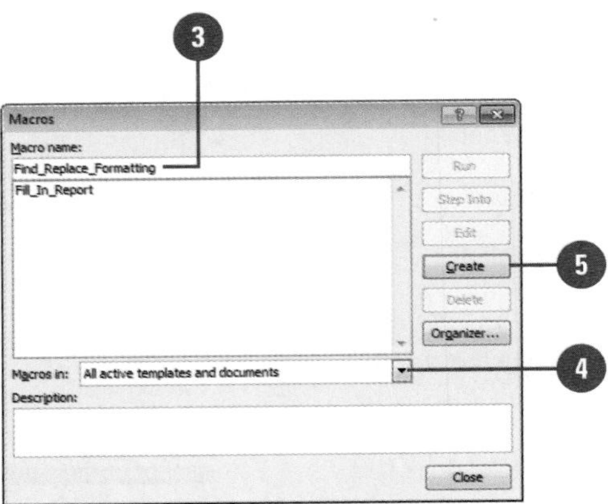

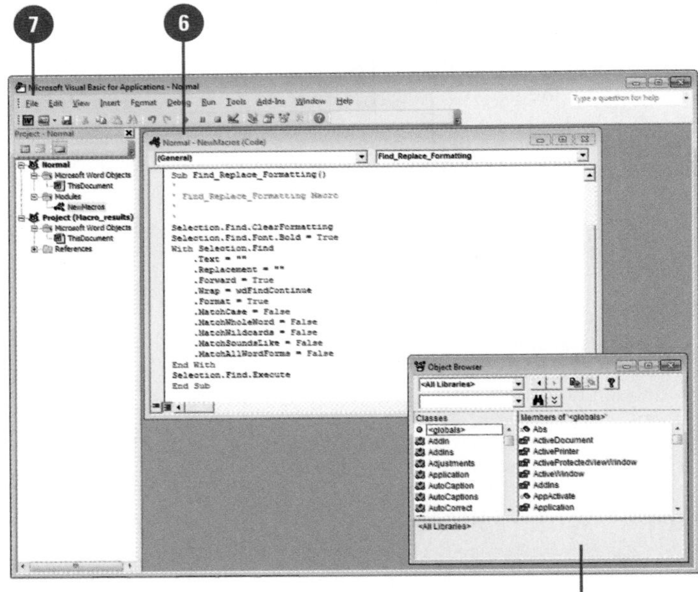

Object Browser helps you insert commands.

Running a Macro

Running a macro is similar to choosing a command in Word. When you record or edit the macro, you have the choice of making it available through a menu command, a keyboard combination, or even a toolbar button. As with other options in Word, your choice depends on your personal preferences—and you can choose to make more than one option available. Where you store a macro when you save it determines its availability later. Macros stored in the Personal Macro document are always available, and macros stored in any other documents are only available when the document is open.

Run a Macro

1. Click the **Developer** or **View** tab.
2. Click the **Macros** button.
   - If you use the View tab, click **View Macros** on the menu.

   TIMESAVER *Click the Macros button on the Status bar.*
3. Click the macro you want to run.
4. Click **Run**.

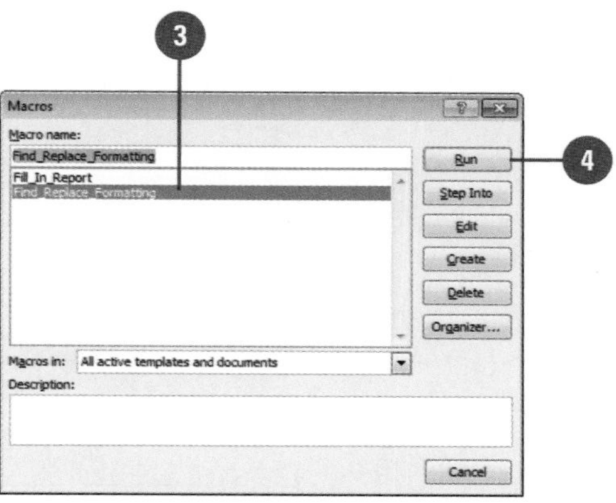

Delete a Macro

1. Click the **Developer** or **View** tab.
2. Click the **Macros** button.
   - If you use the View tab, click **View Macros** on the menu.
3. Click the macro you want to delete.
4. Click **Delete**, and then click **Delete** again to confirm the deletion.

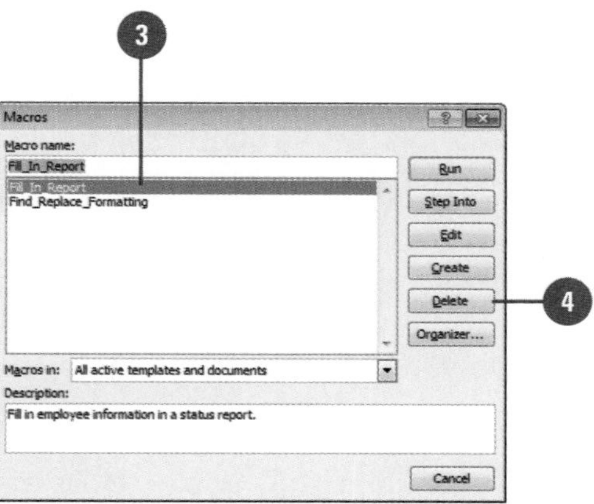

Did You Know?

You can stop a macro. Press Ctrl+Break to stop a macro before it completes its actions.

Controlling a Macro

If a macro doesn't work exactly the way you want it to, you can fix the problem using Microsoft Visual Basic for Applications (VBA). VBA allows you to **debug**, or repair, an existing macro so that you change only the actions that aren't working correctly. All macros for a particular document are stored in a macro module, a collection of Visual Basic programming codes that you can copy to other document files. You can view and edit your Visual Basic modules using the Visual Basic editor. By learning Visual Basic you can greatly increase the scope and power of your programs.

Debug a Macro Using Step Mode

1. Click the **Developer** or **View** tab.
2. Click the **Macros** button.
   - If you use the View tab, click **View Macros** on the menu.
3. Click the macro you want to debug.
4. Click **Step Into**.

   The Microsoft Visual Basic window opens.
5. Click the **Debug** menu, and then click **Step Into** (or press F8) to proceed through each action.
   - You can also use other commands like **Step Over** and **Step Out** to debug the code.
6. When you're done, click the **Save** button, click the **File** menu, and then click **Close and Return to Microsoft Word**.
7. Click **OK** to stop the debugger.

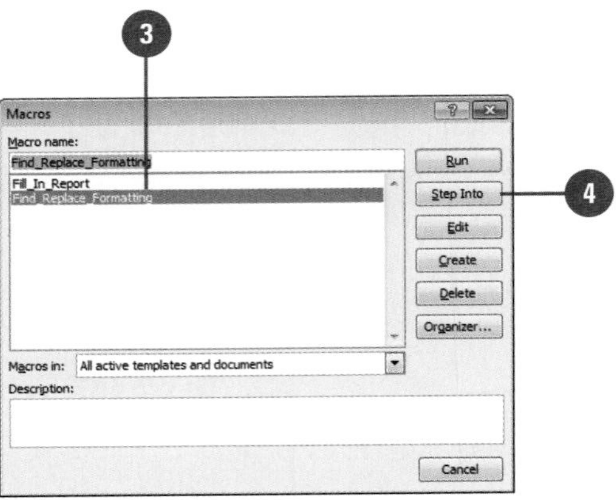

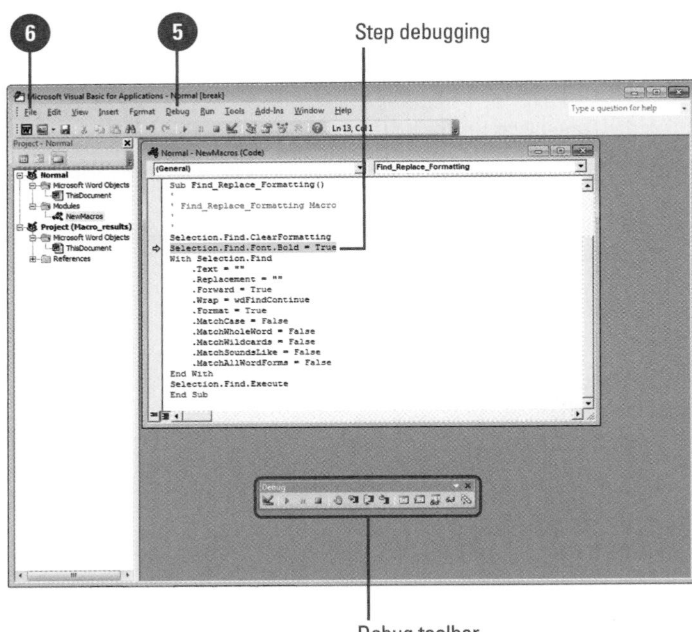

Did You Know?

You can display the Debug toolbar. In the Visual Basic editor, click the View menu, point to Toolbars, and then click Debug.

Edit a Macro

1. Click the **Developer** or **View** tab.
2. Click the **Macros** button.
   - If you use the View tab, click **View Macros** on the menu.
3. To open a macro, click the macro you want to change, and then click the **View Code** button.
4. Click the Module window containing the Visual Basic code for your macro.
5. Type new Visual Basic commands, or edit the commands already present.
6. Click the **Save** button, and then click the program **Close** button.

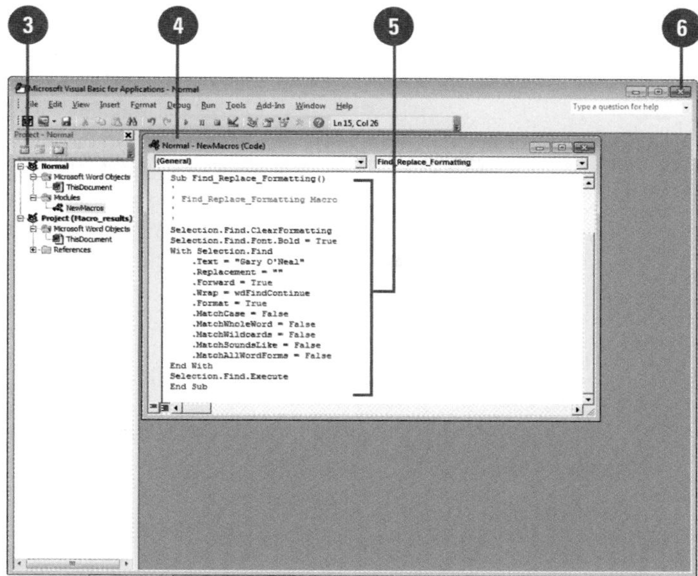

Copy a Macro Module to Another Document

1. Open the document files you want to copy the macro from and to.
2. Click the **Developer** tab.
3. Click the **Visual Basic** button.
4. Click the **View** menu, and then click **Project Explorer**.
5. Drag the module you want to copy from the source document to the destination document.
6. Click the **Save** button, and then click the program **Close** button.

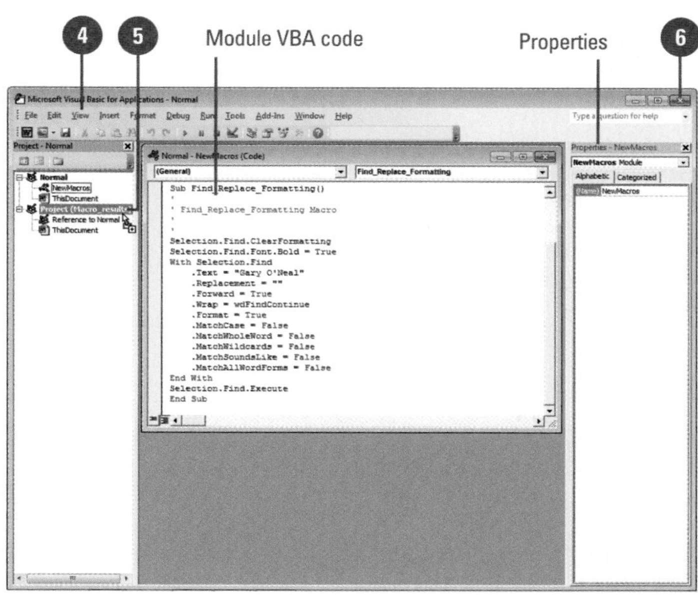

Adding a Digital Signature to a Macro Project

If you want to add a digital signature to a document with a macro, you need to add it using the Visual Basic editor. If you open a document that contains a signed macro project with a problem, the macro is disabled by default and the Message Bar appears to notify you of the potential problem. You can click Options or Enable Content in the Message Bar to view or use it. For more details, you can click Show Signature Details to view certificate. If a digital signature has problems—it's expired, not issued by a trusted publisher, or the document has been altered—the certificate information image contains a red X. When there's a problem, contact the signer to have them fix it, or save the document to a trusted location, where you can run the macro without security checks.

Sign a Macro Project

1. Open the document that contains the macro project, and then click the **Developer** tab.
2. Click the **Visual Basic** button to open the Visual Basic window.
3. Click the **Tools** menu, and then click **Digital Signature**.
4. Click **Choose**.
5. Select a certificate in the list.
6. To view a certificate, click **View Certificate** or a link, and then click **OK**.
7. Click **OK**.
8. Click **OK** again.
9. Click the **Save** button, click the **File** menu, and then click **Close and Return to Microsoft Word**.

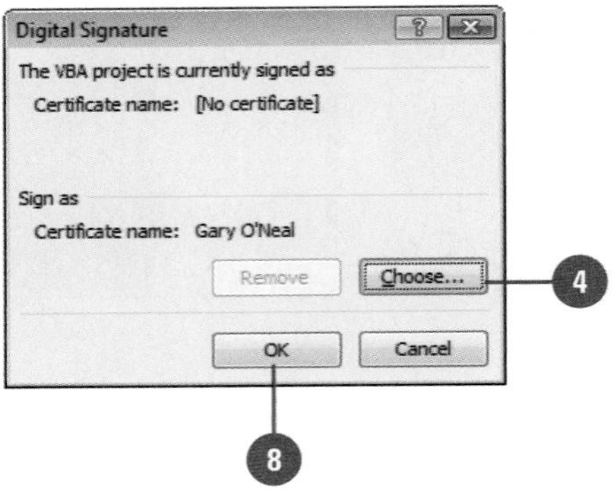

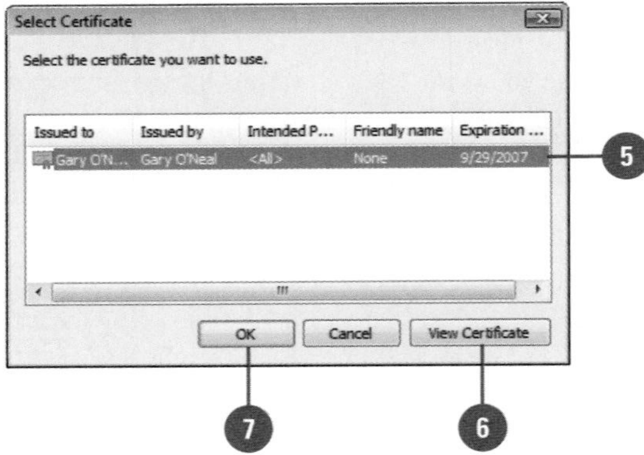

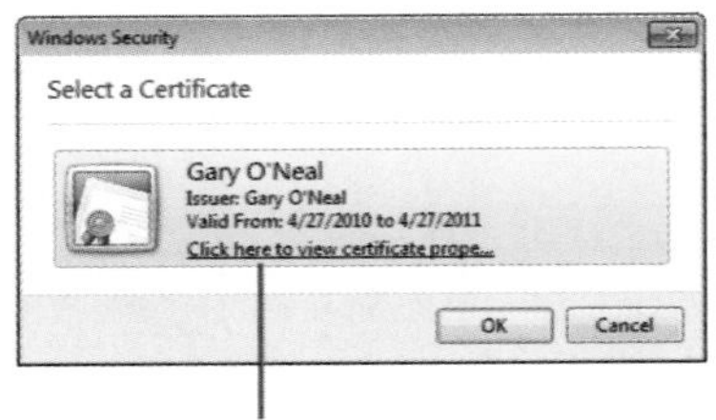

Click the link to view the certificate (Win 7)

Did You Know?

You can create a self-signing certificate for a macro project. Click the Start button, point to All Programs, click Microsoft Office, click Microsoft Office Tools, click Digital Certificate For VBA Projects, enter a name, and then click OK. Office programs trust a self-signed certificate only on the computer that created it.

Assigning a Macro to a Toolbar

After you create a macro, you can add the macro to the Quick Access Toolbar for easy access. When you create a macro, the macro name appears in the list of available commands when you customize the Quick Access Toolbar in Word Options. When you point to a macro button on the Quick Access Toolbar, a ScreenTip appears, displaying Macro: *document name*!*macro name*.

Assign a Macro to a Toolbar

1. Click the **Customize Quick Access Toolbar** list arrow, and then click **More Commands**.
   - You can also click the **File** tab, click **Options**, and then click **Quick Access Toolbar**.
2. Click the **Choose command from** list arrow, and then click **Macros**.
3. Click the **Customize Quick Access Toolbar** list arrow, and then click **For all documents (default)**.
4. Click the macro you want to add (left column).
5. Click **Add**.
6. Click the **Move Up** and **Move Down** arrow buttons to arrange the commands in the order you want them to appear.
7. Click **Modify**.
8. Type a name for the button.
9. Click an icon in the symbol list.
10. Click **OK**.
11. Click **OK**.

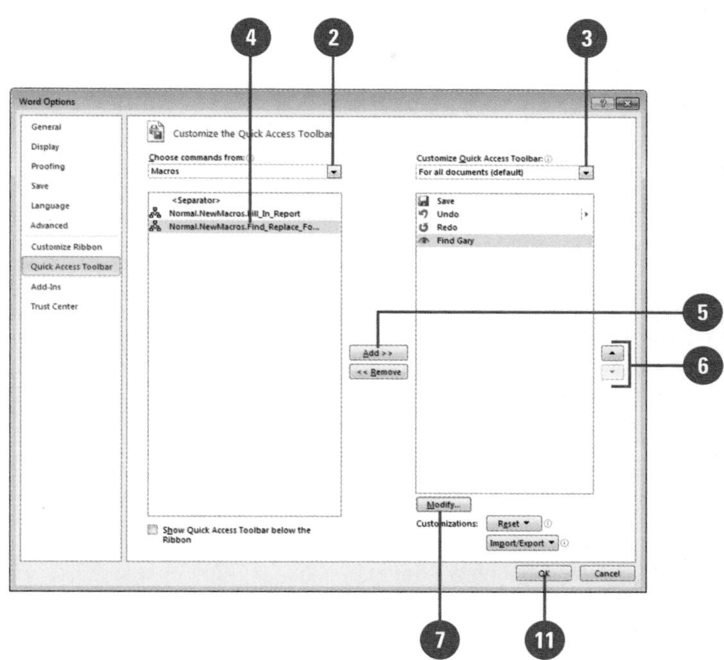

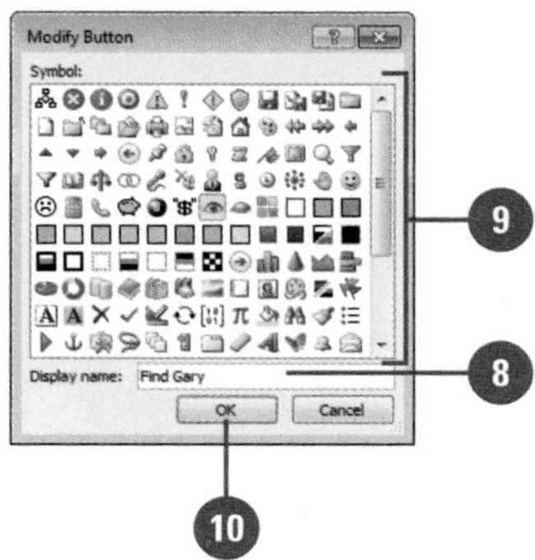

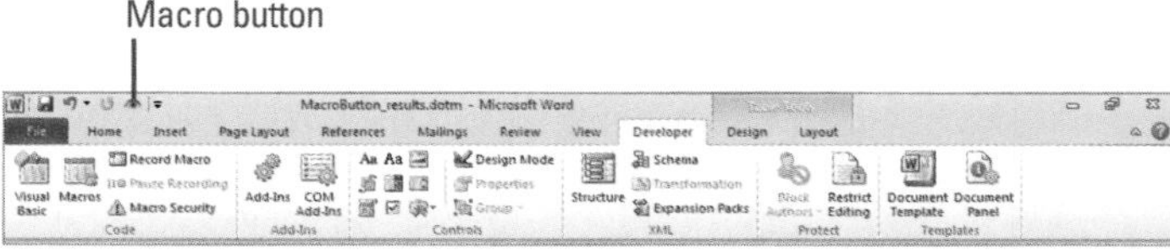

Macro button

See Also

See "Working with Toolbars" on page 6 and "Accessing Commands Not in the Ribbon" on page 396 for information on using the Quick Access Toolbar.

Saving a Document with Macros

Macros are created using Visual Basic for Applications (VBA) code. If you add a macro to a document, you need to save it with a file name extension that ends with an "m", either Word Macro-Enabled Document (.docm), or Word Macro-Enabled Template (.dotm). If you try to save a document containing a macro with a file name extension that ends with an "x" (such as .docx or .dotx), Word displays an alert message, restricting the operation. These Word file types are designated to be VBA code-free.

Save a Document with Macros

1. Click the **File** tab, and then click **Save As**.
2. Click the **Save in** list arrow, and then click the drive or folder where you want to save the file.
3. Type a document file name.
4. If necessary, click the **Save as type** list arrow, and then select the macro format you want:
   - **Word Macro-Enabled Document.** A document (.docm) that contains VBA code.
   - **Word Macro-Enabled Template.** A template (.dotm) that includes preapproved macros.
5. Click **Save**.

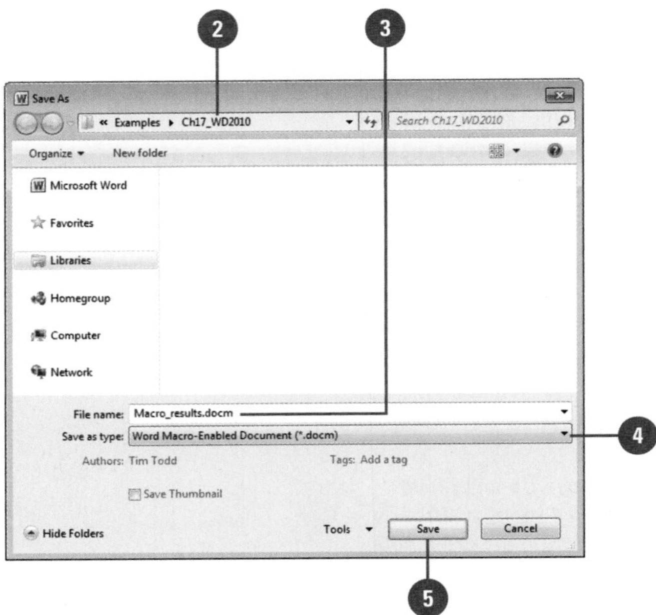

Opening a Document with Macros

When you open a document with a macro, VBA, or other software code, Word displays a security warning to let you know the document might contain potentially harmful code that may harm your computer. If you know and trust the author of the document, you can change security options to enable the macro content and use the document normally. If you don't trust the content, you can continue to block and disable the content and use the document with limited functionality in Protected view (**New!**). If you don't want a security alert to appear, you can change security settings in the Trust Center in Word Options.

Open a Document with Macros

1. Click the **File** tab, and then click **Open**.
2. If necessary, click the **File as type** list arrow, and then the document type that contains a macro.
3. If the file is located in another folder, click the **Look in** list arrow, and then navigate to the file.
4. Click the document with macros you want to open, and then click **Open**.
5. Click the **File** tab, click **Info**, click the **Enable Content** button (**New!**), and then click **Advanced Options**. To enable all content (make trusted), click **Enable All Content** on the menu.
   - You can also click **Enable Content** in the Message Bar with the Security Warning.
6. If you trust the document content, click the **Enable content for this session** option to use it. If you don't trust it, click the **Help protect me from unknown content (recommended)** option to block and disable the macros.
7. Click **OK**.

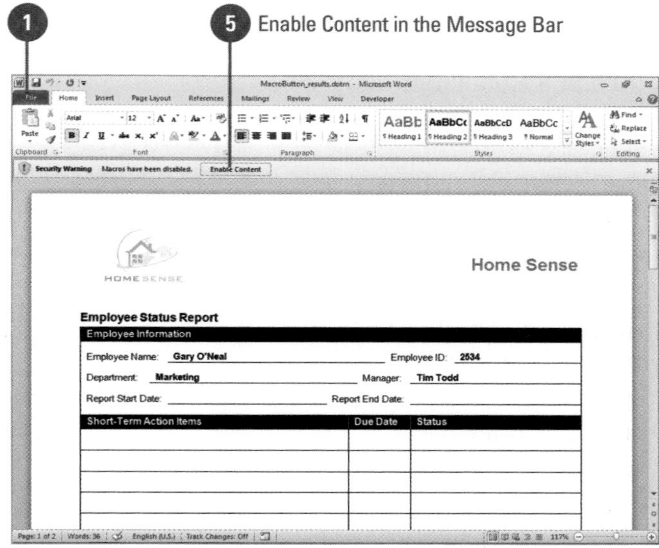

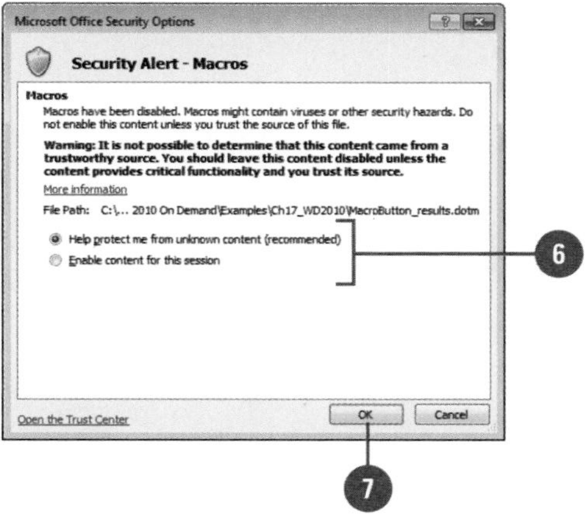

Using Content Controls to Create Documents

Forms are an easy way for you to interact with users of your documents, either online or in print, and gain information and feedback from them in the process. Controls—either Content, Form, and ActiveX—are predefined fields or set of fields that contain information you can use throughout a document. Word includes many different types: text boxes for typed entries, date picker, combo boxes, drop-down lists, and check boxes. The fields display information you provided in Document Properties or a placeholder, which you can fill in. After you insert the fields you want, you can change field properties to customize the form. Word uses Content controls and Quick Parts as part of the program to build page covers, headers and footers, pull quotes, and side bar to name a few.

Add Controls to a Document

1. Click the **Developer** tab.
2. Position the insertion point where you want to insert a control.
3. Use the buttons in the Controls group to insert controls.
   - **Rich Text** or **Text.** Click to insert a text box where you can enter text.
   - **Picture.** Click to insert a placeholder where you can insert a picture.
   - **Combo Box.** Click to insert a combo box control.
   - **Drop Down List.** Click to insert a drop down list control where you can select from a list.
   - **Date Picker.** Click to insert a control to select a date from a pop-up calendar.
   - **Building Block Gallery.** Click to insert a Quick Part control where you can specify the information you want.
   - **Legacy Tools.** Click to select form and ActiveX controls.
   - **Group.** Select contents you want to protect; prevents changes to document.

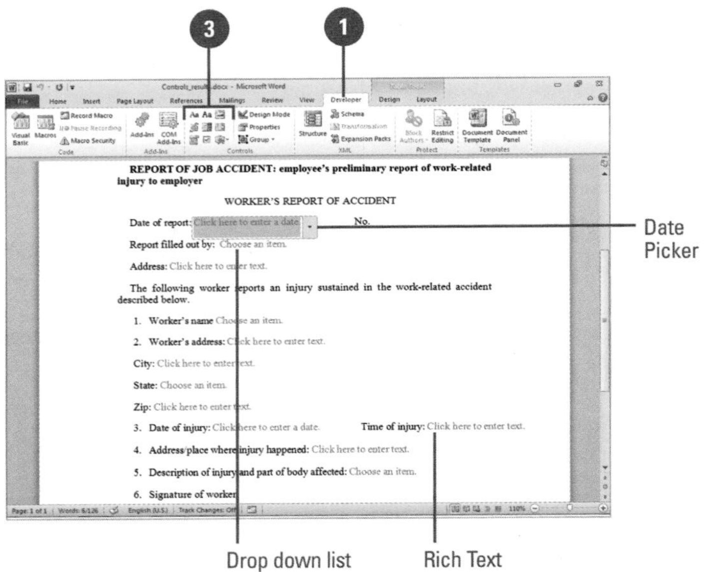

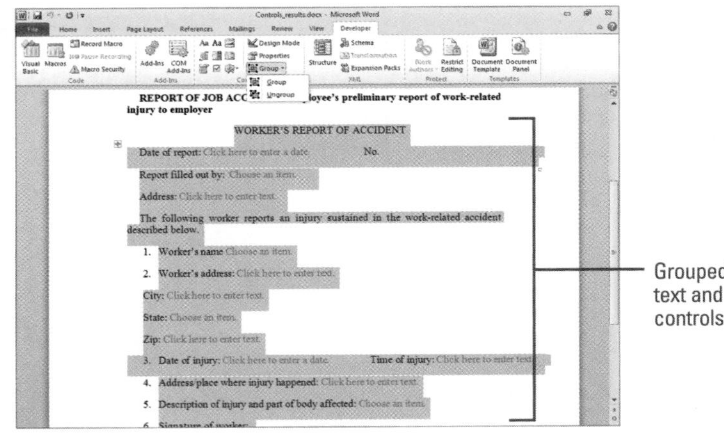

Set or Change Control Properties

1. Click the **Developer** tab.
2. Select the control you want to set or change properties.
3. Click the **Properties** button.
4. Select the new options you want for the form field.
5. Click **OK**.

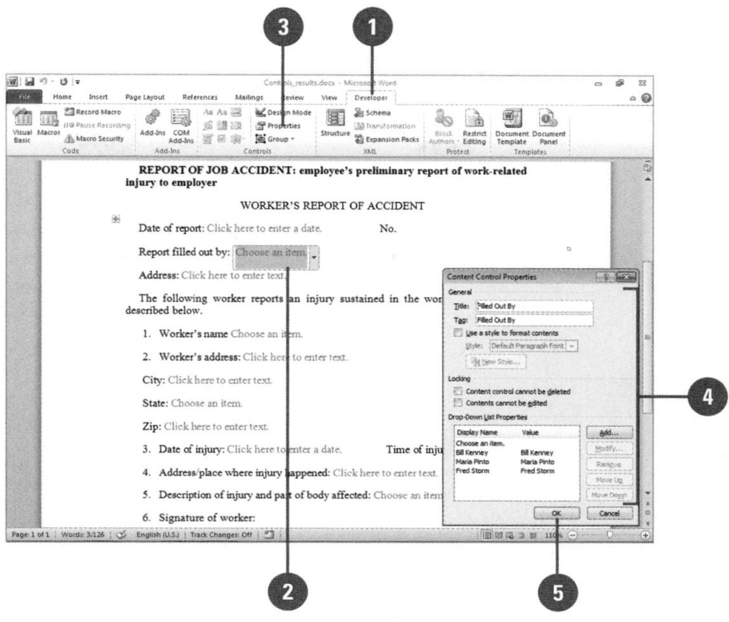

Did You Know?

You can prevent any changes to a document except content controls. Open the document with content controls, click the Developer tab, select the text you don't want to get changed, click the Group button, and then click Group. You can not change any of the grouped text. However, you can enter text or specify options using the content controls. To remove the protection, click the Group button, and then click Ungroup.

You can protect a form or document. Click the Restrict Editing button on the Developer tab, and then Restrict Formatting and Editing to prevent users of the form from being able to edit its content (not their answers, but the questions and choices themselves).

For Your Information

Mapping Content Controls to XML Data

You can map most content controls to elements in XML data attached to a document. XML data is stored in document parts using the Office XML file formats; for Word the XML file format is .docx. Document parts help define sections of the overall contents of the file. The file format consists of many different types of document parts, including custom XML data part. All document content associated with an XML element maps to data in a custom XML data part. This separation of the XML from the document formatting and layout—known as the Open Packaging Convention—makes it easier to access data. To view the document parts (which is a compressed zip package), add **.zip** to the end of the document name after the .docx, and then double-click the renamed file. The contents of the file appear, displaying a tree structure of individual document parts. You can move the custom.xml document part out of the zip file to open and modify it. You can attach the XML file to other Office documents to reuse data. When you're done changing the XML file, you can move it back into the zip file and use it with the original file.

Inserting ActiveX Controls

An ActiveX control is a software component that adds functionality to an existing program. An ActiveX control is really just another term for an OLE (Object Linking and Embedding) object, known as a Component Object Model (COM) object. An ActiveX control supports a customizable, programmatic interface. Word includes several pre-built ActiveX controls on the Developer tab, including a label, text box, command button, image, scroll bar, check box, option button, combo box, list box, and toggle button. To create an ActiveX control, click the Insert button on the Developer tab, click the ActiveX control you want, and then drag to insert it with the size you want. If there is a problem with an ActiveX control, Word disables it to protect the program and your data. When a problem does occur, a security alert dialog box appears, displaying information about the problem and options you can choose to leave it disabled in Protected view (**New!**) or enable it.

Insert ActiveX Controls

1. Display the document where you want to place the ActiveX control.
2. Click the **Developer** tab.
3. Click the **Design Mode** button (highlighted).
4. Click the **Legacy Tools** button arrow, and then click the button with the ActiveX control you want to use.

   See the next page for a list and description of each ActiveX control.
5. Drag (pointer changes to a plus sign) to draw the ActiveX control the size you want.
6. To resize the control, drag a resize handle (circles) to the size you want.
7. To add Visual Basic code to the ActiveX control, right-click the control, click **View Code**, or to change display properties, click the **Properties** button. To exit, click the **Save** and **Close** buttons.
8. Click the **Design Mode** button (not highlighted) to exit.

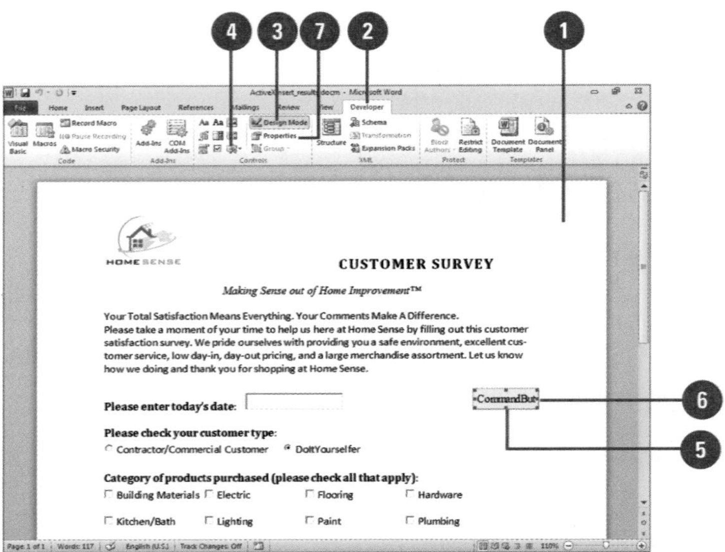

For Your Information

Using Form Controls

Form controls are objects that users can interact with to enter or manipulate data. For example, you can add a Check box control to your document so that users can turn an option on and off. You can select a control from the Developer tab and drag to create the control directly on your document just like an ActiveX control. For an example on using form controls, see project downloads for Office 2010 On Demand available on the Web at *www.perspection.com*.

Deal with an ActiveX Control Security Alert

1. Click the **File** tab, and then click **Open**.
2. Click the **File as type** list arrow, and then click the document type that contains the ActiveX control.
3. If the file is located in another folder, click the **Look in** list arrow, and then navigate to the file.
4. Click the document with the ActiveX control you want to open, and then click **Open**.
5. Click the **File** tab, click **Info**, click the **Enable Content** button (**New!**), and then click **Advanced Options**. To enable all content (make trusted), click **Enable All Content** on the menu.
   - You can also click **Enable Content** in the Message Bar with the Security Warning.
6. If you trust the document content, click the **Enable content for this session** option to use it. If you don't trust it, click the **Help protect me from unknown content (recommended)** option to block and disable the macros.
7. Click **OK**.

See Also

See "Setting ActiveX Security Options" on page 333 for more information about setting options that trigger the ActiveX security alert.

See "Setting ActiveX Control Properties" on page 425 for more information about setting ActiveX display properties.

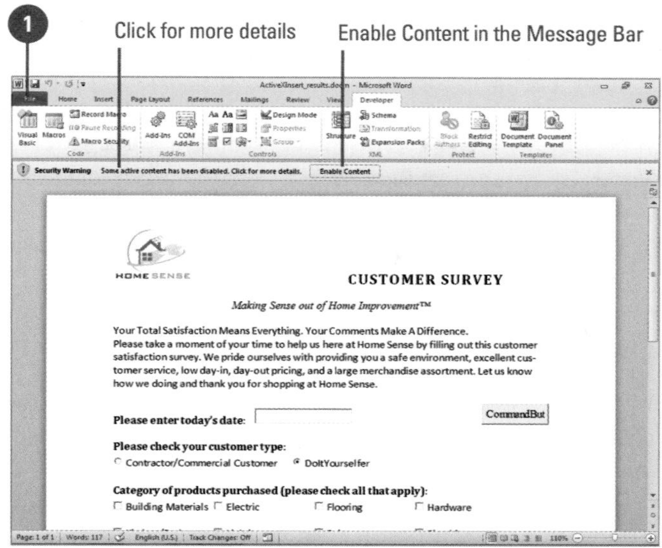

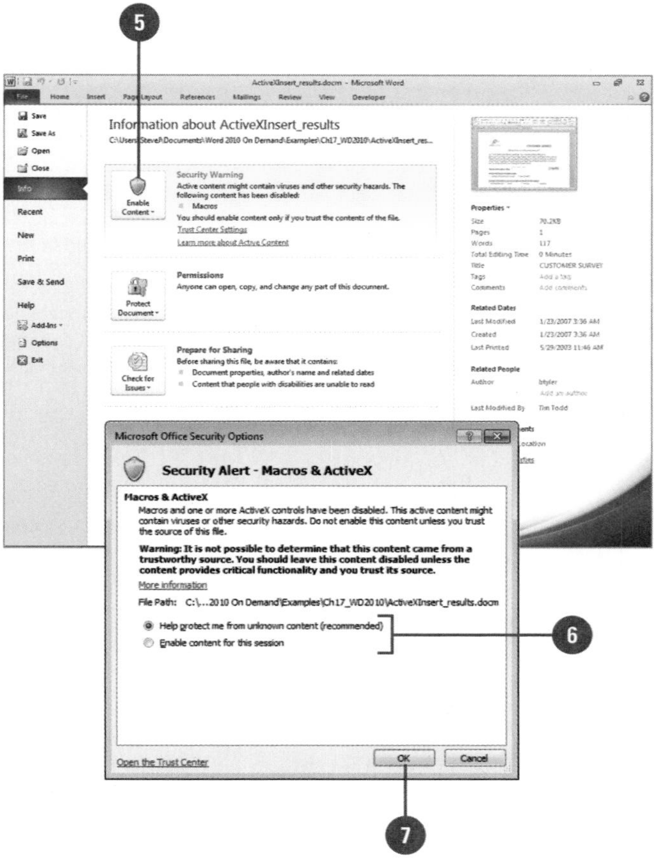

Using ActiveX Controls

ActiveX Controls		
Button	**Name**	**Description**
	Label	This button creates a text label. Because the other controls already include a corresponding label, use this button to create labels that are independent of other controls.
	Text Box	This button creates a text box in which the user can enter text (or numbers). Use this control for objects assigned to a text or number data type.
	Spin Button	This button creates a box in which the user can click arrows to increase or decrease numbers in a box. Use this control assigned to a number data type.
	Command Button	This button creates a button that runs a macro or Microsoft Visual Basic function when the user clicks the button in the form.
	Image	This button inserts a frame, in which you can insert a graphic in your form. Use this control when you want to insert a graphic, such as clip art or a logo.
	Scroll Bar	This button creates a scroll bar pane in which the user can enter text (or numbers) in a scrollable text box. Use this control for objects assigned to a text or number data type.
	Check Box	This button creates a check box that allows a user to make multiple yes or no selections. Use this control for fields assigned to the yes/no data type.
	Option Button	This button creates an option button (also known as a radio button) that allows the user to make a single selection from at least two choices. Use this control for fields assigned to the yes/no data type.
	Combo Box	This button creates a combo box in which the user has the option to enter text or select from a list of options. You can enter your own options in the list, or you can display options stored in another table.
	List Box	This button creates a list box that allows a user to select from a list of options. You can enter your own options in the list, or can have another table provide a list of options.
	Toggle Button	This button creates a button that allows the user to make a yes or no selection by clicking the toggle button. Use this control for fields assigned to the yes/no data type.
	More Controls	Click to display other controls, such as Adobe Acrobat Control for ActiveX, Microsoft Forms 2.0, Microsoft Office InfoPath controls, and Microsoft Web Browser.

Setting ActiveX Control Properties

Every ActiveX control has properties, or settings, that determine its appearance and function. You can open a property sheet that displays all the settings for that control in alphabetic or category order directly from Word. The ActiveX controls appear in the Properties window in two columns: the left column displays the name of the control, and the right column displays the current value or setting for the control. When you select either column, a list arrow appears in the right column, allowing you to select the setting you want. After you set properties, you can add VBA code to a module to make it perform.

Set ActiveX Control Properties

1. Click the **Developer** tab.
2. Click the **Design Mode** button (highlighted).
3. Select the control whose properties you want to modify.
4. Click the **Properties** button.
5. To switch controls, click the **Controls** list arrow (at the top), and then select the one you want.
6. Click the **Alphabetic** or **Categorized** tab to display the control properties so you can find the ones you want.
7. Click the property box for the property you want to modify, and then do one of the following:
   - Type the value or information you want to use, such as the control name.
   - If the property box contains a list arrow, click the arrow and then click a value in the list.
   - If a property box contains a dialog button (...), click it to open a dialog box to select options or insert an object, such as a picture.
8. When you're done, click the **Close** button on the Properties window.
9. Click the **Design Mode** button (not highlighted) to exit.

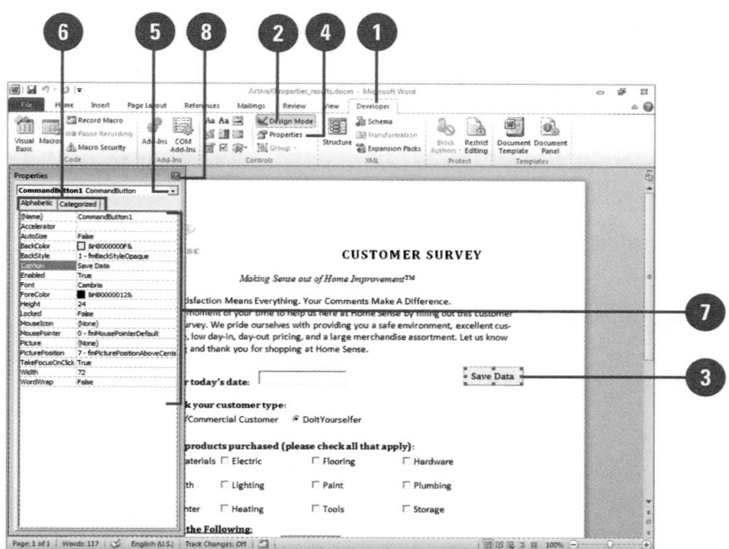

Adding VBA Code to an ActiveX Control

After you add controls and set properties, you can add VBA code to a module to determine how the controls respond to user actions. All controls have a predefined set of events. For example, a command button has a Click event that occurs when the user clicks the button. When you select a control in Design Mode and then click the View Code button, the Visual Basic Editor opens with a Code window, displaying the start of a procedure that runs when the event occurs. The top of the Code window displays the active object and event procedure. The Object list displays the ActiveX control, such as *CommandButton1*, and the Procedure list displays the trigger event, such as *Click*.

Add VBA Code to an ActiveX Control

1. Click the **Developer** tab.
2. Click the **Design Mode** button (highlighted).
3. Select the control to which you want to add VBA code.
4. Right-click the control, and then click **View Code**.

   The Visual Basic Editor window opens.
5. To show the Properties window, click the **Properties window** button.
6. To help with scripting commands, click the **Object Browser** button on the toolbar.
7. Click in the Code window between the beginning and ending line of the procedure, and then type VBA code to perform the task you want.

   The Object list is set to *CommandButton1*, and the Procedure list is set to *Click*.
8. When you're done, click the **Save** button on the toolbar.
9. Click the program **Close** button.
10. Click the **Design Mode** button (not highlighted) to exit.

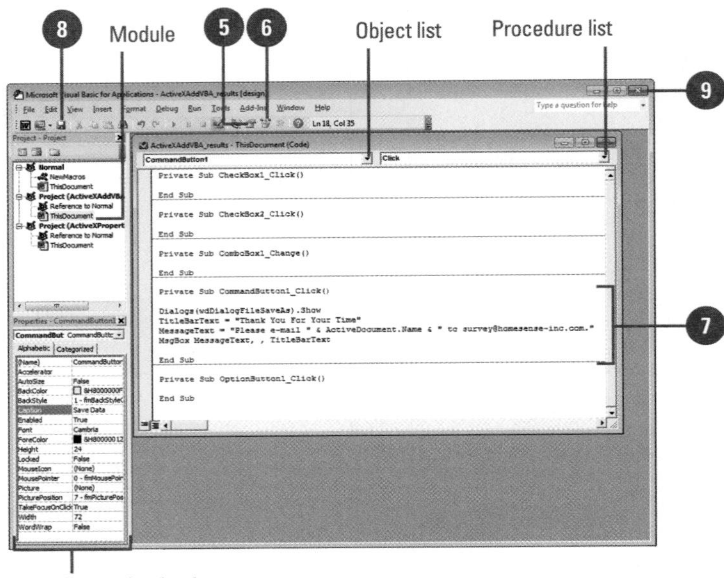

Playing a Movie Using an ActiveX Control

Although you cannot insert a Flash movie into an Word document, you can play one using an ActiveX control and the Flash player. Before you can use the control, the ActiveX control and Flash player need to be installed on your computer. You can get the ActiveX control at *http://activex.microsoft.com/activex/activex/*. To play the Flash (.swf) movie, you add the Shockwave Flash Object ActiveX control to the document and create a link to the file. If a movie doesn't play, check ActiveX security options in the Trust Center in Word Options.

Play a Flash Movie

1. Save the Flash file to a Flash movie file (.swf) using the Flash software.
2. Click the **Developer** tab.
3. Click the **Design Mode** button (highlighted).
4. Click the **Legacy Tools** button, and then click the **More Controls** button.
5. Click **Shockwave Flash Object**.
6. Click **OK**.
7. Drag to draw the movie control.
8. Right-click the Shockwave Flash Object, and then click **Properties**.
9. Click the **Alphabetic** tab.
10. Click the **Movie** property, click in the value column next to Movie, type full path and file name (c:\MyFolder\Movie.swf), or the URL to the Flash movie you want.
11. To set specific options, choose any of the following:
    - To play the file automatically when the document appears, set the Playing property to True.
    - To embed the Flash file, set the EmbedMovie property to True.
12. When you're done, click the **Close** button.
13. Click the **Design Mode** button (not highlighted) to exit.

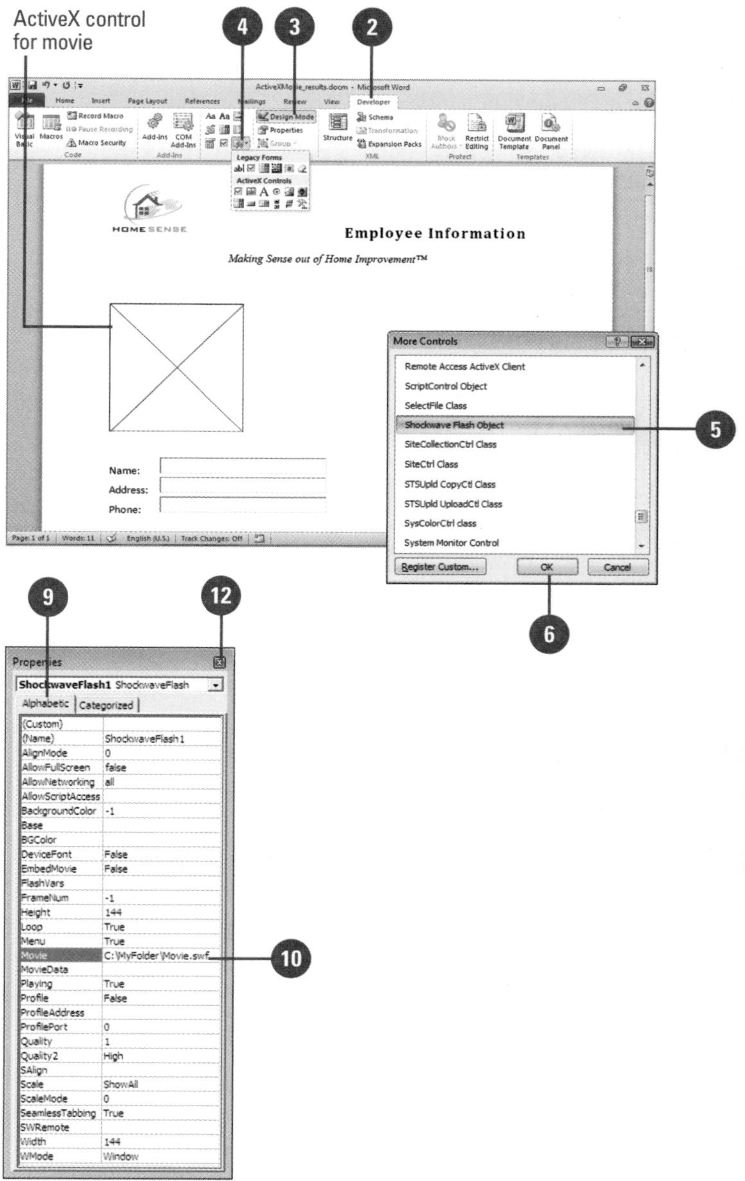

Changing the Document Information Panel

The Document Information Panel helps you manage and track document property information—also known as metadata—such as title, author, subject, keywords, category, and status. The Document Information Panel displays an XML-based mini-form using an InfoPath Form Template (.xsn) file developed in Microsoft InfoPath. By using an XML InfoPath form, you can create your own form templates to edit the document property data and perform data validation.

Select a Document Information Panel Template

1. Click the **Developer** tab.
2. Click the **Document Panel** button.
3. Click **Browse**, locate and select the custom template you want, and then click **Open**.
   - **URL.** Short for Uniform Resource Locator. The address of resources on the Web.

     http://www.perspection.com/index.htm
   - **UNC.** Short for Uniform or Universal Naming Convention. A format for specifying the location of resources on a local-area network (LAN).

     \\server-name\shared-resource-pathname
   - **URN.** Short for Uniform Resource Name.
4. Click the **Display by default** list arrow, and then select the default properties you want.
5. Select the **Always show Document Information Panel on document open and initial save** check box.
6. Click **OK**.

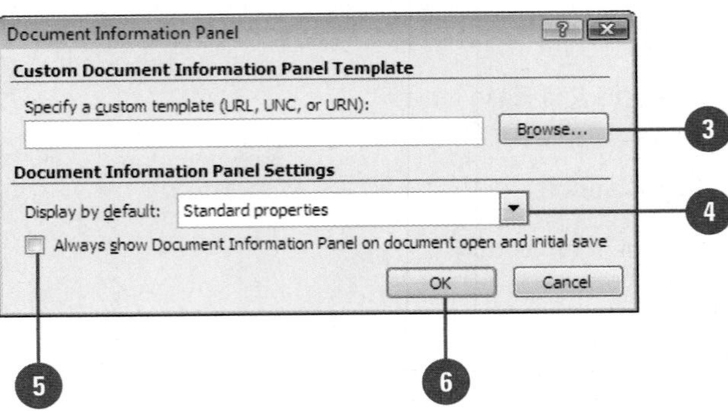

Working Together on Office Documents

18

Introduction

Instead of storing and working on Office documents on your desktop, you can store them on the Web and work on them with an Office Web App. An Office Web App allows you to work with an Office document in a browser. The process of using the Web instead of a desktop as a base of operation is known as cloud computing.

Windows Live is a cloud computing Web site, where you can store and share information, such as contacts, e-mail (using hotmail), photos, and files. Windows Live is a free service provided by Microsoft, which is available at *www.live.com* with a Windows Live ID.

When you store an Office document on the Windows Live SkyDrive or on a Microsoft SharePoint server configured with Office Web Apps, you can view or edit the document in a browser using the same look and feel as an Office 2010 program. To make storing files on the SkyDrive quick and easy, Office 2010 programs provide a Save to Web command on the Save & Send screen on the File tab for you to save Office documents directly to a SkyDrive folder.

If you have access to a SharePoint server, you can save documents directly to the site from your Office program, in a similar way that you save documents on your hard disk. With Microsoft SharePoint Workspace, a program that comes along with your Office programs, you can create your own personal copy of a SharePoint server so you can access it whether or not you are connected to your network. In addition to SharePoint, you can also connect to a Groove workspace, or create a shared folder in Windows.

If you have a Windows Mobile 6.5 phone, you can use Office Mobile 2010 to work with your files from anywhere. If you have a touch screen device, you can intuitively scroll through menus and navigation documents.

What You'll Do

Getting Started with Office Web Apps

Introduction

Any Office document that resides on Windows Live or a SharePoint server can be accessed from any computer that has an Internet connection and browser using an Office Web App (**New!**). Office Web Apps work in a variety of browsers, including Internet Explorer, Firefox, and Safari for the Macintosh, and are compatible with most operating systems. This means you can also view Office documents using other web-enabled devices, such as smartphones or PDAs. An Office Web App provides a subset of the features in the desktop version. For example, in the Excel Web App, you can apply standard formatting, such as fonts, fills, and borders, but you can't apply more sophisticated formatting, such as table styles, cell styles, and conditional formatting.

You can use an Office Web App in your browser on Windows Live or a SharePoint server with Office Web Apps installed. Windows Live is a Web site with Office Web Apps already installed, where you can store and share information, such as contacts, e-mail (using hotmail), photos, and files. Windows Live provides drive space, called a **SkyDrive**, for you to store files and photos in a folder, just like your computer drive, where others with permission can access them using a browser.

Understanding File Compatibility

Before you get started working with Office Web Apps, it's important to note that the Office Web Apps aren't fully compatible with all types of Office documents. If you want to edit an Office document with an Office Web App, you need to use the Office Open XML file format. This includes the Office 2007 or Office 2010 or Windows or Office 2008 for Mac. If you want to view an Office document with an Office Web App, you need to use the Office 97 or later file format.

When you edit or view an Office document with an Office Web App, the file format doesn't change or affect the content of the file. In other words, you can upload an Office file to the Web, make changes using an Office Web App, download the file back to your desktop, and then make changes to it using your desktop Office App without any problems. This is called **roundtripping**. Any unsupported features in the Office Web App doesn't affect the Office file during a roundtrip.

Viewing the Office Web App Interface

Each Office Web App comes with a scaled-down version of the desktop Ribbon and Quick Access Toolbar. The Web Apps Ribbon typically comes with a File tab, Home tab, and Insert tab. Within each tab, you get a subset of commands on the desktop Ribbon. There are no contextual tabs in the Office Web Apps. The Quick Access Toolbar appears above the Ribbon and contains just the Undo and Redo buttons. The content area for each of the Office Web Apps is similar to the desktop version.

Preparing to Use Office Web Apps

Before you can use an Office Web App on the Web, you need a Web browser with the Microsoft Silverlight browser add-in and have access to a Windows Live account or SharePoint 2010 site user account.

Office Web Apps support the following browsers: Internet Explorer 7 and 8 or Firefox 3.5 running on Windows 7, Windows Vista, or Windows XP, and Firefox 3.5 or Safari 4 running on Mac OS X 10.4 or later. You can also use the iPhone's Mobile Safari browser. If you use another browser, such as Google Chrome, it doesn't mean you can't use it with an Office Web App; it's just not officially supported as of yet. Give it time.

Windows Live is a Web site, where you can store and share information, such as contacts, e-mail (using hotmail), photos, and files. Windows Live is a free service provided by Microsoft, which is available at *www.live.com* with a Windows Live ID.

You can improve the performance of the Office Web Apps by installing Microsoft Silverlight. This is a cross-platform browser add-in that takes some of the processing burden off the server and puts it locally on your browser and provides powerful tools and controls for developers of Web applications. The Silverlight add-in works on all supported browsers and the following operating systems: Windows 7, Windows Vista, Windows XP (Service Pack 2 or later), Windows 2000 (Service Pack 4 or later), Windows Server 208, Mac OS X 10.4.8 or later, Linux, FreeBSD, and Solaris OS.

Using Office Desktop and Web Apps

When you're working in an Office Desktop App and want to save a document to your SkyDrive, you can use the Save to Web command on the Save & Send screen on the File tab to save Office documents directly to a SkyDrive folder using a Windows Live account. Once the Office documents are stored on the SkyDrive, or a Microsoft SharePoint server as another option, you can view or edit them in a browser using a Microsoft Office Web App, which is installed and provided by Windows Live.

An Office Web App provides a subset of the features in the desktop version. For example, in the Word Web App, you can apply standard formatting, such as fonts, paragraphs, and styles, but you can't apply more sophisticated formatting, such as text effects and conditional formatting.

When you're working in an Office Web App, and want to switch to your desktop Office App, you can use the Open in <Program> button (such as Open in Word) on the Home tab to close the document in the Office Web App and reopen it in the desktop version.

Setting Up to Use Office Web Apps

Before you can use an Office Web App on the Web in your browser, you need to create a Windows Live account. Windows Live is a Web site, where you can store and share information, such as contacts, e-mail (using hotmail), photos, and files. Windows Live is a free service provided by Microsoft, which is available at *www.live.com* with a Windows Live ID. If you already have a Hotmail, Messenger, or Xbox LIVE account, you already have a Windows Live ID. In addition to your browser, you can improve the performance of Office Web Apps by installing Microsoft Silverlight (**New!**). This is a cross-platform browser add-in that takes some of the processing burden off the server and puts it locally on your browser and provides powerful tools and controls for developers of Web applications.

Set Up a Windows Live Account

1. Open your browser, and then go to *https://signup.live.com*.
2. If you already have a Hotmail, Messenger, or Xbox LIVE account, click the **Sign in** link. You already have a Windows Live ID. Use your e-mail address, and password to complete the sign in.
3. Enter the information required for the Windows Live ID.
   - **E-mail address.** Use your own e-mail address or click the **Or get a Windows Live e-mail address** link to get a free e-mail address.
   - **Password.** Enter a password with at least 6-characters; the password is case sensitive (meaning upper- and lower-case sensitive).
   - **Personal Info.** Enter your name, location, gender, and birth year.
   - **Characters.** Enter the characters in the preview box for security purposes.
4. Click the **I accept** button.

   Windows Live creates an ID for you.

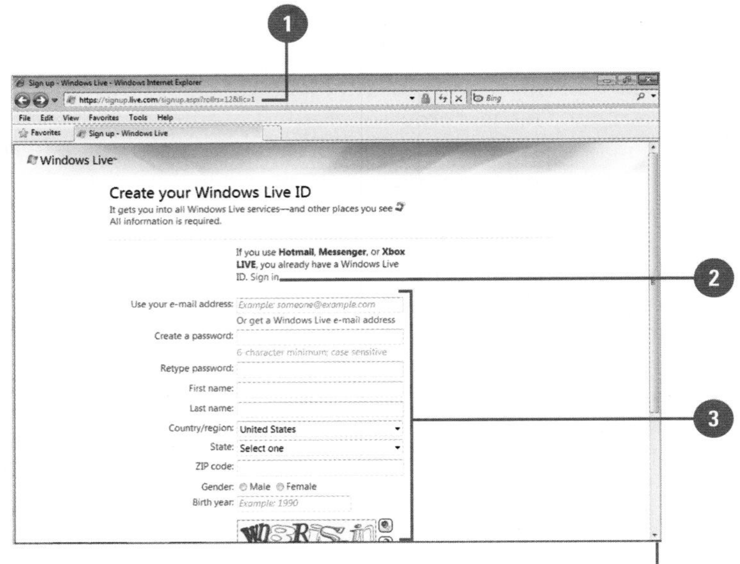

Sign in to Windows Live

1. Open your browser, and go to *www.live.com.*
2. Enter your Windows Live ID and password.
3. Select the **Remember me** and/or **Remember my password** check boxes to speed up sign in process in the future. However, it opens the door for others who have access to your computer to sign in.
4. Click **Sign in**.

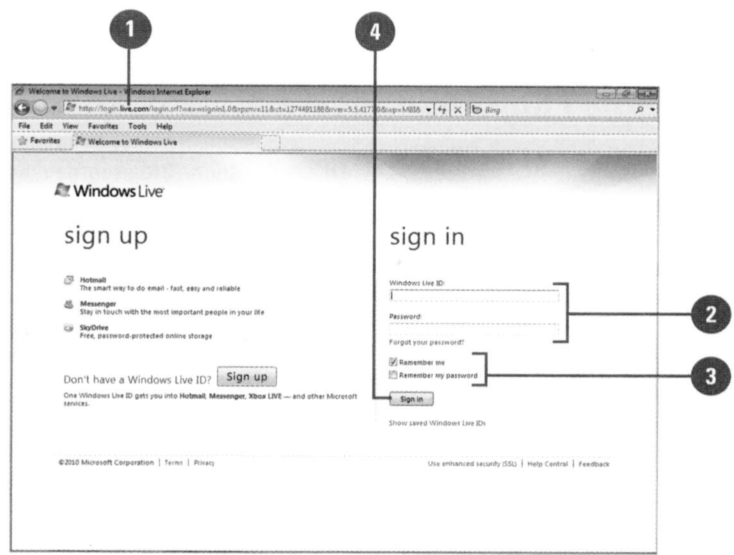

Install Microsoft Silverlight

1. Open your browser, and go to *www.microsoft.com/ silverlight/.*
2. Click the **Download Silverlight** link, and then click any additional links to start the download and install for the browser plug-in.
   - Microsoft checks your computer to determine if Silverlight is installed, and if so, what version. It's important to get the latest version.
3. When prompted, run the installer; options vary depending on your browser.
4. Click **Install now**, and then step through the installation steps to complete the process; steps vary depending on your browser.
5. Upon completion, click **Close**, and then restart your browser.

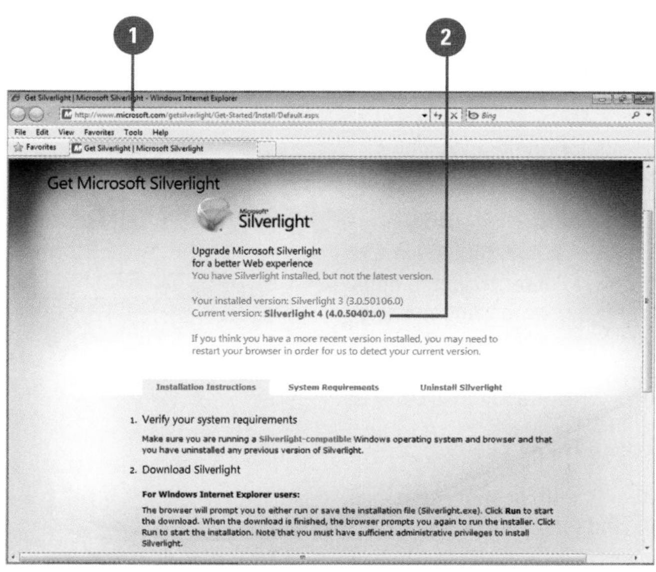

Saving and Opening Documents with Windows Live

Windows Live is a Web site, where you can store and share information, such as contacts, e-mail (using hotmail), photos, and files. Windows Live is a free service provided by Microsoft. Windows Live provides drive space, called a SkyDrive, for you to store files and photos in a folder, just like your computer drive, where others with permission can access them using a browser. To make storing files on the SkyDrive quick and easy, Office 2010 programs provide a Save to Web command (**New!**) on the Save & Send screen for you to save Office documents directly to a SkyDrive folder (**New!**) using a Windows Live account. Once the Office documents are stored on the SkyDrive, or a Microsoft SharePoint server as another option, you can view or edit them in a browser using a Microsoft Office Web App (**New!**), which is installed and provided by Windows Live.

Save an Office Document to Windows Live

1. In an Office Desktop App, open the document you want to save to the Web.
2. Click the **File** tab, click **Save & Send**, and then click **Save to Web**.
3. If necessary, click the **Sign In** button, enter your Windows Live ID e-mail address and password, and then click **OK**.
4. Select a folder on the Windows Live Web site, either a personal or shared folder.
   - To create a new folder, click the **New Folder** button to open your browser to Windows Live, type a name, select a Share with location, click **Next**, and then complete the instructions.
5. Click the **Save As** button.
6. Use the default location, specify a name, and then click **Save**.
7. To open Windows Live Web site, click the **Windows Live** link.

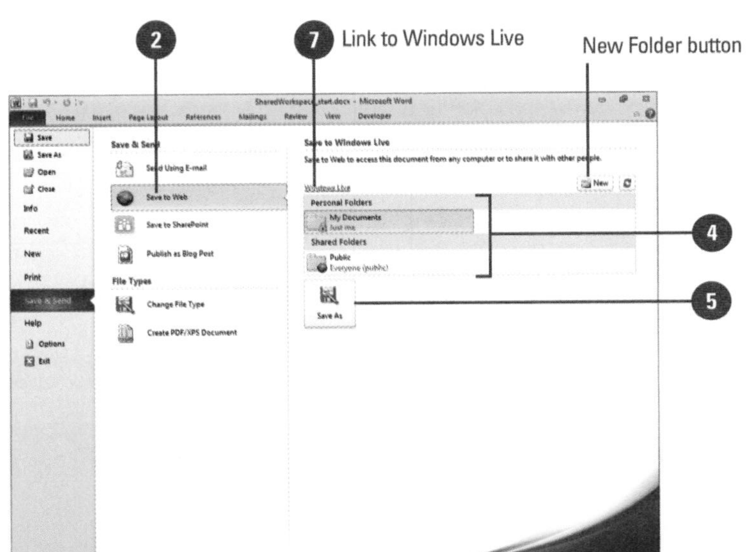

Open an Office Document Directly from Windows Live

1. In an Office Desktop App, click the **File** tab, and then click **Open**.
   - To access a recently used file stored on Windows Live, click the **File** tab, click **Recent**, and then click the recent file or recent folder to open it.
2. Navigate to the Windows Live SkyDrive.
3. Select the file you want to open.
4. Click **Open**.
5. If necessary, enter your Windows Live ID e-mail address and password, and then click **OK**.

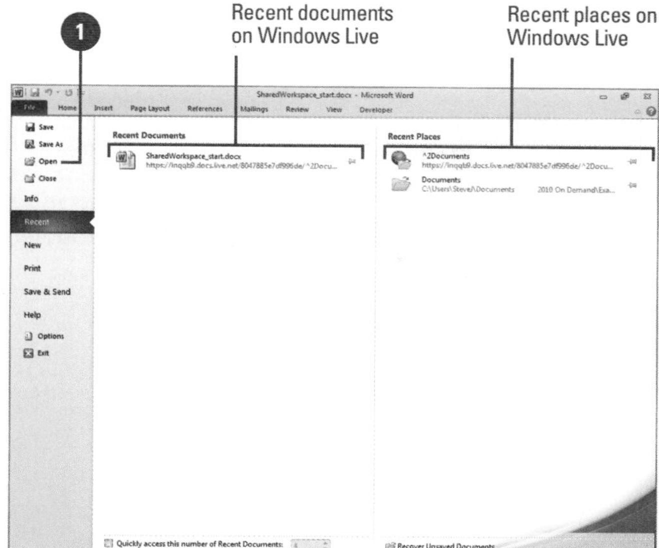

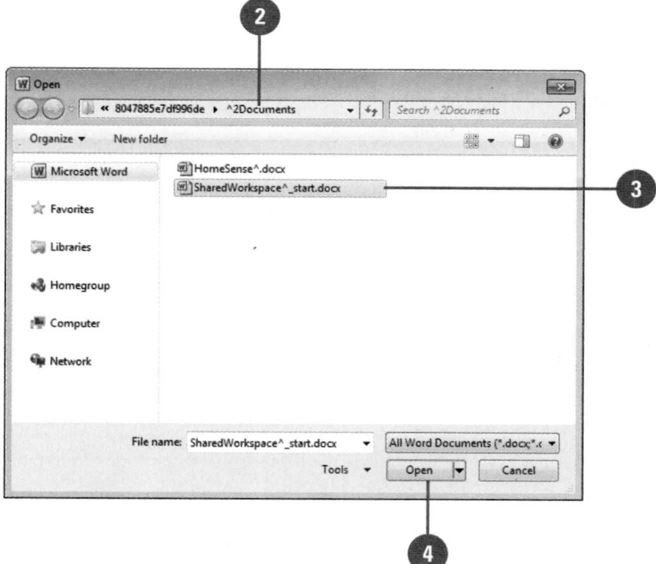

Comparing the Desktop App to Web App

Each Office Web App (**New!**) comes with a scaled-down version of the desktop Ribbon and Quick Access Toolbar. The Web Apps Ribbon typically comes with a File tab, Home tab, and Insert tab. Within each tab, you get a subset of commands on the desktop Ribbon.

There are no contextual tabs in the Office Web Apps. The Quick Access Toolbar appears above the Ribbon and contains just the Undo and Redo buttons. The content area for each of the Office Web Apps is similar to the desktop version.

Desktop App

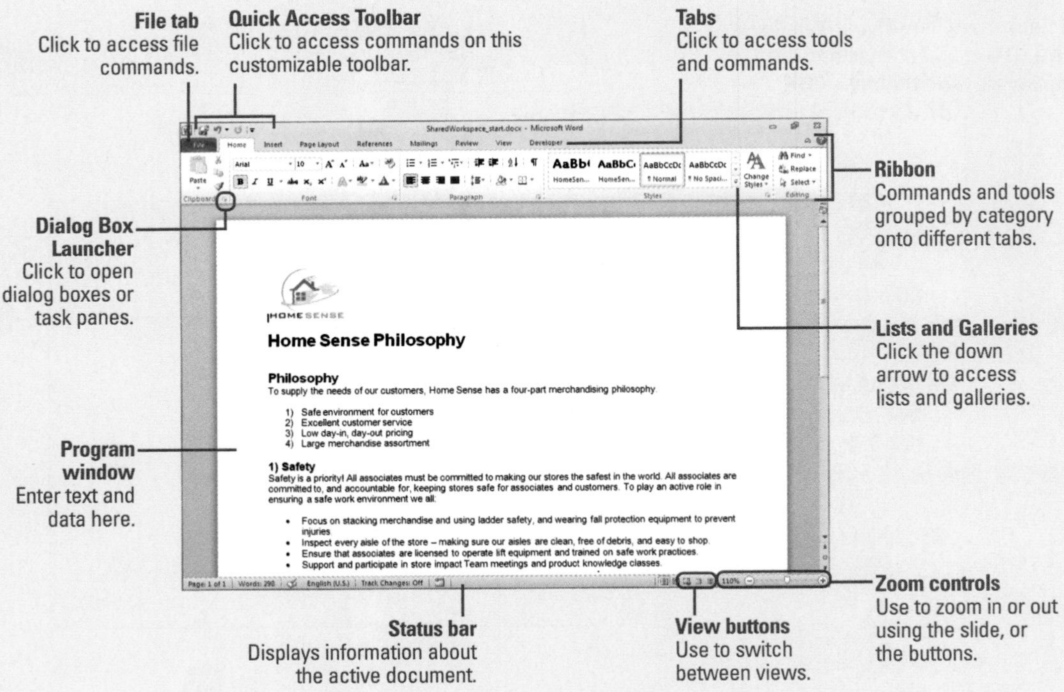

Web App (Edit in Browser)

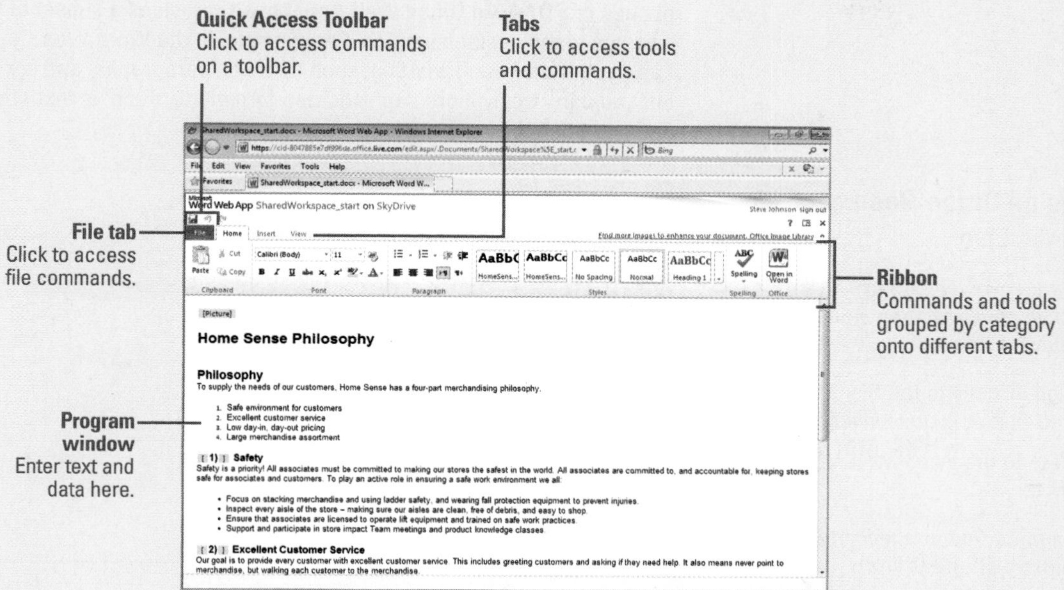

Web App (View in Browser)

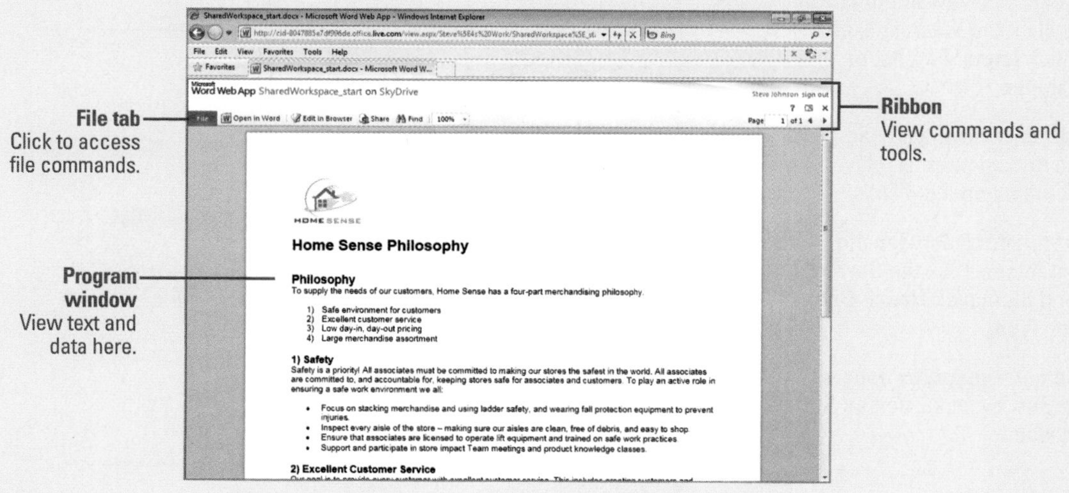

Accessing Documents on Windows Live

Any Office document that resides on Windows Live or a SharePoint server can be accessed from any computer that has an Internet connection. Office Web Apps (**New!**) work in a variety of browsers, including Internet Explorer, Firefox, and Safari for the Macintosh, and are compatible with most operating systems. This means you can also view Office documents using other web-enabled devices, such as smartphones or PDAs. An Office Web App (**New!**) provides a subset of the features in the desktop version. For example, in the Word Web App, you can apply standard formatting, such as fonts, paragraphs, and styles, but you can't apply more sophisticated formatting, such as text effects and conditional formatting.

Browse to an Office Document on Windows Live

1. Open your browser, go to *www.live.com*, and then sign in to Windows Live.
   - To go directly to the SkyDrive, go to *http://skydrive.live.com*.
2. Navigate to the Windows Live SkyDrive.
3. Click a folder icon to navigate to the folder with the Office document.
4. To navigate back to a previous location, click a navigation link.
5. To change the view in the current folder, click the **View:** link, and then click **Icons**, **Details**, or **Thumbnails**.
   - In Details view, you can point to a document to display document specific links.
6. To sort the documents in the current folder, click the **Sort by:** link, and then click **Name**, **Date**, **Size**, or **Type**.
   - The current sort by appears in the Sort by: link, such as Sort by: Name.

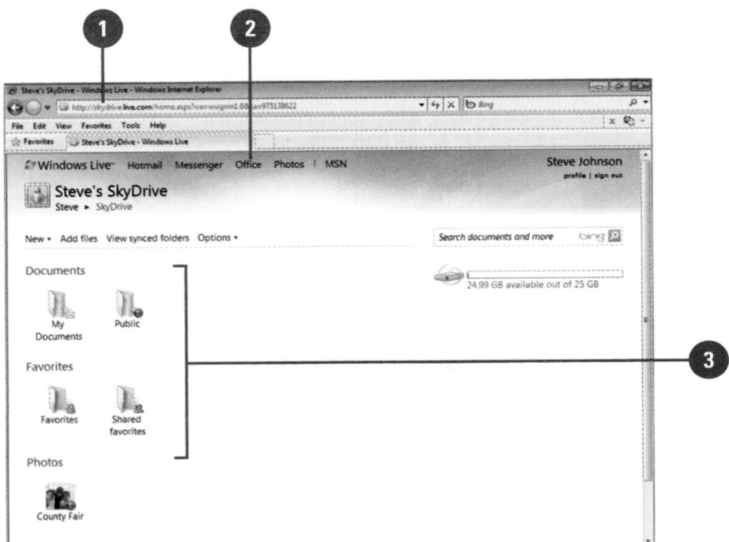

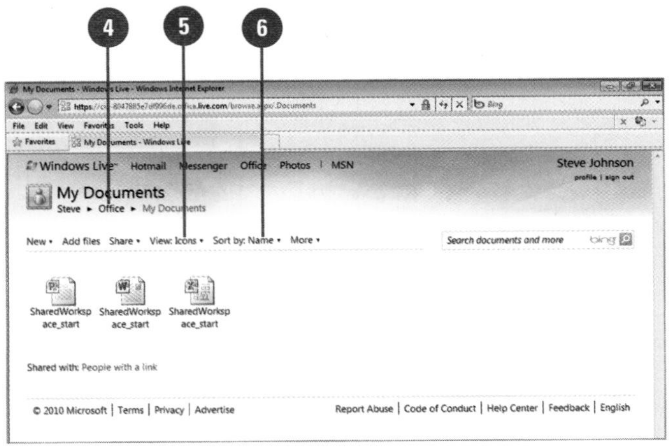

Open an Office Document in a Browser on Windows Live

1. Open your browser, go to *www.live.com*, and then sign in to Windows Live.

   - To go directly to the SkyDrive, go to *http://skydrive.live.com.*

2. Navigate to the Windows Live SkyDrive.

3. Click a folder icon to navigate to the folder with the Office document you want to open.

4. Click the Office document icon.

   - In Details view, you can point to a document, and then click the **Edit in Browser** link.

   The Office Web App opens in view mode, where you can edit it in your browser or open it in the Office Desktop App.

5. Click the **Edit in Browser** button.

6. Use the Ribbon tabs to make changes to the Office document; any changes in an Office Web App are automatically saved.

7. To close the Office document online, use any of the following:

   - **Close document.** Click the **File** tab, and then click **Close**.
   - **Close document and switch to the Office Desktop App.** Click the **File** tab, and then click **Open in <Program>**.
     - You can also click the **Open in <Program>** button on the Home tab.

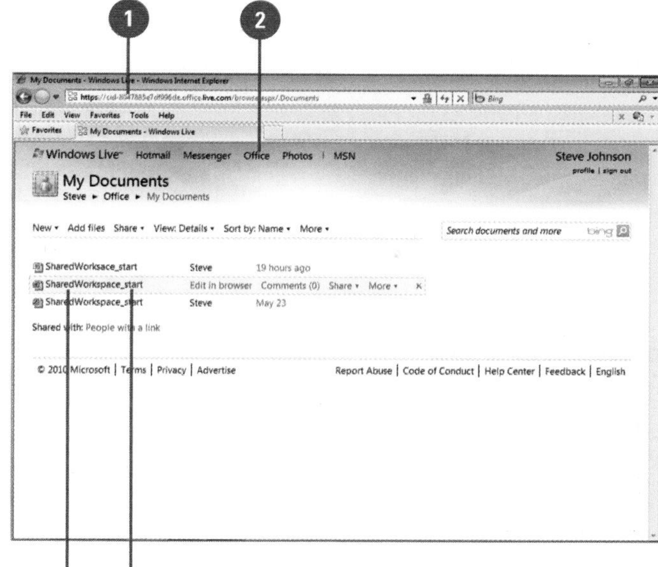

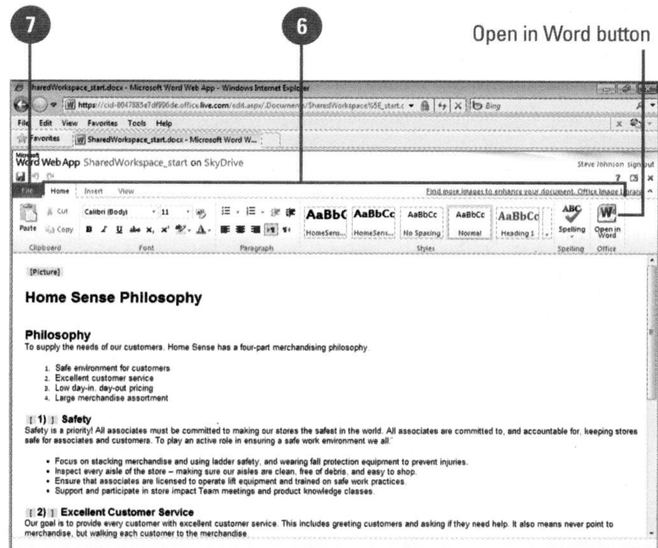

Working with Folders on Windows Live

The SkyDrive on Windows Lives comes with four default folders: My Documents, Favorites, Shared Favorites, and Public. The My Documents and Public folders store documents, while the Favorites and Shared Favorites folders store links to Web sites. The My Documents and Favorites folders are private for your eyes only, while the Shared Favorites and Public folders are viewable by everyone in your Windows Live network. If you want to share your documents with others, then add or move them to the Public folder. Instead of using the default folders, you can create and use your own and then specify permissions for access. If you no longer need a folder, you can delete it. You cannot rename a default folder, however, you can rename the ones you create.

Create a SkyDrive Folder

1. Open your browser, go to *www.live.com*, and then sign in to Windows Live.
   - To go directly to the SkyDrive, go to *http://skydrive.live.com*.
2. Navigate to the Windows Live SkyDrive.
3. Click a folder icon to navigate to the folder where you want to create a folder.
4. Click the **New** link, and then click **Folder**.
5. Type a name for the folder.
6. To change the share permissions, click the **Share with** link, select an option: **Everyone (public), My friends and their friends, Friends, Some friends, Just me**, or **Add Specific people**.
7. Click **Next**.

   The new folder opens.
8. To add files to the new folder, click the **Add files** link, drag or select the you want, and then click **Continue**.

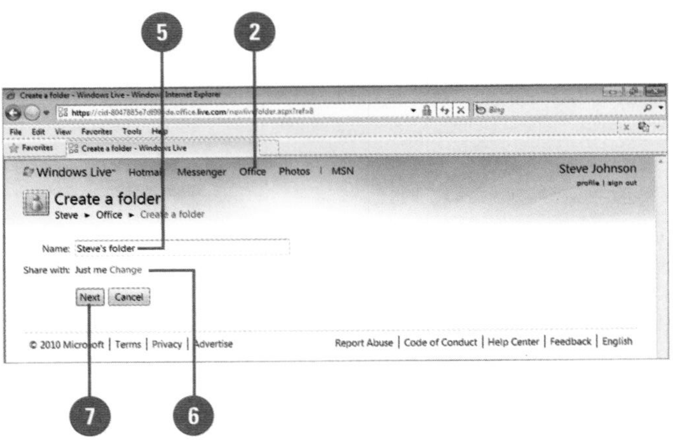

Added file

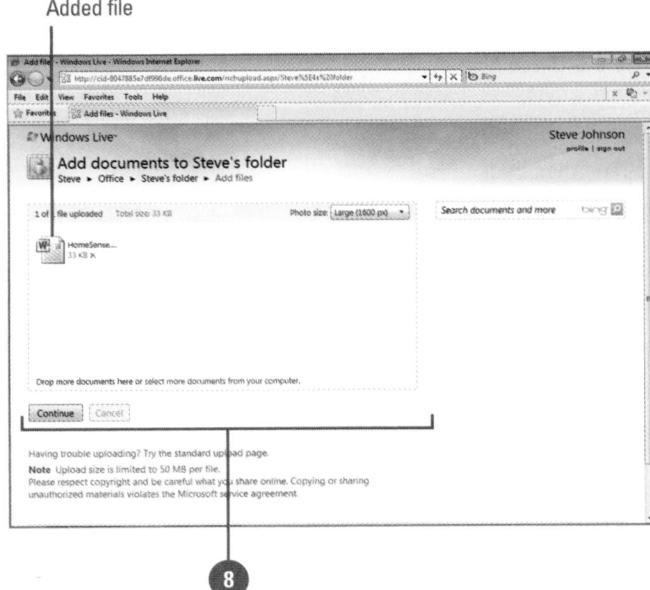

Rename a SkyDrive Folder

1. Open your browser, go to *www.live.com*, and then sign in to Windows Live.
   - To go directly to the SkyDrive, go to *http://skydrive.live.com.*
2. Navigate to the Windows Live SkyDrive.
3. Click a folder icon to navigate to the folder you want to rename.
4. Click the **More** link, and then click **Rename**.
5. Enter a new name for the folder.
6. Click **Save**.

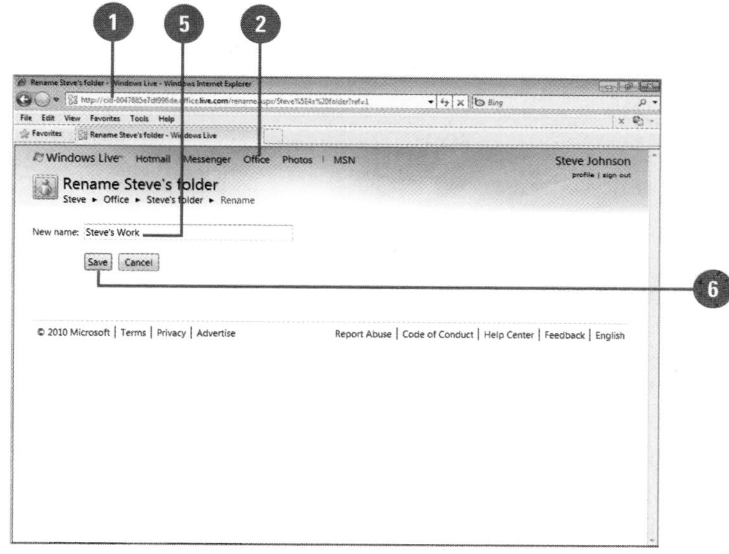

Delete a SkyDrive Folder

1. Open your browser, go to *www.live.com*, and then sign in to Windows Live.
   - To go directly to the SkyDrive, go to *http://skydrive.live.com.*
2. Navigate to the Windows Live SkyDrive.
3. Click a folder icon to navigate to the folder you want to delete.
4. Click the **More** link, and then click **Delete**.
5. Click **OK** to confirm the deletion of the folder and all of its contents.

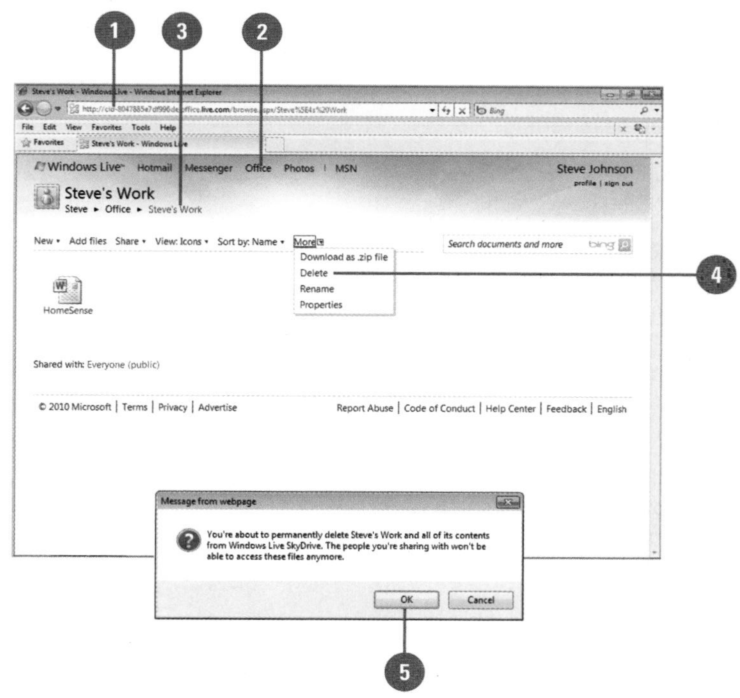

Setting Folder Permissions on Windows Live

Permissions are special properties applied to a folder that allows access to specified groups of people. You can set folder permissions that allow everyone to access a folder, a specified network of people to access a folder, or individuals to access a folder. If you want to set permissions for a group of users, you can create a user category, and then set the permissions you want. You can assign two levels of permissions, either Can Add, Edit Details, and Delete Files or Can View Files.

Edit Permissions on a SkyDrive Folder

1. Open your browser, go to *www.live.com*, and then sign in to Windows Live.
   - To go directly to the SkyDrive, go to *http://skydrive.live.com*.
2. Navigate to the Windows Live SkyDrive.
3. Click a folder icon to navigate to the folder where you want to change permissions.
4. Click the **Share** link, and then click **Edit permissions**.
5. To clear current settings, click the **Clear these settings** link
6. Drag the slider to any of the following permissions:
   - **Everyone (public).** Select to allows everyone access to this public folder.
   - **My friends and their friends, Friends, Some Friends, or Just me.** Select to allow specific groups to access this folder.
7. Click the **Permission Level** list arrow, and then click **Can view files** or **Can add, edit details, and delete files**.
8. To allow individual user, specify a name, e-mail address or select a contact, and then press Enter.
9. Click **Save**.

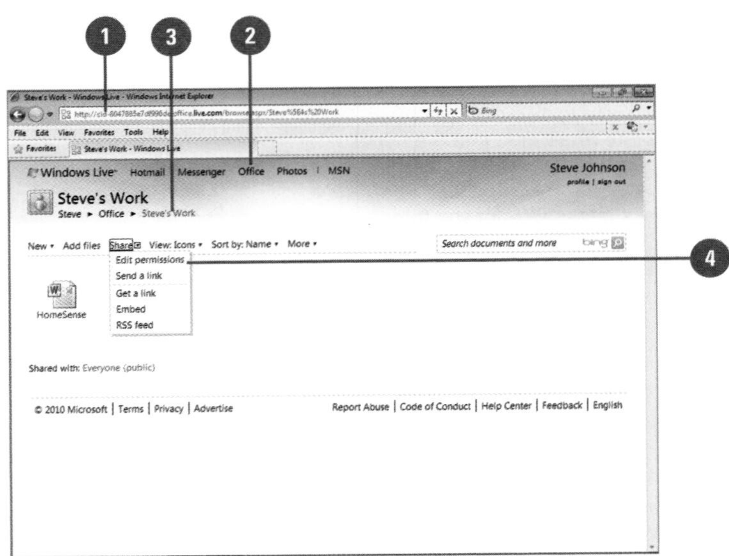

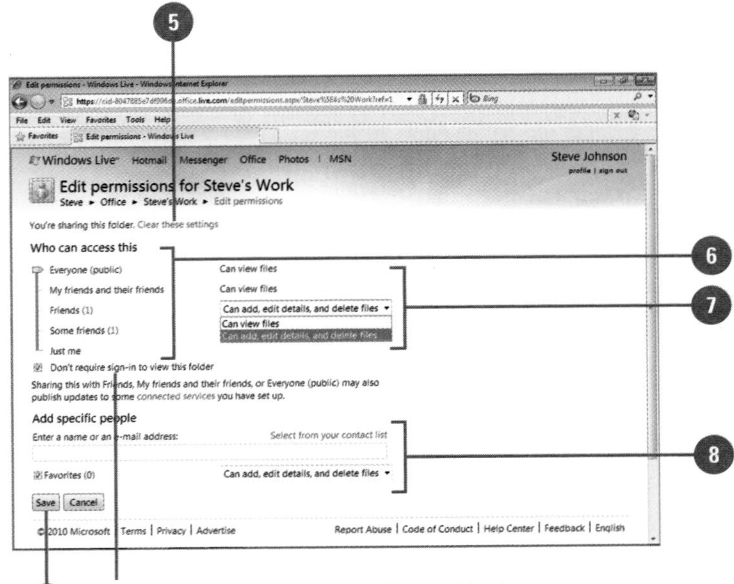

Select to not require sign-in to Windows Live for access

Creating Office Documents on Windows Live

When you're working on Windows Live, you create a new Office document (**New!**). You can create an Excel workbook, a PowerPoint presentation, a Word document, or an OneNote notebook. This option allows you to create a new Office document on a computer that doesn't have the Microsoft Office software. So, if you're working on a different computer while you're on the road that doesn't have the Office programs installed and you need to create a new document to get some work done, you can do it online at Windows Live.

Create Office Documents on a SkyDrive Folder

1. Open your browser, go to *www.live.com*, and then sign in to Windows Live.
   - To go directly to the SkyDrive, go to *http://skydrive.live.com.*
2. Navigate to the Windows Live SkyDrive.
3. Click a folder icon to navigate to the folder where you want to create an Office document.
4. Click the **New** link, and then click a document option:
   - **Word document.**
   - **Excel workbook.**
   - **PowerPoint presentation.**
   - **OneNote notebook.**
5. Type a name for the document.
6. Click **Save**.

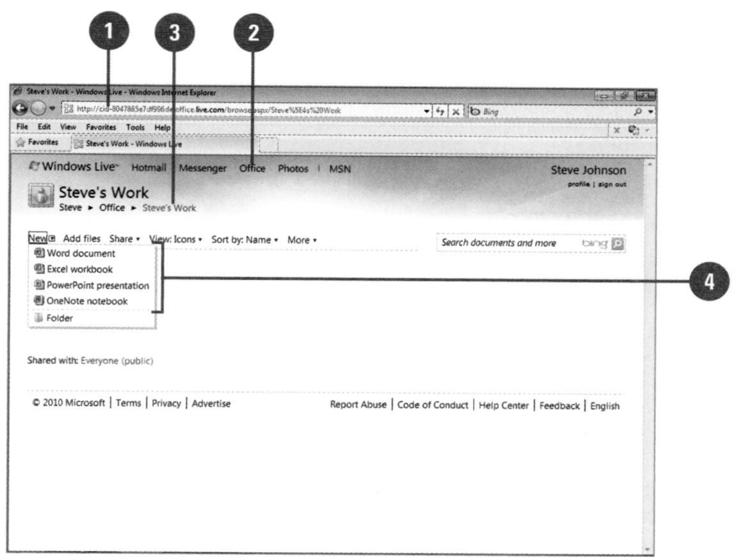

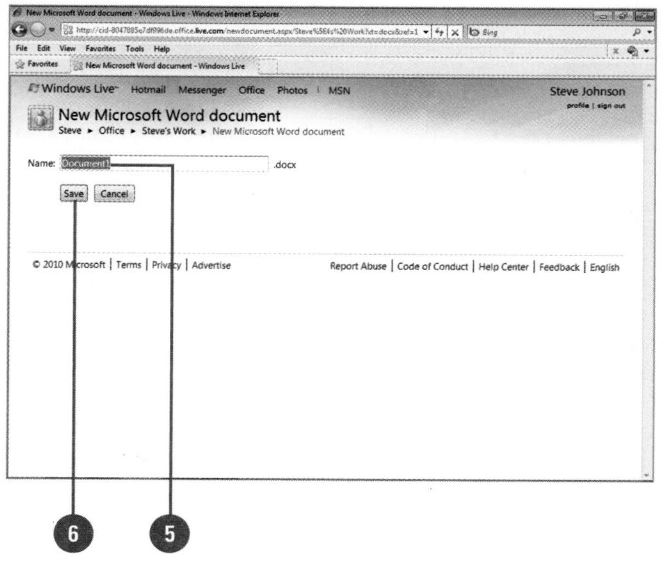

Working with Documents on Windows Live

When you're working on Windows Live, you can add files to a SkyDrive folder. You can add files from your computer drive by using the Add files link or while you create a new folder. You can add files from your computer by using two methods: (1) by dragging files from Windows Explorer (with the Windows Explorer and your browser window side by side) or (2) by using the Select files from your computer link. Once a document is stored on Windows Live, you can copy, move, or rename the file. If you no longer need the document, you can delete it to save space.

Add Files to a SkyDrive Folder

1. Open your browser, go to *www.live.com*, and then sign in to Windows Live.
   - To go directly to the SkyDrive, go to *http://skydrive.live.com*.
2. Navigate to the Windows Live SkyDrive.
3. Click a folder icon to navigate to the folder where you want to add files.
4. Click the **Add files** link.
5. Drag files from Windows Explorer to the selected area, or click the **Select documents from your computer** link, select the files to upload, and then click **Open**.
6. Click **Continue**.

See Also

See "Saving and Opening Documents with Windows Live" on page 434 for more information on saving documents to Windows Live from the Office Desktop App.

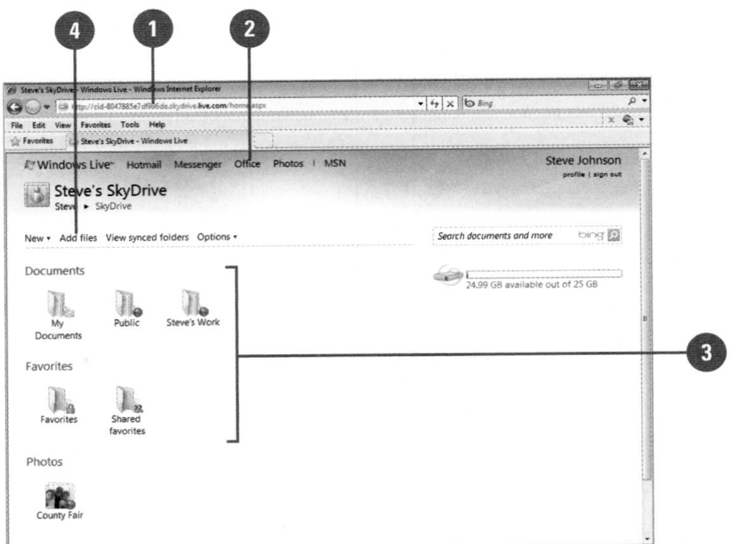

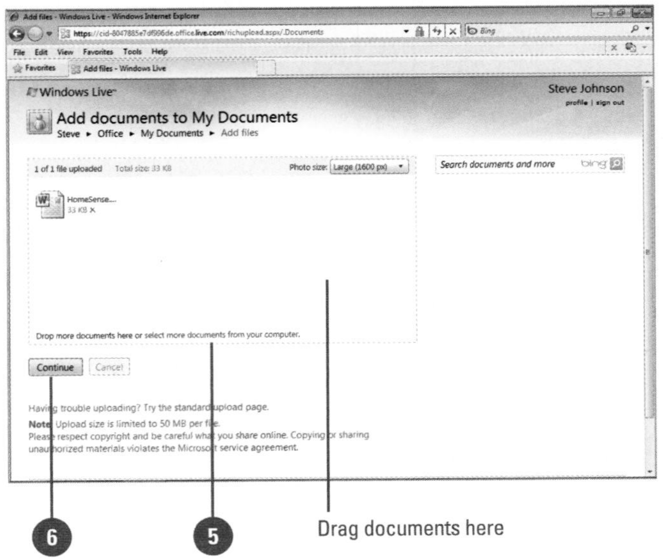

Copy, Move, Rename a Document

1. Open your browser, go to *www.live.com*, and then sign in to Windows Live.
2. Navigate to the Windows Live SkyDrive.
3. Click a folder icon to navigate to the document.
4. In Details view, point to the document you want, click the **More** link, and then use any of the following:
   - **Move.** Click **Move**, click a folder, and then click **Move this file into *foldername*.**
   - **Copy.** Click **Copy**, click a folder, and then click **Copy this file into *foldername*.**
   - **Rename.** Click **Rename**, enter a new name, and then click **Save**.

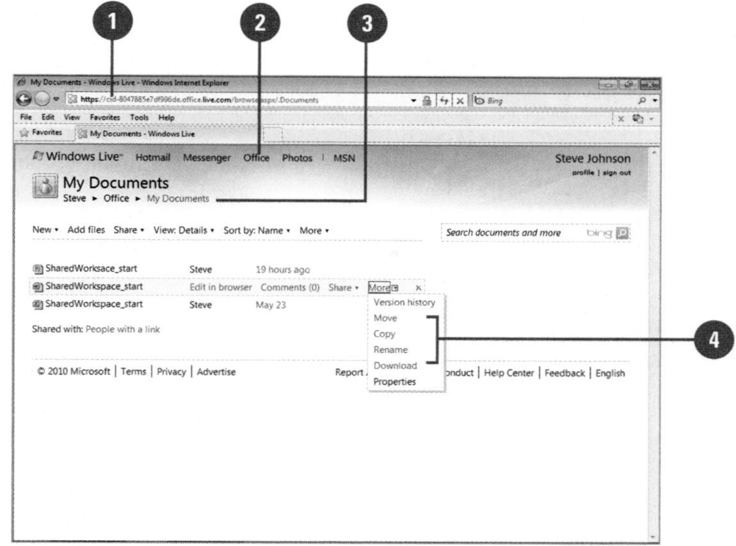

Delete a Document

1. Open your browser, go to *www.live.com*, and then sign in to Windows Live.
2. Navigate to the Windows Live SkyDrive.
3. Click a folder icon to navigate to the document you want to delete.
4. In Details view, point to the document you want to delete, and then click the **Delete** link.
5. Click **OK** to confirm the deletion of the file.

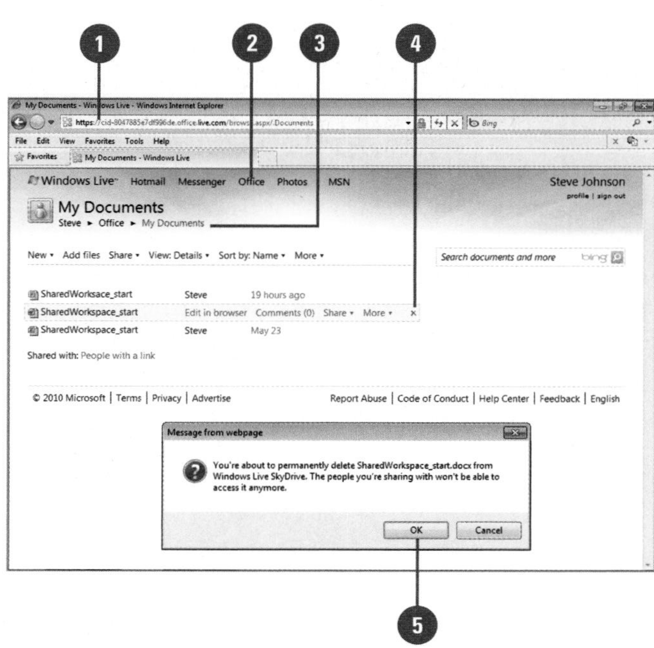

Downloading Documents from Windows Live

When you no longer want a document or folder of documents on Windows Live or you want to share them with others, you can download them to your local drive on your computer. You can download individual files one at a time in their native Office file format, such as .docx, or an entire folder of documents as a zipped file. The .zip file format compresses all the files in the folder into a single file. You can open a zipped file on Microsoft Windows by double-clicking it and then using an Extract button or by using the Winzip.exe software, which you can download for free from the Web at one of many download sites, such as *www.download.com*.

Download a File from a SkyDrive Folder

1. Open your browser, go to *www.live.com*, and then sign in to Windows Live.
   - To go directly to the SkyDrive, go to *http://skydrive.live.com*.
2. Navigate to the Windows Live SkyDrive.
3. Click a folder icon to navigate to the document you want to download.
4. In Details view, point to the document you want, click the **More** link, and then click **Download**.
5. Click **Save**.
6. Navigate to the location where you want to download the file, and then click **Save**.

   The document is downloaded to the specified folder in the native Office file format.

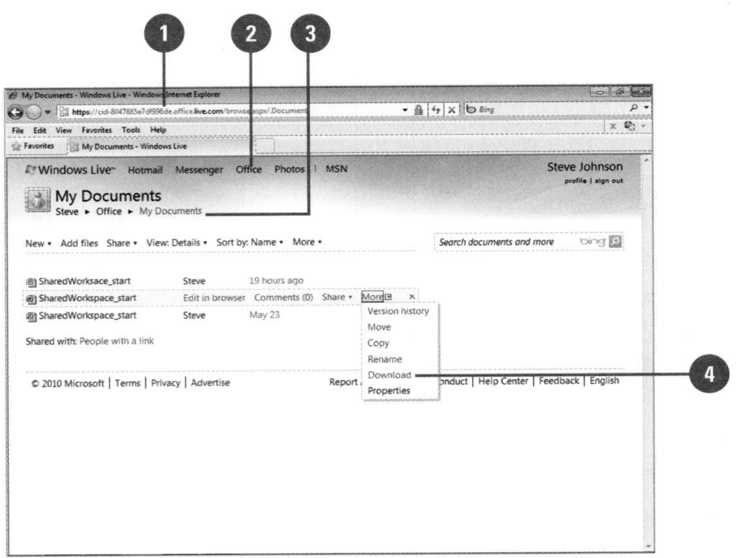

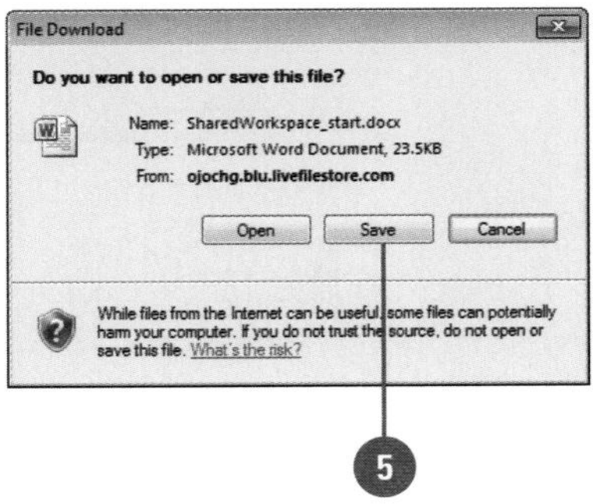

Download a Folder of Files from a SkyDrive Folder

1. Open your browser, go to *www.live.com*, and then sign in to Windows Live.
   - To go directly to the SkyDrive, go to *http://skydrive.live.com*.
2. Navigate to the Windows Live SkyDrive.
3. Click a folder icon to navigate to the folder of files you want to download.
4. Click the **More** link, and then click **Download as .zip file**.
5. Click **Save**.
6. Navigate to the location where you want to download the file, and then click **Save**.

   All the documents in the folder are zipped and downloaded to the specified folder in the .zip file format.

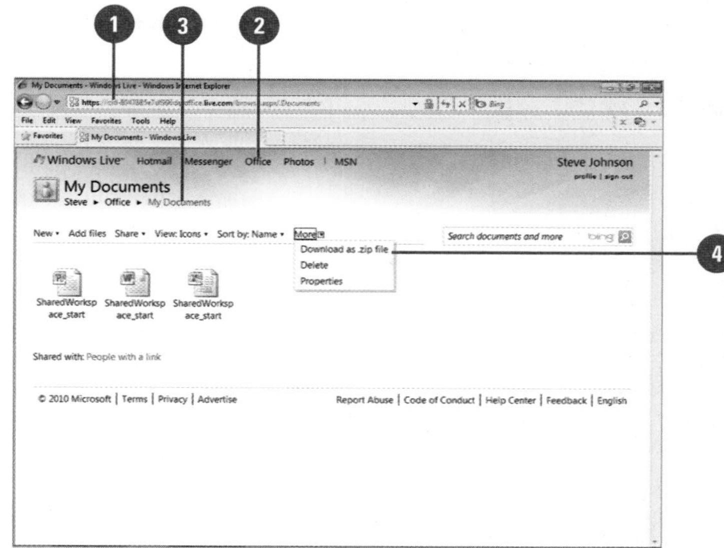

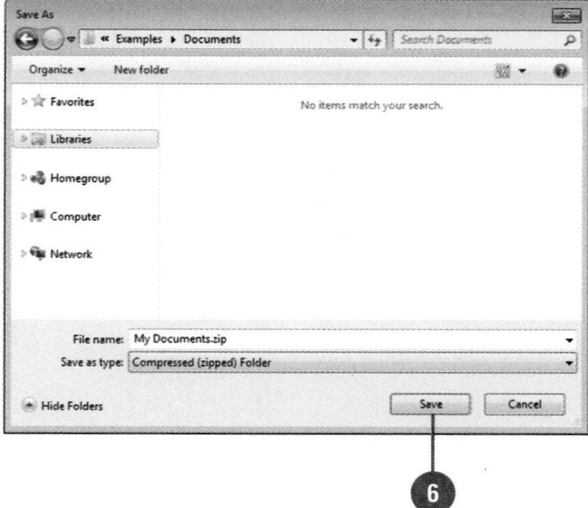

Did You Know?

You can view document properties for a file in a SkyDrive folder. In Windows Live SkyDrive, click a folder icon to navigate to the file you want, point to a document in Details view, click the More link, and then click Properties.

You can add a comment to a file in a SkyDrive folder. In Windows Live SkyDrive, click a folder icon to navigate to the file you want, point to a document in Details view, click the Comments link, enter a comment, and then click Add.

Downloading or Saving Documents in Office Web Apps

If you're viewing a document in an Office Web App (**New!**), you can download a copy of a file to your hard drive on your computer or save it with another name (Excel) in the current SkyDrive folder on Windows Live. When you download a file, you can specify the location on your local hard drive where you want to store it. In Excel, when you save a file with another name in the current SkyDrive folder on Windows Live, you can specify whether you want to overwrite an existing file with the same name. The download and save as options may vary or change in the Office Web Apps.

Download a File in an Office Web App

1. Open your browser, go to *www.live.com*, and then sign in to Windows Live.
   - To go directly to the SkyDrive, go to *http://skydrive.live.com*.
2. Navigate to the Windows Live SkyDrive.
3. Click a folder icon to navigate to the document you want to download, and then click the document icon.
4. To download a snapshot in Excel, click the **Edit in Browser** button.
5. Click **File** tab, and then click a download option (options vary depending on the Office Web App):
   - **Download a Copy.** Downloads the entire document to your computer.
   - **Download a Snapshot.** In Excel (edit in browser), downloads a copy of a workbook containing only the values and formatting.
6. Click **Save**.
7. Navigate to the location where you want to download the file, and then click **Save**.

View in browser

Save a File with a New Name in an Office Web App

1. Open your browser, go to *www.live.com*, and then sign in to Windows Live.
   - To go directly to the SkyDrive, go to *http://skydrive.live.com*.
2. Navigate to the Windows Live SkyDrive.
3. Click a folder icon to navigate to the document you want to save, and then click the document icon.
4. In Excel, click the **File** tab, and then click **Save a Copy**.
   - **Edit in Browser.** If you're working in edit mode, click the **File** tab, and then click **Save As**.
5. Type a name for the file.
6. To overwrite existing files in the folder, select the **Overwrite existing files** check box.
7. Click **Save**.

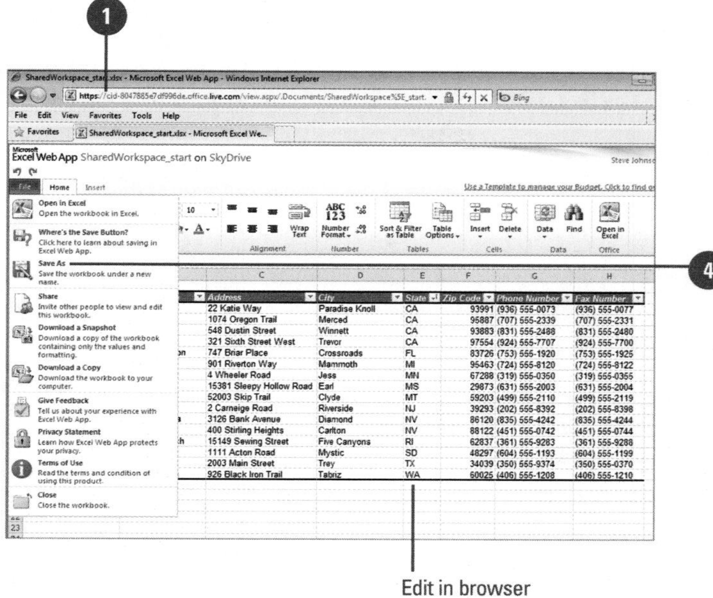

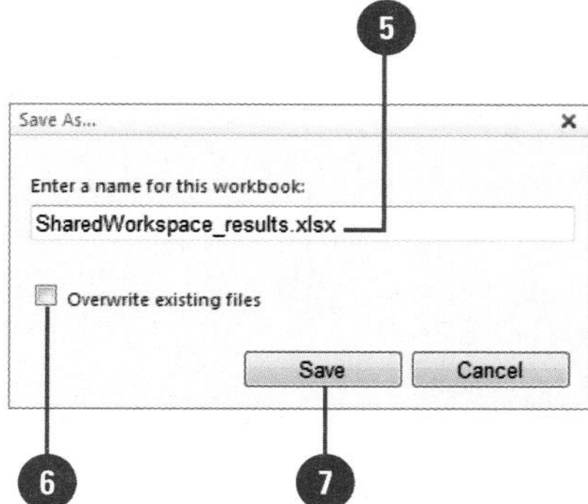

Collaborating with Documents on Windows Live

After you upload your Office documents to a SkyDrive folder and configure the folder permissions, you can start to collaborate on an Office document. With Office Web Apps you can simultaneously edit documents, known as co-authoring (**New!**). Co-authoring allows two or more people to work on a document at the same time in real-time without the need to save and reject or accept changes, known as sharing. If two people edit the same thing, each Office Web App deals with differently. Before you can co-author a document, you need to send a link in e-mail to those you want to share the folder that contains the document or embed a link in a blog or Web page, so others can access the folder. The folder permissions provide security access to the folder.

Send a Link to Share a Folder

1. Open your browser, go to *www.live.com*, and then sign in to Windows Live.
   - To go directly to the SkyDrive, go to *http://skydrive.live.com*.
2. Navigate to the Windows Live SkyDrive.
3. Click a folder icon to navigate to the folder with the documents you want to share.
4. Click the **Share** link, and then click **Send a link**.
   - To copy a link to share, click the **Share** link, click **Get a link**, click the Copy link, and then click **Done**.
5. Specify the recipients to whom you want to send a link.
6. Select or clear the **Require recipients to sign in with Windows Live ID** check box.
7. Click **Send**.
8. In the e-mail message a recipient, click the **View folder** button.
   - In Windows Live for a recipient, you can also open the shared folder to access a document.
9. Click a document, and then edit or co-edit it in the Office Web App.

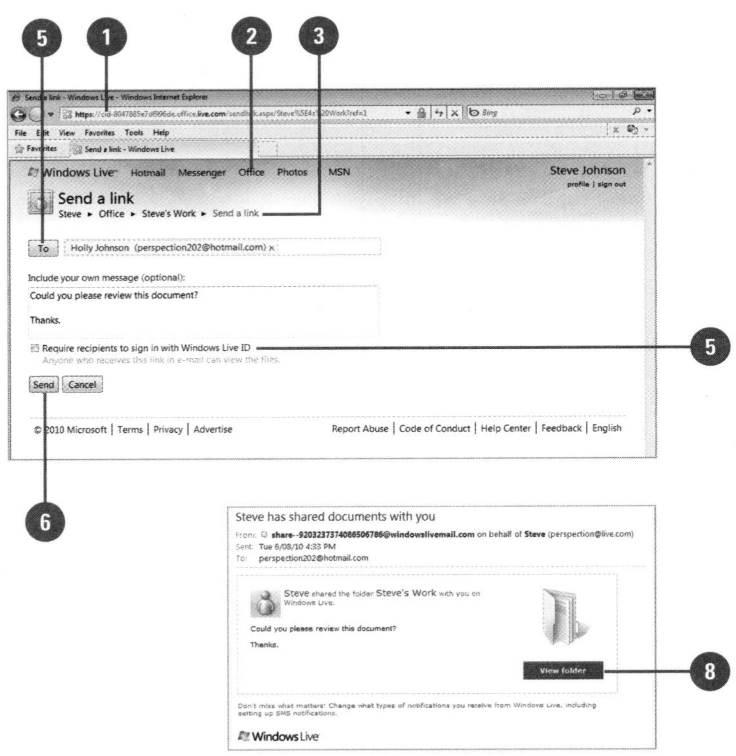

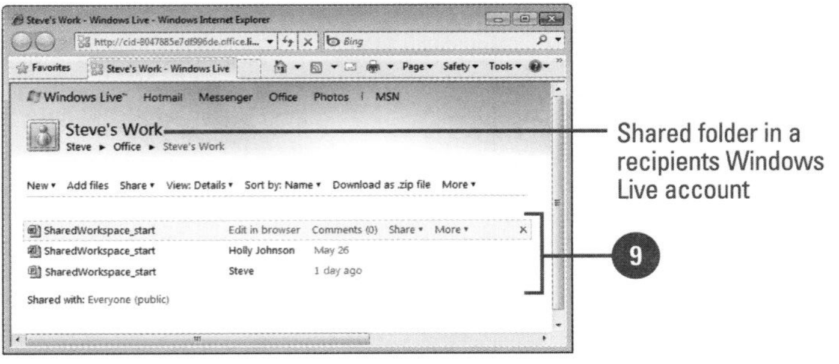

Embed a Link to Share a Folder or Document in a Blog or Web Page

1. Open your browser, go to *www.live.com*, and then sign in to Windows Live.
   - To go directly to the SkyDrive, go to *http://skydrive.live.com*.
2. Navigate to the Windows Live SkyDrive.
3. Click a folder icon to navigate to the folder with the documents you want to share.
4. Click the **Share** link, and then click **Embed**.
   - To embed a document, point to it in Details view, click the **Share** link, and then click **Embed**.
5. Click the **Copy** link, and then click **Allow access**.

   The embed code is copied to the Clipboard.
6. Click **Done**.
7. Paste the code into a blog post or Web page.
   - **Blog.** Create a blog post in a blogger, such as Windows Live Writer, and then paste the code.
   - **Web Page.** Open a Web page in an HTML editor, and then paste the code.
8. Open your browser, display the blog post or Web page, and then click the link to the shared folder or document on Windows Live.
9. Open a document, and then edit or co-edit it in the Office Web App.

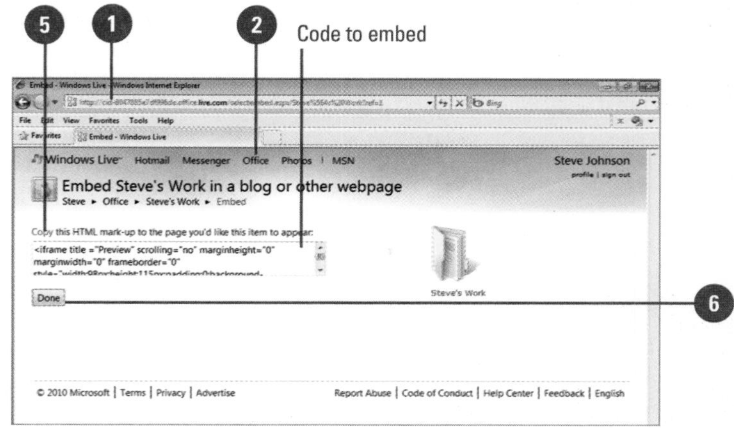

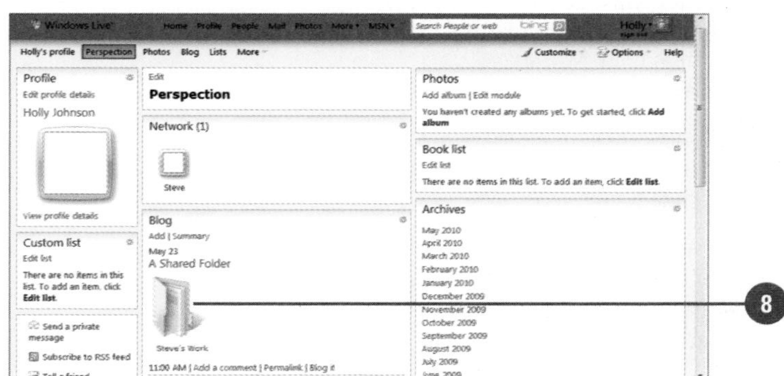

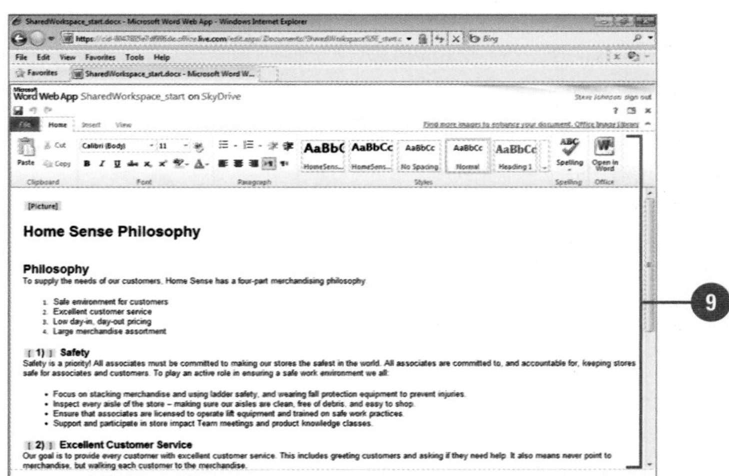

Working with SharePoint Workspaces

A SharePoint workspace is your own personal copy of the SharePoint server, or selected lists and libraries you want to take offline and synchronize. A SharePoint workspace is useful when you want access to a SharePoint server whether or not you are connected to your network. You are the only member of the workspace and share content updates with other SharePoint members. In addition to SharePoint, you can also connect to a Groove workspace, or create a shared folder in Windows. SharePoint is a centralized server based sharing solution, while Groove is a local computer based sharing solution. When you start Microsoft SharePoint Workspace 2010 (**New!**), the Launchbar opens, where you can create and work with workspaces and contacts. SharePoint and Groove workspaces open in Workspace Explorer while shared folders open in a special layout in Windows Explorer.

Work with a Shared Folder

1. Click the **Start** button, point to **All Programs**, click **Microsoft Office**, and then click **Microsoft SharePoint Workspace 2010**.
   - On first use, use the wizard to create an account or select an existing one.
2. To create a shared folder, click the **New** button, click **Shared Folder**, type a name, and then click **Create**.
3. To work with the shared folder in the Launchbar, right-click it, and then select an option.
4. To open the shared folder in the Launchbar, double-click it.
5. In Windows Explorer, use the available options to work with people and files.
6. To add a contact in the Launchbar, click the **Add Contact** button, and then select a contact from the server list. Click the Contacts bar to display and work with them.

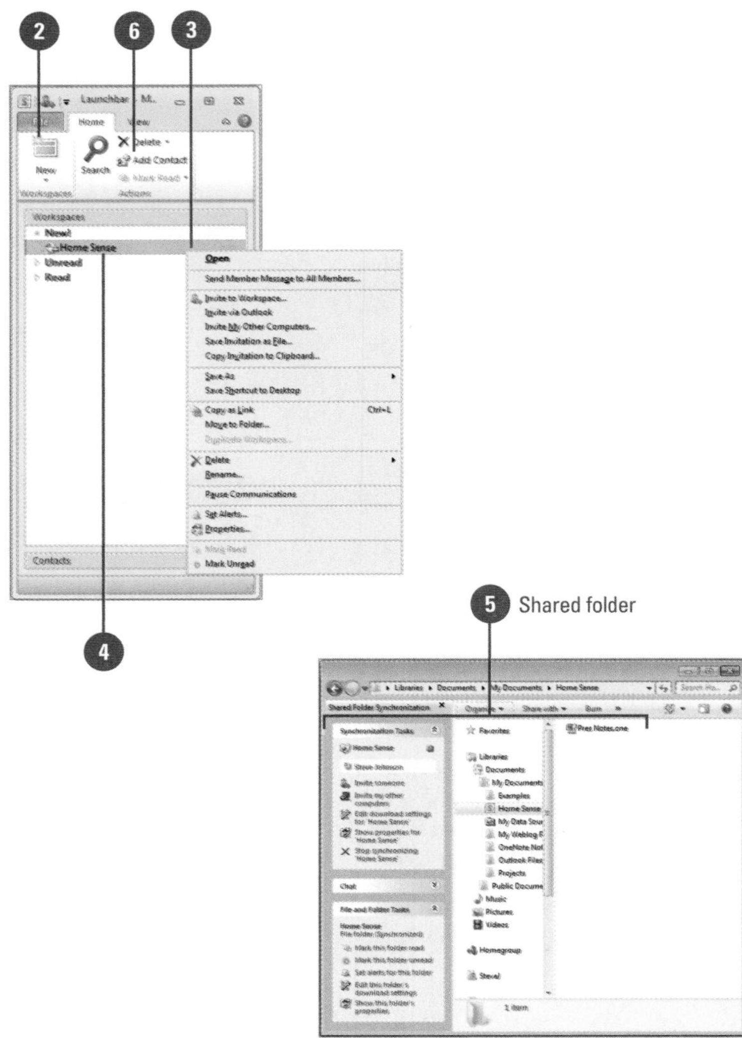

Work with SharePoint or Groove Workspaces

1. Click the **Start** button, point to **All Programs**, click **Microsoft Office**, and then click **Microsoft SharePoint Workspace 2010**.
   - On first use, use the wizard to create an account or select an existing one.
2. To create a server workspace, click the **New** button, and then click **SharePoint Workspace** or **Groove Workspace**.
   - **SharePoint Workspace.** Specify a location, and then click **OK**.
   - **Groove Workspace.** Type a name for the Groove workspace, and then click **Create**. To specify a Groove workspace version, click **Options**.
3. To work with a workspace in the Launchbar, right-click it, and then select an option.
4. To open a workspace in the Launchbar, double-click it.
5. In the Workspace, use the available tabs and options to work with people and files.
6. To add a contact in the Launchbar, click the **Add Contact** button, and then select a contact from the server list. Click the Contacts bar to display and work with them.

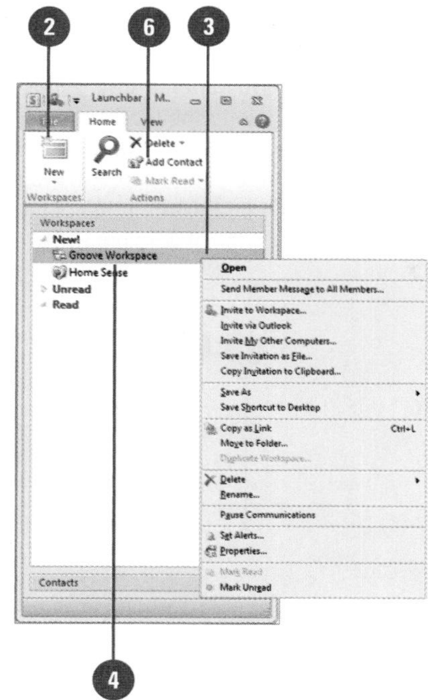

Groove workspace

See Also

See "Saving a Document to a SharePoint Server" on page 456 for more information on saving and opening a document using a workspace from Microsoft SharePoint Workspace.

Sharing Documents in a Groove Workspace

The Documents Tool in Groove allows you to share and collaborate on different types of files, including files from Microsoft Office programs. All team members of a workspace can open files that appear in the Documents Tool. When a team member opens, changes, and saves a file to the workspace, Groove automatically updates the file for all other team members. When several team members work on the same file at the same time, the first person to save changes to the workspace updates the original file. If another team member saves changes to the original version, Groove creates a second copy with the editor's name.

Share Documents in a Workspace

1. In SharePoint Workspace 2010 (**New!**), double-click the Groove workspace you want to use.
2. Click the **Documents** tool.
3. Click the **Add Documents** button on the Home tab.
4. Locate and select the files you want to add to the workspace.
5. Click **Open**.

   The selected files appear in the file list in the workspace.

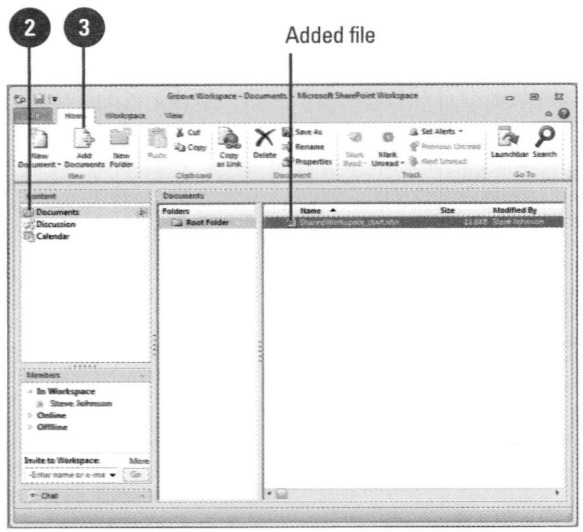

Manage Document Tools

- **New Files.** Select a folder, click the **Home** tab, click the **New Document** button, click a file type, type a name, and then click **OK**.
- **Open Files.** Double-click file, make and save changes, and then click **Yes** or **No** to save changes.
- **Delete Files.** Right-click file, and then click **Delete**.
- **New Folder.** Select a folder, click the **Home** tab, click the **New Folder** button, type a name, and then press Enter.
- **Alerts.** Right-click a folder or file, click **Properties**, click the **Alerts** tab, drag slider, and then click **OK**.

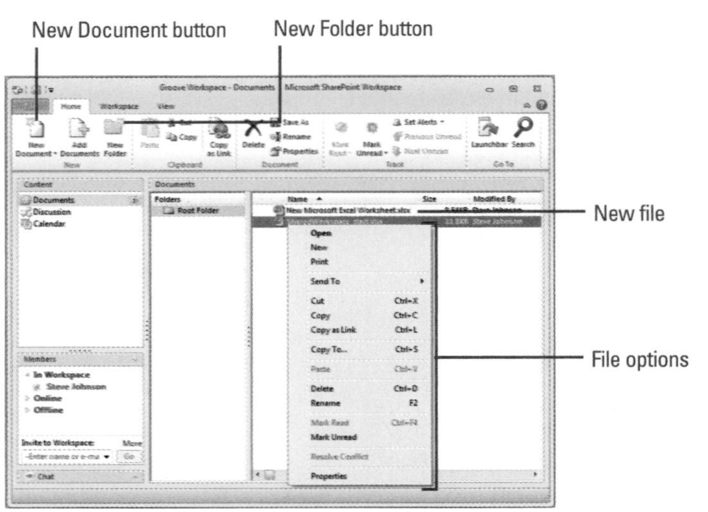

Inviting Others to a Groove Workspace

Before you can invite someone to a Groove workspace, they need to be a Groove user. Each person you invite to a Groove workspace needs to have a role, either Manager, Participant, or Guest. Each role comes with a set of permissions that allow a user to perform certain tasks. Mangers can invite others, edit existing files, and delete files or the entire workspace. Participants can edit and delete files. Guests can view existing data, but not make changes. After you send an invitation to join a workspace, check for Groove alerts in the notification area to see if the user has accepted your invitation.

Invite Users to a Workspace

1. In SharePoint Workspace 2010 (**New!**), double-click the Groove workspace you want to use.
2. Click the **Workspace** tab.
3. Click the **Invite Members** button.
4. Click the **To** list arrow, and then select a user.

   If the user you want is not there, click **Add More**, click **Search for User**, type part of the user's name, click **Find**, select the user's name you want, click **Add**, and then click **OK**.
5. Click the **Role** list arrow, and then click a role: **Manager**, **Participant**, or **Guest**.
6. Enter a message.
7. Select the **Require acceptance confirmation** check box as a security recommendation.
8. Click **Invite**.

   Monitor your Groove alerts for status and acceptance.

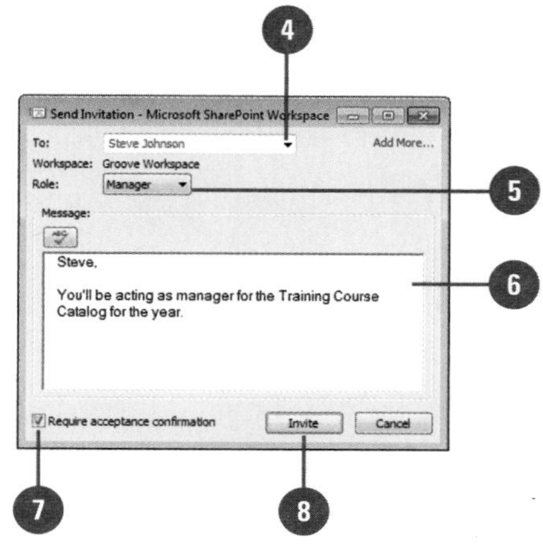

Groove alert with invitation

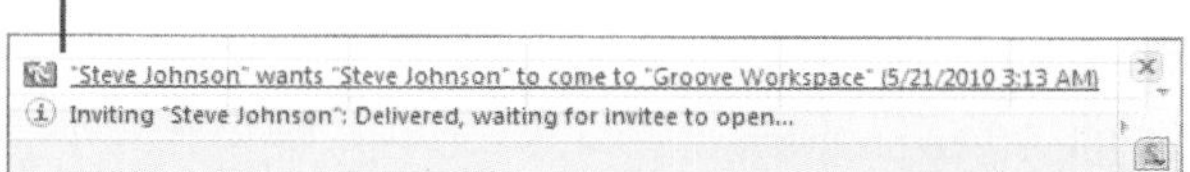

Did You Know?

You can change workspace roles and permissions. Click the Workspace tab, click Properties, click the Permissions tab, adjust permissions, and then click OK.

Saving a Document to a SharePoint Server

You can save documents to a Document Management Server, such as a Document Library on a SharePoint site, in a similar way that you save documents on your hard disk. After you save the document for the first time using the Save to SharePoint command (**New!**), you can click the Save button on the Quick Access Toolbar as you do for any document to update the document on the site. If you save a file to a library that requires you to check documents in and out, the SharePoint site checks it out for you. However, you need to check the document in when you're done with it. If the site stores multiple content types, you might be asked to specify the content type.

Save an Office Document to a SharePoint Server

1. Open the Office document you want to save to a Document Management Server.
2. Click the **File** tab, click **Save & Send**, and then click **Save to SharePoint**.
3. Click the **Save As** button.
4. Navigate to the network folder location on the SharePoint server where you want to save the file.
   - If you set up a local version of a SharePoint workspace with Microsoft SharePoint Workspace 2010 (**New!**), you can click the Office program name in the left pane, and then click Workspaces to access it.
5. Type a document file name.
6. If necessary, click the **Save as type** list arrow, and then click the file format you want.
7. Click **Save**.

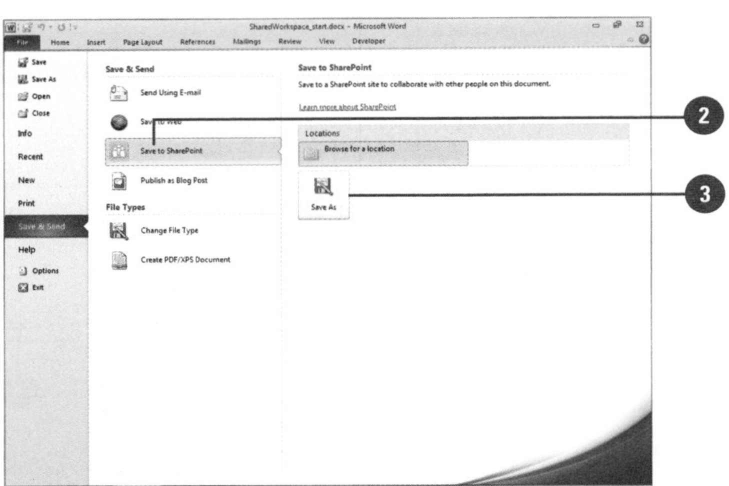

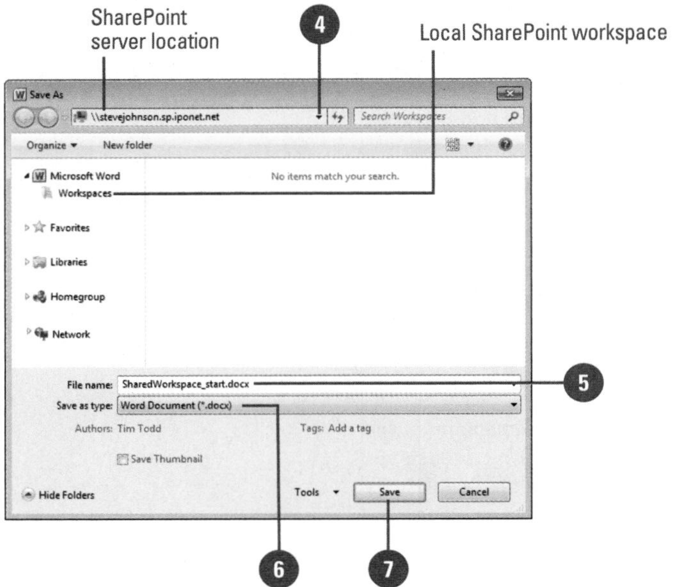

Open an Office Document from a SharePoint Server

1. Click the **File** tab, and then click **Open**.
2. Navigate to the network folder location on the SharePoint server where you want to save the file.
   - If you set up a local version of a SharePoint workspace with Microsoft SharePoint Workspace 2010 (**New!**), you can click the Office program name in the left pane, and then click Workspaces to access it.
3. Select the document.
4. Click **Open**.

Did You Know?

You can access SharePoint resources. After you save or publish an Office document to a SharePoint Server site, you can click the File tab, click Save & Send, and then click Save To SharePoint to access other server related commands.

See Also

See "Working with SharePoint Workspaces" on page 452 for more information on setting up a local version of a SharePoint server.

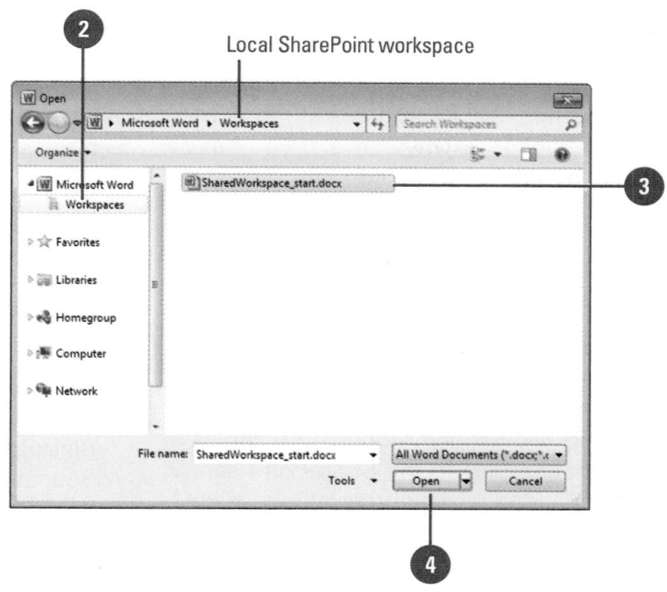

For Your Information

Co-authoring Office Documents with SharePoint

If you have a Microsoft SharePoint server, you can have multiple authors work on the same Office document from the server at the same time. When multiple authors are working on the same document, you can see who is editing the document and where they are working in the Status bar or on the File tab Info screen (**New!**). Any changes made by other authors get merged into the main document where you can review and modify them.

Using Office Mobile 2010

If you have a Windows Mobile 6.5 phone, you can use Office Mobile 2010 (**New!**) to work with your files from anywhere. If you have a touch screen device, you can intuitively scroll through menus and navigation documents.

You can use an Office Mobile 2010 program to view and edit Office documents stored on your phone, sent to you as e-mail attachments, or stored on a Microsoft SharePoint server through SharePoint Workspace Mobile 2010. When you use the SharePoint Workspace Mobile, you can save document changes to the SharePoint server or sync changes when you're offline. If you need a secondary monitor, you can connect your phone to your computer using Bluetooth, and use your phone as a secondary monitor to deliver a document or presentation slide show.

Don't Have Office Mobile 2010

You can view Office files even if your phone doesn't have Office Mobile 2010. With Mobile Viewers for Microsoft Office, you can use your browser-enabled cell phone to read Microsoft Excel, Microsoft PowerPoint, and Microsoft Word files in organizations that have installed and configured Microsoft Office Web Apps on a SharePoint 2010 server.

The following devices provide support for Mobile Viewers for Office: Windows Mobile, BlackBerry, iPhone, iPod Touch, Android, Nokia S60, and Japan feature phones including docomo, SoftBank and KDDI by au phones. Over time, this list of supported devices will expand and grow. Check online at Office.com and search for cell phone use of Office Web Apps.

Workshops

Introduction

The Workshops are all about being creative and thinking outside of the box. These workshops will help your right-brain soar, while making your left-brain happy; by explaining why things work the way they do. Exploring possibilities is great fun; however, always stay grounded with knowledge of how things work.

Getting and Using the Project Files

Each project in the Workshops includes a start file to help you get started with the project, and a final file to provide you with the results of the project so you can see how well you accomplished the task.

Before you can use the project files, you need to download them from the Web. You can access the files at *www.perspection.com* in the software downloads area. After you download the files from the Web, uncompress the files into a folder on your hard drive to which you have easy access from Microsoft Word 2010.

Project 1: Creating a Form with Content Controls

Skills and Tools: Use content controls to create a form

Forms are an easy way for you to interact with users of your documents, either online or in print, and gain information and feedback from them in the process. Content controls are predefined fields or set of fields that contain information you can use throughout a document. Word includes many different types: text boxes (Rich Text and Text), picture, date picker, combo boxes, drop-down lists, and building block gallery. The fields display information you provided in Document Properties or a placeholder, which you can fill in. After you insert the fields you want, you can change field properties to customize the form. When you're done with the form, you can group the document text to the content controls to prevent a user from accidentally making changes to the document text.

The Project

In this project, you'll learn how to create a form, add content controls, change properties, and group the results to protect the document text, yet allow the content controls to change.

The Process

1. Open Word 2010, open **Form_start.dotx**, and then save it as **Form_results.dotx**.
2. Click the **Developer** tab.
   - To turn on the Developer tab, click the **File** tab, click **Options**, click **Custom Ribbon** in the left pane, select the **Developer** check box in the left column, and then click **OK**.
3. Click the **Design Mode** button.
4. Click to place the insertion point to the right of the text *Date of report:*
5. Click the **Date Picker** button in the Controls group.
6. Click to place the insertion point to the right of the text *Report filled out by:*
7. Click the **Drop-Down List** button in the Controls group.
8. Click to place the insertion point to the right of the text *Address:*
9. Click the **Rich Text** button in the Controls group.
10. Use the Rich Text button and the Date Picker button to insert a text or date control for the rest of the elements in the form that end with a colon.
    - If you need to delete a control, right-click the control, and then click Remove Content Control.
11. Select the text *Click here to enter a date* in the control to the right of the text *Date of report:*
12. Type **Report Date**.

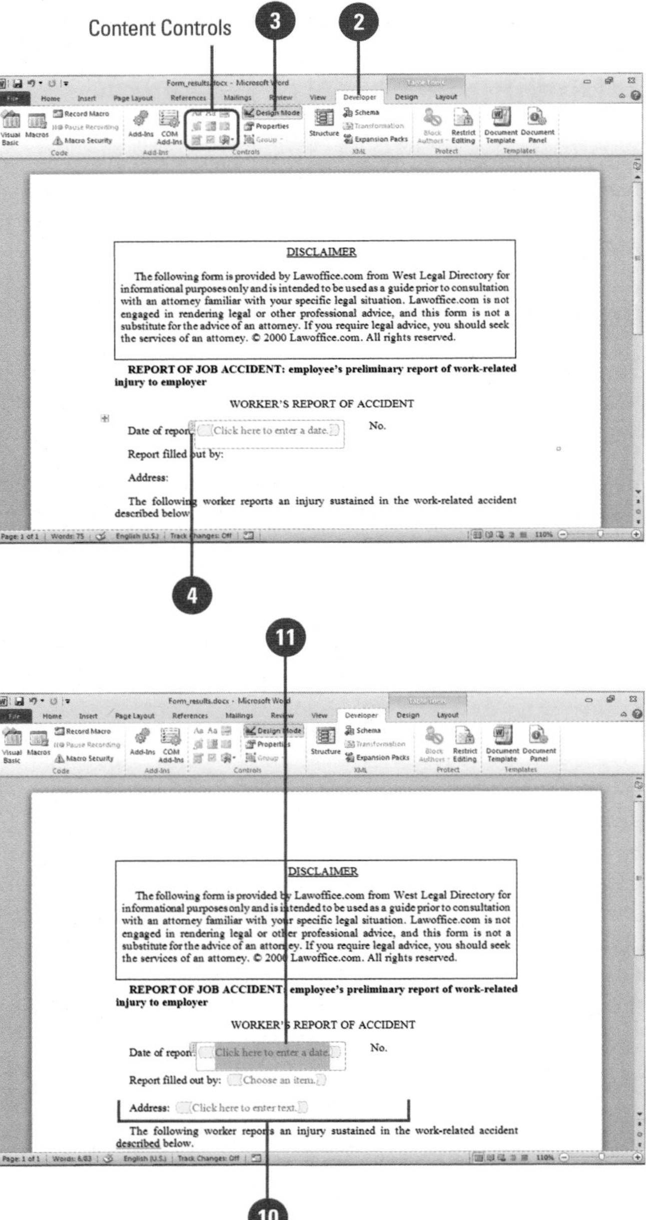

13. Select the text in each one of the controls and enter an appropriate name for the data item.

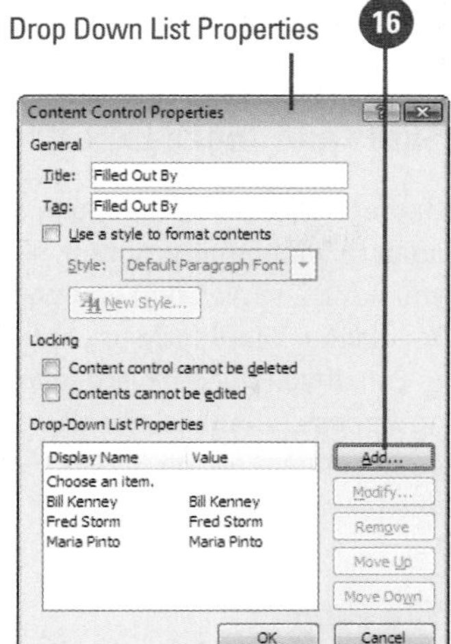

14. Select the control next to the text *Report filled out by:*
15. Click the **Properties** button.
16. Click **Add**, and enter a display name of your choice for the drop-down list, and then click **OK**. Add in two other names of your choice. When you're done adding names, click **OK**.
17. Set properties for all the controls providing a title and XML tag (label) for each one. For the date controls, you can also specify the format you want.
18. Select all the text in the document.
19. Click the **Group** button, and then click **Group**.
20. When you're done, click the **Design Mode** button.
21. Enter information of your choice in the content controls for the form. Try to change the standard text in the document. Grouping the text and controls provides a protection against anyone from accidentally changing the text.

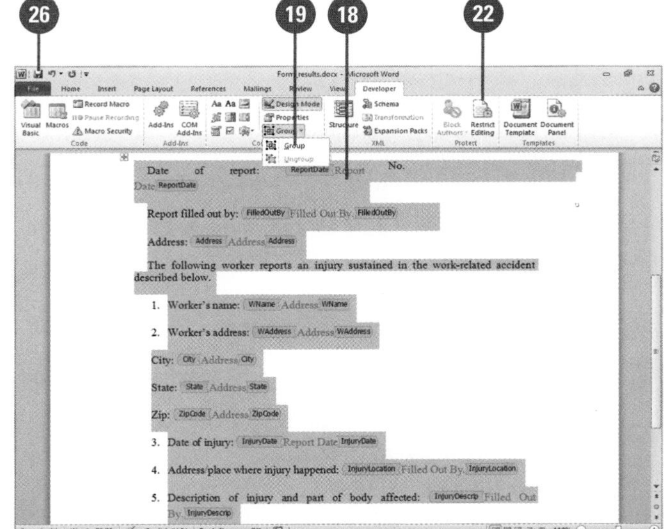

22. Click the **Restrict Editing** button.
23. Select the **Allow only this type of editing in the document** check box.
24. In the list of editing restrictions, select **Filling in forms**, and then click **Yes, Start Enforcing Protection**.
25. If you want to assign a password enter it; if not, leave the password boxes blank, and then click **OK**.
26. Click the **Save** button on the Quick Access Toolbar.

The Results

Finish: Compare your completed project file with the results file **FormControls_results.dotx**.

Project 2: Exporting Form Data to Access or Excel

Skills and Tools: Export form data from Word to Access or Excel

Gathering form information in a Word document is an easy way to get the data that you can further analyze in another program, such as Microsoft Access or Microsoft Excel. For example, suppose you have a survey that you want filled out by customers who don't have access to your network. You send a Word form to your customers in e-mail, ask them to complete it and e-mail the form back to you. If you don't have to many forms, you can export the Word form data and then import it into an Access database or an Excel worksheet. If you have a large number of forms, you can create a code connection to the database or spreadsheet to automate the data transfer process; however this takes some programming.

The Project

In this project, you'll learn how to export form data from Word and import it into Access database or Excel worksheet.

The Process

1. Open Word 2010, open FormDataTransfer_start.docx, and then save it as **FormDataTransfer_results.docx**.
2. Click the **File** tab, click **Options**, and then click **Advanced** in the left pane.
3. Select the **Save form data as delimited text file** check box.
4. Click **OK**.
5. Click the **File** tab, and then click **Save**.
6. Select **Plain Text (.txt)** as the Save as type, and then click **Save**.

   The File Conversion dialog box opens. There are commas between each separate data item, which is surrounded by quotes.
7. Click **OK**.

   Now, you can import this data into a database or spreadsheet.

Import the Data into Access

1. Open Access 2010, create a new database or open an existing one.
   - To create a new database, click the **File** tab, click **New**, click **Blank database**, type a name for the database, select a location to store it, and then click **Create**.
2. Click the **External Data** tab.
3. Click the **Text File** button.

4. Click **Browse**, navigate to and select the file with the exported Word form data, and then click **Open**.
5. Click the **Import the source data into a new table in the current database** option, if necessary.
6. Click **OK**.

   The Import Text Wizard opens.
7. Click the **Delimited** option, and then click **Next**.
8. Click the **Comma** option, and then click **Next**.
9. Specify information about each of the fields, and then click **Next**.
10. Click the **Let Access add primary key** option, and then click **Next**.
11. Type **FormDataTransfer** to name the imported table, click **Finish**, and then click **Close**.

    The Word form data appears in the table.

Import the Data into Excel

1. Open Excel 2010, create a new spreadsheet or open an existing one.
2. Click the **Data** tab.
3. Click the **From Text** button.
4. Navigate to and select the file with the exported Word form data, and then click **Import**.

   The Import Text Wizard opens.
5. Click the **Delimited** option, and then click **Next**.
6. Select the **Comma** check box and deselect all others, and then click **Next**.
7. Select the default **General** option for the column data format, and then click **Finish**.
8. Specify a worksheet location where you want to put the data, and then click **OK**.

   The Word form data appears in the worksheet.

The Results

Finish: Compare your completed project file with the results file **FormDataTransfer_results.docx**.

Project 3: Viewing XML Data in a Document

Skills and Tools: View XML data in a Word document

XML data is stored in document parts using the Office XML file formats; for Word the XML file format is .docx. Document parts help define sections of the overall contents of the file. The file format consists of many different types of document parts, including custom XML data part. All document content associated with an XML element maps to data in a custom XML data part. This separation of the XML from the document formatting and layout—known as the Open Packaging Convention—makes it easier to access data. To view the document parts (which is a compressed zip package), add .zip to the end of the document name after the .docx, and then double-click the renamed file. The contents of the file appear, displaying a tree structure of individual document parts.

The Project

In this project, you'll learn how to view the XML data in an Office document by opening the ZIP package.

The Process

1. Open Word 2010, open **ViewXML_start.docx**, and then save it as **ViewXML_results.docx**.
2. Exit Word and navigate to the location where you saved the file ViewXML_results.docx.
3. Right-click the file, and then click **Rename**.
4. Add **.zip** to the end of the file name. (ViewXML_results.docx.zip), and then press Enter.
   - Make sure a Zip utility is installed on your computer, and the .zip extension is associated with the program.
5. Double-click the file with the .zip extension.

   The ZIP utility opens and you can see the document parts that are included in the file. The folder structure contains different types of files.

   - The *_rels* folder contains a .rels file that defines the root relationship within the package.
   - The *docProps* folder contains files for the document properties (core.xml) and application properties (app.xml), which includes author name, word count, and software version.
   - The *word* folder (application specific) contains application-specific, document component files.

     The document.xml file contains the data (text) in the document.
   - The *Content_Types.xml* file provides a listing of the content types for the other parts that are contained in the package.

Sample file structure for a Word document

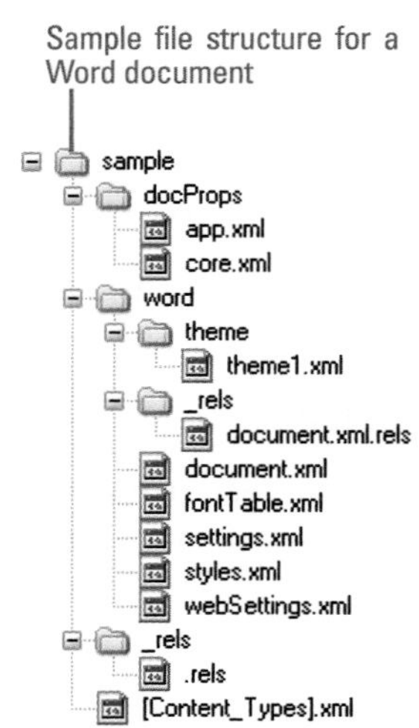

6. Navigate through the folders to locate the document.xml file.
7. Double-click the document.xml file to view the XML contents in the associated viewer. In this case, Internet Explorer.

   You can see the data entered while in Word in XML form.
8. Close Internet Explorer.

The Results

Finish: Compare your completed project file with the results file **ViewXMLData_results.docx**.

Want More Projects

You can access and download more workshop projects and related files at *www.perspection.com* in the software downloads area. After you download the files from the Web, uncompress the files into a folder on your hard drive to which you have easy access from your Microsoft Office program.

Get Everything on DVD

Instead of downloading everything from the Web, which can take a while depending on your Internet connection speed, you can get all the files used in this book and much more on the Microsoft Office 2010 On Demand DVD. The DVD contains task and workshop files, tips and tricks, keyboard shortcuts, transition helpers from 2003 or 2007 to 2010, and other goodies from the author.

To get the Microsoft Office 2010 On Demand DVD, go to *www.perspection.com.*

W

New! Features

Microsoft Word 2010

Microsoft Word 2010 is a powerful word-processing program that enables you to easily compose and edit documents for print or online use. Word 2010 contains many new tools specifically designed to improve the way you interact with the program, and the way you collaborate with one another in preparing documents. With enhancements to the user interface, and the addition of advanced tools, page layout, SmartArt graphics, Office themes and Quick Styles for text, shapes, tables, and pictures, you can accomplish a variety of business or personal tasks more easily in Word 2010.

Only New Features

If you're already familiar with Microsoft Word 2007, you can access and download all the tasks in this book with Microsoft Word 2010 New Features to help make your transition to the new version simple and smooth. The Microsoft Word 2010 New Features as well as other 2007 to 2010 transition helpers are available on the Web at *www.perspection.com.*

What's New

If you're searching for what's new in Word 2010, just look for the icon: New!. The new icon appears in the table of contents and throughout this book so you can quickly and easily identify a new or improved feature in Word 2010. The following is a brief description of each new feature and it's location in this book.

Office 2010

- **64-bit Office programs (p. 2)** The 64-bit version of an Office program is built specifically for 64-bit computers. For example, in the 64-bit version of Word, you can break through the physical memory (RAM) limitation of 2 GB that exists with the 32-bit version, and crunch numbers with ease.
- **File tab and Backstage view (p. 4, 5, 402)** The File tab replaces the Office button from Office 2007 and provides access to Backstage view, which lets you access common file management tasks, such as opening, saving, and sharing files. When add-ins are enabled, you can use the Add-ins button on the File tab to use them.

- **Customize Ribbon (p. 4, 6-7)** In the Options dialog box, you can customize the Ribbon by adding tabs, groups, and command buttons. You can also show and hide the Developer tab.
- **Recently Used Files (p. 12-13)** For easy access, you can add recently used documents to the File tab. In addition to Recent Documents, you can also access files on the Recent Places list.
- **Protected view (p. 12, 328, 330-331, 419, 422-423)** Office documents with a potentially unsafe location, such as the Internet or an e-mail attachment, or active content, such as macros, data connections or ActiveX controls, are opened with editing functions disabled in Protected view.
- **Compatibility Checker (p. 15, 26)** The Compatibility Checker generates a report that provides a summary of the potential losses and the number of occurrences in the workbook. You can also specify what versions to show compatibility issues. There is a compatibility mode for Word 97-2003 and Word 2007.
- **Accessibility Checker (p. 27)** The Accessibility Checker identifies potential difficulties that people with disabilities might have reading or interactive with an Office document. In addition to the Accessibility Checker, you can also add alternative text (also known as alt text) to objects and other items to provide information for people with visual impairments who may be unable to easily or fully see it.
- **Auto Recovered (p. 30-31)** You can select the Keep the last Auto Recovered file if I close without saving check box in Options as a safe guard to protect your unsaved work. You can use the Manage Versions button on the Info screen on the File tab to open any available recovered unsaved files.
- **Live Preview of Paste Options (p. 52, 3600, 369, 371)** When you point to an option on a Paste menu, a live preview of the paste contents appears in the document. When you point to a paste option, use the ScreenTip to determine the option.
- **Actions (p. 58-59, 403)** Actions, a replacement for smart tags, help you integrate actions typically performed in other programs directly in Word. For example, you can insert a financial symbol to get a stock quote. To use an action, you right-click an item to view any custom actions associated with it.
- **Math AutoCorrect (p. 60)** If you use math symbols in your work, you can use Math AutoCorrect to make it easier to insert them. It works just like AutoCorrect.
- **More Themes and Styles (p. 101)** Office comes with more themes and styles.
- **Office.com (p. 110, 132, 392)** In the Clip Art task pane, you can select the Include Office.com content check box to access clip content on the Web at Office.com. In the Options dialog box, you can set an option to show or hide customer submitted Office.com content.
- **Screenshot (p. 112)** With the Screenshot button, you can capture a screenshot of your computer and insert it into an Office document. As you capture screens, the Screenshot gallery stores them, so you can use them later.
- **Artistic Quick Style Gallery (p. 113)** With the Artistic Quick Style gallery, you can change the look of a picture to a sketch, drawing, or painting.

- **Crop to Shape Gallery (p. 115)** The Crop to Shape gallery makes it easy to choose the shape you want to use.
- **Compress a Picture (p. 120)** Office allows you to compress pictures in order to minimize the file size of the image. In doing so, however, you may lose some visual quality, depending on the compression setting.
- **Correct a Picture (p. 121)** The brightness and contrast controls change a picture by an overall lightening or darkening of the image pixels. In addition, you can sharpen and soften pictures by a specified percentage.
- **Recolor a Picture (p. 122)** The Color Picture Quick Style gallery provides a variety of different recolor formatting combinations.
- **Crop a Picture (p. 124-125)** Use the Crop button to crop an image by hand. In addition, you can crop a picture while maintaining a selected resize aspect ratio or crop a picture based on a fill or fit.
- **Remove Picture Background (p. 126)** With the Remove Background command, you can specify the element you want in a picture, and then remove the background.
- **SmartArt Graphic Types (p. 132, 140)** Office provides more built-in SmartArt graphic types: picture and Office.com. With SmartArt graphic layouts, you can insert pictures in the SmartArt shapes. If you no longer want to use a SmartArt graphic or want to share it with others, you can also convert SmartArt graphics to shapes.
- **Record Macros with Chart Elements (p. 163, 411)** When you use the macro recorder with charts, it now records formatting changes to charts and other objects.
- **Unlimited Points in a Data Series (p. 167)** In previous Office versions, you were limited to 32,000 data points in a data series for 2-D charts. Now you can have as much as your memory to store.
- **Gradient Fills (p. 191)** The Gradient Fills dialog box allows you to adjust the brightness of a gradient. In Word, you can also apply gradients to text like you can for shapes and other objects.
- **Shape Effects Formatting (p. 192-193)** Office provides improved formatting effects to shapes, including Font Color Gradient, Shadow, Outline, Reflection, Glow, and 3-D.
- **Mini-Translator (p. 278-279)** In Word, Outlook, PowerPoint, or OneNote, you can enable the Mini Translator that translates words or phrases in a small window when you point to them.
- **Language Preferences (p. 280)** You can set language preferences for editing, display, ScreenTip, and Help languages. If you don't have the keyboard layout or related software installed, you can click links to add or enable them.
- **Print and Preview Screen (p. 288-289)** Instead of a dialog box, you can preview a document and choose printing options together on the same Print screen on the File tab; it detects the type of printer that you choose—either color or black and white—and then prints the appropriate version.

- **Trust Center (p. 328, 330-331, 419, 422-423)** The Trust Center provides new security and privacy settings for Trusted Documents, Protected view, and File Block Settings. In Trusted Documents, you can set options to open trusted documents without any security prompts for macros. Protected view provides a place to open potentially dangerous files, without any security prompts, in a restricted mode to help minimize harm to your computer. In File Block Settings, you can select the Open and Save check boxes to prevent each file type from opening, or just opening in Protected view, and from saving.
- **Linked OneNotes (p. 375)** In PowerPoint and Word, you can create and open linked notes directly from OneNote by using the Linked Notes button on the Review tab.
- **Office Web Apps (p. 430-439, 443, 448-451)** After you store Office documents on the Windows Live SkyDrive, or a Microsoft SharePoint server, you can view, edit, or share them in a browser using a Microsoft Office Web App.
- **Save to Web (p. 434-435)** Office programs provide a Save to Web command on the Save & Send screen to save Office documents directly to a Windows Live SkyDrive folder using a Windows Live account.
- **SharePoint Workspaces (p. 452-453)** An Office program that allows you to create and work with local versions of workspaces (SharePoint and Groove, or shared folders) and contacts.
- **SharePoint and Groove Workspaces (p. 452-455)** The Ribbon replaces menus, toolbars, and most of the task panes in SharePoint Workspaces 2010. The Ribbon is comprised of tabs with buttons and options that are organized by task.
- **Save to SharePoint (p. 456-457)** Office programs provide a Save to SharePoint command on the Save & Send screen to save Office documents directly to a SharePoint server or workspace.
- **Co-authoring with SharePoint (p. 457)** If you have a Microsoft SharePoint server, you can have multiple authors work on the same Office document at the same time. When multiple authors are working on the same document, you can see who is editing the document and where they are working in the Status bar or on the File tab Info screen.
- **Office Mobile (p. 458)** You can use an Office Mobile 2010 program to view and edit Office documents stored on your phone, sent to you as e-mail attachments, or stored on a Microsoft SharePoint server through SharePoint Workspace Mobile 2010.

Word 2010

- **Full Screen Reading View (p. 16, 18-19)** In the Full Screen Reading view, you can display the Navigation pane with the Browse Heading or Browse Pages tab to quickly jump to different parts of your document.
- **Navigation Pane (p. 18-19, 46, 54-55, 216)** If you have a long document with headings or you're searching for keywords, you can use the Navigation pane to find your way around it.

- **Text Effects Formatting (p. 66-67, 187, 388)** Word provides additional formatting effects to text, including Font Color Gradient, Shadow, Outline, Reflection, Glow, and 3-D. You can also apply gradients to text like you can for shapes and other objects.
- **Character Spacing (p. 68)** You can set text formatting for OpenType/TrueType fonts that include a range of ligature settings (where two or three letters combine into a single character), number spacing and forms, and stylistic sets (added font sets in a given font).
- **Numbering List (p. 80-81)** You can insert a customize numbering list style—including fixed-digits, such as 001, 002, etc.
- **Watermarks (p. 172)** More Watermarks are available from Office.com.
- **Text Boxes (p. 180-181)** More Text Boxes are available from Office.com.
- **Cover Pages (p. 223)** More Cover Pages are available from Office.com.
- **AutoText (p. 228-229)** You can insert AutoText with the Quick Parts button on the Insert tab.
- **Word Options (p. 274, 383, 386, 392, 395)** The Word Options dialog box includes some additional options. In the Proofing section, you can set Spanish modes for proofing and working with the Spanish language. In the Advanced section, you can disable hardware graphics acceleration, show AutoComplete suggestions, and show customer submitted Office.com content. In the Research Options dialog box, you can select a research service as your favorite.
- **Document Inspector (p. 314-315)** The inspector modules to find and remove any hidden data and personal information specific to each of these modules that you might not want to share with others.

What Happened To . . .

- **Format tab under Text Box Tools** In Word 2010, the Format tab under Text Box Tools has been integrated with the Format tab under Drawing Tools. If you're working with a document in compatibility mode, the Format tab under Text Box Tools is still available.
- **Smart tags** Smart tags are not supported in Word 2010. Smart tag indicators (such as the purple triangles in the corners of cells) are no longer displayed in the worksheet when you select a cell or move the pointer over the cell. Instead, you can right-click a cell to view any custom actions associated with its contents by clicking Additional actions on the shortcut menu. Additional actions are disabled by default, but you can enable or disable this functionality on the Actions tab of the AutoCorrect dialog box.

  ➤ Click the **File** tab, click **Options**, click the **Proofing** category, click **AutoCorrect Options** button, and then click the **Actions** tab.
- **SmartArt Pattern Fills** The pattern fills interface for shape objects, such as chart elements, was not provided with the new SmartArt technology in Word 2007, causing display issues when pattern fills were used in earlier versions of Word. In Word 2010, SmartArt provides the pattern fills interface so that you can

n

apply a pattern fill to shape objects. Shape objects that contain pattern fills in Word 97-2003 workbooks will also be displayed correctly when those workbooks are opened in Word 2010.

In Word 2010, in addition to shape objects, the following controls and objects are converted to the new SmartArt technology: Form controls, Microsoft ActiveX objects, OLE objects, and Camera tool objects

It is important to note that shape objects drawn in earlier versions of Word that are not upgraded to Word 2010 SmartArt format cannot be grouped with shape objects that are created in or upgraded to Word 2010 SmartArt format. Mixed shape objects will be layered, with the earlier versions of shape objects drawn on top of all later versions. This also means that Word 2010 charts cannot be shown on dialog sheets that were created in an earlier version of Word. You won't be able to access the new shape objects by clicking Select Objects on the Select button menu on the Home tab. To select the newer shape objects, you must use the Select Multiple Objects command, which you can add to a Ribbon by using the Custom Ribbon category in Word Options.

- **Clip Art task pane** The Search in box is no longer available, which means that you can no longer limit your search to specific collections of content. To narrow your search, you can use multiple search terms in the Search for box. The Organize clips link is no longer available. To open Microsoft Clip Organizer from Windows 7, Windows Vista, or Windows XP, click the Windows Start button, click All Programs, click Microsoft Office, click Microsoft Office 2010 Tools, and then click Microsoft Clip Organizer.
- **Clip Organizer** Clip Organizer is a tool that arranges and catalogs clip art and other media files stored on your hard disk. As described earlier in this article, Clip Organizer is no longer accessible directly from the Clip Art task pane in Microsoft Office programs.
    - **Automatic organization** Clip Organizer is a tool that arranges and catalogs clip art and other media files stored on your hard disk. As described earlier in this article, Clip Organizer is no longer accessible directly the Clip Art task pane in Microsoft Office programs.
    - **Send to e-mail recipient as attachment** The command for sending a clip as an attachment in e-mail messages is no longer available.
    - **Delete from collection** Although you can delete clips from Clip Organizer, you can no longer delete a clip from a specific collection.
    - **Find similar style** The command that allowed you to find clips of a similar style is no longer available.
    - **List and Details views** The List and Details views are no longer available. Instead, all clips appear as thumbnails in the Clip Organizer window.

Microsoft Certified Applications Specialist

C

About the MCAS Program

The Microsoft Certified Applications Specialist (MCAS) certification is the globally recognized standard for validating expertise with the Microsoft Office suite of business productivity programs. Earning an MCAS certificate acknowledges you have the expertise to work with Microsoft Office programs. To earn the MCAS certification, you must pass a certification exam for the Microsoft Office desktop applications of Microsoft Word, Microsoft Excel, Microsoft PowerPoint, Microsoft Outlook, or Microsoft Access. (The availability of Microsoft Certified Applications Specialist certification exams varies by program, program version, and language. Visit *www.microsoft.com* and search on *Microsoft Certified Applications Specialist* for exam availability and more information about the program.) The Microsoft Certified Applications Specialist program is the only Microsoft-approved program in the world for certifying proficiency with Microsoft Office programs.

What Does This Logo Mean?

It means this book has been approved by the Microsoft Certified Applications Specialist program to be certified courseware for learning Microsoft Word 2010 and preparing for the certification exam. This book will prepare you for the Microsoft Certified Applications Specialist exam for Microsoft Word 2010. Each certification level has a set of objectives, which are organized into broader skill sets. The Microsoft Certified Applications Specialist objectives and the specific pages throughout this book that cover the objectives are available on the Web at *www.perspection.com.*

Microsoft Certified Application Specialist

WD10S-1.1
WD10S-2.2

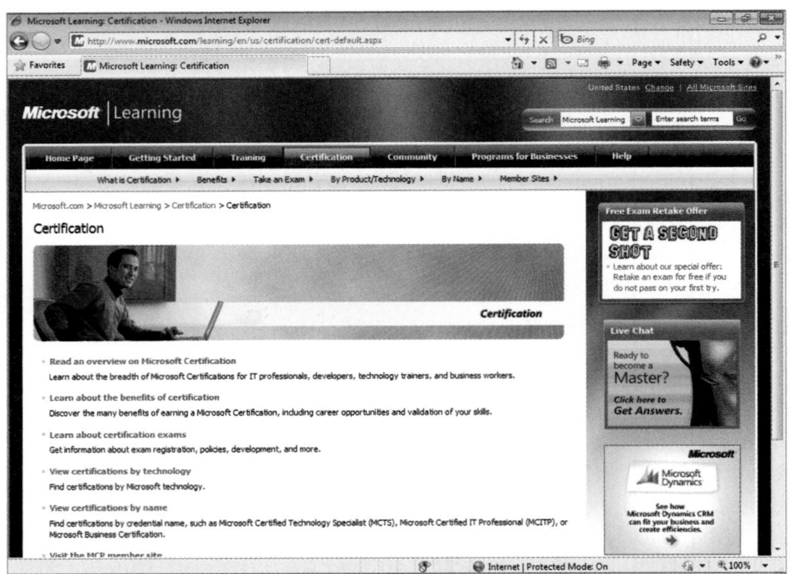

Preparing for a MCAS Exam

Every Microsoft Certified Applications Specialist certification exam is developed from a list of objectives based on how Microsoft Office programs are actually used in the workplace. The list of objectives determine the scope of each exam, so they provide you with the information you need to prepare for MCAS certification. Microsoft Certified Applications Specialist Approved Courseware, including the On Demand series, is reviewed and approved on the basis of its coverage of the objectives. To prepare for

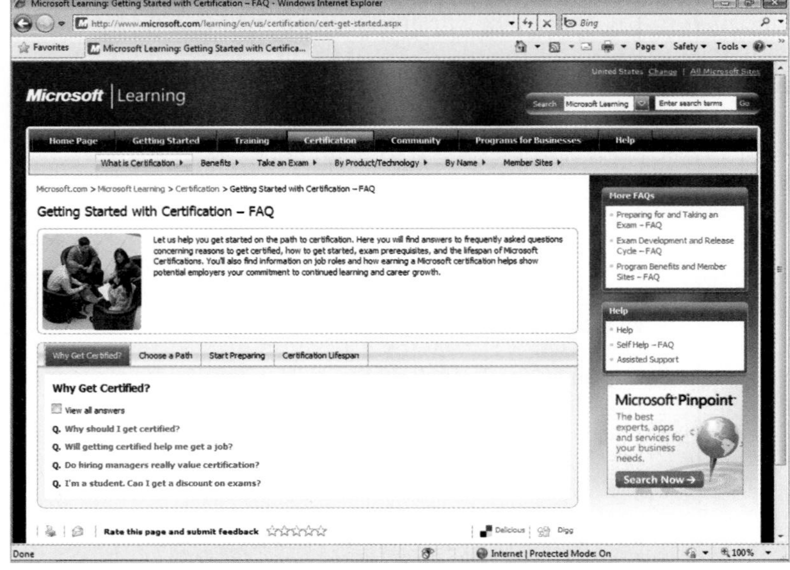

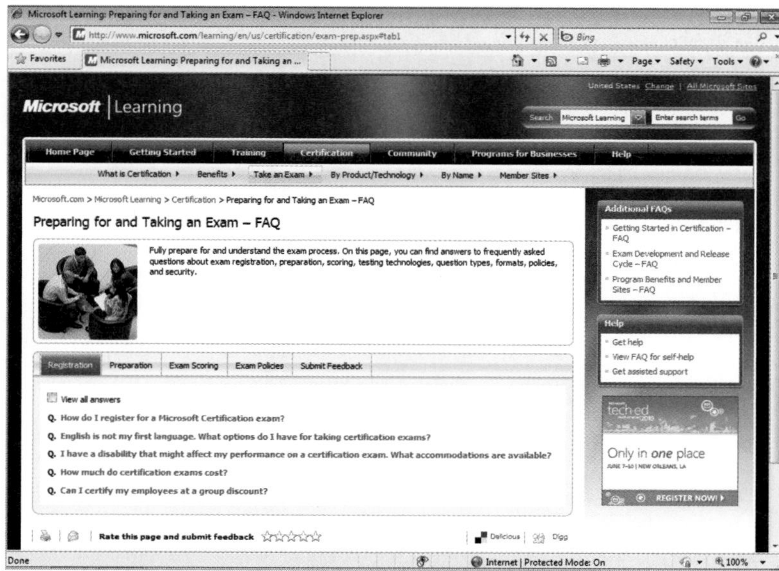

the certification exam, you should review and perform each task identified with a MCAS objective to confirm that you can meet the requirements for the exam.

Taking a MCAS Exam

The Microsoft Certified Applications Specialist certification exams are not written exams. Instead, the exams are performance-based examinations that allow you to interact with a "live" Office program as you complete a series of objective-based tasks.

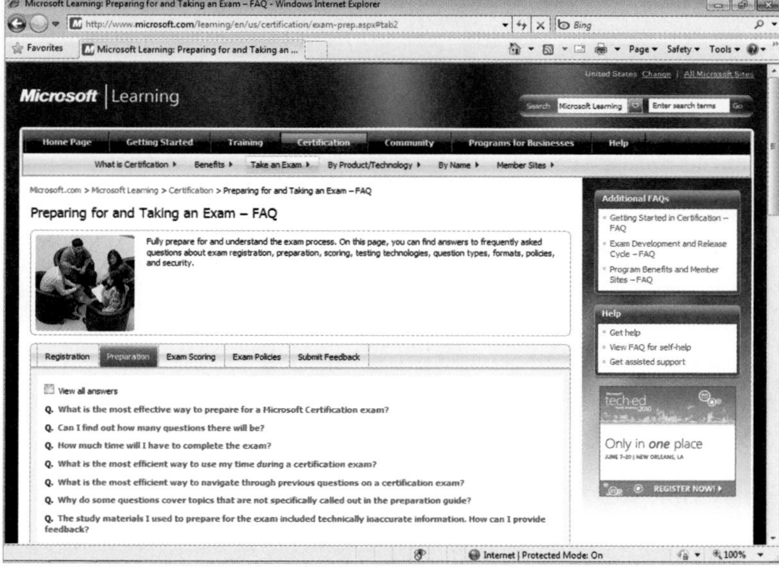

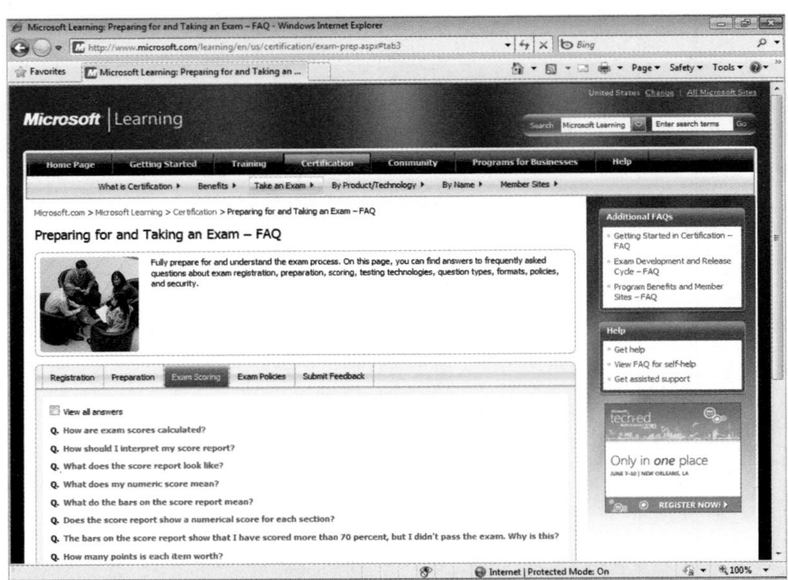

All the standard ribbons, tabs, toolbars, and keyboard shortcuts are available during the exam. Microsoft Certified Applications Specialist exams for Office 2010 programs consist of 25 to 35 questions, each of which requires you to complete one or more tasks using the Office program for which you are seeking certification. A typical exam takes from 45 to 60 minutes. Passing percentages range from 70 to 80 percent correct.

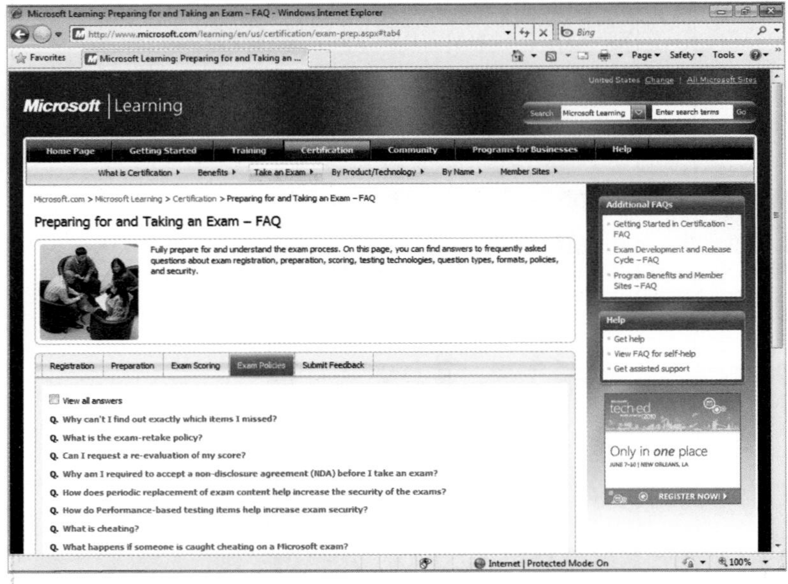

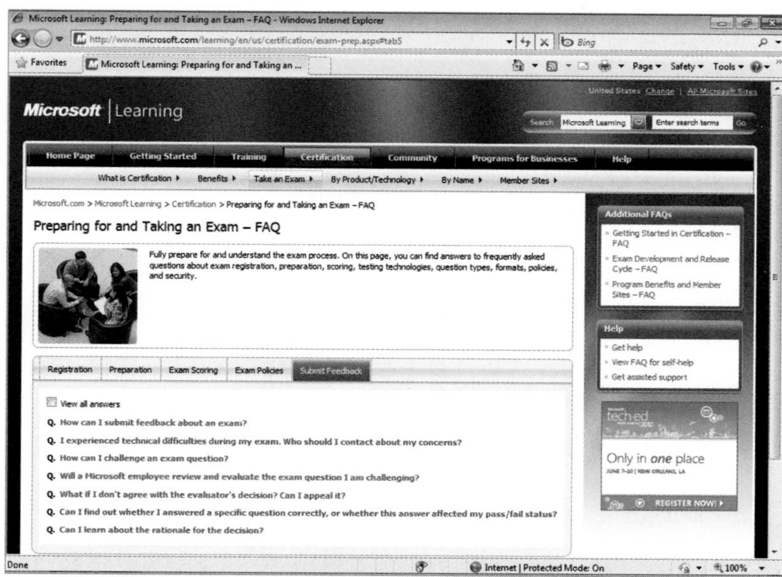

The Exam Experience

After you fill out a series of information screens, the testing software starts the exam and the Office program. The test questions appear in the exam dialog box in the lower right corner of the screen.

- The timer starts when the first question appears and displays the remaining exam time at the top of the exam dialog box. If the timer and the counter are distracting, you can click the timer to remove the display.
- The counter at the top of the exam dialog box tracks how many questions you have completed and how many remain.
- If you think you have made a mistake, you can click the Reset button to restart the question. The Reset button does not restart the entire exam or extend the exam time limit.
- When you complete a question, click the Next button to move to the next question. It is not possible to move back to a previous question on the exam.
- If the exam dialog box gets in your way, you can click the Minimize button in the upper right corner of the exam dialog box to hide it, or you can drag the title bar to another part of the screen to move it.

Tips for Taking an Exam

- Carefully read and follow all instructions provided in each question.
- Make sure all steps in a task are completed before proceeding to the next exam question.
- Enter requested information as it appears in the instructions without formatting unless you are explicitly requested otherwise.

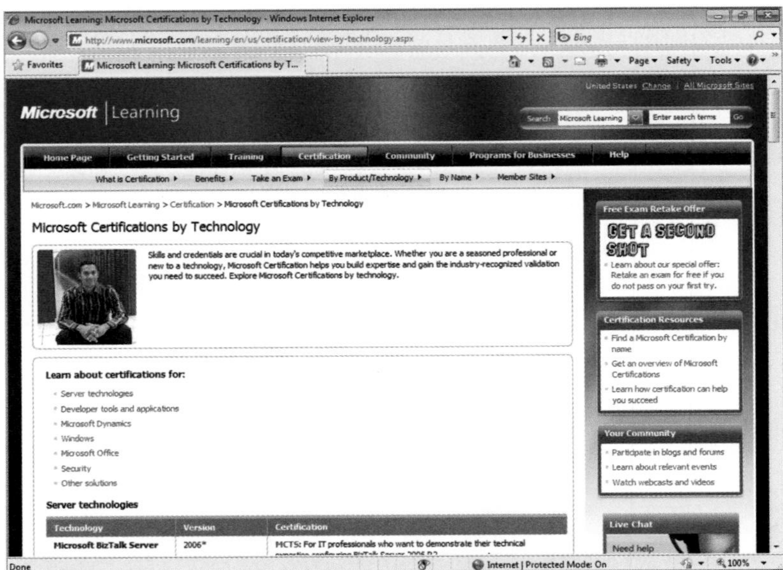

- Close all dialog boxes before proceeding to the next exam question unless you are specifically instructed otherwise.
- Do not leave tables, boxes, or cells “active” unless instructed otherwise.
- Do not cut and paste information from the exam interface into the program.
- When you print a document from an Office program during the exam, nothing actually gets printed.
- Errant keystrokes or mouse clicks do not count against your score as long as you achieve the correct end result. You are scored based on the end result, not the method you use to achieve it. However, if a specific method is explicitly requested, you need to use it to get credit for the results.
- The overall exam is timed, so taking too long on individual questions may leave you without enough time to complete the entire exam.
- If you experience computer problems during the exam, immediately notify a testing center administrator to restart your exam where you were interrupted.

Exam Results

At the end of the exam, a score report appears indicating whether you passed or failed the exam. An official certificate is mailed to successful candidates in approximately two to three weeks.

Getting More Information

To learn more about the Microsoft Certified Applications Specialist program, read a list of frequently asked questions, and locate the nearest testing center, visit:

www.microsoft.com

For a more detailed list of Microsoft Certified Applications Specialist program objectives, visit:

www.perspection.com

Index

A

B

C

D

E

F

G

H

I

J

K

L

M

P

Q

R

S

T

U

V

W

X

Z